interactive SCIENCE

Go to MyScienceOnline.com to experience science in a whole new way.

Interactive tools such as My Planet Diary connect you to the latest science happenings.

MY PLANET DIARY

- Search **Earth's Journal** for important science news from around the world.

- Use **Earth's Calendar** to find out when cool scientific events occur.

- Explore science **Links** to find even more exciting information about our planet.

- Visit **Jack's Blog** to be the first to know about what is going on in science!

SAVVAS
LEARNING COMPANY

Virginia

You're an author!

As you write in this science book, your answers and personal discoveries will be recorded for you to keep, making this book unique to you. That is why you are one of the primary authors of this book.

✎ **In the space below, print your name, school, town, and state. Then write a short autobiography that includes your interests and accomplishments.**

YOUR NAME _____

SCHOOL _____

TOWN, STATE _____

AUTOBIOGRAPHY _____

_____

_____

_____

Your Photo

ISBN-13: 978-0-13-319783-9
ISBN-10:   0-13-319783-2
15 20

ON THE COVER
Robotics
Students at Virginia Tech developed this robot to introduce other students and researchers to robotics. Users are encouraged to change their robot's hardware and software to make it do new things. For example, since it can see colors, the robot could be programmed to say "Hello" when shown a blue square or even go find, pick up, and throw a red ball!

Program Authors

KATHRYN THORNTON, Ph.D.
Professor and Associate Dean, School of Engineering and Applied Science, University of Virginia, Charlottesville, Virginia
Selected by NASA in May 1984, Dr. Kathryn Thornton is a veteran of four space flights. She has logged more than 975 hours in space, including more than 21 hours of extravehicular activity. As an author on the *Scott Foresman Science* series, Dr. Thornton's enthusiasm for science has inspired teachers around the globe.

DON BUCKLEY, M.Sc.
Information and Communications Technology Director, The School at Columbia University, New York, New York
A founder of New York City Independent School Technologists (NYCIST) and long-time chair of New York Association of Independent Schools' annual IT conference, Mr. Buckley has taught students on two continents and created multimedia and Internet-based instructional systems for schools worldwide.

ZIPPORAH MILLER, M.A.Ed.
Associate Executive Director for Professional Programs and Conferences, National Science Teachers Association, Arlington, Virginia
Ms. Zipporah Miller is a former K–12 science supervisor and STEM coordinator for the Prince George's County Public School District in Maryland. She is a science education consultant who has overseen curriculum development and staff training for more than 150 district science coordinators.

MICHAEL J. PADILLA, Ph.D.
Associate Dean and Director, Eugene P. Moore School of Education, Clemson University, Clemson, South Carolina
A former middle school teacher and a leader in middle school science education, Dr. Michael Padilla has served as president of the National Science Teachers Association and as a writer of the National Science Education Standards. He is professor of science education at Clemson University.

MICHAEL E. WYSESSION, Ph.D.
Associate Professor of Earth and Planetary Science, Washington University, St. Louis, Missouri
An author on more than 50 scientific publications, Dr. Wysession was awarded the prestigious Packard Foundation Fellowship and Presidential Faculty Fellowship for his research in geophysics. Dr. Wysession is an expert on Earth's inner structure and has mapped various regions of Earth using seismic tomography. He is known internationally for his work in geoscience education and outreach.

Instructional Design Author

GRANT WIGGINS, Ed.D.
President, Authentic Education, Hopewell, New Jersey
Dr. Wiggins is a co-author with Jay McTighe of *Understanding by Design, 2nd Edition* (ASCD 2005). His approach to instructional design provides teachers with a disciplined way of thinking about curriculum design, assessment, and instruction that moves teaching from covering content to ensuring understanding.

UNDERSTANDING BY DESIGN® and UbD® are trademarks of ASCD, and are used under license.

Planet Diary Author

JACK HANKIN
Science/Mathematics Teacher, The Hilldale School, Daly City, California, Founder, Planet Diary Web site
Mr. Hankin is the creator and writer of Planet Diary, a science current events Web site. He is passionate about bringing science news and environmental awareness into classrooms and offers numerous Planet Diary workshops at NSTA and other events to train middle and high school teachers.

ELL Consultant

JIM CUMMINS, Ph.D.
Professor and Canada Research Chair, Curriculum, Teaching and Learning department at the University of Toronto
Dr. Cummins focuses on literacy development in multilingual schools and the role of technology in promoting student learning across the curriculum. *Interactive Science* incorporates essential research-based principles for integrating language with the teaching of academic content based on his instructional framework.

Reading Consultant

HARVEY DANIELS, Ph.D.
Professor of Secondary Education, University of New Mexico, Albuquerque, New Mexico
Dr. Daniels is an international consultant to schools, districts, and educational agencies. He has authored or coauthored 13 books on language, literacy, and education. His most recent works are *Comprehension and Collaboration: Inquiry Circles in Action* and *Subjects Matter: Every Teacher's Guide to Content-Area Reading*.

Virginia

Contributing Writers

Edward Aguado, Ph.D.
Professor, Department of
  Geography
San Diego State University
San Diego, California

Elizabeth Coolidge-Stolz, M.D.
Medical Writer
North Reading, Massachusetts

Donald L. Cronkite, Ph.D.
Professor of Biology
Hope College
Holland, Michigan

Jan Jenner, Ph.D.
Science Writer
Talladega, Alabama

Linda Cronin Jones, Ph.D.
Associate Professor of Science and
  Environmental Education
University of Florida
Gainesville, Florida

T. Griffith Jones, Ph.D.
Clinical Associate Professor
  of Science Education
College of Education
University of Florida
Gainesville, Florida

Andrew C. Kemp, Ph.D.
Teacher
Jefferson County Public Schools
Louisville, Kentucky

Matthew Stoneking, Ph.D.
Associate Professor of Physics
Lawrence University
Appleton, Wisconsin

R. Bruce Ward, Ed.D.
Senior Research Associate
Science Education Department
Harvard-Smithsonian Center for
  Astrophysics
Cambridge, Massachusetts

Content Reviewers

Paul D. Beale, Ph.D.
Department of Physics
University of Colorado at Boulder
Boulder, Colorado

Jeff R. Bodart, Ph.D.
Professor of Physical Sciences
Chipola College
Marianna, Florida

Joy Branlund, Ph.D.
Department of Earth Science
Southwestern Illinois College
Granite City, Illinois

Marguerite Brickman, Ph.D.
Division of Biological Sciences
University of Georgia
Athens, Georgia

Bonnie J. Brunkhorst, Ph.D.
Science Education and Geological
  Sciences
California State University
San Bernardino, California

Michael Castellani, Ph.D.
Department of Chemistry
Marshall University
Huntington, West Virginia

Charles C. Curtis, Ph.D.
Research Associate Professor
  of Physics
University of Arizona
Tucson, Arizona

Diane I. Doser, Ph.D.
Department of Geological
  Sciences
University of Texas
El Paso, Texas

Rick Duhrkopf, Ph.D.
Department of Biology
Baylor University
Waco, Texas

Alice K. Hankla, Ph.D.
The Galloway School
Atlanta, Georgia

Mark Henriksen, Ph.D.
Physics Department
University of Maryland
Baltimore, Maryland

Chad Hershock, Ph.D.
Center for Research on Learning
  and Teaching
University of Michigan
Ann Arbor, Michigan

Jeremiah N. Jarrett, Ph.D.
Department of Biology
Central Connecticut State
  University
New Britain, Connecticut

Scott L. Kight, Ph.D.
Department of Biology
Montclair State University
Montclair, New Jersey

Jennifer O. Liang, Ph.D.
Department of Biology
University of Minnesota–Duluth
Duluth, Minnesota

Joseph F. McCullough, Ph.D.
Physics Program Chair
Cabrillo College
Aptos, California

Heather Mernitz, Ph.D.
Department of Physical Science
Alverno College
Milwaukee, Wisconsin

Sadredin C. Moosavi, Ph.D.
Department of Earth and
  Environmental Sciences
Tulane University
New Orleans, Louisiana

David L. Reid, Ph.D.
Department of Biology
Blackburn College
Carlinville, Illinois

Scott M. Rochette, Ph.D.
Department of the Earth Sciences
SUNY College at Brockport
Brockport, New York

Karyn L. Rogers, Ph.D.
Department of Geological
  Sciences
University of Missouri
Columbia, Missouri

Laurence Rosenhein, Ph.D.
Department of Chemistry
Indiana State University
Terre Haute, Indiana

Sara Seager, Ph.D.
Department of Planetary Sciences
  and Physics
Massachusetts Institute of
  Technology
Cambridge, Massachusetts

Tom Shoberg, Ph.D.
Missouri University of Science
  and Technology
Rolla, Missouri

Patricia Simmons, Ph.D.
North Carolina State University
Raleigh, North Carolina

William H. Steinecker, Ph.D.
Research Scholar
Miami University
Oxford, Ohio

Paul R. Stoddard, Ph.D.
Department of Geology and
  Environmental Geosciences
Northern Illinois University
DeKalb, Illinois

John R. Villarreal, Ph.D.
Department of Chemistry
The University of Texas–Pan
  American
Edinburg, Texas

John R. Wagner, Ph.D.
Department of Geology
Clemson University
Clemson, South Carolina

Jerry Waldvogel, Ph.D.
Department of Biological Sciences
Clemson University
Clemson, South Carolina

Donna L. Witter, Ph.D.
Department of Geology
Kent State University
Kent, Ohio

Edward J. Zalisko, Ph.D.
Department of Biology
Blackburn College
Carlinville, Illinois

Museum of Science.

Special thanks to the Museum of
Science, Boston, Massachusetts,
and Ioannis Miaoulis, the
Museum's president and director,
for serving as content advisors for
the technology and design strand
in this program.

Virginia **Table of Contents**

CHAPTER 1

Using Scientific Inquiry

The Big Question .... **xxxviii**
How do science and society affect each other?

Vocabulary Skill: Identify Multiple Meanings 2
Reading Skills 3

LESSON 1
How Scientists Work 4
△ Inquiry Skill: Observe 5, 6
do the math! Calculate 7

LESSON 2
The Characteristics of Scientific Knowledge ... 10
△ Inquiry Skill: Interpret Data 12

LESSON 3
Designing an Experiment 18
△ Inquiry Skill: Develop Hypotheses 20
do the math! Graphing Data 23

LESSON 4
Scientific Literacy 28
△ Inquiry Skill: Interpret Data 31
Explore the Big Question 33
Answer the Big Question 33

Study Guide & Review and Assessment 34
Review the Big Question 34
Apply the Big Question 36
Virginia SOL Test Prep 37

Science Matters 38
• Seismic-Safe Buildings • Engineering Solutions

Enter the Lab zone for hands-on inquiry.

△ **Chapter Lab Investigation:**
  • Directed Inquiry: Piecing Information Together
  • Open Inquiry: Piecing Information Together

△ **Inquiry Warm-Ups:** • How Does a Scientist Think? • Developing a Theory • What's the Question? • Posing Questions

△ **Quick Labs:** • Scientific Skills • Activities of Science • Scientific Thinking • Science and Its Methods • It Starts With a Question • How Can You Explain It? • Scientific Literacy Survey • Analyzing Claims • Sources of Information

my science online.com

Go to MyScienceOnline.com to interact with this chapter's content. Keyword: Using Scientific Inquiry

> **PLANET DIARY**
• Using Scientific Inquiry

> **INTERACTIVE ART**
• Inquiry Diagram

> **REAL-WORLD INQUIRY**
• Where's the Evidence? • When Science Sparks Controversy

> **VIRTUAL LAB**
• What Is Scientific Inquiry?

CHAPTER 2

Mathematics and Models in Science

The Big Question **40**
How do scientists use measurement and mathematics?

    Vocabulary Skill: High-Use Academic Words **42**
    Reading Skills **43**

LESSON 1
Scientific Measurement **44**
    do the math! Calculating Using SI Units **46**
    Inquiry Skill: Measure **48, 49**

LESSON 2
Mathematics and Scientific Thinking **54**
    Inquiry Skill: Interpret Data **55**
    Explore the Big Question **60**
    Answer the Big Question **61**

LESSON 3
Using Graphs in Science **62**
    Inquiry Skill: Graph .63, 64, 65

LESSON 4
Models and Systems **68**
    Inquiry Skill: Make Models **72**

LESSON 5
Safety in the Science Laboratory **76**
    Inquiry Skill: Observe **77**

Study Guide & Review and Assessment **82**
    Review the Big Question **82**
    Apply the Big Question **84**
    Virginia SOL Test Prep **85**

Science Matters **86**
    • The Race to be Faster • Aquanauts

 Lab zone® Enter the Lab zone for hands-on inquiry.

Chapter Lab Investigation:
• Directed Inquiry: Selecting Models
• Open Inquiry: Selecting Models

Inquiry Warm-Ups: • What Is Scientific Measurement? • How Do Math and Science Work Together? • What's in a Graph? • Models in Science • Can You Name the Safety Equipment?

Quick Labs: • Measuring With SI • A Unit of SI • Is It Accurate? • Math Tools in Science • Recognizing Trends • Working With Models • Characteristics of Systems • Be Prepared to Be Safe in the Field • How Would You Respond to These Emergencies?

my science online.com

Go to MyScienceOnline.com to interact with this chapter's content. **Keyword:** Mathematics and Models in Science

> **UNTAMED SCIENCE**
• Measuring Up

> **PLANET DIARY**
• Mathematics and Models in Science

> **INTERACTIVE ART**
• The Need for Numbers • Plotting a Line Graph • Modeling a System

> **VIRTUAL LAB**
• How Are Units Useful?

CHAPTER 3

Introduction to Matter

The Big Question 88
How is matter described?

Vocabulary Skill: Prefixes 90
Reading Skills 91

LESSON 1
Describing Matter 92
Inquiry Skill: Classify 95

LESSON 2
Classifying Matter 96
Inquiry Skill: Infer 97

LESSON 3
Measuring Matter 102
Inquiry Skill: Calculate 104, 105, 106, 107

LESSON 4
Changes in Matter 108
Inquiry Skill: Draw Conclusions 115
do the math! Analyzing Data 115
Explore the Big Question 116
Answer the Big Question 117

Study Guide & Review and Assessment 118
Review the Big Question 118
Apply the Big Question 120
Virginia SOL Test Prep 121

Science Matters 122
• Long Ago in a Faraway Land... • An Antiuniverse?

 Enter the Lab zone for hands-on inquiry.

Chapter Lab Investigation:
• Directed Inquiry: Making Sense of Density
• Open Inquiry: Making Sense of Density

Inquiry Warm-Ups: • How Do You Describe Matter? • What Is a Mixture? • Which Has More Mass? • Is a New Substance Formed?

Quick Labs: • Observing Physical Properties • Modeling Atoms and Molecules • Separating Mixtures • Calculating Volume • What Is a Physical Change? • Demonstrating Tarnishing • Where Was the Energy?

my science online

Go to MyScienceOnline.com to interact with this chapter's content.
Keyword: Introduction to Matter

> **UNTAMED SCIENCE**
• What's the Matter?

> **PLANET DIARY**
• Introduction to Matter

> **INTERACTIVE ART**
• Conservation of Matter • Properties of Matter

> **ART IN MOTION**
• What Makes Up Matter?

> **VIRTUAL LAB**
• How Do You Measure Weight and Volume?
• Will It Float? Density of Solids and Liquids

CHAPTER 4

Solids, Liquids, and Gases

 The Big Question 124
Why does a substance change states?

Vocabulary Skill: Suffixes 126
Reading Skills 127

LESSON 1
States of Matter 128
Inquiry Skill: Infer 132
do the math! Using Formulas 134

LESSON 2
Changes of State 136
Explore the Big Question 142
Answer the Big Question 143
Inquiry Skill: Predict 143

LESSON 3
Gas Behavior 144
Inquiry Skill: Graph 149
do the math! Analyzing Data 149

Study Guide & Review and Assessment 150
Review the Big Question 150
Apply the Big Question 152
Virginia SOL Test Prep 153

Science Matters 154
• Scuba Diving • A Shocking State • Growing Snow

Lab zone® **Enter the Lab zone for hands-on inquiry.**

Chapter Lab Investigation:
• Directed Inquiry: Melting Ice
• Open Inquiry: Melting Ice

Inquiry Warm-Ups: • What Are Solids, Liquids, and Gases? • What Happens When You Breathe on a Mirror? • How Can Air Keep Chalk From Breaking?

Quick Labs: • Modeling Particles • As Thick as Honey • How Do the Particles in a Gas Move? • Keeping Cool • Observing Sublimation • How Are Pressure and Temperature Related? • Hot and Cold Balloons • It's a Gas

my science online.com

Go to MyScienceOnline.com to interact with this chapter's content. Keyword: Solids, Liquids, and Gases

> **UNTAMED SCIENCE**
• Building a House of Snow

> **PLANET DIARY**
• Solids, Liquids, and Gases

> **INTERACTIVE ART**
• Gas Laws • States of Matter

> **VIRTUAL LAB**
• Solid to Liquid to Gas: Changes of State

CHAPTER 5

Elements and the Periodic Table

The Big Question **156**
How is the periodic table organized?

Vocabulary Skill: Greek Word Origins **158**
Reading Skills **159**

LESSON 1
Introduction to Atoms **160**
Inquiry Skill: Make Models **164**

LESSON 2
Organizing the Elements **168**
Inquiry Skill: Predict **170, 171, 175**

LESSON 3
Metals **176**
Inquiry Skill: Infer **179, 183**
do the math! Analyzing Data **181**

LESSON 4
Nonmetals and Metalloids **184**
Inquiry Skill: Classify **191**
Explore the Big Question **192**
Answer the Big Question **193**

LESSON 5
Radioactive Elements **194**
Inquiry Skill: Calculate **199**
do the math! Analyzing Data **199**

Study Guide & Review and Assessment **202**
Review the Big Question **202**
Apply the Big Question **204**
Virginia SOL Test Prep **205**

Science Matters **206**
• Discovery of the Elements • Elements of the Human Body

Lab zone® Enter the Lab zone for hands-on inquiry.

Chapter Lab Investigation:
• Directed Inquiry: Copper or Carbon? That Is the Question
• Open Inquiry: Copper or Carbon? That Is the Question

Inquiry Warm-Ups: • What's in the Box?
• Which Is Easier? • Why Use Aluminum?
• What Are the Properties of Charcoal? • How Much Goes Away?

Quick Labs: • Visualizing an Electron Cloud
• How Far Away Is the Electron? • Classifying
• Using the Periodic Table • Expanding the Periodic Table • Finding Metals • Carbon—A Nonmetal • Finding Nonmetals • What Happens When an Atom Decays? • Modeling Beta Decay • Designing Experiments Using Radioactive Tracers

MY SCIENCE ONLINE.com

Go to MyScienceOnline.com to interact with this chapter's content. Keyword: Elements and the Periodic Table

> **PLANET DIARY**
• Elements and the Periodic Table

> **INTERACTIVE ART**
• Periodic Table • Investigate an Atom

> **ART IN MOTION**
• Types of Radioactive Decay

> **VIRTUAL LAB**
• Which Element Is This?

CHAPTER

6

Atoms and Bonding

The Big Question 208
How can bonding determine the properties
of a substance?

Vocabulary Skill: High-Use Academic Words 210
Reading Skills 211

LESSON 1
Atoms, Bonding, and the Periodic Table 212
△ Inquiry Skill: Predict 215

LESSON 2
Ionic Bonds 218
△ Inquiry Skill: Interpret Data 223

LESSON 3
Covalent Bonds 226
△ Inquiry Skill: Graph 230
do the math! Analyzing Data 230
? Explore the Big Question 232
? Answer the Big Question 233

LESSON 4
Bonding in Metals 234
△ Inquiry Skill: Classify 238

Study Guide & Review and Assessment 240
? Review the Big Question 240
? Apply the Big Question 242
⬎ Virginia SOL Test Prep 243

Science Matters 244
• Pharmacists: Chemists at Work • The Superhero of Glues
• Sci-Fi Metal

**Enter the Lab zone
for hands-on inquiry.**

△ **Chapter Lab Investigation:**
• Directed Inquiry: Shedding Light on Ions
• Open Inquiry: Shedding Light on Ions

△ **Inquiry Warm-Ups:** • What Are the Trends
in the Periodic Table? • How Do Ions Form?
• Covalent Bonds • Are They "Steel" the
Same?

△ **Quick Labs:** • Element Chemistry • Ion
Formation • How Do You Write Ionic
Names and Formulas? • Sharing Electrons
• Properties of Molecular Compounds
• Attraction Between Polar Molecules • Metal
Crystals • What Do Metals Do?

my science ONLINE.COM

Go to MyScienceOnline.com to
interact with this chapter's content.
Keyword: Atoms and Bonding

▷ **UNTAMED SCIENCE**
• The Elements of Hockey

▷ **PLANET DIARY**
• Atoms and Bonding

▷ **INTERACTIVE ART**
• Periodic Table • Investigate Ionic
Compounds • Table Salt Dissolving in Water

▷ **ART IN MOTION**
• Bonding in Polar Molecules

▷ **VIRTUAL LAB**
• Will It React?

CHAPTER

7

Chemical Reactions

The Big Question 246
How is matter conserved in a chemical reaction?

Vocabulary Skill: Identify Multiple Meanings 248
Reading Skills 249

LESSON 1

Observing Chemical Change 250
Inquiry Skill: Graph 257
do the math! Analyzing Data 257

LESSON 2

Describing Chemical Reactions 258
Inquiry Skill: Make Models 260, 261
do the math! Balancing Equations 265
Explore the Big Question 266
Answer the Big Question 267

LESSON 3

Controlling Chemical Reactions 270
do the math! Finding Surface Area 273
Inquiry Skill: Predict 274

Study Guide & Review and Assessment 276
Review the Big Question 276
Apply the Big Question 278
Virginia SOL Test Prep 279

Science Matters 280
• Look, Ma, Warm Hands • Can You Be Clean and Green?

**Enter the Lab zone
for hands-on inquiry.**

Chapter Lab Investigation:
• Directed Inquiry: Where's the Evidence?
• Open Inquiry: Where's the Evidence?

Inquiry Warm-Ups: • What Happens When
Chemicals React? • Did You Lose Anything?
• Can You Speed Up or Slow Down a Reaction?

Quick Labs: • Observing Change
• Information in a Chemical Equation • Is
Matter Conserved? • Categories of Chemical
Reactions • Modeling Activation Energy
• Effect of Temperature on Chemical Reactions

my science online

**Go to MyScienceOnline.com to
interact with this chapter's content.
Keyword: Chemical Reactions**

> **UNTAMED SCIENCE**
• Chemical Reactions to the Rescue

> **PLANET DIARY**
• Chemical Reactions

> **INTERACTIVE ART**
• Physical or Chemical Change?
• Conservation of Matter • Balancing
Equations

> **ART IN MOTION**
• Activation Energy

> **VIRTUAL LAB**
• Energy and Chemical Changes

CHAPTER

8 Acids, Bases, and Solutions

The Big Question **282**
What determines the properties of a solution?

Vocabulary Skill: Identify Related Word Forms ... 284
Reading Skills 285

LESSON 1
Understanding Solutions **286**
Inquiry Skill: Interpret Data 291
do the math! Analyzing Data 291

LESSON 2
Concentration and Solubility **292**
Inquiry Skill: Calculate 294, 295, 297
do the math! Calculating Concentration 294
Explore the Big Question 298
Answer the Big Question 299

LESSON 3
Describing Acids and Bases **300**
Inquiry Skill: Predict 302, 304, 305

LESSON 4
Acids and Bases in Solution **306**
Inquiry Skill: Measure 308

Study Guide & Review and Assessment **312**
Review the Big Question 312
Apply the Big Question 314
Virginia SOL Test Prep 315

Science Matters **316**
• Limestone and Acid Drainage • Vinegar

 Enter the Lab zone for hands-on inquiry.

Chapter Lab Investigation:
• Directed Inquiry: Speedy Solutions
• Open Inquiry: Speedy Solutions

Inquiry Warm-Ups: • What Makes a Mixture a Solution? • Does It Dissolve? • What Color Does Litmus Paper Turn? • What Can Cabbage Juice Tell You?

Quick Labs: • Scattered Light • Measuring Concentration • Predicting Rates of Solubility • Properties of Acids • Properties of Bases • pHone Home • The Antacid Test

my science online.com

Go to MyScienceOnline.com to interact with this chapter's content. Keyword: Acids, Bases, and Solutions

> UNTAMED SCIENCE
• What's the Solution?

> PLANET DIARY
• Acids, Bases, and Solutions

> INTERACTIVE ART
• Table Salt Dissolving in Water • Classifying Solutions • The pH Scale

> VIRTUAL LAB
• Acid, Base, or Neutral?

CHAPTER 9

Motion

The Big Question **318**
How do you describe the motion of an object?

Vocabulary Skill: High-Use Academic Words **320**
Reading Skills **321**

LESSON 1
Describing Motion **322**
△ Inquiry Skill: Measure **325**

LESSON 2
Speed and Velocity **326**
△ Inquiry Skill: Calculate **328, 329, 331**
❓ Explore the Big Question **331**
❓ Answer the Big Question **331**

LESSON 3
Acceleration **334**
do the math! Calculate Acceleration **337**
△ Inquiry Skill: Graph **338, 339**

Study Guide & Review and Assessment **340**
❓ Review the Big Question **340**
❓ Apply the Big Question **342**
🌀 Virginia SOL Test Prep **343**

Science Matters **344**
• The Race for Speed • Stop Sign

 Enter the Lab zone for hands-on inquiry.

△ **Chapter Lab Investigation:**
• Directed Inquiry: Stopping on a Dime
• Open Inquiry: Stopping on a Dime

△ **Inquiry Warm-Ups:** • What Is Motion?
• How Fast and How Far? • Will You Hurry Up?

△ **Quick Labs:** • Identifying Motion • Velocity
• Motion Graphs • Describing Acceleration
• Graphing Acceleration

my science ONLINE.com

**Go to MyScienceOnline.com to interact with this chapter's content.
Keyword: Motion**

▷ **UNTAMED SCIENCE**
• The Adventures of Velocity Girl

▷ **PLANET DIARY**
• Motion

▷ **INTERACTIVE ART**
• Speed and Acceleration

▷ **INTERACTIVE ART**
• Graphing Motion

▷ **ART IN MOTION**
• Relative Motion

▷ **VIRTUAL LAB**
• How Can You Measure Acceleration?

CHAPTER
10

Forces

The Big Question 346
How do objects react to forces?

Vocabulary Skill: Latin Word Origins 348
Reading Skills 349

LESSON 1
The Nature of Force 350
Inquiry Skill: Make Models 352

LESSON 2
Friction and Gravity 354
Inquiry Skill: Design Experiments 358

LESSON 3
Newton's Laws of Motion 362
Inquiry Skill: Infer 363
do the math! Calculate Acceleration 365
Explore the Big Question 368
Answer the Big Question 369

LESSON 4
Momentum 370
Inquiry Skill: Calculate 371

LESSON 5
Free Fall and Circular Motion 374
Inquiry Skill: Create Data Tables 375

Study Guide & Review and Assessment 378
Review the Big Question 378
Apply the Big Question 380
Virginia SOL Test Prep 381

Science Matters 382
• Safety Restraints • Superlubricity

 Lab zone Enter the Lab zone for hands-on inquiry.

Chapter Lab Investigation:
• Directed Inquiry: Sticky Sneakers
• Open Inquiry: Sticky Sneakers

Inquiry Warm-Ups: Is the Force With You?
• Observing Friction • What Changes Motion?
• How Pushy Is a Straw? • What Makes an Object Move in a Circle?

Quick Labs: • What Is Force? • Modeling Unbalanced Forces • Calculating • Around and Around • Newton's Second Law • Interpreting Illustrations • Colliding Cars • Which Lands First? • Orbiting Earth

my science online.com

Go to MyScienceOnline.com to interact with this chapter's content.
Keyword: Forces

> **UNTAMED SCIENCE**
• Sir Isaac Visits the Circus

> **PLANET DIARY**
• Forces

> **INTERACTIVE ART**
• Balanced and Unbalanced Forces
• Conservation of Momentum

> **ART IN MOTION**
• Types of Friction

> **VIRTUAL LAB**
• Investigating Newton's Laws of Motion

CHAPTER 11
Work and Machines

The Big Question 384
How do machines make it easier to do work?

Vocabulary Skill: Identify Multiple Meanings 386
Reading Skills 387

LESSON 1
Work and Power 388
△ Inquiry Skill: Calculate 391, 393
do the math! Calculate Power 393

LESSON 2
Understanding Machines 394
do the math! Interpret Graphs 399
△ Inquiry Skill: Predict 400

LESSON 3
Inclined Planes and Levers 402
△ Inquiry Skill: Infer 407

LESSON 4
Putting Machines Together 410
△ Inquiry Skill: Classify 411, 412, 413
Explore the Big Question 415
Answer the Big Question 415

Study Guide & Review and Assessment 416
Review the Big Question 416
Apply the Big Question 418
Virginia SOL Test Prep 419

Science Matters 420
• Good Things Come in Small Packages • A New Set of Wheels
• Science Athletes: Let the Games Begin

Enter the Lab zone for hands-on inquiry.

△ **Chapter Lab Investigation:**
• Directed Inquiry: Angling for Access
• Open Inquiry: Angling for Access

△ **Inquiry Warm-Ups:** • Pulling at an Angle
• Is It a Machine? • Inclined Planes and Levers
• Machines That Turn

△ **Quick Labs:** • What Is Work? • Investigating Power • Going Up • Mechanical Advantage
• Friction and Efficiency • Modeling Levers
• Building Pulleys • Machines in the Kitchen

my science online

Go to MyScienceOnline.com to interact with this chapter's content.
Keyword: **Work and Machines**

> **UNTAMED SCIENCE**
• Remodeling Stonehenge

> **PLANET DIARY**
• Work and Machines

> **INTERACTIVE ART**
• Types of Pulleys • Work

> **ART IN MOTION**
• Levers

> **REAL-WORLD INQUIRY**
• Bicycle Racing and Efficiency

CHAPTER
12

Energy

The Big Question 422
How is energy conserved in a transformation?

Vocabulary Skill: Identify Multiple Meanings 424
Reading Skills 425

LESSON 1
What Is Energy? 426
do the math! Calculate Kinetic Energy 429
△ Inquiry Skill: Calculate 429

LESSON 2
Forms of Energy 432
△ Inquiry Skill: Classify 436

LESSON 3
Energy Transformations and Conservation 438
Explore the Big Question 442
Answer the Big Question 443
△ Inquiry Skill: Infer 443

Study Guide & Review and Assessment 444
Review the Big Question 444
Apply the Big Question 446
Virginia SOL Test Prep 447

Science Matters 448
• Charge It! • Catch and No Release

 Enter the Lab zone for hands-on inquiry.

△ **Chapter Lab Investigation:**
• Directed Inquiry: Can You Feel the Power?
• Open Inquiry: Can You Feel the Power?

△ **Inquiry Warm-Ups:** • How High Does a Ball Bounce? • What Makes a Flashlight Shine? • What Would Make a Card Jump?

△ **Quick Labs:** • Mass, Velocity, and Kinetic Energy • Determining Mechanical Energy • Sources of Energy • Soaring Straws • Law of Conservation of Energy

my science online.com

Go to MyScienceOnline.com to interact with this chapter's content.
Keyword: Energy

> **UNTAMED SCIENCE**
• The Potential for Fun

> **PLANET DIARY**
• Energy

> **ART IN MOTION**
• Kinetic and Potential Energy

> **INTERACTIVE ART**
• Types of Energy

> **INTERACTIVE ART**
• Energy Transformations

> **VIRTUAL LAB**
• Exploring Potential and Kinetic Energy

CHAPTER
13

Thermal Energy and Heat

 The Big Question 450
How does heat flow from one object to another?

Vocabulary Skill: Identify Multiple Meanings 452
Reading Skills 453

LESSON 1
Temperature, Thermal Energy, and Heat 454
△ Inquiry Skill: Communicate 457

LESSON 2
The Transfer of Heat 458
Explore the Big Question 460
Answer the Big Question 461
△ Inquiry Skill: Infer 461

LESSON 3
Thermal Properties 462
△ Inquiry Skill: Calculate 464, 465
do the math! Calculate Thermal Energy 464

Study Guide & Review and Assessment 466
Review the Big Question 466
Apply the Big Question 468
Virginia SOL Test Prep 469

Science Matters 470
• Aerogel Windows • Thermal Expansion

Lab zone® Enter the Lab zone for hands-on inquiry.

△ **Chapter Lab Investigation:**
• Directed Inquiry: Build Your Own Thermometer
• Open Inquiry: Build Your Own Thermometer

△ **Inquiry Warm-Ups:** • How Cold Is the Water? • What Does It Mean to Heat Up? • Thermal Properties

△ **Quick Labs:** • Temperature and Thermal Energy • Visualizing Convection Currents • Frosty Balloons

my science ONLINE.com

Go to MyScienceOnline.com to interact with this chapter's content. Keyword: Thermal Energy and Heat

▶ **UNTAMED SCIENCE**
• Why Is This Inner Tube So Hot?

▶ **PLANET DIARY**
• Thermal Energy and Heat

▶ **INTERACTIVE ART**
• Heat Transfer

▶ **ART IN MOTION**
• Temperature and Thermal Energy
• Conductors and Insulators

▶ **VIRTUAL LAB**
• Temperature or Heat? What's the Difference?

CHAPTER 14 Characteristics of Waves

The Big Question 472
What are the properties of waves?

Vocabulary Skill: Identify Multiple Meanings 474
Reading Skills 475

LESSON 1
What Are Waves? 476
Inquiry Skill: Predict 480, 481

LESSON 2
Properties of Waves 482
Inquiry Skill: Calculate 486
do the math! Calculate 486
Explore the Big Question 487
Answer the Big Question 487

LESSON 3
Interactions of Waves 488
Inquiry Skill: Observe 491, 493

Study Guide & Review and Assessment 496
Review the Big Question 496
Apply the Big Question 498
Virginia SOL Test Prep 499

Science Matters 500
• Wall of Water • An Operatic Superpower

Enter the Lab zone for hands-on inquiry.

Chapter Lab Investigation:
• Directed Inquiry: Making Waves
• Open Inquiry: Making Waves

Inquiry Warm-Ups: • What Are Waves?
• What Do Waves Look Like? • How Does a Ball Bounce?

Quick Labs: • What Causes Mechanical Waves? • Three Types of Waves • Properties of Waves • What Affects the Speed of a Wave? • Wave Interference • Standing Waves

my science online.com

Go to MyScienceOnline.com to interact with this chapter's content. Keyword: Characteristics of Waves

> **UNTAMED SCIENCE**
• Extreme Wave Science!

> **PLANET DIARY**
• Characteristics of Waves

> **INTERACTIVE ART**
• Wave Interference • Properties of Waves

> **ART IN MOTION**
• Wave and Energy Movement

> **VIRTUAL LAB**
• Bouncing and Bending Light

Sound

The Big Question 502
What determines the pitch and loudness
of sound?

Vocabulary Skill: Identify Multiple Meanings 504
Reading Skills 505

LESSON 1
The Nature of Sound 506
△ Inquiry Skill: Graph 509
do the math! Analyzing Data 510

LESSON 2
Properties of Sound 512
△ Inquiry Skill: Make Models 513
Explore the Big Question 517
Answer the Big Question 517

LESSON 3
Music 518
△ Inquiry Skill: Predict 521

LESSON 4
Hearing Sound 522
△ Inquiry Skill: Observe 523

LESSON 5
Using Sound 526
△ Inquiry Skill: Calculate 528

Study Guide & Review and Assessment 530
Review the Big Question 530
Apply the Big Question 532
Virginia SOL Test Prep 533

Science Matters 534
• Can You Hear Me Now? • Noisy Occupations

Lab® zone **Enter the Lab zone for hands-on inquiry.**

△ **Chapter Lab Investigation:**
• Directed Inquiry: Changing Pitch
• Open Inquiry: Changing Pitch

△ **Inquiry Warm-Ups:** • What Is Sound?
• How Does Amplitude Affect Loudness?
• What Is Music? • Hearing Sound • How Can
You Use Time to Measure Distance?

△ **Quick Labs:** • Understanding Sound
• Ear to the Sound • Listen to This • Pipe
Sounds • How Can You Change Pitch?
• Design and Build Hearing Protectors
• Designing Experiments

my science online.com

**Go to MyScienceOnline.com to interact with this chapter's content.
Keyword: Sound**

> **UNTAMED SCIENCE**
• Was That a Whale I Heard?

> **PLANET DIARY**
• Sound

> **INTERACTIVE ART**
• Musical Instruments • Exploring
Sound Waves

> **ART IN MOTION**
• Observing the Doppler Effect

> **REAL-WORLD INQUIRY**
• How Can Sound Solve a Problem?

CHAPTER 16
Electromagnetic Waves

The Big Question **536**
What kinds of waves make up the
electromagnetic spectrum?

Vocabulary Skill: Greek Word Origins **538**
Reading Skills **539**

LESSON 1
The Nature of Electromagnetic Waves **540**
Inquiry Skill: Calculate **541**

LESSON 2
Waves of the Electromagnetic Spectrum **544**
Inquiry Skill: Communicate **549**
Explore the Big Question **551**
Answer the Big Question **551**

LESSON 3
Wireless Communication **552**
Inquiry Skill: Interpret Data **555**
do the math! Analyzing Data **555**

Study Guide & Review and Assessment **560**
Review the Big Question **560**
Apply the Big Question **562**
Virginia SOL Test Prep **563**

Science Matters **564**
• Channel Surfin' on an Infrared Wave • Healing
With Magnetism?

 Lab zone Enter the Lab zone
for hands-on inquiry.

Chapter Lab Investigation:
• Directed Inquiry: Build a Crystal Radio
• Open Inquiry: Build a Crystal Radio

Inquiry Warm-Ups: • How Fast Are
Electromagnetic Waves? • What Is White
Light? • How Can Waves Change?

Quick Labs: • What Is an Electromagnetic
Wave Made Of? • Waves or Particles?
• Differences Between Waves • Parts of the
Electromagnetic Spectrum • How Cell Phones
Work • How Does GPS Work?

my science online.com

Go to MyScienceOnline.com to
interact with this chapter's content.
Keyword: **Electromagnetic Waves**

> **UNTAMED SCIENCE**
• The Day the Waves Died

> **PLANET DIARY**
• Electromagnetic Waves

> **INTERACTIVE ART**
• Electromagnetic Waves • Modulating
Electromagnetic Waves

> **ART IN MOTION**
• Invisible Information • Global Positioning
System (GPS)

> **VIRTUAL LAB**
• Wave or Particle? Exploring the Properties
of Light

CHAPTER 17 Light

The Big Question 566
How does light interact with matter?

    Vocabulary Skill: Use Prefixes 568
    Reading Skills 569

LESSON 1
Light and Color 570
    Inquiry Skill: Predict 573

LESSON 2
Reflection and Mirrors 576
    Inquiry Skill: Classify 581

LESSON 3
Refraction and Lenses 582
    Inquiry Skill: Interpret Data 584
    do the math! Analyzing Data 584
    Explore the Big Question 585
    Answer the Big Question 586

LESSON 4
Seeing Light 590
    Inquiry Skill: Observe 591

LESSON 5
Using Light 594
    Inquiry Skill: Infer 595

Study Guide & Review and Assessment 598
    Review the Big Question 598
    Apply the Big Question 600
    Virginia SOL Test Prep 601

Science Matters 602
    • Seeing Double • Hiding in Plain Sight

 Enter the Lab zone for hands-on inquiry.

Chapter Lab Investigation:
• Directed Inquiry: Changing Colors
• Open Inquiry: Changing Colors

Inquiry Warm-Ups: • How Do Colors Mix?
• How Does Your Reflection Wink? • How
Can You Make an Image Appear? • Can You
See Everything With One Eye? • How Does a
Pinhole Camera Work?

Quick Labs: • Developing Hypotheses
• Observing • Mirror Images • Bent Pencil
• Looking at Images • True Colors • What
a View!

my science online.com

Go to MyScienceOnline.com to
interact with this chapter's content.
Keyword: Light

> **UNTAMED SCIENCE**
• Why Is the Ocean Blue?

> **PLANET DIARY**
• Light

> **INTERACTIVE ART**
• Mirrors and Lenses • Refracting and
Reflecting Telescopes

> **ART IN MOTION**
• Refraction, Reflection, and Rainbows

> **VIRTUAL LAB**
• Color in Light

CHAPTER 18

Electricity

The Big Question **604**
How does an electric circuit work?

Vocabulary Skill: Latin Word Origins **606**
Reading Skills **607**

LESSON 1
Electric Charge and Static Electricity **608**
Inquiry Skill: Draw Conclusions **609, 610, 614**

LESSON 2
Electric Current **616**
Inquiry Skill: Classify **619**

LESSON 3
Electric Circuits **624**
do the math! Calculate Resistance and Voltage **626**
Inquiry Skill: Make Models **627, 628, 629**
Explore the Big Question **630**
Answer the Big Question **631**

LESSON 4
Electric Power and Safety **632**
Inquiry Skill: Calculate **633**
do the math! Calculate Current **633**

Study Guide & Review and Assessment **636**
Review the Big Question **636**
Apply the Big Question **638**
Virginia SOL Test Prep **639**

Science Matters **640**
• Something for Nothing • Going Green

Lab zone® Enter the Lab zone for hands-on inquiry.

Chapter Lab Investigation:
• Directed Inquiry: Build a Flashlight
• Open Inquiry: Build a Flashlight

Inquiry Warm-Ups: • Can You Move a Can Without Touching It? • How Can Current Be Measured? • Do the Lights Keep Shining? • How Can You Make a Bulb Burn More Brightly?

Quick Labs: • Drawing Conclusions • Sparks Are Flying • Producing Electric Current • Conductors and Insulators • Modeling Potential Difference • Ohm's Law • Calculating Electric Power and Energy Use • Electric Shock and Short Circuit Safety

my science online

Go to MyScienceOnline.com to interact with this chapter's content.
Keyword: **Electricity**

> **PLANET DIARY**
• Electricity

> **INTERACTIVE ART**
• Series and Parallel Circuits • Current Flow

> **ART IN MOTION**
• Static Charge

> **VIRTUAL LAB**
• Discovering Ohm's Law

> **REAL-WORLD INQUIRY**
• Energy Conservation

CHAPTER 19
Magnetism and Electromagnetism

The Big Question **642**
How are electricity and magnetism related?

Vocabulary Skill: Use Context to
Determine Meaning **644**
Reading Skills **645**

LESSON 1
What Is Magnetism? **646**
△ Inquiry Skill: Infer **649**

LESSON 2
Magnetic Fields **650**
△ Inquiry Skill: Observe **653**
do the **math!** Analyze Data **655**

LESSON 3
Electromagnetic Force **656**
△ Inquiry Skill: Predict **661**

LESSON 4
Electricity, Magnetism, and Motion **662**
△ Inquiry Skill: Graph **665**
do the **math!** Interpret Graphs **665**

LESSON 5
Electricity From Magnetism **668**
Explore the Big Question **673**
Answer the Big Question **673**
△ Inquiry Skill: Make Models **674**
do the **math!** Calculate Ratios **675**

Study Guide & Review and Assessment **676**
Review the Big Question **676**
Apply the Big Question **678**
Virginia SOL Test Prep **679**

Science Matters **680**
• Magnetic Pictures • A Shocking Message!

Appendices, English/Spanish Glossary, Index **682**

**Enter the Lab zone
for hands-on inquiry.**

△ **Chapter Lab Investigation:**
 • Directed Inquiry: Detecting Fake Coins
 • Open Inquiry: Detecting Fake Coins

△ **Inquiry Warm-Ups:** • Natural Magnets
 • Predict the Field • Electromagnetism • How
Are Electricity, Magnets, and Motion Related?
 • Electric Current Without a Battery

△ **Quick Labs:** • Magnetic Poles • Spinning
in Circles • Earth's Magnetic Field • Electric
Current and Magnetism • Magnetic Fields
From Electric Current • Electromagnet • Can a
Magnet Move a Wire? • How Galvanometers
Work • Parts of an Electric Motor • Inducing
an Electric Current • How Generators Work
 • How Transformers Work

my science online.com

**Go to MyScienceOnline.com to
interact with this chapter's content.
Keyword:** Magnetism and
Electromagnetism

> **PLANET DIARY**
• Magnetism and Electromagnetism

> **INTERACTIVE ART**
• Magnetic Fields • Motors and Generators

> **ART IN MOTION**
• Maglev Train

> **REAL-WORLD INQUIRY**
• Exploring Electromagnetism

Untamed Science™

Video Series: Chapter Adventures

Untamed Science created this captivating video series for **interactive** SCIENCE featuring a unique segment for every chapter of the program.

Featuring videos such as

Chapter 1   **Principles of Scientific Principles**
Chapter 2   **Measuring Up**
Chapter 3   **What's the Matter?**
Chapter 4   **Building a House of Snow**
Chapter 5   **Organizing Like Mendeleev**
Chapter 6   **The Elements of Hockey**
Chapter 7   **Chemical Reactions to the Rescue**
Chapter 8   **What's the Solution?**
Chapter 9   **The Adventures of Velocity Girl**
Chapter 10 **Sir Isaac Visits the Circus**
Chapter 11 **Remodeling Stonehenge**
Chapter 12 **The Potential for Fun**
Chapter 13 **Why Is This Inner Tube So Hot?**
Chapter 14 **Extreme Wave Science!**
Chapter 15 **Was That a Whale I Heard?**
Chapter 16 **The Day the Waves Died**
Chapter 17 **Why Is the Ocean Blue?**
Chapter 18 **Shining Some Light on Lightning**
Chapter 19 **Magnetism: What's the Attraction?**

Virginia

inter**active**
SCIENCE

Interactive Science

Virginia Interactive Science is a program that features 3 pathways to match the way you learn.

- The write-in student edition enables you to become an active participant as you read about science.

- A variety of hands-on activities will not only engage you but also provide you with a deep understanding of the Virginia Standards of Learning.

- Go to MyScienceOnline.com to access a wide array of digital resources built especially for Virginia students like you!

 Interact with your textbook.

 Interact with inquiry.

 Interact online.

HOW CAN **WIND** KEEP YOUR **LIGHTS ON?**

What are some of Earth's energy sources?

This man is repairing a wind turbine at a wind farm in Texas. Most wind turbines are at least 30 meters off the ground where the winds are fast. Wind speed and blade length help determine the best way to capture the wind and turn it into power. Develop Hypotheses Why do you think people are working to increase the amount of power we get from wind?

_____
_____
_____
_____

UNTAMED SCIENCE Watch the **Untamed Science** video to learn more about energy resources.

78   Energy and Energy Resources

 Focus on the Virginia Standards
Each chapter begins with a Big Question ❓ . This Big Question sets a clear learning target and helps you develop a deeper understanding of the Virginia Standards of Learning. . . . .

Built for Virginia

Fully aligned to the Virginia Standards of Learning, Virginia Interactive Science provides comprehensive support to prepare you for the SOL test!

Build Reading, Inquiry, and Vocabulary Skills

- In every lesson you will learn new Reading and Inquiry skills to help you read and think like a scientist.

- Go online to MyScienceOnline.com and click on My Reading Web to get additional reading at your level.

Go Online!

At MyScienceOnline.com, you will find a variety of engaging digital resources such as the Untamed Science videos. Follow the Untamed Science video crew as they travel the globe exploring the Big Ideas of Science.

Unlocking the Virginia Standards

my science online.com

Go to MyScienceOnline.com to access a wide array of digital resources such as Virtual Labs, additional My Planet Diary activities, and Got It? assessments with instant feedback.

Focus on the Virginia Standards

Each lesson starts with key concept questions to help you unlock the chapter's Big Question ❓. The Virginia Standards of Learning are tied to the key concept questions. That means when you see a key ✦, you are learning your Virginia Standards.

My Planet Diary

At the start of each lesson, My Planet Diary will introduce you to amazing events, significant people, and important discoveries in science or help you to overcome common misconceptions about science concepts.

apply it!

Elaborate further with the Apply It activities. This is your opportunity to take what you've learned and apply those skills to new situations.

Explore the Virginia Standards Through Inquiry

Look for the Lab Zone triangle throughout your lesson. This means that it's time to do a hands-on inquiry lab. There's a Lab Zone activity for each key question—that means you can learn each Virginia content standard as well as the process standards through hands-on inquiry! • • • • • • • • • • •

ertile area becomes depleted
become a desert. The
eas that previously were
t uh fih KAY shun).
. For example, a **drought**
alls in an area. During
r, the exposed soil easily
y cattle and sheep and
se desertification, too.
People cannot grow crops
n has occurred. As a result,
Desertification is severe in
there are moving to the
rt themselves on the land.

Key
- Existing desert
- High-risk area
- Moderate-risk area

in areas where there
a on the map to support

tification, what are some
its effects?

Land Reclamation Fortunately, it is possible to replace land damaged by erosion or mining. The process of restoring an area of land to a more productive state is called **land reclamation**. In addition to restoring land for agriculture, land reclamation can restore habitats for wildlife. Many different types of land reclamation projects are currently underway all over the world. But it is generally more difficult and expensive to restore damaged land and soil than it is to protect those resources in the first place. In some cases, the land may not return to its original state.

FIGURE 4 • • • • • • • • • • • • • • • • •
Land Reclamation
These pictures show land before and after it was mined.

🖋 **Communicate** Below the pictures, write a story about what happened to the land.

🔖 Assess Your Understanding

1a. Review Subsoil has (less/more) plant and animal matter than topsoil.

b. Explain What can happen to soil if plants are removed?

c. Apply Concepts Wha
that could prevent
land reclamation?

got it?

○ **I get it!** Now I know that soil management is important because

○ **I need extra help** with

Go to MY SCIENCE 🌐 COACH *online for help with this subject.*

Lab zone — Do the Quick Lab *Modeling Soil Conservation.*

got it?

Evaluate Your Progress

After answering the Got It question, think about how you're doing. Did you get it or do you need a little help? Remember, **MY SCIENCE ⓢ COACH** is there for you if you need extra help.

Assessing the Virginia Standards

Explore the Big Question

At one point in the chapter, you'll have the opportunity to take all that you've learned to further explore the Big Question.

Pollution and Solutions

EXPLORE THE BIG ?

What can people do to use resources wisely?

FIGURE 4 ....

REAL-WORLD INQUIRY All living things depend on land, air, and water. Conserving these resources for the future is important. Part of resource conservation is identifying and limiting sources of pollution.

✎ **Interpret Photos** On the photograph, write the letter from the key into the circle that best identifies the source of pollution.

Land
Describe at least one thing your community could do to reduce pollution on land.

_____
_____
_____

Air
Describe at least one thing your community could do to reduce air pollution.

_____
_____
_____

Water
Describe at least one thing your community could do to reduce water pollution.

_____
_____
_____

Pollution Sources

A. Sediments

B. Municipal solid waste

C. Runoff from development

Lab zone Do the Q
Getting C

⬛ **Assess Your Understa**

1a. Define What are sediments?

b. Explain How can bacteria help cle
spill in the ocean?

c. ANSWER What can people do to use
resources wisely?

d. CHALLENGE Why might a compan
to recycle the waste they produce
would reduce water pollution?

got it? ....

○ I get it! Now I know that water
can be reduced by _____

○ I need extra help with _____

Go to MY SCIENCE 🌐 COACH onli
with this subject.

ANSWER THE BIG ?

Answer the Big Question ....

Now it's time to show what you know and answer the Big Question.

Review What You've Learned

Use the Chapter Study Guide to review the Big Question and prepare for the test.

CHAPTER 4 Review and Assessment

LESSON 4 Water Pollution and Solutions

11. Why is fresh water a limited resource?
   a. because most water on Earth is in lakes
   b. because most water on Earth is in clouds
   c. because most water on Earth is in the ground
   d. because most water on Earth is salt water

12. A _____ is a chemical that kills crop-destroying organisms.

13. Draw Conclusions Rain may wash fertilizers into bodies of water, such as ponds. How might fertilizer affect a pond?

What can people do to use resources wisely?

17. Every individual, including young people, can make decisions to use resources wisely. Use the terms *reduce*, *reuse*, and *recycle* to explain how the students in the picture below can help minimize solid waste.

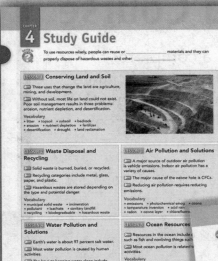

CHAPTER 4 Study Guide

To use resources wisely, people can reuse or _____ materials and they can properly dispose of hazardous wastes and other _____.

LESSON 1 Conserving Land and Soil

Three uses that change the land are agriculture, mining, and development.

Without soil, most life on land could not exist. Poor soil management results in three problems: erosion, nutrient depletion, and desertification.

Vocabulary
• litter • topsoil • subsoil • bedrock
• erosion • nutrient depletion • fertilizer
• desertification • drought • land reclamation

LESSON 2 Waste Disposal and Recycling

Solid waste is burned, buried, or recycled.

Recycling categories include metal, glass, paper, and plastic.

Hazardous wastes are stored depending on the type and potential danger.

Vocabulary
• municipal solid waste • incineration
• pollutant • leachate • sanitary landfill
• recycling • biodegradable • hazardous waste

LESSON 3 Air Pollution and Solutions

A major source of outdoor air pollution is vehicle emissions. Indoor air pollution has a variety of causes.

The major cause of the ozone hole is CFCs.

Reducing air pollution requires reducing emissions.

Vocabulary
• emissions • photochemical smog • ozone
• temperature inversion • acid rain
• radon • ozone layer • chlorofluoro...

LESSON 4 Water Pollution and Solutions

Earth's water is about 97 percent salt water.

Most water pollution is caused by human activities.

The keys to keeping water clean include cleaning oil spills, proper sewage treatment, and the reduction of pollutants.

Vocabulary
• groundwater • pesticide • sewage • sediment

LESSON 5 Ocean Resources

Resources in the ocean include _____ such as fish and nonliving things such...

Most ocean pollution is related to _____ activities.

Vocabulary
• nodule • upwelling

168 Land, Air, and Water Resources

Review and Assessment

MY SCIENCE | Land, Water, and Air Resources | MY SCIENCE COACH | PRACTICE TEST

LESSON 1 Conserving Land and Soil

1. What is an agricultural use of land?
   a. growing crops on land
   b. collecting water on land
   c. building structures on land
   d. removing minerals from land

2. Plant roots absorb nutrients and water from the layer of soil called _____.

3. Relate Cause and Effect What type of land use can result in nutrient depletion? Explain.

LESSON 2 Waste Disposal and Recycling

4. What is one benefit of recycling?

LESSON 3 Air Pollution and Solutions

7. Which of the following describes a pollutant that has been released into the air?
   a. sewage   b. leachate
   c. sediment   d. emissions

8. The _____ in the upper atmosphere prevents some of the sun's ultraviolet radiation from reaching Earth.

9. Predict Do you think the hole in the ozone layer will increase or decrease in size? Why?

10. Solve Problems Describe two ways a large city can reduce air pollution.

169

Practice the Virginia Standards

Practice key concepts at the end of each chapter in the SOL test format to prepare you for the "big test."

Virginia SOL Test Prep

Read each question and choose the best answer.

1 What might be one reason scientists would build a model of Earth like the one shown here?

   A to show the color of the continents
   B to show the depths of Earth's oceans
   C to show the layers of Earth
   D to show pressure inside Earth

2 Nicole measured the height of her locker as 39.8 cm, 42.3 cm, 42.0 cm, and 43.1 cm. The locker is actually 45.5 cm. Which best describes Nicole's measurements?
   F They were accurate.
   G They were precise.
   H They were both accurate and precise.
   J They were neither accurate nor precise.

3 Which SI unit would you use to measure the volume of a tomato?
   A gram
   B grams per cubic meter
   C cubic centimeter
   D newton

4 The median for the data set 32, 40, 38, 41, 36 is
   F 9
   G 38
   H 93.5
   J 187

5 Suppose you are cleaning up after a scientific investigation in the laboratory. As you are cleaning a glass container, it slips from your hands and breaks in the sink. What should you do?
   A Pick up the broken glass.
   B Leave the broken glass in the sink.
   C Tell your teacher or another adult in the room.
   D Recycle the broken glass.

6 What kind of trend do the data show?

   F linear
   G positive
   H no trend
   J nonlinear

85

Assess the Virginia Standards Online

Go to MyScienceOnline.com to show what you know and get extra help. Through Savvas Successnet®, you can take benchmark assessments online. Activities are assigned to you immediately based on your performance on each Virginia Standard of Learning.

SAVVAS SuccessNet   Help   Close

Jennifer Smith, Grade 6
Benchmark Test 2: Unit 1, Part 2

Test Report

Your score is 29 out of 33 : 87.88%

Successfully completed:

Apply knowledge of word origins
Distinguish fact
Analyze tone
Make generalizations
Describe how the author's perspective affects the text
Analyze, interpret, and evaluate information, ideas, organization, and language from textbooks
Distinguish between the facts found in documents, narratives, charts, maps, tables and other sources and the generalizations and interpretations that are drawn from them
Recognize symbolism
Understand and use parts of speech correctly
Verify facts

You need to continue working on :

Use/understand homophones

Question Number

= Correct   = Incorrect

my science online.com

159

xxxi

Explore Your Complete Online Virginia Course

Virginia *MyScienceOnline.com* is a complete online course featuring exciting Untamed Science Videos, Interactive Art Simulations, and innovative personalized learning solutions like My Science Coach and My Reading Web.

> INTERACTIVE ART

At MyScienceOnline.com, many of the beautiful visuals in your book become interactive so you can extend your learning.

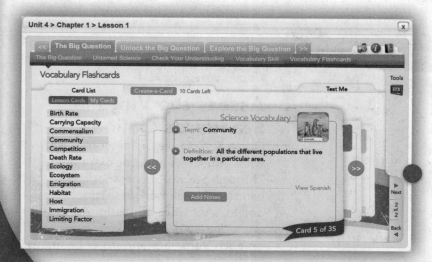

> VOCAB FLASH CARDS

Practice chapter vocabulary with interactive flash cards. Each card has an image, definitions in English and Spanish, and space for your own notes.

VIRTUAL LAB

Get more practice with realistic virtual labs. Interact with on-line labs without costly equipment or clean-up.

Your Virginia Online Student Edition

Create an online notebook! Highlighted important information and post-it notes are saved in your profile.

? BIG IDEAS OF SCIENCE

Have you ever worked on a jigsaw puzzle? Usually a puzzle has a theme that leads you to group the pieces by what they have in common. But until you put all the pieces together you can't solve the puzzle. Studying science is similar to solving a puzzle. The big ideas of science are like puzzle themes. To understand big ideas, scientists ask questions. The answers to those questions are like pieces of a puzzle. Each chapter in this book asks a big question to help you think about a big idea of science. By answering the big questions, you will get closer to understanding the big idea.

✏ **Before you read each chapter, write about what you know and what more you'd like to know.**

BIGIDEA

Scientists use scientific inquiry to explain the natural world.

Firefighters use science to put out fires. For example, they must know what types of chemicals to use on different types of fires.

What do you already know about how science affects your everyday life? ✏ **What more would you like to know?**

_____

_____

_____

Big Question:

? How do science and society affect each other? Chapter 1

✏ **After reading the chapter, write what you have learned about the Big Idea.**

_____

_____

_____

BIGIDEA

Scientists use mathematics in many ways.

Scientists rely on estimates when they cannot obtain exact data. Estimating is a quick way of determining how many birds are in this photo.

Which math skills have you used to study science? ✏ **Which math skills do you need to practice?**

_____

_____

_____

Big Question:

? How do scientists use measurement and mathematics? Chapter 2

✏ **After reading the chapter, write what you have learned about the Big Idea.**

_____

_____

_____

BIGIDEA

Atoms are the building blocks of matter.

Many ionic compounds form crystals. Some crystals have a cubic shape, like these crystals of halite, or sodium chloride.

Na⁺

Cl⁻

If the building blocks of matter are the same, then what makes everything different?

✏️ **What more would you like to know?**

_____

_____

_____

Big Questions:

❓ How is matter described? Chapter 3

❓ How is the periodic table organized? Chapter 5

❓ How can bonding determine the properties of a substance? Chapter 6

✏️ **After reading the chapter, write what you have learned about the Big Idea.**

_____

_____

BIGIDEA

Mass and energy are conserved during physical and chemical changes.

Over the years, the Statue of Liberty has changed from a shiny copper to this bluish-green color because of its exposure to oxygen in the air. During these changes, the total mass and energy of the statue's atoms have been conserved.

If you burn a candle, gradually the candle becomes smaller. What happens to the part of the candle that burns away? Does it cease to exist?

✏️ **What more would you like to know?**

_____

_____

Big Questions:

❓ Why does a substance change state? Chapter 4

❓ How is matter conserved during a chemical reaction? Chapter 7

❓ What determines the properties of a solution? Chapter 8

✏️ **After reading the chapter, write what you have learned about the Big Idea.**

_____

_____

BIGIDEA

A net force causes an object's motion to change.

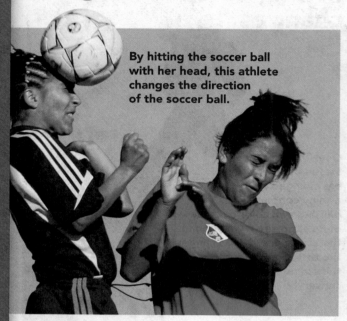

By hitting the soccer ball with her head, this athlete changes the direction of the soccer ball.

What do you already know about how the force of one object can affect the movement of another object? ✎ **What more would you like to know?**

_____
_____
_____
_____

Big Questions:

❓ How do you describe the motion of an object? Chapter 9

❓ How do objects react to forces? Chapter 10

✎ **After reading the chapters, write what you have learned about the Big Idea.**

_____
_____
_____
_____

BIGIDEA

Energy can take different forms but is always conserved.

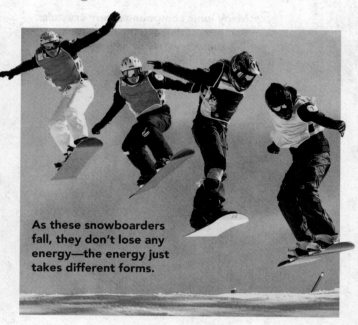

As these snowboarders fall, they don't lose any energy—the energy just takes different forms.

What do you already know about what happens to the mass and energy of a candle as it burns? ✎ **What more would you like to know?**

_____
_____
_____
_____

Big Questions:

❓ How do machines make it easier to do work? Chapter 11

❓ How is energy conserved in a transformation? Chapter 12

❓ How does heat flow from one object to another? Chapter 13

✎ **After reading the chapters, write what you have learned about the Big Idea.**

_____
_____
_____

BIGIDEA

Waves transmit energy.

What do you already know about waves and how they travel from one place to another?

✏️ **What more would you like to know?**

_____

_____

_____

_____

Big Questions:

❓ What are the properties of waves?
Chapter 14

❓ What determines the pitch and loudness of sound? Chapter 15

❓ What kinds of waves make up the electromagnetic spectrum? Chapter 16

❓ How does light interact with matter?
Chapter 17

❓ How does an electric circuit work?
Chapter 18

❓ How are electricity and magnetism related?
Chapter 19

✏️ **After reading the chapters, write what you have learned about the Big Idea.**

_____

_____

_____

The light and heat that lightning gives off travels in the form of electromagnetic waves.

HOW COULD POLLUTION FROM ASIA AFFECT PEOPLE IN THE ARCTIC?

How do science and society affect each other?

These children are sledding in Igloolik, Nunavut, in northern Canada. The sky is so blue and clear that you would think that the cold arctic air would be fresh and clean. However, pollution generated thousands of kilometers away affects the air, snow, water, wildlife, and people of the Arctic. Pollutants from burning fossil fuels migrate north. High concentrations of chemicals that evaporate from televisions, paints, and pesticides in countries worldwide, have been found in the people that live in small Arctic towns like Igloolik.

Develop Hypotheses **How do you think pollution produced thousands of kilometers away ends up in the Arctic?**

_____

_____

_____

_____

> UNTAMED SCIENCE Watch the **Untamed Science** video to learn more about scientific inquiry.

Using Scientific Inquiry

Science Standards of Learning

PS.1f, PS.1g, PS.1i, PS.1j, PS.1k, PS.1l, PS.1m, PS.1n

1 Getting Started

Check Your Understanding

1. **Background** Read the paragraph below and then answer the question.

> Emi studied hard to prepare for her science lab investigation. She was concerned because her **research** was complex. However, it was also well **organized**. Emi wanted to use her lab report as a **sample** of her science work.

> **Research** is information collected from careful study of a subject.

> To be **organized** is to be arranged in an orderly way.

> A **sample** is a portion of something that is used to represent the whole thing.

• Why would being organized help Emi prepare for her lab investigation?

_____

_____

_____

> MY READING WEB If you have trouble completing the question above, visit **My Reading Web** and type in *Using Scientific Inquiry.*

Vocabulary Skill

Identify Multiple Meanings Words you use every day may have different meanings in science. Look at the different meanings of the words below.

Word	Everyday Meaning	Scientific Meaning
model	*n.* A person who poses for an artist Example: Julio worked as a *model* for a sculptor in Daytona Beach.	*n.* A representation of an object or process Example: A globe is a *model* of Earth.
cost	*n.* The price paid by someone for a certain object or service Example: The *cost* of the train ticket was $35.	*n.* An undesirable outcome of a decision Example: Dirty air might be one *cost* of not using "clean" energy.

2. **Quick Check** Circle the sentence below that uses the scientific meaning of the word *cost*.

• The cost of repairing the highway was $12 million.

• One cost of building a new highway might be more cars on the road.

science

subjective reasoning

controlled experiment

A B C

opinion

Chapter Preview

LESSON 1
- science • observing
- quantitative observation
- qualitative observation
- classifying • inferring
- predicting • analyzing
- 🔁 Identify Supporting Evidence
- 🔺 Observe

LESSON 2
- skepticism • data
- empirical evidence
- objective reasoning
- subjective reasoning
- pseudoscience
- 🔁 Outline
- 🔺 Interpret Data

LESSON 3
- scientific inquiry • hypothesis
- independent variable
- dependent variable
- controlled experiment • bias
- repeated trial • replication
- scientific explanation
- 🔁 Summarize
- 🔺 Develop Hypotheses

LESSON 4
- scientific literacy
- evidence • opinion
- 🔁 Summarize
- 🔺 Interpret Data

 VOCAB FLASH CARDS For extra help with vocabulary, visit **Vocab Flash Cards** and type in *Using Scientific Inquiry.*

How Scientists Work

my planet Diary

The Road to Discovery

Today, paclitaxel is one of the most effective drugs against cancer. But it was not well known until Dr. Susan Horwitz's work drew attention to it. Horwitz went to college to study history, but after taking a biology class, she became fascinated with how scientists form and test their ideas. After graduating with a biology degree, she went on to a graduate program in biochemistry. At the time, there were very few women in graduate schools, but that didn't stop Dr. Horwitz. Armed with a doctorate degree, Horwitz eventually moved to her current position at Albert Einstein School of Medicine. It was there that she discovered how paclitaxel stopped the growth of cancer cells. Her work convinced pharmaceutical companies to turn paclitaxel into a medicine that now saves many lives.

BIOGRAPHY

Model of the paclitaxel molecule

Write your answers to each question below.

1. Why did Susan Horwitz decide to become a scientist?

_____

_____

_____

_____

2. What do you think is the difference between the way historians and scientists think?

_____

_____

_____

_____

▶ PLANET DIARY Go to **Planet Diary** to learn more about how scientists work.

Lab zone Do the Inquiry Warm-Up
How Does a Scientist Think?

Vocabulary

- science • observing • quantitative observation
- qualitative observation • classifying • inferring
- predicting • analyzing

Skills

↻ **Reading:** Identify Supporting Evidence
△ **Inquiry:** Observe

How Do Scientists Explore the Natural World?

Paclitaxel is one of the many great success stories of science. **Science** is a way of learning about the natural world. Science is also the knowledge gained through this exploration. 🔑 **Scientists explore the natural world by using skills such as observing, classifying, making models, inferring, and predicting. They form and test their ideas through scientific investigation.**

Observing Paclitaxel is a drug made from the bark of the Pacific yew tree, shown in **Figure 1.** The seeds and leaves of all yew trees are poisonous, but Native Americans found that they could make teas from the bark and needles. They observed that drinking the tea sometimes made people who were sick feel better. **Observing** means using one or more of your senses to gather information. Native Americans observed the effects of the tea on sick people and decided that the tea could help treat headaches and other health problems. Observing also means using tools, such as a microscope, to help your senses.

Observations can be quantitative or qualitative. A **quantitative observation** deals with numbers, or amounts. For example, seeing that a person has a fever of 101 degrees Fahrenheit is a quantitative observation. A **qualitative observation** deals with descriptions that cannot be expressed in numbers. Feeling that a person's head is warm is a qualitative observation.

FIGURE 1 ···
What Do You Observe?
The photo shows the berries and bark of the slow-growing and ancient Pacific yew tree.

✏️ △ **Observe** Write one quantitative observation and one qualitative observation about the tree.

_____

_____

_____

5

Organizing Data

In 1962, plant biologists collected samples of different types of trees. They were searching for a cure to cancer. They sent the samples back to a laboratory that ran tests to see what effect these samples had on cancer cells. Then the samples were classified according to their results. **Classifying** is grouping together items that are alike in some way. Paclitaxel, from the yew tree sample, was classified as having anticancer effects. **Figure 2** shows a test that can be used to classify samples.

Making Models

Once people realized that paclitaxel had an effect on cancer cells, they needed to figure out what it was made of. They built a model that showed the arrangement of atoms in a molecule of paclitaxel. Making models involves creating representations of complex objects or processes. Some models can be made of actual objects, such as balls and sticks. Others are in the form of drawings or mathematical equations. Models help people study things that can't be observed directly. By using models, scientists were able to better understand the properties of paclitaxel.

Inferring

Susan Horwitz examined how paclitaxel affected cancer cells. The invention of the electron microscope allowed scientists to observe how cells divide. From her observations, Horwitz inferred that paclitaxel stopped cancer cells from dividing.

When you explain or interpret things that you observe, you are **inferring**. Making an inference is not guessing. Inferences are based on reasoning from your prior knowledge and from what you observe. By making inferences about how paclitaxel worked, Horwitz was able to show that paclitaxel could be an effective anticancer drug.

FIGURE 2 ···

Classifying Cancer Colonies

Scientists observed the effects of different tree samples on cancer cells. Each petri dish began with 10 colonies of cancer cells. The diagrams show the results after being treated with the tree samples.

✏ **Complete these tasks.**

1. **Observe** Count and record the number of cancer cell colonies below each petri dish.

2. **Infer** What can you infer about each of the samples from the petri dishes that were treated?

_____

_____

_____

3. **Classify** Which sample(s) should be classified as possible cancer treatment(s)? Explain.

_____

Predicting Paclitaxel only kills some kinds of cancer cells. After running tests on mice, scientists made predictions about what types of human cancer paclitaxel might treat. **Predicting** means making a statement or a claim about what will happen in the future based on past experience or evidence.

Scientists planted human tumors onto mice. Then they gave the mice paclitaxel. The mice with breast tumors showed signs of recovery. From this observation, scientists predicted that paclitaxel could help treat breast cancer.

Predictions and inferences are related. While inferences are attempts to explain what has already happened, predictions are forecasts about what will happen. If you see a puddle of water on the floor, you might infer that a glass spilled. If, however, you see someone bump into a glass, you can predict that it's about to make a mess.

Identify Supporting Evidence Determine if the statement below is a prediction or an inference. Then underline the sentence in the text that supports your answer. "The alarm clock is blinking 12:00 because the electricity went out temporarily."

do the math!

Only a small amount of paclitaxel can be produced from the bark of a single Pacific yew. It requires 120 kilograms of paclitaxel to treat 60,000 patients with 2 grams each of the drug per year.

❶ Calculate If 1 kilogram of bark can produce about 0.015 kilogram of paclitaxel, how much bark is needed to make 120 kilograms of paclitaxel?

_____

_____

❷ CHALLENGE You need to cut down 3 trees to get about 5 kilograms of bark. About how many trees do you have to cut down each year to make enough paclitaxel for 60,000 patients?

_____

_____

❸ Evaluate the Impact on Society Some people think that the destruction of so many trees and the habitat of forest animals was too high a price to pay for paclitaxel. Explain why you agree or disagree with this opinion.

_____

_____

_____

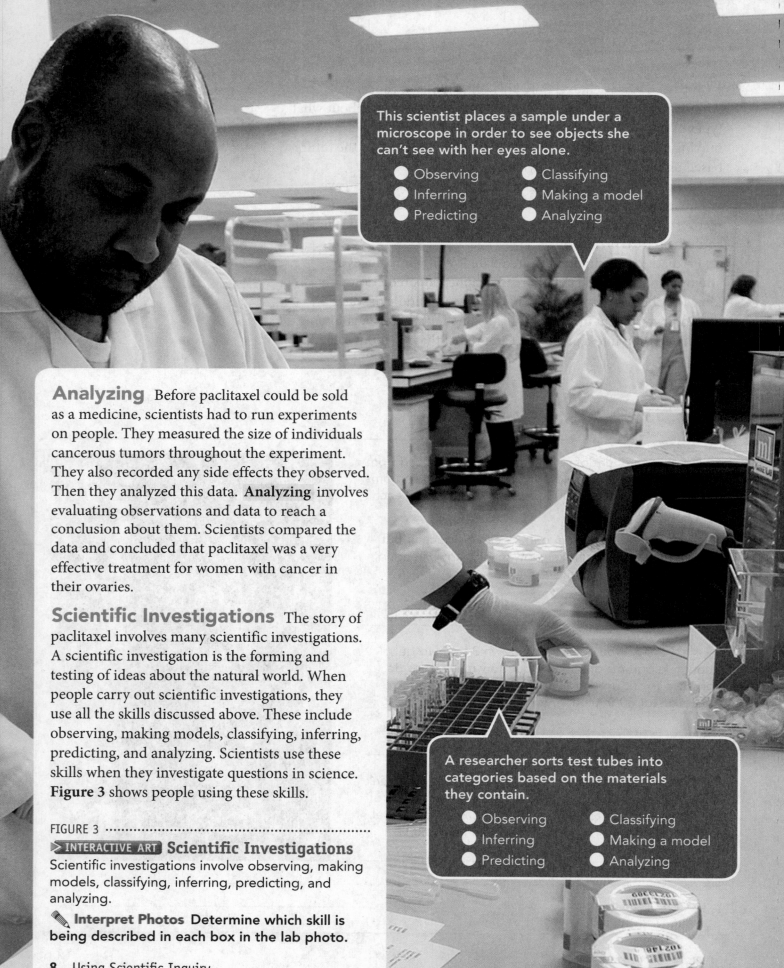

This scientist places a sample under a microscope in order to see objects she can't see with her eyes alone.

- ● Observing
- ● Inferring
- ● Predicting
- ● Classifying
- ● Making a model
- ● Analyzing

Analyzing Before paclitaxel could be sold as a medicine, scientists had to run experiments on people. They measured the size of individuals cancerous tumors throughout the experiment. They also recorded any side effects they observed. Then they analyzed this data. **Analyzing** involves evaluating observations and data to reach a conclusion about them. Scientists compared the data and concluded that paclitaxel was a very effective treatment for women with cancer in their ovaries.

Scientific Investigations The story of paclitaxel involves many scientific investigations. A scientific investigation is the forming and testing of ideas about the natural world. When people carry out scientific investigations, they use all the skills discussed above. These include observing, making models, classifying, inferring, predicting, and analyzing. Scientists use these skills when they investigate questions in science. **Figure 3** shows people using these skills.

FIGURE 3 ···

▶ INTERACTIVE ART **Scientific Investigations**
Scientific investigations involve observing, making models, classifying, inferring, predicting, and analyzing.

✎ **Interpret Photos** Determine which skill is being described in each box in the lab photo.

A researcher sorts test tubes into categories based on the materials they contain.

- ● Observing
- ● Inferring
- ● Predicting
- ● Classifying
- ● Making a model
- ● Analyzing

Scientists often use whiteboards to draw sketches of molecules or other objects they observe in order to study them more closely.

- ● Observing
- ● Inferring
- ● Predicting
- ● Classifying
- ● Making a model
- ● Analyzing

After data have been collected, this researcher examines them to find results and draw conclusions.

- ● Observing
- ● Inferring
- ● Predicting
- ● Classifying
- ● Making a model
- ● Analyzing

Communicate Describe a time you used one or more scientific skills to answer a question about the natural world. Then, discuss your answer with a classmate.

_____

_____

_____

_____

Lab® Do the Quick Lab *Scientific Skills.*
zone

🔑 Assess Your Understanding

1a. Define A (qualitative/quantitative) observation is a property that is observed in a science investigation, but cannot be expressed with numbers.

b. Explain Describe three skills people use to conduct scientific investigations.

_____

_____

_____

_____

_____

_____

_____

_____

c. Pose Questions Ask a question about the natural world that you would like to test.

_____

_____

_____

got it? ....

○ **I get it!** Now I know that scientists test their ideas using skills including _____

_____

_____

_____

○ **I need extra help with** _____

_____

_____

_____

Go to **MY SCIENCE ⓢ COACH**
online for help with this subject.

The Characteristics of Scientific Knowledge

UNLOCK THE BIG ?

🔑 **What Do Scientific Investigations Involve?**
PS.1f, PS.1g, PS.1i, PS.1j, PS.1k, PS.1l

🔑 **What Are Scientific and Pseudoscientific Thinking?**
PS.1j

🔑 **What Characterizes Science and Its Methods?**
PS.1j

MY PLANET DIARY

BIOGRAPHY

A Scientific Success

Dr. Percy Lavon Julian (1899–1975) was a renowned research chemist who grew up and studied in Indiana. His first experiments isolated simple compounds found in plants. He used this knowledge to later develop drugs to treat glaucoma, slow down the effects of Alzheimer's disease, and prevent miscarriages. Julian also created aerofoam, a flame retardant that saved the lives of countless sailors during World War II.

Dr. Percy Julian became the first African-American chemist inducted into the National Academy of Sciences in 1973.

Communicate Discuss the question with a partner. Write your answer below.

Why do you think it's important for scientists like Dr. Julian to be curious?

_____

_____

_____

_____

Lab zone® Do the Inquiry Warm-Up *Developing a Theory.*

> **PLANET DIARY** Go to **Planet Diary** to learn more about scientific investigations.

Vocabulary

- skepticism • data • empirical evidence
- objective reasoning • subjective reasoning
- pseudoscience

Skills

↻ Reading: Outline

△ Inquiry: Interpret Data

What Do Scientific Investigations Involve?

As you just read, scientists use certain skills, such as observing and inferring, in scientific investigations. They also bring important attitudes to investigations. These attitudes include curiosity, honesty, creativity, and open-mindedness, or the willingness to accept new ideas. But scientists are also skeptical. Their **skepticism**, which is an attitude of having doubt, keeps scientists from accepting faulty ideas and may lead to new understandings.

🔑 **In addition to the skills and attitudes of scientists, scientific investigations involve collecting evidence in a scientific way and using that evidence to make inferences and to reach conclusions.** Figure 1 shows an investigation that researchers performed with crows to find out if crows could recognize an individual human face. To test their idea, researchers wore caveman masks while they trapped, banded, and released several of the crows living in a group in a specific area. During this process, the captured crows cawed loudly. Later, researchers walked among the group of crows to observe how the banded crows reacted. On different walks, the researchers wore the caveman masks, different masks, or no masks.

FIGURE 1 ···

Cause and Effect

Researchers wanted to see if crows could recognize a specific human face.

✏️ **Complete these tasks.**

1. **Classify** Read the two statements below. Write *O* next the statement that is an observation. Write *I* next to the statement that is an inference.

   _____ The crow caws because it does not like to be handled.

   _____ The crow caws when it is banded.

2. **Observe** Use the evidence from the During Capture picture to circle the banded crows in the After Capture picture.

3. **Identify** Look at the After Capture picture. What are some other ways besides cawing that the crows reacted?

   _____

   _____

During Capture

After Capture

Collecting Empirical Evidence In the crow investigation, the researchers walking among the crows recorded their observations in notebooks. The information they recorded is called data. **Data** (singular: *datum*) are facts, figures, and other evidence collected during a scientific investigation.

When data are collected in a precise, logical, and consistent manner, the data are called empirical evidence. **Empirical evidence** is data that are collected using scientific processes that describe particular observations. All scientific investigations involve the collection of relevant empirical evidence. **Figure 2** shows some of the data that the crow researchers collected on some of their walks.

FIGURE 2 ....

> REAL-WORLD INQUIRY **Conclusions and Empirical Evidence**

The table below uses tally marks to show the number of times that a banded crow had a specific type of reaction to two different researchers at a certain site.

✎ **Answer the questions on each notebook page.**

1. **Make Generalizations** Why might a scientist choose to use a table to record this kind of data?

_____

_____

A Banded Crow's Reactions	Researcher Wearing Caveman Mask	Researcher Wearing Different Mask
No reaction	—	ⅢⅢ Ⅰ
Looking at researcher	Ⅱ	—
Looking at and cawing at researcher	Ⅲ	—
Cawing and following researcher	Ⅲ Ⅰ	—

2. **Interpret Data** Using the data from the table, make a bar graph in the space below, or on a computer or calculator. Label the x- and y-axes of your graph.

☐ Wearing Caveman Mask

☐ Wearing Different Mask

Analyzing Empirical Evidence

After scientists collect empirical evidence, they carefully look for patterns in it that allow them to make inferences and predict trends. Once they have collected a lot of data that show the same patterns, they use logic and reasoning to state a conclusion. In the crow investigation, the researchers studied all the data they collected. Each set of data showed a similar pattern. Crows banded by the researchers cawed at and followed researchers wearing caveman masks more often than other researchers without masks or with different masks. Therefore, the researchers concluded that crows can recognize an individual human face.

3. **Infer** Based on the information in the graph, make an inference about whether or not crows can recognize an individual human face. Explain the reasoning that led to your inference.

Crow Study

Inference: _____

_____

Reasoning: _____

_____

_____

_____

_____

_____

_____

_____

_____

Do the Quick Lab Activities of Science.

🔑 Assess Your Understanding

1a. Review (Empirical evidence/Logical reasoning) is data collected using scientific processes that describe particular observations.

b. Relate Evidence and Explanation What evidence allowed the crow researchers to conclude that crows can recognize an individual human face?

_____

_____

_____

_____

_____

_____

_____

c. Apply Concepts Some people might tell stories about an animal recognizing them. How might skepticism about such stories lead to new explanations?

_____

_____

_____

_____

_____

_____

got it? ....

○ **I get it!** Now I know scientific investigations involve _____

_____

_____

_____

○ **I need extra help with** _____

_____

Go to **MY SCIENCE ⑤ COACH** *online for help with this subject.*

What Are Scientific and Pseudoscientific Thinking?

Recall that the crow researchers used reasoning to review their data. Then the researchers drew a logical conclusion from their data. Scientific thinking requires a logical way of reasoning based on gathering and evaluating evidence. Look at **Figure 3.** Scientific thinking can be divided into two general types of reasoning: objective reasoning and subjective reasoning.

Objective and Subjective Reasoning

Objective reasoning is reasoning that is based on evidence. Because scientific reasoning relies on gathering and evaluating evidence, it is objective reasoning.

In contrast, **subjective reasoning** is reasoning that is based on personal feelings or personal values. For instance, you might think crows are stupid. As a result, you might conclude crows could not possibly recognize humans. If you based your conclusion on your personal feelings, you could reach the wrong conclusion.

Look at the photograph in **Figure 3.** By being able to distinguish between objective and subjective reasoning, you can distinguish between strong scientific claims and less reliable assertions.

✎ **Outline** Read the text and complete the outline.

1. _____
   a. Based on evidence
   b. Example: _____
   _____
2. Subjective Reasoning
   a. _____
   _____
   b. Example: Crows are stupid.

FIGURE 3 ....

Subjective Reasoning
Personal feelings can be misleading. In science, conclusions are based on objective reasoning.

✎ **Look at the photograph of a horseshoe crab and answer the questions.**

1. **Describe** What words would you use to describe horseshoe crabs? Are your words based on opinion or on objective reasoning?

_____
_____
_____
_____

2. **Apply Concepts** The blood of horseshoe crabs is often used to ensure that some vaccines do not contain potentially deadly contamination from bacteria. Knowing this, what new words would you use to describe this animal?

_____
_____
_____

Science Versus Pseudoscience For thousands of years, people imagined that patterns in the stars looked like humans, animals, or objects. What does the star pattern in **Figure 4** look like to you? Perhaps you know that astronomy is the scientific study of stars. But do you know what astrology is? It is the use of stars to predict the course of human events. Unlike astronomy, astrology is not a science.

Astrologists claim that the course of human life in part depends on the stars. They make use of data regarding the positions of the stars. But they base their predictions on subjective reasoning rather than empirical evidence. So astrology can be classified as a pseudoscience. A **pseudoscience** is a set of beliefs that may make use of science. But the conclusions and predictions of a pseudoscience are not based on observation, objective reasoning, or scientific evidence.

🔑 **Science is based on empirical evidence and well-reasoned interpretation of data. Pseudoscience may make use of scientific data. But the conclusions of pseudoscience are based on subjective reasoning, faulty reasoning, or faulty beliefs, not on careful examination of evidence.**

Taurus

Aldebaran

FIGURE 4 ···

Starry-Eyed
Scientists make use of empirical evidence and relevant data to draw conclusions. People who practice pseudoscience do not.

✏️ **Identify Faulty Reasoning Look at the outline above of the star pattern called Taurus (also known as "the bull"). Identify whether each statement below is based on science (S) or on pseudoscience (P).**

_____ People whose zodiac sign is Taurus tend to be loyal.

_____ Aldebaran is the brightest star in the constellation Taurus.

_____ Each year, Taurus reaches its highest point in the sky in January.

_____ Taurus is a constellation, or pattern of stars.

_____ Scientists know that bulls are colorblind. So many people whose zodiac sign is Taurus cannot tell green and red apart.

15

Nonscientific Ways of Knowing

The study of science provides a logical, well-reasoned understanding of the natural world. But understanding other aspects of the world requires training outside of science. Look at **Figure 5.** Many artists apply their understanding of mathematics when they use points, lines, angles, shapes, and sizes to define spaces. But knowing mathematics would not provide you with a complete understanding of the meaning of an abstract painting. You would need training in the history and principles of art to fully understand the aesthetics, or beauty, of such a painting.

The study of science can also provide only a partial understanding of subjects such as philosophy and history. For example, scientists do not claim to be able to explain the meaning of life. Nor do scientists seek to explain the circumstances that led to major historic events.

"Untitled" (1920) by George Grosz.
© 2009 VAGA

FIGURE 5 ···

Eyes of the Beholder

Many artists create beauty in their art by using the science of defining spaces in a series of lines, angles, and shapes.

✎ CHALLENGE Find three simple shapes in the painting and outline them. How does your appreciation of this piece of art relate to the science of shapes? How does it relate to your personal sense of beauty?

_____

_____

_____

_____

 Do the Quick Lab *Scientific Thinking.*

🔑 Assess Your Understanding

2a. Summarize The conclusions of (science/pseudoscience) are based on subjective reasoning.

b. Identify Faulty Reasoning Is palm-reading a science or a pseudoscience? Explain.

_____

_____

_____

_____

got it?

○ **I get it!** Now I know that science is based on empirical evidence. Although pseudoscience makes use of scientific data, the conclusions of pseudoscience are based on _____

_____

○ **I need extra help with** _____

_____

Go to MY SCIENCE ⬣ COACH *online for help with this subject.*

What Characterizes Science and Its Methods?

Science Standards of Learning

PS.1j Make valid conclusions after analyzing data.

🔑 **Science is characterized by an ordered approach to learning about the world.** This approach relies on using skills to collect empirical data, analyzing the data to find patterns that lead to inferences and trends, and using objective reasoning to reach conclusions. Because scientific investigations are ordered, other scientists can repeat them.

apply it!

Scientists once thought that coral reefs thrive only in shallow water because sunlight can easily reach them. But in 1999, scientists discovered a reef off Florida's southwest coast that lies at depths between 60 and 80 meters. Scientists think that this reef thrives because the water around it is extremely clear so sunlight can reach it.

1 Summarize How did scientists revise their original thinking to explain where coral reefs can thrive?

_____

_____

2 Discuss How does the revised idea illustrate the nature of science?

_____

_____

_____

Coral at Florida's Pulley Ridge

Although science is based on empirical evidence and objective reasoning, its results are open to change. Sometimes, scientific investigations produce data that show new patterns. If the new patterns do not contradict existing ones, scientists keep their existing conclusions, or perhaps revise them slightly. However, sometimes, new patterns contradict existing patterns. Scientists must then throw out their old conclusions.

 Lab zone Do the Quick Lab *Science and Its Methods.*

🔑 **Assess Your Understanding**

got it?.....................

○ **I get it!** Now I know that science is characterized by _____

_____

○ **I need extra help with** _____

Go to **MY SCIENCE COACH** online for help with this subject.

Designing an Experiment

UNLOCK THE BIG ?

🔑 **What Is Scientific Inquiry?**
PS.1k

🔑 **How Do You Design an Experiment?**
PS.1f, PS.1g, PS.1i, PS.1j, PS.1k, PS.1n

🔑 **What Is a Scientific Explanation?**
PS.1f, PS.1n

MY PLANET DiARY

DISCOVERY

A Galactic Garden

Orbiting Earth is an amazing experience. But eating dehydrated space food can be boring and unappetizing. So, scientists conducted an experiment to see whether they could grow vegetables in space. They picked an old Thanksgiving favorite: sweet potatoes. They grew some cuttings onboard a shuttle and some cuttings on Earth. The cuttings were placed under similar conditions in space and on Earth for five days. They discovered that the number of roots that sprouted were the same in both places. But the roots of those in space actually grew faster! The cuttings that grew in space had more sugar and starch than those on Earth. Astronauts, however, hope that space potatoes taste just as good!

Write your answers to each question below.

1. What was the purpose of the experiment?

_____

_____

_____

_____

2. Why do you think the scientists grew cuttings both in space and on Earth?

_____

_____

_____

_____

_____

_____

> PLANET DIARY Go to **Planet Diary** to learn more about designing experiments.

Lab zone® Do the Inquiry Warm-Up What's the Question?

Vocabulary

- scientific inquiry • hypothesis • independent variable
- dependent variable • controlled experiment • bias
- repeated trial • replication • scientific explanation

Skills

↻ **Reading:** Summarize

△ **Inquiry:** Develop Hypotheses

What is Scientific Inquiry?

It's Monday morning. You drag yourself out of bed and go to the kitchen. You pour yourself a bowl of cereal with milk and eat a spoonful. Yuck! Something tastes awful. The milk has gone sour. What happened? Your questioning is the beginning of the **scientific inquiry** process. **Scientific inquiry is the process of gathering evidence about the natural world and proposing explanations based on this evidence.**

Posing Questions and Defining a Problem

Scientific inquiry often begins with a question that leads to an observation. Your observation about the sour milk may lead you to ask a question: What made the milk go bad so quickly? Questions come from your experiences, observations, and natural curiosity. Look at **Figure 1** to pose a question about the strawberries.

Once you've posed your question, you should define a problem that can be tested. It is possible that others have already investigated the same problem. You can do research to find what information is known about the topic before you try to answer your question.

Science Standards of Learning

PS.1k Use research methods to investigate practical problems and questions.

Look for the milk icon to follow the steps of the scientific inquiry.

✎ **Identify** In the text, circle the question posed about the sour milk.

FIGURE 1 ···

Posing Questions

Scientific inquiry starts with a question.

✎ **Pose Questions** Observe the photo. Then pose a question you could test about the strawberries.

_____

_____

_____

Develop Hypotheses
Underline an explanation about souring milk in the text. Then write your own explanation about why the milk went sour.

_____
_____
_____

Developing a Hypothesis
How could you answer your question about the milk becoming sour? You start by developing a hypothesis. A **hypothesis** (plural: *hypotheses*) is a possible answer to a scientific question. It is also a possible explanation. For example, you know that you bought the milk five days ago. You also know that you left the milk out overnight. So, you may suspect that the temperature at which the milk is kept contributes to how quickly the milk goes sour. Your hypothesis might be that milk turns sour more quickly if it is left at room temperature for too long. Use **Figure 2** to practice developing a hypothesis.

Hypotheses are not facts. In science, a fact is an observation or description that has been confirmed repeatedly. For example, that milk has calcium is a fact that describes something found in milk. However, a hypothesis is one possible explanation to answer a question.

In science, you must be able to test a hypothesis. Researchers perform investigations and collect data that either support or fail to support a hypothesis.

FIGURE 2 ···
Developing a Hypothesis
Adam wonders why he has been sleeping less than usual.

Develop Hypotheses Write an explanation that might answer Adam's question.

_____
_____
_____

Lab zone® Do the Quick Lab *It Starts With a Question.*

🔑 Assess Your Understanding

1a. Pose Questions Write a testable question about what causes cavities.

_____
_____

b. Develop Hypotheses Write another possible explanation for why milk sours.

_____
_____

got it?

○ **I get it!** Now I know that scientific inquiry is

_____
_____
_____
_____

○ **I need extra help with** _____

Go to **MY SCIENCE** ⬤ᔆ **COACH** online for help with this subject.

How Do You Design an Experiment?

Once you have a hypothesis, you need to test it. 🔑 **You can design an experiment that follows reliable scientific principles to test a hypothesis.** To test a hypothesis that milk will sour quicker if left out at room temperature than at colder temperatures, you could smell the milk periodically when it is left out at room temperature. But how do you know that the milk wouldn't turn sour in the refrigerator? You cannot know unless you smell the milk periodically when it is left in the refrigerator, as well.

Controlling Variables Suppose you want to test the temperature. You could observe how milk smells when it is kept at different temperatures over time. All other variables, or factors that can change in an experiment, must be the same. This includes variables such as the type of milk used and the container it's kept in. By keeping these variables the same, you will know that any differences in the odor of the milk are due to temperature alone.

The one factor that is purposely changed to test a hypothesis is the **independent variable.** In this experiment, the independent variable is air temperature. The factor that may change in response to the independent variable is the **dependent variable.** Here, the dependent variable is the time it takes the milk to sour. Look at **Figure 3**.

FIGURE 3 ···

Controlling Variables

A student wants to test whether shampoo cleans oily hair better than water alone. The student mixes oil with water in one test tube and oil with soapy water in another test tube. She watches to see when the mixture separates.

 Use the data table to complete the activities.

1. **Classify** What is the independent variable? What is the dependent variable?

_____

_____

2. **Identify** Name two other possible variables in this experiment.

_____

_____

3. **Draw Conclusions** Write a summary of what was observed in this experiment. What can you conclude?

_____

_____

Science Standards of Learning

PS.1f Identify independent and dependent variables, constants, controls, and repeated trials.

PS.1g Construct and interpret data tables showing the independent and dependent variables, derived quantities, and the number of trials.

PS.1i Construct and interpret frequency distributions, scatterplots, line plots, and histograms.

PS.1j Make valid conclusions after analyzing data.

PS.1k Use research methods to investigate practical problems and questions.

PS.1n Use current applications of physical science concepts.

✏️ **Name** In the text, circle the independent variable and underline the dependent variable for the milk experiment.

Amount of Soap in Water (mL)	Time of Oil and Water Separation (seconds)
0	15
1.5	105

21

Summarize Explain how bias can affect an experiment.

_____

_____

_____

_____

_____

Designing a Controlled Experiment A scientific experiment in which only one variable is changed at a time is called a **controlled experiment.** You decide to test the milk at three different temperatures, as shown in **Figure 4.** All other variables are kept the same. If your experiment were to have more than one independent variable, there would be no way to tell which variable influenced your results.

For example, in this experiment you are testing the effect of three temperatures on the time it takes milk to sour. You will keep all variables the same, except temperature. However, if you were to use different types of milk for each of your samples or kept each sample in a different kind of container, then you would not know which variable caused the milk to sour quickly. Was it temperature? Was it the type of milk? For this reason, you can only test one variable at a time in a controlled experiment.

Experimental Bias In any experiment there is a risk of introducing experimental **bias,** an error in the design of the experiment. The error may make a particular result more likely. For example, without meaning to, you might use a carton of milk that is beyond its expiration date.

FIGURE 4 ·······················
▷ VIRTUAL LAB **A Controlled Experiment**
In this experiment, the temperatures must be different enough that your results can only be due to temperature.

✎ **Complete the activities.**

1. **Design Experiments** Label each milk sample with the temperature at which it could be tested. (*Hint:* Average room temperature is 22°C.)

2. **Apply Concepts** What is another variable that must be kept the same for each milk sample?

_____

_____

3. **Analyze Sources of Error** How could testing milk that is past its expiration date introduce experimental bias?

_____

_____

_____

Collecting and Interpreting Data

You are almost ready to begin your experiment. You decide to test the milk every 12 hours. Before starting your experiment, determine what observations you will make and what data you will gather. Recall that data are the facts, figures, and other information gathered through qualitative and quantitative observations. A helpful tool to use while collecting data is a data table. A data table is an organized way to collect and record your observations.

After your data have been collected, they need to be interpreted. Tools such as diagrams, graphs, and models can help you interpret data. They can reveal patterns or trends. For example, you might organize the data for the milk experiment in a graph. You could use the graph to compare the time it took for each sample to sour.

do the math!

Information organized in a data table can be made into a graph. This data table shows the percent of students who finished testing over a period of time.

❶ Graph Plot the data on the graph. Identify the independent and dependent data.

Students Finished (%)	Time (min)
0	30
2	45
50	60
98	75

_____

_____

_____

_____

_____

Percent of Students Finished Testing Over Time

❷ Read Graphs Describe the difference in the percent of students finished testing between 30 and 45 minutes and between 45 and 60 minutes.

_____

_____

_____

_____

❸ CHALLENGE After about how many minutes would you predict that all the students will finish their testing?

_____

✎ **Identify the Main Idea**
Underline the sentence(s) in
the text that summarize what
to consider when you draw a
conclusion.

Drawing Conclusions Once you've collected your data, you can draw a conclusion. A conclusion is a summary of what you have learned from an experiment. When drawing a conclusion, examine the data objectively to see if the results support or fail to support your hypothesis. Also, consider whether the data allow you to draw a conclusion at all based on the results.

You may decide that the data support your hypothesis. The milk at room temperature smelled sour sooner than the milk kept refrigerated. Now, repeat your experiment to see if you get the same results. A conclusion is unreliable if it comes from the results of one experiment. Many trials are needed before a hypothesis can be accepted as true. A **repeated trial** is a repetition of an experiment.

Sometimes your data won't support your hypothesis. When this happens, check your experiment for errors, or bias, and for improvements. Maybe you could have tested the milk every 6 hours. Sometimes you cannot draw a firm conclusion from your data. For example, you might discover that milk left at room temperature, 22°C, soured sooner than milk left at 35°C.

Hypotheses are valuable even when they are not supported by the data. They can lead to further investigation. For example, you may decide to test whether milk's exposure to light has an effect on how quickly it sours. How would you design an experiment to test your new hypothesis?

A student dipped squares of nylon, polyester, and cotton in water and hung them up to dry. He then measured the amount of time the squares took to dry.

❶ Analyze Experimental Results Before the experiment, the student hypothesized that nylon dries the fastest. Do the data support his hypothesis? Explain.

_____

_____

Fabric	Trial 1	Trial 2	Trial 3	Trial 4
Nylon	28 min	25 min	27 min	33 min
Polyester	17 min	19 min	19 min	25 min
Cotton	44 min	45 min	45 min	51 min

❷ Identify Experimental Bias Are the results from one trial different from the others? If so, how might the student have introduced bias that resulted in the different results?

_____

_____

_____

❸ Apply Concepts Based on these results, what kind of socks would you want to wear on a fishing trip?

_____

Communicating

Scientists communicate, or share their results with others through writing and speaking. They give talks at meetings, exchange information on the Internet, or publish articles in scientific journals.

When scientists share the results of their research, they describe their procedure and data so that others can repeat their experiments. A **replication** is an attempt by a different group of scientists to conduct the same experiment. Different groups of scientists must run replications and obtain similar results before these results can be used as evidence to support a hypothesis. Even after results are accepted, ongoing skepticism can lead to new understanding of a scientific replication.

Sometimes, scientists from around the world work together on scientific inquiries that are part of a larger project. For example, the International Space Station is one of the largest international scientific projects in history. Sixteen nations participate in it. The goal is to conduct experiments in unusual conditions, such as near-weightlessness. On such a large project, scientists must share their ideas and results regularly.

Scientific results must be published in written form using appropriate international standards and formats so that other scientists around the world can replicate the results.

✎ **Communicate**
You conclude that milk left at room temperature (22°C) sours quicker than refrigerated milk. Write a catchy newspaper headline that communicates this to other scientists.

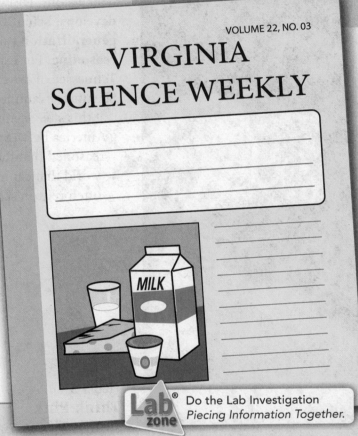

VOLUME 22, NO. 03

VIRGINIA SCIENCE WEEKLY

Lab zone® Do the Lab Investigation
Piecing Information Together.

🔑 Assess Your Understanding

2a. Identify At the beach, a student tests the effectiveness of three sunscreens, each with a different sun protection factor. What is the independent variable in her experiment?

_____

_____

b. Design Experiments Controlling _____ and eliminating _____ are important parts of designing an experiment.

got it? . . . .

○ I get it! Now I know that you design an experiment _____

_____

○ I need extra help with _____

Go to MY SCIENCE ⓢ COACH *online for help with this subject.*

PS.1f Identify independent and dependent variables, constants, controls, and repeated trials.

PS.1n Use current applications of physical science concepts.

What Is a Scientific Explanation?

If you are studying chemistry or physics, you can usually design and conduct controlled experiments, as shown in **Figure 5.** If you are studying astronomy or geology, however, it can be difficult or even impossible to carry out controlled experiments.

When you study astronomy or geology, you are often trying to understand how things happened in the past. You must make observations and then use what you already know to draw conclusions. Drawing a conclusion from observations is a way to develop a **scientific explanation.** **A scientific explanation is a generalization that makes sense of observations by using logical reasoning.** For example, in 2000, workers digging a road in Tennessee discovered a layer of black soil filled with bones. Scientists examined the bones to find out what animals had lived at this site. Scientists knew these animals had lived in North America between 4 and 7 million years ago. Using this data, they reasoned that the site must be the same age! Things in the natural world that cannot be studied through a controlled experiment often rely on scientific explanation.

FIGURE 5 ···

Think Pink

Baby flamingos are born with white feathers, but over time they turn bright pink. Sometimes the feathers of adult flamingos fade back to white. Why does this happen?

✏️ **Design Experiments** Plan an investigation to determine if something in their diet causes flamingos' feathers to turn pink.

❶ Question

Does a flamingo's diet of shrimp affect the color of its feathers?

❷ Hypothesis

_____

_____

Do the Quick Lab *How Can You Explain It?*

Variables

Independent Variable

_____

_____

Dependent Variable

_____

_____

Factors to Control

_____

_____

_____

_____

④ Procedure

_____

_____

_____

_____

_____

_____

⑤ Analyze Information

Scientific Skills Used

_____

_____

_____

Possible Sources of Error

_____

_____

_____

Alternative Explanations

_____

Assess Your Understanding

3a. Review What is one problem that studying the past causes for a geologist?

_____

_____

_____

_____

_____

b. Summarize How does a scientist explain something when a controlled experiment cannot be carried out?

_____

_____

_____

_____

_____

_____

c. Make Generalizations What types of sources might a scientist use to investigate a question about flamingos before designing an experiment?

_____

_____

_____

_____

_____

got it? ....

○ **I get it!** Now I know that a scientific

explanation is _____

_____

○ **I need extra help with** _____

Go to my science ⑤ coach *online for help with this subject.*

27

Scientific Literacy

UNLOCK THE BIG ?

🔑 **Why Is Scientific Literacy Important?**
PS.1k, PS.1n

🔑 **How Do You Analyze Scientific Claims?**
PS.1j, PS.1k, PS.1n

🔑 **How Do You Research Scientific Questions?**
PS.1k, PS.1n

MY PLANET DIARY

DNA Detective

If you watch TV crime programs, then you know that investigators often use DNA testing to solve a case. How does DNA testing help? Scientists can identify people by examining their DNA. A person's DNA is unique, like a person's fingerprint.

In the future, you may need more information about DNA evidence than what is given in TV programs. For example, if you are selected to sit on a jury in a trial that uses DNA evidence, you will want to know scientific details about DNA to make your decision.

FUN FACTS

Communicate Discuss the question with a partner. Then write your answer below.

A DNA sample links an accused suspect to a crime. Suppose there is a one in ten million chance that the DNA sample comes from someone else. How would this affect your decision as a juror?

_____

_____

_____

_____

▷ PLANET DIARY Go to **Planet Diary** to learn more about scientific literacy.

Lab zone® Do the Inquiry Warm-Up *Posing Questions.*

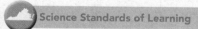
Science Standards of Learning

PS.1k Use research methods to investigate practical problems and questions.

PS.1n Use current applications of physical science concepts.

Why Is Scientific Literacy Important?

Suppose someone asks you to sign a petition to protect the Canada geese in your town. "People are trying to keep the geese away from our parks!" he says. A person standing nearby says, "But the geese make an awful mess." You're confused. You know you need to learn more about the issue.

Vocabulary
- scientific literacy
- evidence
- opinion

Skills
- Reading: Summarize
- Inquiry: Interpret Data

Scientific Literacy To understand the many issues you encounter, you need scientific literacy. **Scientific literacy** means understanding scientific terms and principles well enough to ask questions, evaluate information, and make decisions. 🔑 **By having scientific literacy, you will be able to identify good sources of scientific information, evaluate them for accuracy, and apply the knowledge to questions or problems in your life.**

Evidence and Opinion To evaluate scientific information, you must first distinguish between evidence and opinion. In science, **evidence** includes observations and conclusions that have been repeated. Evidence may or may not support a scientific claim. An **opinion** is an idea that may be formed from evidence but has not been confirmed by evidence. In **Figure 1,** try separating evidence from opinion.

Summarize In your own words, summarize the second paragraph.

_____
_____
_____
_____
_____
_____
_____
_____
_____

FIGURE 1 .....

Evidence and Opinion
Should your town try to keep Canada geese away from the parks?

✏️ **Distinguish Evidence and Opinion** Under each statement in the boxes, label the statement as evidence or opinion.

Geese spend up to 12 hours a day eating grass and roots.
_____

Geese are too messy.
_____

 Do the Quick Lab *Scientific Literacy Survey.*

🔑 Assess Your Understanding

got it? .....

O **I get it!** Now I know that by having scientific literacy _____
_____

O **I need extra help with** _____

Go to MY SCIENCE COACH *online for help with this subject.*

29

How Do You Analyze Scientific Claims?

Scientific literacy gives you the tools to analyze scientific claims. Scientific reasoning gives you the process. **You can use scientific reasoning to analyze scientific claims by looking for bias and errors in the research, evaluating data, and identifying faulty reasoning.**

FIGURE 2 ···

Analyzing Scientific Claims

✎ Read about this research and think about the researcher's conclusion. Then answer the question in each box.

A researcher needs to find out if people in a town have good computer skills. The researcher advertises online for participants to take the test. He offers a free thumb drive as a payment.

Twenty people take the test. Everyone gets a perfect score.

The researcher concludes that the town's residents have excellent computer skills.

Identify Experimental Bias What is an important source of experimental bias in this research?

_____

_____

_____

Analyze Sources of Error What is an important source of error in this research?

_____

_____

_____

_____

apply it!

Read the sample advertisement. Then use scientific reasoning to analyze its claims.

1 ⚠ **Interpret Data** How many subjects were in the study?

_____

2 **Evaluate Scientific Claims** Do the research results support the claim that using *KnowHow* helps people get better grades? Explain your answer.

_____

_____

_____

_____

3 [CHALLENGE] Was Subject B's score actually 25% higher than Subject A's score? Calculate.

_____

_____

Lab zone® Do the Quick Lab *Analyzing Claims.*

🔑 Assess Your Understanding

1a. Identify What is one way to use scientific reasoning to analyze scientific claims?

_____

_____

_____

b. Make Generalizations Would a scientific claim based on one test be a good claim? Why or why not?

_____

_____

got it?

○ **I get it!** Now I know that I can analyze scientific claims by _____

_____

_____

○ **I need extra help with** _____

Go to MY SCIENCE ⓢ COACH *online for help with this subject.*

How Do You Research Scientific Questions?

Chances are you will need to answer scientific questions to make decisions in your life. For example, suppose you injure your knee and the doctor gives you a choice of treatments. You need to do research before deciding. In science, you also need to do research to design an experiment.

🔑 **To make decisions and design experiments, you need relevant and reliable background information.** Relevant information is knowledge that relates to the question. Reliable, or consistent and truthful, information comes from a person or organization that is not biased. Generally, universities, museums, and government agencies are sources of reliable information. So are many nonfiction books, magazines, and educational Web sites. Look at the sources in **Figure 3**.

Vocabulary Use Context to Determine Meaning
Underline the phrase in the text that helps you understand the word *relevant*.

FIGURE 3 ·······························

Evaluating Sources of Information

✎ **Evaluate Data Reliability** Circle the most relevant and reliable source of information for your research about water use in your community. Explain your choice below.

_____

_____

_____

🌐 World Wide Web

File   Edit   View   Help

http://www.|

Water Usage   Search

All About Water Use
How much do you know about the water you use? Take this quiz. By
Mr. Pickle's 6th-Grade Class

Effect of Water Rate Increases on Reducing Water Usage in Sydney
NSW Government, Australia

Water Usage by County
Your State Government Office of Water Resources and Conservation

EXPLORE THE BIG ? All Bottled Up!

How do science and society affect each other?

1 Clear plastics that could be used to make light, cheap bottles were invented.

2 Manufacturers made many plastic bottles for many beverages, which people buy.

3 Empty plastic bottles became litter. Bottle deposit laws encouraged recycling empty bottles.

4 Ways to recycle bottles into new, safe products were invented.

5 People bought products made from recycled bottles.

6 Bottles that use 30% less plastic were designed.

FIGURE 4 ·······

▷ REAL-WORLD INQUIRY Science and society are interconnected.

✎ **Infer** Circle the boxes that show the work of science. Then explain below how the statements in boxes 3 and 4 show how science and other aspects of society affect each other.

_____
_____
_____
_____

Lab® zone Do the Quick Lab *Sources of Information.*

🔑 **Assess Your Understanding**

2a. Review What is information that relates to a question called?
_____

b. How do science and society affect each other?
_____
_____
_____
_____
_____

got it? ·······

○ **I get it!** Now I know that to make informed decisions and design experiments, you

need _____

_____

○ **I need extra help with** _____

Go to **MY SCIENCE ⓢ COACH** *online for help with this subject.*

REVIEW THE BIG ?

Science affects society by allowing individuals, communities, and countries to analyze the _____ and _____ of a decision.

LESSON 1 How Scientists Work

🔑 Scientists explore the natural world by using skills such as observing, classifying, making models, inferring, and predicting. They form and test their ideas through scientific investigation.

Vocabulary
- science • observing
- quantitative observation
- qualitative observation
- classifying • inferring
- predicting • analyzing

LESSON 2 The Characteristics of Scientific Knowledge

🔑 Scientific investigations involve collecting and using evidence.

🔑 Science is based on empirical evidence and well-reasoned interpretation of data.

🔑 Science is characterized by an ordered approach to learning about the world.

Vocabulary • skepticism • data
- empirical evidence • objective reasoning
- subjective reasoning • pseudoscience

LESSON 3 Designing an Experiment

🔑 Scientific inquiry is the process of gathering evidence and proposing explanations.

🔑 You can design an experiment that follows reliable scientific principles to test a hypothesis.

🔑 A scientific explanation is a generalization about observations by using logical reasoning.

Vocabulary • scientific inquiry • hypothesis
- independent variable • dependent variable
- controlled experiment • bias
- repeated trial • replication • scientific explanation

LESSON 4 Scientific Literacy

🔑 By having scientific literacy, you will be able to identify good sources of scientific information, evaluate them for accuracy, and apply the knowledge to questions or problems in your life.

🔑 You can use scientific reasoning to analyze scientific claims by looking for bias and errors in the research, evaluating data, and identifying faulty reasoning.

🔑 To make decisions and design experiments, you need relevant and reliable background information.

Vocabulary
- scientific literacy • evidence • opinion

Review and Assessment

LESSON 1 **How Scientists Work**

1. When scientists group information into categories, they are

   a. analyzing.   **b.** making models.

   c. classifying.   **d.** observing.

2. Finding that the length of a caterpillar is 4.5 centimeters is a(n) _____ observation.

3. Infer What inference might a scientist make if she observed an increase in her energy after eating an afternoon snack?

_____

_____

_____

_____

LESSON 2 **The Characteristics of Scientific Knowledge**

4. Empirical evidence is data and observations that have been collected through

   a. the Internet.   **b.** inferring.

   c. scientific processes.   **d.** the imagination.

5. An attitude of doubt toward ideas is

_____.

6. Write About It Neurology is, in part, the study of the brain's functions to determine how the brain controls the human nervous system. Phrenology is the study of the shape of a person's skull to determine that person's personality. Both neurology and phrenology are based on evidence that specific areas of the brain control specific functions. Which is a science? Which is a pseudoscience? Explain.

LESSON 3 **Designing an Experiment**

7. What is often the first step in scientific inquiry?

   a. developing a hypothesis

   b. posing a question

   c. designing an experiment

   d. collecting data

8. The variable that is purposely changed in order to be tested is the _____

_____

9. Compare and Contrast How are repetition and replication of an experiment different?

_____

_____

_____

10. Why is it important to have only one independent variable?

_____

_____

_____

_____

_____

11. How do tools such as diagrams, graphs, and models help you understand the results of an experiment?

_____

_____

_____

12. A scientific explanation makes sense of observations using _____ reasoning.

LESSON 4 **Scientific Literacy**

13. Being able to understand basic scientific terms and principles well enough to apply them to your life is called

    a. evidence.   **b.** opinion.

    c. scientific literacy.   **d.** scientific questioning.

14. When you perform scientific research, you should look for information that is _____

15. **Pose Questions** A scientific study proves that frozen fruit is more nutritious than canned fruit. What questions would you want answered before you accept this claim?

    _____

    _____

    _____

    _____

    _____

16. **Evaluate Data Reliability** You are working on a science fair project and need to gather research on your topic. Where will you look for reliable information? Identify at least three different sources.

    _____

    _____

    _____

    _____

    _____

    _____

 APPLY THE BIG ? **How do science and society affect each other?**

17. Scientists are studying the effects that melting ice might have on rising sea levels. Describe how the results of these studies might affect society.

    _____

    _____

    _____

    _____

    _____

    _____

    _____

    _____

    _____

    _____

    _____

    _____

    _____

    _____

    _____

    _____

Mark only one answer for each question.

1 Lia tested the effect of temperature on plant growth. Before the experiment, she hypothesized that plants grow better in warm temperatures. The results of the experiment are shown below.

How would you *best* describe the results of Lia's experiment?

A The results support the hypothesis.

B The results fail to support the hypothesis.

C No conclusion can be drawn from the results.

D The results are inaccurate.

2 Drew made observations while visiting the pet store. Which of the following is a quantitative observation he may have made?

F The store sells hamsters.

G The dogs are fed at 4:00 in the afternoon.

H The store's employees wear blue aprons.

J There are ten more cats than rabbits.

3 A controlled experiment—

A introduces bias

B tests several variables at once

C tests only one variable and is free of bias

D changes no variables

4 Jamie is testing how caffeine intake affects heart rate. In the experiment, what is the amount of caffeine consumed called?

F the dependent variable

G the independent variable

H the hypothesis

J the repeated trial

5 Determining that the moon is the same age as Earth based on comparison of the age of moon rocks to the age of Earth rocks is an example of—

A a scientific explanation

B a qualitative observation

C an estimate

D anomalous data

6 A scientist measured the distance that a stream of lava from a volcano flowed over 5 minutes. Which statement is *best* supported by the scientist's data?

F The lava flowed faster with time.

G The lava flowed at a constant rate.

H The lava flowed slower with time.

J The lava will reach 100 m at 6 min.

Seismic-SAFE BUILDINGS

Suppose you are on the highest floor of a tall building in your town. An earthquake strikes. What features might help the building withstand the powerful effects of an earthquake?

Tension ties firmly "tie" the floors and ceilings of the building to the walls, and work to absorb and scatter earthquake energy.

Base isolators are pads under the first floor that separate, or isolate, the building from its foundation. The pads stop some of an earthquake's energy from entering the building.

Cross braces form a network of steel on the outside of the building to stiffen its frame.

Dampers work like shock absorbers in a car, absorbing some of the energy of seismic waves.

Design It Use cardboard, craft sticks, and modeling clay to build a model of a seismic-safe building. Place your model on a table, and drop a heavy book next to it. Then try bumping the table to shake the model sideways. How well does your building stand up? What changes could you make to improve your structure's stability?

PS.1k, PS.1m

▲ Cross braces on the outside of the building help to support the frame.

ENGINEERING SOLUTIONS

There is no such thing as a typical day for Lisa Short. As a chemical engineer for the United States government, Lisa uses her knowledge of biochemistry to improve the way new medications are developed. Some days she may build, and install, equipment in a biotechnology lab. Or you might find Lisa researching better, faster, and less expensive techniques for producing medications. Other days Lisa works in the lab, analyzing data from experiments.

In high school, Lisa focused on science and math. In college, she majored in chemical engineering, where she learned how to set up experiments, used lab equipment, and studied chemistry and biochemistry. Today she uses that knowledge to improve technology for making medications.

Chemical engineers work in factories, labs, or offices. They work to improve processes and tools for making products from raw materials. These products include medications, cleaning products, paints, cosmetics, and just about anything else that is made by combining ingredients to create a new substance. They are problem solvers who use chemistry to improve how things work. So next time you use soap or hand lotion, or watch someone fill a vehicle with gasoline, realize that a chemical engineer worked to make these products better.

Chemical engineers use laboratory equipment, such as the centrifuge shown here. A centrifuge separates solid or liquid particles in a mixture.

Research It Chemical engineers use chemistry to improve materials. Identify a problem you have experienced with a material that does not do what it is supposed to do. (One example might be plastic wrap that doesn't cling tightly enough.) Write a letter to the company describing the problem and stating how the product should be improved.

 PS.1k

39

HOW CAN SCIENCE SPEED UP A JET?

How do scientists use measurement and mathematics?

This is a model of an F-16XL jet. The model represents just four percent of the jet's actual size. The model is being tested in a wind tunnel where fans blow air towards the jet. Smoke and lasers are then used to show how the air moves around the jet. The scientists are looking for smooth airflow around the jet to increase the jet's performance and reduce engine noise.

Infer Why do you think scientists would make a model of a jet and wind test it before building it?

_____

_____

_____

_____

> **UNTAMED SCIENCE** Watch the **Untamed Science** video to learn more about how scientists use mathematics.

Mathematics and Models in Science

Science Standards of Learning

PS.1a, PS.1b, PS.1c, PS.1d, PS.1e, PS.1g, PS.1h,
PS.1i, PS.1j, PS.1k, PS.1l, PS.1m, PS.1n, PS.7a

2 Getting Started

Check Your Understanding

1. **Background** Read the paragraph below and then answer the question.

> Jane worked as a scientific **researcher** in the field of genetics. She designed experiments that provided **evidence** certain families can be at higher risk for specific diseases. Joan learned that genetics has had a great impact on how **society** treats diseases.

> A **researcher** is anyone who studies a scientific problem.

> **Evidence** is any object or result that indicates a certain theory is true.

> **Society** is an organization of individuals, forming a larger unit such as a city or town.

- What is one activity a scientific researcher does?

_____

> **MY READING WEB** If you have trouble completing the question above, visit **My Reading Web** and type in *Mathematics and Models in Science.*

Vocabulary Skill

High-Use Academic Words High-use academic words are words that are used frequently in academic reading, writing, and discussions. These words are different from key terms because they appear in many subject areas.

Word	Definition	Example
trend	*n.* a general tendency or direction	An increase in song downloads shows a *trend* in the way people purchase music.
periodically	*adv.* at regular intervals	Scientists update their research *periodically* throughout their experiments.

2. **Quick Check** Complete each sentence with the correct high-use academic word.

- Melting glaciers show a _____ toward rising temperatures.

- Birds return to the nest _____ to tend to their chicks.

weight

estimate

model

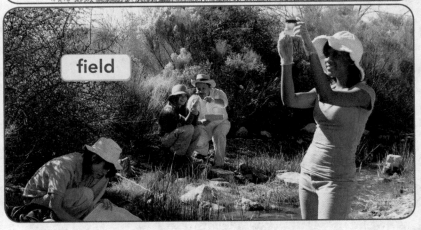

field

Chapter Preview

LESSON 1
- metric system
- International System of Units (SI)
- mass • weight • volume
- meniscus • density

↻ **Ask Questions**
△ **Measure**

LESSON 2
- estimate • accuracy • precision
- significant figures • mean
- median • mode • range
- scientific notation
- anomalous data • percent error

↻ **Identify the Main Idea**
△ **Interpret Data**

LESSON 3
- graph • linear graph
- nonlinear graph • outlier

↻ **Relate Cause and Effect**
△ **Graph**

LESSON 4
- model • system • input
- process • output • feedback

↻ **Identify the Main Idea**
△ **Make Models**

LESSON 5
- field

↻ **Sequence**
△ **Observe**

▷ **VOCAB FLASH CARDS** For extra help with vocabulary, visit **Vocab Flash Cards** and type in *Mathematics and Models in Science.*

43

Scientific Measurement

UNLOCK THE BIG ?

🔑 **Why Do Scientists Use a Standard Measurement System?**
PS.1c

🔑 **What Are Some SI Units of Measure?**
PS.1b, PS.1c, PS.1d, PS.7a

— **610 meters**

MY PLANET DIARY

Tallest or Deepest?

Misconception: The world's tallest structures must be built on land.

Until 2008, the world's tallest structure was the Petronius Compliant Tower, which was built on the ocean floor. This 610-meter-high tower is an oil platform in the Gulf of Mexico located 210 kilometers southeast of New Orleans. The pumps on the tower remove oil and natural gas from the Petronius oil field. Today, the 828-meter-high Burj Khalifa built on land in the city of Dubai, completed in 2010, is the tallest building in the world.

AR MS
• Shreveport
AL GA
TX LA
Lafayette ★ Baton Rouge
• New Orleans □ Petronius Tower FL
Gulf of Mexico

MISCONCEPTION

Communicate Discuss the questions with a partner. Then write your answers below.

1. Name one measurement you think builders had to make when they were constructing the Petronius Compliant Tower.

_____
_____
_____
_____

2. What is the tallest building where you live?

_____
_____

> **PLANET DIARY** Go to **Planet Diary** to learn more about scientific measurement.

Lab zone Do the Inquiry Warm-Up *What Is Scientific Measurement?*

Drawing of the Petronius Compliant Tower

— **0 meters**

Vocabulary
- metric system
- International System of Units (SI)
- mass
- weight
- volume
- meniscus
- density

Skills
- Reading: Ask Questions
- Inquiry: Measure

Why Do Scientists Use a Standard Measurement System?

A standard measurement system enables scientists to share information or repeat experiments done by other scientists. Modern scientists use a version of the metric system called the International System of Units (SI)—from the French *Systéme International d'Unités*. Suppose you decided to measure length using your foot. Your friend decided to measure length using her hand. How would you be able to compare the length of a 5-foot object to a 7-hand one? Without a standard measurement system, it would be hard to share information about the world.

The **metric system** is a standard measurement system based on the number 10. Modern scientists use a version of the metric system called the **International System of Units (SI).** Using SI as the standard system of measurement allows scientists to compare data and communicate with each other about the results of scientific investigations. Mass, length, and many other properties are measured using SI units. All SI units use the same set of prefixes. For example, a paper clip has a mass of about 1 gram. An object with ten times more mass than a paper clip has a mass of 10 grams, or 1 dekagram. A child could be 1 meter tall. A tree that is ten times taller than the child has a height of 10 meters, or 1 dekameter. **Figure 1** shows some common SI prefixes.

Science Standards of Learning

PS.1c Convert among metric units and apply appropriate prefixes.

Ask Questions Write a question you want to know about the SI system.

_____

_____

_____

FIGURE 1 ....

> **VIRTUAL LAB** Prefixes of SI Units

The man in this photo is one of the tallest men in the world at 2.46 meters, or 246 centimeters.

Name Complete the column in the table using the meter, which is the SI unit for length, as the base.

Common SI Prefixes

Prefix	Meaning	Example
kilo- (k)	1,000	_____
deka- (da)	10	_____
no prefix	1	meter
centi- (c)	0.01 (one hundredth)	_____
milli- (m)	0.001 (one thousandth)	_____
micro- (μ)	0.000001 (one millionth)	_____
nano- (n)	0.000000001 (one billionth)	_____

45

do the math!

SI prefixes show how measurements increase or decrease by powers of 10. Use the table of SI prefixes in **Figure 1** to answer the questions.

① Calculate A picnic blanket is 1 meter across. An ant is 1 centimeter in length. How many ants of the same length would fit end-to-end across the length of the picnic blanket?

_____

② Explain The length of the grassy park where the ant lives is 1 kilometer. How many times longer than the ant is the park? Explain your answer.

_____

_____

_____

③ CHALLENGE How could you convert the length of the ant from centimeters to kilometers? How long is the ant in kilometers?

_____

_____

_____

_____

Do the Quick Lab
Measuring With SI.

🔑 Assess Your Understanding

1a. Review The International System of Units, or

_____ , is based on the _____ system.

b. Apply Concepts A nickel coin weighs 5 grams. How many milligrams does it weigh?

_____

c. Calculate Suppose the mass of a dog is 90 pounds. If 1 kilogram is equal to 2.2 pounds, what is the mass of the dog in kilograms?

_____

d. Make Generalizations What might occur if the scientists in one country started to use a different system of measurement than the system used by scientists in the rest of the world?

_____

_____

_____

_____

_____

_____

_____

got it?

○ **I get it!** Now I know that scientists use SI to _____

_____

○ **I need extra help with** _____

   Go to **MY SCIENCE** ⓢ **COACH** online for help with this subject.

What Are Some SI Units of Measure?

Scientists measure length, mass, volume, density, temperature, and time using SI units.

Length Length is the distance from one point to another.
🔑 **The basic SI unit for measuring length is the meter (m).** One meter is about the distance from the floor to a doorknob. Metric rulers are used to measure lengths smaller than a meter, such as a centimeter (cm), or millimeter (mm). A kilometer (km) is 1,000 times longer than a meter. **Figure 2** shows two organisms that can be measured with a ruler.

Conversions for Length

1 km	= 1,000 m
1 m	= 100 cm
1 m	= 1,000 mm
1 cm	= 10 mm

FIGURE 2 ·····························
Wing Length

You can use a metric ruler to measure the length of small objects. Line up one end of the object with the zero mark. Read the number at the other end of the object to find the length.

✏️ **Use the rulers to find the lengths of the bird and butterfly wings. Then complete the activities below.**

1. **Measure** What is the length of each wing?

   _____
   _____

2. **Apply Concepts** Using the table in Figure 1, convert the length of each wing from centimeters to micrometers (μm).

   _____
   _____

Conversions for Mass

1 kg	= 1,000 g
1 g	= 1,000 mg

Mass

Mass is the measure of the amount of matter in an object. **The basic SI unit for measuring mass is the kilogram (kg).** The mass of dogs, people, cars, and other large objects is measured in kilograms. The mass of birds, cell phones, and other small objects is measured in grams (g) or milligrams (mg). Electronic and triple-beam balances are used to measure mass in grams.

When you step on a scale, you are measuring your weight. **Weight** is the measure of the force of gravity acting on an object. The basic SI unit for measuring weight is a measure of force called the newton (N). The pound is a non-SI unit commonly used in the United States to measure weight. When you stand on a scale, gravity pulls down on you and the springs in the scale compress. Gravity has a greater pull on objects with more mass, so these objects weigh more than objects with less mass. Weight changes as gravity changes, so you would weigh less on the moon because it has weaker gravity than Earth. However, an object's mass does not change with a change in gravity. **Figure 3** shows tools for measuring an object's mass and weight.

FIGURE 3 ·······································

Comparing Apples and Oranges

Triple-beam balances use weights to determine an object's mass. A spring scale is used to measure an object's weight.

1. **Measure** Find the mass of the apple by adding the masses of each weight on the balance.

   _____

2. **Define** The spring scale measures the weight of the oranges, which is a measure of the _____ on the oranges.

3. **Infer** Suppose the oranges weigh 16.7 newtons on Earth. How would their weight change if they were on the moon?

   _____

   _____

Volume

Volume A microwave oven takes up space on a countertop. A jug of milk takes up space in the refrigerator. Air spreads out to take up space in a room. **Volume** is the amount of space taken up by an object or substance. 🔑 **The basic SI unit for measuring volume is the cubic meter (m³).** Other units include the liter (L) and cubic centimeter (cm³). Liters are used to measure liquids. Cubic meters or cubic centimeters are used to measure solid objects. Use this page to practice measuring volume.

Conversions for Volume	
1 L	= 1,000 mL
1 L	= 1,000 cm³
1 mL	= 1 cm³

Volume of Liquids

Use a graduated cylinder or beaker to measure the volume of liquids. Pour the liquid into one of these containers and read the level at the bottom of the **meniscus,** or curve of the liquid.
✏️ **Measure What is the total volume of the liquid and berry in this photo?**

_____

Volume of Rectangular Solids

Use a ruler or meterstick to find the volume of rectangular solids. Measure the length, width, and height of the solid. Multiply these three values to get the volume.
✏️ **Calculate What is the volume of the crate?**

_____

30 cm
28 cm
42 cm

Volume of Irregular Solids

You can use the displacement of water to measure the volume of an irregular solid, like a rock or a berry. Fill a graduated cylinder partially full with water. Measure the volume of the water. Now place the berry in the water. Measure the volume of the water again. To get the volume of the berry, subtract the original volume of the water from the volume of water that included the berry.
✏️ **Infer Why would you get a more accurate measure of the volume of an irregular solid by using displacement instead of measuring with a ruler?**

_____

_____

_____

25ml
20
15
10
5

Density A foam brick and a clay brick can be the same size. If you pick them up, the clay brick feels heavy and the foam brick feels light. This is because the clay brick has a higher density than the foam brick. **Density** is the measure of how much mass is contained in a given volume. Units of mass are divided by units of volume to express the density of objects. **The SI unit for density is kilograms per cubic meter (kg/m³), but scientists commonly use grams per milliliter (g/mL) or grams per cubic centimeter (g/cm³) to express density.** Look at **Figure 4** to compare the density of the balls in the picture.

FIGURE 4 ·······························

Predicting Density
Density determines if an object floats or sinks.

✎ **Predict** Circle the ball you think has the lower density. Explain your choice.

_____

_____

_____

_____

_____

_____

Table tennis ball

Golf ball

To find the actual value of an object's density, you can use a mathematical formula for calculating density. Once you have taken measurements to find both the mass and volume of an object, calculate its density using the following formula.

$$\text{Density} = \frac{\text{Mass}}{\text{Volume}}$$

apply it!

Once you find the volume and mass of an object, calculate its density using the formula.

❶ **Identify** Draw a line from the word *Meniscus* to the meniscus of each graduated cylinder.

❷ **Observe** What is the volume of water in each graduated cylinder? What is the volume of the bolt?

_____

_____

❸ **Calculate** The mass of the bolt is 101 grams. Find its density.

_____

_____

Meniscus

Using Density

The density of a pure substance is always the same, no matter how much of the substance you have. For example, the density of fresh water is always 1.0 g/cm^3, whether you have a drop of water or a whole lake. Figure 5 shows the density of some common substances.

When you know the density of an object, you also know whether it will sink or float in water. If an object's density is less than 1.0 g/cm^3, it will float. If its density is greater than 1.0 g/cm^3, the object will sink. If you have an object made out of an unknown substance, you can tell whether its density is greater than or less than 1.0 g/cm^3 by dropping the object in water!

FIGURE 5 ·····················

Using Density

The planet Saturn could float in water because its density is less than 1.0 g/cm^3.

✏️ **Infer** In the table, circle the liquids or solids that would float in water. Put a star next to those that would sink in water.

Densities of Common Substances	
Substance	Density (g/cm³)
Gold	19.3
Gasoline	0.7
Milk	1.03
Water	1.0
Iron	7.8
Air	0.001
Ice	0.9
Aluminum	2.7

✏️ **CHALLENGE** Find the density of the surfboard and determine if the board should float. The surfboard's mass is 14 kg and its volume is 0.0875 m^3. (*Hint:* The density of salt water is equal to about 1,025 kg/m^3.)

_____

_____

Time

How long would it take you to run 100 meters? Did you know that the fastest time recorded for running 100 meters is under 10 seconds? 🔑 **The second (s) is the SI unit used to measure time.** Seconds can be divided into smaller units, such as milliseconds (ms). Sixty seconds make up a minute. Sixty minutes make up an hour. So there are 3,600 seconds in an hour ($60 \times 60 = 3{,}600$).

Time is measured by clocks or stopwatches. A clock can measure time to the nearest second. Stopwatches like the one shown in **Figure 6** can measure time to the nearest hundredth of a second. The official timers used in the Olympics and other sports events can measure time to the nearest thousandth of a second!

FIGURE 6 ·······································

The Race Is On

The stopwatch shows the winning time in the last race at a school swim meet.

✎ **Answer the following questions about the race times.**

1. **Calculate** Jessica swims the last race in 22.56 seconds. By how much time did she lose the race?

_____

_____

2. **Analyze Sources of Error** Why would machine-operated stopwatches be used at sports events instead of hand-operated stopwatches?

_____

_____

_____

_____

_____

Temperature

Did you need a jacket today, or could you wear shorts? You probably checked the temperature to find out. Temperature is a measure of the energy of motion of the particles in a substance. When molecules in air are moving fast and bouncing into each other, temperature is high and you feel hot. When these molecules slow down, temperature is lower and you feel cooler. Temperature affects the properties of some substances. For example, rising temperature can change a substance from a solid to a liquid to a gas.

Probeware and thermometers are instruments that measure temperature. Probeware thermometers consist of digital probes or sensors and accompanying software that can collect and record data on temperature. Thermometers can have different temperature scales. Scientists commonly use thermometers with the Celsius temperature scale to measure temperature. On this scale, water freezes at 0°C and boils at 100°C. Scientists also use thermometers with the Kelvin scale to measure temperature. **Kelvin (K) is the official SI unit for temperature. The Kelvin scale starts at 0 K (absolute zero) and only goes up.** Units on the Kelvin scale are the same size as units on the Celsius scale. Use **Figure 7** to compare the Celsius and Kelvin scales.

FIGURE 7 ·······································

Kelvin and Celsius Scales

Liquid in a thermometer moves up or down as temperature changes.

✎ **Use the thermometer diagrams to complete the tasks.**

1. **Identify** Color in the Celsius thermometer to show how it would look when immersed in boiling water.

2. **Predict** Color in the Kelvin thermometer to show how it would look when immersed in ice water.

3. **CHALLENGE** Use the conversion chart to label the Kelvin thermometer with temperatures that correspond to the boiling point and freezing point of water.

Celsius (°C) Kelvin (K)

Conversions for Temperature

0°C	= 273 K
100°C	= 373 K

Lab zone Do the Quick Lab *A Unit of SI.*

Assess Your Understanding

2a. Identify An SI unit used to measure volume is the (cubic centimeter/millimeter).

b. Sequence What steps would you take to determine the density of a rubber eraser?

_____

_____

_____

_____

_____

got it?

○ **I get it!** Now I know that the SI units for length, mass, volume, density, time, and temperature are _____

_____

_____

○ **I need extra help with** _____

Go to **MY SCIENCE** Ⓢ **COACH** *online for help with this subject.*

Mathematics and Scientific Thinking

🔑 **What Math Skills Do Scientists Use?**
PS.1j

🔑 **What Math Tools Do Scientists Use?**
PS.1e, PS.1h, PS.1j, PS.1k

MY PLANET DIARY

Math in the Environment

For what job do you need to be able to solve for *x* and find the area of a polygon? You may be surprised to learn that people other than math teachers need to have these skills.

Rachel Sweeney is a coastal restoration project manager. Her job involves restoring barrier islands. She helps plan how to prevent erosion by building dikes. Dikes are long walls that help stop flooding.

Rachel uses math in her job every day. She uses estimation to determine the size of a grain of sand. Then she uses equations to calculate the volume of sand she needs to fill the dikes and what the mass of the sand will be. Without these math skills, Rachel's work in saving the environment would not be possible.

CAREER

Answer the questions below.

1. What are two math skills Rachel uses in her job?

_____

_____

2. Think about a job that interests you. How would that job use math?

_____

_____

_____

▷ **PLANET DIARY** Go to **Planet Diary** to learn more about mathematics and science.

With the help of people like Rachel Sweeney, barrier islands such as the ones shown may be saved from erosion.

Rachel Sweeney

Lab zone® Do the Inquiry Warm-Up *How Do Math and Science Work Together?*

Vocabulary

- estimate - accuracy - precision - significant figures
- mean - median - mode - range - scientific notation
- anomalous data - percent error

Skills

- ↻ Reading: Identify the Main Idea
- △ Inquiry: Interpret Data

What Math Skills Do Scientists Use?

The size of a grizzly bear, the number of bees in a hive, and the distance a kangaroo can jump are just a few of the interesting things that scientists investigate. Good math skills are essential as scientists collect and analyze data about their subject. ☞ **When collecting data, scientists use math skills that include estimation, accuracy and precision, and significant figures.**

Science Standards of Learning

PS.1j Make valid conclusions after analyzing data.

Estimation White blood cells help the human body fight disease. When a person's blood is tested, lab technicians count the number of white blood cells in a drop of the patient's blood. Doctors then use this count in their estimate of the total number of white blood cells in all of the patient's blood. An **estimate** is an approximation of a number based on reasonable assumptions. The estimated white blood cell count helps a doctor determine if the patient has an infection. Estimates are useful when it is impossible to count every individual or object. They are also useful when the thing being estimated, such as the distance of a star, cannot be measured directly. Use **Figure 1** to practice estimation.

FIGURE 1 ···
Estimating
This microscopic view shows red and white blood cells.

✎ **Use the photograph to complete these tasks.**

1. **Estimate** How many white blood cells (WBC) are in

   the microscopic field? _____

2. **Calculate** The sample is 500 times smaller than a microliter. A microliter is one millionth of a liter. Estimate the number of white blood cells in a microliter of the patient's blood.

   Number of WBC counted × 500 = _____ WBC per microliter

3. △ **Interpret Data** Patients with white blood cell counts greater than 10,500 WBC per microliter may have an infection. Could this patient have an infection? Explain.

   _____

   _____

55

Accuracy and Precision

When scientists make measurements, they want to be both accurate and precise. **Accuracy** refers to how close the measurement is to the true or accepted value. **Precision** refers to how close a group of measurements are to each other.

Scientists try to use the highest quality tools to take measurements. They also measure the same object more than once. By repeating measurements with high-quality tools, scientists obtain the most accurate and precise results possible. Look at **Figure 2** to determine the accuracy and precision of the measurements.

⊙ **Identify the Main Idea** In the text, underline the main idea that describes how scientists are accurate and precise.

FIGURE 2 ···

Accuracy and Precision

Three teams measured the mass of the turtle below.

✎ **Interpret Diagrams** Determine how accurate and precise each team's measurements are. Circle your answers in the boxes.

Team One	Team Two	Team Three
Measurements	**Measurements**	**Measurements**
1. 172.5 g	1. 154.5 g	1. 153.7 g
2. 172.8 g	2. 121.7 g	2. 153.6 g
3. 172.6 g	3. 177.0 g	3. 153.9 g
This team was (accurate/not accurate).	This team was (accurate/not accurate).	This team was (accurate/not accurate).
This team was (precise/not precise).	This team was (precise/not precise).	This team was (precise/not precise).

Significant Figures

Measurements are never completely precise. For example, a centimeter ruler allows you to measure centimeters precisely because these units are marked evenly with lines. If you want to measure a portion of a centimeter, you have to estimate that measurement between the lines. **Significant figures** communicate how precise measurements are. The significant figures in a measurement include all digits measured exactly, plus one estimated digit. If the measurement has only one digit, you can assume that it is estimated. Look at **Figure 3.**

FIGURE 3 ....

Significant Figures

An encyclopedia is 3.2 cm across its spine. The measurement *3.2 cm* has 2 significant figures, or sig figs. The *3* is a precise measurement. The *2* is an estimate.

✎ **Calculate** Read the boxes below and answer the questions.

Adding or Subtracting Measurements

When you add or subtract measurements, the answer must have the same number of digits after the decimal point as the measurement with the fewest number of digits after the decimal point. If you add an encyclopedia to a row of books that is 42.12 cm, how long will the row be?

  42.12 cm (2 places after the decimal)

+ 3.2 cm (1 place after the decimal)

  45.32 cm ⟶ 45.3 cm (1 place after the decimal)

If you remove an encyclopedia from a row of books that is 42.12 cm, what will the new length of the row be?

_____

_____

Multiplying or Dividing Measurements

When you multiply or divide measurements, the answer must have the same number of significant figures as the measurement with the fewest number of significant figures. What is the area of a shelf that has a height of 33 cm and a width of 111 cm?

   111 cm (3 sig figs)

× 33 cm (2 sig figs)

3,663 cm² ⟶ 3,700 cm² (2 sig figs)

Zeroes at the end of a number, but before a decimal point, are not sig figs. What is the area of a desk in the library that is 115 cm long and 45 cm wide?

_____

_____

Lab zone® Do the Quick Lab *Is It Accurate?*

🔑 Assess Your Understanding

got it? ....

○ **I get it!** Now I know that scientists use math skills when they collect data that include_____

_____

○ I need extra help with _____

Go to **my science COACH** *online for help with this subject.*

Science Standards of Learning

PS.1e Express numbers in scientific notation where appropriate.

PS.1h Construct and interpret data tables for descriptive statistics showing specific measures of central tendency, the range of the data set, and the number of repeated trials.

PS.1j Make valid conclusions after analyzing data.

PS.1k Use research methods to investigate practical problems and questions.

What Math Tools Do Scientists Use?

Scientists use math to analyze data and draw conclusions about experimental results. 🔑 **Scientists use many math tools to analyze data. Some of these tools include mean, median, mode, and range. Scientists also use percent error and other math tools to determine if the values of data points are reasonable.**

Mean, Median, Mode, and Range To understand a set of data, scientists use math tools. These tools help organize and summarize scientific data. Use **Figure 4** to learn more about mean, median, mode, and range.

FIGURE 4 ....

Precipitation in South Bend The table below shows the average monthly precipitation in South Bend, Indiana.
✏️ **Use the table to calculate the mean, median, mode, and range of the rainfall data.**

Average Precipitation, South Bend	
Month	Average Precipitation (cm)
Jan	5.8
Feb	4.6
March	6.4
April	8.1
May	9.4
June	8.9
July	9.7
Aug	10.2
Sept	8.6
Oct	8.6
Nov	7.9
Dec	6.9

Mean The **mean** is the numerical average of a set of data. To find the mean, add all the numbers in the data set. Then divide by the total number of items that you added.

Mean of the rainfall data: _____

Median The **median** is the middle number in an ordered set of data. To find the median, list all the numbers in order from least to greatest. If the list has an odd number of entries, the median is the middle entry. If the list has an even number of entries, the median is the mean of the two middle entries.

Median of the rainfall data: _____
_____
_____

Mode The **mode** is the number that appears most often in a list of numbers.

Mode of the rainfall data: _____

Range The **range** of a data set is the difference between the greatest value in the set and the least value.

Range of the rainfall data: _____

Scientific Notation

Scientists often work with data that is very large or very small. **Scientific notation** is the method scientists use to write these numbers. Each number is written as the product of a number between 1 and 10 and a power of 10. Positive powers are used for large numbers and negative powers are used for numbers less than 1. The exponent indicates how many places to move the decimal point when writing the number in standard form. For example, the circumference of Earth is approximately 40,000,000 m. This can be written in scientific notation as 4.0×10^7 m.

Reasonable and Anomalous Data

Scientists must always ask themselves whether their data make sense and are reasonable. There is always an acceptable range of variation in collected data. However, some variation may not be acceptable. For example, suppose that a scientist is studying the wind speed of a strong hurricane. A wind speed measured at 56 km/hr is far lower than expected. The scientist is likely to check the wind speed recorder.

Human or equipment error can produce **anomalous data,** or data that do not fit with the data set. If a scientist sees a data point that is different from others, he or she will examine it for errors. If no errors were made, the anomalous data might be due to an unknown variable. Investigating the reason for anomalous data can lead scientists to new discoveries.

Adult female black bears have masses from about 50 kilograms to 125 kilograms. Adult male black bears have masses from about 60 kilograms to 250 kilograms. Researchers measured the masses of five adult female black bears in their natural habitat. You can see their results in the table.

1 Identify Which mass is anomalous data?

_____

2 Solve Problems How could the researcher check the anomalous data?

_____

_____

3 CHALLENGE What might have produced the anomalous data?

_____

_____

Adult Female Black Bear Masses

Bear	Mass (in kg)
A	79
B	73
C	74
D	155
E	70

Adding It Up

How do scientists use measurement and mathematics?

FIGURE 5 ·······································

>INTERACTIVE ART Two lab partners measured the mass and volume of a sample of quartz four times. They recorded their measurements in the table at the right.

✎ **Answer the questions.**

1. Draw Conclusions How do you think the partners measured the sample's mass and volume?

_____

_____

_____

2. Infer Are the students' measurements precise? Explain.

_____

_____

FIGURE 6 ·················

Percent Error
A Nobel Prize medal is plated with gold. The density of gold is 19.3 g/cm³.

✎ **Calculate A worker finds the density of the Nobel medal's plating to be 20.1 g/cm³. What is the percent error of his measurement?**

_____

_____

_____

_____

_____

Percent Error Some properties of substances never change. For example, the density of pure silver is always 10.5 g/cm³, no matter the size of the sample. However, when you measure an object made of pure silver, you may get a density of 10.75 g/cm³. The difference between the two density values might be due to an error you made when you measured the mass or volume of the silver. It could also be due to the accuracy of your measuring equipment. The percent difference between the known value of a substance and its measured value is called the **percent error.** A low percent error means that the experimental results were accurate. The formula below calculates percent error in the silver sample.

$$\text{Percent Error} = \frac{\text{experimental value} - \text{true value}}{\text{true value}} \times 100\%$$

$$\% \ E = \frac{10.75 \ \text{g/cm}^3 - 10.5 \ \text{g/cm}^3}{10.5 \ \text{g/cm}^3} \times 100\%$$

$$\% \ E = \frac{0.25 \ \text{g/cm}^3}{10.5 \ \text{g/cm}^3} \times 100\% = 2.38$$

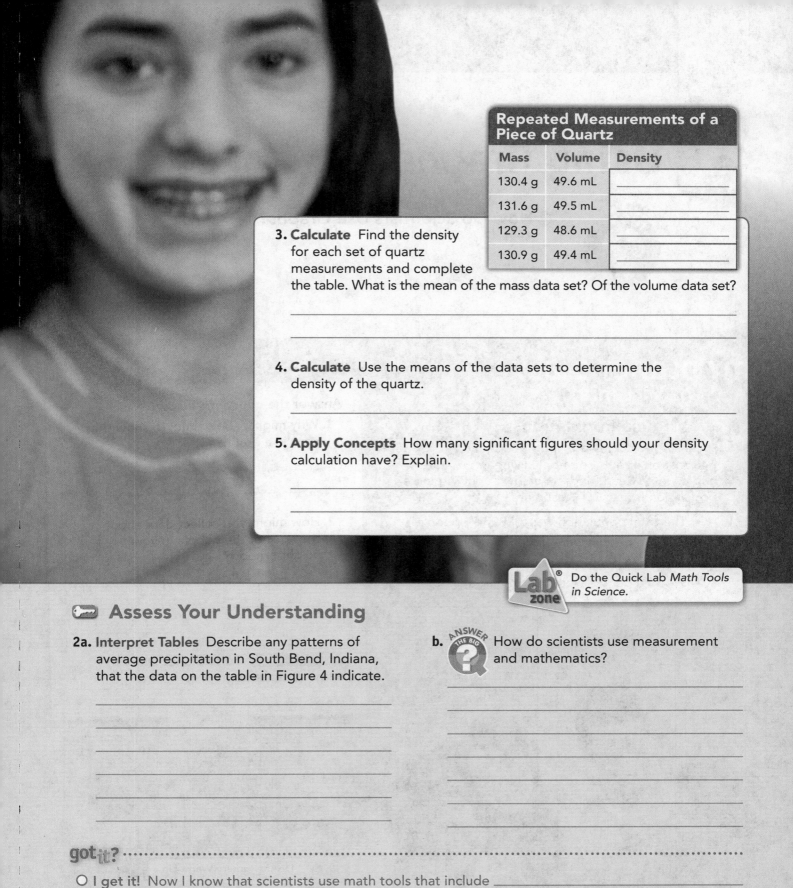

Repeated Measurements of a Piece of Quartz

Mass	Volume	Density
130.4 g	49.6 mL	_____
131.6 g	49.5 mL	_____
129.3 g	48.6 mL	_____
130.9 g	49.4 mL	_____

3. **Calculate** Find the density for each set of quartz measurements and complete the table. What is the mean of the mass data set? Of the volume data set?

_____

_____

4. **Calculate** Use the means of the data sets to determine the density of the quartz.

_____

5. **Apply Concepts** How many significant figures should your density calculation have? Explain.

_____

_____

Lab zone® Do the Quick Lab *Math Tools in Science.*

🔑 Assess Your Understanding

2a. Interpret Tables Describe any patterns of average precipitation in South Bend, Indiana, that the data on the table in Figure 4 indicate.

_____

_____

_____

_____

_____

b. ANSWER THE BIG ? How do scientists use measurement and mathematics?

_____

_____

_____

_____

_____

_____

got it? ···

○ **I get it!** Now I know that scientists use math tools that include _____

_____

○ **I need extra help with** _____

Go to MY SCIENCE ⑤ COACH *online for help with this subject.*

Virginia
LESSON
3 Using Graphs in Science

 How Do Scientists Use Graphs?
PS.1g, PS.1i, PS.1j, PS.1l, PS.1n

my planet Diary for Virginia

Virginia Population

A census is a survey that individuals take. It provides information about the people living in the state and country. Read the facts below about Virginia's population from a 2009 estimate.

- The total population was 7,882,590 people.
- 536,016 people were under five years old.
- 1,844,526 people were under the age of 18.
- 961,676 people were over the age of 65.

SCIENCE STATS

Answer the questions below.

1. Why might it be helpful to show these data in a graph?

_____

_____

2. How might you collect data about the ages of the people in your neighborhood?

_____

_____

_____

> PLANET DIARY Go to **Planet Diary** to learn more about graphs.

 Lab zone® Do the Inquiry Warm-Up *What's in a Graph?*

Vocabulary
- graph • linear graph
- nonlinear graph • outlier

Skills
- ⤷ Reading: Relate Cause and Effect
- △ Inquiry: Graph

How Do Scientists Use Graphs?

Have you ever been to an event that started off with a jet plane flyby? If so, you probably noticed that you could see the jets before you heard the roar of their engines. That is because sound travels slower than light. The speed of sound is also affected by the temperature of the medium it's traveling through, as shown by the data in **Figure 1.** To help understand what the data mean, you can use a graph. A **graph** is a "picture" of your data.

Kinds of Data Graphs can illustrate different types of data. ⊂⊐ **Scientists use graphs to identify trends, make predictions, and recognize anomalous, or inconsistent, data.** Graphs display categorical and numerical data. Categorical data can be grouped into categories. For example, census information can be categorized by age group. Numerical data, such as temperature and the speed of sound, are continuous, ranging from small to large amounts. Different kinds of graphs are used to display these two kinds of data.

Kinds of Graphs Line graphs are used to display numerical data that are continuous, such as the data in **Figure 1.** They may show how a dependent variable changes in response to an independent variable. Scientists control changes in the independent variable. Then they collect data about how the dependent variable responded to those changes. Bar graphs can be used to display both numerical and categorical data.

Science Standards of Learning

PS.1g Construct and interpret data tables showing the independent and dependent variables, derived quantities, and the number of trials.

PS.1i Construct and interpret frequency distributions, scatterplots, line plots, and histograms.

PS.1j Make valid conclusions after analyzing data.

PS.1l Present experimental results in appropriate written form.

PS.1n Use current applications of physical science concepts.

⤷ **Relate Cause and Effect**
In the text, underline the cause and circle the effect of variables when scientists use them.

FIGURE 1 ••••••••••••••••••••••••••••••••••••••

Graphing the Speed of Sound

As temperatures rise, so does the speed at which sound travels through the air.

✎ **Graph Make a line graph by plotting the data from the table on the grid.**

Temp. (°C)	Speed of Sound (m/s)
−15	322
0	331
15	340
30	349
45	358

Speed of Sound as Temperature Changes

(Graph axes: Speed of Sound (m/s) on y-axis from 320 to 360; Temperature (°C) on x-axis from −15 to 45)

know?

Graphs are not limited to two dimensions. Many types of graphs can be plotted in three dimensions, using an x-axis, y-axis, and z-axis. This graph displays the depth of an area of the ocean floor.

Ocean Depth

FIGURE 2

> INTERACTIVE ART **Sea Life Diving Data**

The diving depths of several sea creatures were measured and recorded in the data table.

1. **Graph** Arrange the animals in order from shallowest to deepest divers in a bar graph. Label the x-axis with the animals' initials and title the graph.

2. **Draw Conclusions** What trend does the graph show?

_____

_____

_____

Linear and Nonlinear Graphs

As you saw in the line graph in **Figure 1,** temperature and the speed of sound are related. Line graphs are powerful tools because they show how different sets of data are related. The line graph shows that as temperature increases, the speed of sound increases in a predictable way.

A line graph in which the data points yield a straight line is a **linear graph.** The relationship between temperature and the speed of sound can be shown by a linear graph. A graph in which the data points do not fall along a straight line is a **nonlinear graph.** Changes in population can be shown by a nonlinear graph.

If most points do not fall exactly along a line, a graph can still show a trend. A point that is not part of the trend is an anomalous data point called an **outlier.** When a graph does not have a clear trend, it usually means the variables are not related.

Maximum Dive Depths of Sea Animals		
Animal	Dive Depths (meters)	Average Mass (kg)
Leatherback sea turtle (LST)	1200	575
Emperor penguin (EP)	565	30
Elephant seal (ES)	1529	2000
King penguin (KP)	343	12

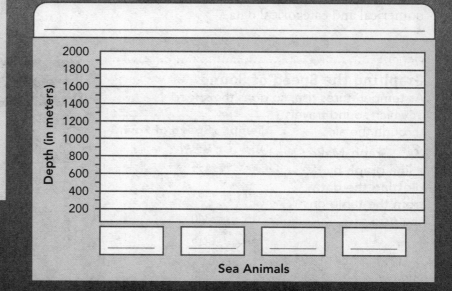

Scatterplots A scatterplot is a graph that shows data plotted as points, like a line graph. Scatterplots are a good choice to display data when you are trying to show that two variables might be related to each other. The relationship between the two variables is called their correlation.

The correlation between two variables can be analyzed in terms of its strength. The more the points in a scatterplot approximate a line, the stronger the correlation between the two variables. The less they approximate a line, the weaker the correlation. If the points are scattered all over the graph, then there is no correlation.

Like a line graph's trend, a scatterplot can also show positive and negative relationships in terms of its direction. If an increase in one variable corresponds to an increase in the other variable, then the variables have a positive correlation, or upward trend. If an increase in one variable corresponds to a decrease in the other variable, then the variables have a negative correlation, or downward trend.

Vocabulary High-Use Academic Words When a graph shows a trend, you can make predictions about data beyond the axes of the graph. Which word below is a synonym for the word *trend*?

○ origin
○ course
○ point

apply it!

In 2003, scientists studying the waters around Antarctica wanted to know if there were a correlation between the surface temperature of the water and the concentration of phytoplankton chlorophyll. The data was collected and displayed in a scatterplot.

❶ **Interpret Graphs** Does the scatterplot show a positive or negative correlation? Is the correlation weak or strong?

_____

_____

❷ **Draw Conclusions** What conclusion can you draw about the relationship between chlorophyll concentration and the surface temperature of the water based on the data? _____

_____

_____

Southern Ocean, October 2003

Sea Surface Temperature (C°) vs. Chlorophyll Concentration (mg/m³)

Frequency Distributions Scientists often collect data that involve recording the frequency of particular observations. Frequency refers to the number of times an event occurs in a given period. For example, a scientist might study the kinds of birds that live in a particular habitat. She might record data about the number of each species of bird that she observes during a given period of time.

Scientists use frequency distributions to summarize and display these kinds of data. A frequency table is constructed by arranging data values with their corresponding frequencies. These tables can show either categorical or numerical data.

Line Plots A line plot is a type of graph used to show frequency distributions. It consists of a number line and X's to show the frequency of each data value. Since each data value is listed on the line plot, they are most useful when there is small numbers of data.

FIGURE 3 ···

Frequency Tables and Line Plots

The Golden eagle (*Aquila chrysaetos*) is a bird of prey known to overwinter in Virginia along the Appalachians. Biologists studying the Golden eagle in Virginia captured, measured, and then released eagles. The frequency distribution table shows data for the wingspans of a sample of eagles.

1. **Identify** Complete the frequency distribution table by listing the frequency for each wingspan.

2. **Graph** Using the data in the table, complete the line plot. Write the values for the wingspans on the number line. For each occurrence in the table, place an X above the appropriate wingspan value.

3. **Interpret Data** Look at the line plot. What generalization can you make about the wingspans of the sample?

_____

_____

Wingspan of Golden Eagles

Wingspan (cm)	Tally	Frequency
198	II	
199	III	
200	II	
201	IIII	
202	HHT I	
203	HHT	

Wingspan (cm)

Histograms

Histograms also can be used to visually display frequency distributions. A histogram looks similar to a bar graph, but it is used to display and analyze continuous numerical data that are grouped. For example, a histogram could be used to display the heights of all students in your class. After determining the height of each student, you would group the heights in continuous ranges, such as 100–120 cm, 120–140 cm, 140 cm–160 cm. Then count the number, or frequency, of students that fit in each height category and plot your data in bar form on a graph.

Scientists use histograms when they need to organize and analyze a large number of observations. Whereas a line plot lists each data value alone, a histogram divides the total range of the values into equal continuous groups.

FIGURE 4 ···

Histograms

Histogram A shows the number of instruments, such as the Chandra telescope, that were or will be launched by NASA since 1990.

1. **Read Graphs** Look at Histogram A. In which period did NASA launch the most instruments?

_____

2. **Graph** Use the data from Histogram A to complete Histogram B.

3. **Compare and Contrast** What effect does the range of the groups have on the picture of the data?

_____

_____

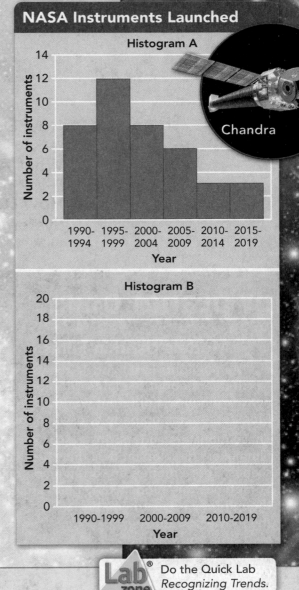

NASA Instruments Launched

Histogram A

Chandra

Histogram B

Do the Quick Lab
Recognizing Trends.

🔑 Assess Your Understanding

1a. Compare and Contrast How are linear and nonlinear graphs alike? Different?

_____

_____

b. Apply Concepts What does a scatterplot with no correlation indicate about the variables?

_____

got it?···

○ **I get it!** Now I know that scientists use graphs _____

_____

○ **I need extra help with** _____

Go to MY SCIENCE COACH online for help with this subject.

Models and Systems

UNLOCK THE BIG ?

🗝 **How Do Scientists Use Models?**
PS.1k, PS.1m, PS.1n

🗝 **What Are the Characteristics of a System?**
PS.1m, PS.1n

🗝 **How Do Models Help Scientists Understand Systems?**
PS.1k, PS.1m, PS.1n

my PLANeT DiaRY   SCIENCE AND TECHNOLOGY

Models Used in Films

As the lights in the movie theater dim, your excitement about the latest hit movie builds. For the next two hours, a different world flashes in front of you. Monsters snatch up people, or alien robots invade Earth.

These monsters and robots are not actual objects. Instead, filmmakers develop models that they incorporate into the scenes. These models are often made on the computer. Sometimes, the models they build are very small, even though they appear huge on the movie screen. The next time you watch a movie, can you tell which things are real and which are models?

Answer the questions below.

1. How do models help filmmakers?

_____

_____

_____

2. What might you need to make a model of if you were filming a movie at your school?

_____

_____

_____

▶ PLANET DIARY Go to **Planet Diary** to learn more about making models.

Lab zone ®   Do the Inquiry Warm-Up *Models in Science.*

Vocabulary
- model
- process
- system
- output
- input
- feedback

Skills
- Reading: Identify the Main Idea
- Inquiry: Make Models

How Do Scientists Use Models?

Many department stores use mannequins to show customers how certain outfits might look. A mannequin is a model. A **model** is any representation of an object or a process. You use models in your daily life without even realizing it. For example, you might use a globe to find a country. A globe is a model of Earth.

Scientists work with models for a specific purpose. **Scientists use models to test their ideas about things they cannot observe directly.** Scientists often build models to create a reasonable representation of things that are either very small or very large. These kinds of models are physical models—drawings (like the one in **Figure 1**) or three-dimensional objects. But many models are not physical objects. For example, many models are models of a process. A computer program might be used to model the movement of the stars as seen from Earth.

Science Standards of Learning

PS.1k Use research methods to investigate practical problems and questions.

PS.1m Construct and use models and simulations to illustrate and explain phenomena.

PS.1n Use current applications of physical science concepts.

FIGURE 1 ···

Connecting the Dots

This model shows how networks (drawn as dots) connect to each other on the Internet. The bigger the dot, the more Internet traffic the network handles.

✎ **Explain** Suppose all networks in the center of the model became unavailable for 24 hours. How can scientists use this model to predict how Internet traffic will be affected?

_____

_____

_____

Do the Quick Lab
Working With Models

🔑 Assess Your Understanding

got it? ··

○ I get it! Now I know that scientists use models to _____

_____

○ I need extra help with _____

Go to MY SCIENCE **COACH** *online for help with this subject.*

Science Standards of Learning

PS.1m Construct and use models and simulations to illustrate and explain phenomena.

PS.1n Use current applications of physical science concepts.

What Are the Characteristics of a System?

Models are often used to represent systems. A **system** is a group of parts that work together to carry out a function. You may recall that Earth is a system that consists of air, life, water, ice, and rock. But look at **Figure 2**. Many things you use in your daily life are systems. A bicycle pump, a toaster, and a flashlight all contain parts that work together while performing a function.

Systems have common characteristics. **All systems have at least one input, at least one process, and at least one output.** An **input** is a material or the energy that goes into the system. A **process** is an action or series of actions that happen within the system. An **output** is the material or energy that comes out of a system. To understand input, process, and output, think of a toaster. The input is electricity. The process is heating the bread. The output is hot toast.

Handle

Cylinder

Piston

Valve

FIGURE 2

▶ INTERACTIVE ART **An Everyday System**
In a bicycle pump, many parts work together as a system. ✎ Chart **Look at the pump and use what you know to fill in the chart.**

A Bicycle Pump as a System

Parts	Inputs	Outputs

Look at **Figure 3.** The harder you ride a bike, the more oxygen your muscles need. As a result, your circulatory system provides information to your heart indicating that you need more oxygen. So your heart starts beating faster. By beating faster, your heart provides more oxygen to your muscles. **Feedback** is output that changes a system in some way. When you exercise, your heart receives feedback that makes your heart pump faster.

You exercise.

Your _____ pumps harder, providing more oxygen.

Your _____ use oxygen in your blood.

Your _____ provides information to your _____ that your muscles need oxygen.

FIGURE 3 ··

Feedback
When you exercise, your body's circulatory system feeds back information to your heart.
✎ **Fill in the blanks of the graphic organizer.**
Identify What is the input and output for this system?

_____
_____
_____
_____
_____

Lab zone® Do the Quick Lab *Characteristics of Systems.*

🔑 Assess Your Understanding

1a. Identify A (model/system) is a group of parts that work together to perform a function.

b. Apply Concepts Is a handheld can opener a system? Explain.

_____
_____
_____
_____

c. Infer What is the input when you use a can opener?

_____
_____
_____
_____
_____

got**it?**···

○ **I get it!** Now I know that all systems have _____
and some systems have feedback.

○ **I need extra help with** _____

Go to **my science s coach** *online for help with this subject.*

PS.1k Use research methods to investigate practical problems and questions.

PS.1m Construct and use models and simulations to illustrate and explain phenomena.

PS.1n Use current applications of physical science concepts.

How Do Models Help Scientists Understand Systems?

It's easy to identify the materials and energy that make up the inputs and outputs of a system. But observing a system's process can be difficult. Models can help scientists understand a system's process. **Scientists build models to represent a process. They test whether the input and output from the model match the input and output of the system in the natural world.**

Scientists use models to predict changes in a natural system as a result of feedback or input changes. A natural system is a system in the natural world. For example, scientists have tried to restore the Everglades, which is a natural system. To do this, they need to understand how a rise in water levels might affect plant and animal survival. Water levels can rise as a result of climate change. So scientists construct models showing how water levels affect the Everglades. Then they can predict what changes to the Everglades might result from a change in water levels.

apply it!

The Cape Sable seaside sparrow nests in certain areas of the Everglades. In one model of the sparrow's nesting habits, the sparrows start to mate when water levels drop to 5 cm. After they mate, the sparrows need approximately 43 consecutive days during which the water level is lower than 16 cm. If water levels rise to 16 cm or higher during this time, the sparrows will abandon their nest.

Nest not drawn to scale

Nest not drawn to scale

2 CHALLENGE How might scientists use the information from your model to save the species?

_____

_____

_____

_____

1 Make Models Shade in the water levels on each meterstick to show how Cape Sable seaside sparrow nests vary according to water levels.

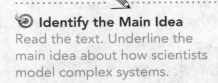

Modeling Simple and Complex Systems
Some systems that scientists study are simple. There may be only a few parts in the system or a few steps in the process. A toaster is one example of a system that is made up of only a few parts. **Figure 4** shows another example of a simple system.

However, some systems are more complex. Many parts and many variables, or factors that can vary, interact in these systems. Often scientists may use a computer to keep track of the variables. For example, weather systems are very complex. Many factors affect weather, such as oceans, mountains and valleys, wind patterns, and the angle of the sun's rays. These factors can interact in many ways. As a result, scientists have a difficult time predicting when and where rain or snow will fall. Because such systems are difficult to model, scientists may model the specific part of the system that they wish to study. For instance, a hurricane is a complex natural system. To predict where a hurricane will make landfall, scientists might try to model winds that affect the hurricane's path.

Identify the Main Idea
Read the text. Underline the main idea about how scientists model complex systems.

FIGURE 4
The Mercury Cycle
Materials that contain the element mercury can be harmful to fish that eat them.

Look at the diagram and then complete the activities.

1. **Identify** On the diagram, label the inputs, processes, and outputs of the system.

2. **Predict** Suppose you want less mercury to end up in fish. How might you change the inputs of the system?

_____

_____

_____

_____

Mercury released in burning of wastes and fossil fuels
_____

Air

Rain

Mercury released from rocks and soil
_____

Water

Mercury dissolves.
_____

Mercury sinks to bottom.
_____

Small organisms eat sediment.
_____

Fish eat organisms.
_____

High concentration of mercury in fish
_____

Sediment

The lion is nicknamed the "King of the Jungle." But in open savannas, female lions do most of the hunting.

Testing Assumptions

When scientists construct a model of a system, they begin with certain assumptions. For example, an astronomer might assume that in order for a planet to support life, the planet must have water.

Scientists check their assumptions. They compare the input and output of the model to the input and output in the natural world. If they match, then the assumptions are correct. If they do not match, scientists must change one or more assumptions. The revised model more accurately represents the natural world.

Sometimes scientists make assumptions to simplify the model. A scientist who wants to study how energy flows through a certain environment might use a model called a food chain. A food chain is a series of diagrams that shows what animals eat in a certain environment. For example, in a savanna, or grassy plain, a lion eats zebras and many other animals. Zebras eat grass. But the model may assume that lions eat only zebras. So the process that is shown in the model is somewhat simpler than the process that takes place in the natural world. Yet the model still accurately shows the relationship between the parts of the system. A food web, which you can draw in **Figure 5,** is a slightly more complex model of how energy flows through an environment.

FIGURE 5 ·······································

Food Webs

Scientists use food webs to model how energy flows through a particular environment. In a food web, lines connect organisms that eat other organisms. For any two organisms, the organism that eats the other is always shown higher up on the food web. ✎ **Analyze Models and Systems** Construct a food web based on the images in the Picture Bank below. (*Hint:* Zebras and giraffes eat grass or leaves. Lions eat zebras and giraffes. Vultures eat lions, zebras, and giraffes.) Then answer the questions on the next page.

✏ **Infer** What are the assumptions of this model?

_____

_____

_____

_____

_____

CHALLENGE How could you test this model to see if your assumptions are correct?

_____

_____

_____

_____

_____

_____

Do the Lab Investigation _Selecting Models._

🗝 **Assess Your Understanding**

2a. Review Scientists check _____ by comparing the inputs and outputs of a model to inputs and outputs of a natural system.

b. Explain A certain astronomer assumes that a planet must have water to support life. How does the astronomer's assumption help the astronomer search for life in the universe?

_____

_____

_____

_____

_____

c. Predict What might make the astronomer change the assumption made in the previous question?

_____

_____

_____

_____

_____

got it? . . . .

○ **I get it!** Now I know models help scientists understand natural systems by allowing scientists to test _____

_____

_____

and compare them to those of the natural world.

○ **I need extra help with** _____

_Go to_ **MY SCIENCE** ᔆ **COACH** _online for help with this subject._

LESSON 5

Safety in the Science Laboratory

UNLOCK THE BIG

🔑 **Why Prepare for a Scientific Investigation?**
PS.1a

🔑 **What Should You Do if an Accident Occurs?**
PS.1a

MY PLANET DIARY
for Virginia

Posted by: Ruby

Location: King George, Virginia

My teacher was going to show us an experiment, but before we started she told each and every one of us that we had to wear goggles if we wanted to participate. I grabbed my goggles and put them on. Here came the moment. She smashed the rock and tiny pieces went all over the place. So, no wonder she told us we needed goggles.

Lab zone® Do the Inquiry Warm-Up *Can You Name the Safety Equipment?*

BLOG

Write your answer to the question on the lines below.
What are some steps you can take to create a safe lab environment?

_____

_____

_____

▷ **PLANET DIARY** Go to **Planet Diary** to learn more about lab safety.

Science Standards of Learning

PS.1a Safely use chemicals and equipment.

Why Prepare for a Scientific Investigation?

How do you prepare for a long trip? You probably find and reserve a place to stay weeks or months in advance. A few days before your trip, you begin to pack. You check the area's weather forecast and use the information to choose the appropriate clothes. After you make these preparations, you are ready to relax and enjoy your trip.

Vocabulary
- field

Skills
- Reading: Sequence
- Inquiry: Observe

Preparing for an Investigation

Good preparation helps you have a safe, enjoyable trip. It can also help you perform a successful scientific investigation. 🔑 **Good preparation helps to keep you and your classmates safe when you perform a scientific investigation. It also keeps any living things you use safe.** To prepare for an investigation, read the procedures carefully. If you do not understand any part of the investigation, ask your teacher questions before you start. Make sure you know where all the safety equipment is located in the laboratory.

Working Safely in the Field

Although you will do many of your investigations in the laboratory, you may do some investigations in the field. The **field** is any area outside a science laboratory. The field may be a nearby forest, park, or beach. Good preparation is important in the field because there are additional safety hazards, such as wild animals, poisonous plants, or severe weather, that you may encounter. Wear appropriate clothing, including hats and sunglasses, and bring appropriate equipment, such as gloves and safety goggles. Treat plants and animals with proper care and respect. Always work in the field with another person and an adult.

apply it!

These students are working in the field.

1 ⚠ **Observe** What clothing items protect these students?

_____

_____

_____

2 CHALLENGE Suppose the students are caught in a sudden rainstorm. How can they stay safe during the storm?

_____

Conducting the Investigation Safely

Whenever you perform a scientific investigation, your primary concern should be your safety and the safety of others. Keep in mind this rule: *Always follow your teacher's instructions and the directions exactly.* If you have an idea that you would like to try, ask your teacher before doing it.

There are certain safety measures you should take before, during, and after an investigation. Before you do any investigation, first make sure you know its safety symbols. Safety symbols alert you to possible sources of accidents in the investigation. Familiarize yourself with any equipment you will be using. Then, clean and organize your work area. Finally, label any containers you will be using. Look at **Figure 1** to see safety symbols and learn ways to be safe during and after a scientific investigation.

FIGURE 1 ·····················

Safety in the Laboratory

To be safe, there are a number of things you should do during and after a scientific investigation.

✐ **Relate Text and Visuals** For each scene shown, circle any safety equipment the students are using. Then, write in the boxes the names of four safety symbols that apply to that investigation.

During the investigation:

- Wear safety goggles to protect your eyes from chemical splashes, glass breakage, and sharp objects.
- Wear an apron to protect yourself and your clothes from chemicals.
- Wear heat-resistant gloves when handling hot objects.
- Wear plastic gloves to protect your skin when handling animals, plants, or chemicals.
- Handle live animals and plants with care.

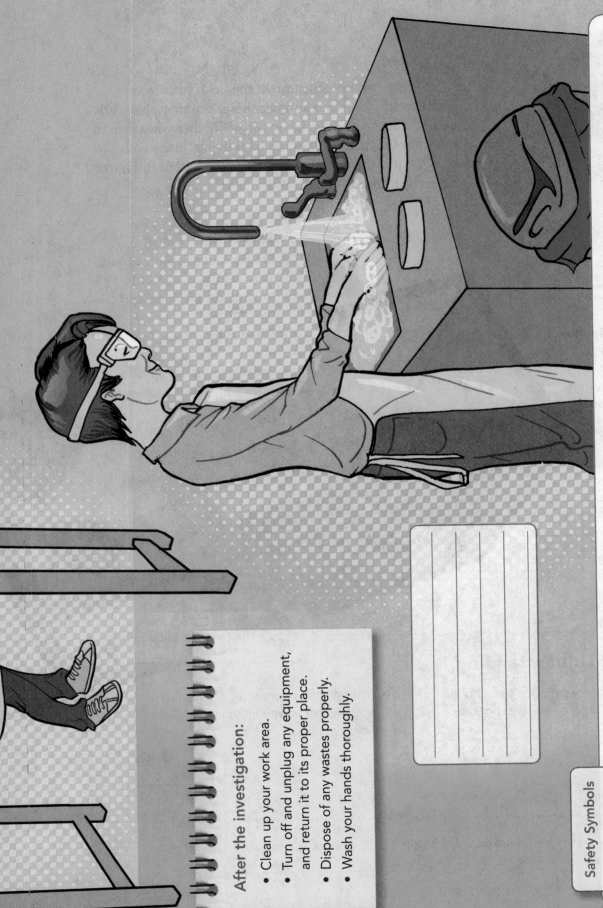

After the investigation:

- Clean up your work area.
- Turn off and unplug any equipment, and return it to its proper place.
- Dispose of any wastes properly.
- Wash your hands thoroughly.

Safety Symbols

Animal safety

Disposal

Breakage

Heat-Resistant Gloves

Plastic Gloves

Corrosive chemical

Sharp Object

Safety Goggles

Plant safety

Lab Apron

Hand Washing

Flames

Caring for Plants and Animals Properly When you are performing an investigation in the field, you are very likely to encounter plants and animals there. You may also work with plants and animals in the laboratory. Whether you are in the laboratory or in the field, you should treat living things with care and respect. Follow the animal care instructions listed in **Figure 2** when you are working with animals in the laboratory.

Proper Animal Care
- Provide animals with enough space in their cage or terrarium.
- Provide proper food and clean drinking water.
- Clean the cages or terrariums regularly.
- Handle animals with care.

FIGURE 2 ·······························

Animal Care
You must treat the animals you use in an investigation properly and humanely.

✎ **Interpret Photos** What information should you know about this turtle to care for it properly?

_____
_____
_____
_____
_____

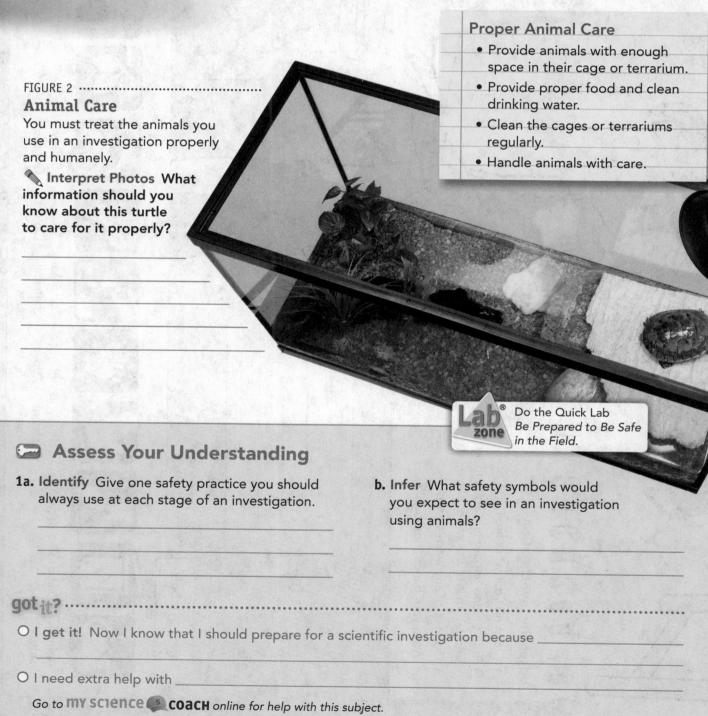

Lab zone Do the Quick Lab *Be Prepared to Be Safe in the Field.*

🔑 Assess Your Understanding

1a. Identify Give one safety practice you should always use at each stage of an investigation.

_____
_____
_____

b. Infer What safety symbols would you expect to see in an investigation using animals?

_____
_____

got it? ···

○ **I get it!** Now I know that I should prepare for a scientific investigation because _____
_____

○ **I need extra help with** _____

Go to **MY SCIENCE ⓈCOACH** *online for help with this subject.*

What Should You Do If an Accident Occurs?

Even with careful preparation, sometimes accidents occur during an investigation. In the event of an accident, what should you do? 🗝 **Always alert your teacher first. Then follow your teacher's directions, and carry them out quickly.** If your teacher is not available, then find and alert the nearest adult. Familiarize yourself with the location and the proper use of all the emergency equipment in your laboratory. You can use some of the equipment shown in **Figure 3.** Knowing safety and first-aid procedures beforehand will prepare you to handle accidents properly.

Science Standards of Learning

PS.1a Safely use chemicals and equipment.

✎ **Sequence** Underline the steps you should take when an accident occurs.

FIGURE 3 ·····································

Emergency Equipment
Use the emergency equipment shown in case of a fire or an injury.

✎ **Identify** In each box, write how the equipment can help you in an emergency.

Lab zone Do the Quick Lab *How Would You Respond to These Emergencies?*

🗝 **Assess Your Understanding**

got it? ·······································

○ **I get it!** Now I know that in case of an accident I should _____
_____
_____
_____

○ **I need extra help with** _____

Go to **MY SCIENCE COACH** online for help with this subject.

81

Study Guide

Scientists use _____ to communicate how precise their measurements are.

LESSON 1 Scientific Measurement

🔑 The SI system allows scientists to compare data and communicate with each other about the results of scientific investigations.

🔑 SI units for length, mass, weight, volume, density, time, and temperature include meters, kilograms, newtons, cubic meters, kilograms per cubic meter, seconds, and kelvins.

Vocabulary
• metric system   • International System of Units (SI)
• mass   • weight   • volume   • meniscus   • density

LESSON 2 Mathematics and Scientific Thinking

🔑 Scientists use estimation, accuracy and precision, and significant figures.

🔑 Scientists use math tools including mean, median, mode, range, and percent error.

Vocabulary
• estimate   • accuracy   • precision
• significant figures   • mean   • median   • mode
• range   • scientific notation   • anomalous data
• percent error

LESSON 3 Using Graphs in Science

🔑 Scientists use graphs to identify trends, make predictions, and recognize anomalous data.

Vocabulary
• graph
• linear graph
• nonlinear graph
• outlier

LESSON 4 Models and Systems

🔑 Scientists use models to test their ideas about things they cannot observe directly.

🔑 All systems have input, process, and output.

🔑 Scientists build models to represent a process. They test whether the input and output from the model match the input and output of the system in the natural world.

Vocabulary
• model   • system   • input   • process   • output
• feedback

LESSON 5 Safety in the Science Laboratory

🔑 Good preparation helps to keep you and your classmates safe when you perform a scientific investigation. It also keeps any living things you use safe.

🔑 In the event of an accident, always alert your teacher first. Then follow your teacher's directions, and carry them out quickly.

Vocabulary
• field

Review and Assessment

LESSON 1 Scientific Measurement

1. A newton is the SI unit for

a. mass.　　　　b. density.

c. volume.　　　d. weight.

2. The SI system of measurement is based on the

_____

3. Calculate Find the volume of the object at the right. Explain your method.

_____

_____

_____

_____

4. Apply Concepts Will an object with a volume of 77 grams per cubic centimeter and a mass of 65 grams float or sink in water? Explain.

_____

_____

_____

5. Write About It Your friend sends you an e-mail about an experiment that she read about. She mentions that the results from the experiment work best at −2 K. Write an e-mail back to your friend explaining why she must be mistaken about the temperature.

LESSON 2 Mathematics and Scientific Thinking

6. How close a measurement is to its true or accepted value is

a. accuracy.　　　b. estimation.

c. precision.　　　d. range.

7. Nineteen is the _____ for the data set 25, 19, 18, 31, 19, 22.

8. Interpret Data How many significant figures are in the measurement 230 kg?

_____

9. Calculate You measure the mass of a model car to be 230 grams. The actual mass is 218 grams. What is your percent error?

_____

_____

10. A bacterium has a mass of 0.00000000000095 g. What is this number in scientific notation?

_____

Use the table below to answer Question 11.

Month and Year	Number of Ducks
Nov. 2009	356,000
Dec. 2009	656,000
Jan. 2010	976,000

11. Interpret Tables The table shows the estimated number of ducks counted in an area over several months. Why are the counts only estimates?

_____

_____

_____

_____

LESSON 3 Using Graphs in Science

12. Anomalous data shows on a graph as a(n)

   a. nonlinear graph.   **b.** trend.

   c. linear graph.   **d.** outlier.

13. A histogram can be used to display

_____ .

14. **math!** Plot a line graph using this data table from a summer science camp. Determine if the graph is linear or nonlinear and label any outliers.

Year	Number of Campers
1	52
2	60
3	63
4	41
5	70

LESSON 4 Models and Systems

15. A model is any representation of an object or

   a. an opinion.   **b.** a process.

   c. an investigation.   **d.** data.

16. A system is a group of parts that work

together to _____ .

17. **Explain** Meteorologists use models to help them predict the weather, but their predictions are not always correct. Explain why this is so.

_____

_____

_____

_____

_____

_____

LESSON 5 Safety in the Science Laboratory

18. What safety equipment should you use when you handle live animals?

   a. sunglasses   **b.** heat-resistant gloves

   c. plastic container   **d.** plastic gloves

19. You should always work in the _____ with another person and an adult.

20. **Infer** You have volunteered to take care of your classroom's mouse for the week. To care for the mouse properly, what must you do?

_____

_____

_____

_____

 How do scientists use measurement and mathematics?

21. Suppose a scientist wants to measure the lengths of twenty queen bees from twenty different hives. How would the scientist find the mean of the data set? Why might the scientist choose to compare the queens' lengths in a bar graph?

_____

_____

_____

_____

_____

_____

Virginia SOL Test Prep

Read each question and choose the best answer.

1 What might be one reason scientists would build a model of Earth like the one shown here?

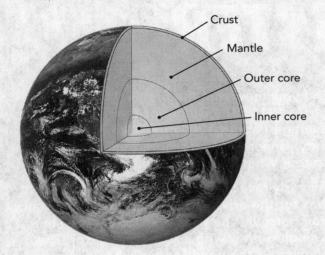

- Crust
- Mantle
- Outer core
- Inner core

- **A** to show the color of the continents
- **B** to show the depths of Earth's oceans
- **C** to show the layers of Earth
- **D** to show pressure inside Earth

2 Nicole measured the height of her locker as 39.8 cm, 42.3 cm, 42.0 cm, and 43.1 cm. The locker is actually 45.5 cm. Which *best* describes Nicole's measurements?

- **F** They were accurate.
- **G** They were precise.
- **H** They were both accurate and precise.
- **J** They were neither accurate nor precise.

3 Which SI unit would you use to measure the volume of a tomato?

- **A** gram
- **B** grams per cubic meter
- **C** cubic centimeter
- **D** newton

4 The median for the data set 32, 40, 38, 41, 36 is—

- **F** 9
- **G** 38
- **H** 93.5
- **J** 187

5 Suppose you are cleaning up after a scientific investigation in the laboratory. As you are cleaning a glass container, it slips from your hands and breaks in the sink. What should you do?

- **A** Pick up the broken glass.
- **B** Leave the broken glass in the sink.
- **C** Tell your teacher or another adult in the room.
- **D** Recycle the broken glass.

6 What kind of trend do the data show?

- **F** linear
- **G** positive
- **H** no trend
- **J** nonlinear

THE RACE TO BE FASTER

Did you know that the first Indianapolis 500 ran in 1911? The winner of the first race only averaged about 120 km/h (75 mph). Today Indy winners average more than twice that speed! What changed in all that time?

All early racecars were two-seaters. One seat was for the driver and one was for a mechanic. Ray Harroun, the winner in 1911, raced in a single-seater with a rear-view mirror. This eliminated the need for a mechanic—as well as the additional weight!

As technology progressed, the engines and exteriors of cars were manufactured from lightweight metal alloys and polymers. Engines became smaller, lighter, and more powerful. The cars became more aerodynamic. New designs decreased the resistance from air when traveling at high speeds, called drag. Race cars also switched fuels from gasoline to ethanol, allowing for smaller gas tanks. These modifications made the cars faster—and the races more exciting!

Design It Design a toy race car that is built for speed. Brainstorm potential design solutions. Document your ideas with labeled drawings and choose the best design. Build a prototype and measure how fast the car can travel on a set course without pushing it. Present your data using graphs or tables. Using this information, redesign your prototype to make the car faster.

 PS.1j, PS.1k, PS.1m

AQUANAUTS

Science has sent people to the moon and robots to Mars. But vast amounts of Earth's surface—the parts that are deep underwater—remain unexplored.

Aquarius, the world's first underwater research station, is located more than 18 meters below the ocean's surface off the southern tip of Florida. The scientists and crew who work in *Aquarius* are called aquanauts.

Aquanauts are marine biologists and oceanographers. While on board *Aquarius*, the aquanauts may study nearby coral reefs or test new technology for marine exploration. *Aquarius* has allowed scientists to study and observe undersea life in ways that were previously impossible. Aquanaut missions are also helping the National Aeronautics and Space Administration (NASA). Because the undersea habitat is similar to a space station, NASA uses *Aquarius* to explore the challenges of living in space.

Design It Find out more about *Aquarius* and the missions it supports. Then write a news article to tell the public about the underwater research station, its missions, and the people who work on it. Remember to write an attention-grabbing headline and exciting lead paragraph. Use visuals as well as specific data to support your article.

PS.1j, PS.1k

Warm and dry inside Aquarius, an aquanaut looks out at the ocean. ▼

WHAT ARE ALL OF THESE THINGS MADE OF?

How is matter described?

Imagine a warm day at Waikiki Beach on the island of Oahu, Hawaii. You can feel the warm breeze, the hot sand, and the cool water. Palm trees, hotels, shops, and the volcanic crater called Diamond Head, are all a part of the scenery around you. People swimming, surfing, and sailing are enjoying the ocean.

Classify **Categorize the items found at Waikiki Beach by what they are made of.**

_____

_____

_____

_____

_____

> **UNTAMED SCIENCE** Watch the **Untamed Science** video to learn more about matter.

Introduction to Matter

Science Standards of Learning

PS.1b, PS.1c, PS.1i, PS.1j, PS.1k, PS.1n, PS.2a, PS.2b,
PS.2c, PS.2d, PS.2e, PS.2f, PS.5a, PS.5b, PS.6b, PS.7d

3 Getting Started

Check Your Understanding

1. **Background** Read the paragraph below and then answer the question.

On a hot day, Jorge decides to make a pitcher of cold lemonade. He combines **pure** water with lemon juice in a **ratio** of six to one. He adds sugar and ice and stirs all the ingredients together. The **properties** of the lemonade are that it is cold, yellow, and sweet.

A **pure** material is not mixed with any other matter.

A **ratio** tells you the relationship between two or more things.

A **property** is a characteristic that belongs to a person or thing.

• How would the properties of the lemonade change if the ratio of pure water to lemon juice were three to one? Assume the amount of sugar is the same.

_____

_____

> MY READING WEB If you had trouble completing the question above, visit **My Reading Web** and type in **Introduction to Matter.**

Vocabulary Skill

Prefixes A prefix is a word part that is added at the beginning of a root word to change the word's meaning. The prefixes below will help you understand some of the vocabulary in this chapter.

Prefix	Meaning	Example
endo-	in, within	endogenous, *adj.* describes something that arises from inside an organism's tissues or cells
exo-	out	exoskeleton, *n.* an outer shell or outer skeleton that protects animals, such as crustaceans

2. **Quick Check** The Greek root *therm* means "heat." Predict the meaning of the term *endothermic change.*

_____

_____

substance

mixture

density

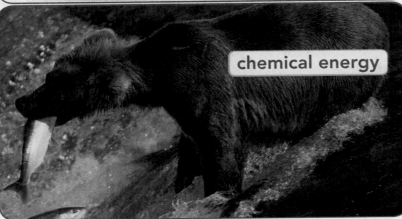
chemical energy

Chapter Preview

LESSON 1
- matter
- chemistry
- substance
- physical property
- chemical property

🔄 **Summarize**
🔺 **Classify**

LESSON 2
- element
- atom
- chemical bond
- molecule
- compound
- chemical formula
- mixture

🔄 **Compare and Contrast**
🔺 **Infer**

LESSON 3
- weight
- mass
- International System of Units
- volume
- density

🔄 **Identify the Main Idea**
🔺 **Calculate**

LESSON 4
- physical change
- chemical change
- law of conservation of mass
- temperature
- thermal energy
- endothermic change
- exothermic change
- chemical energy

🔄 **Relate Cause and Effect**
🔺 **Draw Conclusions**

> **VOCAB FLASH CARDS** For extra help with vocabulary, visit **Vocab Flash Cards** and type in *Introduction to Matter.*

91

Describing Matter

🔑 **What Properties Describe Matter?**
PS.1n, PS.2d, PS.2e, PS.2f

my planet Diary

CAREER

Art Conservation Scientist

Science and art may seem like two very different interests, but they are both part of the job for an art conservation scientist. Over time, art can fade, decay, or get dirty. Conservation scientists find ways to restore art by examining its properties. They look at texture, color and age of the paint, the condition of the canvas, and materials used to make the paint. Then, the scientists can determine chemical properties of the painting. For example, they can predict how the painting will react to light, changes in temperature, and the use of chemicals for cleaning. Thanks to art conservation scientists, masterpieces of art can be enjoyed for many years.

Before

After

Write your answers to the questions below.

1. Why is it important for an art conservation scientist to study the properties of a painting before it's repaired?

_____

_____

_____

_____

2. Name another career that combines science with another interest.

_____

_____

> PLANET DIARY Go to **Planet Diary** to learn more about matter.

Medusa by Caravaggio, about 1598. Uffizi Gallery, Florence, Italy

Lab®
zone
Do the Inquiry Warm-Up *How Do You Describe Matter?*

Vocabulary
- matter • chemistry
- substance • physical property
- chemical property

Skills
 Reading: Summarize
⚠ Inquiry: Classify

What Properties Describe Matter?

You have probably heard the word *matter* used many times. "As a matter of fact…" or "Hey, what's the matter?" In science, **matter** is anything that has mass and takes up space. All the "stuff" around you is matter, and you are matter too. Air, plastic, metal, wood, glass, paper, and cloth are all matter.

Even though air and paper are both matter, you know they are different materials. Matter can have many different properties, or characteristics that can be used to identify and classify it. Materials can be hard or soft, hot or cold, liquid, solid, or gas. Some materials catch fire easily, but others do not burn. **Chemistry** is the study of matter and how matter changes.

Substances Some types of matter are substances and some are not. In chemistry, a **substance** is a single kind of matter that is pure, meaning it always has a specific makeup, or composition. For example, table salt has the same composition and properties whether it comes from seawater or a salt mine. **Figure 1** shows two examples of water that appear to be very different. Water is a substance. Pure water is always the same, whether it comes from a glacier or from a geyser.

> **Science Standards of Learning**
>
> **PS.1n** Use current applications of physical science concepts.
> **PS.2d** Investigate and understand physical properties of matter.
> **PS.2e** Investigate and understand chemical properties of matter.
> **PS.2f** Investigate and understand characteristics of types of matter based on physical and chemical properties.

Summarize How are matter and substances related?

_____

_____

_____

_____

_____

_____

_____

FIGURE 1 ···

Properties of Matter

✎ **Compare and Contrast** Complete the Venn diagram with the properties of water from a glacier and from a geyser.

Glacier   **Geyser**

Physical and Chemical Properties of Matter

Matter is described by its properties. 🔑 **Every form of matter has two kinds of properties—physical properties and chemical properties.** A **physical property** is a characteristic of a substance that can be observed without changing it into another substance.

Some properties of matter can't be seen just by observation or touch. A **chemical property** is a characteristic of a substance that describes its ability to change into different substances. To observe the chemical properties of a substance, you must try to change it into another substance. Physical and chemical properties are used to classify matter.

Basketball Hoop Two physical properties of metals are luster, or shine, and the ability to conduct electric current and heat. Another physical property is flexibility, which is the ability to be bent into shapes.

Mark all the objects that are flexible.
- ◯ Aluminum can
- ◯ Copper sheeting
- ◯ Brick house
- ◯ Glass window
- ◯ Silver spoon
- ◯ Wood drumstick

What do all of the flexible objects have in common?

_____

What physical property makes metal pots good for cooking?

_____

Water A physical property of water is that it freezes at 0°C. When liquid water freezes, it changes to ice, but it is still water. The temperatures at which substances boil and melt are also physical properties.

Rusty Metal Chain A chemical property of iron is that it combines slowly with oxygen in the air to form a different substance, rust. Silver reacts with sulfur in the air to form tarnish. In contrast, a chemical property of gold is that it does not react easily with oxygen or sulfur.

Frozen Fruit Bar Hardness, texture, temperature, and color are examples of physical properties. When you describe a material as a solid, a liquid, or a gas, you are describing its state of matter. State of matter is another physical property.

Describe three properties of a frozen fruit bar, including its state of matter.

_____

_____

Will any of these properties change after a couple of hours in the sun? Explain.

_____

_____

_____

Charcoal Briquettes Fuels, like charcoal, can catch fire and burn. When a fuel burns, it combines with oxygen in the air and changes into the substances water and carbon dioxide. The ability to burn, or flammability, is a chemical property.

How do you know that flammability is a chemical property?

_____

_____

_____

 Do the Quick Lab *Observing Physical Properties.*

apply it!

The wax in a burning candle can be described by both physical and chemical properties.

❶ Describe What are the physical properties of the wax in a burning candle?

_____

_____

_____

❷ CHALLENGE Why is melting a physical property of the wax, but flammability is a chemical property?

_____

_____

_____

_____

_____

🔑 Assess Your Understanding

1a. Classify The melting point of table salt is 801°C. Is this a physical or chemical property?

_____

b. Draw Conclusions Helium does not usually react with other substances. Does this mean that helium has no chemical properties? Explain.

_____

_____

got it?

○ **I get it!** Now I know that matter is described by its _____

_____

_____

○ **I need extra help with** _____

_____

Go to **MY SCIENCE** Ⓢ **COACH** *online for help with this subject.*

95

Virginia

LESSON

2 Classifying Matter

UNLOCK THE BIG Q?

🔑 **What Is Matter Made Of?**
PS.1n, PS.2a, PS.2b

🔑 **What Are Two Types of Mixtures?**
PS.2b

MY PLANET DIARY

Smaller Than Small

What's the smallest thing you can think of? A grain of sand? A speck of dust? If you look at these items under a powerful microscope, you'll see that they're made up of smaller and smaller pieces. All matter is made up of very tiny particles called atoms. Atoms are so small, there is a special unit of measure used to describe them called a nanometer (nm). A nanometer is equal to 1/1,000,000,000 or one-billionth of a meter!

At least 50,000 of these tiny compounds called nanobouquets could fit on the head of a pin.

SCIENCE STATS

Write your answers to the questions below.

1. A nickel is about 2 millimeters thick, or 2/1,000 of a meter. How many nanometers is this?

   _____
   _____

2. Imagine being the size of an atom. Describe how something like a red blood cell might look to you.

   _____
   _____
   _____

▶ **PLANET DIARY** Go to **Planet Diary** to learn more about atoms.

Common Objects in Nanometers (nm)

Object	Approximate Size
Compact disc diameter	120,000,000 nm
Grain of sand	3,000,000 nm
Grain of pollen	500,000 nm
Human hair diameter	100,000 nm
Red blood cell	7000 nm
Length of 3–10 atoms lined up	1 nm

Lab zone® Do the Inquiry Warm-Up *What Is a Mixture?*

Vocabulary
- element • atom • chemical bond
- molecule • compound • chemical formula
- mixture

Skills
↻ Reading: Compare and Contrast
△ Inquiry: Infer

What Is Matter Made Of?

What is matter? Why is one kind of matter different from another kind of matter? Around 450 B.C., a Greek philosopher named Empedocles attempted to answer these questions. He proposed that all matter was made of four "elements"—air, earth, fire, and water. Empedocles thought that all other matter was a combination of these elements. The idea of four elements was so convincing that people believed it for more than 2,000 years.

Elements In the late 1600s, experiments by early chemists began to show that matter was made up of many more than four elements. 🔑 Scientists know that all matter in the universe is made of more than 100 different substances, called elements. An **element** is a substance that cannot be broken down into any other substances by chemical or physical means. Elements are the simplest substances. Each element can be identified by its specific physical and chemical properties. You may already be familiar with some elements such as aluminum or tin. Elements are represented by one- or two-letter symbols, such as C for carbon, O for oxygen, and Ca for calcium.

> **Science Standards of Learning**
>
> **PS.1n** Use current applications of physical science concepts.
>
> **PS.2a** Investigate and understand the particle theory of matter.
>
> **PS.2b** Investigate and understand elements and compounds.

apply it!

The elements make up all the matter in the universe.

1 Explain How can you tell one element from another?

_____

_____

_____

2 △ Infer Match the pictures on this page of items containing common elements to the element's name.

A) helium   B) gold   C) copper
D) iron   E) neon

3 CHALLENGE Choose another element that you are familiar with and describe its properties.

_____

_____

_____

Atoms Imagine tearing a piece of aluminum foil in half over and over again. Would you reach a point where you had the smallest possible piece of aluminum? The answer is yes. The particle theory of matter explains that all matter is made of atoms. An **atom** is the basic particle from which all elements are made. An atom has a positively charged center, or nucleus, containing smaller particles. The nucleus is surrounded by a "cloud" of negative charge. The elements have different properties because their atoms are different.

Molecules Atoms of most elements are able to combine with other atoms. When atoms combine, they form a **chemical bond**, which is a force of attraction between two atoms. In many cases, atoms combine to form larger particles called molecules. A **molecule** (MAHL uh kyool) is a group of two or more atoms held together by chemical bonds. A molecule of water, for example, is made up of an oxygen atom chemically bonded to two hydrogen atoms. Two atoms of the same element can also combine to form a molecule. Oxygen molecules are made up of two oxygen atoms. **Figure 1** shows models of some common molecules.

✎ **Compare and Contrast** How are atoms and molecules the same? How are they different?

_____

_____

_____

_____

_____

_____

FIGURE 1 ·······································

Atoms and Molecules

Molecules are made up of groups of atoms.

✎ **Use the molecule models to complete the activities.**

1. **Interpret Diagrams** Count the number of atoms of each element in the molecules and write it on the lines below.

2. CHALLENGE On the bottom line, write a representation for each molecule using letters and numbers.

Key

C = Carbon
H = Hydrogen
O = Oxygen
N = Nitrogen

Carbon dioxide

_____

_____

_____

CHALLENGE

_____

Water

_____

_____

_____

Oxygen

_____

_____

_____

Ammonia

_____

_____

_____

Compounds Water, ammonia, and carbon dioxide are all compounds. A **compound** is a substance made of two or more elements that are chemically combined in a set ratio. A compound is represented by a **chemical formula,** which shows the elements in the compound and the ratio of atoms. For example, the chemical formula for carbon dioxide is CO_2. The 2 below the O for oxygen tells you that the ratio of carbon atoms to oxygen atoms is 1 to 2. If there is no number after an element's symbol, it is understood that the number is 1. A different number of atoms in a formula represents a different compound. For example, the formula for carbon monoxide is CO. Here, the ratio of carbon atoms to oxygen atoms is 1 to 1.

When elements chemically combine, they form compounds with properties different from those of the elements. **Figure 2** shows that the element sulfur is a yellow solid and the element copper is a shiny metal. When copper and sulfur combine, they form a compound called copper sulfide. The new compound has different properties from both copper and sulfur.

FIGURE 2 ....

> ART IN MOTION **Compounds From Elements**
When elements combine, the compound that forms has different properties than the original elements.

✎ **Describe** List the properties of copper, sulfur, and copper sulfide.

Copper

Sulfur

Copper Sulfide

Lab® Do the Quick Lab *Modeling*
zone *Atoms and Molecules.*

🔑 **Assess Your Understanding**

1a. Review What holds the hydrogen and oxygen atoms together in a water molecule?

_____

b. Identify Table sugar has the chemical formula $C_{12}H_{22}O_{11}$. What is the ratio of carbon atoms to oxygen atoms in this compound?

_____

_____

c. Draw Conclusions Two formulas for compounds containing hydrogen and oxygen are H_2O and H_2O_2. Do these formulas represent the same compound? Explain.

_____

_____

_____

_____

_____

got it? ....

○ **I get it!** Now I know that all matter is made up of _____

_____

○ **I need extra help with** _____

Go to MY SCIENCE ⑤ COACH *online for help with this subject.*

Science Standards of Learning

PS.2b Investigate and understand elements, compounds, mixtures, acids, bases, and salts.

What Are Two Types of Mixtures?

Elements and compounds are substances, but most materials are mixtures. **Figure 3** shows some common mixtures. A **mixture** is made of two or more substances that are together in the same place, but their atoms are not chemically bonded. Mixtures differ from compounds. Each substance in a mixture keeps its own properties. Also, the parts of a mixture are not combined in a set ratio.

Think of a handful of sand. If you look closely at the sand, you will see particles of rock, bits of shells, maybe even crystals of salt.

Heterogeneous Mixtures There are two types of mixtures. **A mixture can be heterogeneous or homogeneous.** In a heterogeneous mixture (het ur oh JEE nee us), you can usually see the different parts and they can easily be separated out. The sand described above is a heterogeneous mixture. So is a salad. Think of how easy it is to see the pieces of lettuce, tomatoes, onions, and other ingredients that can be mixed in countless ways.

Homogeneous Mixtures The substances involved in a homogeneous mixture (hoh moh JEE nee us), are so evenly mixed that you can't see the different parts. It is difficult to separate the parts of a homogeneous mixture. Air is a homogeneous mixture of gases. You know that oxygen is present in the air because you are able to breathe, but you cannot identify where the oxygen is in the air. A solution is another example of a homogeneous mixture. Solutions can be liquids, gases, or even solids.

Vocabulary Prefixes The prefix *homo-* comes from a Greek word that means "the same or alike." Predict the meaning of the prefix *hetero-*.
- more than one
- different
- equal

FIGURE 3 ································

Mixtures

Many foods are mixtures.

✎ **Interpret Photos** Label each food as a heterogeneous or homogeneous mixture.

Honey

Guacamole

Soy sauce

Ketchup

CHALLENGE Is ketchup a heterogeneous or homogeneous mixture? Explain your reasoning.

_____
_____
_____
_____

Separating Mixtures

Since the substances in a mixture keep their properties, you can use those properties to separate a mixture into its parts. Methods used to separate the parts of a mixture, including distillation, evaporation, filtration, and magnetic attraction, are shown in **Figure 4.**

FIGURE 4 ·····················

Separating a Mixture
Different methods can be used to separate mixtures.

✎ **Identify** Name the type of separation method being used in each photo.

Solids can be separated from liquids by pouring the mixture through a filter.

Sulfur and water mixture

Water

Iron objects can be separated from a mixture using a magnet.

When left in the open air, liquid solutions can change to gas, leaving solid components behind.

Salt water → Table salt

Liquids can be separated from each other by heating them up to the temperature at which one of the liquids boils. The liquid boils into a gas. Then the gas cools, forming the separated liquid.

Water vapor rises.

Solution boils.

Water vapor cools inside the tube.

Pure liquid water drips into a flask.

Lab zone® Do the Quick Lab *Separating Mixtures.*

🔑 Assess Your Understanding

got it? ··

○ **I get it!** Now I know that the two types of mixtures are _____

_____

○ **I need extra help with** _____

Go to MY SCIENCE ⬢ COACH *online for help with this subject.*

Measuring Matter

UNLOCK THE BIG ?

🗝 **What Units Are Used to Express Mass and Volume?**
PS.1b, PS.1c

🗝 **How Is Density Determined?**
PS.1b, PS.1j

MY PLANET DIARY

FIELD TRIP

Site: Lake Assal
Location: Djibouti, Republic of Djibouti

Travel to the eastern coast of Africa and you will find the country of Djibouti. There, you can visit one of the saltiest bodies of water in the world. Lake Assal is ten times saltier than the ocean. Its crystal white beaches are made up of salt. While on your visit to Lake Assal, be sure to take a dip in the clear blue waters. Take a book or magazine with you to read. Wait … what? Take a book into a lake? It might seem strange, but bodies of water with high salt contents, like Lake Assal or the Dead Sea in the Middle East, allow you to float so well that it's nearly impossible to sink below the surface of the water.

Salt water is denser than fresh water. Less-dense liquids float on top of more-dense liquids. You, too, will float on top of the salty water. In fact, it will be difficult even to swim, so what else can you do? Read a book while you float along!

Floating in the Dead Sea

Communicate Write your answers to the questions below. Then discuss your answers with a partner.

What water activities might be easier to do in Lake Assal's salty water? What activities could be more difficult?

_____

_____

_____

▶ PLANET DIARY Go to **Planet Diary** to learn more about density.

Lab zone® Do the Inquiry Warm-Up *Which Has More Mass?*

Vocabulary

- weight • mass
- International System of Units
- volume • density

Skills

- ↻ Reading: Identify the Main Idea
- △ Inquiry: Calculate

What Units Are Used to Express Mass and Volume?

Science Standards of Learning

PS.1b Accurately measure mass, volume, and weight.

PS.1c Convert among metric units and apply appropriate prefixes.

Here's a riddle for you: Which weighs more, a pound of feathers or a pound of sand? If you answered "a pound of sand," think again. Both weigh exactly the same—one pound.

There are all sorts of ways to measure matter, and you use these measurements every day. Scientists rely on measurements as well. In fact, scientists work hard to make sure their measurements are as accurate as possible.

Weight Your **weight** is a measure of the force of gravity on you. On another planet, the force of gravity will be more if the planet is more massive than Earth and less if the planet is less massive than Earth. On the moon, you would weigh only about one sixth of your weight on Earth. On Jupiter, you would weigh more than twice your weight on Earth.

To find the weight of an object, you could place it on a scale like the ones shown in **Figure 1.** The object's weight pulls down on the mechanisms inside the scale. These mechanisms cause beams or springs inside the scale to move. The amount of movement depends on the weight of the object. From the movement of the beams, the scale displays the weight to you.

↻ **Identify the Main Idea**
Underline the sentence(s) that describe how weight can be affected by location.

FIGURE 1 ······························

Measuring Weight

✎ **Complete the tasks below.**

1. **Estimate** Use the weight of the first scale to estimate the weight of the fish on the other scales. Draw in the pointers.

2. **Describe** How would their weight change on a small planet like Mercury? Or a large planet like Neptune?

_____

_____

_____

_____

With 10 seconds left on the clock, John makes the play at the 9.144-meter line.

9.144

If we always used the metric system

Mass How can you weigh less on the moon than on Earth when nothing about you has changed? Your weight is dependent on the gravity of the planet you are visiting. The amount of matter in an object is its **mass,** which does not change with location even if the force of gravity changes. If you travel to the moon, the amount of matter in your body—your mass—does not change. You are the same size. For this reason, scientists prefer to describe matter in terms of mass rather than weight. The mass of an object is a physical property.

To measure the properties of matter, scientists use a system called the **International System of Units** (abbreviated SI for the French name, *Système International d'Unités*). **The SI unit of mass is the kilogram (kg).** If you weigh 90 pounds on Earth, your mass is about 40 kilograms. Often, a smaller unit is used to measure mass, the gram (g). There are 1,000 grams in a kilogram, or 0.001 kilograms in a gram. The table in **Figure 2** lists the masses of some common items.

Mass of Common Objects

Object	Mass (g)	Mass (kg)
Nickel	5	0.005
Baseball	150	_____
Pineapple	1,600	_____
Full can of soda	390	_____
Inflated balloon	3	_____

FIGURE 2 ·······························

Measuring Mass
The SI system uses grams and kilograms to measure mass.

✎ **Complete the following tasks about mass.**

1. **Calculate** In the table, convert the mass of each object from grams to kilograms.

2. **CHALLENGE** Suppose you are taking a flight to Europe. You are only allowed a 23-kg suitcase. How much is that in pounds? (*Hint:* 1 kg = 2.2 lbs.)

   ○ 50.6 lbs   ○ 46.2 lbs   ○ 10.5 lbs

Volume

All matter has mass and takes up space. The amount of space that matter occupies is called its **volume.** It's easy to see that solids and liquids take up space, but gases have volume, too.

🔑 **The SI unit of volume is the cubic meter (m³).** Other common SI units of volume include the cubic centimeter (cm³), the liter (L), and the milliliter (mL). Common plastic soda bottles hold 2 liters of liquid. A milliliter is 1/1,000 of a liter and is exactly the same volume as 1 cubic centimeter. A teaspoonful of water has a volume of about 5 milliliters. In a lab, volumes of liquid are often measured with a graduated cylinder.

Calculating Volume

Suppose you want to know the volume of a rectangular object, like one of the suitcases shown in **Figure 3.** First, measure the length, width, and height (or thickness) of the suitcase. Then, multiply the measurements together.

Volume = Length × Width × Height

When you multiply the three measurements, you must also multiply the units.

Units = cm × cm × cm = cm³

63.5 cm

23 cm

43 cm

FIGURE 3 ·······························
> VIRTUAL LAB **Calculating Volume**
△ **Calculate** Find the volume of the suitcase.

_____

_____

Measuring Irregular Objects

How do you measure the volume of an irregular object, such as a key or a raspberry? One way is to submerge the object in a liquid in a graduated cylinder. The liquid level will rise by an amount that is equal to the volume of the object in milliliters.

Labzone® Do the Quick Lab
Calculating Volume.

🔑 Assess Your Understanding

1. Explain Why is mass more useful than weight for measuring matter?

_____

_____

_____

_____

_____

got it? ···

○ **I get it!** Now I know that the SI unit for
mass is _____
and the SI unit for volume is _____

_____

○ **I need extra help with** _____

_____

Go to **MY SCIENCE** ⑤ **COACH** *online for help with this subject.*

How Is Density Determined?

Remember the riddle about the sand and the feathers? Although they weigh the same, a kilogram of sand takes up much less space than a kilogram of feathers. The volumes differ because sand and feathers have different densities—an important property of matter.

Calculating Density **Density** is a measure of the mass of a material in a given volume. Density can be expressed as the number of grams in one cubic centimeter (g/cm^3). For example, the density of water at room temperature is stated as "one gram per cubic centimeter" ($1 \ g/cm^3$). Recall that volume can also be measured in milliliters. So the density of water can also be expressed as 1 g/mL. 🔑 **You can determine the density of a sample of matter by dividing its mass by its volume.**

$$Density = \frac{Mass}{Volume}$$

Sinking or Floating? Suppose you have a block of wood and a block of iron of equal mass. When you drop both blocks into a tub of water, you see that the wood floats and the iron sinks. You know the density of water is $1 \ g/cm^3$. Objects with densities greater than that of water will sink. Objects with lesser densities will float.

Watch a bottle of oil and vinegar salad dressing after it has been shaken. You will see the oil slowly form a separate layer above the vinegar. This happens because oil is less dense than vinegar.

apply it!

Liquids can form layers based on density.

❶ **Apply Concepts** Label the layers of colored liquid in the column according to their densities.

Water: 1.00 g/mL   Honey: 1.36 g/mL   Dish soap: 1.03 g/mL
Corn syrup: 1.33 g/mL   Vegetable oil: 0.91 g/mL

❷ **Calculate** What is the density of a liquid with a mass of 17.4 g and a volume of 20 mL? Where would this liquid be in the column?

_____

_____

❸ [CHALLENGE] In which layer(s) would a solid cube with 6-cm sides and a mass of 270 g float? Explain.

_____

_____

Using Density
Suppose you are a gold miner in the 1800s, like the men in **Figure 4**. One day, while panning through the sediment in a stream, you come across a shiny golden rock. How do you know if the rock is real gold? Since density is a physical property of a substance, it can be used to identify an unknown substance. You can measure the mass and volume of the rock and find its density. If it matches 19.3 g/cm³, the density of gold, then you have struck it rich!

FIGURE 4 ....

 Using Density
Density can be used to identify substances.

✎ **Estimate** Hypothesize which rock sample is gold. Then, calculate the density of each sample. Circle the rock that is real gold.

My hypothesis is that the gold rock is:

○ A   ○ B   ○ C

A   Mass = 108 g
Volume = 12 cm³

Density = _____

B   Mass = 126 g
Volume = 15 cm³

Density = _____

C   Mass = 386 g
Volume = 20 cm³

Density = _____

 Do the Lab Investigation
Making Sense of Density.

⚷ Assess Your Understanding

2a. Identify Maple syrup will (float/sink) in water because its density is greater than 1 g/cm³.

b. ✎ **Calculate** What is the mass of a sample of a substance with a volume of 120 mL and a density of 0.75 g/mL?

_____

c. [CHALLENGE] Liquid water and ice are the same substance, H₂O. How would you explain why ice floats in water?

_____

_____

_____

got it? ....

○ **I get it!** Now I know density is calculated by _____

_____

○ **I need extra help with** _____

Go to MY SCIENCE ˢ COACH *online for help with this subject.*

Virginia

LESSON

4 Changes in Matter

UNLOCK THE BIG ❓

🔑 **What Happens to a Substance in a Physical Change?**
PS.2c, PS.5a

🔑 **What Happens to a Substance in a Chemical Change?**
PS.1k, PS.5b

🔑 **How Are Changes in Energy and Matter Related?**
PS.1b, PS.1i, PS.1j, PS.1k, PS.6b, PS.7d

MY PLANET DIARY

BLOG

Posted by: Dylan
Location: Fountain Valley, California

Whenever I go to the beach, I spend a majority of my time building a sand castle. I try to build it after a high tide comes. That way I have a lot of time to build up the walls and they will not be destroyed as quickly by the water.

Even though the waves will eventually destroy the castle and take the sand with them back to the ocean, the sand could be easily separated from the ocean. At the end of the day when I leave and kick and stomp on my sand castle, it is still sand. Only its appearance changes.

Write your answers to the questions below.

1. Describe the differences in the ways the sand castle is changed by an ocean wave and by Dylan stomping on it.

_____
_____
_____
_____

2. Dylan changed a formless pile of sand into a sand castle. What other natural materials can be changed into art?

_____
_____

▶ PLANET DIARY Go to **Planet Diary** to learn more about changes in matter.

Lab® zone Do the Inquiry Warm-Up
Is a New Substance Formed?

Vocabulary

- physical change
- chemical change
- law of conservation of mass
- temperature
- thermal energy
- endothermic change
- exothermic change
- chemical energy

Skills

- Reading: Relate Cause and Effect
- Inquiry: Draw Conclusions

Science Standards of Learning

PS.2c Investigate and understand solids, liquids, and gases.

PS.5a Investigate and understand physical changes in matter and how they relate to the Law of Conservation of Matter and Energy.

What Happens to a Substance in a Physical Change?

How can matter change? A **physical change** alters the form or appearance of matter but does not turn any substance in the matter into a different substance. In **Figure 1,** a butter artist has changed a formless block of butter into artwork. Although it looks different, the sculpture is still butter. **A substance that undergoes a physical change is still the same substance after the change.** Many physical changes, such as snow melting into water, occur in nature.

Changes of State As you may know, matter occurs in three familiar states—solid, liquid, and gas. Suppose you leave a small puddle of liquid water on the kitchen counter. When you come back two hours later, the puddle is gone. Has the liquid water disappeared? No, a physical change happened. The liquid water changed into water vapor (a gas) and mixed with the air. A change in state, such as from a solid to a liquid or from a liquid to a gas, is an example of a physical change.

FIGURE 1 ···

Change of State

Changes between solids, liquids, and gases are physical changes.

✎ **Predict** Describe the changes the butter sculpture will undergo in a few hours if it is left out in the sun.

_____

_____

_____

_____

_____

Changes in Shape or Form Is there a physical change when you dissolve a teaspoon of table sugar in water? To be sure, you would need to know whether or not the sugar has been changed to a different substance. For example, you know that a sugar solution tastes sweet, just like the undissolved sugar. If you pour the sugar solution into a pan and let the water dry out, the sugar will remain as a crust at the bottom of the pan. The crust may not look like the sugar before you dissolved it, but it's still sugar. So, dissolving is also a physical change. Other examples of physical changes are bending, crushing, breaking, and chopping. Any change that alters only the shape or form of matter is a physical change. The methods of separating mixtures, such as filtration and distillation, also involve physical changes.

FIGURE 2 ··
Changes in Appearance
The Japanese art of origami paper folding involves physical changes.

✎ **Complete the following tasks.**

1. **Make Models** Using the corner of this page or a separate sheet, make two physical changes to the paper.

2. **Communicate** Ask a classmate to identify and list below the changes you made.

_____

_____

3. CHALLENGE Is it correct to say that dissolving a packet of juice powder in water makes a new substance, fruit punch, so it must not be a physical change?

_____

_____

_____

_____

Lab zone® Do the Quick Lab *What Is a Physical Change?*

🔑 **Assess Your Understanding**

1a. Classify Mark all the processes that are physical changes.

○ drying wet clothes
○ lighting a match from a matchbook
○ cutting snowflakes out of paper
○ melting butter for popcorn

b. Apply Concepts Describe three physical changes that occur in nature.

_____

_____

_____

_____

got it? ···

○ **I get it!** Now I know that a substance that undergoes a physical change is _____

_____

○ **I need extra help with** _____

Go to MY SCIENCE ⬤S COACH *online for help with this subject.*

What Happens to a Substance in a Chemical Change?

Another kind of change occurs when a substance transforms into another substance. A change in matter that produces one or more new substances is a chemical change, or chemical reaction. In some chemical changes, a single substance breaks down into two or more other substances. For example, hydrogen peroxide breaks down into water and oxygen gas when it's poured on a cut on your skin. In other chemical changes, two or more substances combine to form different substances. Photosynthesis is a natural chemical change. Several compounds combine with energy from the sun to produce new substances.

Figure 3 shows chemical changes that are used in forensics to collect evidence. To make fingerprints more visible, a chemical found in super-strong glues is heated. Vapors from the glue react with sweat or other body chemicals in a fingerprint to form a white powder making the print visible. Luminol is a chemical that reacts with blood. It combines with traces of blood that are too small to see with the naked eye to form a new substance that glows in the dark. The footprint in Figure 3 has been treated with luminol. ● Unlike a physical change, a chemical change produces new substances with new and different properties.

Science Standards of Learning

PS.1k Use research methods to investigate practical problems and questions.

PS.5b Investigate and understand chemical changes in matter and how they relate to the Law of Conservation of Matter and Energy.

FIGURE 3 ·······················
Chemical Changes
The prints are visible because of chemical change.

apply it!

You are a detective investigating a robbery. When you arrive at the scene, there are not many clues that you can see to help solve the crime. You're able to write down a few observations.

Solve Problems
Determine how you would use chemical changes to gather evidence at the crime scene.

An empty jewelry box is knocked over on a table.

Chemical treatment: _____
_____
_____

An open box of bandages is on the floor. Bandage wrappers are found nearby.

Chemical treatment: _____
_____
_____

Shattered glass from a window is scattered across the floor.

Chemical treatment: _____
_____
_____

111

Copper: before

Copper: after

Examples of Chemical Change One common chemical change is the burning of natural gas on a gas stove. Natural gas is mostly made up of the compound methane (CH_4). When it burns, methane combines with oxygen in the air and forms new substances. These new substances include carbon dioxide gas (CO_2) and water vapor (H_2O). Both of these substances can be identified by their properties, which are different from those of methane. The chemical change that occurs when fuels, such as natural gas, candle wax, or wood, burn in air is called combustion. Other processes resulting in chemical change include electrolysis, oxidation, and tarnishing. The table in **Figure 4** describes each of these types of chemical change.

FIGURE 4 ·······················

Types of Chemical Change
The copper in the Statue of Liberty is exposed to oxygen in the air.

✎ **Observe** What chemical change did the Statue of Liberty likely undergo? Describe the properties before and after the chemical change.

_____

_____

_____

_____

_____

_____

Examples of Chemical Change

Chemical Change	Description	Example
Combustion	Rapid combination of a fuel with oxygen; produces heat, light, and new substances	Gas, oil, or coal burning in a furnace
Electrolysis	Use of electricity to break a compound into elements or simpler compounds	Breaking down water into hydrogen and oxygen
Oxidation	Combination of a substance with oxygen	Rusting of an iron fence
Tarnishing	Slow combination of a bright metal with sulfur or another substance, producing a dark coating on the metal	Tarnishing of brass

Conservation of Mass Water may seem to "disappear" when it evaporates, but scientists long ago proved otherwise. In the 1770s, a French chemist, Antoine Lavoisier, measured mass both before and after a chemical change. His data showed that no mass was lost or gained during the change. The fact that matter is not created or destroyed in any chemical or physical change is called the **law of conservation of mass.** This law is also called the law of conservation of matter since mass is a measurement of matter.

Suppose you could measure all of the carbon dioxide and water produced when methane burns. You would find that it equals the mass of the original methane plus the mass of the oxygen from the air that was used in the burning. **Figure 5** demonstrates that during a chemical change, atoms are not lost or gained, only rearranged.

FIGURE 5 ·······························
> INTERACTIVE ART

Conservation of Mass
✎ **Interpret Diagrams** Count the atoms of each element before and after the chemical change. Is mass conserved in this reaction? Explain.

_____
_____
_____
_____

| Methane molecule | Two oxygen molecules | | Carbon dioxide molecule | Two water molecules |

☐ Carbon atom(s)   ☐ Hydrogen atom(s)   ☐ Oxygen atom(s)   ☐ Carbon atom(s)   ☐ Hydrogen atom(s)   ☐ Oxygen atom(s)

Lab zone Do the Quick Lab
Demonstrating Tarnishing.

🔑 Assess Your Understanding

2a. Name A chemical reaction is another name for a chemical (combustion/change).

b. Predict What kind of chemical change do you think occurs when a banana peel turns brown in the open air? Explain.

_____
_____

c. CHALLENGE Assuming no mass escapes, explain why the mass of a rusted nail is greater than the mass of a nail before it rusted.

_____
_____
_____
_____

got it? ···

○ **I get it!** Now I know that when a substance undergoes a chemical change, _____
_____

○ **I need extra help with** _____
   Go to MY SCIENCE ⓢ COACH *online for help with this subject.*

113

Science Standards of Learning

PS.1b Accurately measure density.

PS.1i Construct and interpret line plots.

PS.1j Make valid conclusions after analyzing data.

PS.1k Use research methods to investigate practical problems and questions.

PS.6b Investigate and understand mechanical, chemical, electrical, thermal, radiant, and nuclear energy and how they can be transferred and transformed.

PS.7d Investigate and understand applications of thermal energy transfer.

How Are Changes in Energy and Matter Related?

Do you feel as if you are full of energy today? Energy is the ability to do work or cause change. 🔑 **Every chemical and physical change in matter includes a change in energy.** A change as simple as bending a paper clip takes energy. When ice changes to liquid water, it absorbs energy from the surrounding matter. When candle wax burns, it gives off energy as light and heat.

Like matter, energy is conserved in a chemical change. Energy is never created or destroyed. It can only be transformed from one form to another.

Temperature and Thermal Energy

Think of how it feels when you walk inside an air-conditioned building from the outdoors on a hot day. Whew, what a difference in temperature! **Temperature** is a measure of how hot or cold something is. It is related to the energy of motion of the particles of matter. The particles of gas in the warm outside air have greater average energy of motion than the particles of air inside the cool building.

Thermal energy is the total energy of the motion of all of the particles in an object. Usually, you experience thermal energy when you describe matter as feeling hot or cold. Temperature and thermal energy are not the same thing, but the amount of thermal energy an object has is related to its temperature. Thermal energy naturally flows from warmer matter to cooler matter.

FIGURE 6 ···

Thermal Energy

✎ **Apply Concepts** Shade in the arrow that indicates which direction energy will flow between the people and the icy water or warm mud pit.

Energy

Energy

Energy

Energy

Thermal Energy and Changes in Matter

Thermal energy is a form of energy that is often released or absorbed when matter changes. For example, ice absorbs thermal energy from its surroundings when it melts, leaving the surroundings feeling cold. That's why you can pack food and drinks in an ice-filled picnic cooler. The melting of ice is an **endothermic change,** a change in which energy is absorbed. Changes in matter can also occur when energy is given off. An **exothermic change** releases energy. Combustion is a chemical change that releases thermal energy and light.

Transforming Chemical Energy
The energy stored in the chemical bonds between atoms is a form of energy called **chemical energy.** Chemical energy is stored in foods, fuels, and even the cells of your body. Animals, like the bear in **Figure 7,** gain chemical energy from food.

Burning fuels transforms chemical energy and releases some of it as thermal energy. When you ride a bike up a hill, chemical energy from foods you ate changes into energy of motion. Chemical energy can change into other forms of energy, and other forms of energy can change into chemical energy.

Relate Cause and Effect
Underline the sentence that describes how your hand would be affected if you made a snowball or held a frozen treat.

FIGURE 7 ....
Transforming Chemical Energy
Chemical energy from food can be transformed into other types of energy needed for activity.

do the math! Analyzing Data

A student records the temperature of two reactions once per minute. Her data are plotted on the graph.

1 Calculate What was the change in temperature for each reaction after 10 minutes?

_____

_____

2 Draw Conclusions On the graph, label each reaction as exothermic or endothermic. How can you tell?

_____

_____

_____

_____

Temperature of Two Reactions

Reaction A
Reaction B

Time (minutes)

115

INDIANA JANE
AND THE
INVESTIGATION OF MATTER

EXPLORE THE BIG ?

How is matter described?

FIGURE 8 ·····················

> **INTERACTIVE ART** Indiana Jane is hunting for lost treasures of matter. Join her in following clues to describe different types of matter.

✎ **Review** Answer questions about Indiana's findings along the way. Then, complete the logbook with information you've gathered about the properties of matter.

Tarnished coins I found these coins near the opening of a foul-smelling cave. I believe they were a shiny metal at one point, perhaps silver, platinum, or aluminum. I've determined the mass of each coin to be 315 g and the volume to be 30 cm³.

What element are the coins made of?
- ○ Aluminum (density = 2.7 g/cm³)
- ○ Silver (density = 10.5 g/cm³)
- ○ Platinum (density = 21.5 g/cm³)

Arrowhead This arrowhead, most likely carved by an ancient hunter, was discovered in a pile of rocks.
Describe the type of mixture the arrowhead was found in.

_____
_____
_____
_____
_____

Mummy The mummy we found today is badly decayed, probably because its sarcophagus is not sealed airtight. I translated a scroll found nearby that says the mummy and case originally had a mass of 200 kg. The mass is now 170 kg.
Explain how the mummy and its sarcophagus decreased in mass if the law of conservation of mass must be obeyed.

_____
_____
_____
_____
_____
_____
_____
_____
_____

Yellowed, torn map
Field notes: The paper of this ancient map has suffered from changes over the years making it nearly impossible to read.—IJ

Indiana Jane has to bring all the artifacts back to the museum. Describe each object's properties and the physical or chemical changes it underwent.

Object	Properties	Changes Undergone
1. Clay pot		
2. Coins		
3. Map		

Broken clay pot Field notes: I've come across some clay pots. Many have been broken or cracked over time.—IJ

Wax statue I believe we have found the remains of the famous Carved Dove wax statue. It would have been a valuable artifact, but all that's left is a puddle of liquid.
Describe at least two changes the wax has undergone over time.

_____
_____
_____

Lab zone® Do the Quick Lab *Where Was the Energy?*

Assess Your Understanding

3a. Identify What energy transformation takes place when you exercise?

_____
_____

b. ANSWER THE BIG ? How is matter described?

_____
_____
_____
_____
_____
_____
_____
_____
_____

got it? ....

○ I get it! Now I know that every chemical and physical change includes _____
_____

○ I need extra help with _____
_____

Go to **MY SCIENCE COACH** *online for help with this subject.*

Study Guide

Water is a _____ . A _____ property of water is that it boils at 100°C. The _____ of water is 1 g/cm³.

LESSON 1 Describing Matter

🔑 Every form of matter has two kinds of properties—physical properties and chemical properties.

Vocabulary
• matter
• chemistry
• substance
• physical property
• chemical property

LESSON 2 Classifying Matter

🔑 Scientists know that all matter in the universe is made of more than 100 different substances, called elements.

🔑 A mixture can be heterogeneous or homogeneous.

Vocabulary
• element   • atom
• chemical bond   • molecule   • compound
• chemical formula   • mixture

LESSON 3 Measuring Matter

🔑 The SI unit of mass is the kilogram (kg).

🔑 The SI unit of volume is the cubic meter (m³).

🔑 You can determine the density of a sample of matter by dividing its mass by its volume.

Vocabulary
• weight   • mass   • International System of Units
• volume   • density

LESSON 4 Changes in Matter

🔑 A substance that undergoes a physical change is still the same substance after the change.

🔑 Unlike a physical change, a chemical change produces new substances with new and different properties.

🔑 Every chemical and physical change in matter includes a change in energy.

Vocabulary
• physical change   • chemical change   • law of conservation of mass
• temperature   • thermal energy   • endothermic change
• exothermic change   • chemical energy

Review and Assessment

LESSON 1   Describing Matter

1. Which of the following is an example of a chemical property?

   a. density   **b.** flammability

   c. hardness   **d.** luster

2. A substance can be classified by its physical properties, which are properties that

_____

_____

_____

_____

_____

3. Classify Which of the following is a substance: table salt, seawater, or sand? Explain how you know.

_____

_____

_____

_____

4. Interpret Tables Write a title that describes the table below.

Helium	Colorless; less dense than air
Iron	Attracted to magnets; melting point of 1,535°C
Oxygen	Odorless; gas at room temperature

5. **Write About It** Write an e-mail to a friend explaining why the melting point of a substance is a physical property but flammability is a chemical property. Use examples to explain.

LESSON 2   Classifying Matter

6. Which of the following is an element?

   a. water   **b.** carbon dioxide

   c. oxygen   **d.** ammonia

7. Four methods that can be used to separate mixtures are _____

_____

_____

Use the diagrams to answer Questions 8–10. Each diagram represents a different kind of matter. Each ball represents an atom. Balls of the same color are the same kind of atom.

8. Interpret Diagrams Which diagram or diagrams represent a single element? Explain.

_____

_____

9. Compare and Contrast How do the atoms in Diagram A differ from those in Diagram D?

_____

_____

_____

10. Apply Concepts Which diagram or diagrams represent a mixture? Explain.

_____

_____

_____

3 Review and Assessment

LESSON 3 Measuring Matter

11. What is the SI unit of mass?

   a. milliliter   **b.** kilogram

   c. pound   **d.** cubic centimeter

12. The density of a substance is calculated by

_____

_____

13. Make Judgments Which measurement shown in the diagram is not needed to find the volume of the box? Explain.

_____

_____

_____

14. math! A piece of metal has a volume of 38 cm³ and a mass of 277 g. Calculate the density of the metal and identify it based on the information in the table below.

Density of Common Metals	
Iron	7.9 g/cm³
Lead	11.3 g/cm³
Tin	7.3 g/cm³
Zinc	7.1 g/cm³

LESSON 4 Changes in Matter

15. Which of the following is a physical change?

   a. burning   **b.** rusting

   c. freezing   **d.** oxidation

16. The law of conservation of mass states that

_____

_____

_____

17. Solve Problems How could you prove that dissolving table salt in water is a physical change, not a chemical change?

_____

_____

_____

_____

_____

APPLY THE BIG ? How is matter described?

18. Choose a substance you're familiar with. What are its physical and chemical properties? How would you measure its density? What are some physical and chemical changes it can undergo?

_____

_____

_____

_____

_____

_____

_____

_____

_____

_____

Virginia SOL Test Prep

Read each question and choose the best answer.

1 Each diagram below represents a different kind of matter. Each ball represents an atom. Balls of the same size and shade are the same atom. Which diagram *best* represents a mixture of two kinds of molecules?

A

B

C

D

A Diagram A   B Diagram B
C Diagram C   D Diagram D

2 The fact that matter is neither created nor destroyed in any chemical or physical change is called the —

F law of exothermic change
G law of endothermic change
H law of thermal matter
J law of conservation of mass

3 The density of a substance equals its mass divided by its volume. The density of sulfur is 2.0 g/cm³. What is the mass of a sample of sulfur with a volume of 6.0 cm³?

A 3.0 g   B 4.0 g
C 8.0 g   D 12 g

4 The abilities to dissolve in water and to conduct electric current are examples of —

F physical properties
G chemical properties
H physical changes
J chemical bonding

5 Which two pieces of laboratory equipment would be the *most* useful for measuring the mass and volume of a rectangular block?

A a metric ruler and a stopwatch
B a balance and a metric ruler
C a graduated cylinder and a metric ruler
D a balance and a stop watch

6 A student mixes two liquids of the same temperature together. The graph above shows the change in temperature after the liquids mix. Based on the data in the graph, which of the following conclusions can you draw about the reaction?

F The reaction was exothermic because the temperature decreased over time.

G The reaction was neither exothermic nor endothermic because the temperature did not change.

H The reaction was endothermic because the temperature increased over time.

J The reaction was exothermic because the temperature increased over time.

121

Science and History

Long Ago in a Faraway Land...

In an old German tale, a strange little man named Rumpelstiltskin spins straw into gold. Sounds far-fetched, right? It wouldn't have sounded that strange to someone in the fourteenth century. Hundreds of years ago, alchemists searched for a way to turn metals, like lead, into gold. They also tried to make medicines that would cure all diseases and allow people to live for a long time. They thought they needed just one ingredient to do all of this—the philosopher's stone.

Nowadays, we know that a magic ingredient will not change the chemical and physical properties of elements. We have learned that different elements have different properties. But alchemists did make valuable contributions to people's understanding of the physical world. Alchemists discovered alcohol and mineral acids, and recorded their observations of how these acids reacted with other substances. They worked in laboratories heating base metals and observing interactions and changes in color. They recorded their conclusions about these experiments. Their goal may have been impossible, but their research helped build the foundation of chemistry today.

Research It Throughout history, scientists have increased our understanding of the natural world by learning from those before them. Research how the fields of chemistry and medicine have developed from the experiments of alchemists. Write an essay describing the progression.

 PS.1k, PS.2b

An Antiuniverse?

What if the entire universe had a mirror or negative image? Would everything happen backward? Or, would there be an opposite you? Scientists working in the field of particle physics think there just might be a mirror universe, but they don't really expect it to be the stuff of science fiction movies.

A little over a hundred years ago, scientists thought that the smallest part of matter—a part not made up of anything else—was the atom. That wasn't true. An atom is made up of a nucleus that contains protons and neutrons, surrounded by electrons. A physicist named Paul Dirac added an interesting twist to this knowledge. He correctly predicted that the electron might have a reverse twin, which he called a positron. (He won the Nobel Prize for this leap of genius back in 1933.) The positron has the same mass as an electron but the opposite charge—it's the antielectron.

Electrons, neutrons, and protons all have these antiparticles, or at least they did when the particles formed. Scientists have been able to study them in the laboratory. Inside particle accelerators, scientists can even use positrons and electrons to form entirely new atoms. But outside of the controlled laboratory environment, where are these antiparticles? Are they now part of an antiuniverse somewhere? Physicists are hoping to find the answers in the twenty-first century— your century!

Research It Write down three questions you have about particle physics and antimatter. Research to find out the answers. Articles about the CERN laboratory in Switzerland would be a good place to start. Answer your questions in one or two paragraphs.

 PS.1k

Paul Dirac predicted that positrons might exist as the opposites of electrons. ▼

◀ Inside a special chamber, two invisible photons enter and produce a pair of electrons (colored green) and antielectrons (colored red).

HOW DID THIS BUILDING TURN TO ICE?

Why does a substance change states?

Firefighters sprayed water on a blaze in this historic building in Maine. The air temperature was −14°F, which was uncomfortably cold. This made it difficult for firefighters to battle the flames. The building was in danger of falling down because it was covered in ice 6 to 10 inches thick. **Infer** How did this building get covered in ice?

_____

_____

_____

_____

_____

> UNTAMED SCIENCE Watch the **Untamed Science** video to learn more about changing states.

Solids, Liquids, and Gases

Virginia

CHAPTER

4

Science Standards of Learning

PS.1b, PS.1c, PS.1f, PS.1g, PS.1i, PS.1j, PS.1k,
PS.1m, PS.1n, PS.2a, PS.2c, PS.2d, PS.2f, PS.7a,
PS.7b, PS.11a, PS.11b

4 Getting Started

Check Your Understanding

1. **Background** Read the paragraph below and then answer the question.

The air **temperature** outside has been below freezing all week. The local pond has frozen over and is ready for ice skating. Ronnesia is excited just thinking about all the things she can do on the **ice.** She eats a good breakfast to get the **energy** she needs for ice skating.

> **Temperature** is a measure of the average energy of random motion of particles of matter.
>
> **Ice** is water in the solid form.
>
> **Energy** is the ability to do work or cause change.

• Why is the pond ready for ice skating?

_____

_____

> **MY READING WEB** If you had trouble completing the question above, visit **My Reading Web** and type in *Solids, Liquids, and Gases.*

Vocabulary Skill

Suffixes A suffix is a letter or group of letters added to the end of a word to change its meaning and often its part of speech. In this chapter, you will learn vocabulary words that end in the suffixes *-ation*, *-ine*, and *-sion*.

Suffix	Meaning	Example
-ation	State of, process of, act of	Vaporization, evaporation, condensation, sublimation
-ine	Consisting of	Crystalline solid
-sion	State of, process of, act of	Surface tension

2. **Quick Check** *Vapor* is another word for gas. Use the table above to predict the meaning of *vaporization*. Revise your definition as needed.

_____

_____

liquid

surface tension

 melting

sublimation

Chapter Preview

LESSON 1
- solid
- crystalline solid
- amorphous solid
- liquid
- fluid
- surface tension
- viscosity
- gas
- pressure

  ↻ **Relate Cause and Effect**
  ▲ **Infer**

LESSON 2
- melting
- melting point
- freezing
- vaporization
- evaporation
- boiling
- boiling point
- condensation
- sublimation

  ↻ **Compare and Contrast**
  ▲ **Predict**

LESSON 3
- Charles's Law
- directly proportional
- Boyle's Law
- inversely proportional

  ↻ **Identify the Main Idea**
  ▲ **Graph**

▶ VOCAB FLASH CARDS For extra help with vocabulary, visit **Vocab Flash Cards** and type in *Solids, Liquids, and Gases*.

States of Matter

UNLOCK
THE BIG
?

🔑 **How Do You Describe a Solid?**
PS.2a, PS.2c, PS.2d, PS.2f

🔑 **How Do You Describe a Liquid?**
PS.2a, PS.2c, PS.2d, PS.2f

🔑 **How Do You Describe a Gas?**
PS.1b, PS.1c, PS.2a, PS.2c, PS.2d, PS.2f

MY PLANET DIARY

Liquid Crystals

Have you ever wondered why some television sets are referred to as LCD TVs? *LCD* stands for "liquid crystal display." An LCD is a thin, flat screen. LCDs have replaced the picture tubes in many computer monitors and television sets because they are lighter and use less power. LCDs are also found in cell phones and clock radio faces.

Liquid crystals are neither solid nor liquid—instead they fall somewhere in between. But it takes just a small amount of thermal energy to change a liquid crystal to a liquid. As a result, LCDs tend to be very sensitive to heat.

FUN FACTS

Communicate Discuss these questions with a classmate. Write your answers below.

1. List some things that contain LCDs.

_____

_____

_____

2. Why might you not want to leave a cell phone or a laptop computer outside on a hot day?

_____

_____

_____

_____

> PLANET DIARY Go to **Planet Diary** to learn more about solids, liquids, and gases.

Lab zone® Do the Inquiry Warm-Up *What Are Solids, Liquids, and Gases?*

LCD display with crystals cooling (background)

Vocabulary
- solid • crystalline solid • amorphous solid • liquid
- fluid • surface tension • viscosity • gas • pressure

Skills
↻ Reading: Relate Cause and Effect
△ Inquiry: Infer

How Do You Describe a Solid?

Look at the bowl in **Figure 1.** It contains the metal bismuth. Notice that the shape and size of the piece of bismuth are different from the bowl's shape and size. What would happen if you took the bismuth out of the bowl and placed it on a tabletop? Would it become flatter? What would happen if you put it in a larger bowl? Would it become larger? Of course not, because it's a solid. A **solid** has a definite shape and a definite volume. Your pencil is another example of a solid. If your pencil has a cylindrical shape and a volume of 6 cubic centimeters, it will keep this shape and volume in any position in any container.

Particles in a Solid The particles that make up a solid are packed very closely together. Also, each particle is tightly fixed in one position. 🔑 **This fixed, closely packed arrangement of particles in a solid causes it to have a definite shape and volume.** Do the particles that make up a solid move at all? Yes, but not much. The particles in a solid are closely locked in position and can only vibrate in place. This means that the particles move back and forth slightly, like a group of people running in place.

> **Science Standards of Learning**
>
> **PS.2a** Investigate and understand the particle theory of matter.
> **PS.2c** Investigate and understand solids, liquids, and gases.
> **PS.2d** Investigate and understand physical properties of matter.
> **PS.2f** Investigate and understand characteristics of types of matter based on physical properties.

Place a check in each category that describes a solid.

	Definite	Indefinite
Shape	_____	_____
Volume	_____	_____

Particles in a solid

FIGURE 1 ·······························
Solid
A solid does not take the shape or volume of its container.
✎ **Interpret Diagrams** Describe the arrangement of particles in a solid.

_____

_____

_____

FIGURE 2 ················

Types of Solids
Solids are either crystalline or amorphous. Butter is an amorphous solid. The mineral fluorite is a crystalline solid.

✎ **Compare and Contrast** Use the Venn diagram to compare the characteristics of amorphous and crystalline solids.

Types of Solids In many solids, the particles form a regular, repeating pattern. These patterns create crystals. Solids that are made up of crystals are called **crystalline solids** (KRIS tuh lin). Salt, sugar, and snow are examples of crystalline solids. The fluorite crystal shown in **Figure 2** is an example of a colorful crystalline solid. When a crystalline solid is heated, it melts at a distinct temperature.

In **amorphous solids** (uh MAWR fus), the particles are not arranged in a regular pattern. Unlike a crystalline solid, an amorphous solid does not melt at a distinct temperature. Instead, it may become softer and softer or change into other substances. Glass is an example of an amorphous solid. A glass blower can bend and shape glass that has been heated. Plastics and rubber are other examples of amorphous solids.

Amorphous   Both   Crystalline

Lab zone® Do the Quick Lab
Modeling Particles.

🔑 **Assess Your Understanding**

1a. Identify The two types of solids are
_____ and _____.

b. Explain Are the particles in a solid motionless? Explain your answer.

_____

_____

c. Draw Conclusions Candle wax gradually loses its shape as it is heated. What type of solid is candle wax? Explain.

_____

_____

_____

_____

got it? ···

○ I get it! Now I know that a solid has a definite shape and volume because_____

_____

○ I need extra help with _____

    Go to MY SCIENCE ⬤ᔆ COACH online for help with this subject.

How Do You Describe a Liquid?

Without a container, a liquid spreads into a wide, shallow puddle. Like a solid, however, a liquid does have a constant volume. A **liquid** has a definite volume but no shape of its own. **Figure 3** shows equal volumes of iced tea in two different containers. The shape of a liquid may change with its container, but its volume remains the same.

Particles in a Liquid In general, the particles in a liquid are packed almost as closely together as those in a solid. However, the particles in a liquid move around one another freely. You can compare this movement to the way you might move a group of marbles around in your hand. Like the particles of a liquid, the marbles slide around one another but still touch. **Because its particles are free to move, a liquid has no definite shape. However, it does have a definite volume.** These freely moving particles allow a liquid to flow from place to place. For this reason, a liquid is also called a **fluid,** meaning a "substance that flows."

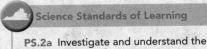

Science Standards of Learning

PS.2a Investigate and understand the particle theory of matter.

PS.2c Investigate and understand solids, liquids, and gases.

PS.2d Investigate and understand physical properties of matter.

PS.2f Investigate and understand characteristics of types of matter based on physical properties.

Relate Cause and Effect
Underline the cause and circle the effect in the boldface sentences.

Place a check in each category that describes a liquid.

	Definite	Indefinite
Shape	_____	_____
Volume	_____	_____

Particles in a liquid

FIGURE 3 ••••••••••••••••••••••

Liquid
Each container contains 300 cm^3 of iced tea. The iced tea takes the shape of its container, but its volume does not change.

✎ **Interpret Diagrams** Describe the arrangement of particles in a liquid.

_____

_____

_____

_____

FIGURE 4 ·····················

Surface Tension

Infer **Circle the correct answer.**
Water beads up on the surface of
the leaves because water molecules
(attract/repel) each other strongly.

Properties of Liquids One characteristic property
of liquids is surface tension. **Surface tension** is an inward
force, or pull, among the molecules in a liquid that brings
the molecules on the surface closer together. You may
have noticed that water forms droplets and can bead up on
many surfaces, such as the leaves shown in **Figure 4.** That's
because water molecules attract one another strongly. These
attractions cause molecules at the water's surface to be
pulled slightly toward the water molecules beneath its surface. Due to surface tension, the surface of water can act like
a sort of skin. For example, a sewing needle floats when you
place it gently on the surface of water, but it quickly sinks if
you push it below the surface. Surface tension lets an insect
called a water strider walk on the calm surface of a pond.

Another characteristic property of liquids is **viscosity**
(vis KAHS uh tee), or a liquid's resistance to flowing. A
liquid's viscosity depends on the size and shape of its
particles and the attractions between the particles. Some
liquids flow more easily than others. Liquids with high
viscosity flow slowly. Honey is an example of a liquid with a
very high viscosity. Liquids with low viscosity flow quickly.
Water and vinegar have relatively low viscosities.

Lab zone Do the Quick Lab *As Thick as Honey.*

Assess Your Understanding

2a. Name A substance that flows is called a

_____

b. Describe Why is a liquid able to flow?

_____

_____

c. Compare and Contrast How do liquids with
a high viscosity differ from liquids with a low
viscosity?

_____

_____

_____

got it? ···

O **I get it!** Now I know that a liquid has a definite volume but not a definite shape because _____

_____

_____

O **I need extra help with** _____

  Go to **MY SCIENCE** **COACH** *online for help with this subject.*

How Do You Describe a Gas?

Like a liquid, a gas is a fluid. Unlike a liquid, however, a **gas** has neither a definite shape nor a definite volume. If a gas is in a closed container such as the flask in **Figure 5,** the gas particles will move and spread apart as they fill the container.

If you could see the particles that make up a gas, you would see them moving in all directions. **As gas particles move, they spread apart, filling all the space available. Thus, a gas has neither definite shape nor definite volume.** When working with a gas, it is important to know its volume, temperature, and pressure. So what exactly do these measurements mean?

Volume Remember that volume is the amount of space that matter fills. Volume is measured in cubic centimeters (cm³), cubic meters (m³), milliliters (mL), liters (L), and other units. Because gas particles move and fill all of the space available, the volume of a gas is the same as the volume of its container. For example, a large amount of helium gas can be compressed—or pressed together tightly—to fit into a metal tank. When you use the helium to fill balloons, it expands to fill many balloons that have a total volume much greater than the volume of the tank.

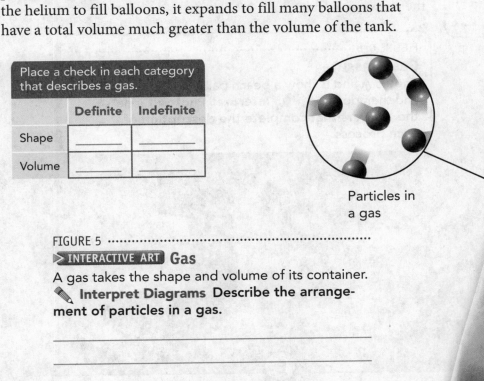

Place a check in each category that describes a gas.

	Definite	Indefinite
Shape		
Volume		

Particles in a gas

FIGURE 5

▷ INTERACTIVE ART **Gas**

A gas takes the shape and volume of its container.

✎ **Interpret Diagrams** Describe the arrangement of particles in a gas.

_____

_____

_____

_____

_____

133

Calculating Pressure

When calculating pressure, force is measured in newtons (N). If the area is measured in square meters (m^2), pressure is expressed in pascals (Pa), where $1 \text{ Pa} = 1 \text{ N/m}^2$. Suppose a gas exerts a force of 252 N on a piston having an area of 0.430 m^2. What is the pressure on the piston in Pascals?

$$\text{Pressure} = \frac{\text{Force}}{\text{Area}}$$

$$= \frac{252 \text{ N}}{0.430 \text{ m}^2}$$

$$= 586 \text{ Pa}$$

Practice Problem A gas exerts a force of 5,610 N over an area of 0.342 m^2. What pressure does the gas exert in Pa?

_____

_____

_____

Pressure Gas particles constantly collide with one another and with the walls of their container. As a result, the gas pushes on the walls of the container. The **pressure** of the gas is the force of its outward push divided by the area of the walls of the container. Pressure is measured in units of pascals (Pa) or kilopascals (kPa) (1 kPa = 1,000 Pa).

$$\text{Pressure} = \frac{\text{Force}}{\text{Area}}$$

The firmness of a gas-filled object comes from the pressure of the gas. For example, the air inside an inflated ball has a higher pressure than the air outside. This higher pressure is due to the greater concentration of gas particles inside the ball than in the surrounding air. Concentration is the number of gas particles in a given unit of volume.

Why does a ball leak even when it has only a tiny hole? The higher pressure inside the ball results in gas particles hitting the inner surface of the ball more often. Therefore, gas particles inside the ball reach the hole and escape more often than gas particles outside the ball reach the hole and enter. Thus, many more particles go out than in. The pressure inside drops until it is equal to the pressure outside.

FIGURE 6 ···

Gas Pressure
Photos A and B show a beach ball being inflated and then deflated. ✎ **Interpret Photos** Circle the answers that complete the description of each process.

A The concentration of gas particles inside the beach ball (increases/decreases). The gas pressure inside the beach ball (increases/decreases).

B The concentration of gas particles inside the beach ball (increases/decreases). The gas pressure inside the beach ball (increases/decreases).

Faster-moving, hot gas particles

Slower-moving, cool gas particles

Temperature

The balloonists in **Figure 7** are preparing the balloon for flight. To do this, they use a propane burner to heat the air inside the balloon. Once the temperature of the air is hot enough, the balloon will start to rise. But what does the temperature tell you? Recall that all particles of matter are constantly moving. Temperature is a measure of the average energy of random motion of the particles of matter. The faster the particles are moving, the greater their energy and the higher the temperature. You might think of a thermometer as a speedometer for particles.

Even at room temperature, the average speed of particles in a gas is very fast. At about 20°C, the particles in a typical gas travel about 500 meters per second—more than twice the cruising speed of a jet plane!

FIGURE 7 ··

Temperature of a Gas

✏ **Explain** Why are the hot gas particles moving faster than the cool gas particles?

_____

_____

_____

Lab zone® Do the Quick Lab *How Do the Particles in a Gas Move?*

🔑 Assess Your Understanding

3a. Describe Describe how the motions of gas particles are related to the pressure exerted by the gas.

_____

_____

_____

_____

_____

b. Relate Cause and Effect Why does pumping more air into a basketball increase the pressure inside the ball?

_____

_____

_____

_____

_____

got it? ···

○ **I get it!** Now I know that a gas has neither a definite shape nor definite volume because_____

_____

○ **I need extra help with** _____

Go to MY SCIENCE ⬤ᔆ COACH *online for help with this subject*

Changes of State

LESSON

2

Virginia

UNLOCK THE BIG ?

🔑 **What Happens to the Particles of a Solid as It Melts?**
PS.1j, PS.2a, PS.2c, PS.2d, PS.7b

🔑 **What Happens to the Particles of a Liquid as It Vaporizes?**
PS.2a, PS.2c, PS.2d, PS.7b

🔑 **What Happens to the Particles of a Solid as It Sublimes?**
PS.1j, PS.2a, PS.2c, PS.2d, PS.7b

MY PLANET DiARY

SCIENCE STATS

On the Boil

You might have noticed that as an uncovered pot of water boils, the water level slowly decreases. The water level changes because the liquid is changing to a gas. As you heat the water, the thermal energy of its molecules increases. The longer you leave the pot on the hot stove, the more energy is absorbed by the water molecules. When the water molecules gain enough energy, they change state from a liquid to a gas.

The graph shows the temperature of a small pot of water on a stove set to high heat. The starting temperature of the water is 20°C.

Liquid to a Gas

Answer the following questions.

1. How long does it take for the water to start boiling? At what temperature does the water boil?

_____

_____

_____

2. Does it take more energy to heat the water to 100°C or to boil it?

_____

_____

_____

▷ PLANET DIARY Go to **Planet Diary** to learn more about changes of state.

 Do the Inquiry Warm-Up *What Happens When You Breathe on a Mirror?*

136 Solids, Liquids, and Gases

Vocabulary

- melting • melting point • freezing • vaporization
- evaporation • boiling • boiling point • condensation
- sublimation

Skills

↻ **Reading: Compare and Contrast**

▲ **Inquiry: Predict**

What Happens to the Particles of a Solid as It Melts?

Particles of a liquid have more thermal energy than particles of the same substance in solid form. As a gas, the particles have even more thermal energy. A change from a solid to a liquid involves an increase in thermal energy. As you might guess, a change from a liquid to a solid is just the opposite: It involves a decrease in thermal energy.

Melting The change in state from a solid to a liquid is called **melting**. In pure, crystalline solids, melting occurs at a specific temperature, called the **melting point**. Because the melting point is a characteristic property of a substance, chemists often compare melting points when trying to identify an unknown material. The melting point of pure water, for example, is 0°C at sea level.

What happens to the particles of a solid as it melts? Think of an ice cube taken from the freezer. The energy needed to melt the ice comes mostly from the air in the room. At first, the added thermal energy makes the water molecules vibrate faster, raising their temperature. **At a solid's melting point, its particles vibrate so fast that they break free from their fixed positions.** At 0°C, the temperature of the ice stops increasing. Any added energy continues to change the arrangement of the water molecules from ice crystals into liquid water. The ice melts.

Science Standards of Learning

PS.1j Make valid conclusions after analyzing data.

PS.2a Investigate and understand the particle theory of matter.

PS.2c Investigate and understand solids, liquids, and gases.

PS.2d Investigate and understand physical properties of matter.

PS.7b Investigate and understand phase change, freezing point, melting point, boiling point, vaporization, and condensation.

FIGURE 1 ·······························

Melting

✎ **Relate Diagrams and Photos** Draw a line matching each illustration of water molecules to either ice or liquid water. Then describe how ice and liquid water differ in the arrangement of their molecules.

_____

_____

_____

_____

Freezing The change of state from a liquid to a solid is called **freezing.** It is just the reverse of melting. **At a liquid's freezing point, its particles are moving so slowly that they begin to take on fixed positions.**

When you put liquid water into a freezer, for example, the water loses energy to the cold air in the freezer. The water molecules move more and more slowly as they lose energy. Over time, the water becomes solid ice. When water begins to freeze, its temperature stays at 0°C until freezing is complete. The freezing point of water, 0°C, is the same as its melting point.

apply it!

In metal casting, a liquid metal is poured into a container called a mold. The mold gives a shape to the metal when it cools and hardens.

1 Explain How does metal casting make use of the different characteristics of liquids and solids?

_____
_____
_____
_____
_____

2 | CHALLENGE | The melting point of copper is 1084°C. How does the energy of the particles in a certain amount of liquid copper compare to the energy of the molecules in the same amount of liquid water? Why?

_____
_____
_____
_____
_____

> **Lab** zone® Do the Lab Investigation
> *Melting Ice.*

Assess Your Understanding

1a. Identify The change in state from a solid to a liquid is called _____

b. Compare and Contrast How does what happens to the particles in a substance during melting differ from what happens in freezing?

_____
_____
_____
_____
_____

got it? ....

O **I get it!** Now I know that melting occurs when the particles in a solid_____
_____
_____

O **I need extra help with** _____

Go to **MY SCIENCE** ⬤ᔆ **COACH** *online for help with this subject.*

What Happens to the Particles of a Liquid as It Vaporizes?

Have you ever wondered how clouds form or why puddles dry up? To answer these questions, you need to look at what happens when changes occur between the liquid and gas states.

Evaporation and Boiling The change in state from a liquid to a gas is called **vaporization** (vay puhr ih ZAY shun). 🔑 **Vaporization occurs when the particles in a liquid gain enough energy to move independently.** There are two main types of vaporization—evaporation and boiling.

Vaporization that takes place only on the surface of a liquid is called **evaporation** (ee vap uh RAY shun). A shrinking puddle is an example. Water in the puddle gains energy from the ground, the air, or the sun. The added energy enables some of the water molecules on the surface of the puddle to escape into the air, or evaporate.

Vaporization that takes place both below and at the surface of a liquid is called **boiling.** When water boils, vaporized water molecules form bubbles below the surface. The bubbles rise and eventually break the surface of the liquid. The temperature at which a liquid boils is called its **boiling point.** As with melting points, chemists use boiling points to help identify unknown substances.

Science Standards of Learning

PS.2a Investigate and understand the particle theory of matter.

PS.2c Investigate and understand solids, liquids, and gases.

PS.2d Investigate and understand physical properties of matter.

PS.7b Investigate and understand phase change, freezing point, melting point, boiling point, vaporization, and condensation.

✎ **Compare and Contrast**
Compare and contrast the two types of vaporization.

_____
_____
_____
_____
_____
_____
_____

FIGURE 2 ················

Types of Vaporization
Liquid water changes to water vapor by either evaporation or boiling.

✏ **Interpret Diagrams** Label the type of vaporization occurring in each flask. Then draw arrows to indicate the paths of water molecules leaving each flask.

Suppose there is the same amount of water in both of the flasks. ▲**Predict** Which flask does water vaporize from first? Why?

_____
_____
_____
_____

139

Condensation

Condensation is the reverse of vaporization. The change in state from a gas to a liquid is called **condensation.** You can observe condensation by breathing onto a mirror. When warm water vapor in your breath reaches the cooler surface of the mirror, the water vapor condenses into liquid droplets. **Condensation occurs when particles in a gas lose enough thermal energy to form a liquid.**

Clouds typically form when water vapor in the atmosphere condenses into tiny liquid droplets. When the droplets get heavy enough, they fall to the ground as rain. Water vapor is a colorless gas that you cannot see. The steam you see above a kettle of boiling water is not water vapor, and neither are clouds or fog. What you see in those cases are tiny droplets of liquid water suspended in air.

Vocabulary Suffixes Complete the sentences using the correct forms of the word *condense.*

_____ is the change in state from a gas to a liquid. Clouds form because water vapor _____

FIGURE 3 ·······························
Foggy Mirror
Explain Why does a mirror fog up after a hot shower?

_____
_____
_____
_____
_____
_____

Lab zone® Do the Quick Lab *Keeping Cool.*

Assess Your Understanding

2a. Identify The change in state from a liquid to a gas is called _____

b. Apply Concepts How does the thermal energy of water vapor change as the vapor condenses?

_____
_____

c. Relate Cause and Effect Why do clouds form before it rains?

_____
_____
_____
_____
_____

got it? ···

○ **I get it!** Now I know that vaporization occurs when the particles in a liquid _____
_____

○ **I need extra help with** _____

Go to **my science COACH** online for help with this subject.

What Happens to the Particles of a Solid as It Sublimes?

In places where the winters are cold, the snow may disappear even when the temperature stays well below freezing. This change is the result of sublimation. **Sublimation** occurs when the surface particles of a solid gain enough energy that they form a gas. ⚷ **During sublimation, particles of a solid do not pass through the liquid state as they form a gas.**

One example of sublimation occurs with dry ice. Dry ice is the common name for solid carbon dioxide. At ordinary atmospheric pressures, carbon dioxide cannot exist as a liquid. So instead of melting, solid carbon dioxide changes directly into a gas. As it sublimes, the carbon dioxide absorbs thermal energy. This property helps keep materials near dry ice cold and dry. For this reason, using dry ice is a way to keep the temperature low when a refrigerator is not available. Some fog machines use dry ice to create fog in movies or at concerts, as shown in **Figure 4.** When dry ice becomes a gas, it cools water vapor in the nearby air. The water vapor then condenses into a liquid, forming fog near the dry ice.

Science Standards of Learning

PS.1j Make valid conclusions after analyzing data.

PS.2a Investigate and understand the particle theory of matter.

PS.2c Investigate and understand solids, liquids, and gases.

PS.2d Investigate and understand physical properties of matter.

PS.7b Investigate and understand phase change, freezing point, melting point, boiling point, vaporization, and condensation.

did you know?

Mosquitos are attracted to the carbon dioxide gas you exhale during breathing. A mosquito trap baited with dry ice can attract up to four or five times as many mosquitos as traps baited with a light source alone.

FIGURE 4

Dry Ice

A fog machine uses dry ice to create fog at this rock concert. ✏ **Explain** Why does fog form near dry ice?

_____

_____

_____

_____

_____

Dry ice subliming

The Changing States of Water

Why does a substance change states?

FIGURE 5 ....

VIRTUAL LAB Four examples of how water changes states—by melting, freezing, vaporization, and condensation—are shown here.

✎ **Review** Use what you have learned about states of matter to answer the questions.

FREEZING

This lake has frozen over due to the cold weather. As liquid water freezes, its molecules (gain/lose) thermal energy. How does the motion of the water molecules change during freezing?

_____

_____

_____

_____

Freezing ←

Melting →

Low Thermal Energy

MELTING

The air outside is so warm that this snow-man is melting. During melting, the water molecules (gain/lose) thermal energy. How does the motion of the molecules change during melting?

_____

_____

_____

_____

_____

VAPORIZATION

These wet footprints are disappearing due to evaporation. As water evaporates, its molecules (gain/lose) thermal energy. How does the motion of the molecules change during evaporation?

_____
_____
_____
_____
_____

High Thermal Energy

← Condensation

Vaporization →

CONDENSATION

During the night, water vapor in the air condensed on this spider web. As water vapor condenses, its molecules (gain/lose) thermal energy. How does the motion of the molecules change during condensation?

_____
_____
_____
_____

 Lab zone Do the Quick Lab *Observing Sublimation.*

⊶ Assess Your Understanding

3a. Identify What is dry ice?

_____
_____

b. Predict If you allowed dry ice to stand in a bowl at room temperature for several hours, what would be left?

_____
_____

c. ANSWER THE BIG ? Why does a substance change states?

_____
_____
_____
_____
_____

got it? ....

○ **I get it!** Now I know that sublimation occurs when the particles in a solid_____
_____
_____

○ **I need extra help with** _____

Go to **MY SCIENCE** ⁵ **COACH** *online for help with this subject.*

Gas Behavior

UNLOCK THE BIG ?

🔑 **How Are Pressure and Temperature of a Gas Related?**
PS.2a, PS.2c, PS.2d

🔑 **How Are Volume and Temperature of a Gas Related?**
PS.1g, PS.1j, PS.2a, PS.2c, PS.2d, PS.7a

🔑 **How Are Pressure and Volume of a Gas Related?**
PS.1f, PS.1g, PS.1i, PS.1j, PS.2a, PS.2c, PS.2d

MY PLANET DIARY

BIOGRAPHY

Jacques Charles (1746–1823)

French scientist Jacques Charles is best known for his work on gases. But he also made contributions to the sport of ballooning. On August 27, 1783, Charles released the first hydrogen-filled balloon, which was about 4 meters in diameter. This balloon, which did not carry any people, rose to a height of 3,000 feet. Charles also improved the design of hot-air balloons. He added a valve line that allowed the pilot to release gas from the balloon. He also added a wicker basket that attached to the balloon with ropes. Charles was elected to the French Academy of Sciences in 1785.

Communicate Discuss this question with a classmate. Write your answer below.

What sport or hobby inspires you to want to know more about science? Why?

_____

_____

_____

> **PLANET DIARY** Go to **Planet Diary** to learn more about gases.

Lab zone Do the Inquiry Warm-Up *How Can Air Keep Chalk From Breaking?*

How Are Pressure and Temperature of a Gas Related?

If you dropped a few grains of sand onto your hand, you would hardly feel them. But what if you were caught in a sandstorm? Ouch! The sand grains fly around very fast, and they would sting if they hit you. Although gas particles are much smaller than sand grains, a sandstorm is a good model for gas behavior. Like grains of sand in a sandstorm, gas particles travel at high speeds. The faster the gas particles move, the greater the force with which they collide with the walls of their container.

Vocabulary
- Charles's law
- directly proportional
- Boyle's law
- inversely proportional

Skills
- Reading: Identify the Main Idea
- Inquiry: Graph

Consider a gas in a closed, rigid container. If you heat the gas, its particles will move faster on average. They will collide with the walls of their container with greater force. The greater force over the same area results in greater pressure. **When the temperature of a gas at constant volume is increased, the pressure of the gas increases. When the temperature is decreased, the pressure of the gas decreases.**

On long trips, especially in the summer, a truck's tires can become very hot. As the temperature increases, so does the pressure of the air inside the tire. If the pressure becomes greater than the tire can hold, the tire will burst. For this reason, truck drivers need to monitor and adjust tire pressure on long trips.

Gas at low temperature — No heat

Gas at high temperature — Heat added

FIGURE 1

Temperature and Gas Pressure
When a gas is heated in a closed, rigid container, the particles move faster and collide more often.

Infer Draw an arrow in each pressure gauge to show the change in pressure of the gas.

Do the Quick Lab
How Are Pressure and Temperature Related?

Assess Your Understanding

got it? ....

O **I get it!** Now I know that when the temperature of a gas at a constant volume increases, _____

_____

O **I need extra help with** _____

Go to **my science coach** *online for help with this subject.*

| A gas-filled balloon is at room temperature, 20°C. | The balloon is lowered into liquid nitrogen at −196°C. | The balloon shrinks as gas volume decreases. | When the balloon is removed, the gas warms and the balloon expands. | The balloon is again at room temperature. |

FIGURE 2 ....

Cooling a Balloon

The volume of a gas-filled balloon decreases as temperature decreases and then increases as temperature increases.

FIGURE 3 ....

Charles's Law

A gas in a cylinder with a movable piston is slowly heated.

✎ **Predict** Draw the piston and gas particles when the temperature reaches 200°C and 400°C.

How Are Volume and Temperature of a Gas Related?

Figure 2 shows what happens when a balloon is slowly lowered into liquid nitrogen at nearly −200°C and then removed. As the air inside the balloon cools, its volume decreases. When the air inside warms up again, its volume increases. The pressure remains more or less constant because the air is in a flexible container.

Charles's Law French scientist Jacques Charles examined the relationship between the temperature and volume of a gas that is kept at a constant pressure. He measured the volume of a gas at various temperatures in a container that could change volume. (A changeable volume allows the pressure to remain constant.) 🔑 **When the temperature of a gas at constant pressure is increased, its volume increases. When the temperature of a gas at constant pressure is decreased, its volume decreases.** This principle is called **Charles's law.**

| No heat | Some heat added | More heat added |

Graphing Charles's Law

Graphing Charles's Law Suppose you do an experiment to test Charles's law. The experiment begins with 50 mL of gas in a cylinder with a movable piston similar to the one in **Figure 3.** The gas is slowly heated. Each time the temperature increases by 10°C, the gas volume is recorded. The data are recorded in the data table in **Figure 4.** Note that the temperatures in the data table have been converted to kelvins, the SI unit of temperature. To convert from Celsius degrees to kelvins (K), add 273.

As you can see in the graph of the data, the data points form a straight line. The dotted line represents how the graph would look if the gas could be cooled to 0 K. Notice that the line passes through the point (0, 0), called the origin. When a graph of two variables is a straight line passing through the origin, the variables are said to be **directly proportional** to each other. The graph of Charles's law shows that the volume of a gas is directly proportional to its kelvin temperature at constant pressure.

Temperature		Volume
(°C)	(K)	(mL)
0	273	50
20	293	54
40	313	58
60	333	62
80	353	66
100	373	70
120	393	74

Charles's Law Graph

FIGURE 4 ··

Temperature and Gas Volume

✎ In an experiment, a gas is heated at a constant pressure. The data shown in the table are plotted on the graph.

1. **Draw Conclusions** What happens to the volume of a gas when the temperature is increased at constant pressure?

_____

2. **CHALLENGE** Suppose the data formed a line with a steeper slope. For the same change in temperature, how would the change in volume compare?

_____

_____

 Do the Quick Lab
Hot and Cold Balloons.

🔑 Assess Your Understanding

1a. Identify The graph of Charles's law shows that the volume of a gas is

_____ to its

kelvin temperature at constant pressure.

b. Predict Suppose the gas in **Figure 4** could be cooled to 100 K (−173°C). Predict the volume of the gas at this temperature.

_____

got it? ···

○ **I get it!** Now I know that when the temperature of a gas is decreased at constant pressure _____

_____

○ **I need extra help with** _____

Go to MY SCIENCE ⑤ **COACH** online for help with this subject.

Identify the Main Idea
Underline the main idea in the text under the red heading "Boyle's Law."

How Are Pressure and Volume of a Gas Related?

Suppose you use a bicycle pump to inflate a tire. By pressing down on the plunger, you force the gas inside the pump through the rubber tube and out of the nozzle into the tire. What happens to the volume of air inside the pump cylinder as you push down on the plunger? What happens to the pressure?

Boyle's Law In the 1600s, the scientist Robert Boyle carried out experiments to try to improve air pumps. He measured the volumes of gases at different pressures. Boyle's experiments showed that gas volume and pressure were related. **When the pressure of a gas at constant temperature is increased, the volume of the gas decreases. When the pressure is decreased, the volume increases.** This relationship between the pressure and the volume of a gas is called **Boyle's law.**

Boyle's law describes situations in which the volume of a gas is changed. The pressure then changes in the opposite way. For example, as you push down on the plunger of a bicycle pump, the volume of air inside the pump cylinder gets smaller, and the pressure inside the cylinder increases. The increase in pressure forces air into the tire.

FIGURE 5 ···

> **INTERACTIVE ART** **Boyle's Law**
As weights are added to the top of each piston, the piston moves farther down in the cylinder. **Interpret Diagrams** First, rank the pressure in each of the cylinders. Then rank the volume. A ranking of 1 is the greatest. A ranking of 3 is the lowest.

1a. _____ pressure **1b.** _____ pressure **1c.** _____ pressure

2a. _____ volume **2b.** _____ volume **2c.** _____ volume

do the math! Analyzing Data

In an experiment, the volume of a gas was varied at a constant temperature. The pressure of the gas was recorded after each 50-mL change in volume. The data are in the table below.

① **Graph** Use the data to make a line graph. Plot volume on the horizontal axis. Plot pressure on the vertical axis. Write a title for the graph at the top.

② **Control Variables** The manipulated variable in this experiment is _____. The responding variable is _____.

③ **Make Generalizations** What happens to the pressure of a gas when the volume is decreased at a constant temperature?

_____

Volume (mL)	Pressure (kPa)
300	20
250	24
200	30
150	40
100	60
50	120

Graphing Boyle's Law Look at the graph that you made above. Notice that the points lie on a curve and not a straight line. The curve is steep at lower volumes, but it becomes less steep as volume increases. If you multiply the two variables at any point on the curve, you will find that the product does not change.

$$300 \text{ mL} \times 20 \text{ kPa} = 6{,}000 \text{ mL·kPa}$$
$$250 \text{ mL} \times 24 \text{ kPa} = 6{,}000 \text{ mL·kPa}$$

When the product of two variables is constant, the variables are **inversely proportional** to each other. The graph for Boyle's law shows that gas pressure is inversely proportional to volume at constant temperature.

Do the Quick Lab
It's a Gas.

🔑 Assess Your Understanding

2a. Identify The graph of Boyle's law shows that the gas pressure is

_____ to volume at constant temperature.

b. Read Graphs Use the graph that you made in Analyzing Data above to find the pressure of the gas when its volume is 125 mL.

_____

got it? ···

○ **I get it!** Now I know that when the pressure of a gas at a constant temperature is increased, _____

_____

○ **I need extra help with** _____

Go to **MY SCIENCE COACH** online for help with this subject.

Study Guide

A substance (gains/loses) thermal energy when it melts or vaporizes.

A substance (gains/loses) thermal energy when it freezes or condenses.

LESSON 1 States of Matter

The fixed, closely packed arrangement of particles causes a solid to have a definite shape and volume.

Because its particles are free to move, a liquid has no definite shape. However, it does have a definite volume.

As gas particles move, they spread apart, filling all the space available. Thus, a gas has neither definite shape nor definite volume.

Vocabulary
- solid   • crystalline solid   • amorphous solid   • liquid
- fluid   • surface tension   • viscosity   • gas   • pressure

LESSON 2 Changes of State

At a solid's melting point, its particles vibrate so fast that they break free from their fixed positions.

Vaporization occurs when the particles in a liquid gain enough thermal energy to move independently.

During sublimation, particles of a solid do not pass through the liquid state as they form a gas.

Vocabulary
- melting   • melting point   • freezing   • vaporization   • evaporation
- boiling   • boiling point   • condensation   • sublimation

LESSON 3 The Behavior of Gases

When the temperature of a gas at constant volume is increased, the pressure of the gas increases.

When the temperature of a gas at constant pressure is increased, its volume increases.

When the pressure of a gas at constant temperature is increased, the volume of the gas decreases.

Vocabulary
- Charles's law   • directly proportional   • Boyle's law
- inversely proportional

20°C

No heat

Review and Assessment

LESSON 1 States of Matter

1. A substance with a definite shape and definite volume is a

   a. solid   **b.** liquid

   c. gas   **d.** fluid

2. Rubber is considered a(n) _____ solid because it does not melt at a distinct temperature.

3. Compare and Contrast Why do liquids and gases take the shape of their containers while solids do not?

_____

_____

_____

_____

_____

4. Predict What happens to the gas particles in an inflated ball when it gets a hole? Why?

_____

_____

_____

_____

_____

_____

5. math! Earth's atmosphere exerts a force of 124,500 N on a kitchen table with an area of 1.5 m². What is the pressure in pascals?

_____

_____

_____

6. Write About It Write a short essay in which you create an analogy to describe particle motion. Compare the movements and positions of people dancing with the motions of water molecules in liquid water and in water vapor.

LESSON 2 Changes of State

7. A puddle dries up by the process of

   a. melting   **b.** freezing

   c. condensation   **d.** evaporation

8. When you see fog or clouds, you are seeing water in the _____ state.

9. Classify Label the correct change of state on top of the arrows in the diagram below.

Gas

Solid

Liquid

10. Draw Conclusions At room temperature, table salt is a solid and mercury is a liquid. What conclusion can you draw about the melting points of these substances?

_____

_____

_____

_____

11. Apply Concepts When you open a solid room air freshener, the solid slowly loses mass and volume. How do you think this happens?

_____

_____

_____

_____

_____

151

LESSON 3 **The Behavior of Gases**

12. According to Boyle's law, the volume of a gas increases when its

    a. pressure increases.   **b.** pressure decreases.

    c. temperature falls.   **d.** temperature rises.

13. According to Charles's law, when the temperature of a gas is increased at a constant pressure, its volume _____

14. **Relate Cause and Effect** How does heating a gas in a rigid container change its pressure?

  _____

  _____

15. **Interpret Data** Predict what a graph of the data in the table would look like. Volume is plotted on the *x*-axis. Pressure is plotted on the *y*-axis.

Volume (cm³)	Pressure (kPa)
15	222
21	159
31	108
50	67

  _____

  _____

  _____

  _____

  _____

16. **Relate Cause and Effect** Explain why placing a dented table-tennis ball in boiling water is one way to remove the dent in the ball. (Assume the ball has no holes.)

  _____

  _____

  _____

  _____

APPLY THE BIG **Why does a substance change states?**

17. A fog forms over a lake. What two changes of state must occur to produce the fog? Do the water molecules absorb or release energy during these changes of state? What happens to the motion of the water molecules as a result?

  _____

  _____

  _____

  _____

  _____

  _____

  _____

  _____

  _____

  _____

  _____

  _____

  _____

  _____

Virginia SOL Test Prep

Read each question and choose the best answer.

1 The graph below shows changes in 1 g of a solid as energy is added.

What is the total amount of energy absorbed by the substance as it completely changes from a solid at 40°C to a gas at 200°C?

A   3 kJ   B   6 kJ
C   12 kJ   D   18 kJ

2 Which of the following correctly describes a solid?

F   The particles do not move at all.
G   The particles are closely locked in position and can only vibrate in place.
H   The particles are free to move about independently, colliding frequently.
J   The particles are closely packed but have enough energy to slide past one another.

3 A gas exerts a force of 1,000 N on a surface with an area of 5.0 m². What is the pressure on the area?

A   200 Pa
B   500 Pa
C   2,000 Pa
D   5,000 Pa

4 A gas at constant temperature is in a cylinder with a movable piston. The piston is pushed into the cylinder, decreasing the volume of the gas. The pressure increases. What are the variables in this experiment?

F   temperature and time
G   time and volume
H   volume and pressure
J   pressure and temperature

5 A wet towel is hanging on a clothesline in the sun. The towel dries by the process of—

A   boiling
B   condensation
C   evaporation
D   sublimation

6 The diagrams represent the molecules of water before and after a change of state. What change of state has occurred?

Before   After

F   solid to liquid
G   liquid to gas
H   liquid to solid
J   gas to liquid

SCUBA DIVING

When you swim to the bottom of a pool, you can feel the pressure of the water around you. That pressure increases rapidly during a deeper dive.

To make really deep dives, people use SCUBA (self-contained underwater breathing apparatus) gear. The SCUBA tank is filled with air at very high pressure. Boyle's law states that as pressure increases under conditions of constant temperature, the volume of the gas decreases. In other words, more air will fit into the tank when the pressure is high.

Breathing air straight from the tank could damage the diver's lungs. The pressure of the air entering the diver's lungs needs to match the pressure of the gases already inside the diver's body. Valves on the tank adjust the pressure of the air as it is released to match the pressure of the water around the diver, so that when it enters the diver's body, it matches the pressure of the gases in the body.

Write About It Make an instruction card for new divers explaining that it is dangerous for divers to hold their breath during a deep dive or ascent. Use Boyle's law to explain why this is true.

PS.1j, PS.1m, PS.1n, PS.2a, PS.2c, PS.2d, PS.2f, PS.5a

◀ The regulator adjusts the pressure to match the surrounding water pressure.

A Shocking State

You touch a plasma globe, and lightning crackles. *Zap!* A plasma globe is a glass globe filled with partially ionized gas (that's the plasma!) and pumped full of high voltage power.

What's the Matter?

Plasma is different! In plasma, the electrons have been separated from the neutral atoms, so that they're no longer bound to an atom or molecule. Because positive and negative charges move independently, plasma can conduct electricity—causing the shocking light displays in a plasma globe. Plasma is its own state of matter. Like a gas, it has no shape or volume until it is captured in a container. Unlike a gas, it can form structures and layers, like the bolts in a plasma globe, or a bolt of lightning. It's shocking!

Find It Research and make a list of plasma objects. Compare your list with a partner, and discuss how plasma changes state to become a gas.

 PS.1k, PS.2a, PS.2d, PS.2f, PS.11a, PS.11b

Growing Snow

You may have heard that no two snowflakes look the same. Writers use the unique structures of snowflakes as a metaphor for things that are one-of-a-kind, and impossible to reproduce. And it's probably true! A snowflake forms when water begins to freeze around small particles of dust inside a cloud. The exact shape of the crystal depends on humidity and temperature, and because there are tiny variations in both of these factors, each snowflake will differ slightly from every other snowflake.

All snowflakes share a common shape, though. The hexagonal shape of a snow crystal forms as molecules come together during the phase change from liquid to solid. The oxygen atom has a partial negative charge and the hydrogen atoms a partial positive charge, so the atoms are attracted to one another.

Graphing Research to find out how the exact shape of snow crystals change as temperature and humidity change. Draw a line graph that illustrates your findings.

 PS.1i, PS.1j, PS.1k, PS.2c, PS.2d, PS.2f

The most stable arrangement of water molecules occurs when six molecules form a ring.

HOW WOULD YOU SORT OUT THIS MESS?

How is the periodic table organized?

Maybe you know someone with a messy room like this one. Imagine how difficult it would be to find things that you need. For example, what if you had misplaced your homework in this room? Where would you look for it? You might have to search for a long, long time! **Classify** **If this were your room, how would you organize the things inside it?**

_____

_____

_____

_____

_____

> **UNTAMED SCIENCE** Watch the **Untamed Science** video to learn more about organizing matter.

Elements and the Periodic Table

Science Standards of Learning

PS.1g, PS.1i, PS.1j, PS.1k, PS.1m, PS.1n,
PS.2a, PS.2b, PS.2d, PS.2e, PS.2f, PS.3a,
PS.3b, PS.4a, PS.4b, PS.5c, PS.6b, PS.11d

5 Getting Started

Check Your Understanding

1. Background Read the paragraph below and then answer the question.

Katherine and her family are having a barbecue. They are burning charcoal in the grill to provide heat to cook their food. Charcoal is one form of the **element** carbon. As the charcoal burns, it reacts with oxygen **molecules** in the air. Each oxygen molecule contains two **atoms.**

An **element** is a pure substance that cannot be broken down into any other substances by chemical or physical means.

A **molecule** is a group of two or more atoms held together by chemical bonds.

An **atom** is the basic particle from which all elements are made.

- How can oxygen be both an element and a molecule?

_____

_____

> **MY READING WEB** If you had trouble completing the question above, visit **My Reading Web** and type in *Elements and the Periodic Table.*

Vocabulary Skill

Greek Word Origins Many science words in English come from Greek. For example, the word *autograph* comes from the Greek words *auto,* meaning "self," and *graph,* meaning "written." An *autograph* is one's name written in one's own handwriting. Look at the Greek origins and their meanings below.

Greek Origin	Meaning	Key Words
atomos	Cannot be cut, indivisible	Atom, atomic number, atomic mass
di	Two, double	Diatomic molecule

2. Quick Check Predict the meaning of *diatomic molecule.*

_____

_____

periodic table

corrosion

semiconductor

noble gas

Chapter Preview

LESSON 1
- atom • electron • nucleus
- proton • energy level
- neutron • atomic number
- isotope • mass number

 Compare and Contrast
△ Make Models

LESSON 2
- atomic mass • periodic table
- chemical symbol • period
- group

 Relate Text and Visuals
△ Predict

LESSON 3
- metal • luster • malleable
- ductile • thermal conductivity
- electrical conductivity • reactivity
- corrosion • alkali metal
- alkaline earth metal
- transition metal

 Ask Questions
△ Infer

LESSON 4
- nonmetal • diatomic molecule
- halogen • noble gas • metalloid
- semiconductor

 Summarize
△ Classify

LESSON 5
- radioactive decay
- nuclear reaction • radioactivity
- alpha particle • beta particle
- gamma ray • half-life
- radioactive dating • tracer

 Relate Cause and Effect
△ Calculate

> VOCAB FLASH CARDS For extra help with vocabulary, visit **Vocab Flash Cards** and type in *Elements and the Periodic Table.*

Introduction to Atoms

UNLOCK THE BIG **?**

🔑 **How Did Atomic Theory Develop?**
PS.1m, PS.2a, PS.2b, PS.3a

🔑 **What Is the Modern Model of the Atom?**
PS.1m, PS.2a, PS.2b, PS.3b, PS.4a

MY PLANET DIARY

DISCOVERY

Nanowhiskers

What's more than 16,000 times thinner than a human hair, and, when added to fabric, able to repel spills, stains, and the smell of the sweatiest of socks? It's a nanowhisker!

Nanowhiskers are tiny threads that measure about 10 nanometers (nm) in length and 1.5 nanometers in diameter (1 nm equals 0.000000001 m). They are often made of carbon or silver atoms. Scientists have found a way to bond nanowhiskers to individual threads of cloth. The nanowhiskers are so small and so close together that they form a barrier that prevents substances from ever touching the fabric. Nanowhiskers made from silver can even kill bacteria on your feet and stop socks from smelling!

Communicate Write your answer to each question below. Then discuss your answers with a partner.

1. Why are nanowhiskers used to repel stains on fabrics?

_____

_____

_____

_____

_____

2. What uses for nanowhiskers can you imagine?

_____

_____

▶ PLANET DIARY Go to **Planet Diary** to learn more about atomic structure.

Lab zone® Do the Inquiry Warm-Up *What's in the Box?*

Vocabulary
- atom • electron • nucleus • proton • energy level
- neutron • atomic number • isotope • mass number

Skills
↻ Reading: Compare and Contrast
△ Inquiry: Make Models

How Did Atomic Theory Develop?

If you could see a single atom, what would it look like? Studying atoms is difficult because atoms are so small. The smallest visible speck of dust may contain 10 million billion atoms! Scientists have created models to describe atoms because they are so small. Models of the atom have changed many times.

Around 430 B.C., the Greek philosopher Democritus proposed that matter was formed of small pieces that could not be cut into smaller parts. He used the word *atomos*, meaning "uncuttable," for these smallest possible pieces. In modern terms, an **atom** is the smallest particle that still can be considered an element.

The idea of atoms began to develop again in the 1600s. As people did experiments, atomic theory began to take shape. ☞ **Atomic theory grew as a series of models that developed from experimental evidence. As more evidence was collected, the theory and models were revised.**

Dalton's Atomic Theory Using evidence from many experiments, John Dalton, an English chemist, inferred that atoms had certain characteristics. Dalton thought that atoms were like smooth, hard balls that could not be broken into smaller pieces. The main ideas of Dalton's theory are summarized in **Figure 1**.

Science Standards of Learning

PS.1m Construct and use models and simulations to illustrate and explain phenomena.

PS.2a Investigate and understand the particle theory of matter.

PS.2b Investigate and understand elements, compounds, mixtures, acids, bases, and salts.

PS.3a Investigate and understand the contributions of Dalton, Thomson, Rutherford, and Bohr in understanding the atom.

FIGURE 1 ·······················

Dalton's Model
Dalton thought that atoms were smooth, hard balls.

✎ **Predict** Read the summary of Dalton's theory. Based on this theory, would you expect a carbon atom to have the same mass as an oxygen atom? Explain.

_____

_____

_____

Dalton's Atomic Theory
- All elements consist of atoms that cannot be divided.
- All atoms of the same element are exactly alike and have the same mass. Atoms of different elements are different and have different masses.
- An atom of one element cannot be changed into an atom of a different element by a chemical reaction.
- Compounds are formed when atoms of more than one element combine in a specific ratio.

Thomson's Model

Dalton's atomic theory has some similarities to today's models, but there are many differences. One important change is that atoms are now known to be made of even smaller parts. In 1897, J.J. Thomson discovered that atoms contain negatively charged particles called **electrons.** Yet scientists knew that atoms themselves had no electrical charge. So Thomson reasoned that atoms must also contain some sort of positive charge. This positive charge must balance the negative charge of the electrons.

Thomson proposed a model like the one shown in **Figure 2.** He described an atom that had electrons scattered throughout a ball of positive charge—something like seeds in a watermelon.

Rutherford's Model

In 1911, one of Thomson's former students, Ernest Rutherford, found evidence that challenged Thomson's model. Rutherford's research team aimed a beam of positively charged particles at a thin sheet of gold foil. A diagram of the experiment is shown in **Figure 3.** Rutherford and his team predicted that, if Thomson's model were correct, the charged particles would pass straight through the foil. They also predicted that the paths of some particles would bend, or deflect, slightly. The particles would be only slightly deflected because the positive charge was thought to be spread out in the gold atoms.

Rutherford observed that most of the particles passed straight through the foil with little or no deflection. But to everyone's surprise, a few particles were deflected by the gold foil at very large angles. Based on the results of his experiment, Rutherford suggested that the atom is mostly empty space but has a positive charge at its center.

FIGURE 2 ·····································
Thomson's Model
Thomson suggested that atoms had negatively charged electrons set in a positive sphere. Each electron is represented above by the symbol e⁻.

FIGURE 3 ·····································
Rutherford's Gold Foil Experiment
Rutherford was surprised that a few particles were deflected strongly.
✎ **Interpret Diagrams** Place a check (✔) to show the paths of the particles that were not predicted by Thomson's atomic model.

Beam of particles — Thin gold foil

Screen

Source of positively charged particles

Like charges repel each other. So Rutherford inferred that an atom's positive charge must be packed within a small region in its center, called the **nucleus** (NOO klee us). (The plural of *nucleus* is *nuclei*.) Any particle that was deflected strongly had been repelled by a gold atom's nucleus. Rutherford's new model of the atom, which is shown in **Figure 4,** is like a cherry. The pit models the nucleus of the atom. The rest of the fruit is the space taken up by the electrons. Later research suggested that the nucleus was made up of one or more positively charged particles. Rutherford called the positively charged particles in an atom's nucleus **protons.**

FIGURE 4 ·······················
Rutherford's Model
According to Rutherford's model, an atom was mostly open space. The "6+" in the model means that there are six protons in the nucleus.

apply it!

Use the diagrams below to compare the expected and observed results of Rutherford's gold foil experiment. Part **a** shows the expected paths of the charged particles through the atoms of the gold foil. In part **b**, draw the observed paths of the charged particles. Show at least one particle that is deflected strongly.

a Expected result

Gold atoms

Positive particles

b Observed result

Nucleus of gold atom

Bohr's Model One of Rutherford's students was Niels Bohr, a Danish scientist. In 1913, Bohr revised the atomic model again. Bohr suggested that electrons are found only in specific orbits around the nucleus. The orbits in Bohr's model look like planets orbiting the sun or the rings of a tree, as shown in **Figure 5.** Each possible electron orbit in Bohr's model has a fixed energy.

FIGURE 5 ·······························
Bohr's Model
Niels Bohr suggested that electrons move in specific orbits around the nucleus of an atom.

6+

6e⁻

Cloud Model In the 1920s, the atomic model changed again. Scientists determined that electrons do not orbit the nucleus like planets, as Bohr suggested. Instead, electrons move rapidly within a cloudlike region around the nucleus. Look at **Figure 6.** The orange "cloud" is a visual model. It represents where electrons are likely to be found. An electron's movement is related to its **energy level,** or the specific amount of energy it has. Electrons at different energy levels are likely to be found in different places.

FIGURE 6 ···
Cloud Model
Electrons move rapidly in different directions around the nucleus.

apply it!

Scientists have used models to help them understand atoms. You can too!

❶ ✏ **Make Models** Match each object with the atomic model the object most closely represents.

❷ [CHALLENGE] An object is missing for one of the atomic models listed. In the space provided, draw an object that represents this model.

Dalton's Model

Thomson's Model

Bohr's Model

Cloud Model

Lab zone® Do the Quick Lab
Visualizing an Electron Cloud.

🔑 Assess Your Understanding

1a. Define An atom is _____
_____ .

b. Describe Bohr's model of the atom consisted of a central _____ surrounded by electrons moving in specific _____ .

c. 🔄 Compare and Contrast How is the cloud model of the atom different from Bohr's model?

_____
_____
_____
_____
_____

got it? ··

○ **I get it!** Now I know that atomic theory changed with time because _____
_____

○ **I need extra help with** _____

Go to MY SCIENCE ⓢ COACH online for help with this subject.

What Is the Modern Model of the Atom?

In 1932, English scientist James Chadwick showed that another particle exists in the nucleus of atoms. This particle, called a **neutron,** was hard to find because it has no electric charge.

Scientists have learned more about the atom since then. One modern model of the atom is shown in **Figure 7.** **At the center of the atom is a tiny, dense nucleus containing protons and neutrons. Surrounding the nucleus is a cloudlike region of moving electrons.**

Most of an atom's volume is the space in which the electrons move. This space is huge compared to the space taken up by the nucleus. Imagine holding a pencil while standing in the middle of a stadium. If the nucleus were the size of the pencil's eraser, the electrons would reach as far away as the top row of seats!

New research supports the modern model of the atom. However, scientists still don't know the details of the smallest scales of matter. Who will develop the next model of the atom? Maybe it will be you!

Science Standards of Learning

PS.1m Construct and use models and simulations to illustrate and explain phenomena.

PS.2a Investigate and understand the particle theory of matter.

PS.2b Investigate and understand elements, compounds, mixtures, acids, bases, and salts.

PS.3b Investigate and understand the modern model of atomic structure.

PS.4a Investigate and understand symbols, atomic numbers, atomic mass, chemical families (groups), and periods on the periodic table of elements.

FIGURE 7 ....

Modern Model of an Atom
A carbon atom has a nucleus made up of positively charged protons and neutral neutrons. The nucleus is surrounded by a cloud of negatively charged electrons.

✎ **Identify** How many protons are in the carbon atom?

_____

Cloud of electrons

$6e^-$

Nucleus

Proton

Neutron

Particle Charges In **Figure 7,** protons are shown by a plus sign (+). Electrons are shown by the symbol e^-. According to the scale used for measuring charge in atoms, protons have a charge of +1. Electrons have exactly the opposite charge. So electrons have a charge of −1. If you count the number of protons in **Figure 7,** you'll see there are six. The number of protons equals the number of electrons. As a result, the positive charge from the protons equals the negative charge from the electrons. The charges balance, making the atom neutral. Neutrons don't affect the charge of an atom because they have a charge of zero.

.... ✎ ....
⤵ **Compare and Contrast**

A proton has a charge of _____.

An electron has a charge of _____.

A neutron has a charge of _____.

165

Comparing Particle Masses Although electrons may balance protons charge for charge, they can't compare when it comes to mass. It takes almost 1,840 electrons to equal the mass of one proton. A proton and a neutron are about equal in mass. Together, the protons and neutrons make up almost all the mass of an atom.

Figure 8 compares the charges and masses of the three atomic particles. Atoms are too small to be described by everyday units of mass, such as grams or kilograms. Sometimes scientists use units known as atomic mass units (amu). A proton or a neutron has a mass equal to about one amu.

Atomic Number Every atom of an element has the same number of protons. For example, every carbon atom has 6 protons and every iron atom has 26 protons. The number of protons in the nucleus of an atom is the **atomic number** of that atom's element. The definition of an element is based on its atomic number. Carbon's atomic number is 6 and iron's is 26.

Hey, pipsqueak... You're only 4 kg. I'm 8,000 kg! HA!

Relative to an elephant, I'm about the same mass as an electron is relative to a proton. Meow!

FIGURE 8 ···

> INTERACTIVE ART **Particles in an Atom**

An atom is made up of protons, neutrons, and electrons.

✏️ **Review** Complete the table by filling in the correct charge for each atomic particle.

Particles in an Atom

Particle	Symbol	Charge	Mass (amu)	Model
Proton	p^+	_____	1	●
Neutron	n	_____	1	●
Electron	e^-	_____	$\dfrac{1}{1,840}$	●

Isotopes All atoms of an element have the same number of protons. The number of neutrons can vary. Atoms with the same number of protons and different numbers of neutrons are called **isotopes** (EYE suh tohps). **Figure 9** shows three isotopes of carbon.

An isotope is identified by its **mass number,** which is the sum of the protons and neutrons in the atom. The most common isotope of carbon has a mass number of 12 (6 protons + 6 neutrons) and may be written as "carbon-12." About 99 percent of naturally occurring carbon is carbon-12. Two other isotopes are carbon-13 and carbon-14. Despite their different mass numbers, all three carbon isotopes react the same way chemically.

FIGURE 9 ·······························
Isotopes of Carbon
All isotopes of carbon contain 6 protons. They differ in the number of neutrons.
✎ **Relate Text and Visuals Fill in the missing information for each isotope below.**

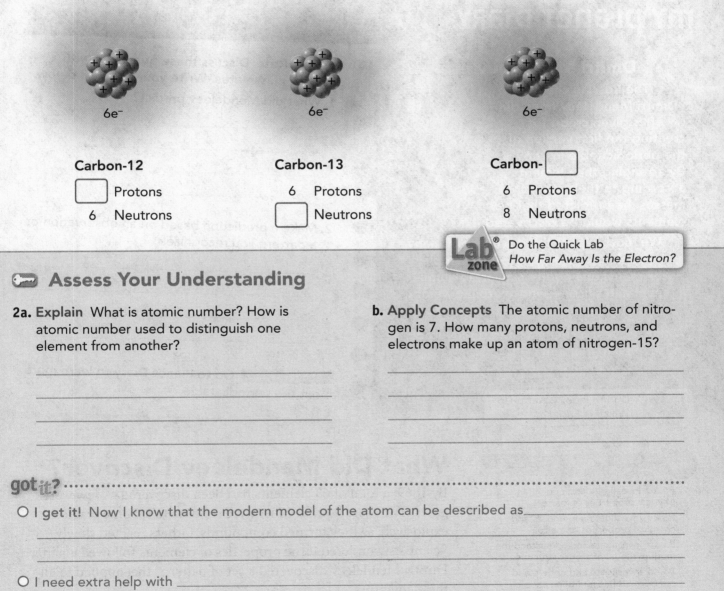

6e⁻   6e⁻   6e⁻

Carbon-12   **Carbon-13**   **Carbon-☐**

☐ Protons   6 Protons   6 Protons

6 Neutrons   ☐ Neutrons   8 Neutrons

Lab zone ® Do the Quick Lab
How Far Away Is the Electron?

🔑 Assess Your Understanding

2a. Explain What is atomic number? How is atomic number used to distinguish one element from another?

_____

_____

_____

b. Apply Concepts The atomic number of nitrogen is 7. How many protons, neutrons, and electrons make up an atom of nitrogen-15?

_____

_____

_____

got it? ··

○ **I get it!** Now I know that the modern model of the atom can be described as_____

_____

_____

○ **I need extra help with** _____

Go to MY SCIENCE ⬤ COACH online for help with this subject.

Organizing the Elements

🔑 **What Did Mendeleev Discover?**
PS.2d, PS.2e, PS.3b, PS.4a

🔑 **What Information Does the Periodic Table Contain?**
PS.1j, PS.2b, PS.4a, PS.4b

🔑 **How Is the Periodic Table Useful?**
PS.2b, PS.4a, PS.4b

my planeT DiaRY

VOICES FROM HISTORY

Dmitri Mendeleev

The Russian chemist Dmitri Mendeleev (men duh LAY ef) is given credit for creating the first version of the periodic table in 1869. By arranging the elements according to their atomic masses, he predicted that new elements would be discovered:

We must expect the discovery of many yet unknown elements—for example, elements analogous [similar] to aluminum and silicon—whose atomic weight [mass] would be between 65 and 75.

Within 17 years, chemists had discovered these missing elements.

Communicate Discuss these questions with a group of classmates. Write your answers below.

1. What did Mendeleev predict?

_____

_____

_____

_____

2. Make a prediction based on an observation or a pattern you recognize.

_____

_____

_____

_____

▶ **PLANET DIARY** Go to **Planet Diary** to learn more about the periodic table.

Do the Inquiry Warm-Up
Which Is Easier?

Science Standards of Learning

PS.2d Investigate and understand physical properties of matter.

PS.2e Investigate and understand chemical properties of matter.

PS.3b Investigate and understand the modern model of atomic structure.

PS.4a Investigate and understand symbols, atomic numbers, atomic mass, and chemical families (groups).

What Did Mendeleev Discover?

By 1869, a total of 63 elements had been discovered. A few were gases. Two were liquids. Most were solid metals. Some reacted explosively as they formed compounds. Others reacted slowly. Scientists wondered if the properties of elements followed a pattern. Dmitri Mendeleev discovered a set of patterns that applied to all the elements.

Vocabulary

- atomic mass
- chemical symbol
- group
- periodic table
- period

Skills

- Reading: Relate Text and Visuals
- Inquiry: Predict

Mendeleev's Work Mendeleev knew that some elements had similar chemical and physical properties. For example, silver and copper are both shiny metals. Mendeleev thought these similarities were important clues to a hidden pattern.

To find that pattern, Mendeleev wrote each element's melting point, density, and color on an individual card. He also included the element's atomic mass. The **atomic mass** of an element is the average mass of all the isotopes of that element. Mendeleev tried arranging the cards in different ways.

Mendeleev noticed that a pattern of properties appeared when he arranged the elements in order of increasing atomic mass. He found that the properties repeated regularly. For example, lithium, sodium, and potassium showed several common properties. As you can see from **Figure 1,** these elements react with water in a similar way. (The letters *amu* mean "atomic mass units.") Mendeleev lined up the cards for these elements to form their own group. He did the same with other elements that shared similar properties.

FIGURE 1 ·····························

Metals That React With Water

Lithium, sodium, and potassium all react with water.

✎ **Observe** Write down your observations of each reaction.

Lithium
Atomic mass = 7 amu

_____

_____

_____

Sodium
Atomic mass = 23 amu

_____

_____

_____

Potassium
Atomic mass = 39 amu

_____

_____

_____

Relate Text and Visuals
Using **Figure 2**, predict an element that would react with water as lithium (Li), sodium (Na), and potassium (K) did. Explain.

_____

_____

_____

_____

_____

The Periodic Table

Mendeleev created the first periodic table in 1869. A **periodic table** is an arrangement of elements showing the repeating pattern of their properties. (The word *periodic* means "in a regular, repeated pattern.") The periodic table shown in **Figure 2** was an improved version published in 1871.

As scientists discovered new elements and learned more about atomic structure, the periodic table changed. It is now known that the number of protons in the nucleus, given by the atomic number, determines the chemical properties of an element. Modern periodic tables are arranged in order of increasing atomic number.

Group I	Group II	Group III	Group IV	Group V	Group VI	Group VII	Group VIII
H = 1							
Li = 7	Be = 9.4	B = 11	C = 12	N = 14	O = 16	F = 19	
Na = 23, K = 39	Mg = 24, Ca = 40	Al = 27.3, — = 44	Si = 28, Ti = 48	P = 31, V = 51	S = 32, Cr = 52	Cl = 35.5, Mn = 55	Fe = 56, Co = 59, Ni = 59, Cu = 63.
(Cu = 63), Rb = 85	Zn = 65, Sr = 87	— = 68, Yt = 88	— = 72, Zr = 90	As = 75, Nb = 94	Se = 78, Mo = 96	Br = 80, — = 100	
(Ag = 108), Cs = 133	Cd = 112, Ba = 137	In = 113, Di = 138	Sn = 118, Ce = 140	Sb = 122, —	Te = 125, —	I = 127	Ru = 104, Rh = 104, Pd = 106, Ag = 108.
(—), —	—, —	—, Er = 178	—, La = 180	—, Ta = 182	—, W = 184	—	— — — —
(Au = 199), —	Hg = 200	Tl = 204, —	Pb = 207, Th = 231	Bi = 208, —	U = 240		Os = 195, Ir = 197, Pt = 198, Au = 199.

FIGURE 2 ·············
Mendeleev's Periodic Table
In his periodic table, Mendeleev left blank spaces. He predicted that the blank spaces would be filled by elements that had not yet been discovered. He even correctly predicted the properties of those new elements.

Lab zone
Do the Quick Lab
Classifying.

Assess Your Understanding

1a. Review In what order did Mendeleev arrange the elements in his periodic table?

_____

_____

b. Predict How could Mendeleev predict the properties of elements that had not yet been discovered?

_____

_____

_____

got it?·····························

○ **I get it!** Now I know that when Mendeleev arranged the elements in order of increasing atomic mass, _____

_____

_____

○ **I need extra help with** _____

Go to MY SCIENCE ⓢ COACH online for help with this subject.

What Information Does the Periodic Table Contain?

The periodic table contains information about each of the known elements. 🔑 **In this book, the periodic table includes the atomic number, chemical symbol, name, and atomic mass for each element.** The information that the periodic table lists about potassium is shown below in **Figure 3**.

❶ **Atomic Number** The first piece of information is the number 19, the atomic number of potassium. Every potassium atom has 19 protons in its nucleus.

❷ **Chemical Symbol** Just below the atomic number is the letter K—the **chemical symbol** for potassium. Chemical symbols contain either one or two letters. Often, an element's symbol is an abbreviation of the element's name in English. Other elements have symbols that are abbreviations of their Latin names.

❸ **Atomic Mass** The last piece of information is the average atomic mass. For potassium, this value is 39.098 amu (atomic mass units). The atomic mass is an average because most elements consist of a mixture of isotopes.

The modern periodic table is shown in **Figure 4** on the next two pages. Can you find potassium?

☁ **Science Standards of Learning**

PS.1j Make valid conclusions after analyzing data.

PS.2b Investigate and understand elements, compounds, mixtures, acids, bases, and salts.

PS.4a Investigate and understand symbols, atomic numbers, atomic mass, chemical families (groups), and periods on the periodic table of elements.

PS.4b Investigate and understand the classification of elements as metals, metalloids, and nonmetals.

FIGURE 3 ·······························
Potassium
Potassium has an atomic number of 19 and an atomic mass of 39.098 amu. Bananas are rich in potassium.

apply it!

The entry for silicon (Si) in the periodic table looks like this. ➡

❶ The atomic number of silicon is _____.

❷ 🔺 **Predict** Without looking at the periodic table, do you think that any other element has the same atomic number as silicon? Explain.

_____
_____
_____
_____
_____
_____
_____
_____

171

Key
- Metal
- Metalloid
- Nonmetal

Group

Period

Lanthanides

Actinides

The lanthanides and the actinides are placed off the table to save space and to make the rest of the table easier to read. Follow the line to see how they fit in the table.

Many periodic tables include a zigzag line that separates the metals from the nonmetals. Metalloids, found on either side of the line, share properties of both metals and nonmetals.

13	14	15	16	17	18
					2 **He** Helium 4.0026
5 **B** Boron 10.81	6 **C** Carbon 12.011	7 **N** Nitrogen 14.007	8 **O** Oxygen 15.999	9 **F** Fluorine 18.998	10 **Ne** Neon 20.179
13 **Al** Aluminum 26.982	14 **Si** Silicon 28.086	15 **P** Phosphorus 30.974	16 **S** Sulfur 32.06	17 **Cl** Chlorine 35.453	18 **Ar** Argon 39.948
31 **Ga** Gallium 69.72	32 **Ge** Germanium 72.59	33 **As** Arsenic 74.922	34 **Se** Selenium 78.96	35 **Br** Bromine 79.904	36 **Kr** Krypton 83.80
49 **In** Indium 114.82	50 **Sn** Tin 118.69	51 **Sb** Antimony 121.75	52 **Te** Tellurium 127.60	53 **I** Iodine 126.90	54 **Xe** Xenon 131.30
81 **Tl** Thallium 204.37	82 **Pb** Lead 207.2	83 **Bi** Bismuth 208.98	84 **Po** Polonium (209)	85 **At** Astatine (210)	86 **Rn** Radon (222)
113 ***Uut** Ununtrium (284)	114 ***Uuq** Ununquadium (289)	115 ***Uup** Ununpentium (288)	116 ***Uuh** Ununhexium (292)	117 ***Uus** Ununseptium (292)	118 ***Uuo** Ununoctium (294)

The discoveries of elements 113 and above have not yet been officially confirmed. Atomic masses in parentheses are those of the most stable isotopes.

66 **Dy** Dysprosium 162.50	67 **Ho** Holmium 164.93	68 **Er** Erbium 167.26	69 **Tm** Thulium 168.93	70 **Yb** Ytterbium 173.04
98 **Cf** Californium (251)	99 **Es** Einsteinium (252)	100 **Fm** Fermium (257)	101 **Md** Mendelevium (258)	102 **No** Nobelium (259)

FIGURE 4 ....

> **INTERACTIVE ART** **The Periodic Table**

The periodic table is one of the most valuable tools to a chemist. ✎ **Interpret Tables** Find the element identified by the atomic number 25 on the periodic table. Use the information to fill in the blanks below.

Name of element: ....

Chemical symbol: ....

Atomic mass: ....

 Lab zone® Do the Quick Lab *Using the Periodic Table.*

🔑 Assess Your Understanding

2a. Compare and Contrast Describe two differences between Mendeleev's periodic table and the modern periodic table.

_____

_____

_____

_____

_____

b. Interpret Tables An atom of which element has 47 protons in its nucleus?

_____

got it? ....

○ **I get it!** Now I know that information found in the periodic table for each element includes _____

_____

_____

○ **I need extra help with** _____

Go to **MY SCIENCE** ⑤ **COACH** *online for help with this subject.*

Science Standards of Learning

PS.2b Investigate and understand elements.

PS.4a Investigate and understand symbols, atomic numbers, atomic mass, chemical families (groups), and periods on the periodic table of elements.

PS.4b Investigate and understand the classification of elements as metals, metalloids, and nonmetals.

ELEMENT SCRAMBLE

Rearrange the chemical symbols to form a word.

Example:

⁵³ I	³ Li	¹ H	⁶ C

C H I Li

⁵⁶ Ba	⁵ B	²⁰ Ca	³² Ge

¹ H	⁴⁹ In	¹⁵ P	⁸⁹ Ac	¹⁶ S

¹⁸ Ar	⁴⁷ Ag	¹⁵ P	¹⁶ S	³³ As	⁹² U

Answers: CaBBaGe, SPInAcH, AsPArAgUS

How Is the Periodic Table Useful?

Look at the periodic table on the previous two pages. Notice that the atomic numbers increase from left to right. Also notice that each color-coded region corresponds to a different class of elements—metals, nonmetals, and metalloids.

As you look across a row, the elements' properties change in a predictable way. **An element's properties can be predicted from its location in the periodic table.** This predictability is the reason that the periodic table is so useful to chemists.

Periods The periodic table is arranged in rows called **periods.** A period contains a series of different elements. From left to right, the properties of the elements change in a pattern. Metals are shown on the left of the table and nonmetals are located on the right. Metalloids are found between the metals and nonmetals. This pattern is repeated in each period. **Figure 5** shows the elements of Period 3.

FIGURE 5 ···

Elements of Period 3

The properties of the Period 3 elements change as you move across the period.

Classify Use three different colors to fill in the key below. Then color in each element in Period 3 according to your key.

11 **Na** Sodium 22.990	12 **Mg** Magnesium 24.305	13 **Al** Aluminum 26.982	14 **Si** Silicon 28.086	15 **P** Phosphorus 30.974	16 **S** Sulfur 32.06	17 **Cl** Chlorine 35.453	18 **Ar** Argon 39.948

Key

☐ Metal

☐ Metalloid

☐ Nonmetal

Groups The modern periodic table has 7 periods, which form 18 columns. The elements in a column form a **group.** Groups are also known as families. The groups are numbered from Group 1 on the left of the table to Group 18 on the right.

The pattern of properties repeats in each period, so the elements in each group have similar characteristics. For example, except for hydrogen, the elements in Group 1 are all metals that react violently with water. Group 17 elements are very reactive, but Group 18 elements are generally nonreactive. The elements of Group 10 are shown in **Figure 6.**

FIGURE 6 ·····················

Elements of Group 10
The elements of Group 10 include nickel (Ni), palladium (Pd), platinum (Pt), and darmstadtium (Ds). Darmstadtium is not found in nature, but scientists believe it exhibits properties similar to the other Group 10 metals.

✏️ CHALLENGE Look at the photos of nickel, palladium, and platinum. What properties would you predict for darmstadtium?

_____

_____

Lab zone Do the Quick Lab *Expanding the Periodic Table.*

🔑 Assess Your Understanding

3a. Name The rows in the periodic table are called _____. The columns in the periodic table are called _____.

b. Describe What do elements in the same group in the periodic table have in common?

_____

_____

c. Predict Use the periodic table to name two elements that you would expect to have properties very much like those of calcium (Ca).

_____

_____

_____

_____

got it? ·························

○ **I get it!** Now I know that the periodic table is useful because _____

_____

○ **I need extra help with** _____

Go to **MY SCIENCE COACH** online for help with this subject.

LESSON 3 Metals

🔑 **What Are the Properties of Metals?**
PS.2d, PS.2e, PS.2f, PS.4b

🔑 **How Are Metals Classified?**
PS.1j, PS.2d, PS.2e, PS.2f, PS.4a, PS.4b

my planet Diary

Recycling Metals

You can find metals in many items that you use every day, including cell phones, computers, appliances, and money. In 2006, the supply of metal in the United States was more than 150 million metric tons. (One metric ton equals 1,000 kilograms.) Many of these metals can be recycled. Recycling helps conserve energy and reduces the amount of waste in landfills.

Metal	Percent of U.S. Supply That Came From Recycling
Aluminum	43
Copper	32.3
Iron and steel	48
Nickel	43
Zinc	24.5

SCIENCE STATS

Communicate **Answer the question below. Then discuss your answer with a partner.**

Beverage cans contain mostly aluminum. Estimate the percent of beverage cans that you recycle. What other objects that contain metal do you think can be recycled?

_____
_____
_____
_____
_____

▷ **PLANET DIARY** Go to **Planet Diary** to learn more about recycling.

Lab zone Do the Inquiry Warm-Up *Why Use Aluminum?*

Vocabulary

- metal • luster • malleable • ductile • thermal conductivity
- electrical conductivity • reactivity • corrosion • alkali metal
- alkaline earth metal • transition metal

Skills

↺ **Reading:** Ask Questions

△ **Inquiry:** Infer

What Are the Properties of Metals?

It's hard to imagine modern life without metals. The cars and buses you ride in are made of steel, which is mostly iron (Fe). Airplanes are covered in aluminum (Al). Copper (Cu) wires carry electric current to lamps, stereos, and computers. Can you identify the objects that contain metals in **Figure 1** below?

Elements can be classified by their properties, including melting temperature, density, hardness, and thermal and electrical conductivity. **Metals** are elements that are good conductors of electric current and heat. They also tend to be shiny and bendable—like copper wire, for instance. The majority of elements in the periodic table are metals. The metals begin on the left side and extend across the periodic table.

Science Standards of Learning

PS.2d Investigate and understand physical properties of matter.

PS.2e Investigate and understand chemical properties of matter.

PS.2f Investigate and understand characteristics of types of matter based on physical and chemical properties.

PS.4b Investigate and understand the classification of elements as metals, metalloids, and nonmetals.

FIGURE 1 ·····················

Metals

Many of the objects around you contain metals.

✎ **Communicate** Circle the objects that will set off the metal detector. Then, with a partner, look around your classroom and make a list of the objects you see that contain metals.

_____

_____

_____

This stone, called magnetite, is made out of a compound of iron.

_____

_____

Gold can be pounded into coins.

_____

_____

Copper is often used for electrical wires.

_____

_____

FIGURE 2 ···

Physical Properties of Metals

Metals have certain physical properties.

✎ **Interpret Photos** After reading about the physical properties of metals below, identify the property or properties of metals exhibited by each of the objects above.

Physical Properties **Figure 2** shows some common metal objects. 🔑 **The physical properties of metals include luster, malleability, ductility, and conductivity.** A material that has a high **luster** is shiny and reflective. A **malleable** (MAL ee uh bul) material is one that can be hammered or rolled into flat sheets or other shapes. A **ductile** material is one that can be pulled out, or drawn, into long wires. Copper is both malleable and ductile. It can be made into thin sheets or drawn into wires.

Thermal conductivity is the ability of an object to transfer heat. The ability of an object to carry electric current is called **electrical conductivity.** Most metals are good thermal conductors and electrical conductors. Metals also generally have low specific heats. Recall that specific heat is the amount of energy required to raise the temperature of 1 gram of a material by 1 kelvin. This means that only a small amount of thermal energy is required to raise the temperature of a metal.

Some metals are magnetic. Iron, cobalt (Co), and nickel (Ni) are attracted to magnets and can be made into magnets. Most metals are solids at room temperature. Only mercury (Hg) is a liquid at room temperature.

Chemical Properties The ease and speed with which an element combines, or reacts, with other substances is called its **reactivity.** Metals usually react by losing electrons to other atoms. Some metals are very reactive. For example, sodium (Na) reacts strongly with water. By comparison, gold (Au) and platinum (Pt) do not react easily with other substances.

The reactivities of other metals fall somewhere between those of sodium and gold. Iron, for example, reacts slowly with oxygen in the air, forming iron oxide, or rust. The iron chain in **Figure 3** is coated with reddish brown rust. The deterioration of a metal due to a chemical reaction in the environment is called **corrosion.**

FIGURE 3 ·······················

Reactivity of Metals
This iron chain is coated with rust after being exposed to air and water.

apply it!

The forks shown are made of silver (Ag).

❶ Some of the silver forks shown have lost their luster—they have become tarnished. This is an example of _____.

❷ ▲Infer What properties of gold and platinum make these metals desirable for jewelry?

_____

_____

_____

Lab zone® Do the Lab Investigation *Copper or Carbon? That Is the Question.*

🔑 Assess Your Understanding

1a. Explain What does the term *thermal conductivity* mean?

_____

_____

_____

_____

b. ▲Infer What property of metals led to the use of plastic or wooden handles on many metal cooking utensils? Explain.

_____

_____

_____

_____

got it? ··

○ **I get it!** Now I know that the physical properties of metals include _____

_____

○ **I need extra help with** _____

Go to MY SCIENCE ⬤ COACH online for help with this subject.

Potassium
39.098

FIGURE 4 ·····································

Fireworks
Compounds containing potassium are used in fireworks.

FIGURE 5 ·····································

X-Ray of Healthy Bones
Calcium compounds are an essential part of teeth and bones.

20

Ca

Calcium
40.08

How Are Metals Classified?

The metals in a group have similar properties. Properties within a group change gradually as you look across the periodic table. For example, the reactivity of metals tends to decrease from left to right across the table. 🔑 **In the periodic table, metals are classified as alkali metals, alkaline earth metals, transition metals, metals in mixed groups, lanthanides, and actinides.**

Alkali Metals
The metals of Group 1, from lithium (Li) to francium (Fr), are called the **alkali metals.** These metals are the most reactive metals in the periodic table. Alkali metals are so reactive that they are never found as uncombined elements in nature. They are found only in compounds. Compounds that contain potassium (K) are used in fireworks, such as those shown in **Figure 4.**

In the laboratory, chemists can isolate alkali metals from their compounds. As pure, uncombined elements, some of the alkali metals are shiny and so soft you can cut them with a plastic knife. These elements have low densities and melting points. For example, sodium melts at 98°C and has a density of 0.97 g/cm^3—less than water.

✏️ Shade in the alkali metals on the periodic table.

Alkaline Earth Metals
The metals of Group 2 are called the **alkaline earth metals.** These metals are harder and denser, and melt at higher temperatures than the alkali metals. For example, magnesium (Mg) is a hard metal that melts at 648.8°C.

Alkaline earth metals are very reactive, though not as reactive as the alkali metals. These metals are also never found uncombined in nature. Calcium (Ca) is one of the most common alkaline earth metals. Calcium compounds are essential for bone health. **Figure 5** shows an X-ray of healthy bones.

✏️ Shade in the alkaline earth metals on the periodic table.

do the math! Analyzing Data

Melting Points in a Group of Elements

Properties of elements in a single group in the periodic table often change according to a certain pattern. The graph shows the melting points of the Group 1 elements, or the alkali metals.

1 Read Graphs The melting points of the alkali metals (increase/decrease) from lithium to francium.

2 Interpret Data Which of the alkali metals are liquids at 50°C?

3 CHALLENGE If element 119 were discovered, it would fall below francium in Group 1. Predict the approximate melting point of element 119.

Melting Points of Alkali Metals

Melting Point (°C) vs Alkali Metal (Li, Na, K, Rb, Cs, Fr)

Transition Metals

The elements in Groups 3 through 12 are called the **transition metals.** The transition metals include iron, copper, nickel, gold, and silver. Most of these metals are hard and shiny solids. However, mercury is a liquid at room temperature. Except for mercury, the transition metals often have high melting points and high densities. They are also good conductors of heat and electric current, and are very malleable. As shown in **Figure 6**, gold is sometimes used to coat an astronaut's visor.

The transition metals are less reactive than the metals in Groups 1 and 2. When iron reacts with air, forming rust, it sometimes takes many years to react completely.

Shade in the transition metals on the periodic table.

FIGURE 6
Astronaut Visor
The gold film in an astronaut's visor protects the eyes and face from the sun without interfering with vision.

79
Au
Gold
196.97

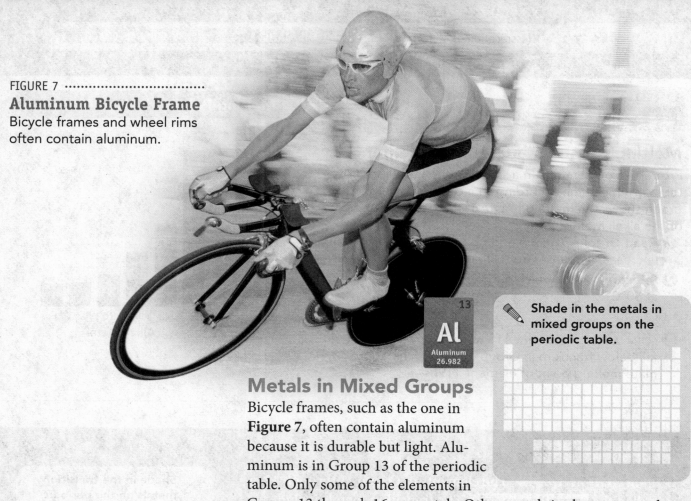

FIGURE 7 ·····

Aluminum Bicycle Frame
Bicycle frames and wheel rims often contain aluminum.

| 13 |
| Al |
| Aluminum |
| 26.982 |

✏️ Shade in the metals in mixed groups on the periodic table.

Metals in Mixed Groups

Bicycle frames, such as the one in **Figure 7**, often contain aluminum because it is durable but light. Aluminum is in Group 13 of the periodic table. Only some of the elements in Groups 13 through 16 are metals. Other metals in these groups that you may be familiar with are tin (Sn) and lead (Pb). A thin coating of tin protects steel from corrosion in some cans of food. Lead was once used in paints and water pipes. Lead is no longer used for these purposes because it was found to be poisonous. Now its most common use is in automobile batteries.

✏️ Shade in the lanthanides and actinides on the periodic table.

Lanthanides and Actinides

Two rows of elements are placed below the main part of the periodic table. The elements in the top row are the lanthanides (LAN thuh nydz). Compounds containing neodymium (Nd), a lanthanide, are used to make laser light. These lasers are used for surgery, for cutting metals, and in laser range finders, such as the one shown in **Figure 8.**

The elements below the lanthanides are called actinides (AK tuh nydz). Many of these elements are not found in nature but are made artificially in laboratories.

| 60 |
| Nd |
| Neodymium |
| 144.24 |

FIGURE 8 ·····

Laser Range Finder
A compound containing neodymium is used to produce the laser light in a range finder. The range finder uses a laser beam to determine the distance to an object.

Transuranium Elements Elements that follow uranium (U) in the periodic table are transuranium elements. These elements are made, or synthesized, when nuclear particles are forced to crash into one another. They are sometimes called synthetic elements. For example, plutonium (Pu) is synthesized by bombarding nuclei of uranium-238 with neutrons in a nuclear reactor.

To make elements with atomic numbers above 95, scientists use devices called particle accelerators that move atomic nuclei at extremely high speeds. If these nuclei crash into the nuclei of other elements with enough energy, the particles can combine into a single nucleus. An example of a particle accelerator is shown in **Figure 9.**

In general, the difficulty of synthesizing new elements increases with atomic number. So new elements have been synthesized only as more powerful particle accelerators have been built. Elements in the periodic table with atomic numbers greater than 111 do not yet have permanent names or symbols. In the future, scientists around the world will agree on permanent names and symbols for these elements.

Ask Questions Before reading about transuranium elements, ask a *What* or *How* question. As you read, write the answer to your question.

_____

_____

_____

_____

_____

_____

FIGURE 9 ·······················
Particle Accelerator
The heaviest synthetic elements are synthesized using particle accelerators.

Lab ® Do the Quick Lab
zone *Finding Metals.*

Assess Your Understanding

2a. Identify Which family of elements in the periodic table contains the most reactive metals?

_____

b. Infer Period 4 of the periodic table contains the elements potassium, calcium, and copper. Which is the least reactive?

_____

c. Apply Concepts How is plutonium made?

_____

_____

_____

got it? ·······································

○ **I get it!** Now I know that metals are classified in the periodic table as _____

_____

_____

_____

_____

○ **I need extra help with** _____

_____

Go to **MY SCIENCE** ⓢ **COACH** *online for help with this subject.*

Nonmetals and Metalloids

UNLOCK THE BIG ?

🔑 **What Are the Properties of Nonmetals?**
PS.1j, PS.2d, PS.2e, PS.2f, PS.4b

🔑 **What Are the Families Containing Nonmetals?**
PS.1j, PS.2d, PS.2e, PS.2f, PS.4a, PS.4b, PS.11d

my planet diary

Something in the Air

A common misconception is that the air in the atmosphere is mostly oxygen.

Fact: At sea level, air is actually only about 21 percent oxygen by volume. Nitrogen makes up about 78 percent of the atmosphere. The remaining one percent is made up of several gases, including argon and carbon dioxide.

Evidence: Oxygen is actually toxic at high concentrations. If you breathed in pure oxygen, you would eventually get very sick.

MISCONCEPTION

Communicate Write your answer to each question below. Then discuss your answers with a partner.

1. Why don't scuba divers fill their tanks with pure oxygen?

_____

_____

_____

_____

_____

2. Can you think of anything else that is good for you in small amounts but bad for you in large amounts?

_____

_____

_____

_____

▶ PLANET DIARY Go to **Planet Diary** to learn more about nonmetals.

 Do the Inquiry Warm-Up What *Are the Properties of Charcoal?*

Vocabulary
- nonmetal • diatomic molecule • halogen
- noble gas • metalloid • semiconductor

Skills
↺ Reading: Summarize
△ Inquiry: Classify

What Are the Properties of Nonmetals?

Life on Earth depends on many nonmetals. For example, carbon (C), nitrogen (N), phosphorus (P), hydrogen (H), and oxygen (O) are all nonmetal elements found in your body's DNA. A model of DNA is shown in **Figure 1.** While many compounds made with nonmetals are essential to life, some nonmetals are poisonous and highly reactive. Still others are nonreactive. Compared to metals, nonmetals have a much wider variety of properties. However, nonmetals do have several properties in common.

Physical Properties A **nonmetal** is an element that lacks most of the properties of a metal. Except for hydrogen, the nonmetals are found on the right side of the periodic table. ⊙━ **In general, most nonmetals are poor conductors of electric current and heat. Solid nonmetals tend to be dull and brittle.** If you were to hit most solid nonmetals with a hammer, they would break or crumble into a powder. Also, nonmetals usually have lower densities than metals.

Many nonmetals are gases at room temperature. The air you breathe contains mostly nitrogen and oxygen. Some nonmetal elements, such as carbon, sulfur (S), and iodine (I), are solids at room temperature. Bromine (Br) is the only nonmetal that is a liquid at room temperature.

FIGURE 1 ···

DNA
DNA, which is made up of atoms of nonmetals, is essential to life.

✎ Identify **Can you think of other substances essential to life that contain nonmetals?**

_____

_____

_____

Science Standards of Learning

PS.1j Make valid conclusions after analyzing data.

PS.2d Investigate and understand physical properties of matter.

PS.2e Investigate and understand chemical properties of matter.

PS.2f Investigate and understand characteristics of types of matter based on physical and chemical properties.

PS.4b Investigate and understand the classification of elements as metals, metalloids, and nonmetals.

Key
- Hydrogen
- Carbon
- Nitrogen
- Oxygen
- Phosphorus

Chemical Properties Atoms of nonmetals usually gain or share electrons when they react with other atoms. When nonmetals and metals react, electrons move from the metal atoms to the nonmetal atoms. For example, when sodium and chlorine react to form table salt (NaCl), an electron moves from the sodium atom to the chlorine atom.

Many nonmetals can form compounds with other nonmetals. In these types of compounds, the atoms share their electrons to form bonds. When two or more atoms bond this way, they form a molecule. A water (H_2O) molecule consists of two hydrogen atoms and one oxygen atom.

apply it!

Most properties of nonmetals are the opposite of the properties of metals.

❶ Compare and Contrast Complete the table about the properties of metals and nonmetals.

❷ Observe Sulfur, shown at the right, is a nonmetal. What properties can you observe from the photo? What additional properties can you predict?

_____

_____

_____

_____

Properties of Metals	Properties of Nonmetals
Shiny	Dull
Malleable	_____
Good conductors of electric current	_____ _____
_____ _____	Poor conductors of heat

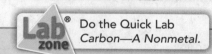
Do the Quick Lab
Carbon—A Nonmetal.

Assess Your Understanding

1a. Identify What property of nonmetals is the opposite of being *malleable* and *ductile*?

_____

b. Make Generalizations What happens to the atoms of most nonmetals when they react with other elements?

_____

_____

_____

_____

got it?

○ **I get it!** Now I know that the physical properties of nonmetals are that _____

_____

_____

_____

○ **I need extra help with** _____

Go to MY SCIENCE ⑤ COACH *online for help with this subject.*

What Are the Families Containing Nonmetals?

Look back at the periodic table. There are nonmetals in Group 1 and in Groups 14–18. 🔑 **The families containing nonmetals include the carbon family, the nitrogen family, the oxygen family, the halogen family, the noble gases, and hydrogen.**

Science Standards of Learning

PS.1j Make valid conclusions after analyzing data.

PS.2d Investigate and understand physical properties of matter.

PS.2e Investigate and understand chemical properties of matter.

PS.2f Investigate and understand characteristics of types of matter based on physical and chemical properties.

PS.4a Investigate and understand symbols, atomic numbers, atomic mass, chemical families (groups), and periods on the periodic table of elements.

PS.4b Investigate and understand the classification of elements as metals, metalloids, and nonmetals.

PS.11d Investigate and understand semiconductors.

Before you read about the families containing nonmetals, refer to the periodic table to complete the table below.

Family	Group	Nonmetals in Family
Carbon family	14	
Nitrogen family	15	
Oxygen family	16	
Halogen family	17	
Noble gases	18	
Hydrogen	1	

The Carbon Family
In Group 14, only carbon is a nonmetal. Carbon is especially important in its role in the chemistry of life. Proteins, DNA, and fats all contain carbon.

Most of the fuels that are burned to yield energy contain carbon. Coal contains large amounts of carbon. Gasoline is made from crude oil, a mixture of carbon compounds with one carbon atom to chains of several hundred carbon atoms. A diamond, which is shown in **Figure 2**, is made of pure carbon.

6
C
Carbon
12.011

✏️ **Shade in the nonmetal in Group 14 on the periodic table.**

FIGURE 2 ••••••••••••••••••
Diamond
Diamonds are made of pure carbon.

The Nitrogen Family

Group 15, the nitrogen family, contains two nonmetals, nitrogen and phosphorus. Nitrogen makes up about 78 percent of Earth's atmosphere by volume. In nature, nitrogen exists as two nitrogen atoms bonded together to form a diatomic molecule, N_2. A **diatomic molecule** is made up of two atoms. In this form, nitrogen is not very reactive.

Shade in the nonmetals in Group 15 on the periodic table.

Although living things need nitrogen, most of them are unable to use nitrogen from the air. However, certain kinds of bacteria can use the nitrogen from the air to form compounds. This process is called nitrogen fixation. Plants can then take in these nitrogen compounds formed by the bacteria in the soil. Farmers also add nitrogen compounds to the soil in the form of fertilizers. Lightning, shown in **Figure 3,** also converts nitrogen in the atmosphere into a form that can be used by plants.

Phosphorus is the other nonmetal in the nitrogen family. Much more reactive than nitrogen, phosphorus in nature is always found in compounds.

FIGURE 3 ....

Lightning

The energy released in the atmosphere in the form of lightning is able to break the bonds between nitrogen atoms, causing them to react with oxygen. Plants are able to use the nitrogen in this form.

 CHALLENGE **How do you get the nitrogen you need?**

_____

_____

7

N

Nitrogen
14.007

The Oxygen Family

Group 16, the oxygen family, contains three nonmetals—oxygen, sulfur, and selenium (Se). Oxygen is a gas at room temperature, whereas sulfur and selenium are both solids.

You are using oxygen right now. With every breath, oxygen travels into your lungs. There, it is absorbed into your bloodstream, which distributes it all over your body. Like nitrogen, oxygen (O_2) is a diatomic molecule. Oxygen is relatively reactive, so it can combine with almost every other element.

If you have ever smelled the odor of a rotten egg, then you are already familiar with the smell of some sulfur compounds. Sulfur is used in the manufacturing of rubber for rubber bands and automobile tires, like the one shown in **Figure 4.**

✏️ Shade in the nonmetals in Group 16 on the periodic table.

FIGURE 4 ·················
Rubber Tires
Automobile tires are made out of rubber that contains sulfur compounds.

> 16
> **S**
> Sulfur
> 32.06

The Halogen Family

Group 17 contains the nonmetals fluorine (F), chlorine (Cl), bromine, and iodine. These elements are also known as the **halogens,** which means "salt forming." The properties of astatine (At) are unknown because it is extremely rare.

All of the halogens are very reactive. Fluorine is the most reactive of all the elements. It is so reactive that it reacts with almost every known substance, including water. Chlorine gas is extremely dangerous, but it is used in small amounts to kill bacteria in water supplies.

✏️ Shade in the nonmetals in Group 17 on the periodic table.

Though the halogen elements are dangerous, many of the compounds that halogens form are quite useful. Compounds of fluorine make up the nonstick coating on cookware. Fluorine compounds are also found in toothpaste, which is shown in **Figure 5,** because they help prevent tooth decay.

> 9
> **F**
> Fluorine
> 18.998

FIGURE 5 ·····························
Toothpaste
Toothpastes often contain fluorine compounds.

✏️ **Vocabulary** If the word *halogen* means "salt forming," what do you think the Greek word *hals* means?

_____

_____

_____

He Ne Ar Kr Xe

FIGURE 6 ·······································

Neon Lights

Glowing electric lights are often called "neon lights" even though they are usually filled with other noble gases or mixtures of them. The lights above show the symbols for helium (He), neon (Ne), argon (Ar), krypton (Kr), and xenon (Xe).

The Noble Gases

The elements in Group 18 are known as the **noble gases.** They do not ordinarily form compounds because atoms of noble gases do not usually gain, lose, or share electrons. As a result, the noble gases are usually nonreactive. Even so, scientists have been able to synthesize some noble gas compounds in the laboratory.

Shade in the noble gases on the periodic table.

You have probably seen a floating balloon filled with helium (He). Noble gases are also used in glowing electric lights, such as the ones shown in **Figure 6**.

Hydrogen

Alone in the upper left corner of the periodic table is hydrogen—the element with the simplest atoms. The chemical properties of hydrogen are very different from those of the other elements, so it cannot be grouped in with a family.

Hydrogen makes up more than 90 percent of the atoms in the universe. Stars—like the sun, shown in **Figure 7**—contain massive amounts of hydrogen. But, hydrogen makes up only 1 percent of the mass of Earth's crust, oceans, and atmosphere. Hydrogen is rarely found on Earth as a pure element. Most hydrogen is combined with oxygen in water.

Shade in hydrogen on the periodic table.

FIGURE 7 ·····················

The Sun

The sun fuses hydrogen atoms together to form helium.

Explain Why isn't hydrogen considered an alkali metal?

1

H

Hydrogen
1.0079

FIGURE 8 ··············
Solar Cells
The solar cells
on the International
Space Station transform energy
from the sun into electrical energy.
Some solar cells contain silicon,
which is a semiconductor.

14
Si
Silicon
28.086

Shade in the metalloids
on the periodic table.

Metalloids Between the metals
and the nonmetals in the periodic table
lie the metalloids. The **metalloids** have
some properties of metals and some properties
of nonmetals. All metalloids are solids at room temperature. The
metalloids are brittle, hard, and somewhat reactive.

The most common metalloid is silicon (Si). Ordinary sand,
which is mostly silicon dioxide, (SiO_2) is the main component of
glass. A compound of boron (B) and oxygen is added during the
process of glassmaking to make heat-resistant glass.

A metalloid's most useful property is the ability to conduct
electric current. The conductivity of a metalloid can depend on
temperature, exposure to light, or the presence of impurities.
For this reason, metalloids such as silicon and germanium (Ge) are
used to make semiconductors. **Semiconductors** are substances that
can conduct electric current under some conditions but not under
other conditions. Semiconductors are used to make computer
chips, transistors, and lasers. Semiconductors are also used in solar
cells, such as the ones shown in **Figure 8**.

⟳ **Summarize** Summarize the
properties of the metalloids.

_____
_____
_____
_____
_____
_____
_____

apply it!

Use this portion of the periodic table to answer the questions.

❶ **Classify** List the chemical symbols of the nonmetals:
_____. The remaining
elements are classified as _____

❷ Selenium has properties similar to (sulfur/bromine)
because they are in the same (period/group).

14	15	16	17
Si	**P**	**S**	**Cl**
Silicon 28.086	Phosphorus 30.974	Sulfur 32.06	Chlorine 35.453
32	**33**	**34**	**35**
Ge	**As**	**Se**	**Br**
Germanium 72.59	Arsenic 74.922	Selenium 78.96	Bromine 79.904

Alien Periodic Table

How is the periodic table organized?

FIGURE 9 ···

▷ VIRTUAL LAB   Imagine that inhabitants of another planet send a message to Earth that contains information about 30 elements. However, the message contains different names and symbols for these elements than those used on Earth. ✎ Infer Using the clues provided, fill in the periodic table with these "alien" names.

Alien Elements

The noble gases are **bombal** (Bo), **wobble** (Wo), **jeptum** (J), and **logon** (L). Among these gases, wobble has the greatest atomic mass and bombal the least. Logon is lighter than jeptum.

The most reactive group of metals are **xtalt** (X), **byyou** (By), **chow** (Ch), and **quackzil** (Q). Of these metals, chow has the lowest atomic mass. Quackzil is in the same period as wobble.

Apstrom (A), **vulcania** (Vc), and **kratt** (Kt) are non-metals in Group 17. Vulcania is in the same period as quackzil and wobble.

The metalloids are **ernst** (E), **highho** (Hi), **terriblum** (T), and **sississ** (Ss). Sississ is the metalloid with the greatest atomic mass. Ernst is the metalloid with the lowest atomic mass. Highho and terriblum are in Group 14. Terriblum has more protons than highho. **Yazzer** (Yz) touches the zigzag line, but it's a metal, not a metalloid.

The lightest element of all is called **pfsst** (Pf). The heaviest element in the group of 30 elements is **eldorado** (El). The most chemically active non-metal is apstrom. Kratt reacts with byyou to form table salt.

					18
13	14	15	16	17	

The element **doggone** (D) has only 4 protons in its atoms.

Floxxit (Fx) is important in the chemistry of life. It forms compounds made of long chains of atoms. **Rhaatrap** (R) and **doadeer** (Do) are metals in the fourth period, but rhaatrap is less reactive than doadeer.

Magnificon (M), **goldy** (G), and sississ are all members of Group 15. Goldy has fewer electrons than magnificon.

Urrp (Up), **oz** (Oz), and **nuutye** (Nu) are in Group 16. Nuutye is found as a diatomic molecule and has the same properties as a gas found in Earth's atmosphere. Oz has a lower atomic number than urrp.

The element **anatom** (An) has atoms with a total of 49 electrons. **Zapper** (Z) and **pie** (Pi) are both members of Group 2. Zapper has fewer protons than pie.

 Do the Quick Lab *Finding Nonmetals.*

Assess Your Understanding

2a. List What are the nonmetals in Group 16 of the periodic table?

_____

_____

_____

b. Compare and Contrast How do the chemical properties of the halogens compare to those of the noble gases?

_____

_____

_____

_____

c. ANSWER THE BIG ? How is the periodic table organized?

_____

_____

_____

_____

_____

_____

_____

_____

_____

_____

got it? ·····························

○ **I get it!** Now I know that the families containing nonmetals include _____

_____

_____

_____

○ **I need extra help with** _____

Go to MY SCIENCE COACH *online for help with this subject.*

Radioactive Elements

UNLOCK THE BIG Q?

- **What Happens to an Atom During Radioactive Decay?**
  PS.5c

- **What Does Radioactive Decay Produce?**
  PS.3b, PS.5c

- **How Are Radioactive Isotopes Useful?**
  PS.1g, PS.1n, PS.5c, PS.6b

my planet diary   FUN FACTS

Running on Radioactive Isotopes

Did you know that the *Cassini* spacecraft, which is being used to explore Saturn, runs on batteries? The batteries are called radioisotope thermoelectric generators (RTGs).

The batteries you can buy in the store use chemical reactions to generate electrical energy. However, RTGs produce electrical energy by using radioactive decay. RTGs contain unstable isotopes, which are called radioactive isotopes. Heat is released as the radioactive isotopes lose particles from their atoms. The heat is then converted into electrical energy. A single RTG contains several pounds of radioactive material. This is enough fuel to provide power for up to 23 years!

Communicate Write your answer to each question below. Then discuss your answers with a partner.

1. How are RTGs different from the batteries you buy at a store?

_____

_____

_____

_____

_____

2. Imagine being on a spacecraft traveling to distant planets. What are some of the things you might see?

_____

_____

_____

_____

> **PLANET DIARY** Go to **Planet Diary** to learn more about radioactive decay.

 Lab zone Do the Inquiry Warm-Up *How Much Goes Away?*

Vocabulary

- radioactive decay • nuclear reaction • radioactivity
- alpha particle • beta particle • gamma ray
- half-life • radioactive dating • tracer

Skills

↻ Reading: Relate Cause and Effect

△ Inquiry: Calculate

What Happens to an Atom During Radioactive Decay?

Suppose you could find a way to turn dull, cheap lead into valuable gold. More than a thousand years ago, many people tried, but nothing worked. As the young scientist in **Figure 1** will soon discover, there is no chemical reaction that converts one element into another. Even so, elements do sometimes change into other elements. For example, atoms of carbon can become atoms of nitrogen. How are these changes possible?

Radioactive Decay Recall that atoms with the same number of protons and different numbers of neutrons are called isotopes. Some isotopes are unstable, so their nuclei do not hold together well. These unstable isotopes are also called radioactive isotopes. In a process called **radioactive decay,** the atomic nuclei of radioactive isotopes release fast-moving particles and energy. ⬤━ **During radioactive decay, the identity of an atom changes.**

Radioactive decay is an example of a nuclear reaction. **Nuclear reactions** involve the particles in the nucleus of an atom. Nuclear fission, a process in which an atom's nuclei split apart, and nuclear fusion, the process in which atomic nuclei join together, are both nuclear reactions. These physical processes make it possible for scientists to turn one element into another.

Science Standards of Learning

PS.5c Investigate and understand nuclear reactions and how they relate to the Law of Conservation of Matter and Energy.

Goldy, it won't work because
_____
_____
_____
_____
_____
_____

FIGURE 1 ································

Trying to Turn Lead Into Gold

Goldy is furiously trying to turn lead into gold in the chemistry lab. Meanwhile, her lab partner Lucy is trying to convince her that it can't be done with a chemical reaction.

✎ **Communicate** Use what you know about nuclear and chemical reactions to complete Lucy's argument.

Discovery of Radioactive Decay

In 1896, the French scientist Henri Becquerel accidentally discovered the effects of radioactive decay. He observed that when a mineral containing uranium was exposed to sunlight, it gave off an energy that could fog photographic film plates. Becquerel thought that sunlight was necessary for the energy release. So, on a cloudy day, he put away the mineral in a desk drawer next to a photographic plate wrapped in paper. Later, when Becquerel opened his desk to retrieve his materials, he found an image of the mineral on the photographic plate. Sunlight wasn't necessary after all. Becquerel hypothesized that uranium gives off energy, called radiation, all the time.

Becquerel presented his findings to a young Polish researcher, Marie Curie, and her husband, French chemist Pierre Curie. The Curies showed that a reaction was taking place within the uranium nuclei. The uranium was able to spontaneously emit radiation. Marie Curie called this property **radioactivity.** The Curies, along with Becquerel, won the Nobel Prize in physics for their work on radioactivity. Marie Curie, shown in **Figure 2,** was later awarded the Nobel Prize in chemistry for her research on radioactive elements. She eventually died of cancer, a result of her years of exposure to radium.

FIGURE 2 ···

Marie Curie

Marie Curie was the first scientist to win the Nobel Prize in two different subject areas (physics and chemistry). She was also the first woman ever to receive a Nobel Prize.

 Do the Quick Lab *What Happens When an Atom Decays?*

🔑 Assess Your Understanding

1a. Define The spontaneous emission of radiation by an unstable atomic nucleus is called

_____

b. Apply Concepts What caused the fogging of the photographic plates that Becquerel observed in 1896?

_____

_____

_____

got it?

○ I get it! Now I know that during radioactive decay _____

_____

_____

○ I need extra help with _____

_____

_____

Go to MY SCIENCE ⓢ COACH online for help with this subject.

What Does Radioactive Decay Produce?

Figure 3 illustrates the three major forms of radiation produced during the decay of an unstable nucleus. **Radioactive decay can produce alpha particles, beta particles, and gamma rays.**

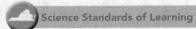
Science Standards of Learning

PS.3b Investigate and understand the modern model of atomic structure.

PS.5c Investigate and understand nuclear reactions and how they relate to the Law of Conservation of Matter and Energy.

FIGURE 3 ···

> **ART IN MOTION** **Radioactive Decay**

Radioactive elements give off particles and energy during radioactive decay. ✎ **Compare and Contrast Identify the change (if any) that occurs in an unstable nucleus during each form of radioactive decay.**

Alpha Decay

An **alpha particle** consists of two protons and two neutrons. It is positively charged. The release of an alpha particle by an atom during alpha decay decreases the atomic number by 2 and the mass number by 4. For example, a thorium-232 nucleus decays to produce an alpha particle and a radium-228 nucleus.

Radioactive nucleus

Alpha particle

2 protons lost
2 neutrons lost

Beta Decay

During beta decay, a neutron in an unstable nucleus changes into a negatively charged beta particle and a proton. A **beta particle** is a fast-moving electron given off by a nucleus during radioactive decay. The new proton remains inside the nucleus. The nucleus is then left with one less neutron and one more proton. Its mass number remains the same but its atomic number increases by one. For example, a carbon-14 nucleus decays to produce a beta particle and a nitrogen-14 nucleus.

Radioactive nucleus

Beta particle

[   ] proton(s) (lost/gained)

[   ] neutron(s) (lost/gained)

Gamma Radiation

Alpha and beta decay are almost always accompanied by gamma radiation. **Gamma rays** consist of high-energy waves, similar to X-rays. Gamma rays (also called gamma radiation) have no charge and do not cause a change in either the atomic mass or the atomic number.

Radioactive nucleus

Gamma rays

[   ] proton(s) (lost/gained)

[   ] neutron(s) (lost/gained)

Effects of Nuclear Radiation

Effects of Nuclear Radiation **Figure 4** depicts a radioactive source that emits alpha particles, beta particles, and gamma rays. Alpha particles move very fast, they can be blocked by just a sheet of paper. Alpha radiation can cause an injury to human skin that is much like a bad burn.

Beta particles are much faster and more penetrating than alpha particles. They can pass through paper. But, they are blocked by an aluminum sheet 5 millimeters thick. Beta particles can also travel into the human body and damage its cells.

Gamma radiation is the most penetrating. You would need a piece of lead several centimeters thick or a concrete wall about a meter thick to stop gamma rays. They can pass right through a human body. Gamma rays deliver intense energy to cells and can cause severe damage.

FIGURE 4 ····································

The Effects of Nuclear Radiation
The three main types of nuclear radiation vary in their ability to penetrate materials.

✎ **Apply Concepts** Use the key to complete the paths of the alpha particle, beta particle, and gamma ray emitted by the radioactive sample. Each path should end at the point where the radiation is blocked.

Key
— Alpha particle
---- Beta particle
〜〜 Gamma ray

Radioactive sample

Lead box

Paper

Aluminum sheet

Concrete

Lab zone® Do the Quick Lab Modeling Beta Decay.

🔑 Assess Your Understanding

2a. Identify What is the name of the particle produced by radioactive decay that consists of 2 protons and 2 neutrons?

_____

b. Compare and Contrast Rank the three major types of nuclear radiation from 1 (most penetrating) to 3 (least penetrating).

_____ Alpha _____ Beta _____ Gamma

c. Predict What are the identity and mass number of the nucleus formed during the beta decay of magnesium-28?

_____

got it?

○ **I get it!** Now I know that the three major forms of radiation produced during radioactive decay are _____

_____

_____

_____

○ **I need extra help with** _____

_____

Go to **MY SCIENCE** 🔍 **COACH** *online for help with this subject.*

How Are Radioactive Isotopes Useful?

Radioactive isotopes have many uses in science and industry. In some cases, the energy released by radioactive isotopes is itself useful. In other cases, radiation is useful because it can be easily detected. ⚷ **Uses of radioactive isotopes include determining the ages of fossils, tracing the steps of chemical reactions and industrial processes, diagnosing and treating disease, and providing sources of energy.**

Radioactive Dating Radioactive isotopes decay at different rates. The **half-life** of a radioactive isotope is the length of time needed for half of the atoms of a sample to decay. The half-life is different for each radioactive isotope. Half-lives can range from less than a second to billions of years!

Fossils are traces or remains of living things that have been preserved. For fossils millions or billions of years old, ages are found from radioactive isotopes with very long half-lives, like uranium. For much younger fossils, carbon-14 is often used. As plants grow, they use carbon dioxide (CO_2) from the air. A fraction of all carbon dioxide contains the radioactive isotope carbon-14. This becomes part of a plant's structures. After the plant dies, it stops taking in carbon dioxide. If the plant's remains are preserved, the amount of carbon-14 present can be measured. Scientists can calculate how many half-lives have passed since the plant died and estimate the age of the fossil. This process is called **radioactive dating.**

do the math!

Data from a fossil of a mammoth tooth shows that carbon-14 has been decaying in the tooth for five half-lives.

1 Calculate Calculate the age of the tooth.

_____ half-lives × _____ years/half-life = _____ years.

2 CHALLENGE What fraction of the amount of carbon-14 that was in the mammoth's tooth when it died is left after five half-lives?

$$\left(\frac{1}{2}\right)^5 = \underline{\quad} \times \underline{\quad} \times \underline{\quad} \times \underline{\quad} \times \underline{\quad} = \underline{\quad}$$

Half-Lives of Some Radioactive Isotopes

Element	Half-Life
Polonium-216	0.16 second
Sodium-24	15 hours
Iodine-131	8.07 days
Phosphorus-32	14.3 days
Cobalt-60	5.26 years
Radium-226	1,600 years
Carbon-14	5,730 years
Chlorine-36	310,000 years
Uranium-235	710 million years
Uranium-238	4.5 billion years

Why are radioactive isotopes useful for following the steps of a chemical reaction?

_____

_____

_____

_____

_____

_____

Uses in Science and Industry

A radioactive isotope, like a lighthouse flashing in the night, "signals" where it is by emitting radiation that can be detected. **Tracers** are radioactive isotopes that can be followed through the steps of a chemical reaction or an industrial process. Tracers behave chemically like nonradioactive forms of an element. For example, phosphorus is used by plants in small amounts for healthy growth. The plant in **Figure 5** will absorb radioactive phosphorus-32 just as it does the nonradioactive form. Radiation will be present in any part of the plant that contains the isotope. In this way, biologists can learn where and how plants use phosphorus.

Tracers are used to find weak spots in metal pipes, especially in oil pipelines. When added to a liquid, tracers can be easily detected if they leak out of the pipes. Gamma rays can pass through metal and be detected by photographic film. The gamma ray images allow structural engineers to detect small cracks in the metal of bridges and building frames before a disaster occurs.

FIGURE 5

Radioactive Tracers

Phosphorus-32 added to soil is absorbed through a plant's roots. The tracer can be detected in any plant structures in which phosphorus is used. ✎ **Explain Write a short caption under each figure to explain what is happening.**

Gamma radiation

Uses in Medicine Doctors use radioactive isotopes to detect medical problems and to treat some diseases. Tracers are injected into the body and travel to organs and other structures in which that chemical is normally used. Technicians make images of the bone, blood, vessel, or organ affected using equipment that detects radiation.

Cancer tumors are sometimes treated from outside the body with high-energy gamma rays. Gamma radiation directed toward a cancer tumor damages the cancer cells so that they can no longer function.

Nuclear Energy Many power plants, like the one shown in **Figure 6,** use radioactive isotopes as fuel. Both nuclear fission and nuclear fusion release huge amounts of energy when they react. In a nuclear reactor, atoms of uranium-235 are split under controlled conditions. The energy produced heats water to produce steam. The steam turns a turbine. This generates electricity. Nuclear power plants provide electrical energy in many parts of the world. Nuclear reactions also provide the energy for large submarines and other types of ocean vessels.

FIGURE 6 ⋯⋯⋯⋯⋯⋯⋯⋯⋯⋯⋯⋯⋯⋯⋯⋯⋯⋯⋯⋯
Nuclear Power Plant
The cooling tower of a nuclear power plant helps control the temperature inside the reactor. The power plant converts thermal energy to electrical energy.

 Do the Quick Lab *Designing Experiments Using Radioactive Tracers.*

🔑 Assess Your Understanding

3a. Explain Why is half-life useful to an archaeologist?

_____

_____

_____

b. 🔁 **Relate Cause and Effect** Why are radioactive isotopes that emit gamma rays useful for treating some forms of cancer?

_____

_____

_____

got it? ⋯⋯⋯⋯⋯⋯⋯⋯⋯⋯⋯⋯⋯⋯⋯⋯⋯⋯⋯⋯⋯⋯⋯⋯⋯⋯

○ **I get it!** Now I know that four uses of radioactive isotopes are _____

_____

_____

○ **I need extra help with** _____

Go to MY SCIENCE 🅢 COACH *online for help with this subject.*

In the periodic table, the elements are organized in order of _____ atomic number. The properties of the elements repeat in each _____.

LESSON 1 Introduction to Atoms

🔑 Atomic theory grew as a series of models that developed from experimental evidence.

🔑 At the center of the atom is a tiny, dense nucleus containing protons and neutrons. Surrounding the nucleus is a cloudlike region of moving electrons.

Vocabulary
- atom • electron • nucleus • proton
- energy level • neutron • atomic number
- isotope • mass number

LESSON 2 Organizing the Elements

🔑 Mendeleev noticed a pattern of properties in elements arranged by increasing atomic mass.

🔑 The periodic table includes each element's atomic number, symbol, name, and atomic mass.

🔑 The properties of an element can be predicted from its location in the periodic table.

Vocabulary
- atomic mass • periodic table
- chemical symbol • period • group

LESSON 3 Metals

🔑 The physical properties of metals include luster, malleability, ductility, and conductivity.

🔑 Metals are classified as alkali metals, alkaline earth metals, transition metals, metals in mixed groups, lanthanides, and actinides.

Vocabulary
- metal • luster • malleable • ductile
- thermal conductivity • electrical conductivity
- reactivity • corrosion • alkali metal
- alkaline earth metal • transition metal

LESSON 4 Nonmetals and Metalloids

🔑 In general, most nonmetals are poor conductors. Solid nonmetals tend to be dull and brittle.

🔑 The families containing nonmetals include the carbon family, the nitrogen family, the oxygen family, the halogen family, the noble gases, and hydrogen.

Vocabulary
- nonmetal • diatomic molecule • halogen
- noble gas • metalloid • semiconductor

LESSON 5 Radioactive Elements

🔑 During radioactive decay, the identity of an atom changes.

🔑 Radioactive decay can produce alpha particles, beta particles, and gamma rays.

🔑 Uses of radioactive isotopes include determining the ages of fossils, tracing the steps of chemical and industrial processes, and providing sources of energy.

Vocabulary
- radioactive decay • nuclear reaction • radioactivity • alpha particle
- beta particle • gamma ray • half-life • radioactive dating • tracer

Review and Assessment

LESSON 1 Introduction to Atoms

1. The atomic number of an element is determined by the number of

   a. protons.   **b.** electrons.

   c. neutrons.   **d.** isotopes.

2. Two isotopes of an element have the same number of _____ but different numbers of _____ .

3. Relate Cause and Effect How can an atom be electrically neutral when it contains particles that are charged?

_____

_____

_____

4. Relate Evidence and Explanation How did Rutherford's experimental evidence lead to the development of a new atomic model?

_____

_____

_____

_____

_____

_____

5. [Write About It] Write a letter that Thomson might have sent to another scientist explaining why an atom must contain positive charges as well as negative charges. The letter should also explain why Thomson proposed the atomic model that he did.

LESSON 2 Organizing the Elements

6. The rows in the periodic table are called

   a. groups.   **b.** periods.

   c. nonmetals.   **d.** metals.

7. Dmitri Mendeleev constructed the first periodic table, which is _____

_____

_____

_____

8. Apply Concepts Below is an entry taken from the periodic table. Identify the type of information given by each labeled item.

_____

_____

_____

9. Make Generalizations Why aren't the atomic masses of most elements whole numbers?

_____

_____

_____

10. [Write About It] Write an advertisement that you could use to sell copies of Mendeleev's periodic table to chemists in 1869. Be sure to emphasize the benefits of the table to the chemical profession. Remember, the chemists have never seen such a table.

LESSON 3 Metals

11. Of the following, the group that contains elements that are the most reactive is the

   a. alkali metals.   **b.** alkaline earth metals.

   c. carbon family.   **d.** noble gases.

12. A property of metals is high thermal conductivity, which is _____

_____ .

13. **Predict** Using the periodic table, predict which element—potassium, aluminum, or iron—is most reactive. Explain your answer.

_____

_____

_____

_____

LESSON 4 Nonmetals and Metalloids

14. Unlike metals, solid nonmetals are

   a. good conductors of heat and electric current.

   b. malleable.

   c. dull and brittle.

   d. ductile.

15. Two elements that have properties similar to those of chlorine are _____

_____ .

16. **Infer** What property of the materials used in computer chips makes them useful as switches that turn electricity on and off?

_____

_____

_____

_____

LESSON 5 Radioactive Elements

17. Unstable atomic nuclei that release fast-moving particles and energy are

   a. radioactive.   **b.** alloys.

   c. isotopes.   **d.** alpha particles.

18. A radioactive isotope that can be followed through a chemical reaction or industrial process is called a(n) _____ .

19. **Classify** What type of radioactive decay results in uranium-238 becoming thorium-234?

_____

20. **Write About It** Suppose you could go back in time to interview Henri Becquerel on the day he discovered radioactivity. From his perspective, write an account of the discovery.

APPLY THE BIG ? How is the periodic table organized?

5	6	7	8
B Boron 10.81	**C** Carbon 12.011	**N** Nitrogen 14.007	**O** Oxygen 15.999
13	14	15	16
Al Aluminum 26.982	**Si** Silicon 28.086	**P** Phosphorus 30.974	**S** Sulfur 32.06

21. A portion of the periodic table is shown above. Which element on the periodic table has properties that are most similar to those of nitrogen (N)? Explain.

_____

_____

_____

_____

Virginia SOL Test Prep

Read each question and choose the best answer.

1 A portion of the periodic table is shown below.

8	9	10
O Oxygen 15.999	**F** Fluorine 18.998	**Ne** Neon 20.179
16	17	18
S Sulfur 32.06	**Cl** Chlorine 35.453	**Ar** Argon 39.948

Which elements are noble gases?

A oxygen, fluorine, and neon

B sulfur, chlorine, and argon

C fluorine and chlorine

D neon and argon

2 Why is the mass of a carbon atom greater than the total mass of its protons and electrons?

F The mass of a proton is greater than the mass of an electron.

G A proton is positively charged and an electron is negatively charged.

H Most of the atom's volume is the sphere-shaped cloud of electrons.

J The neutrons in the nucleus add mass to the atom.

3 Elements that are gases at room temperature are likely to be classified as which of the following?

A metals

B nonmetals

C metalloids

D semiconductors

4 Which property of aluminum makes it a suitable metal for soft-drink cans?

F It has good electrical conductivity.

G It can be hammered into a thin sheet (malleability).

H It can be drawn into long wires (ductility).

J It can reflect light (luster).

5 Radioactive isotopes give off radiation that can be detected. This property makes them useful in which of the following ways?

A as tracers in chemical reactions

B in detecting leaks in oil pipelines

C in diagnosing certain medical problems

D all of the above

6 The atomic number of an element represents—

F the number of neutrons in the nucleus

G the number of protons in the nucleus

H the atomic mass of the element

J the density of the element

7 According to the cloud model of the atom, electrons—

A orbit the nucleus like planets orbiting the sun

B are uniformly scattered throughout a positively-charged sphere

C move rapidly within a region around the nucleus

D are packed tightly in the center of the atom

Discovery of the Elements

More than 100 chemical elements have been discovered or created on Earth. The following stories describe some of the spectacular ways in which elements have been discovered:

1669 Phosphorus

In 1669, alchemist Hennig Brand was searching for a way to turn lead into gold. He hypothesized that animal urine might contain a substance that could cause the transformation. In the process of heating the urine to obtain a pure substance, he discovered a material that glowed in the dark. That material is phosphorus, which is important in maintaining a healthy body.

1811 Iodine

As French chemist Barnard Courtois isolated sodium and potassium compounds from seaweed ashes, he accidentally added too much sulfuric acid. The mess he created sent out a cloud of violet-colored gas that condensed on metal surfaces in the room. That gas was iodine. Even today, some iodine is isolated from seaweed. Having enough iodine in your diet can prevent illness and allow for healthy development.

1936 Technetium

Italian chemists Emilio Segrè and Carlo Perrier made technetium in a cyclotron in 1936. This was the first element to be produced artificially. Technetium is similar in appearance to platinum, but is very radioactive. Because it breaks down quickly, technetium is not found in nature.

Flame tests historically helped chemists to identify elements. ▶

Research It Find out more about the discovery of the following elements: helium, copper, americium, aluminum, and silicon. Then, create a timeline that shows when each element was discovered and how that discovery affected human life.

 PS.1j, PS.2b, PS.2d, PS.2e, PS.2f

Elements of the Human Body

It's elemental! Atoms of only five different elements make up 98 percent of the mass of the human body.

Oxygen and Hydrogen About two thirds of the body consists of water. So, in terms of mass, more than half of the body is oxygen atoms, and another 10 percent is hydrogen atoms. Both oxygen and hydrogen are also present in other body parts.

Carbon The key element in organic molecules is carbon. Organic molecules make up all body tissues, including muscles.

Calcium and Phosphorus The hard, strong parts of bones are built mostly of calcium phosphate crystals, which contain calcium, phosphorus, and oxygen.

Trace Elements Some elements exist in the body in small amounts, but play important roles. For example, chemical reactions inside body organs require enzymes that contain magnesium. The thyroid gland needs iodine to control growth. The element iron makes up less than one twentieth of 1 percent of the body, yet is an extremely important part of the hemoglobin molecule. Red blood cells use hemoglobin to carry oxygen throughout the body.

Graph It Research how the human body acquires these elements. Then use the data from the table of Elements in the Human Body to create a circle graph that shows the relative percentages of each element in the body.

 PS.1i, PS.1k, PS.2b

Elements in the Human Body

Element	Approximate mass (%)
Oxygen	65
Carbon	18
Hydrogen	10
Nitrogen	3
Calcium	1
Phosphorus	1
Potassium, Sulfur, Sodium, Chlorine	0.1–0.3 percent each
Copper, Magnesium, Zinc, Iron, Selenium, Molybdenum, Fluorine, Iodine, Manganese, Cobalt	less than 0.1 percent each

WHAT IS GROWING IN THIS CAVE?

How can bonding determine the properties of a substance?

Mexico's Cave of Crystals contains the world's largest natural crystals. These rocks are made of the mineral gypsum. They grew under water for as many as 500,000 years. The water was pumped out to reveal thousands of giant crystals up to 11 meters in length and 50,000 kilograms in mass. The cave might appear to be a fun place to climb around, but temperatures inside can reach 65°C (hotter than a desert afternoon). This makes it deadly for human exploration without specialized equipment. **Form Operational Definitions** Based on the photograph of the Cave of Crystals, how would you define a crystal?

_____

_____

_____

> UNTAMED SCIENCE Watch the **Untamed Science** video to learn more about chemical bonding.

Atoms and Bonding

Science Standards of Learning

PS.1f, PS.1g, PS.1i, PS.1j, PS.1k, PS.1m, PS.2d,
PS.2e, PS.2f, PS.3b, PS.4a, PS.4b, PS.4c, PS.5a, PS.5b

6 | Getting Started

Check Your Understanding

1. Background Read the paragraph below and then answer the question.

Marcy fills an ice cube tray with water and places it in a freezer. The temperature in the freezer is −18°C, which is lower than the **melting point** of water (0°C). When Marcy opens the freezer a few hours later, she finds that the water has frozen into **solid** ice cubes.

> The **melting point** of a substance is the temperature at which the substance changes from a solid to a liquid.
>
> A **solid** has a definite shape and a definite volume.

- What will happen to an ice cube if it is left outside on a warm, sunny day? Explain.

_____

_____

_____

> **MY READING WEB** If you had trouble answering the question above, visit **My Reading Web** and type in **Atoms and Bonding**.

Vocabulary Skill

High-Use Academic Words High-use academic words are words you are likely to encounter while reading textbooks. Look for the following words in context as you read this chapter.

Word	Definition	Example Sentence
stable	*adj.* not easily or quickly changed from one state to another	Gold is a *stable* metal that does not rust or tarnish.
symbol	*n.* a written sign that stands for something else	The *symbol* for the element oxygen is O.

2. Quick Check Choose the word that best completes the sentence.

- The letter H is the _____ for hydrogen.
- Platinum jewelry lasts a long time because the metal is very

_____

electron dot diagram

Li·   Be·   ·B·

Lithium   Beryllium   Boron

ionic compound

$CaCO_3$

crystal

I want it!

I want it more!

polar bond

Chapter Preview

LESSON 1
- valence electron
- electron dot diagram
- chemical bond
- ↻ **Relate Cause and Effect**
- △ **Predict**

LESSON 2
- ion
- polyatomic ion
- ionic bond
- ionic compound
- chemical formula
- subscript
- crystal
- ↻ **Relate Text and Visuals**
- △ **Interpret Data**

LESSON 3
- covalent bond
- molecule
- double bond
- triple bond
- molecular compound
- nonpolar bond
- polar bond
- ↻ **Compare and Contrast**
- △ **Graph**

LESSON 4
- metallic bond
- alloy
- ↻ **Identify the Main Idea**
- △ **Classify**

> VOCAB FLASH CARDS For extra help with vocabulary, visit **Vocab Flash Cards** and type in *Atoms and Bonding.*

211

Atoms, Bonding, and the Periodic Table

UNLOCK THE BIG ?

🗝 **What Determines an Element's Chemistry?**

PS.1j, PS.1m, PS.3b, PS.4a, PS.4b, PS.4c, PS.5b

my planeT DiaRY

FUN FACTS

Elemental Effects

Many people enjoy fireworks displays. Did you know that chemistry plays a big part in the beauty and the noise? The different colors and effects produced depend on the properties of the elements in the chemical compounds used in each firework rocket. These compounds produce smoke, color bursts, loud noises, or a combination of these effects when they are detonated.

The table below lists some elements found in the compounds used in rockets. It shows the effects these elements produce.

Using what you know about the periodic table, answer the questions below. After you finish the lesson, check your answers.

What elements do you think were used to produce the fireworks display in the photo? What groups of the periodic table do these elements belong to?

_____

_____

_____

Element	Effect
Strontium	Red color
Barium	Green color
Copper	Blue color
Sodium	Yellow color
Magnesium or aluminum	White color
Potassium or sodium	Whistling sound
Potassium and sulfur	White smoke

▷ PLANET DIARY Go to **Planet Diary** to learn more about elements.

Lab zone

Do the Inquiry Warm-Up *What Are the Trends in the Periodic Table?*

Vocabulary
- valence electron
- electron dot diagram
- chemical bond

Skills
↻ Reading: Relate Cause and Effect
△ Inquiry: Predict

What Determines an Element's Chemistry?

How do atoms combine to form compounds? The answer has to do with electrons and their energy levels.

Valence Electrons The number of protons in a neutral atom equals the number of electrons. The electrons of an atom are found in different energy levels. Electrons at higher energy levels have higher amounts of energy. The **valence electrons** (VAY luns) of an atom are those electrons that have the highest energy. Valence electrons are involved in chemical bonding. ⚷ **The number of valence electrons in each atom helps determine the chemical properties of that element.**

Electron Dot Diagrams Each atom of an element has a certain number of valence electrons. The number of valence electrons is specific to that element. Different elements can have from 1 to 8 valence electrons. **Figure 1** demonstrates one way to show the number of valence electrons in an element. An **electron dot diagram** includes the symbol for the element surrounded by dots. Each dot stands for one valence electron.

Bonding Atoms tend to be more stable if they have 8 valence electrons. Atoms of neon (Ne), argon (Ar), krypton (Kr), and xenon (Xe) have 8 valence electrons. These elements are nonreactive, or stable. Helium (He) is stable with 2 electrons.

Atoms tend to form bonds so that they have 8 valence electrons and become more stable. Hydrogen needs only 2 to be stable. When atoms bond, valence electrons may be transferred from one atom to another. Or they may be shared between the atoms. A **chemical bond** is the force of attraction that holds atoms together as a result of the rearrangement of electrons between them.

H·   ·Ċ·   ·Ö:

Hydrogen   Carbon   Oxygen

Neon

FIGURE 1 ·······················

Electron Dot Diagrams
The valence electrons of an atom are shown as dots around the symbol of the element.

✏ **Interpret Diagrams** Complete the electron dot diagram for neon by drawing the correct number of dots.

213

Group 1
Alkali metals
Valence electrons: _____

Group 2
Alkaline earth metals
Valence electrons: _____

Group 14
Carbon family
Valence electrons: _____

Group 18
Noble gases
Valence electrons: _____

*The names and symbols for elements 113 and above have not yet been decided.

Lanthanides

Actinides

FIGURE 2 ·······························
>INTERACTIVE ART **Periodic Table of the Elements**
The periodic table is arranged in order of increasing atomic number. The number of valence electrons also increases from left to right across a period.

✎ **Interpret Tables** As you read the lesson, fill in the number of valence electrons for each group circled above.

Applying the Periodic Table The periodic table is shown in **Figure 2.** It gives you information about the valence electrons in atoms. The table is organized into rows, called periods, and columns, called groups. The atomic number of an element is the number of protons in each atom of that element.

The elements in the periodic table are in order by increasing atomic number. The number of valence electrons increases from left to right across each period. Each period begins with an element that has 1 valence electron. Except for Period 1, a given period ends with an element that has 8 valence electrons. This repeating pattern means that the elements within a group (except for Period 1) always have the same number of valence electrons. As a result, the elements in each group have similar properties.

Each element in Periods 2 and 3 has one more valence electron than the element to its left. Group 1 elements have 1. Group 2 elements have 2. Group 13 elements have 3 valence electrons. Group 14 elements have 4, and so on. (Elements in Groups 3 to 12 follow a slightly different pattern.)

apply it!

The symbols for the elements in Periods 2 and 3 are shown below. The correct electron dot diagrams are shown for only half of the elements.

1 Complete the electron dot diagrams for nitrogen, oxygen, fluorine, sodium, magnesium, aluminum, silicon, and argon.

2 Fluorine (F) and Chlorine (Cl) are in Group ____. A fluorine atom has _____ valence electrons. A chlorine atom has _____ valence electrons.

3 Predict How many valence electrons does a bromine (Br) atom have? _____

Li·   Be·   ·B·   ·Ç·

Lithium   Beryllium   Boron   Carbon

N   O   F   :Ne:

Nitrogen   Oxygen   Fluorine   Neon

Na   Mg   Al   Si

Sodium   Magnesium   Aluminum   Silicon

·P: ·S: ·Çl: Ar

Phosphorus   Sulfur   Chlorine   Argon

Noble Gases The Group 18 elements are the noble gases. Atoms of the noble gases have 8 valence electrons, except for helium, which has 2. Atoms with 8 valence electrons (or 2, in the case of helium) are stable. They are unlikely to gain or lose electrons or to share electrons with other atoms. Noble gases do not react easily with other elements. Some don't react at all. But, chemists have been able to make some noble gases form compounds with a few other elements.

FIGURE 3 ·······················
Camera Flashes
Argon, a noble gas, is used to produce camera flashes.

Vocabulary Use the word *stable* to explain why the alkali metals tend to lose 1 valence electron.

_____

_____

_____

_____

_____

_____

↻ **Relate Cause and Effect**
Underline the cause and circle the effect in the paragraph at the right.

Metals The metals are the elements in the blue section of the periodic table in **Figure 2**. Metal atoms react by losing their valence electrons. In general, the reactivity of a metal depends on how easily its atoms lose valence electrons. The reactivity of metals decreases from left to right across the periodic table.

At the far left side of the periodic table is Group 1, the alkali metals. Each alkali metal is the most reactive element in its period. Atoms of the alkali metals have 1 valence electron. Except for lithium (Li), when a Group 1 atom loses an electron, it is left with a stable arrangement of 8 electrons in the highest energy level. These electrons are in a lower energy level than the 1 valence electron that was lost. (Lithium atoms are left with a stable arrangement of 2 electrons.) The alkali metals are so reactive that they can cause an explosion when added to water!

Nonmetals The elements in the orange section of the periodic table in **Figure 2** are the nonmetals. Nonmetal atoms become stable when they gain or share enough electrons to have 8 valence electrons. (Hydrogen atoms are left with a stable arrangement of 2 electrons.)

The nonmetals usually combine with metals by gaining electrons. Nonmetals can also combine with other nonmetals and metalloids by sharing electrons.

Atoms of Group 17, the halogens, have 7 valence electrons. A gain of one more electron gives these atoms a stable 8 electrons. The halogens react easily with other elements. **Figure 4** shows the reaction of bromine (Br), a halogen, with aluminum (Al).

FIGURE 4
▷ VIRTUAL LAB **Reactivity of Bromine**
Aluminum reacts violently with bromine to produce aluminum bromide.

✎ CHALLENGE **What would happen if an alkali metal was combined with a halogen? Explain.**

_____

_____

_____

_____

Complete the table about groups of elements in the periodic table.

Group Number	Group Name	Number of Valence Electrons	Reactivity (High/Low)
1	Alkali metals	_____	_____
17	Halogens	_____	_____
18	Noble gases	_____	_____

Metalloids The metalloids lie along the zigzag line in the periodic table, between the metals and the nonmetals. Atoms of the metalloids can either lose or share electrons when they combine with other elements. Each metalloid has some of the properties of metals and some of the properties of nonmetals.

Hydrogen Hydrogen (H) is placed in Group 1 in the periodic table because it has 1 valence electron, but hydrogen is considered to be a nonmetal. The properties of hydrogen are very different from the properties of the alkali metals. Hydrogen shares its electron when forming compounds with other nonmetals to obtain a stable arrangement of 2 electrons.

FIGURE 5 ....
Computer Chip
Silicon, a metalloid, is one of the most abundant elements on Earth. It is used to make computer processor chips.

Lab zone® Do the Quick Lab
Element Chemistry.

🔑 Assess Your Understanding

1a. Define What are valence electrons?

_____

_____

b. Explain Why do the properties of elements change in a regular way across a period?

_____

_____

_____

c. 🔄 **Relate Cause and Effect** Explain the reactivity of the noble gases in terms of valence electrons.

_____

_____

_____

_____

_____

got it? ....

○ **I get it!** Now I know that the chemical properties of an element are determined by _____

_____

○ **I need extra help with** _____

Go to MY SCIENCE ⓢ COACH online for help with this subject.

217

Ionic Bonds

UNLOCK THE BIG ?

🔑 **How Do Ions Form?**
PS1.j, PS.1m, PS.3b, PS.4c, PS.5b

🔑 **How Are the Formulas and Names of Ionic Compounds Written?**
PS.1j, PS.1m, PS.3b, PS.4c, PS.5b

🔑 **What Are Properties of Ionic Compounds?**
PS.1j, PS.1m, PS.2f, PS.3b, PS.4c, PS.5b

MY PLANET DIARY

The Periodic Palette

Imagine calling the colors of the rainbow cadmium, chromium, cobalt, and manganese. These may not sound like the typical colors of the rainbow to you, but they do to many artists and painters!

The "colors" listed above are transition metal elements. These metals can form compounds known as ionic compounds. Many transition metal compounds are brightly colored. They can be used to make the pigments found in oil, acrylic, and watercolor paints. For example, cadmium and chromium compounds are used for red, orange, yellow, or green paints. Cobalt and manganese compounds are used for blue and violet paints.

FUN FACTS

Communicate Write your answer to each question below. Then discuss your answers with a partner.

1. Why are transition metal compounds often used in paint pigments?

_____

_____

_____

2. Some of the compounds used in paint pigments may cause serious health problems. Do you think that using these types of paints is worth the possible health risks? Why or why not?

_____

_____

_____

▶ PLANET DIARY Go to **Planet Diary** to learn more about ionic compounds.

Lab zone® Do the Inquiry Warm-Up *How Do Ions Form?*

Vocabulary
- ion • polyatomic ion • ionic bond • ionic compound
- chemical formula • subscript • crystal

Skills
- Reading: Relate Text and Visuals
- Inquiry: Interpret Data

 Science Standards of Learning

PS.1j Make valid conclusions after analyzing data.

PS.1m Construct and use models and simulations to illustrate and explain phenomena.

PS.3b Investigate and understand the modern model of atomic structure.

PS.4c Investigate and understand the formation of compounds through ionic and covalent bonding.

PS.5b Investigate and understand chemical changes in matter and how they relate to the Law of Conservation of Matter and Energy.

How Do Ions Form?

You and a friend walk past a market that sells apples for 40 cents each and pears for 50 cents each. You have 45 cents and want an apple. Your friend also has 45 cents but wants a pear. If you give your friend a nickel, she will have 50 cents and can buy a pear. You will have 40 cents left to buy an apple. Transferring the nickel gets both of you what you want. In a simple way, your actions model what can happen between atoms.

Ions An **ion** (EYE ahn) is an atom or group of atoms that has an electric charge. **When a neutral atom loses a valence electron, it loses a negative charge. It becomes a positive ion. When a neutral atom gains an electron, it gains a negative charge. It becomes a negative ion.** This is shown in **Figure 1.**

Metal atoms are likely to lose electrons. These atoms lose enough electrons to have a stable arrangement of 8 valence electrons at a lower energy level. A potassium (K) atom easily loses its 1 valence electron to become more stable. Nonmetal atoms are likely to gain electrons. These atoms gain enough electrons so that they have 8 valence electrons. A fluorine (F) atom gains 1 electron to have a stable arrangement of 8 valence electrons.

FIGURE 1 ·········

How Ions Form

An atom that loses one of its electrons becomes a positively charged ion. The atom that gains the electron becomes a negatively charged ion.

Interpret Diagrams
Complete the electron dot diagrams for potassium (K) and fluorine (F) before and after the electron is transferred.

✎ **Relate Text and Visuals**
Using the cartoon in **Figure 1,** explain why the potassium atom becomes positively charged and the fluorine atom becomes negatively charged.

_____
_____
_____
_____
_____
_____

FIGURE 2

> INTERACTIVE ART **Ions**

Ions have electric charges.

Common Ions and Their Charges

Name	Charge	Symbol or Formula
Lithium	1+	Li^+
Sodium	1+	Na^+
Potassium	1+	K^+
Ammonium	1+	NH_4^+
Calcium	2+	Ca^{2+}
Magnesium	2+	Mg^{2+}
Aluminum	3+	Al^{3+}
Fluoride	1–	F^-
Chloride	1–	Cl^-
Iodide	1–	I^-
Bicarbonate	1–	HCO_3^-
Nitrate	1–	NO_3^-
Oxide	2–	O^{2-}
Sulfide	2–	S^{2-}
Carbonate	2–	CO_3^{2-}
Sulfate	2–	SO_4^{2-}

Common Ions **Figure 2** lists the names of some common ions. Notice that some ions are made of several atoms. The ammonium ion is made of 1 nitrogen atom and 4 hydrogen atoms. Ions that are made of more than 1 atom are called **polyatomic ions** (pahl ee uh TAHM ik). The prefix *poly-* means "many," so *polyatomic* means "many atoms." Like other ions, polyatomic ions have an overall positive or negative charge.

Ionic Bonds When atoms that easily lose electrons react with atoms that easily gain electrons, valence electrons are transferred from one type of atom to another. The transfer gives each type of atom a more stable arrangement of electrons. Look at **Figure 3** to see how sodium atoms and chlorine atoms react to form sodium chloride (table salt).

① The sodium atom has 1 valence electron. The chlorine atom has 7 valence electrons.

② The valence electron of the sodium atom is transferred to the chlorine atom. Both atoms become ions. The sodium atom becomes a positive ion (Na^+). The chlorine atom becomes a negative ion (Cl^-).

③ Oppositely charged particles attract, so the positive Na^+ ion and the negative Cl^- ion attract. An **ionic bond** is the attraction between two oppositely charged ions. The resulting compound is called an **ionic compound.** It is made up of positive and negative ions. In an ionic compound, the total positive charge of all the positive ions equals the total negative charge of all the negative ions.

FIGURE 3

Formation of an Ionic Bond

Follow the steps to see how an ionic bond forms between a sodium atom and a chlorine atom.

✎ **Infer** Complete the electron dot diagrams for the sodium and chlorine atoms and their ions.

▲ Sodium metal

▲ Chlorine gas

Transfer of an electron

Sodium ion   Chloride ion

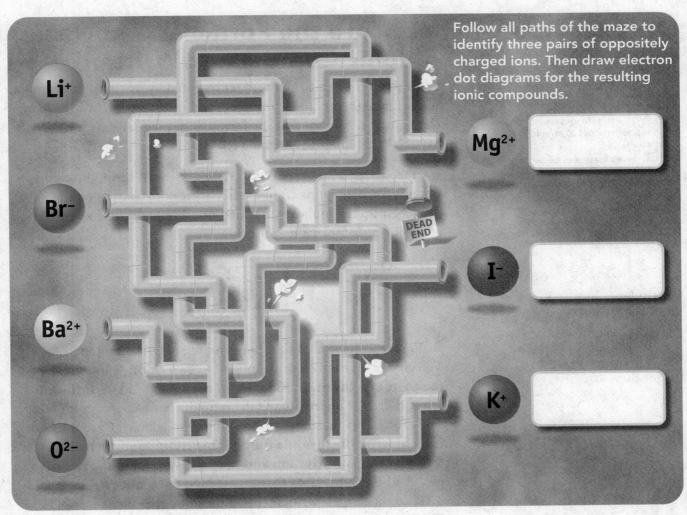

Follow all paths of the maze to identify three pairs of oppositely charged ions. Then draw electron dot diagrams for the resulting ionic compounds.

Li⁺

Br⁻

Ba²⁺

O²⁻

Mg²⁺

DEAD END

I⁻

K⁺

Do the Quick Lab
Ion Formation.

🔑 Assess Your Understanding

1a. Review An atom that loses a valence electron becomes a (positive/negative) ion. An atom that gains a valence electron becomes a (positive/negative) ion.

b. Apply Concepts Write the symbols for the ions that form when potassium and iodine react to form the ionic compound potassium iodide.

_____

c. Relate Cause and Effect Why is potassium iodide electrically neutral?

_____
_____
_____
_____
_____

got it? ....

○ I get it! Now I know ions form when _____

_____

○ I need extra help with _____

Go to MY SCIENCE ⓢ COACH online for help with this subject.

PS.1j Make valid conclusions after analyzing data.

PS.1m Construct and use models and simulations to illustrate and explain phenomena.

PS.3b Investigate and understand the modern model of atomic structure.

PS.4c Investigate and understand the formation of compounds through ionic and covalent bonding.

PS.5b Investigate and understand chemical changes in matter and how they relate to the Law of Conservation of Matter and Energy.

Vocabulary Choose the word that best completes the following sentence.

Mg is the _____ for magnesium.

How Are the Formulas and Names of Ionic Compounds Written?

You will often see a compound represented by its chemical formula. A **chemical formula** is a group of symbols that shows the ratio of elements in a compound. The formula for magnesium chloride is $MgCl_2$. What does this formula tell you?

Formulas of Ionic Compounds When ionic compounds form, the ions combine to balance the charges on the ions. The chemical formula for the compound reflects this balance. Look at the formula for magnesium chloride.

Chemical symbols → MgCl₂ ← Subscript

Figure 2 shows that the charge on the magnesium ion is 2+. The charge on each chloride ion is 1−. Two chloride ions balance the charge on the magnesium ion. The number "2" in the formula is a subscript. **Subscripts** tell the ratio of elements in a compound. The ratio of magnesium ions to chloride ions in $MgCl_2$ is 1 to 2. **To write the formula for an ionic compound, write the symbol of the positive ion and then the symbol of the negative ion. Add the subscripts that are needed to balance the charges.**

If no subscript is written, it is understood that the subscript is 1. The formula NaCl tells you that there is a 1-to-1 ratio of sodium ions to chloride ions. Formulas for compounds of polyatomic ions are written in a similar way. Calcium carbonate has the formula $CaCO_3$. There is one calcium ion (Ca^{2+}) for each carbonate ion (CO_3^{2-}).

FIGURE 4 ....

Coral Reefs

Corals make calcium carbonate, which helps protect them. When coral dies, its calcium carbonate shell remains and adds structure to the reef.

✎ **Identify** Circle the part of the formula representing the carbonate ion. Then identify the charge of each ion in the compound.

CaCO₃

Naming Ionic Compounds

Magnesium chloride, sodium bicarbonate, sodium oxide—where do these names come from? **For an ionic compound, the name of the positive ion comes first, followed by the name of the negative ion.** The name of the positive ion is usually the name of a metal. But, a few positive polyatomic ions exist, such as the ammonium ion (NH_4^+). If the negative ion is a single element, the end of its name changes to *-ide*. For example, MgO is named magnesium oxide. If the negative ion is polyatomic, its name usually ends in *–ate* or *–ite*. Ammonium nitrate (NH_4NO_3) is a common fertilizer for plants.

did you know?

Calcium oxide (CaO), also known as lime, gives off a white light when heated. Theaters once used special lamps to focus this bright light on a single actor. So, the expression *in the limelight* describes a person who receives favorable attention.

apply it!

Chemists refer to compounds by either their names or their chemical formulas.

Interpret Data Use the periodic table and **Figure 2** to fill in the table.

Name	Positive Ion	Negative Ion	Formula
Magnesium chloride	Mg^{2+}	Cl^-	$MgCl_2$
Sodium bromide	_____	_____	_____
_____	_____	_____	Li_2O
_____	Mg^{2+}	S^{2-}	_____
Aluminum fluoride	_____	_____	_____
_____	_____	_____	KNO_3
_____	NH_4^+	Cl^-	_____

Lab zone® Do the Quick Lab *How Do You Write Ionic Names and Formulas?*

Assess Your Understanding

2a. Explain The formula for sodium sulfide is Na_2S. Explain what this formula means.

_____

_____

_____

b. Apply Concepts Write the formula for calcium chloride. Explain how you determined this formula.

_____

_____

_____

got it?

○ **I get it!** Now I know that to write the formula for an ionic compound, _____

_____

_____

○ **I need extra help with** _____

Go to **MY SCIENCE COACH** *online for help with this subject.*

PS.1j Make valid conclusions after analyzing data.

PS.1m Construct and use models and simulations to illustrate and explain phenomena.

PS.2f Investigate and understand the characteristics of types of matter based on physical and chemical properties.

PS.3b Investigate and understand the modern model of atomic structure.

PS.4c Investigate and understand the formation of compounds through ionic and covalent bonding.

PS.5b Investigate and understand chemical changes in matter and how they relate to the Law of Conservation of Matter and Energy.

FIGURE 5 ⋯⋯⋯⋯⋯⋯⋯⋯⋯⋯
Halite
The ions in ionic compounds are arranged in specific three-dimensional shapes called crystals. Some crystals have a cubic shape, like these crystals of halite, or sodium chloride.

What Are Properties of Ionic Compounds?

Compounds have properties that are different from their component elements. You have already read about the properties of metals and nonmetals, but what are the properties of the ionic compounds that form when metals and nonmetals react? **In general, ionic compounds form hard, brittle crystals that have high melting points. They conduct electric current when dissolved in water or melted.**

Ionic Crystals Ionic compounds form solids by building up repeating patterns of ions. **Figure 5** shows a chunk of halite, which is how sodium chloride occurs naturally. Pieces of halite have a cubic shape. Equal numbers of Na^+ and Cl^- ions in halite are attracted in an alternating pattern, as shown in the diagram. The ions form an orderly, three-dimensional arrangement called a **crystal**.

Every ion in an ionic compound is attracted to ions of an opposite charge that surround it. The pattern formed by the ions is the same no matter what the size of the crystal. In a single grain of salt, the crystal pattern extends for millions of ions in every direction. Many crystals of ionic compounds are hard and brittle. This is due to the strength of their ionic bonds and the attractions among all the ions.

High Melting Points The ions in the crystal have to break apart for an ionic compound to melt. It takes a huge amount of energy to separate the ions in a crystal, because the attraction between the positive and negative ions is so great. As a result, ionic compounds have very high melting points. The melting point of sodium chloride is 801°C.

apply it!

Galena, or lead sulfide (PbS), has a structure similar to that of table salt.

1 Infer The chemical formula of lead sulfide tells you that it contains _____ S^{2-} ion(s) for every Pb^{2+} ion.

2 What holds the ions together in galena?

_____

_____

3 CHALLENGE If the pattern of ions shown here for galena is expanded in every direction, how many sulfide ions would surround each lead ion? _____ How many lead ions would surround each sulfide ion? _____

S^{2-}
Pb^{2+}

FIGURE 6 ·······
Glowing Pickle
Electric current can be conducted through a pickle because pickles contain salt water. After a time, the pickle becomes hot and begins to glow. ✏ **Communicate** **Discuss with a partner what ions you think are present in solution inside the pickle.**

Electrical Conductivity
Electric current is the flow of charged particles. When ionic crystals dissolve in water, the ions are free to move about, and the solution can conduct current. This is why the electric current can pass through the pickle in **Figure 6**. Likewise, when an ionic compound melts, the ions are able to move freely, and the liquid conducts current. In contrast, ionic compounds in solid form do not conduct current well. The ions in the solid crystal are tightly bound to each other and cannot move from place to place. If charged particles cannot move, there is no current.

POWER
OFF   ON
V
FUSE 20A
OUTPUT:0-130V AC 60Hz

TRANSFORMER
MODEL NO:TDG KM
MAX:2000VA
INPUT:110V 60Hz

MADE CHINA

Lab® zone Do the Lab Investigation *Shedding Light on Ions.*

🔑 Assess Your Understanding

3a. Review Ionic bonds are strong enough to cause almost all ionic compounds to be _____ at room temperature.

b. Relate Cause and Effect Solid table salt does not conduct electric current. How does dissolving salt in water allow electric current to flow?

_____
_____
_____

got it? ·······

○ **I get it!** Now I know that properties of ionic compounds include _____

_____
_____
_____

○ **I need extra help with** _____

_____

Go to **MY SCIENCE** ⓢ **COACH** *online for help with this subject.*

Covalent Bonds

UNLOCK THE BIG ?

🔑 **How Are Atoms Held Together in a Covalent Bond?**
PS.1m, PS.3b, PS.4c, PS.5b

🔑 **What Are Properties of Molecular Compounds?**
PS.1f, PS.1g, PS.1i, PS.2f, PS.3b, PS.4c, PS.5b

🔑 **How Do Bonded Atoms Become Partially Charged?**
PS.1j, PS.3b, PS.4c

MY PLANET DIARY

Sticky Feet

Have you ever seen a gecko climbing up a wall or running across a ceiling? Geckos seem to defy gravity. They have tiny hairs that cover the pads of their feet. These hairs branch out into hundreds of smaller structures, called *spatulae*. When a gecko climbs a wall, billions of spatulae on its feet come into contact with the surface. Scientists believe that geckos can stick to surfaces because of the billions of small attractive forces, called van der Waals forces, between the molecules of the spatulae and the molecules on the surface. Now, scientists are developing adhesives that can copy the characteristics of the spatulae.

FUN FACTS

Communicate Answer the following questions. Then discuss your answers with a partner.

1. Why is it important that billions of spatulae come into contact with the surface the gecko is climbing?

_____

_____

_____

_____

_____

_____

2. What uses do you think you could find for an adhesive that works like the gecko's foot?

_____

_____

_____

_____

_____

> **PLANET DIARY** Go to Planet Diary to learn more about attractions between molecules.

 Lab® zone Do the Inquiry Warm-Up *Covalent Bonds.*

Vocabulary
- covalent bond • molecule • double bond • triple bond
- molecular compound • nonpolar bond • polar bond

Skills
- Reading: Compare and Contrast
- Inquiry: Graph

How Are Atoms Held Together in a Covalent Bond?

You and a friend walk past a bakery that sells giant chocolate chip cookies for one dollar each. But each of you has only 50 cents. If you combine your money, you can buy a cookie and split it. So, you can afford a cookie by sharing your money. Similarly, 2 atoms can form a bond by sharing electrons. The chemical bond formed when 2 atoms share electrons is called a **covalent bond.** Covalent bonds usually form between nonmetal atoms. Ionic bonds usually form when a metal combines with a nonmetal.

Electron Sharing Nonmetals can bond to other nonmetals by sharing electrons. Atoms of some nonmetals can bond with each other. **Figure 1** shows how 2 fluorine atoms can react by sharing a pair of electrons. By sharing electrons, each fluorine atom is surrounded by 8 valence electrons. **The attractions between the shared electrons and the protons in the nucleus of each atom hold the atoms together in a covalent bond.** The 2 bonded fluorine atoms form a **molecule.** A molecule is a neutral group of atoms joined by covalent bonds.

> **Science Standards of Learning**
>
> **PS.1m** Construct and use models and simulations to illustrate and explain phenomena.
>
> **PS.3b** Investigate and understand the modern model of atomic structure.
>
> **PS.4c** Investigate and understand the formation of compounds through ionic and covalent bonding.
>
> **PS.5b** Investigate and understand chemical changes in matter and how they relate to the Law of Conservation of Matter and Energy.

apply it!

Apply Concepts Draw electron dot diagrams to show how 2 iodine atoms bond together to form a molecule.

FIGURE 1 ....
Sharing Electrons
By sharing 2 electrons in a covalent bond, each fluorine atom gains a stable set of 8 valence electrons.

✎ **Interpret Diagrams** Circle the shared electrons that form a covalent bond between the 2 fluorine atoms.

Fluorine atom   Fluorine atom

Fluorine molecule

Single Bonds	Double Bond	Triple Bond

Hydrogen + Oxygen + Hydrogen
atom   atom   atom

Water molecule

Oxygen + Oxygen
atom   atom

Oxygen molecule

Nitrogen + Nitrogen
atom   atom

Nitrogen molecule

FIGURE 2 ···

Covalent Bonds

Atoms can form single, double, and triple covalent bonds by sharing one or more pairs of electrons.

How Many Bonds? Look at the electron dot diagrams in **Figure 2.** Count the valence electrons around each hydrogen and oxygen atom. Hydrogen has 1 valence electron. Oxygen has 6 valence electrons. In a water molecule, oxygen forms one covalent bond with each of 2 hydrogen atoms. As a result, the oxygen atom has a stable arrangement of 8 valence electrons. Each hydrogen atom forms one bond because it needs only 2 electrons to be stable.

Look at the electron dot diagram of the oxygen molecule (O_2) in **Figure 2.** This time the 2 atoms share 2 pairs of electrons, forming a **double bond.** Atoms of some elements, such as nitrogen, can share 3 pairs of electrons, forming a **triple bond.** The electron dot diagram for the nitrogen molecule (N_2) is also shown in **Figure 2.**

CHALLENGE In a carbon dioxide (CO_2) molecule, the carbon atom forms a double bond with each of the 2 oxygen atoms. Draw the electron dot diagram for carbon dioxide below.

Do the Quick Lab
Sharing Electrons.

🔓 Assess Your Understanding

got it? ···

○ **I get it!** Now I know that the atoms in a covalent bond are held together by _____

_____

○ **I need extra help with** _____

Go to MY SCIENCE ⓢ COACH *online for help with this subject.*

What Are Properties of Molecular Compounds?

Water, oxygen, and sucrose (table sugar, $C_{12}H_{22}O_{11}$) are all examples of molecular compounds. A **molecular compound** is a compound that is made up of molecules. The molecules of a molecular compound contain atoms that are covalently bonded. Ionic compounds are made up of ions and do not form molecules. **Unlike ionic compounds, molecular compounds usually do not conduct electric current when melted or dissolved in water. Also, compared to ionic compounds, molecular compounds generally have lower melting points and boiling points.**

Poor Conductivity
Most molecular compounds do not conduct electric current. Molecular compounds do not contain charged particles that are available to move, so there is no current. Have you ever noticed that some wires are insulated with plastic or rubber? These materials are made up of molecular compounds. Even as liquids, molecular compounds are poor conductors. Pure water does not conduct electric current. Neither does table sugar when it is melted or dissolved in pure water.

Low Melting Points and Boiling Points
Forces hold the molecules close to one another in a molecular solid. But the forces between molecules are much weaker than the forces between ions. Compared with an ionic solid, less heat must be added to a molecular solid to separate the molecules and change it from a solid to a liquid. For example, table salt melts at 801°C, but table sugar melts at about 190°C.

Science Standards of Learning

PS.1f Identify independent and dependent variables, constants, controls, and repeated trials.

PS.1g Construct and interpret data tables showing the independent and dependent variables, derived quantities, and the number of trials.

PS.1i Construct and interpret frequency distributions, scatterplots, line plots, and histograms.

PS.2f Investigate and understand the characteristics of types of matter based on physical and chemical properties.

PS.3b Investigate and understand the modern model of atomic structure.

PS.4c Investigate and understand the formation of compounds through ionic and covalent bonding.

PS.5b Investigate and understand chemical changes in matter and how they relate to the Law of Conservation of Matter and Energy.

FIGURE 3

Headphones
Wires, such as the ones found on your headphones, are insulated with plastic or rubber to prevent electric current from flowing between the wires. The insulation also allows you to touch the wires without being shocked or electrocuted.

✎ **Observe** What are some other objects that have insulated wires?

_____

_____

_____

_____

229

do the math! Analyzing Data

Molecular and Ionic Compounds

The table shows the melting points and boiling points of a few molecular compounds and ionic compounds.

1 ⚑ **Graph** In the space below, draw a bar graph of the melting points of these compounds. Arrange the bars in order of increasing melting point. Label each bar with the chemical formula of the compound.

2 The melting points of molecular compounds are (lower/higher) than those of ionic compounds.

3 The boiling points of molecular compounds are (lower/higher) than those of ionic compounds.

Substance	Formula	Melting Point (°C)	Boiling Point (°C)
Calcium chloride	$CaCl_2$	775	1,935
Isopropyl alcohol	C_3H_8O	−87.9	82.3
Octane	C_8H_{18}	−56.8	125.6
Sodium chloride	NaCl	800.7	1,465
Water	H_2O	0	100

▭ Molecular compound   ▭ Ionic compound

4 **Predict** Ammonia (NH_3) has a melting point of −78°C and a boiling point of −34°C. These data suggest that ammonia is a(n) (molecular/ionic) compound.

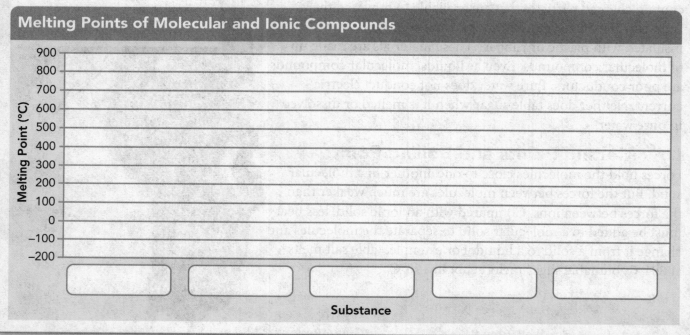

Melting Points of Molecular and Ionic Compounds

Melting Point (°C) axis: 900, 800, 700, 600, 500, 400, 300, 200, 100, 0, −100, −200

Substance

Lab zone® Do the Quick Lab *Properties of Molecular Compounds.*

🔑 Assess Your Understanding

got it? ....

○ **I get it!** Now I know that properties of molecular compounds include _____

_____

○ **I need extra help with** _____

Go to MY SCIENCE ⓢ COACH *online for help with this subject.*

How Do Bonded Atoms Become Partially Charged?

Have you ever played tug-of-war? If you have, you know that when one team pulls the rope with more force than the other team, the rope moves toward the side of the stronger team. The same is true of electrons in a covalent bond. Atoms of some elements pull more strongly on the shared electrons of a covalent bond than do atoms of other elements. As a result, the electrons are shared unequally. **Unequal sharing of electrons causes covalently bonded atoms to have slight electric charges.**

Nonpolar Bonds and Polar Bonds
If 2 atoms pull equally on the electrons, neither atom becomes charged. This happens when identical atoms are bonded. A covalent bond in which electrons are shared equally is a **nonpolar bond.** The hydrogen molecule (H_2) shown in **Figure 4** has a nonpolar bond.

When electrons in a covalent bond are shared unequally, the atom with the stronger pull gains a slightly negative charge. The atom with the weaker pull gains a slightly positive charge. A covalent bond in which electrons are shared unequally is a **polar bond.** Hydrogen fluoride (HF), also shown in **Figure 4,** has a polar bond.

Science Standards of Learning

PS.1j Make valid conclusions after analyzing data.

PS.3b Investigate and understand the modern model of atomic structure.

PS.4c Investigate and understand the formation of compounds through ionic and covalent bonding.

Compare and Contrast
In a nonpolar bond electrons are shared (equally/unequally).
In a polar bond electrons are shared (equally/unequally).

FIGURE 4 ....

> ART IN MOTION **Nonpolar and Polar Bonds**
Hydrogen forms a nonpolar bond with another hydrogen atom. In hydrogen fluoride, fluorine attracts electrons more strongly than hydrogen does. The bond formed is polar.

Round 1: H_2

Round 2: HF

I want it!

I want it more!

Communicate Imagine you're a sportscaster. Write a commentary describing each of the "tug-of-war" matchups below.

Round 1: Hydrogen (H_2)

_____

_____

_____

_____

Round 2: Hydrogen Fluoride (HF)

_____

_____

_____

_____

231

Nonpolar Molecule
Carbon dioxide

Opposite pulling cancels.

Polar Molecule
Water

Electrons pulled
toward oxygen

FIGURE 5 ·······································

Nonpolar and Polar Molecules

Both carbon dioxide and water molecules
contain polar bonds. However, only water is
a polar molecule.

✎ **Interpret Diagrams** Draw a positive (+)
sign next to the atoms that gain a slight positive charge. Draw a negative (–) sign next to the
atoms that gain a slight negative charge.

Polar Bonds in Molecules A molecule
is polar if it has a positively charged end and a
negatively charged end. However, not all molecules containing polar bonds are polar overall.
In a carbon dioxide molecule, the oxygen atoms
attract electrons more strongly than the carbon
atom does. The bonds between the oxygen
and carbon atoms are polar. But, as you can see
in **Figure 5,** a carbon dioxide molecule has a
straight-line shape. The two oxygen atoms pull
with equal strength in opposite directions.
The attractions cancel out, so the molecule
is nonpolar.

A water molecule, with its two polar bonds,
is itself polar. As you can see in **Figure 5,** a water
molecule has a bent shape. The two hydrogen
atoms are at one end of the molecule. The oxygen atom is at the other end of the molecule. The
oxygen atom attracts electrons more strongly than
do the hydrogen atoms. As a result, the end of
the molecule with the oxygen atom has a slight
negative charge. The end of the molecule with the
hydrogen atoms has a slight positive charge.

EXPLORE THE BIG ?

A Sea of Bonding

How can bonding determine the properties of a substance?

FIGURE 6 ·······································

▶ INTERACTIVE ART The Dead Sea is a
saltwater lake in the Middle East. It is
so salty that neither fish nor plants can
survive in it. The water contains many
dissolved compounds, including sodium
chloride, magnesium chloride, and
potassium chloride.

✎ **Review** Answer the questions
about water and sodium chloride.

Water (H₂O)

Water is an example of a(n)
(ionic/molecular) compound.

This type of bond forms when _____
_____
_____

Properties of these compounds
include _____
_____
_____
_____

Close-up of salt

Attractions Between Molecules

Opposite charges attract. Polar molecules are connected to each other by weak attractions between their slight negative and positive charges. These attractions are called van der Waals forces. The negatively charged oxygen ends of the polar water molecules attract the positively charged hydrogen ends of nearby water molecules. Van der Waals forces pull water molecules toward each other. They are also the reason a gecko's feet can grip onto smooth surfaces, such as glass.

The properties of polar and nonpolar compounds are different because of differences in attractions between their molecules. The melting point and boiling point of water are much higher than the melting point and boiling point of oxygen. The attractions between the polar water molecules require more energy to overcome than the attractions between the nonpolar oxygen molecules.

Sodium Chloride (NaCl)

Sodium chloride is an example of a(n) (ionic/molecular) compound.

This type of bond forms when _____
_____
_____

Properties of these compounds include _____
_____
_____
_____

Do the Quick Lab
Attraction Between
Polar Molecules.

Assess Your Understanding

1a. Review What type of bonds are formed when atoms share electrons unequally?
_____

b. Predict Would carbon dioxide or water have a higher boiling point? Explain.
_____
_____
_____
_____
_____
_____

c. ANSWER THE BIG ? How can bonding determine the properties of a substance?
_____
_____
_____
_____
_____
_____
_____
_____
_____

got it? ....

O **I get it!** Now I know that some atoms in covalent bonds become slightly negative or slightly positive when _____
_____
_____

O **I need extra help with** _____
_____

Go to MY SCIENCE COACH *online for help with this subject.*

233

Virginia
LESSON

4 Bonding in Metals

UNLOCK THE BIG

 What Is the Structure of a Metal Crystal?
PS.3b, PS.4b, PS.4c, PS.5b

 What Are Properties of Metals?
PS.2d, PS.2e, PS.2f, PS.3b, PS.4b, PS.4c, PS.5b

my planet diary

Superconductors

In 1911, physicist Heike Kamerlingh Onnes made a remarkable discovery. When he cooled mercury to −269°C (4 kelvins), the mercury no longer resisted the flow of electric current! The cooled mercury became the world's first superconductor. A superconductor is a material that has no resistance to the flow of electric current.

Certain metals and alloys become superconductors as they are cooled to very low temperatures. This means they can carry electric currents for long periods of time without losing energy as heat. Superconductors can also be used to produce very powerful magnetic fields. These magnetic fields can be used to levitate and move high-speed trains.

DISCOVERY

Communicate Write your answers to each question below. Then discuss your answers with a partner.

1. How is a superconductor different from a regular conductor?

_____

_____

_____

_____

2. Power lines lose 10 to 15 percent of the electric current they carry to heat. Why might scientists want to create superconducting power lines?

_____

_____

_____

_____

> PLANET DIARY Go to **Planet Diary** to learn more about metals.

 Do the Inquiry Warm-Up
Are They "Steel" the Same?

Vocabulary
- metallic bond
- alloy

Skills
- Reading: Identify the Main Idea
- Inquiry: Classify

What Is the Structure of a Metal Crystal?

The properties of solid metals can be explained by the structure of metal atoms and the bonding among those atoms. When metal atoms combine chemically with atoms of other elements, they usually lose valence electrons. They then become positively charged metal ions. Metal atoms lose electrons easily because they do not hold onto their valence electrons very strongly.

The loosely held valence electrons in metal atoms result in a type of bonding that happens in metals. Most metals are crystalline solids. **A metal crystal is composed of closely packed, positively charged metal ions. The valence electrons drift among the ions.** Each metal ion is held in the crystal by a **metallic bond**—an attraction between a positive metal ion and the electrons surrounding it. **Figure 1** illustrates the metallic bonds that hold together aluminum foil.

Science Standards of Learning

PS.3b Investigate and understand the modern model of atomic structure.

PS.4b Investigate and understand the classification of elements as metals, metalloids, and nonmetals.

PS.4c Investigate and understand the formation of compounds through ionic and covalent bonding.

PS.5b Investigate and understand chemical changes in matter and how they relate to the Law of Conservation of Matter and Energy.

FIGURE 1 ....

Metallic Bonding
The positively charged metal ions are embedded in a "sea" of valence electrons.

✎ **Infer** Why would nonmetals be unlikely to have the type of bonding shown here?

_____

_____

_____

Lab zone® Do the Quick Lab *Metal Crystals.*

☞ Assess Your Understanding

got it? ....

○ **I get it!** Now I know that a metal crystal consists of _____

_____

○ **I need extra help with** _____

Go to MY SCIENCE ⬤ COACH *online for help with this subject.*

Identify the Main Idea
Underline the main idea of this section on the properties of metals. As you read, circle the supporting details.

What Are Properties of Metals?

You know a piece of metal when you see it. It's usually hard, dense, and shiny. Almost all metals are solids at room temperature. They can be hammered into sheets or drawn out into thin wires. Electronics such as stereos, computers, and MP3 players have metal parts because metals conduct electric current. Metallic bonding explains many of the common physical properties of metals.

🔑 **Properties of metals include a shiny luster, and high levels of malleability, ductility, electrical conductivity, and thermal conductivity.** Each of these properties is related to the behavior of valence electrons in metal atoms.

Luster Some of the parts of the motorcycle shown in **Figure 2** are covered in chromium, which is shiny. Polished metals have a shiny and reflective luster, called metallic luster. The luster of a metal is due to its valence electrons. When light strikes these electrons, they absorb the light and then re-emit the light.

The fender protects the rider from dirt and debris. Metals can be used to form a fender because they are

Metal fins cool a motorcycle by heat to the outside.

Malleability and Ductility

Metals are ductile. They can be bent easily and pulled into thin strands or wires. Metals are also malleable. They can be rolled into thin sheets, as with aluminum foil, or beaten into complex shapes. Metals act this way because the positive metal ions are attracted to the loose electrons all around them rather than to other metal ions. These ions can be made to change position. However, the metallic bonds between the ion and the surrounding electrons keep the metal ions from breaking apart from one another.

Thermal Conductivity

Thermal energy is the total energy of motion of all the particles in an object. Thermal energy flows from warmer matter to cooler matter. The greater energy of the particles in the warmer parts of the material is transferred to the particles in the cooler parts. This transfer of thermal energy is known as heat. Metals conduct heat easily because the valence electrons within a metal are free to move. Electrons in the warmer part of the metal can transfer energy to electrons in the cooler part of the metal.

FIGURE 2 ·······

Properties of Metals

The unique properties of metals result from the ability of their valence electrons to move about freely.

✎ **Interpret Photos** Complete each sentence with the correct term.

When the metal parts of the motorcycle are polished, they exhibit a

_____

Electrical Conductivity   Charged particles that are free to move can conduct an electric current. Metals conduct electric current easily because the valence electrons in a metal can move freely among the atoms. Electrical wires are made out of metal. Circuit boards, such as the one shown in **Figure 3,** contain metal strips that conduct electric current throughout the circuit.

apply it!

Many objects that are made out of metal take advantage of one or more properties of metals.

① **Classify** Draw arrows from each physical property listed below to the object or objects you think best exhibit that particular property.

Luster

Malleability

Ductility

Thermal Conductivity

Electrical Conductivity

② **Communicate** Compare your answers with a classmate's. Did your answers match? If not, discuss the differences in your answers.

③ CHALLENGE   Name an example of a metal object that shows both luster and malleability.

_____

_____

_____

FIGURE 3 ·······················

Electrical Conductivity
Metal strips on a circuit board inside this MP3 player conduct electric current throughout the circuit.

FIGURE 4 ···
Alloys
A steel suit prevents the diver from being injured by a shark.

✎ **List** What other objects do you think contain steel?

_____

_____

_____

Alloys Very few of the "metals" you use every day are made up of just one element. Most of the metallic objects you see and use are made of alloys. An **alloy** is a mixture made of two or more elements, at least one of which is a metal. Alloys are generally stronger and less reactive than the pure metals from which they are made.

Pure gold is shiny, but it is soft and easily bent. For that reason, gold jewelry is made of an alloy of gold mixed with a harder element, such as copper or silver. Gold alloys are much harder than pure gold but still retain its beauty and shine.

Iron is a strong metal, but iron objects rust when they are exposed to air and water. For this reason, iron is often alloyed with one or more other elements to make steel. Objects made of iron alloys, such as the shark suit worn by the diver in Figure 4, are much stronger than iron and resist rust much better. Forks and spoons made of stainless steel can be washed over and over again without rusting. That's because stainless steel—an alloy of iron, carbon, nickel, and chromium—does not react with air and water as iron does.

Lab ® Do the Quick Lab
zone *What Do Metals Do?*

🔑 Assess Your Understanding

1a. Identify What accounts for the properties of metals?

_____

_____

b. Explain Explain why metals are good conductors of electric current.

_____

_____

c. Apply Concepts Why is it safer to use a non-metal mixing spoon when cooking something on the stove?

_____

_____

_____

_____

_____

got it? ···

⭕ **I get it!** Now I know that properties of metals include _____

_____

⭕ **I need extra help with** _____

Go to MY SCIENCE ⓢ COACH *online for help with this subject.*

6 Study Guide

REVIEW
THE BIG
?

Compared to molecular compounds, ionic compounds have _____ melting points.

Ionic compounds conduct electric current when _____

LESSON 1 Atoms, Bonding, and the Periodic Table

🔑 The number of valence electrons in each atom of an element helps determine the chemical properties of that element.

Vocabulary
• valence electron
• electron dot diagram
• chemical bond

Carbon

LESSON 2 Ionic Bonds

🔑 When a neutral atom loses or gains a valence electron, it becomes an ion.

🔑 For an ionic compound, the name of the negative ion follows the name of the positive ion.

🔑 Ionic compounds have high melting points.

Vocabulary
• ion • polyatomic ion   • ionic bond
• ionic compound   • chemical formula
• subscript • crystal

LESSON 3 Covalent Bonds

🔑 Attractions between the shared electrons and the protons in the nucleus of each atom hold the atoms together in a covalent bond.

🔑 Molecular compounds have low melting points and do not conduct electric current.

🔑 Unequal sharing of electrons causes bonded atoms to have slight electric charges.

Vocabulary
• covalent bond • molecule • double bond • triple bond
• molecular compound • nonpolar bond • polar bond

LESSON 4 Bonding in Metals

🔑 A metal crystal is composed of closely packed, positively charged metal ions. The valence electrons drift among the ions.

🔑 Properties of metals include a shiny luster, and high levels of malleability, ductility, electrical conductivity, and thermal conductivity.

Vocabulary
• metallic bond
• alloy

Review and Assessment

LESSON 1 Atoms, Bonding, and the Periodic Table

1. An electron dot diagram shows an atom's number of

   a. protons.   **b.** electrons.

   c. valence electrons.   **d.** chemical bonds.

2. When atoms react, they form a chemical bond, which is defined as _____

_____

_____

Use the diagrams to answer Questions 3 and 4.

Calcium   Argon   Sodium

Nitrogen   Oxygen   Chlorine

3. Infer Which of these elements can become stable by losing 1 electron? Explain.

_____

_____

_____

4. Draw Conclusions Which of these elements is least likely to react with other elements? Explain.

_____

_____

5. ~~Write About It~~ Go to your local grocery store and observe how the products on the shelves are organized. Write a paragraph comparing how food products are organized in a grocery store and how elements are organized in the periodic table.

LESSON 2 Ionic Bonds

6. When an atom loses or gains electrons, it becomes a(n)

   a. ion.   **b.** formula.

   c. crystal.   **d.** subscript.

7. Magnesium chloride is an example of an ionic compound, which is a compound composed of

_____

8. Classify Based on their chemical formulas, which of these compounds is not likely to be an ionic compound: KBr, SO_2, or $AlCl_3$? Explain your answer.

_____

_____

_____

9. Interpret Tables Use the periodic table to find the number of valence electrons for calcium (Ca), aluminum (Al), rubidium (Rb), oxygen (O), sulfur (S), and iodine (I). Then use that information to predict the formula for each of the following compounds: calcium oxide, aluminum iodide, rubidium sulfide, and aluminum oxide.

_____

_____

_____

_____

10. ~~Write About It~~ Pretend that you are the size of an atom and you are observing a reaction between a potassium ion and a fluorine atom. Describe how an ionic bond forms as the atoms react. Tell what happens to the valence electrons in each atom and how each atom is changed by losing or gaining electrons.

LESSON 3 **Covalent Bonds**

11. A covalent bond in which electrons are shared equally is called a

a. double bond. b. triple bond.

c. polar bond. d. nonpolar bond.

12. The formulas N_2, H_2O, and CO_2 all represent molecules, which are defined as _____

_____

_____

13. Infer A carbon atom can form four covalent bonds. How many valence electrons does a carbon atom have?

_____

14. Classify Identify each molecule below as either a polar molecule or a nonpolar molecule. Explain your reasoning.

Oxygen   Carbon dioxide

_____

_____

_____

_____

_____

_____

_____

_____

_____

LESSON 4 **Bonding in Metals**

15. The metal atoms in iron are held together by

a. ionic bonds. b. polar bonds.

c. covalent bonds. d. metallic bonds.

16. Polished metals have a metallic luster, which means that _____

_____

17. Apply Concepts Why does an aluminum horseshoe bend but not break when a blacksmith pounds it into shape with a hammer?

_____

_____

_____

_____

_____

 How can bonding determine the properties of a substance?

18. An ice cube and a scoop of table salt are left outside on a warm, sunny day. Explain why the ice cube melts and the salt does not.

_____

_____

_____

_____

_____

Virginia SOL Test Prep

Read each question and choose the best answer.

1 The table below lists some ions and their charges.

Ions and Their Charges

Name	Charge	Symbol/Formula
Sodium	1+	Na^+
Calcium	2+	Ca^{2+}
Chloride	1–	Cl^-
Phosphate	3–	$PO_4{}^{3-}$

How many sodium ions are needed to balance the charge of one phosphate ion?

A 1
B 2
C 3
D 4

2 The chemical formula for a glucose molecule is $C_6H_{12}O_6$. The subscripts represent the

F mass of each element.
G number of atoms of each element in a glucose molecule.
H total number of bonds made by each atom.
J number of valence electrons in each atom.

3 Elements that have the same number of valence electrons are—

A within the same group of the periodic table.
B within the same period of the periodic table.
C called noble gases.
D called metalloids.

4 When an atom loses an electron, it

F becomes a negative ion.
G becomes a positive ion.
H forms a covalent bond.
J gains a proton.

5 All of the following are characteristics that result from metallic bonding EXCEPT—

A the tendency to form hard, brittle crystals.
B the ability to conduct electric current.
C the ability to be hammered into sheets.
D luster.

Use the electron dot diagrams to help you answer Question 6.

Magnesium

Fluorine

6 Which of the following shows the formula for the combination of magnesium and fluorine?

F Mg_2F
G MgF_2
H Mg_2F_2
J Mg_2F_7

Pharmacists
Chemists at Work

Interested in science—specifically in chemistry? Your local drugstore pharmacist is a highly trained chemist.

Pharmacists work with medications. All pharmacists earn an advanced degree in pharmacy. They must also take an exam in their state before they can receive their license.

Retail pharmacists dispense medications from behind a pharmacy counter at a drugstore. They work with customers to make sure the customers' medications are safe for them to take. This means knowing how medications interact with each other, and which are safe to take at the same time.

But drugstore pharmacies aren't the only places you'll find pharmacists. Research pharmacists develop and test new medications in labs. These medicines may improve and save lives, lives of people you know.

Research It Find out more about what a research pharmacist or a retail pharmacist does, and create an informational poster about this person's work.

 PS.1k

Pharmacists are trained to be experts in handling medications. ▶

THE SUPERHERO OF GLUES

It bonds instantly to put together a broken dish, close a hole in a fish's skin, or stick a ton of concrete to a metal beam! Magic? No, it's cyanoacrylate, a special glue. Just three square centimeters of cyanoacrylate can hold more than one ton of just about anything to any surface.

Cyanoacrylate ($C_5H_5NO_2(l)$) forms strong bonds when it comes into contact with hydroxide ions ($OH^-(g)$), found in water. Almost the moment you squeeze it out of the tube, the adhesive comes into contact with water vapor in the air and hardens, changing from liquid to solid.

Cyanoacrylate's powerful electron-attracting groups form chains of molecules, linked together. These chains form a rigid, plastic net that holds any molecules it comes into contact with! You have one super sticky situation.

Design It Design a cartoon strip explaining how the cyanoacrylate molecule forms chains to produce super bonds.

 PS.1k, PS.3b, PS.4c, PS.5b

◀ Cyanoacrylate glue is used to attach a researcher's tag to a loggerhead sea turtle.

Sci-Fi Metal

Scientists in California have produced an amorphous, or glassy, metal that acts like plastic but is stronger than titanium. To produce the metal, elements are mixed and melted together, and then cooled very quickly.

A glassy metal is stronger than other metals because its atoms do not cool into a crystalline pattern. Instead, it has a random arrangement of atoms, which makes it able to transfer energy faster and last longer than other metals.

Research It Research the advantages and disadvantages of using glassy metals. What impact might glassy metals have on industry and society?

 PS.1k, PS.4b, PS.5a, PS.5b

▲ NASA has used amorphous metal, which has a mirrored surface, to make solar wind collector tiles.

HOW DO BEES MAKE HONEY?

How is matter conserved in a chemical reaction?

Honeybees drink nectar from flowers. They store the nectar in a honey sac found inside their bodies. Nectar begins changing into honey in the honey sac. Nectar is mostly water, which evaporates during the honey-making process.

▷ UNTAMED SCIENCE Watch the **Untamed Science** video to learn more about chemical reactions.

After collecting nectar, the honeybees return to the hive where they spit the nectar into the mouths of house bees. Chemicals in the mouths of the house bees continue changing the nectar into honey until it is ready to be stored in the honeycomb.

✐ Draw Conclusions **Explain why the amount of nectar that bees collect is larger than the amount of honey they produce.**

_____

_____

_____

Chemical Reactions

Science Standards of Learning

PS.1b, PS.1f, PS.1g, PS.1i, PS.1j, PS.1k,
PS.1m, PS.4c, PS.5a, PS.5b

7 Getting Started

Check Your Understanding

1. Background Read the paragraph below and then answer the question.

Alex is doing an experiment to see how vinegar reacts with **ionic compounds.** He measures the **mass** of a sample of baking soda. Alex records the measurement in his lab book next to the **chemical formula** for baking soda, $NaHCO_3$.

> An **ionic compound** consists of positive and negative ions.
>
> **Mass** is the amount of material in an object.
>
> A **chemical formula** shows the ratio of elements in a compound.

- Which substance is an ionic compound in the experiment that Alex is conducting?

_____

> **MY READING WEB** If you had trouble completing the question above, visit **My Reading Web** and type in *Chemical Reactions*.

Vocabulary Skill

Identify Multiple Meanings Some familiar words have more than one meaning. Words you use every day may have different meanings in science.

Word	Everyday Meaning	Scientific Meaning
matter	*n.* a subject of discussion, concern, or action **Example:** We had an important *matter* to discuss in the meeting.	*n.* anything that has mass and takes up space **Example:** Solids, liquids, and gases are states of *matter*.
product	*n.* anything that is made or created **Example:** Milk and cheese are dairy *products*.	*n.* a substance formed as a result of a chemical reaction **Example:** In a chemical reaction, substances can combine or split up to form *products*.

2. Quick Check Circle the sentence below that uses the scientific meaning of the word *product*.

- She brought napkins and other paper **products** to the picnic.
- Table salt is the **product** of the reaction of sodium and chlorine.

chemical change

precipitate

open system

replacement

Chapter Preview

LESSON 1

- physical change
- chemical change
- reactant
- product
- precipitate
- exothermic reaction
- endothermic reaction

↻ **Relate Cause and Effect**

△ **Graph**

LESSON 2

- chemical equation
- law of conservation of mass
- open system
- closed system
- coefficient
- synthesis
- decomposition
- replacement

↻ **Summarize**

△ **Make Models**

LESSON 3

- activation energy
- concentration
- catalyst
- enzyme
- inhibitor

↻ **Ask Questions**

△ **Predict**

▷ VOCAB FLASH CARDS For extra help with vocabulary, visit **Vocab Flash Cards** and type in *Chemical Reactions.*

Observing Chemical Change

UNLOCK THE BIG ?

🔑 **How Can Changes in Matter Be Described?**
PS.1j, PS.4c, PS.5a, PS.5b

🔑 **How Do You Identify a Chemical Reaction?**
PS.1i, PS.4c, PS.5b

MY PLANET DIARY

PROFILE

Chemistry in the Kitchen

Teen chef Fatoumata Dembele knows that chemical reactions are an important part of cooking great food. In fact, Fatoumata is so skilled at using chemistry in the kitchen that she won an award for her recipes.

Fatoumata knows that to prepare some foods, such as eggs, adding heat is required. Other foods, such as gelatin, need to have heat removed to taste best. Fatoumata says you have to keep a close eye on food while it's cooking. A good chef always pays attention to signs of change. For example, when you cook meat, the color is what tells you when it's ready. A raw steak is red, but a medium steak should be dark brown on the outside and pink in the center. Fatoumata prefers her steak well done. She knows it's ready when the meat is brown all the way through. For chefs like Fatoumata, there is one particular property that matters the most. It's the taste!

Write your answers to the questions below.

1. Energy is required for chemical reactions to take place. What form of energy is used in cooking?

_____

2. Think of something you've cooked before. What changes did you observe in the food?

_____
_____
_____

▶ **PLANET DIARY** Go to **Planet Diary** to learn more about chemical changes.

Lab zone ® Do the Inquiry Warm-Up *What Happens When Chemicals React?*

Vocabulary

- physical change • chemical change
- reactant • product • precipitate
- exothermic reaction • endothermic reaction

Skills

- Reading: Relate Cause and Effect
- Inquiry: Graph

How Can Changes in Matter Be Described?

Picture yourself frying an egg. You crack open the shell, and the yolk and egg white spill into the pan. As the egg heats up, the white changes from a clear liquid to a white solid. The egg, the pan, and the stove are all examples of matter. Recall that matter is anything that has mass and takes up space. An important part of chemistry is describing matter.

Properties of Matter Matter is often described by its characteristics, or properties, and how it changes. There are two kinds of properties of matter—physical properties and chemical properties.

How would you describe the penny in **Figure 1A**? It is solid, shiny, and hard. A physical property is a characteristic of a substance that can be observed without changing the substance into another substance. The temperature at which a solid melts is a physical property. Color, texture, density, and conductivity are other physical properties of matter.

A chemical property is a characteristic of a substance that describes its ability to change into other substances. To observe the chemical properties of a substance, you must try to change it into another substance. For example, **Figure 1B** shows a penny that has turned green. This color change demonstrates a chemical property of the penny's copper coating. When copper is exposed to air, it reacts over time to form a dull, crusty solid. Another chemical property is a material's ability to burn in the presence of oxygen. This property is called flammability.

Science Standards of Learning

PS.1j Make valid conclusions after analyzing data.

PS.4c Investigate and understand formation of compounds through ionic and covalent bonding.

PS.5a Investigate and understand physical changes in matter and how they relate to the Law of Conservation of Matter and Energy.

PS.5b Investigate and understand chemical changes in matter and how they relate to the Law of Conservation of Matter and Energy.

FIGURE 1 ·······························

Properties of Copper
Pennies are coated with copper.

✎ **Complete the following tasks.**

1. **Classify** Check off which properties of copper are physical properties and which are chemical properties.

2. **Communicate** Add two properties to the list and ask a classmate to classify them as physical or chemical.

Copper

Property	Physical	Chemical
• Reddish color	☐	☐
• Reacts with oxygen	☐	☐
• Smooth texture	☐	☐
• Conducts heat	☐	☐
• Not flammable	☐	☐
• _____	☐	☐
• _____	☐	☐

FIGURE 2 ······································

> INTERACTIVE ART **Changes in Matter**
Matter can undergo both physical and chemical changes.

✏️ **Identify** Label each apple with the type of change it has undergone.

Changes in Matter Like properties of matter, there are two types of changes in matter. 🔑 **Changes in matter can be described in terms of physical changes and chemical changes.** A **physical change** is any change that alters the form or appearance of a substance but does not change it into another substance. When you cut an apple in half, as shown in **Figure 2A,** you cause a physical change. In a physical change, some of the physical properties of the material may be altered, but the chemical composition remains the same. Bending, crushing, and cutting are all physical changes. Changes in the state of matter, such as melting, freezing, and boiling, are also physical changes.

Sometimes when matter changes, its chemical composition is changed. For example, when a cut apple is left out in the air, it turns brown, as shown in **Figure 2B**. Compounds in the apple react with the oxygen in the air to form new compounds. A change in matter that produces one or more new substances is a **chemical change,** or chemical reaction. In a chemical change, the atoms rearrange to form new substances. When a substance undergoes a chemical change, it results in different physical properties as well. Burning and rusting are both chemical changes. Substances that undergo the chemical changes are called **reactants.** The new substances that form are the **products.**

apply it!

Changes in matter occur everywhere in your daily life.

1 Apply Concepts Paper that has been (torn/burned) has undergone a chemical change.

2 Interpret Photos Label the change in each set of pictures as a physical or chemical change.

3 CHALLENGE In the correct box, draw or explain how the leaf will look if it undergoes a physical change and if it undergoes a chemical change.

Physical

Chemical

252 Chemical Reactions

Bonding and Chemical Change Chemical changes occur when existing bonds break and new bonds form. As a result, new substances are produced. Atoms form bonds when they share or transfer electrons. The reaction pictured in **Figure 3** involves both the breaking of shared bonds and the transfer of electrons.

Oxygen gas (O_2) in the air consists of molecules made up of two oxygen atoms bonded together. These bonds break when oxygen reacts with magnesium (Mg) and a new ionic bond forms. The compound magnesium oxide (MgO) is produced. Magnesium oxide, a white powder, has properties that differ from those of either shiny magnesium or invisible oxygen gas. For example, while magnesium melts at 650°C, magnesium oxide melts at 2,800°C.

✏️
↪ Relate Cause and Effect
Find and underline the effect caused by breaking and forming bonds.

FIGURE 3 ···

Breaking and Making Bonds

✏️ **Summarize** On the lines below the diagrams, describe what happens to the bonds in each of the steps as oxygen reacts with magnesium.

① $O::O \longrightarrow O: + :O$

_____

_____

② $Mg: + :O: \longrightarrow Mg^{2+}:O:^{2-}$

_____

_____

Lab zone® Do the Quick Lab *Observing Change.*

🔑 Assess Your Understanding

1a. Review The freezing point of water is a (physical/chemical) property. The ability of oxygen to react with iron to cause rust is a (physical/chemical) property.

b. Pose Questions When silver coins are found in ancient shipwrecks, they are coated with a black crust. Ask a question that could help you determine whether the silver underwent a chemical change or physical change. Explain.

_____

_____

_____

got it?

○ **I get it!** Now I know that two ways changes in matter can be described are _____

_____

_____

_____

_____

○ **I need extra help with** _____

Go to **MY SCIENCE** 🔵ˢ **COACH** *online for help with this subject.*

Vocabulary Identify Multiple Meanings Precipitation can mean rain, snow, or hail. In chemistry, precipitation is the formation of a solid from

_____

_____

✎ **Design Experiments** Describe how you would test the best method for separating the precipitate from the liquid in curdled milk.

_____

_____

_____

_____

_____

_____

_____

How Do You Identify a Chemical Reaction?

Look at the images in **Figure 4**. Even without reading the caption, you probably can tell that each image shows a chemical reaction. How can you tell when a chemical reaction occurs? 🔑 **Chemical reactions involve changes in properties and changes in energy that you can often observe.**

Changes in Properties One way to detect chemical reactions is to observe changes in the physical properties of the materials. Changes in properties result when new substances form. For instance, formation of a precipitate, gas production, and a color change are all possible evidence that a chemical reaction has taken place. Many times, physical properties such as texture and hardness may also change in a chemical reaction.

Changes in physical properties can be easy to recognize in a chemical reaction, but what about the chemical properties? During a chemical reaction, reactants interact to form products with different chemical properties. For example, sodium (Na) and chlorine (Cl_2) react to form an ionic compound, sodium chloride (NaCl). Both reactants are very reactive elements. However, the product, sodium chloride, is a very stable compound.

❶ Formation of a Precipitate
The mixing of two liquids may form a precipitate. A **precipitate** (pree SIP uh tayt) is a solid that forms from liquids during a chemical reaction. For example, the precipitate seen in this curdled milk has formed from the liquids milk and lemon juice.

FIGURE 4 ·······
Evidence of Chemical Reactions
Many kinds of change provide evidence that a chemical reaction has occurred.

Although you may observe a change in matter, the change does not always indicate that a chemical reaction has taken place. Sometimes physical changes give similar results. For example, when water boils, the gas bubbles you see are made of molecules of water, just as the liquid was. Boiling is a physical change. The only sure evidence of a chemical reaction is that one or more new substances are produced.

❷ Gas Production

Another observable change is the formation of a gas from solid or liquid reactants. Often, the gas formed can be seen as bubbles.

✎ **Observe** Bread dough rises from gas bubbles produced when yeast reacts with sugar. What evidence in a slice of bread shows the presence of gas?

_____
_____
_____
_____
_____
_____

❸ Color Change

A color change can signal that a new substance has formed. For example, avocados turn brown when they react with oxygen in the air.

✎ **Apply Concepts** Draw or describe evidence of a chemical reaction you have observed in food or in other types of matter. Label the evidence as a color change, formation of a precipitate, or gas production.

✎ **Relate Evidence and Explanation** Adding food coloring to water causes a color change. Is this evidence of a chemical reaction? Explain.

_____
_____
_____
_____
_____
_____
_____

255

Exothermic

Energy
Energy

Changes in Energy Recall that a chemical reaction occurs when bonds break and new bonds form. Breaking bonds between atoms or ions requires energy, while forming bonds releases energy.

In an **exothermic reaction** (ek soh THUR mik), the energy released as the products form is greater than the energy required to break the bonds of the reactants. The energy is usually released as heat. For example, some stoves use natural gas. When natural gas burns, it releases heat. This heat is used to cook your food. Similarly, the reaction between oxygen and other fuels that produce fire, such as wood, coal, oil, or the wax of the candle shown in **Figure 5,** release energy in the form of light and heat.

Endothermic

Energy
Energy

In an **endothermic reaction** (en doh THUR mik), more energy is required to break the bonds of the reactants than is released by the formation of the products. The energy can be absorbed from nearby matter. When energy is absorbed, it causes the surroundings to become cooler. In **Figure 5,** baking soda undergoes an endothermic reaction when it is mixed with vinegar. The reaction absorbs heat from its surroundings, so the reaction feels cold. Not all endothermic reactions result in a temperature decrease. Many endothermic reactions occur only when heat is constantly added, as when you fry an egg. Heat must be applied throughout the entire process in order for the reactions that cook the egg to continue.

FIGURE 5 ···

VIRTUAL LAB **Exothermic and Endothermic Reactions**
Chemical reactions either absorb energy or release energy.

✎ **Complete the following tasks.**

1. **Interpret Photos** Shade in the arrow that indicates the direction the net energy is moving for each reaction.

2. **Infer** How might each reaction feel if you were to put your hands near it?

_____

_____

do the math! Analyzing Data

A student adds magnesium oxide to hydrochloric acid. She measures the temperature of the reaction every minute. Her data are recorded in the table.

1 Graph Plot the data from the table onto the graph. Then name the graph.

2 Interpret Data Is the reaction endothermic or exothermic? Explain.

_____

_____

_____

_____

_____

Time (min)	Temperature (°C)
0	20
1	24
2	27
3	29
4	29

3 Read Graphs In which time interval did the temperature increase the most?

_____

Assess Your Understanding

2a. List What changes in physical properties can be used as evidence that a chemical reaction has occurred?

_____

_____

b. Apply Concepts What evidence of a chemical change is observed when rust forms on iron?

_____

_____

c. Compare and Contrast How are endothermic and exothermic reactions the same? How are they different?

_____

_____

_____

_____

_____

_____

Do the Lab Investigation
Where's the Evidence?

got it? ....

○ **I get it!** Now I know that two kinds of changes you can observe when chemical reactions occur are

_____

○ **I need extra help with** _____

Go to MY SCIENCE COACH online for help with this subject.

Describing Chemical Reactions

🔑 **What Information Does a Chemical Equation Contain?**
PS.1m, PS.4c, PS.5b

🔑 **How Is Mass Conserved During a Chemical Reaction?**
PS.1b, PS.4c, PS.5b

🔑 **What Are Three Types of Chemical Reactions?**
PS.1j, PS.4c, PS.5b

MY PLANET DIARY

Lifesaving Reactions

What moves faster than 300 km/h, inflates in less than a second, and saves lives? An airbag, of course! Did you know that the "air" in an airbag is made by a chemical reaction? A compound called sodium azide (NaN_3) breaks down into sodium metal (Na) and nitrogen gas (N_2). The nitrogen gas fills the airbag and cushions the passengers in an accident.

It's important that the correct amount of sodium azide is used. The mass of sodium azide in the airbag before the collision will equal the mass of sodium and nitrogen that is made by the reaction. If too little or too much nitrogen gas is made, the airbag will not inflate properly.

FUN FACTS

Write your answer to the question below.

What might happen if an airbag doesn't contain the correct amount of sodium azide?

_____

_____

_____

_____

> PLANET DIARY Go to **Planet Diary** to learn more about the law of conservation of mass.

Do the Inquiry Warm-Up
Did You Lose Anything?

Science Standards of Learning

PS.1m Construct and use models and simulations to illustrate and explain phenomena.

PS.4c Investigate and understand formation of compounds through ionic and covalent bonding.

PS.5b Investigate and understand chemical changes in matter and how they relate to the Law of Conservation of Matter and Energy.

What Information Does a Chemical Equation Contain?

Cell phone text messages, like the one shown in **Figure 1,** use symbols and abbreviations to express ideas in shorter form. A type of shorthand is used in chemistry, too. A **chemical equation** is a way to show a chemical reaction, using symbols instead of words. Chemical equations are shorter than sentences, but they contain plenty of information. In chemical equations, chemical formulas and other symbols are used to summarize a reaction.

Vocabulary
- chemical equation • law of conservation of mass
- open system • closed system • coefficient
- synthesis • decomposition • replacement

Skills
↻ Reading: Summarize
△ Inquiry: Make Models

FIGURE 1 ··

Symbols and Abbreviations

Text messages, like chemical equations, let you express ideas in shorter form.

✎ **Interpret Photos** Translate the text message using complete words and sentences.

_____

_____

_____

_____

_____

_____

_____

_____

_____

Formulas in an Equation

You may recall that a chemical formula is a combination of symbols that represents the elements in a compound. For example, CO_2 is the formula for carbon dioxide. The formula tells you that the ratio of carbon atoms to oxygen atoms in this compound is 1 to 2. Carbon dioxide is a molecular compound. Each carbon dioxide molecule has 1 carbon atom and 2 oxygen atoms. **Figure 2** lists the formulas of other familiar compounds.

FIGURE 2 ··

Chemical Formulas

The formula of a compound identifies the elements in the compound and the ratio in which their atoms or ions are present.

✎ **Interpret Tables** Complete the table by filling in the missing chemical formulas.

Formulas of Familiar Compounds

Compound	Formula
Propane	C_3H_8
Sugar (sucrose)	$C_{12}H_{22}O_{11}$
Rubbing alcohol	C_3H_8O
Ammonia	NH_3
Baking soda	$NaHCO_3$
Water	_____
Carbon dioxide	_____
Sodium chloride	_____

FIGURE 3 ··

Modeling a Chemical Equation

Like a skateboard, a chemical equation has a basic structure.

⚠ **Make Models** Complete the equation by filling in the number of the skateboard parts shown. Determine the number of complete skateboards that can be made and draw them as the product.

_____ wheels + _____ trucks + _____ decks ➡ _____ skateboards

Structure of an Equation

Suppose you are building a skateboard. What parts do you need? How many of each part are necessary to build a complete skateboard? **Figure 3** summarizes everything you need to build several skateboards. Similarly, a chemical equation summarizes everything needed to carry out a chemical reaction.

All chemical equations have a basic structure that is followed. 🔑 **A chemical equation tells you the substances you start with in a reaction and the substances that are formed at the end.** The substances you have at the beginning are the reactants. When the reaction is complete, you have new substances, called the products.

The formulas for the reactants are written on the left, followed by an arrow. You read the arrow as "yields," or "reacts to form." The formulas for the products are written to the right of the arrow. When there are two or more reactants, they are separated by plus signs. In a similar way, plus signs are used to separate two or more products. Below is the general structure of a chemical equation.

Reactant + Reactant → Product + Product

The number of reactants and products can vary. Some reactions have only one reactant or product. Other reactions have two, three, or more reactants or products. For example, the reaction that occurs when limestone, or calcium carbonate ($CaCO_3$), is heated has one reactant and two products (CaO and CO_2).

$$CaCO_3 \rightarrow CaO + CO_2$$

apply it!

Molecules of nitrogen (N_2) and hydrogen (H_2) react to form ammonia (NH_3).

1 Identify Indicate the number of H_2 and N_2 molecules needed to yield two molecules of NH_3.

2 Make Models Draw the correct number of reactant molecules in the boxes on the left side of the equation.

_____ N_2 + _____ H_2 ⟶ 2 NH_3

+

3 Describe What bonds of the reactants are broken in this reaction? What bonds are formed in the product?

_____
_____
_____
_____

® Do the Quick Lab *Information in a Chemical Equation.*

🔑 Assess Your Understanding

1a. Explain What do the formulas, arrows, and plus signs tell you in a chemical equation?

_____
_____
_____

_____
_____

b. Interpret Data Write the chemical equation for the following reaction: The elements carbon and oxygen combine to yield the compound carbon dioxide.

_____
_____

got it?

○ **I get it!** Now I know that a chemical equation tells you _____
_____

○ **I need extra help with** _____

Go to MY SCIENCE ⓢ COACH *online for help with this subject.*

did you know?

Antoine Lavoisier is known as the father of modern chemistry, but he was also a lawyer and a tax collector. Despite his support for reform, his connection to tax collection led to his unfortunate beheading in 1794 during the French Revolution.

How Is Mass Conserved During a Chemical Reaction?

Look at the reaction below in **Figure 4.** Iron and sulfur can react to form iron sulfide (FeS). Can you predict the mass of iron sulfide, knowing the mass of the reactants? It might help you to know about a principle first demonstrated by the French chemist Antoine Lavoisier in 1774. This principle, called the **law of conservation of mass,** states that during a chemical reaction, matter is not created or destroyed.

The idea of atoms explains the conservation of mass. 🔑 **In a chemical reaction, all of the atoms present at the start of the reaction are present at the end of the reaction.** Atoms are not created or destroyed. However, they may be rearranged to form new substances. Look again at **Figure 4.** Suppose 1 atom of iron reacts with 1 atom of sulfur. At the end of the reaction, you have 1 iron atom bonded to 1 sulfur atom in the compound iron sulfide (FeS). All the atoms in the reactants are present in the products. The amount of matter does not change. According to the law of conservation of mass, the total mass stays the same before and after the reaction.

FIGURE 4 ....

> **INTERACTIVE ART** **Conservation of Mass**
In a chemical reaction, matter is not created or destroyed.

✎ **Calculate** On the balance, write the mass of iron sulfide produced by this reaction.

Fe	+	S	→	FeS
Iron		Sulfur		Iron sulfide

Open and Closed Systems

At first glance, some reactions may seem to violate the principle of conservation of mass. It's not always easy to measure all the matter involved in a reaction. For example, if you burn a match, oxygen comes into the reaction from the surrounding air, but how much? Likewise, the products escape into the air. Again, how much?

A fish bowl is an example of an open system. It contains different types of matter that are interacting with each other. In an **open system,** matter can enter from or escape to the surroundings. If you want to measure all the matter before and after a reaction, you have to be able to contain it. In a **closed system,** matter does not enter or leave. A chemical reaction that occurs inside a sealed, airtight container is a closed system. The enclosed ecosphere shown in **Figure 5** doesn't allow any mass to enter or escape.

FIGURE 5 ·················

Open and Closed Systems
Matter cannot enter or leave a closed system, as it can in an open system.

✎ **Complete the following tasks.**

1. **Identify** Label each system as open or closed.

2. **Design Experiments** Which system would you use to demonstrate conservation of mass? Why?

_____

_____

_____

_____

3. CHALLENGE Why do you think the fish bowl above is considered a system, but an empty fish bowl is not?

_____

_____

_____

Balancing Chemical Equations The principle of conservation of mass means that the total number of atoms of each element in the reactants must equal the total number of atoms of each element in the products. To be accurate, a chemical equation must show the same number of atoms of each element on both sides of the equation. Chemists say an equation is balanced when conservation of mass is correctly shown. How can you write a balanced chemical equation?

STEP 1 Write the Equation Suppose you want to write a balanced chemical equation for the reaction between hydrogen and oxygen that forms water. To begin, write the correct chemical formulas for both reactants and the product. Place the reactants, H_2 and O_2, on the left side of the arrow, separated by a plus sign. Then write the product, H_2O, on the right side of the arrow.

| Hydrogen | + | Oxygen | ⟶ | Water |

STEP 2 Count the Atoms Count the number of atoms of each element on each side of the equation. Recall that a subscript tells you the ratio of elements in a compound.

____ Hydrogen + ____ Oxygen ⟶ ____ Hydrogen atom(s)
atom(s)   atom(s)   ____ Oxygen atom(s)

After counting, you find 2 atoms of oxygen in the reactants but only 1 atom of oxygen in the product. How can the number of oxygen atoms on both sides of the equation be made equal? You cannot change the formula for water to H_2O_2 because H_2O_2 is the formula for hydrogen peroxide, a completely different compound. So how can you show that mass is conserved?

STEP ③ Use Coefficients to Balance Atoms To balance the equation, use coefficients. A **coefficient** (koh uh FISH unt) is a number placed in front of a chemical formula in an equation. It tells you the amount of a reactant or a product that takes part in a reaction. The coefficient applies to every atom of the formula it is in front of. If the coefficient is 1, you don't need to write it.

Balance the number of oxygen atoms by changing the coefficient of H_2O to 2. Again, count the number of atoms on each side of the equation.

✎

⟳ **Summarize** Describe the steps to balancing a chemical equation.

_____

_____

_____

_____

_____

_____

_____

H_2 + O_2 ⟶ [ ] H_2O

[ ] Hydrogen atom(s) + [ ] Oxygen atom(s) ⟶ [ ] Hydrogen atom(s)

[ ] Oxygen atom(s)

Balancing the oxygen atoms "unbalances" the number of hydrogen atoms. There are now 2 hydrogen atoms in the reactants and 4 in the product. How can you balance the hydrogen? Try changing the coefficient of H_2 to 2. Then, count the atoms again.

[ ] H_2 + O_2 ⟶ 2 H_2O

[ ] Hydrogen atom(s) + [ ] Oxygen atom(s) ⟶ [ ] Hydrogen atom(s)

[ ] Oxygen atom(s)

STEP ④ Look Back and Check Is the number of atoms of each element in the reactants equal to the number of atoms of each element in the products? If so, mass is conserved and the equation is balanced. The balanced equation tells you 2 hydrogen molecules react with 1 oxygen molecule to yield 2 water molecules.

do the math! Sample Problem

Apply Concepts Use the sample problem in the blue box below to help you balance the following equations.

❶ $KClO_3 \rightarrow KCl + O_2$

_____

❷ $NaBr + Cl_2 \rightarrow NaCl + Br_2$

_____

_____

❸ $Na + Cl_2 \rightarrow NaCl$

_____

❶ Write the equation.
$Mg + O_2 \rightarrow MgO$

❷ Count the atoms.
$Mg + O_2 \rightarrow MgO$
   1   2   1 1

❸ Use coefficients to balance.
$2 Mg + O_2 \rightarrow 2 MgO$
   2   2   2 2

❹ Look back and check.

How Can Chemical Reactions Generate *SPEED*?

How is matter conserved in a chemical reaction?

FIGURE 6 ···

> **INTERACTIVE ART** One day, you might be able to drink the exhaust from your car! Sounds gross, right? Well, it could be possible with hydrogen fuel cells. Hydrogen fuel cells use a chemical reaction between hydrogen and oxygen to generate energy for running a car. In the process, water is produced.

✎ **Review** Use what you've learned about chemical reactions to answer questions about fuel cells.

1 **Endothermic or Exothermic?**

The reaction in a fuel cell is used to power cars and other devices. Is it an endothermic or exothermic reaction? Explain.

_____

_____

_____

_____

_____

2 **Conservation of Mass**

Inside a fuel cell, hydrogen is converted into H^+ ions. These ions combine with oxygen to produce energy for the car and water as exhaust. Describe how the fuel cell obeys the law of conservation of mass.

_____

_____

_____

_____

_____

_____

_____

Fuel Cell

An astronaut gathers packets for drinking.

3 Properties of Matter

Hydrogen fuel cells power missions in space. Describe why the product of fuel cells would be more beneficial to space missions than that of other fuels.

_____

_____

_____

_____

_____

_____

4 Balance the Chemical Equation

Hydrogen must be obtained from decomposing fuels like methane (CH_4). Balance the equation for generating hydrogen for fuel cells.

$$CH_4 + H_2O \rightarrow CO + H_2$$

Lab® Do the Quick Lab
zone Is Matter Conserved?

🔑 Assess Your Understanding

2a. Infer If the total mass of the products in a reaction is 90 grams, what was the total mass of the reactants?

_____

b. Apply Concepts Balance the equations.

- $Al + CuO \rightarrow Al_2O_3 + Cu$
- $Fe_2O_3 + C \rightarrow Fe + CO_2$
- $SO_2 + O_2 \rightarrow SO_3$

_____

_____

_____

_____

c. ANSWER THE BIG **?** How is matter conserved in a chemical reaction?

_____

_____

_____

_____

_____

_____

_____

_____

got it? ....

O **I get it!** Now I know that the masses of reactants and products must be _____

_____

O **I need extra help with** _____

Go to MY SCIENCE COACH online for help with this subject.

PS.1j Make valid conclusions after analyzing data.

PS.4c Investigate and understand formation of compounds through ionic and covalent bonding.

PS.5b Investigate and understand chemical changes in matter and how they relate to the Law of Conservation of Matter and Energy.

apply it!

Aluminum (Al) reacts with silver tarnish (Ag_2S) to yield pure silver (Ag) in a baking soda solution.

$$3\ Ag_2S + 2\ Al \rightarrow 6\ Ag + Al_2S_3$$

1 Classify What type of reaction is this?

_____

_____

2 Interpret Data Which element replaces another in the reaction?

_____

_____

_____

3 [CHALLENGE] Use information from the reaction to design an experiment that could be used to remove the tarnish (Ag_2S) from a silver fork.

_____

_____

_____

_____

_____

_____

_____

_____

What Are Three Types of Chemical Reactions?

In a chemical reaction, substances may combine to make a more complex substance. They may break apart to make simpler substances. They may even exchange parts. In each case, new substances are formed. **Three types of chemical reactions are synthesis, decomposition, and replacement.**

Synthesis Some musicians use a machine called a synthesizer. A synthesizer combines different electronic sounds to make music. To synthesize is to put things together. In chemistry, when two or more elements or compounds combine to make a more complex substance, the reaction is classified as **synthesis** (SIN thuh sis). The reaction of phosphorus with oxygen is a synthesis reaction.

$$P_4 + 3\ O_2 \rightarrow P_4O_6$$

Decomposition In contrast to a synthesis reaction, a **decomposition** reaction occurs when compounds break down into simpler products. You probably have a bottle of hydrogen peroxide (H_2O_2) in your house to clean cuts. If you keep such a bottle for a very long time, you'll have water instead. Hydrogen peroxide decomposes into water and oxygen gas.

$$2\ H_2O_2 \rightarrow 2\ H_2O + O_2$$

Replacement When one element replaces another element in a compound, or if two elements in different compounds trade places, the reaction is called a **replacement.** Look at this example.

$$2\ Cu_2O + C \rightarrow 4\ Cu + CO_2$$

Copper metal is obtained by heating copper oxide with carbon. The carbon replaces the copper in the compound with oxygen.

The reaction between copper oxide and carbon is called a *single* replacement reaction because one element, carbon, replaces another element, copper, in the compound. In a *double* replacement reaction, elements in a compound appear to trade places with the elements in another compound. The following reaction is an example of a double replacement.

$$FeS + 2\ HCl \rightarrow FeCl_2 + H_2S$$

FIGURE 7 ···

Types of Reactions

✎ **Complete the following tasks.**

1. Interpret Diagrams Label each type of reaction represented.

2. Explain How are synthesis and decomposition reactions related to each other?

_____

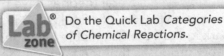 ® Do the Quick Lab *Categories of Chemical Reactions.*

🔑 Assess Your Understanding

3a. Classify What type of chemical reaction is shown in the chemical equation below?

$$Zn + 2\ HCl \rightarrow H_2 + ZnCl_2$$

_____
_____

b. Draw Conclusions The elements iron and oxygen can react to form the compound iron oxide. What type of reaction is this? Explain.

_____
_____
_____
_____

got it? ···

○ **I get it!** Now I know that three types of chemical reactions are _____
_____

○ **I need extra help with** _____

Go to **my science** 🔊 **COACH** *online for help with this subject.*

Controlling Chemical Reactions

UNLOCK THE BIG ?

🔑 **How Do Reactions Get Started?**
PS.1i, PS.4c, PS.5b

🔑 **What Affects the Rate of a Chemical Reaction?**
PS.1f, PS.1g, PS.1i, PS.4c, PS.5b

my planet Diary   DISASTER

Up in Flames

On May 6, 1937, the *Hindenburg* airship was consumed by flames while landing at Lakehurst Naval Air Station in New Jersey. Thirty-five of the 97 people on board and one person on the ground died in the accident.

The cause of the fire, which destroyed the ship within one minute, is still unknown. Most people now believe that an electrical spark started the fire. However, several theories have been proposed to explain what caught fire first. One theory states that the spark ignited the flammable hydrogen inside the blimp. Another theory proposes that the paint on the fabric covering the ship caught fire first, setting off a reaction in the hydrogen.

Write your answer to the task below.

The *Hindenburg* could fly because the hydrogen that filled it was "lighter than air." Yet, hydrogen is incredibly flammable. Describe your own design for the ideal air transport machine.

_____
_____
_____
_____

Lab zone ® Do the Inquiry Warm-Up *Can You Speed Up or Slow Down a Reaction?*

▷ **PLANET DIARY** Go to **Planet Diary** to learn more about controlling chemical reactions.

Vocabulary

- activation energy
- concentration
- catalyst
- enzyme
- inhibitor

Skills

- Reading: Ask Questions
- Inquiry: Predict

How Do Reactions Get Started?

Suppose you're a snowboarder, like the one shown in **Figure 1.** You know that the only way to ride down the mountain is to first get to the top. One way to get there is by riding the chairlift. Once you reach the top of the mountain, you can get off the lift and enjoy the ride down. If you never get to the top, you will never be able to go down the mountain.

Activation Energy Chemical reactions can be like snowboarding. A reaction won't begin until the reactants have enough energy to push them to the "top of the mountain." The energy is used to break the chemical bonds of the reactants. Then the atoms form the new bonds of the products. **Activation energy** is the minimum amount of energy needed to start a chemical reaction. **All chemical reactions need a certain amount of activation energy to get started.** Usually, once a few molecules react, the rest will quickly follow. The first few reactions provide the activation energy for more molecules to react.

Hydrogen and oxygen can react to form water. However, if you just mix the two gases together, nothing happens. For the reaction to start, activation energy must be added. An electric spark or adding heat can provide that energy. A few of the hydrogen and oxygen molecules will react, producing energy. That energy will provide the activation energy needed for even more molecules to react.

Science Standards of Learning

PS.1i Construct and interpret frequency distributions, scatterplots, line plots, and histograms.

PS.4c Investigate and understand formation of compounds through ionic and covalent bonding.

PS.5b Investigate and understand chemical changes in matter and how they relate to the Law of Conservation of Matter and Energy.

Ask Questions Is it clear where chemical reactions get activation energy from? Write a question about this topic that you want answered.

_____

_____

_____

_____

_____

FIGURE 1 ·····················

Activation Energy

A chemical reaction needs a push to the "top of the mountain" to get started.

1. **Infer** Place an arrow at the point where enough activation energy has been added to start the reaction.

2. **Interpret Diagrams** Where does the snowboarder get the activation energy needed to reach the top of the mountain?

_____

Graphing Changes in Energy Every chemical reaction needs activation energy to start. Whether or not a reaction still needs more energy from the environment to keep going depends on whether it is exothermic or endothermic.

Exothermic reactions follow the pattern you can see in **Figure 2A.** The dotted line marks the energy of the reactants before the reaction begins. The peak on the graph shows the activation energy. Notice that at the end of the reaction, the products have less energy than the reactants. This type of reaction results in a release of energy. The burning of fuels, such as wood, natural gas, or oil, is an example of an exothermic reaction.

Exothermic Reaction

Activation energy

Energy

Reactants

Products

Time

A

FIGURE 2 ···

> **ART IN MOTION** **Graphs of Exothermic and Endothermic Reactions**
Each of the graphs shows the amount of energy before and after the reaction.

✎ **Read Graphs** **On each graph, label whether energy is absorbed or released.**

Endothermic Reaction

Energy

Activation energy

Reactants

Products

Time

B

Now look at the graph of an endothermic reaction in **Figure 2B.** Endothermic reactions also need activation energy to get started. In addition, they need energy to continue. Notice that the energy of the products is greater than the energy of the reactants. This means that the reaction must continually absorb energy to keep going. Some endothermic reactions draw energy from the surroundings, leaving the area feeling cold. However, most endothermic reactions require continuous energy. For example, cooking a hamburger requires adding energy constantly until the meat is done.

Lab zone® Do the Quick Lab *Modeling Activation Energy.*

🔑 **Assess Your Understanding**

got it? ···

○ **I get it!** Now I know that in order for reactions to get started _____

_____

○ **I need extra help with** _____

Go to **MY SCIENCE** 🔵 **COACH** *online for help with this subject.*

What Affects the Rate of a Chemical Reaction?

Chemical reactions don't all occur at the same rate. Some, like explosions, are very fast. Others, like the rusting of iron in air, are slow. A particular reaction can occur at different rates depending on the conditions.

If you want to make a chemical reaction happen faster, the particles of the reactants need to collide either more quickly or with more energy. Also, if more particles are available to react, the reaction will happen faster. To slow down a reaction, you need to do the opposite. 🔑 **Factors that can affect rates of reactions include surface area, temperature, concentration, and the presence of catalysts and inhibitors.**

Surface Area Look at the burning building in **Figure 3.** It used to be a sugar factory. The factory exploded when sugar dust ignited in the air above the stored piles of sugar. Although the sugar itself doesn't react violently in air, the dust can. This difference is related to surface area. When a piece of solid substance reacts with a liquid or gas, only the particles on the surface of the solid come into contact with the other reactant. If you break the solid into smaller pieces, more particles are exposed to the surface and the reaction happens faster. Speeding up a reaction by increasing surface area can be dangerous, but it can also be useful. For example, chewing your food breaks it into smaller pieces that your body can digest more easily and quickly.

do the math!

To find the surface area of a cube with 2-cm-long sides, find the area of each face of the cube.

Area = Length × Width

$$4 \text{ cm}^2 = 2 \text{ cm} \times 2 \text{ cm}$$

Then add them together.

$$4 \text{ cm}^2 + 4 \text{ cm}^2 + 4 \text{ cm}^2 + 4 \text{ cm}^2 + 4 \text{ cm}^2 + 4 \text{ cm}^2 = 24 \text{ cm}^2$$

Imagine cutting the cube in half. Find the surface area of each half. Add the values together to get the total surface area.

_____
_____
_____
_____
_____
_____

FIGURE 3 ···

Surface Area and Reaction Rate

Sugar dust can react quickly because it has a greater surface area than a pile of sugar. A chemical reaction that moves quickly can cause an explosion.

apply it!

A chemical reaction takes place in glow sticks. Changing the temperature affects the rate of the reaction.

1 Relate Cause and Effect When the temperature increases, the rate of a chemical reaction (increases/decreases).

2 Predict The brightness of a glow stick's light is affected by temperature. What would happen if the glow stick were placed in boiling water?

_____

_____

_____

3 CHALLENGE The military uses glow sticks for lighting at night. Suggest a method for storing them during the day to maximize their use at night.

_____

_____

_____

_____

_____

Temperature Changing the temperature of a chemical reaction also affects the reaction rate. When you heat a substance, its particles move faster. Faster-moving particles have more energy, which helps reactants get over the activation energy barrier more quickly. Also, faster-moving particles come in contact more often, giving more chances for a reaction to happen.

In contrast, reducing temperature slows down reaction rates. For example, milk contains bacteria, which carry out thousands of chemical reactions as they live and reproduce. You store milk and other foods in the refrigerator because keeping foods cold slows down those reactions, so your foods stay fresh longer.

Concentration Another way to increase the rate of a chemical reaction is to increase the concentration of the reactants. **Concentration** is the amount of a substance in a given volume. For example, adding a small spoonful of sugar to a cup of tea will make it sweet. Adding a large spoonful of sugar makes the tea even sweeter. The cup of tea with more sugar has a greater concentration of sugar molecules.

Increasing the concentration of reactants supplies more particles to react. Look at the tower of bubbles in **Figure 4.** This is the product of the decomposition reaction of a 35 percent hydrogen peroxide solution in water. Hydrogen peroxide that you buy at your local drug store is usually between 3 percent and 12 percent. The high concentration of hydrogen peroxide solution used in this reaction will release huge amounts of oxygen gas more quickly than a lower concentration would.

FIGURE 4 ···

Elephant Toothpaste
This reaction is nicknamed "elephant toothpaste" because of the enormous amount of bubbles it produces.

Predict How would using a lower concentration of hydrogen peroxide affect the rate of reaction?

_____

_____

_____

_____

Catalysts and Inhibitors Another way to control the rate of a reaction is to change the activation energy needed. A **catalyst** (KAT uh list) increases the reaction rate by lowering the activation energy needed. Although catalysts affect a reaction's rate, they are not permanently changed by a reaction and are not considered reactants.

Many chemical reactions can normally only happen at temperatures that would kill living things. Yet, some of these reactions are necessary for life. The cells in your body contain thousands of biological catalysts called **enzymes** (EN zymz) that help these reactions occur at body temperature. Each one is specific to only one chemical reaction. Enzymes provide a surface on which reactions can take place. Since enzymes bring reactant molecules close together, chemical reactions using enzymes require less activation energy and can happen at lower temperatures.

Sometimes it is more useful to slow down a reaction rather than speed it up. A material used to decrease the rate of a chemical reaction is an **inhibitor.** Inhibitors called preservatives are added to food to prevent spoiling.

FIGURE 5 ....
Catalysts
Adding a catalyst speeds up a chemical reaction.

✎ **Graph Draw and label the energy graph for the same chemical reaction when using a catalyst.**

Effects of a Catalyst

Activation energy without a catalyst

Energy

Reactants   Products

Time

Lab zone® Do the Quick Lab *Effect of Temperature on Chemical Reactions.*

🔑 Assess Your Understanding

1a. Describe To slow down a reaction, you can (increase/decrease) the concentration of the reactants.

b. Compare and Contrast What would react more quickly in the air, a pile of grain or a cloud of grain dust? Explain.

_____

_____

c. Explain How do enzymes speed up chemical reactions in your body?

_____

_____

_____

_____

_____

got it? ....

O **I get it!** Now I know that the rate of a chemical reaction can be affected by_____

_____

_____

O **I need extra help with** _____

Go to MY SCIENCE ⓢ COACH online for help with this subject.

The total mass before a chemical reaction equals _____

_____ .

LESSON 1 Observing Chemical Change

🔑 Changes in matter can be described in terms of physical changes and chemical changes.

🔑 Chemical reactions involve changes in properties and changes in energy that you can often observe.

Vocabulary
- physical change • chemical change
- reactant • product • precipitate
- exothermic reaction • endothermic reaction

LESSON 2 Describing Chemical Reactions

🔑 A chemical equation tells you the substances you start with in a reaction and the substances that are formed at the end.

🔑 In a chemical reaction, all of the atoms present at the start of the reaction are present at the end of the reaction.

🔑 Three types of chemical reactions are synthesis, decomposition, and replacement.

Vocabulary
- chemical equation • law of conservation of mass
- open system • closed system • coefficient
- synthesis • decomposition • replacement

$$2\,H_2 \quad + \quad O_2 \quad \longrightarrow \quad 2\,H_2O$$

LESSON 3 Controlling Chemical Reactions

🔑 All chemical reactions need a certain amount of activation energy to get started.

🔑 Factors that can affect rates of reactions include surface area, temperature, concentration, and the presence of catalysts and inhibitors.

Vocabulary
- activation energy
- concentration
- catalyst
- enzyme
- inhibitor

Review and Assessment

LESSON 1 Observing Chemical Change

1. Which of the following results in a chemical change in matter?

   a. bending a straw   b. boiling water

   c. braiding hair   d. burning wood

2. A solid that forms from liquids in a chemical reaction is called a(n)_____

3. **Interpret Photos** What evidence in the photo below tells you that a chemical reaction may have occurred?

   _____

   _____

4. **Solve Problems** Steel that is exposed to water and salt rusts quickly. If you were a shipbuilder, how would you protect a new ship? Explain.

   _____

   _____

   _____

   _____

5. Write About It Suppose you have an Internet friend who is studying chemistry just like you are. Your friend claims the change from liquid water to water vapor is a chemical change. Write a brief e-mail that might convince your friend otherwise.

LESSON 2 Describing Chemical Reactions

6. How can you balance a chemical equation?

   a. Change the coefficients.

   b. Change the products.

   c. Change the reactants.

   d. Change the subscripts.

7. In an open system, such as a campfire, matter can _____

   _____

8. **Classify** Identify each of the balanced equations below as synthesis, decomposition, or replacement.

   $2 Al + Fe_2O_3 \rightarrow 2 Fe + Al_2O_3$

   _____

   $2 Ag + S \rightarrow Ag_2S$

   _____

   $CaCO_3 \rightarrow CaO + CO_2$

   _____

9. **Calculate** Water decomposes into hydrogen (H_2) and oxygen (O_2) when an electric current is applied. How many grams of water must decompose to produce 2 grams of hydrogen and 16 grams of oxygen?

   _____

   _____

10. **math!** Balance the equations.

    $MgO + HBr \rightarrow MgBr_2 + H_2O$

    $N_2 + O_2 \rightarrow N_2O_5$

    $C_2H_4 + O_2 \rightarrow CO_2 + H_2O$

    $Fe + HCl \rightarrow FeCl_2 + H_2$

LESSON 3 **Controlling Chemical Reactions**

11. In general, what happens when you increase the temperature of a reaction?

   a. The heat destroys the reactants.

   b. The rate of the reaction decreases.

   c. The rate of the reaction increases.

   d. The rate of the reaction stays the same.

Graphs A and B represent the same chemical reaction under different conditions. Use the graphs to answer Questions 12 and 13.

12. Interpret Data How does the energy of the products compare with the energy of the reactants?

_____

_____

_____

13. Apply Concepts What change in condition might account for the lower activation energy barrier in the second graph? Explain.

_____

_____

_____

_____

 APPLY THE BIG Q **How is matter conserved in a chemical reaction?**

14. Rust forms when iron metal (Fe) reacts with oxygen (O_2) to produce iron oxide (Fe_2O_3). Write a balanced equation for this reaction. Suppose you find the mass of an iron object, let it rust, and measure the mass again. Predict whether the mass will increase, decrease, or stay the same. Explain your answer in terms of the law of conservation of mass.

_____

_____

_____

_____

_____

_____

_____

_____

_____

_____

_____

_____

_____

_____

_____

Read each question and choose the best answer.

1 The diagram below represents molecules of two different elements. The elements react chemically to produce a compound.

The diagram represents an—

A endothermic reaction in which energy is absorbed

B endothermic reaction in which energy is released

C exothermic reaction in which energy is absorbed

D exothermic reaction in which energy is released

2 Which of the following is the *best* evidence for a chemical reaction?

F change in temperature

G change of state

H formation of a new substance

J gas bubbles

3 Which shows a balanced chemical equation for the decomposition of aluminum oxide (Al_2O_3)?

A $Al_2O_3 \rightarrow 2\,Al + O_2$

B $Al_2O_3 \rightarrow 2\,Al + 3\,O_2$

C $2\,Al_2O_3 \rightarrow 4\,Al + O_2$

D $2\,Al_2O_3 \rightarrow 4\,Al + 3\,O_2$

4 Which of the following would increase the rate of reaction?

F maintain a constant temperature

G increase the concentration of the reactants

H increase the activation energy

J add an inhibitor

5 Which equation describes a synthesis reaction?

A $2\,Na + Cl_2 \rightarrow 2\,NaCl$

B $Mg + CuSO_4 \rightarrow MgSO_4 + Cu$

C $2\,KI \rightarrow 2\,K + I_2$

D $CH_4 + 2\,O_2 \rightarrow CO_2 + 2\,H_2O$

6 The main compound of natural gas is methane. When methane reacts with oxygen gas, carbon dioxide and water vapor are produced. Which shows a balanced equation for this reaction?

Compound	Formula
Carbon dioxide	CO_2
Methane	CH_4
Oxygen	O_2
Water	H_2O

F $CH_4 + O_2 \rightarrow CO_2 + H_2O$

G $CH_4 + 2\,O_2 \rightarrow CO_2 + 2\,H_2O$

H $CO_2 + 2\,O_2 \rightarrow CH_4 + H_2O$

J $H_2O + CH_4 \rightarrow 2\,CO_2 + O_2$

LOOK, MA, WARM HANDS

Winter to many means braving shorter days and blasts of frosty air. Along with heavy clothes, gloves and thick socks, reusable hand warmers can help battle the chill.

Sodium acetate is a salt used in many things, including salt and vinegar chips. The solution in a sodium acetate heat pad is supersaturated. Flexing a metal disk within the heat pad causes a few sodium acetate molecules to come out of solution and form crystals. This causes an exothermic change, which brings the temperature of the solution up to 54°C. (Room temperature is about 22°C.) Placing the heat pad in boiling water causes the crystals to dissolve and become a solution again, so that you can reuse the heat pad. You add heat to dissolve the crystals. When they come out of solution, into their solid state, they release that heat.

So the next time your hands are cold on a chilly day, use a portable warmer and take advantage of the exothermic change!

Design It Design an experiment to determine whether rock salt produces an exothermic or endothermic change when it is placed on icy roads and driveways.

 PS.1k, PS.5b

Safe Moist Heating Pad

To Activate: place pad on flat surface and flex metal disc in corner

To Recharge: place pad on top of cloth in boiling water for 15 minutes or until all crystals are dissolved

note: If crystals form white pad is cooling, recharge

Reusable sodium acetate heat pads use a change of state to generate heat.

Museum of Science

CAN YOU BE CLEAN AND GREEN?

It seems that everything is labeled with something "green" these days. Cleaning products are no exception, but can you make sure that you are both clean and "green"?

The best way to buy green is to read the ingredients list. In order to understand the ingredients and the claims, it helps to know how a product works and what the ingredients do. Detergents and soap work because they contain chemicals called surfactants. Surfactants are long, chain-like molecules. One end of the chain has a strong attraction to oil and dirt, and binds with them. The other end has a strong attraction to water, and binds with water molecules to wash the oil and dirt away. Today, many detergents use petroleum as a basis for surfactants. Petroleum is a nonrenewable resource that can pollute water sources. Some detergents use vegetable oils instead. These oils are renewable resources. Products that use them are more environmentally friendly than those that use petroleum-based surfactants.

Design It Some consumers fight going "green" because they think these products won't work as well. Design a test to compare how well a biodegradable detergent works with one that uses petroleum. Identify the variables and constants in your test.

 PS.1f, PS.1j, PS.1k

HOW DID THIS SINKHOLE APPEAR?

What determines the properties of a solution?

You might be wondering, "What is a sinkhole?" A sinkhole forms when the ground suddenly collapses. Sometimes sinkholes are caused by human activities like mining or by broken water pipes. In this photograph, divers are exploring a sinkhole that happened naturally when the underground rock, called limestone, mixed with slightly acidic water. The water actually dissolved the rock!

▶ UNTAMED SCIENCE Watch the **Untamed Science** video to learn more about solutions.

Infer **Do you think this sinkhole appeared suddenly or gradually over time? Explain your reasoning.**

_____

_____

_____

_____

_____

Acids, Bases, and Solutions

Science Standards of Learning

PS.1f, PS.1j, PS.1k, PS.1m, PS.1n, PS.2b,
PS.2c, PS.2f, PS.4c, PS.5a, PS.5b

Getting Started

Check Your Understanding

1. **Background** Read the paragraph below and then answer the question.

When we breathe, we take in oxygen (O_2) and exhale carbon dioxide (CO_2). The bonds between the oxygen atoms in O_2 are **nonpolar bonds.** The bonds between the carbon and oxygen atoms in CO_2 are **polar bonds.** However, carbon dioxide is a nonpolar molecule.

> A covalent bond in which electrons are shared equally is a **nonpolar bond.**
>
> A covalent bond in which electrons are shared unequally is a **polar bond.**

- Carbon monoxide (CO) is an air pollutant. What type of bonds are in carbon monoxide?

_____

> **MY READING WEB** If you had trouble completing the question above, visit **My Reading Web** and type in *Acids, Bases, and Solutions.*

Vocabulary Skill

Identify Related Word Forms You can expand your vocabulary by learning the related forms of a word. For example, the common verb *to bake* is related to the noun *baker* and the adjective *baked*.

Verb	Noun	Adjective
indicate to show; to point	**indicator** something that shows or points to	**indicative** serving as a sign; showing
saturate to fill up as much as possible	**saturation** the condition of holding as much as possible	**saturated** to be full; to hold as much as is possible

2. **Quick Check** Review the words related to *saturate*. Complete the following sentences with the correct form of the word.

- The _____ sponge could hold no more water.

- He continued to add water to the point of _____

solution

solute

colloid

saturated solution

Chapter Preview

LESSON 1
- solution
- solvent
- solute
- colloid
- suspension

 Identify Supporting Evidence
△ Interpret Data

LESSON 2
- dilute solution
- concentrated solution
- solubility
- saturated solution

Identify the Main Idea
△ Calculate

LESSON 3
- acid
- corrosive
- indicator
- base

Summarize
△ Predict

LESSON 4
- hydrogen ion (H$^+$)
- hydroxide ion (OH$^-$)
- pH scale
- neutralization
- salt

 Relate Cause and Effect
△ Measure

> VOCAB FLASH CARDS For extra help with vocabulary, visit **Vocab Flash Cards** and type in *Acids, Bases, and Solutions.*

Understanding Solutions

 How Are Mixtures Classified?
PS.1m, PS.2b, PS.2c, PS.2f

 How Does a Solution Form?
PS.2b, PS.2c, PS.2f, PS.4c, PS.5b

my PLANeT DiaRY

MISCONCEPTION

Killer Quicksand?

Misconception: You may have watched scenes in a movie like the one below. It's a common misconception that if you fall into a pit of quicksand, it is nearly impossible to escape its muddy clutches.

Fact: Although it is real, quicksand is not as deadly as it's often made out to be. Quicksand is a mixture of sand and water and is rarely more than a few feet deep. It forms when too much water mixes with loose sand. Water molecules surround the individual grains of sand, reducing the friction between them. The sand grains easily slide past each other and can no longer support any weight.

Fortunately, a human body is less dense than quicksand, which means you can float on it. By relaxing and lying on your back, you'll eventually float to the top.

Write your answer to the question below.

Quicksand can be frightening until you understand how it works. Describe something that seemed scary to you until you learned more about it.

_____

_____

_____

_____

_____

_____

_____

▷ PLANET DIARY Go to **Planet Diary** to learn more about solutions.

 Do the Inquiry Warm-Up *What Makes a Mixture a Solution?*

Vocabulary
- solution • solvent
- solute • colloid
- suspension

Skills
- Reading: Identify Supporting Evidence
- Inquiry: Interpret Data

How Are Mixtures Classified?

What do peanut butter, lemonade, and salad dressing have in common? All of these are examples of different types of mixtures. **A mixture is classified as a solution, colloid, or suspension based on the size of its largest particles.**

Solutions Grape juice is one example of a mixture called a solution. A **solution** is a mixture containing a solvent and at least one solute and has the same properties throughout. The **solvent** is the part of a solution usually present in the largest amount. It dissolves the other substances. The **solute** is the substance that is dissolved by the solvent. Solutes can be gases, liquids, or solids. Water is the solvent in grape juice. Sugar and other ingredients are the solutes. A solution has the same properties throughout. It contains solute, molecules or ions that are too small to see.

Water as a Solvent In many common solutions, the solvent is water. Water dissolves so many substances that it is often called the "universal solvent." Life depends on water solutions. Nutrients used by plants are dissolved in water in the soil. Water is the solvent in blood, saliva, sweat, urine, and tears.

Science Standards of Learning

PS.1m Construct and use models and simulations to illustrate and explain phenomena.

PS.2b Investigate and understand elements, compounds, mixtures, acids, bases, and salts.

PS.2c Investigate and understand solids, liquids, and gases.

PS.2f Investigate and understand the characteristics of types of matter based on physical and chemical properties.

apply it!

There are many common solutions in daily life.

A — Soda Water
B — Salt Water
C — Grape Juice

1 Define In a solution, the substance present in the greatest amount is the (solute/solvent).

2 Infer Answer the questions below about the solutions shown above.

Which solution(s) has a gas solute? _____

In which solution(s) is water the solvent? _____

Which solution(s) has two or more solutes? _____

3 CHALLENGE What are some of the solutes in low-fat chocolate milk?

_____

_____

_____

_____

⟲ **Identify Supporting Evidence** Underline evidence in the text that shows water is not the only solvent.

Other Solvents Although water is the most common solvent, it is certainly not the only one. Many solutions are made with solvents other than water, as shown in the table in **Figure 1.** For example, gasoline is a solution of several different liquid fuels. Solvents don't even have to be liquids. A solution may be a combination of gases, liquids, or solids. Air is an example of a solution that is made up of nitrogen, oxygen, and other gases. Solutions can even be made up of solids. Metal alloys like bronze, brass, and steel are solutions of different solid elements.

Sea water is a solution of sodium chloride and other compounds in water.

The air in these gas bubbles is a solution of oxygen and other gases in nitrogen.

The steel of this dive tank is a solution of carbon and metals in iron.

FIGURE 1 ·····

Solutions

Solutions can be made from any combination of solids, liquids, and gases.

✎ **Identify Complete the table by filling in the state of matter of the solvents and solutes.**

Common Solutions

Solute	Solvent	Solution
_____	_____	Air (oxygen and other gases in nitrogen)
_____	_____	Soda water (carbon dioxide in water)
Liquid	_____	Antifreeze (ethylene glycol in water)
_____	Liquid	Dental filling (silver in mercury)
_____	_____	Ocean water (sodium chloride in water)
Solid	_____	Brass (zinc and copper)

Colloids Not all mixtures are solutions. As shown in **Figure 2,** a **colloid** (KAHL oyd) is a mixture containing small, undissolved particles that do not settle out. The particles in a colloid are too small to be seen without a microscope, yet they are large enough to scatter a beam of light. For example, fog is a colloid that is made up of water droplets in air. Fog scatters the headlight beams of cars. Milk, shaving cream, and smoke are some other examples of colloids. Because they scatter light, most colloids are not clear, unlike many solutions.

Colloid

Suspensions If you tried to mix sand in water, you would find that the sand never dissolves completely, no matter how much you stir it. Sand and water make up a suspension. A **suspension** (suh SPEN shun) is a mixture in which particles can be seen and easily separated by settling or filtration. Unlike a solution, a suspension does not have the same properties throughout. It contains visible particles that are larger than the particles in solutions or colloids.

Suspension

FIGURE 2 ··························
Colloids and Suspensions
Colloids and suspensions are classified by the size of their particles.

✎ **Interpret Diagrams
In the circle, draw the particles of a suspension.**

Lab® zone
Do the Quick Lab
Scattered Light.

Assess Your Understanding

1a. Review What is a solution?

_____
_____
_____

b. Compare and Contrast How are colloids and suspensions different from solutions?

_____
_____
_____

c. Infer Suppose you mix food coloring in water to make it blue. Have you made a solution or a suspension? Explain.

_____
_____
_____
_____
_____
_____

got it? ···

○ **I get it!** Now I know that classifying mixtures as solutions, colloids, and suspensions is based on _____

_____

○ **I need extra help with** _____

Go to MY SCIENCE COACH online for help with this subject.

289

Science Standards of Learning

PS.2b Investigate and understand elements, compounds, mixtures, acids, bases, and salts.

PS.2c Investigate and understand solids, liquids, and gases.

PS.2f Investigate and understand the characteristics of types of matter based on physical and chemical properties.

PS.4c Investigate and understand the formation of compounds through ionic and covalent bonding.

PS.5b Investigate and understand chemical changes in matter and how they relate to the Law of Conservation of Matter and Energy.

How Does a Solution Form?

If it were possible to see the particles of a solution, you could see how a solute behaves when it's mixed in a solution. 🔑 **A solution forms when particles of the solute separate from each other and become surrounded by particles of the solvent.**

Ionic and Molecular Solutes **Figure 3** shows an ionic solid, sodium chloride (NaCl), mixed with water. The positive and negative ions of the solute are attracted to the partially charged polar water molecules. Eventually, water molecules will surround all of the ions and the solid crystal will be completely dissolved.

Molecular compounds, such as table sugar, break up into individual neutral molecules in water. The polar water molecules attract the polar sugar molecules. This causes the sugar molecules to move away from each other. The covalent bonds within the molecules remain unbroken.

FIGURE 3 ·······························

▶ **INTERACTIVE ART**

Forming a Solution
✎ **Sequence** Explain what occurs as sodium chloride, an ionic solid, dissolves in water.

do the math!

Analyzing Data

Airplane de-icing fluids are typically solutions of ethylene glycol in water. The freezing point of pure water is 0°C.

1 Explain How is the percent of ethylene glycol in de-icing fluid related to water's freezing point?

_____

_____

_____

2 Read Graphs How much does a 45% solution of de-icing fluid lower the freezing point of water?

_____

3 Interpret Data Would you allow a plane to take off in −20°C weather if it were de-iced with a solution of 30% ethylene glycol? Explain.

_____

_____

Effect of De-icing Fluid on the Freezing Point of Water

Solutes and Conductivity

How could you find out if the solute of a water solution was salt or sugar? Ionic compounds in water conduct electric current, but a solution of molecular compounds may not. If ions are present, electric current will flow and you'll know the solute is salt.

Effects of Solutes

Solutes raise the boiling point of a solution above that of the solvent. As the temperature of a liquid rises, the molecules gain energy and escape as gas. In a liquid solution, the solute particles prevent the solvent molecules' escape. The temperature must go above the boiling point of the solvent in order for the solution to boil. However, the temperature increases only slightly and is not enough to cook food faster.

Solutes lower the freezing point of a solution below that of the solvent alone. When pure liquid water freezes at 0°C, the molecules pack together to form crystals of ice. In a solution, the solute particles get in the way of the water molecules forming ice crystals. The temperature must drop below 0°C in order for the solution to freeze.

 Lab zone ® Do the Lab Investigation *Speedy Solutions.*

🔑 Assess Your Understanding

2. Apply Concepts Why is salt sprinkled on icy roads and sidewalks?

_____

_____

_____

_____

got it?

○ **I get it!** Now I know that in a solution the particles of solute _____

_____

○ **I need extra help with** _____

Go to **MY SCIENCE** Ⓢ **COACH** *online for help with this subject.*

LESSON

2 Concentration and Solubility

UNLOCK THE BIG

🔑 How Is Concentration Changed?
PS.2b, PS.2c, PS.2f, PS.5a

🔑 What Factors Affect Solubility?
PS.2b, PS.2c, PS.2f, PS.5a

my PLANeT DiaRY

DISCOVERY

Even Whales Get the Bends

Decompression sickness, or "the bends" as it's commonly known, is a fear for many scuba divers. Under the extreme pressure of the deep ocean, nitrogen and other gases from the air dissolve in a diver's body tissues. If the diver rises too quickly, the sudden decrease in pressure causes the dissolved gas to bubble out of the tissue. The bubbles can enter a blood vessel and cause intense pain, and sometimes more severe injury.

But what if the diver is a whale? Previously, it was thought that whales did not suffer from the bends. Scientists have discovered evidence in beached whales of nitrogen bubbles expanding and damaging vital organs. It is believed that sonar waves from nearby ships may have frightened the whales, causing them to surface too quickly. This can result in the bends.

Write your answers to the questions below.

1. Scientists have found small gashes in the bones of whale fossils, which are a sign of the bends. What conclusions can you draw from these fossils?

_____
_____
_____
_____
_____

2. Scuba diving is a popular activity. Would you scuba dive knowing the risks of getting the bends?

_____
_____
_____
_____
_____

> PLANET DIARY Go to **Planet Diary** to learn more about solubility.

 Do the Inquiry Warm-Up *Does It Dissolve?*

Vocabulary
- dilute solution • concentrated solution
- solubility • saturated solution

Skills
- Reading: Identify the Main Idea
- Inquiry: Calculate

Science Standards of Learning

PS.2b Investigate and understand elements, compounds, mixtures, acids, bases, and salts.

PS.2c Investigate and understand solids, liquids, and gases.

PS.2f Investigate and understand the characteristics of types of matter based on physical and chemical properties.

PS.5a Investigate and understand physical changes in matter and how they relate to the Law of Conservation of Matter and Energy.

How Is Concentration Changed?

Have you ever had maple syrup on your pancakes? You probably know that it's made from the sap of maple trees. Is something that sweet really made in a tree? Well, not exactly.

The sap of a maple tree and maple syrup differ in their concentrations. That is, they differ in the amount of solute (sugar and other compounds) dissolved in a certain amount of solvent (water). A **dilute solution** is a mixture that has only a little solute dissolved in a certain amount of solvent. A **concentrated solution** is a mixture that has a lot of solute dissolved in the solvent. The sap is a dilute solution and the syrup is a concentrated solution.

Changing Concentration How is sap turned into syrup? **You can change the concentration of a solution by adding solute. You can also change it by adding or removing solvent.** For example, water is removed from the dilute sap to make the more concentrated syrup.

Vocabulary Identify Related Word Forms To *concentrate* is the verb form of the adjective *concentrated*. Write a sentence about solutions using the verb *concentrate*.

_____

_____

_____

FIGURE 1 ·······················
Changing the Concentration of a Solution

A

B

✎ The solution above is made with two droppers of coloring.

1. **Apply Concepts** Show two ways you can make a more concentrated solution by shading in the droppers and water level you would use.

2. **Explain** Describe your methods on the lines.

Calculating Concentration You know that maple syrup is more concentrated than maple sap. What is the actual concentration of either solution? To determine the concentration of a solution, compare the amount of solute to the total amount of solution. You can report concentration as the percent of solute in solution by volume or mass.

do the math! Sample Problem

To calculate concentration, compare the amount of solute to the amount of solution. For example, if a 100-gram solution contains 10 grams of solute, its concentration is 10% by weight.

$$\frac{10 \text{ g}}{100 \text{ g}} \times 100\% = 10\%$$

Calculate Determine the concentration of the contact solution.

_____
_____
_____

10.7 grams hydrogen peroxide
355 grams solution

Contact Solution

10.7 grams hydrogen peroxide
355 grams solution

Do the Quick Lab
Measuring Concentration.

🔑 Assess Your Understanding

1a. Describe What is a concentrated solution?

_____
_____
_____

b. Calculate Find the concentration of a solution with 30 grams of solute in 250 grams of solution.

_____
_____

c. CHALLENGE Solution A has twice as much solute as Solution B. Is it possible for the solutions to have the same concentration? Explain.

_____
_____
_____
_____
_____
_____

got it? ....

○ **I get it!** Now I know that the concentration of a solution can be changed by _____

_____

○ I need extra help with _____

Go to MY SCIENCE 🅢 COACH *online for help with this subject.*

What Factors Affect Solubility?

Suppose you add sugar to a cup of hot tea. Is there a limit to how sweet you can make the tea? Yes, at some point, no more sugar will dissolve. **Solubility** is a measure of how much solute can dissolve in a solvent at a given temperature. 🔑 **Factors that can affect the solubility of a substance include pressure, the type of solvent, and temperature.**

When you've added so much solute that no more dissolves, you have a **saturated solution.** If you can continue to dissolve more solute in a solution, then the solution is unsaturated.

Working With Solubility Look at the table in **Figure 2.** It compares the solubilities of familiar compounds in 100 grams of water at 20°C. You can see that only 9.6 grams of baking soda will dissolve in these conditions. However, 204 grams of table sugar will dissolve in the same amount of water at the same temperature.

Solubility can be used to help identify a substance. It is a characteristic property of matter. Suppose you had a white powder that looked like table salt or sugar. Since you never taste unknown substances, how could you identify the powder? You could measure its solubility in 100 grams of water at 20°C. Then compare the results to the data in **Figure 2** to identify the substance.

Science Standards of Learning

PS.2b Investigate and understand elements, compounds, mixtures, acids, bases, and salts.

PS.2c Investigate and understand solids, liquids, and gases.

PS.2f Investigate and understand the characteristics of types of matter based on physical and chemical properties.

PS.5a Investigate and understand physical changes in matter and how they relate to the Law of Conservation of Matter and Energy.

Solubility in 100 g of Water at 20°C	
Compound	Solubility (g)
Baking soda (sodium bicarbonate, $NaHCO_3$)	9.6
Table salt (sodium chloride, NaCl)	35.9
Table sugar (sucrose, $C_{12}H_{22}O_{11}$)	204

FIGURE 2 ··································

Solubility

Pickling requires saturated solutions of salt in water.

✎ **Calculate** Using the table, determine the amount of sodium chloride you would need to make pickles using 500 grams of water.

_____

_____

Factors Affecting Solubility

You have already read that there is a limit to solubility. By changing certain conditions, you can change a substance's solubility.

Pressure The solubility of a gas solute in a liquid solvent increases as the pressure of the gas over the solution increases. To increase the carbon dioxide concentration in soda water, the gas is added to the liquid under high pressure. Opening the bottle or can reduces the pressure. The escaping gas makes the fizzing sound you hear.

Scuba divers must be aware of the effects of pressure on gases if they want to avoid decompression sickness. Under water, divers breathe from tanks of compressed air. The air dissolves in their blood in greater amounts as they dive deeper. If divers return to the surface too quickly, the gases can bubble out of solution. The bubbles can block blood flow. Divers double over in pain, which is why you may have heard this condition called "the bends."

Solvents Sometimes you just can't make a solution because the solute and solvent are not compatible, as shown in **Figure 3.** This happens with motor oil and water. Have you ever tried to mix oil and water? If so, you've seen how quickly they separate into layers after you stop mixing them. Oil and water separate because water is a polar compound and oil is nonpolar. Some polar and nonpolar compounds do not mix very well.

For liquid solutions, ionic and polar compounds usually dissolve in polar solvents. Nonpolar compounds do not usually dissolve in very polar solvents, but they will dissolve in nonpolar solvents.

◀ Polar water mixed with nonpolar motor oil

FIGURE 3 ···

Solvents and Solubility

Some polar and nonpolar compounds form layers when they are mixed together.

✎ CHALLENGE Determine which of these liquids are polar and which are nonpolar by the way they form layers or mix together. The first answer is given.

A. Polar

B. _____

C. _____

D. _____

E. _____

F. _____

Temperature For most solid solutes, solubility increases as temperature increases. For example, the solubility of table sugar in 100 grams of water at 0°C is 180 grams. However, the solubility increases to 231 grams at 25°C and 487 grams at 100°C.

Cooks use this increased solubility of sugar to make candy. At room temperature, not enough sugar for candy can dissolve in the water. Solutions must be heated for all the sugar to dissolve.

When heated, a solution can dissolve more solute than it can at cooler temperatures. If a heated, saturated solution cools slowly, the extra solute may remain dissolved to become a supersaturated solution. It has more dissolved solute than is predicted by its solubility at the given temperature. If you disturb a supersaturated solution, the extra solute will quickly come out of solution. You can see an example of a supersaturated solution in **Figure 4.**

Unlike most solids, gases become less soluble when the temperature goes up. For example, more carbon dioxide can dissolve in cold water than in hot water. If you open a warm bottle of soda water, carbon dioxide escapes the liquid in greater amounts than if the soda water had been chilled. Why does a warm soda taste "flat" when it's opened? It contains less gas. If you like soda water that's very fizzy, open it when it's cold!

FIGURE 4
Supersaturated Solution
Dropping a crystal of solute into a supersaturated solution causes the extra solute to rapidly come out of solution.

Identify the Main Idea
Underline the sentences on this page that explain how increasing temperature affects the solubility of both solid and gas solutes.

apply it!

Crystallized honey, a supersaturated solution, can be more than 70 percent sugar.

1 **Calculate** How many grams of sugar could be in 50 grams of crystallized honey?

_____

2 **Develop Hypotheses** How would you explain why certain types of honey rarely crystallize?

_____

3 **CHALLENGE** Is there a way to turn crystallized honey back into liquid honey? Explain.

_____
_____
_____
_____
_____

Cooking With Chemistry

What determines the properties of a solution?

FIGURE 5 ···

> **INTERACTIVE ART** At the Solutions Shack Diner, solutions are found everywhere on the menu. In order to serve his customers, the chef must know about the properties of solutions.

✎ **Solve Problems** Use what you know about the properties of solutions to help the chef in the kitchen.

Quick Cooking!

The chef is in a hurry and needs the pasta to cook fast. He adds a handful of salt to the pot of water to raise the boiling point. Explain whether the chef's plan to cook the pasta faster will work or not.

_____

_____

_____

_____

_____

_____

Fizzy!

A customer at the Solutions Shack complains because his soda water is flat. Suggest a reason why this happened.

_____

_____

_____

_____

_____

_____

Mix It Up!

The chef is making salad dressing with vinegar, olive oil, and pepper, but the ingredients are not mixing together. Why?

_____

_____

_____

_____

Yum!

The chef makes the best iced tea. His secret is to make it exactly 15 percent sugar by mass. If he wants to make 3,000 grams of iced tea, how many grams of sugar should he use?

○ 200 grams   ○ 450 grams

○ 20,000 grams   ○ 45,000 grams

Do the Quick Lab
Predicting Rates of Solubility.

🔑 Assess Your Understanding

2a. Review How can you tell when a solution is saturated?

_____

_____

b. Control Variables You are given two white powdery substances. How would you use solubility to identify them?

_____

_____

_____

_____

_____

_____

c. ❓ANSWER THE BIG   What determines the properties of a solution?

_____

_____

_____

_____

_____

_____

_____

got **it?** ....

○ **I get it!** Now I know that the solubility of a substance can be affected by _____

_____

_____

○ **I need extra help with** _____

Go to **MY SCIENCE** ⓢ **COACH** *online for help with this subject.*

Describing Acids and Bases

UNLOCK THE BIG ?

🔑 **What Are the Properties of Acids?**
PS.2b, PS.2c, PS.2f, PS.5b

🔑 **What Are the Properties of Bases?**
PS.2b, PS.2c, PS.2f, PS.5b

my PLANET DiaRY

VOICES FROM HISTORY

Bog Bodies

Even in Shakespeare's time it was known that tanning, the process of making leather, helps preserve body tissues. Hundreds of years later, the body of a 2,300-year-old man was found in the peat bogs of Europe. The man is a bog body. Bog bodies are the remains of human bodies that have been preserved in the highly acidic conditions of peat bogs.

The bog acids are similar in strength to vinegar. They naturally pickle the human bodies. The lack of oxygen and cold temperatures of Northern Europe cause the acids to saturate body tissues before they decay. As a result, the organs, hair, and skin are all preserved. The acids dissolve the bones of the bog bodies, but details like tattoos and fingerprints can still be seen on some of the bodies.

> GRAVE DIGGER. ...A tanner will last you nine year.
>
> HAMLET. Why he, more than another?
>
> GRAVE DIGGER. Why, sir, his hide is so tanned with his trade that he will keep out water a great while, and your water is a sore decayer of your...dead body.
>
> —Shakespeare, *Hamlet*

Write your answers to the questions below.

1. Hypothesize why bog acids react differently with the bones of the bodies than they do with the organs, hair, and skin.

_____
_____
_____
_____
_____
_____

2. How are pickles similar to bog bodies?

_____
_____

▶ **PLANET DIARY** Go to **Planet Diary** to learn more about acids.

Lab zone® Do the Inquiry Warm-Up *What Color Does Litmus Paper Turn?*

Vocabulary
- acid • corrosive
- indicator • base

Skills
- Reading: Summarize
- Inquiry: Predict

What Are the Properties of Acids?

Have you had any fruit to eat recently? If so, an acid was probably part of your meal. Many common items contain acids. **Acids** are compounds with specific characteristic properties. 🔑 **An acid reacts with metals and carbonates, tastes sour, and turns blue litmus paper red.**

Acids are an important part of our lives. Folic acid, found in green, leafy vegetables, is important for cell growth. Hydrochloric acid in your stomach helps with digestion. Phosphoric acid is used to make plant fertilizers. Sulfuric acid drives many types of batteries, giving it the nickname "battery acid."

Reactions With Metals Acids react with certain metals to produce hydrogen gas. Platinum and gold don't react with most acids, but copper, zinc, and iron do. When they react, the metals seem to disappear in the solution. This is one reason acids are described as **corrosive,** meaning they "wear away" other materials.

The purity of precious metals can be determined using acids. **Figure 1** shows a touchstone, which is used to test the purity of gold. The gold object is scraped on the touchstone. Then, acid is poured onto the streak. The more gas bubbles the streak produces, the lower the purity of the gold.

FIGURE 1 ....

Reaction With Metals
Acids are used to test the purity of precious metals.

✎ **Infer** What could you determine about a gold necklace that bubbles when it is exposed to an acid?

_____

_____

_____

_____

Reactions With Carbonates

Acids also react with carbonate ions. Carbonate ions contain carbon and oxygen atoms bonded together with an overall negative charge (CO_3^{2-}). One product of the reaction of an acid with a carbonate is the gas carbon dioxide.

Objects that contain carbonate ions include seashells, eggshells, chalk, and limestone. The sculpture shown in **Figure 2** is carved from limestone. Geologists use this property of acids to identify rocks. If carbon dioxide gas is produced when dilute acid is poured on a rock's surface, then the rock could be made of limestone.

Sour Taste

If you've ever tasted a lemon, you've had firsthand experience with the sour taste of acids. Citrus fruits, such as lemons, grapefruit, and oranges, all contain citric acid. Other foods such as vinegar and tomatoes also contain acids.

Although sour taste is a characteristic of many acids, it is not one you should use to identify a compound as an acid. Scientists don't taste chemicals. It is never safe to taste unknown chemicals.

Reactions With Indicators

Chemists use indicators to test for acids. Litmus paper is an example of an **indicator,** a compound that changes color when it comes in contact with an acid. Acids turn blue litmus paper red.

FIGURE 2 ....
Reactions With Carbonates
Acids react with the carbonates in limestone.

Predict **Describe what a geologist would observe if she poured acid on the sculpture.**

_____
_____
_____
_____
_____

Blue litmus paper turns red in the presence of acid.

Lab zone® Do the Quick Lab *Properties of Acids.*

Assess Your Understanding

1a. Define What is a compound that changes color in an acid called?

◯ metal ◯ indicator ◯ carbonate

b. Explain Why are acids described as corrosive?

_____
_____

c. Draw Conclusions How might you tell if a food contains an acid?

_____
_____
_____
_____

got it? ....

◯ I get it! Now I know that the properties of acids include _____
_____

◯ I need extra help with _____

Go to **MY SCIENCE** ◗ᔆ **COACH** online for help with this subject.

What Are the Properties of Bases?

Bases are another group of compounds that can be identified by their common properties. 🔑 **A base tastes bitter, feels slippery, and turns red litmus paper blue.** The properties of bases are often described as the "opposite" of acids. Bases have many uses. Ammonia is used in fertilizers and household cleaners. Baking soda is a base called sodium bicarbonate, which causes baked goods to rise.

▲ Cocoa beans

Science Standards of Learning

PS.2b Investigate and understand elements, compounds, mixtures, acids, bases, and salts.

PS.2c Investigate and understand solids, liquids, and gases.

PS.2f Investigate and understand the characteristics of types of matter based on physical and chemical properties.

PS.5b Investigate and understand chemical changes in matter and how they relate to the Law of Conservation of Matter and Energy.

Bitter Taste Have you ever tasted tonic water? The base, quinine, causes the slightly bitter taste. Bases taste bitter. Other foods that contain bases include bitter melon, almonds, and cocoa beans, like those shown above.

Slippery Feel Bases have a slippery feel. Many soaps and detergents contain bases. The slippery feeling of your shampoo is a property of the bases it contains.

Just as you avoid tasting an unknown substance, you wouldn't want to touch one either. Strong bases can irritate your skin. A safer way to identify bases is by their other properties.

✏ **Summarize** What are some uses of bases?

_____

_____

_____

FIGURE 3 ....

Acid and Base Properties

✏ **Classify** Draw an arrow from each item to the word "acid" or "base" that describes its properties.

 Window cleaner

 Limes

(ACID)   (BASE)

 Vinegar

 Dish soap

303

Reactions of Bases

Unlike acids, bases don't react with metals. They also don't react with carbonates to form carbon dioxide gas. The lack of a reaction can be a useful property in identifying bases. If you know that a compound doesn't react with metals, you know something about it. For example, you know the compound is probably not an acid. Another important property of bases is how they react with acids in a type of chemical reaction called neutralization, in which acids and bases deactivate one another.

Reactions With Indicators

Since litmus paper can be used to test acids, it can be used to test bases, too, as shown in **Figure 4.** Unlike acids, however, bases turn red litmus paper blue. An easy way to remember this is to think of the letter *b*. **B**ases turn litmus paper **b**lue.

FIGURE 4 ···

Litmus Paper
Litmus paper is used to test if a substance is an acid or a base.

✎ **Look at the apple and soap photos to complete the following tasks.**

1. **Predict** Color or label each strip of litmus paper with the color you would expect to see from the substance.

2. **Infer** What would you infer about a substance that did not change the color of red or blue litmus paper?

_____

_____

FIGURE 5 ···

Properties of Acids and Bases
✎ **Compare and Contrast Complete the table of properties of acids and bases.**

Properties	Acids	Bases
Reaction with metals		
Reaction with carbonates		
Taste		
Reaction with litmus paper		
Uses		

apply it!

Bee venom is slightly acidic, but wasp venom is closer to neutral, meaning it's not an acid or a base. Pure water is another neutral substance.

1 **Predict** Bee venom would taste (bitter/sour).

2 **Apply Concepts** How would bee venom and wasp venom react with litmus paper?

_____

_____

_____

_____

3 **CHALLENGE** One suggestion for treating a bee sting is cleaning it with vinegar. Is this a cure that you would try? Explain.

_____

_____

_____

 Do the Quick Lab
Properties of Bases.

Assess Your Understanding

2a. **Review** The properties of bases are often considered (identical/opposite) to acids.

b. **Apply Concepts** In what products are you most likely to find bases in your home?

_____

_____

_____

_____

c. **Pose Questions** The color of hydrangea flowers depends on the amount of acid or base in the soil. Write a question that helps you determine the cause of a pink hydrangea.

_____

_____

_____

_____

got it? ....

○ **I get it!** Now I know that the properties of bases include _____

_____

○ **I need extra help with** _____

Go to **MY SCIENCE** **COACH** *online for help with this subject.*

Acids and Bases in Solution

UNLOCK THE BIG **?**

🔑 **What Ions Do Acids and Bases Form in Water?**
PS.1m, PS.2b, PS.2c, PS.2f, PS.5b

🔑 **What Are the Products of Neutralization?**
PS.2b, PS.2c, PS.2f, PS.5b

my PLANET DiaRY

FUN FACT

Ocean Stingers

You've probably heard of venomous animals like rattlesnakes and black widow spiders. Did you know that some of the most venomous creatures in the world are jellyfish? Some jellyfish stings can permanently scar and even kill their victims. Jellyfish use their venom to stun and paralyze both prey and predators, including humans. A jellyfish sting can quickly turn a day at the beach into a dash to the hospital. Luckily, most jellyfish stings can be easily treated. The venom of some jellyfish contains bases. Bases can be neutralized, or deactivated, by an acid. The best way to treat some jellyfish stings is to rinse the affected area with vinegar. Vinegar is a solution containing acetic acid, which is a weak acid that is safe for your skin.

Write your answers to the questions below.

1. Stings from other kinds of animals can be acidic. How might you treat a sting that contains an acid?

_____
_____
_____
_____

2. Since jellyfish are nearly invisible, most people never know they're in danger. What advice would you give to a person planning on spending a day at the beach?

_____
_____
_____

▶ PLANET DIARY Go to **Planet Diary** to learn more about neutralization.

Lab zone® Do the Inquiry Warm-Up *What Can Cabbage Juice Tell You?*

Vocabulary
- hydrogen ion (H^+) • hydroxide ion (OH^-)
- pH scale • neutralization • salt

Skills
- Reading: Relate Cause and Effect
- Inquiry: Measure

What Ions Do Acids and Bases Form in Water?

A chemist pours hydrochloric acid into a beaker. Then she slowly adds a base, sodium hydroxide, to the acid. What happens when these two chemicals mix? To answer this question, you must know what happens to acids and bases in solution.

Acids in Solution **Figure 1** lists some common acids. Notice that each formula begins with the letter H, the symbol for hydrogen. In a solution with water, most acids separate into hydrogen ions and negative ions. A **hydrogen ion (H^+)** is an atom of hydrogen that has lost its electron. In the case of hydrochloric acid, for example, hydrogen ions and chloride ions form.

$$HCl \rightarrow H^+ + Cl^-$$

The production of hydrogen ions helps define an acid. **An acid produces hydrogen ions (H^+) in water.** These hydrogen ions are responsible for corroding metals and turning blue litmus paper red. Acids may be strong or weak. Strength refers to how well the acid dissociates, or separates, into ions in water. As shown in **Figure 2,** molecules of a strong acid, such as nitric acid, dissociate to form hydrogen ions in solution. With a weak acid, like acetic acid, very few particles separate to form ions in solution.

FIGURE 1 · · · · · · · · · · · · · · · · ·
Common Acids
The table lists some common acids.

Acid	Formula
Hydrochloric acid	HCl
Nitric acid	HNO_3
Sulfuric acid	H_2SO_4
Acetic acid	$HC_2H_3O_2$

FIGURE 2 ·

Strength of Acids
In solution, strong acids act differently than weak acids do.

✎ **Compare and Contrast** In the empty beaker, use the key to draw how ions of acetic acid would act in solution.

Key

Nitrate ion (NO_3^-)

• Hydrogen ion (H^+)

▶ Acetate ion ($C_2H_3O_2^-$)

Strong Acid

Weak Acid

Bases in Solution

Look at the table in **Figure 3**. Many of the bases shown are made of positive ions combined with hydroxide ions. The **hydroxide ion (OH⁻)** is a negative ion made of oxygen and hydrogen. When some bases dissolve in water, they separate into positive ions and hydroxide ions. Look, for example, at what happens to sodium hydroxide in water.

$$NaOH \rightarrow Na^+ + OH^-$$

Not every base contains hydroxide ions. For example, ammonia (NH_3) does not. In solution, ammonia reacts with water to form hydroxide ions.

$$NH_3 + H_2O \rightarrow NH_4^+ + OH^-$$

Notice that both reactions produce negative hydroxide ions. **A base produces hydroxide ions (OH⁻) in water.** Hydroxide ions are responsible for the bitter taste and slippery feel of bases, and for turning red litmus paper blue. Strong bases, like sodium hydroxide, readily produce hydroxide ions in water. Weak bases, such as ammonia, do not.

Measuring pH

To determine the strength of an acid or base, chemists use a scale called pH. As shown in **Figure 4**, the **pH scale** ranges from 0 to 14. It expresses the concentration of hydrogen ions in a solution.

The most acidic substances are found at the low end of the scale, while basic substances are found at the high end. A low pH tells you that the concentration of hydrogen ions is high and the concentration of hydroxide ions is low. A high pH tells you that the opposite is true.

You can find the pH of a solution using indicator paper, which changes a different color for each pH value. Matching the color of the paper with the colors on the scale tells you the solution's pH. A pH lower than 7 is acidic. A pH higher than 7 is basic. If the pH is 7, the solution is neutral, meaning it's neither an acid nor a base.

Base	Formula
Sodium hydroxide	NaOH
Potassium hydroxide	KOH
Calcium hydroxide	$Ca(OH)_2$
Aluminum hydroxide	$Al(OH)_3$
Ammonia	NH_3
Calcium oxide	CaO

FIGURE 3
Common Bases

FIGURE 4
> INTERACTIVE ART **The pH Scale**
The pH scale helps classify solutions as acidic or basic.

✎ **Use the pH scale to complete the following tasks.**

1. **Measure** Find the approximate pH of each substance shown on the scale.

2. CHALLENGE Each unit of the pH scale represents a tenfold (10x) change in hydrogen ion concentration. What is the difference in hydrogen ion concentration between hydrochloric acid and a lemon?

_____

_____

_____

_____

0
1
2
3
4
5
6
7
8
9
10
11
12
13
14

Hydrochloric acid

pH = _____

Lemon

pH = _____

Vinegar

pH = _____

Banana

pH = _____

Pure water

pH = _____

Blood

pH = _____

Baking soda

pH = _____

Baking Soda

Antacid

pH = _____

CLOG Remover

Drain cleaner

pH = _____

apply it!

You can predict the pH of an acid or base using its properties.

❶ **Estimate** Place each item on the pH scale below.

A Soap

B Tomato

C AMMONIA Ammonia

❷ **Classify** Add your own item to the pH scale based on properties you've experienced.

0 1 2 3 4 5 6 7 8 9 10 11 12 13 14

Lab zone® Do the Quick Lab *pHone Home.*

🔑 **Assess Your Understanding**

1a. Identify What type of solution has a pH of 7?

◯ acidic ◯ basic ◯ neutral

b. Interpret Data Solution A has a pH of 1.6. Solution B has a pH of 4. Which solution has a greater concentration of hydrogen ions? Explain.

_____

_____

_____

_____

got it? ....

◯ **I get it!** Now I know that, in water, acids

produce _____

_____

and bases produce _____

_____

◯ **I need extra help with** _____

Go to MY SCIENCE ⓢ COACH *online for help with this subject.*

309

What Are the Products of Neutralization?

Are you curious about what happens when you mix an acid and a base? Would you be surprised to learn it results in salt water? Look at the equation for the reaction between equal concentrations and amounts of hydrochloric acid and sodium hydroxide.

$$HCl + NaOH \rightarrow H_2O + Na^+ + Cl^-$$

If you tested the pH of the mixture, it would be close to 7, or neutral. In fact, a reaction between an acid and a base is called **neutralization** (noo truh lih ZAY shun).

Reactants After neutralization, an acid-base mixture is not as acidic or basic as the individual starting solutions were. The reaction may even result in a neutral solution. The final pH depends on the volumes, concentrations, and strengths of the reactants. For example, if a small amount of strong base reacts with a large amount of strong acid, the solution will remain acidic, but closer to neutral than the original pH.

FIGURE 5 ·····························

▶VIRTUAL LAB Neutralization

✏ Complete the following tasks.

1. **Interpret Data** Color or write the color of the pH indicator paper on the strip for each solution based on its pH.

2. CHALLENGE Estimate the pH of a mixture of a large amount of weak acid and large amount of strong base. Explain your reasoning.

_____

_____

_____

_____

_____

_____

Acid

Base

pH = 2

pH = 12

When mixed together, acidic and basic solutions produce a more neutral solution.

pH = 8

Products "Salt" may be the familiar name of the stuff you sprinkle on food, but to a chemist, the word refers to a specific group of compounds. A **salt** is any ionic compound that can be made from a neutralization reaction. A salt is made from the positive ion of a base and the negative ion of an acid.

Look at the equation for the neutralization reaction of nitric acid with potassium hydroxide that forms potassium nitrate salt.

$$HNO_3 + KOH \rightarrow H_2O + K^+ + NO_3^-$$
$$\text{(acid)} \quad \text{(base)} \quad \text{(water)} \quad \text{(salt)}$$

🔑 **In a neutralization reaction, an acid reacts with a base to produce a salt and water.** Some common salts are shown in the table in **Figure 6.**

Relate Cause and Effect
Choose all of the following that result from neutralization.
○ Water is produced.
○ pH of the product is closer to 7 than the reactants' pH.
○ Acids turn into bases.

FIGURE 6 ·········
Common Salts
The table lists common salts produced from neutralization reactions.

✏️ **Interpret Tables** Complete the table with the formula for each salt.

Common Salts			
Salt	Neutralization reaction	Salt formula	Use
Sodium chloride	$NaOH + HCl \longrightarrow H_2O + Na^+ + Cl^-$	_____	Table salt
Potassium iodide	$KOH + HI \longrightarrow H_2O + K^+ + I^-$	_____	Disinfectants
Potassium chloride	$KOH + HCl \longrightarrow H_2O + K^+ + Cl^-$	_____	Salt substitute
Calcium carbonate	$Ca(OH)_2 + H_2CO_3 \longrightarrow 2\ H_2O + Ca^{2+} + CO_3^{2-}$	_____	Limestone

Do the Quick Lab
The Antacid Test.

🔑 **Assess Your Understanding**

2a. Define How is the scientific meaning of salt different from the common meaning of salt?

_____
_____
_____

b. Make Generalizations Is the pH of an acid-base neutralization always 7? Why or why not?

_____
_____
_____

got it? ·········

○ **I get it!** Now I know that a neutralization reaction produces _____

_____

○ **I need extra help with** _____

Go to **my science** **coach** *online for help with this subject.*

Solutions contain a _____ and at least one _____ . The solubility of a substance depends on _____ .

LESSON 1 Understanding Solutions

🔑 A mixture is classified as a solution, colloid, or suspension based on the size of its largest particles.

🔑 A solution forms when particles of the solute separate from each other and become surrounded by particles of the solvent.

Vocabulary
• solution • solvent • solute
• colloid • suspension

LESSON 2 Concentration and Solubility

🔑 You can change the concentration of a solution by adding solute. You can also change it by adding or removing solvent.

🔑 Factors that can affect the solubility of a substance include pressure, the type of solvent, and temperature.

Vocabulary
• dilute solution • concentrated solution
• solubility • saturated solution

LESSON 3 Describing Acids and Bases

🔑 An acid reacts with metals and carbonates, tastes sour, and turns blue litmus paper red.

🔑 A base tastes bitter, feels slippery, and turns red litmus paper blue.

Vocabulary
• acid • corrosive • indicator • base

LESSON 4 Acids and Bases in Solution

🔑 An acid produces hydrogen ions (H^+) in water.

🔑 A base produces hydroxide ions (OH^-) in water.

🔑 In a neutralization reaction, an acid reacts with a base to produce a salt and water.

Vocabulary
• hydrogen ion (H^+) • hydroxide ion (OH^-)
• pH scale • neutralization • salt

Review and Assessment

LESSON 1 Understanding Solutions

1. Which of the following is an example of a solution?

   a. fog   **b.** soda water

   c. milk   **d.** mud

2. A mixture of pepper and water is a suspension because _____

   _____

   _____

3. **Apply Concepts** The table below shows the main components of Earth's atmosphere. What is the solvent in air? What are the solutes?

Composition of Earth's Atmosphere	
Compound	**Percent Volume**
Argon (Ar)	0.93
Carbon dioxide (CO_2)	0.03
Nitrogen (N_2)	78.08
Oxygen (O_2)	20.95
Water vapor (H_2O)	0 to 3

   _____

   _____

   _____

   _____

4. **Predict** Suppose you put equal amounts of pure water and salt water into separate ice cube trays of the same size and shape. What would you expect to happen when you put both trays in the freezer? Explain.

   _____

   _____

   _____

   _____

LESSON 2 Concentration and Solubility

5. How can you increase the concentration of a solution?

   a. add solute   **b.** increase temperature

   c. add solvent   **d.** decrease pressure

6. Most gases become more soluble in liquid as the temperature _____

7. **Interpret Diagrams** Which of the diagrams below shows a dilute solution? Which one shows a concentrated solution? Explain.

Solution A   Solution B

Solute particle   Solvent particle

   _____

   _____

   _____

   _____

   _____

   _____

   _____

8. **math!** The concentration of a water and alcohol solution is 25 percent alcohol by volume. Calculate what the volume of alcohol would be in 200 mL of the solution.

LESSON 3 Describing Acids and Bases

9. Which of the following is a property of bases?

a. sour taste

b. slippery feel

c. turns blue litmus paper red

d. reacts with some metals

10. Litmus paper is an example of an indicator because _____

_____

11. Classify Which of the following substances contain bases? Explain your reasoning.

| Lemon | Tonic Water | Soap |

_____

_____

_____

_____

12. Design Experiments Acid rain forms when carbon dioxide (CO_2) in the air reacts with rainwater. How could you test if rain in your town was acid rain?

_____

_____

_____

_____

13. Write About It A bottle of acid is missing from the chemistry lab. Design a "Missing Acid" poster describing the properties of the acid. Include examples of tests that could be done to check if a bottle that is found contains acid.

LESSON 4 Acids and Bases in Solution

14. What is an ion called that is made of hydrogen and oxygen?

a. an acid   b. a base

c. a hydrogen ion   d. a hydroxide ion

15. In water, acids separate into _____

_____

_____

_____

16. Apply Concepts Suppose you have a solution that is either an acid or a base. It doesn't react with any metals. Is the pH of the solution more likely to be 4 or 9? Explain.

_____

_____

_____

_____

APPLY THE BIG ? What determines the properties of a solution?

17. You are given three beakers of unknown liquids. One beaker contains pure water. One contains salt water. One contains sugar water. Without tasting the liquids, how could you identify the liquid in each beaker?

_____

_____

_____

_____

_____

_____

_____

_____

_____

Virginia SOL Test Prep

Read each question and choose the best answer.

1 The graph below shows how the solubility of potassium chloride (KCl) in water changes with temperature.

Thirty grams of potassium chloride are dissolved in 100 grams of water at 60°C. Which *best* describes the solution?

A saturated
B supersaturated
C unsaturated
D acidic

2 Which of the following pH values indicates a solution with the highest concentration of hydrogen ions?

F pH = 1
G pH = 2
H pH = 7
J pH = 14

3 Three sugar cubes are placed in a beaker containing 50 milliliters of water at 20°C. Which action would speed up the rate at which the sugar cubes dissolve in the water?

A Use less water.
B Transfer the contents to a larger beaker.
C Cool the water and sugar cubes to 5°C.
D Heat and stir the contents of the beaker.

4 A scientist observes that an unknown solution turns blue litmus paper red and reacts with zinc to produce hydrogen gas. Which of the following *best* describes the unknown solution?

F a colloid
G an acid
H a base
J a suspension

5 Why is dissolving table salt in water an example of a physical change?

A Neither of the substances changes into a new substance.
B The salt cannot be separated from the water.
C The water cannot become saturated with salt.
D A physical change occurs whenever a substance is mixed with water.

6 How do solutes affect the freezing point of fresh water?

F Solutes slightly increase the freezing point of fresh water.
G Solutes greatly increase the freezing point of fresh water.
H Solutes lower the freezing point of fresh water.
J Solutes have no affect on the freezing point of fresh water.

7 A scientist dissolves a powdered substance in a beaker of water. The resulting mixture is an example of a—

A colloid
B solution
C suspension
D solvent

LIMESTONE AND ACID DRAINAGE

Sport Meets Science

Fifteen-year-old Luke Andraka likes to go kayaking on the Cheat River in West Virginia. On a trip during the summer of 2007, he did more than paddle around. Observing that the water in some areas was orange, Luke began asking questions. He learned that acid runoff from a nearby mine flowed into the stream. The acid changed the chemistry of the stream, causing dead zones, where plants and shellfish could not live and the color of the water changed.

This gave Luke an idea for his science fair project. Luke knew that limestone can neutralize acid rain. He hypothesized that adding limestone to the water could reverse the effects of the runoff from the mine. He experimented to see whether adding small pieces of limestone would work better than adding large pieces of limestone. He proved that limestone could raise the pH level in the stream and clear the stream's pollution without harming the organisms living in the river habitat. Luke also found that limestone sand would work more quickly than an equal mass of limestone rocks.

Write About It Be a keen observer. Research one environmental issue in your community. Identify a possible cause, and present one possible solution. Explain in a letter to your local newspaper how you would research the effectiveness of that solution.

 PS.1k, PS.1n

▶ Acid runoff from mines caused dead zones, where the water in the Cheat River changed color.

vinegar

Pucker Up!

From West Africa, we have chicken yassa—seasoned with malt or cider vinegar. From Japan, we have sushi rice—seasoned with rice vinegar. From Italy we have grilled sea bass with anchovy dressing—seasoned with balsamic vinegar. All the world loves vinegar!

This sour-tasting ingredient is made from the oxidation of ethanol in a liquid. Most vinegar is 3 to 5 percent acetic acid by volume, which is why it curdles with basic ingredients that have a basic pH, such as milk.

Why does vinegar taste so sour? For a long time, scientists weren't sure. Then a team led by scientists at Duke University Medical Center identified two proteins on the surface of our tongues—PKD1L3 and PKD2L1. They also tracked the process that sends an electrical signal to your brain to pucker up. Another study showed that your genes may play a role in how sour something tastes to you.

Design It Work with a partner to design an experiment to find out more about people's taste for sour flavors. How do different people respond to the same sour food and drink? Consider how you can test their reactions. How many people would you need to test? Will repeated trials help you to draw a conclusion?

 PS.1f, PS.1j, PS.1k, PS.2b

◀ PKD1L3 and PKD2L1 are two proteins on the surface of the tongue. They cause vinegar to taste sour.

HOW CAN YOU DESCRIBE THIS COASTER'S MOTION?

 THE BIG ?

How do you describe the motion of an object?

First there is the long, slow climb up the hill. Then the big plunge down. Your body momentarily leaves the seat. The coaster enters a loop the loop and you are upside down! Up and down faster, slower until you finally stop—PHEW!

Classify **What kinds of motion happen during a roller coaster ride?**

_____
_____
_____
_____
_____
_____
_____

> **UNTAMED SCIENCE** Watch the **Untamed Science** video to learn more about motion.

Motion

Science Standards of Learning

PS.1b, PS.1c, PS.1d, PS.1f, PS.1g, PS.1h, PS.1i, PS.1j,
PS.1k, PS.1n, PS.10a, PS.10b, PS.10c, PS.10d

Getting Started

Check Your Understanding

1. Background Read the paragraph below and then answer the question.

> Jenny is watching television. Suddenly, a warning from the National Weather Service appears on the screen. A thunderstorm is heading in her **direction.** At that **instant,** Jenny sees a bolt of lightning in the distant sky. Jenny hopes the storm will be over in **time** for her soccer game.

Direction is the line along which something moves.

Instant is a point or very short space in time.

Time is the period of duration between two events.

• What might happen if the storm were to change direction?

_____

_____

> **MY READING WEB** If you had trouble completing the question above, visit **My Reading Web** and type in *Motion.*

Vocabulary Skill

High-Use Academic Words Knowing these academic words will help you become a better reader in all subject areas. Look for these words as you read this chapter.

Word	Definition	Example
system	*n.* an established way of doing something	People have different *systems* for keeping their music collections organized.
equation	*n.* a statement of equality between two quantities, as shown by the equal sign (=).	The *equation* for the area of a circle is $A = \pi \times r^2$.
conclude	*v.* to decide by reasoning	After investigating the evidence, they *concluded* that everyone should wear a bicycle helmet.

2. Quick Check Choose the word from the table that best completes the sentence.

• After waiting for 20 minutes, he _____ that his friend was not coming.

motion

speed

velocity

acceleration

Chapter Preview

LESSON 1

- motion
- reference point
- International System of Units
- distance

🔄 **Compare and Contrast**

🔺 **Measure**

LESSON 2

- speed
- average speed
- instantaneous speed
- velocity
- slope

🔄 **Identify Supporting Evidence**

🔺 **Calculate**

LESSON 3

- acceleration

🔄 **Identify the Main Idea**

🔺 **Graph**

> **VOCAB FLASH CARDS** For extra help with vocabulary, visit **Vocab Flash Cards** and type in *Motion.*

Describing Motion

🗝 **When Is an Object in Motion?**
PS.1b, PS.1c, PS.10a

MY PLANET DIARY VOICES FROM HISTORY

Nicolaus Copernicus

Why would anyone think that Earth moves around the sun? After all, on a clear day you can see the sun move across the sky. But Polish astronomer Nicolaus Copernicus realized that an object revolving around you from left to right looks the same as an object standing still while you rotate from right to left. In *On the Revolution of the Heavenly Spheres*, he wrote

Every apparent change in respect of position is due to motion of the object observed, or of the observer, or indeed to an unequal change of both.

This book was published in 1543. It was a summary of more than 30 years of Copernicus's studies on the solar system.

Write your answer to the question below.

For thousands of years, many people thought Earth was the center of the universe. Name one possible reason why they thought this.

_____

_____

_____

_____

_____

▷ PLANET DIARY Go to **Planet Diary** to learn more about motion.

Lab zone® Do the Inquiry Warm-Up
What Is Motion?

When Is an Object in Motion?

Deciding if an object is in motion isn't as easy as you might think. For example, you are probably sitting in a chair as you read this book. Are you moving? Parts of you are. Your eyes blink and your chest moves up and down. But you would probably say that you are not moving. An object is in **motion** if its position changes relative to another object. Because your position relative to your chair does not change, you could say that you are not in motion.

Vocabulary
- motion • reference point
- International System of Units • distance

Skills
↻ Reading: Compare and Contrast
△ Inquiry: Measure

Reference Points To decide if you are moving, you use your chair as a reference point. A **reference point** is a place or object used for comparison to determine if something is in motion. 🗝 **An object is in motion if it changes position relative to a reference point.** Objects that are fixed relative to Earth—such as a building, a tree, or a sign—make good reference points.

You may already know what happens if your reference point is moving relative to Earth. Have you ever been in a school bus parked next to another bus? Suddenly, you think that your bus is moving backward. When you look out the window again for a fixed point, you find that your bus isn't moving at all—the other bus is moving forward! Your bus seemed to be moving backward because you had used the other bus as a reference point.

did you know?

Because of Earth's spin, the stars appear to move in circular arcs across the night sky. Only the North Star remains in a fixed position. Historically, sailors have used the North Star to help them navigate.

FIGURE 1 ....

> ART IN MOTION | **Reference Point**

The top photo was taken shortly before the bottom photo.

✎ **Answer the following questions.**

1. **Interpret Photos** Did the car that the boy is in move, or did the car in the background move? Explain your answer.

_____

_____

_____

_____

2. **Identify** What objects in this photo make good reference points?

_____

_____

_____

Compare and Contrast
A tree is (stationary/in motion) relative to Earth. A tree is (stationary/in motion) relative to the sun.

Relative Motion If you use your chair as your reference point as you sit and read, you are not moving. If you choose another object as a reference point, you may be moving.

Suppose you use the sun as a reference point instead of your chair. If you compare your position to the sun, you are moving quite rapidly because you and your chair are on Earth, which revolves around the sun. Earth moves around the sun at a speed of about 30 kilometers every second. So you and everything else on Earth are moving that quickly as well. Going that fast, you could travel from New York City to Los Angeles in about two minutes! Relative to the sun, both you and your chair are in motion. But because you are moving with Earth, you do not seem to be moving.

apply *it!*

The people in the photo are riding on a spinning carousel.

1 Interpret Photos Are the people moving relative to each other? Are they moving relative to objects on the ground? Explain.

_____
_____
_____
_____
_____
_____
_____

2 Explain How is your choice of reference point important when describing the motion of the people?

_____
_____
_____
_____
_____
_____
_____
_____

Measuring Distance

To describe motion completely, you need to use units of measurement. Scientists use a system of measurement called the **International System of Units** or, in French, *Système International* (SI). **Distance** is the length of the path between two points. The SI unit for length is the meter (m). The distance from the floor to a doorknob is about 1 meter.

Scientists use other units to measure distances much smaller or much larger than a meter. For example, the width of the spider shown in **Figure 2** can be measured in centimeters (cm). The prefix *centi-* means "one hundredth." A centimeter is one hundredth of a meter, so there are 100 centimeters in a meter. For lengths smaller than a centimeter, the millimeter (mm) is used. The prefix *milli-* means "one thousandth," so there are 1,000 millimeters in a meter. Distances much longer than a meter can be measured in kilometers (km). The prefix *kilo-* means "one thousand," so there are 1,000 meters in a kilometer. A straight line between San Francisco and Boston would measure about 4,300 kilometers.

FIGURE 2 ·······································

Measuring Distance
The unit of length that you use to measure distance depends on the size of the distance.

✎ **Answer the following questions.**

1. **Review** Fill in the following common conversions for length.

   1 m = _____ mm

   1 m = _____ cm

   1 km = _____ m

2. **Measure** What is the distance in centimeters from points A to B on the spider? _____

3. **CHALLENGE** How many of these spiders would fit side by side in the length of 1 meter?

   _____

   _____

A   B

Lab® Do the Quick Lab
zone *Identifying Motion.*

🗝 Assess Your Understanding

1a. **Review** A _____
   is a place or object used for comparison to determine if something is in motion.

b. **Explain** Why is it important to know if your reference point is moving?

   _____

   _____

   _____

   _____

got it?

○ **I get it!** Now I know that an object is in motion if _____

   _____

   _____

   _____

○ **I need extra help with** _____

   Go to MY SCIENCE ⓢ COACH *online for help with this subject.*

Speed and Velocity

🔑 **How Do You Calculate Speed?**
PS.1h, PS.10a

🔑 **How Do You Describe Velocity?**
PS.1b, PS.1c, PS.1d, PS.10a, PS.10d

🔑 **How Do You Graph Motion?**
PS.1k, PS.10a, PS.10d

MY PLANET DIARY

BLOG

Posted by: Mallory

Location: Fountain Valley, California

Once my sister talked me into going to the roller-skating rink with her. I hate skating, but against my better judgment, I agreed to go. I can skate, but I don't go very fast. At the rink, there were these speed skaters, or, as I like to call them, "assassin skaters." The assassin skaters went ridiculously fast. They were probably going approximately 20 miles per hour in the same direction as me. They zipped past me, just barely missing me.

The worst part about going skating was getting stuck behind a group of skaters or a couple. They went so slowly that you had to speed up to get around them.

Communicate Answer the questions. Discuss your answers with a partner.

1. Do all the skaters in the rink move at the same speed? Explain.

_____

_____

_____

2. Describe a sport or activity in which speed is important.

_____

_____

_____

_____

▶ PLANET DIARY Go to **Planet Diary** to learn more about speed and velocity.

Lab zone Do the Inquiry Warm-Up *How Fast and How Far?*

Vocabulary
- speed
- average speed
- instantaneous speed
- velocity
- slope

Skills
↻ **Reading:** Identify Supporting Evidence
△ **Inquiry:** Calculate

How Do You Calculate Speed?

You might describe the motion of an airplane as fast or the motion of a snail as slow. By using these words, you are describing the object's speed. The **speed** of an object is the distance the object moves per unit of time. Speed is a type of rate. A rate tells you the amount of something that occurs or changes in one unit of time.

Science Standards of Learning

PS.1h Construct and interpret data tables for descriptive statistics showing specific measures of central tendency, the range of the data set, and the number of repeated trials.

PS.10a Investigate and understand speed, velocity, and acceleration.

The Speed Equation **To calculate the speed of an object, divide the distance the object travels by the amount of time it takes to travel that distance.** This relationship can be written as an equation.

$$\text{Speed} = \frac{\text{Distance}}{\text{Time}}$$

The speed equation contains a unit of distance divided by a unit of time. If you measure distance in meters and time in seconds, the SI unit for speed is meters per second, or m/s. (The slash is read as "per.") For example, at its cruising altitude, an airplane might travel at a constant speed of 260 m/s. This means that the airplane will travel a distance of 260 meters in 1 second. The speed of a snail is about 1 mm/s. This means that the snail will travel a distance of 1 millimeter in 1 second. The speed of the airplane is much greater than the speed of the snail because the airplane travels much farther than the snail in the same amount of time.

✎
Vocabulary High-Use Academic Words Complete the following sentence. The relationship between speed, distance, and time can be written as a(n)

_____

apply it!

The cyclist shown in the diagram is moving at a constant speed of 10 m/s during her ride.

1 Identify Draw arrows on the scale to mark how far the cyclist travels after 1, 2, 3, 3.5, and 4 seconds.

2 CHALLENGE How long will it take the cyclist to travel 400 meters?

FIGURE 1 ·······························

Average Speed

Triathletes A and B are competing in a triathlon. The first two legs of the race are swimming and biking.

✎ **Calculate** Use the data in the boxes below to calculate each triathlete's average speed during the swimming and biking legs of the race.

Average Speed

When a plane is at its cruising altitude, it can travel at a constant speed for many hours. But the speed of most moving objects is not constant. In a race known as the triathlon, the competitors (or triathletes) first swim, then bike, and finally run. The speeds of the triathletes change throughout the race. They travel slowest when they swim, a little faster when they run, and fastest when they bike.

Although the triathletes do not travel at a constant speed, they do have an average speed throughout the race. To calculate **average speed,** divide the total distance traveled by the total time. For example, suppose a triathlete swims a distance of 3 kilometers in 1 hour. Then the triathlete bikes a distance of 50 kilometers in 3 hours. Finally, the triathlete runs a distance of 12 kilometers in 1 hour. The average speed of the triathlete is the total distance divided by the total time.

$$\text{Total distance} = 3 \text{ km} + 50 \text{ km} + 12 \text{ km} = 65 \text{ km}$$

$$\text{Total time} = 1 \text{ h} + 3 \text{ h} + 1 \text{ h} = 5 \text{ h}$$

$$\text{Average speed} = \frac{65 \text{ km}}{5 \text{ h}} = 13 \text{ km/h}$$

The triathlete's average speed is 13 kilometers per hour.

Leg 1 *Swimming*

Total distance: 3.0 km
Triathlete A's total time: 0.8 h
Triathlete B's total time: 1.0 h

Triathlete A's average speed =

Triathlete B's average speed =

Leg 2 *Biking*

Total distance: 50.0 km
Triathlete A's total time: 3.0 h
Triathlete B's total time: 2.5 h

Triathlete A's average speed =

Triathlete B's average speed =

Instantaneous Speed   Suppose Triathlete B passes Triathlete A during the biking leg. At that moment, Triathlete B has a greater instantaneous speed than Triathlete A. **Instantaneous speed** is the speed at which an object is moving at a given instant in time. It is important not to confuse instantaneous speed with average speed. The triathlete with the greatest average speed, not the greatest instantaneous speed, wins the race.

apply it!

The triathletes run in the third and final leg of the triathlon.

① **Calculate** Use the data from all three legs to solve for each triathlete's average speed.

> **Leg 3** *Running*
> Total distance: 12.0 km
> Triathlete A's total time: 1.2 h
> Triathlete B's total time: 1.0 h

Total distance =	
Triathlete A's total time =	
Triathlete A's average speed =	
Triathlete B's total time =	
Triathlete B's average speed =	

② **Identify** Which triathlete finishes first? _____

Lab zone® Do the Lab Investigation *Stopping on a Dime.*

🔑 Assess Your Understanding

1a. **Identify** The (instantaneous/average) speed is the speed of the object at a given instant in time. The (instantaneous/average) speed is the speed of the object over a longer period of time.

b. **Apply Concepts** The speedometer in a car gives the car's _____ speed.

got it?

○ **I get it!** Now I know to calculate the speed of an object, I need to _____

_____

○ **I need extra help with** _____

Go to MY SCIENCE COACH *online for help with this subject.*

Identify Supporting Evidence Underline the reason why velocity is important to air traffic controllers.

How Do You Describe Velocity?

Knowing the speed at which something travels does not tell you everything about its motion. To describe an object's motion, you also need to know its direction. For example, suppose you hear that a thunderstorm is traveling at a speed of 25 km/h. Should you prepare for the storm? That depends on the direction of the storm's motion. Because storms usually travel from west to east in the United States, you probably need not worry if you live west of the storm. You probably should take cover if you live east of the storm.

When you know both the speed and direction of an object's motion, you know the velocity of the object. Speed in a given direction is called **velocity.** You know the velocity of the storm when you know that it is moving 25 km/h eastward.

At times, describing the velocity of moving objects can be very important. For example, air traffic controllers must keep close track of the velocities of the aircraft under their control. These velocities change as airplanes move overhead and on the runways. An error in determining a velocity, either in speed or in direction, could lead to a collision.

Velocity is also important to airplane pilots. For example, the stunt pilots in **Figure 2** make spectacular use of their control over the velocity of their aircraft. Stunt pilots use this control to stay in close formation while flying graceful maneuvers at high speeds.

FIGURE 2 ·······················

Velocity

These stunt pilots are performing at an air show.

Explain Why is velocity and not just speed important to these pilots?

_____

_____

_____

_____

_____

_____

_____

_____

EXPLORE THE BIG

Going Somewhere?

Home

Baseball park

How do you describe the motion of an object?

FIGURE 3 ···

Mario is planning on riding his bike from his home to the base-ball park. He looks up the route online. The map shows the route that he will follow. On the map, 1 cm = 100 m.

1. **Measure** Use a metric ruler to determine how far west and how far south Mario has to travel to get to the park.

_____

2. ◢ **Calculate** Suppose Mario is meeting a friend at the park at noon. If he leaves his house at 11:55 A.M., at what average speed does he have to travel to make it there on time? Write your answer in m/s.

_____

_____

_____

_____

Lab zone® Do the Quick Lab Velocity.

🔑 Assess Your Understanding

2. ANSWER THE BIG ? How do you describe the motion of an object?

_____

_____

_____

_____

got it?

○ **I get it!** Now I know that the velocity of an

object is the _____

_____

○ **I need extra help with** _____

Go to MY SCIENCE ⓢ COACH online for help with this subject.

Science Standards of Learning

PS.1k Use research methods to investigate practical problems and questions.

PS.10a Investigate and understand speed, velocity, and acceleration.

PS.10d Investigate and understand technological applications of motion.

How Do You Graph Motion?

The graphs you see in **Figure 4** and **Figure 5** are distance-versus-time motion graphs. 🔑 **You can show the motion of an object on a line graph in which you plot distance versus time.** By tradition, time is shown on the horizontal axis, or *x*-axis. Distance is shown on the vertical axis, or *y*-axis. A point on the line represents the distance an object has traveled during a particular time. The *x* value of the point is time, and the *y* value is distance.

The steepness of a line on a graph is called **slope.** The slope tells you how fast one variable changes in relation to the other variable in the graph. In other words, slope tells you the rate of change. Since speed is the rate that distance changes in relation to time, the slope of a distance-versus-time graph represents speed. The steeper the slope is, the greater the speed. A constant slope represents motion at constant speed.

Calculating Slope You can calculate the slope of a line by dividing the rise by the run. The rise is the vertical difference between any two points on the line. The run is the horizontal difference between the same two points.

$$\text{Slope} = \frac{\text{Rise}}{\text{Run}}$$

In **Figure 4,** using the points shown, the rise is 400 meters and the run is 2 minutes. To find the slope, you divide 400 meters by 2 minutes. The slope is 200 meters per minute.

FIGURE 4 ···

▶ **INTERACTIVE ART** **Constant Speed**

The graph shows the motion of a jogger.

✎ **Use the graph to answer the questions.**

1. **Read Graphs** What is the jogger's speed?

_____

2. **Predict** On the same graph, draw a line that represents the motion of a jogger who moves at a constant speed of 100 m/min.

Motion on Day 1

Slope = $\dfrac{\text{Rise}}{\text{Run}}$ = $\dfrac{400 \text{ m}}{2 \text{ min}}$ = 200 m/min

(6, 1200)

Rise = 400 m

(4, 800)

Run = 2 min

Point (x, y)

Distance (m)

Time (min)

Different Slopes

Most moving objects do not travel at a constant speed. For example, the graph in **Figure 5** shows a jogger's motion on the second day of training. The line is divided into three segments. The slope of each segment is different. From the steepness of the slopes you can tell that the jogger ran fastest during the third segment. The horizontal line in the second segment shows that the jogger's distance did not change at all. The jogger was resting during the second segment.

FIGURE 5 ·····································

Changing Speed

The graph shows how the speed of a jogger varies during her second day of training.

✎ **Read Graphs** Find the rise, the run, and the slope for each segment of the graph. Write the answers in the boxes below.

Motion on Day 2

Distance (m) vs Time (min)

Rise = _____
Run = _____
Slope = _____

Rise = _____
Run = _____
Slope = _____

Rise = _____
Run = _____
Slope = _____

Lab zone ® Do the Quick Lab *Motion Graphs.*

⚷ Assess Your Understanding

3a. Identify The _____ of a distance-versus-time graph shows you the speed of a moving object.

b. Calculate The rise of a line on a distance-versus-time graph is 900 m and the run is 3 min. What is the slope of the line?

_____

_____

c. Apply Concepts Is it possible for a distance-versus-time graph to be a vertical line? Explain.

_____

_____

_____

_____

_____

_____

got it? ·····································

○ **I get it!** Now I know to show the motion of an object on a line graph, you _____

_____

○ **I need extra help with** _____

Go to **my science** ⓢ **coach** *online for help with this subject.*

Acceleration

UNLOCK
THE BIG
?

🗝 **What Is Acceleration?**
PS.1n, PS.10a, PS.10d

🗝 **How Do You Graph Acceleration?**
PS.1f, PS.1g, PS.1j, PS.10a, PS.10d

MY PLANET DIARY

Jumping Spider

A small spider, less than 2 centimeters long, spots an insect. The spider crouches and crawls forward. Then it lifts its front legs and leaps, landing right on its victim!

Amazingly, a jumping spider can jump 10 to 40 times its body length. To capture prey from that far away, it must accurately estimate its initial velocity. Once the spider jumps, the force of gravity controls its motion, causing it to follow a curved path. Its velocity changes at every point along the path until it lands on its prey.

FUN FACT

Write your answer to the question below.

Think of a sport or activity in which the goal is to hit a target from far away. What are some of the challenges?

_____

_____

_____

_____

> PLANET DIARY Go to **Planet Diary** to learn more about acceleration.

 Do the Inquiry Warm-Up *Will You Hurry Up?*

 Science Standards of Learning

PS.1n Use current applications of physical science concepts.
PS.10a Investigate and understand speed, velocity, and acceleration.
PS.10d Investigate and understand technological applications of motion.

What Is Acceleration?

Suppose you are a passenger in a car stopped at a red light. When the light changes to green, the driver steps on the accelerator. As a result, the car speeds up, or accelerates. In everyday language, acceleration means "the process of speeding up."

Acceleration has a more precise definition in science. Scientists define **acceleration** as the rate at which velocity changes. Recall that velocity describes both the speed and direction of an object. A change in velocity can involve a change in either speed or direction—or both. 🗝 **In science, acceleration refers to increasing speed, decreasing speed, or changing direction.**

Vocabulary
• acceleration

Skills
↻ Reading: Identify the Main Idea
△ Inquiry: Graph

Changing Speed Whenever an object's speed changes, the object accelerates. A car that begins to move from a stopped position or speeds up to pass another car is accelerating. People can accelerate too. For example, you accelerate when you coast down a hill on your bike.

Just as objects can speed up, they can also slow down. This change in speed is sometimes called deceleration, or negative acceleration. A car decelerates as it comes to a stop at a red light. A water skier decelerates as the boat slows down.

Changing Direction Even an object that is traveling at a constant speed can be accelerating. Recall that acceleration can be a change in direction as well as a change in speed. Therefore, a car accelerates as it follows a gentle curve in the road or changes lanes. Runners accelerate as they round the curve in a track. A softball accelerates when it changes direction as it is hit.

Many objects continuously change direction without changing speed. The simplest example of this type of motion is circular motion, or motion along a circular path. For example, the seats on a Ferris wheel accelerate because they move in a circle.

↻ **Identify the Main Idea**
Underline the main idea in the section called Changing Speed.

FIGURE 1 ·····················
Acceleration
During the game of soccer, a soccer ball can show three types of acceleration— increasing speed, decreasing speed, and changing direction.

✏ **Interpret Photos** Label the type of acceleration that is occurring in each of the photos.

0.0s   1.0s   2.0s   3.0s

0 m/s   8 m/s   16 m/s   24 m/s

FIGURE 2 ·····································

Acceleration

The airplane is accelerating at a rate of 8 m/s².

✎ **Predict Determine the speed of the airplane at 4.0 s and 5.0 s. Write your answers in the boxes next to each airplane.**

Calculating Acceleration Acceleration describes the rate at which velocity changes. If an object is not changing direction, you can describe its acceleration as the rate at which its speed changes. To determine the acceleration of an object moving in a straight line, you calculate the change in speed per unit of time. This is summarized by the following equation.

$$\text{Acceleration} = \frac{\text{Final Speed} - \text{Initial Speed}}{\text{Time}}$$

If speed is measured in meters per second (m/s) and time is measured in seconds, the SI unit of acceleration is meters per second per second, or m/s². Suppose speed is measured in kilometers per hour and time is measured in hours. Then the unit for acceleration is kilometers per hour per hour, or km/h².

To understand acceleration, imagine a small airplane moving down a runway. **Figure 2** shows the airplane's speed after each second of the first three seconds of its acceleration. To calculate the acceleration of the airplane, you must first subtract the initial speed of 0 m/s from its final speed of 24 m/s. Then divide the change in speed by the time, 3 seconds.

$$\text{Acceleration} = \frac{24 \text{ m/s} - 0 \text{ m/s}}{3 \text{ s}}$$

$$\text{Acceleration} = 8 \text{ m/s}^2$$

The airplane accelerates at a rate of 8 m/s². This means that the airplane's speed increases by 8 m/s every second. Notice in **Figure 2** that after each second of travel, the airplane's speed is 8 m/s greater than its speed in the previous second.

FIGURE 3 ·····································

Deceleration

An airplane touches down on the runway with a speed of 70 m/s. It decelerates at a rate of –5 m/s².

✎ **Predict Determine the speed of the airplane after each second of its deceleration. Write your answers in the table to the right.**

Time (s)	1	2	3	4
Speed (m/s)				

Speed =

Speed =

do the math!

Large accelerations are part of the thrill in many amusement park rides. The problems below are based on actual amusement park rides.

1 Calculate One type of ride falls straight down for 3 seconds. During this time, the ride accelerates from a speed of 0 m/s to a speed of 30 m/s. What is the average acceleration of the ride?

Initial speed = _____ Final speed = _____ Time = _____
Average acceleration =

2 Calculate A roller coaster accelerates from a speed of 4 m/s to 22 m/s in 3 seconds. What is the average acceleration of the ride?

Initial speed = _____ Final speed = _____ Time = _____
Average acceleration =

Lab zone® Do the Quick Lab
Describing Acceleration.

🔑 Assess Your Understanding

1a. Define The rate at which velocity changes is
called _____

b. Infer A softball has a (positive/negative) acceleration when it is thrown. A softball has a (positive/negative) acceleration when it is caught.

c. Explain A girl skates around the perimeter of a circular ice rink at a constant speed of 2 m/s. Is the girl accelerating? Explain.

_____

_____

got it?

○ **I get it!** Now I know that in science
acceleration refers to _____

_____

_____

_____

○ **I need extra help with** _____

Go to **MY SCIENCE COACH** *online for help with
this subject.*

How Do You Graph Acceleration?

Suppose you bike down a long, steep hill. At the top of the hill, your speed is 0 m/s. As you start down the hill, your speed increases. Each second, you move at a greater speed and travel a greater distance than the second before. During the five seconds it takes you to reach the bottom of the hill, you are an accelerating object. 🔑 **You can use both a speed-versus-time graph and a distance-versus-time graph to analyze the motion of an accelerating object.**

FIGURE 4 ·······························

> VIRTUAL LAB **Speed-Versus-Time Graph**
The data in the table show how your speed changes during each second of your bike ride.

✎ **Use the data to answer the questions.**

Time (s)	Speed (m/s)
0	0
1	2
2	4
3	6
4	8
5	10

1. **Graph** Use this data to plot a line graph. Plot time on the horizontal axis. Plot speed on the vertical axis. Give the graph a title.

2. **Calculate** What is the slope of the graph?

Analyzing a Speed-Versus-Time Graph

Look at the speed-versus-time graph that you made in **Figure 4.** What can you learn about your motion by analyzing this graph? First, since the line slants upward, the graph shows that your speed was increasing. Next, since the line is straight, you can tell that your acceleration was constant. A slanted, straight line on a speed-versus-time graph means that the object is accelerating at a constant rate. Your acceleration is the slope of the line.

FIGURE 5 ⋯⋯⋯⋯⋯⋯⋯⋯⋯⋯⋯⋯⋯⋯⋯⋯⋯⋯

▶ **INTERACTIVE ART** **Distance-Versus-Time Graph**

The data in the table show how your distance changes during each second of your bike ride.

✏ **Use the data to answer the questions.**

Time (s)	Distance (m)
0	0
1	1
2	4
3	9
4	16
5	25

1. **Graph** Use this data to create a line graph. Plot time on the horizontal axis. Plot distance on the vertical axis. Give the graph a title.

2. **CHALLENGE** How does the distance change with time?

_____

_____

_____

_____

Analyzing a Distance-Versus-Time Graph

Look at the distance-versus-time graph that you made in **Figure 5**. The curved line tells you that during each second, you traveled a greater distance than the second before. For example, you traveled a greater distance during the third second than you did during the first second.

The curved line in **Figure 5** also tells you that during each second your speed was greater than the second before. Recall that the slope of a distance-versus-time graph is the speed of an object. From second to second, the slope of the line in **Figure 5** gets steeper. Since the slope is increasing, you can conclude that your speed was also increasing. You were accelerating.

Lab ® Do the Quick Lab
zone *Graphing Acceleration.*

🔑 Assess Your Understanding

got it? ⋯⋯⋯⋯⋯⋯⋯⋯⋯⋯⋯⋯⋯⋯⋯⋯⋯⋯⋯⋯⋯⋯⋯⋯⋯

○ **I get it!** Now I know that the two types of graphs that you can use to analyze the motion of an

accelerating object are _____

_____

○ **I need extra help with** _____

Go to **MY SCIENCE** ⑤ **COACH** *online for help with this subject.*

Study Guide

REVIEW THE BIG ?

Which term, speed or velocity, gives you more information about an object's motion? Why?

_____

_____

LESSON 1 Describing Motion

🔑 An object is in motion if it changes position relative to a reference point.

Vocabulary
• motion
• reference point
• International System of Units
• distance

LESSON 2 Speed and Velocity

🔑 To calculate the speed of an object, divide the distance the object travels by the amount of time it takes to travel the distance.

🔑 When you know both the speed and direction of an object's motion, you know the velocity of the object.

🔑 You can show the motion of an object on a line graph in which you plot distance versus time.

Vocabulary
• speed • average speed
• instantaneous speed • velocity • slope

LESSON 3 Acceleration

🔑 In science, acceleration refers to increasing speed, decreasing speed, or changing direction.

🔑 You can use both a speed-versus-time graph and a distance-versus-time graph to analyze the motion of an accelerating object.

Vocabulary
• acceleration

Review and Assessment

LESSON 1 Describing Motion	**LESSON 2** Speed and Velocity

LESSON 1 Describing Motion

1. What is the SI unit of distance?

   a. foot   **b.** meter

   c. mile   **d.** kilometer

2. A change in position with respect to a reference point is _____

3. **Classify** Suppose you are in a train. List some objects that make good reference points to determine whether or not the train is moving.

_____

Use the illustration to answer Questions 4 and 5.

4. **Compare and Contrast** Suppose you are standing on the sidewalk. Describe the direction of your motion relative to the car and the plane.

_____

_____

_____

5. **Compare and Contrast** Suppose you are riding in the plane. Describe the direction of your motion relative to the person standing on the sidewalk and the car.

_____

_____

_____

_____

LESSON 2 Speed and Velocity

6. What quantity can you calculate if you know that a car travels 30 kilometers in 20 minutes?

   a. average speed   **b.** direction

   c. velocity   **d.** instantaneous speed

7. On a graph of distance versus time, the slope of the line indicates the _____ of an object.

The graph shows the motion of a remote-control car. Use the graph to answer Questions 8 and 9.

8. **Read Graphs** During which time period was the car moving the fastest?

_____

_____

9. **Calculate** What was the speed of the car during the first four seconds?

_____

_____

_____

10. **Apply Concepts** A family takes a car trip. They travel for an hour at 80 km/h and then 2 hours at 40 km/h. Find their average speed during the trip.

_____

_____

_____

_____

_____

Acceleration

11. The rate at which velocity changes is

a. acceleration. b. direction.

c. speed. d. velocity.

12. You can calculate the acceleration of an object moving in a straight line by dividing the _____ by the time.

The graph below shows the speed of a downhill skier during a period of several seconds. Use the graph to answer Question 13.

13. Read Graphs What is the skier's acceleration?

_____

_____

_____

14. math! A ball is dropped from a window and takes 2 seconds to reach the ground. It starts from rest and reaches a final speed of 20 m/s. What is the ball's acceleration?

_____

_____

_____

15. Write About It Describe how a baseball player accelerates as he runs around the bases after hitting a home run.

How do you describe the motion of an object?

16. The distance-versus-time graph is for two runners in a 50-meter race. Describe the motion of the runners in as much detail as you can. Which runner won the race? How do you know? Suppose the graph showed the runners' motion until they came to a stop. Describe how the graph would change.

_____

_____

_____

_____

_____

_____

_____

_____

_____

_____

_____

_____

_____

_____

_____

Virginia SOL Test Prep

Read each question and choose the best answer.

1 The graph below shows the motion of a runner.

What could the runner do to make the slope of the line rise?

A stop running

B decrease speed

C maintain the same speed

D increase speed

2 Members of the Fairview Track Running Club are running a 5-kilometer race. What is the distance of the race in meters?

F 0.5 m

G 50 m

H 500 m

J 5000 m

3 What condition is necessary for an object to make a good reference point?

A The object is moving at a constant speed.

B The object is accelerating.

C The object is fixed relative to the motion you are trying to describe.

D The object is large.

4 Two objects traveling at the same speed have different velocities if they—

F start at different times

G travel different distances

H have different masses

J move in different directions

5 Your family is driving to the beach. You travel 200 kilometers in the first two hours. During the next hour, you stop for lunch and only travel 25 kilometers. What was your average speed?

A 60 km/h

B 75 km/h

C 100 km/h

D 225 km/h

6 The graph shows the motion of a person. Based on the graph, which of the following statements is true?

F The person began moving at 10 seconds.

G The person was moving the slowest from 0 to 10 seconds.

H The person's speed was constant from 0 to 10 seconds.

J The person was moving at 15 meters per second for the first 10 seconds.

THE RACE
FOR SPEED

As soon as people started driving automobiles, someone started racing them. We've been trying to go faster ever since.

So how fast can we go? The official top land speed record was set by a man named Andy Green in Blackrock, Nevada, in 1997. Green and his vehicle, named the *Thrust SSC*, reached a speed of 1,288 km/h. That's faster than the speed of sound! In fact, the *Thrust SSC* produced a sonic boom. A sonic boom sounds a lot like an explosion. Thunder is a natural sonic boom.

How did the *Thrust SSC* go so fast? It used two turbo jet engines. So Green's previous experience as a fighter pilot came in handy when he was learning to drive this car.

▲ Andy Green and the jet-propelled *Thrust SSC*.

Graph It There are lots of other speed records. Research the wheel-driven land speed record and the rail speed record, to start. Make a graph or chart that compares all of the speed records you can find. Share your results with your class.

 PS.1i, PS.10a, PS.10d

STOP SIGN

If you've ever watched a movie about jet pilots or race car drivers, you've probably heard someone talk about "pulling Gs." But what does that mean? A G-force is an informal unit of measurement used in aeronautics and space engineering. One G-force is the average acceleration due to gravity at Earth's surface. You experience one G-force all the time.

In the 1940s and 1950s, Colonel John Paul Stapp experienced a lot more than one G-force. At what is now Edwards Air Force Base, Colonel Stapp strapped himself into a device that scientists called the Gee Whiz. This was a rocket sled that hurled volunteers forward before bringing them to a sudden stop along the track. In one of his runs, Colonel Stapp was subjected to 46 Gs! His work had an impact on everything from seat belts to the restraints worn by astronauts.

Share It Research what happens when people experience extreme G-forces. Find out what physical symptoms they are likely to experience and how those symptoms can be prevented. Design a safety pamphlet describing your findings.

 PS.1j, PS.1k, PS.10a, PS.10b, PS.10c, PS.10d

WHY WON'T THIS ACROBAT LAND ON HER HEAD?

How do objects react to forces?

This teen is part of a traveling youth circus that performs in New England. As a circus trouper, she may do stunts such as tumbling and swinging on a trapeze. These stunts often appear to be gravity-defying and dangerous, but the troupers know how to perform in a way that lets them land safely.

 Develop Hypotheses How does this athlete land on her feet?

_____

_____

_____

_____

_____

> UNTAMED SCIENCE Watch the **Untamed Science** video to learn more about forces.

Forces

Science Standards of Learning

PS.1b, PS.1f, PS.1g, PS.1j, PS.1k, PS.1l,
PS.1m, PS.10a, PS.10b, PS.10c, PS.10d

10 Getting Started

Check Your Understanding

1. Background Read the paragraph below and then answer the question.

The dashboard of a car displays your **speed** so that you know how fast you're going. Since this reading doesn't change when you turn, you don't know the car's **velocity.** If the car did show you your change in velocity, you could calculate the car's **acceleration.**

> **Speed** is the distance an object travels per unit of time.
>
> **Velocity** is speed in a given direction.
>
> **Acceleration** is the rate at which velocity changes with time.

• What are three ways to accelerate (change velocity)?

_____

_____

> **MY READING WEB** If you had trouble completing the question above, visit **My Reading Web** and type in *Forces*.

Vocabulary Skill

Latin Word Origins Many science words in English come from Latin. For example, the word *solar*, which means "of the sun," comes from the Latin *sol*, which means "sun."

Latin Word	Meaning of Latin Word	Example
fortis	strong	force, *n.* a push or pull exerted on an object
iners	inactivity	inertia, *n.* the tendency of an object to resist any change in its motion
centrum	center	centripetal force, *n.* a force that causes an object to move in a circle

2. Quick Check Choose the word that best completes the sentence.

• A _____ always points toward the center of a circle.

force

friction

gravity

inertia

Chapter Preview

LESSON 1
- force
- newton
- net force
- 🔁 **Relate Text and Visuals**
- 🔺 **Make Models**

LESSON 2
- friction
- sliding friction
- static friction
- fluid friction
- rolling friction
- gravity
- mass
- weight
- 🔁 **Identify Supporting Evidence**
- 🔺 **Design Experiments**

LESSON 3
- inertia
- 🔁 **Ask Questions**
- 🔺 **Infer**

LESSON 4
- momentum
- law of conservation of momentum
- 🔁 **Identify the Main Idea**
- 🔺 **Calculate**

LESSON 5
- free fall
- satellite
- centripetal force
- 🔁 **Relate Cause and Effect**
- 🔺 **Create Data Tables**

> **VOCAB FLASH CARDS** For extra help with vocabulary, visit **Vocab Flash Cards** and type in *Forces.*

The Nature of Force

UNLOCK
THE BIG
?

🔑 **How Are Forces Described?**
PS.10b, PS.10c

🔑 **How Do Forces Affect Motion?**
PS.1m, PS.10b, PS.10c

mY PLaNeT DiaRY

MISCONCEPTIONS

Forced to Change

Misconception: Any object that is set in motion will slow down on its own.

Fact: A force is needed to change an object's state of motion.

A soccer ball sits at rest. You come along and kick it, sending it flying across the field. It eventually slows to a stop. You applied a force to start it moving, and then it stopped all on its own, right?

No! Forces cause *all* changes in motion. Just as you applied a force to the ball to speed it up from rest, the ground applied a force to slow it down to a stop. If the ground didn't apply a force to the ball, it would keep rolling forever without slowing down or stopping.

Answer the questions below.

1. Give an example of a force you apply to slow something down.

_____

_____

2. Where might it be possible to kick a soccer ball and have it never slow down?

_____

_____

_____

▷ PLANET DIARY Go to **Planet Diary** to learn more about forces.

Lab
zone®

Do the Inquiry Warm-Up
Is the Force With You?

Vocabulary
- force
- newton
- net force

Skills
- Reading: Relate Text and Visuals
- Inquiry: Make Models

How Are Forces Described?

In science, the word *force* has a simple and specific meaning. A **force** is a push or a pull. When one object pushes or pulls another object, the first object exerts a force on the second object. You exert a force on a computer key when you push it. You exert a force on a chair when you pull it away from a table.

 Like velocity and acceleration, a force is described by its strength and by the direction in which it acts. Pushing to the left is a different force from pushing to the right. The direction and strength of a force can be represented by an arrow. The arrow points in the direction of the force, as shown in **Figure 1.** The length of the arrow tells you the strength of the force—the longer the arrow, the greater the force. The strength of a force is measured in the SI unit called the **newton** (N), after scientist Sir Isaac Newton.

Science Standards of Learning

PS.10b Investigate and understand Newton's laws of motion.

PS.10c Investigate and understand work, force, mechanical advantage, efficiency, and power.

FIGURE 1 ··

Describing Forces

Forces act on you whenever your motion changes. In the photos at the right, two men are celebrating an Olympic victory. Forces cause them to pull each other in for a hug, lean over, and fall into the pool.

✎ **Identify** In the box within each photo, draw an arrow that represents the force acting on the person on the right. The first one is done as an example.

 Do the Quick Lab
What Is Force?

🔑 Assess Your Understanding

got it? ··

○ I get it! Now I know that forces are described by _____

_____

○ I need extra help with _____

Go to **my science** ⓢ **coach** online for help with this subject.

FIGURE 2 ....

INTERACTIVE ART **Net Force**

The change in motion of an object is determined by the net force acting on the object.

✏️ **Make Models** **Calculate and draw an arrow for the net force for each situation in the boxes below.**

a Net force _____

b Net force _____

🌐 Science Standards of Learning

PS.1m Construct and use models and simulations to illustrate and explain phenomena.

PS.10b Investigate and understand Newton's laws of motion.

PS.10c Investigate and understand work, force, mechanical advantage, efficiency, and power.

🔄 **Relate Text and Visuals** Use the information in the text to determine the net force of these two force arrows.

3 N   5 N

Circle the net force below.

 8 N

⬅ 2 N

 8 N

How Do Forces Affect Motion?

Often more than one force acts on an object at the same time. The combination of all the forces on an object is called the **net force.** The net force determines if and how an object will accelerate.

You can find the net force on an object by adding together the strengths of all the individual forces acting on the object. Look at **Figure 2a.** The big dog pushes on the box with a force of 16 N to the right. The small dog pushes on the box with a force of 10 N to the right. The net force on the box is the sum of these forces. The box will accelerate to the right. In this situation, there is a nonzero net force. 🗝️ **A nonzero net force causes a change in the object's motion.**

What if the forces on an object aren't acting in the same direction? In **Figure 2b,** the big dog pushes with a force of 20 N. The small dog still pushes with a force of 10 N, but now they're pushing against each other. When forces on an object act in opposite directions, the strength of the net force is found by subtracting the strength of the smaller force from the strength of the larger force. You can still think of this as *adding* the forces together if you think of all forces that act to the right as positive forces and all forces that act to the left as negative forces. The box will accelerate to the right. When forces act in opposite directions, the net force is in the same direction as the larger force.

apply it!

❶ You pull on your dog's leash to the right with a 12 N force. Your dog pulls to the left with a 6 N force. Sketch this situation, including labeled force arrows, below.

C Net force _____

Use what you know about net force to describe the motion of the box in **Figure 2c.** Assume that the box starts at rest.

_____

_____

_____

_____

❷ What is the net force on the leash? Calculate it. Draw and label it in the space above.

_____

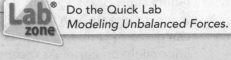 Do the Quick Lab *Modeling Unbalanced Forces.*

🔑 Assess Your Understanding

1a. Calculate You push on a desk with a force of 120 N to the right. Your friend pushes on the same desk with a force of 90 N to the left. What is the net force on the desk?

_____

_____

b. Predict Your friend increases her force on the desk by 30 N. She doesn't change the direction of her push. What happens to the net force on the desk? Will the desk accelerate?

_____

_____

got it? ....

○ I get it! Now I know that changes in motion are caused by _____

_____

○ I need extra help with _____

Go to MY SCIENCE ⓢ COACH *online for help with this subject.*

Friction and Gravity

- 🔑 **What Factors Affect Friction?**
  PS.1f, PS.1g, PS.10b, PS.10c, PS.10d

- 🔑 **What Factors Affect Gravity?**
  PS.10b, PS.10c

MY PLANET DIARY

CAREERS

Space Athletes

Have you ever seen pictures of astronauts playing golf on the moon or playing catch in a space station? Golf balls and baseballs can float or fly farther in space, where gravitational forces are weaker than they are on Earth. Imagine what professional sports would be like in reduced gravity!

You may not have to imagine much longer. At least one company specializes in airplane flights that simulate a reduced gravity environment. Similar to NASA training flights that astronauts use when preparing to go into space, these flights allow passengers to fly around the cabin. In environments with reduced gravity, athletes can perform jumps and stunts that would be impossible on Earth. As technology improves, permanent stadiums could be built in space for a whole new generation of athletes.

Communicate Discuss these questions with a partner and then answer them below.

1. Sports can be more fun in reduced gravity. What jobs could be harder or less fun to do in space? Why?

   _____

   _____

   _____

2. What kinds of sports do you think could be more fun in space? Why?

   _____

   _____

   _____

▷ PLANET DIARY Go to **Planet Diary** to learn more about everyday forces.

 Do the Inquiry Warm-Up *Observing Friction.*

Vocabulary
- friction • sliding friction • static friction
- fluid friction • rolling friction • gravity
- mass • weight

Skills
- Reading: Identify Supporting Evidence
- Inquiry: Design Experiments

What Factors Affect Friction?

If you slide a book across a table, the surface of the book rubs against the surface of the table. The force that two surfaces exert on each other when they rub against each other is called **friction.**

🔑 **Two factors that affect the force of friction are the types of surfaces involved and how hard the surfaces are pushed together.** The football player in **Figure 1** is pushing on a blocking sled. If his coach wanted to make it harder to move the sled, the coach could change the surface of the sled. Covering the bottom of the sled with rubber would increase friction and make the sled harder to move. In general, smooth surfaces produce less friction than rough surfaces.

What would happen if the football player switched to a much heavier sled? He would find the heavier sled harder to push because it pushes down harder against the ground. Similarly, if you rubbed your hands together forcefully, there would be more friction than if you rubbed your hands together lightly. Friction increases when surfaces push harder against each other.

Friction acts in a direction opposite to the direction of the object's motion. Without friction, a moving object will not stop until it strikes another object.

Science Standards of Learning

PS.1f Identify independent and dependent variables, constants, controls, and repeated trials.

PS.1g Construct and interpret data tables showing the independent and dependent variables, derived quantities, and the number of trials.

PS.10b Investigate and understand Newton's laws of motion.

PS.10c Investigate and understand work, force, mechanical advantage, efficiency, and power.

PS.10d Investigate and understand technological applications of work, force, and motion.

Vocabulary Latin Word Origins
Friction comes from the Latin word *fricare*. Based on the definition of friction, what do you think *fricare* means?

○ to burn
○ to rub
○ to melt

FIGURE 1 ....

> ART IN MOTION **Friction and Different Surfaces**
The strength of friction depends on the types of surfaces involved. ✏ **Sequence** Rank the surfaces above by how hard it would be to push a sled over them, from easiest (1) to hardest (3). (Each surface is flat.) What does this ranking tell you about the amount of friction over these surfaces?

_____

_____

Sliding Friction

Sliding friction occurs when two solid surfaces slide over each other. Sliding friction is what makes moving objects slow down and stop. Without sliding friction, a penguin that slid down a hill wouldn't stop until he hit a wall!

✏️ **Classify** **Label five examples of sliding friction and compare with a classmate.**

Friction acts opposite the direction of motion.

Direction of motion →

← Friction

Static Friction

Static friction acts between objects that aren't moving. Think about trying to push a couch across the room. If you don't push hard enough, it won't move. The force that's keeping you from moving it is static friction. Once you push hard enough to overcome static friction, the couch starts moving and there is no more static friction. However, there is sliding friction.

✏️ **Classify** **Label five examples of static friction and compare with a classmate.**

Draw an arrow representing the frictional force at work.

Fluid Friction

Fluids, such as water and air, are materials that flow easily. **Fluid friction** occurs when a solid object moves through a fluid. Fluid friction is easier to overcome than sliding friction. This is why sidewalks become slippery when they get wet.

✏️ **Classify** Label five examples of fluid friction and compare with a classmate.

Draw an arrow representing the frictional force at work.

Rolling Friction

When an object rolls across a surface, **rolling friction** occurs. Rolling friction is much easier to overcome than sliding friction for similar materials. That's why it's easy to push a bike along the sidewalk when the wheels can turn, but much harder to push the bike if you're applying the brakes and the tires slide, not roll.

✏️ **Classify** Label five examples of rolling friction and compare with a classmate.

Draw an arrow representing the frictional force at work.

apply it!

Your family is moving and isn't sure how to best overcome friction while moving furniture. You have a spring scale, wood blocks to represent your furniture, and sandpaper, aluminum foil, marbles, and olive oil as possible surfaces to slide your furniture over.

Design Experiments **Design an experiment that will help you determine which material will reduce friction the most.**

You know that friction occurs between surfaces when they slide against each other. If you measure the applied force required to push something across a surface, you know that your applied force would (increase/decrease) as friction increased.

STEP 1 **Measure** How would you determine your applied force in this experiment?

_____

_____

_____

STEP 2 **Control Variables** What variables would you have to control to keep your results accurate?

_____

_____

_____

STEP 3 **Create Data Tables** Draw the data table you would use when performing this experiment.

 Do the Lab Investigation
Sticky Sneakers.

Assess Your Understanding

1a. List Name four types of friction and give an example of each.

_____

_____

_____

_____

_____

b. Classify What types of friction occur between your bike tires and the ground when you ride over cement, ride through a puddle, and apply your brakes?

_____

got it?

O **I get it!** Now I know that friction is affected by

_____

_____

_____

O **I need extra help with** _____

_____

Go to **MY SCIENCE** **COACH** *online for help with this subject.*

What Factors Affect Gravity?

A skydiver would be surprised if she jumped out of a plane and did not fall. We are so used to objects falling that we may not have thought about why they fall. One person who thought about it was Sir Isaac Newton. He concluded that a force acts to pull objects straight down toward the center of Earth. **Gravity** is a force that pulls objects toward each other.

Universal Gravitation Newton realized that gravity acts everywhere in the universe, not just on Earth. It is the force that makes the skydivers in **Figure 2** fall to the ground. It is the force that keeps the moon orbiting around Earth. It is the force that keeps all the planets in our solar system orbiting around the sun.

What Newton realized is now called the law of universal gravitation. The law of universal gravitation states that the force of gravity acts between all objects in the universe that have mass. This means that any two objects in the universe that have mass attract each other. You are attracted not only to Earth but also to the moon, the other planets in the solar system, and all the objects around you. Earth and the objects around you are attracted to you as well. However, you do not notice the attraction among small objects because these forces are extremely small compared to the force of Earth's attraction.

Science Standards of Learning

PS.10b Investigate and understand Newton's laws of motion.
PS.10c Investigate and understand work, force, mechanical advantage, efficiency, and power.

FIGURE 2 ....
Observing Gravity
Newton published his work on gravity in 1687.

✏️ **Observe** What observations might you make today that would lead you to the same conclusions about gravity? Write down your ideas below.

_____
_____
_____
_____
_____
_____

359

Factors Affecting Gravity

A gravitational force exists between any two objects in the universe. However, you don't see your pencil fly toward the wall the way you see it fall toward Earth. That's because the gravitational force between some objects is stronger than the force between others. You observe only the effects of the strongest gravitational forces. 🔑 **Two factors affect the gravitational attraction between objects: mass and distance.** **Mass** is a measure of the amount of matter in an object. The SI unit of mass is the kilogram.

The more mass an object has, the greater the gravitational force between it and other objects. Earth's gravitational force on nearby objects is strong because the mass of Earth is so large. The more massive planets in **Figure 3** interact with a greater gravitational force than the less massive planets. Gravitational force also depends on the distance between the objects' centers. As distance increases, gravitational force decreases. That's why Earth can exert a visible gravitational force on a pencil in your room and not on a pencil on the moon.

✎ **Identify Supporting Evidence** Underline the factors that determine how strong the gravitational force is between two objects.

FIGURE 3

Gravitational Attraction

Gravitational attraction depends on two factors: mass and distance. Suppose there was a solar system that looked like this.

✎ **Interpret Diagrams** Use the diagram below to compare the gravitational force between different planets and their sun. Assume all planets are made of the same material, so bigger planets have more mass.

1 Circle the object in the outermost orbit that experiences the greatest gravitational pull from the sun.

2 Planet B's force arrow from the sun's gravitational pull should be (longer/shorter) than the arrow from Planet A.

Gravitational force

3 Draw what a planet would look like if it was the same distance from the sun as Planet C but experienced a smaller gravitational pull from the sun.

Earth
60 N

60 N

Moon
____N

?

Mars
____N

?

Weight and Mass

Mass is sometimes confused with weight. Mass is a measure of the amount of matter in an object. **Weight** is a measure of the force of gravity on an object. When you stand on a bathroom scale, it displays the gravitational force Earth is exerting on you.

At any given time, your mass is the same on Earth as it would be on any other planet. But weight varies with the strength of the gravitational force. The dog in **Figure 4** has a different weight at different places in the solar system. On the moon, he would weigh about one sixth of what he does on Earth. On Mars, he would weigh just over a third of what he does on Earth.

FIGURE 4

Weight and Mass

The Mars Phoenix Lander weighs about 3,400 N on Earth. It weighs about 1,300 N on Mars. ✎ **Predict** The first scale shows the dog's weight on Earth. Predict its weight on the moon and on Mars. Enter those weights in the boxes on the other two scales.

Lab zone® Do the Quick Lab *Calculating.*

🔑 Assess Your Understanding

2a. Describe What happens to the gravitational force between two objects when their masses are increased? What happens when the distance between the objects increases?

_____

_____

_____

b. Relate Cause and Effect If the mass of Earth increased, what would happen to your weight? What about your mass?

_____

_____

_____

_____

got it?

○ **I get it!** Now I know that the factors that affect the gravitational force between objects are _____

_____

○ **I need extra help with** _____

Go to **MY SCIENCE** 🔵 **COACH** online for help with this subject.

Newton's Laws of Motion

UNLOCK THE BIG ?

🔑 **What Is Newton's First Law of Motion?**
PS.10b, PS.10c, PS.10d

🔑 **What Is Newton's Second Law of Motion?**
PS.1b, PS.10a, PS.10b, PS.10c, PS.10d

🔑 **What Is Newton's Third Law of Motion?**
PS.10b, PS.10c, PS.10d

my planet Diary

Horse Force

"If a horse draws a stone tied to a rope, the horse (if I may so say) will be equally drawn back towards the stone...."

—Sir Isaac Newton

Scientists have used everyday examples to explain their ideas for hundreds of years. The quotation is from Newton's *Mathematical Principles of Natural Philosophy*, which was first published in the 1680s. Newton used this book to set down his laws of motion. These three simple laws describe much of the motion around you, and they continue to be studied today.

VOICES FROM HISTORY

Answer the question below.
What current scientific discoveries might be taught in schools hundreds of years from now?

_____

_____

_____

_____

_____

> PLANET DIARY Go to **Planet Diary** to learn more about Newton.

 Lab® zone Do the Inquiry Warm-Up *What Changes Motion?*

 Science Standards of Learning

PS.10b Investigate and understand Newton's laws of motion.

PS.10c Investigate and understand work, force, mechanical advantage, efficiency, and power.

PS.10d Investigate and understand technological applications of work, force, and motion.

What Is Newton's First Law of Motion?

You would be surprised if a rock started rolling on its own or a raindrop paused in midair. If an object is not moving, it will not start moving until a force acts on it. If an object is moving, it will continue at a constant velocity until a force acts to change its speed or its direction. 🔑 **Newton's first law of motion states that an object at rest will remain at rest unless acted upon by a nonzero net force. An object moving at a constant velocity will continue moving at a constant velocity unless acted upon by a nonzero net force.**

Vocabulary
• inertia

Skills
↻ **Reading:** Ask Questions
△ **Inquiry:** Infer

Inertia All objects, moving or not, resist changes in motion. Resistance to change in motion is called **inertia** (in UR shuh). Newton's first law of motion is also called the law of inertia. Inertia explains many common events, including why you move forward in your seat when the car you are in stops suddenly. You keep moving forward because of inertia. A force, such as the pull of a seat belt, is needed to pull you back. Roller coasters like the one in **Figure 1** have safety bars for the same reason.

Inertia Depends on Mass Some objects have more inertia than others. Suppose you need to move an empty backpack and a full backpack. The greater the mass of an object, the greater its inertia, and the greater the force required to change its motion. The full backpack is harder to move than the empty one because it has more mass and therefore more inertia.

FIGURE 1 ·······················
Inertia
A roller coaster is hard to stop because it has a lot of inertia. ✎ △ **Infer Use Newton's first law of motion to explain why you feel tossed around whenever a roller coaster goes over a hill or through a loop.**

_____
_____
_____
_____

Lab ® Do the Quick Lab
zone Around and Around.

⚷ Assess Your Understanding

got it? ·······························

○ **I get it!** Now I know that Newton's first law of motion states that _____

_____

○ **I need extra help with** _____

Go to **my science** ⓢ **COACH** *online for help with this subject.*

Science Standards of Learning

PS.1b Accurately measure force.

PS.10a Investigate and understand speed, velocity, and acceleration.

PS.10b Investigate and understand Newton's laws of motion.

PS.10c Investigate and understand work, force, mechanical advantage, efficiency, and power.

PS.10d Investigate and understand technological applications of work, force, and motion.

What Is Newton's Second Law of Motion?

Which is harder to push, a full shopping cart or an empty one? Who can cause a greater acceleration on a shopping cart, a small child or a grown adult?

Changes in Force and Mass Suppose you increase the force on a cart without changing its mass. The acceleration of the cart will also increase. Your cart will also accelerate faster if something falls out. This reduces the mass of the cart, and you keep pushing just as hard. The acceleration of the sled in **Figure 2** will change depending on the mass of the people on it and the force the sled dogs apply. Newton realized these relationships and found a way to represent them mathematically.

Determining Acceleration 🔑 **Newton's second law of motion states that an object's acceleration depends on its mass and on the net force acting on it.** This relationship can be written as follows.

$$\text{Acceleration} = \frac{\text{Net force}}{\text{Mass}}$$

This formula can be rearranged to show how much force must be applied to an object to get it to accelerate at a certain rate.

$$\text{Net force} = \text{Mass} \times \text{Acceleration}$$

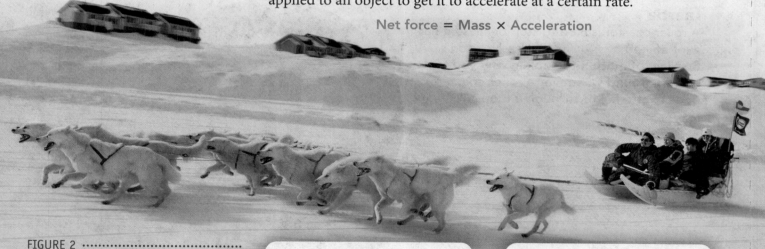

FIGURE 2 ·····················

Newton's Second Law
Suppose that four dogs pull a sled carrying two people.

✏️ **Explain** Use words and fill in the pictures to show how you can change the dog/person arrangement to change the sled's acceleration.

How could you increase the sled's acceleration?
_____
_____
_____
_____

How could you decrease the sled's acceleration?
_____
_____
_____
_____

Acceleration is measured in meters per second per second (m/s^2). Mass is measured in kilograms (kg). Newton's second law shows that force is measured in kilograms times meters per second per second ($kg \cdot m/s^2$). This unit is also called the newton (N), which is the SI unit of force. One newton is the force required to give a 1-kg mass an acceleration of $1\ m/s^2$.

do the math!

Every year in cities around the world, teams create cars, push them across platforms, and hope they will fly. Unfortunately, the cars always end up accelerating down into the water.

1 **Calculate** If a 100-N net force acts on a 50-kg car, what will the acceleration of the car be?

_____

2 After that same car leaves the platform, gravity causes it to accelerate downward at a rate of $9.8\ m/s^2$. What is the gravitational force on the car?

_____

Lab zone® Do the Quick Lab
Newton's Second Law.

🔑 Assess Your Understanding

1a. Review What equation allows you to calculate the force acting on an object?

_____

_____

b. Calculate What is the net force on a 2-kg skateboard accelerating at a rate of $2\ m/s^2$?

_____

_____

c. Predict If the mass of the skateboard doubled but the net force on it remained constant, what would happen to the acceleration of the skateboard?

_____

_____

_____

got it? ···

○ **I get it!** Now I know that Newton's second law of motion describes the relationship _____

_____

○ **I need extra help with** _____

Go to **my science** **COACH** *online for help with this subject.*

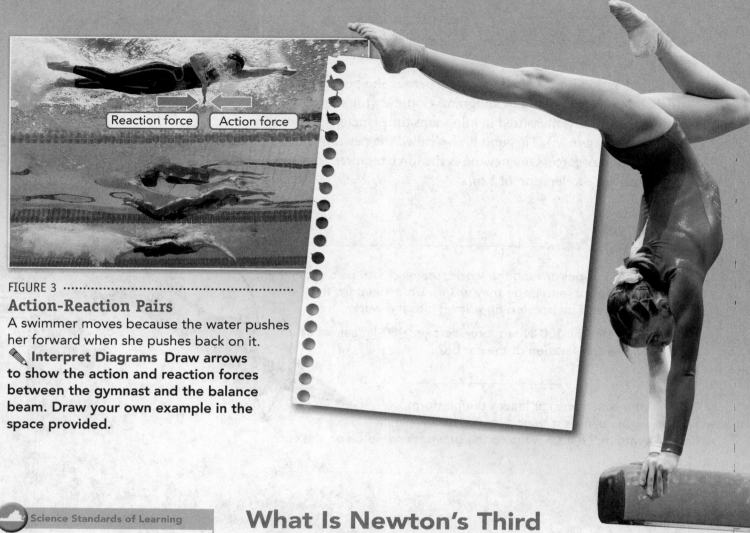

FIGURE 3 ·····················

Action-Reaction Pairs

A swimmer moves because the water pushes her forward when she pushes back on it.

🖊 **Interpret Diagrams Draw arrows to show the action and reaction forces between the gymnast and the balance beam. Draw your own example in the space provided.**

Reaction force   Action force

Science Standards of Learning

PS.10b Investigate and understand Newton's laws of motion.

PS.10c Investigate and understand work, force, mechanical advantage, efficiency, and power.

PS.10d Investigate and understand technological applications of work, force, and motion.

·················· 🖊 ··················

🔄 **Ask Questions** Action and reaction force pairs are all around you, but they aren't always obvious. Write down a question about a situation in which you can't identify what force pairs are at work.

_____

_____

_____

_____

_____

_____

What Is Newton's Third Law of Motion?

If you leaned against a wall and it didn't push back on you, you'd fall through. The force exerted by the wall is equal in strength and opposite in direction to the force you exert on the wall. 🔑 **Newton's third law of motion states that if one object exerts a force on another object, then the second object exerts a force of equal strength in the opposite direction on the first object.** Another way to state Newton's third law is that for every action there is an equal but opposite reaction.

Action-Reaction Pairs Pairs of action and reaction forces are all around you. When you walk, you push backward on the ground with your feet. Think of this as an action force. (It doesn't matter which force is called the "action" force and which is called the "reaction" force.) The ground pushes forward on your feet with an equal and opposite force. This is the reaction force. You can only walk because the ground pushes you forward! In a similar way, the swimmer in **Figure 3** moves forward by exerting an action force on the water with her hands. The water pushes on her hands with an equal reaction force that propels her body forward.

Detecting Motion

If you drop your pen, gravity pulls the pen downward. According to Newton's third law, the pen pulls Earth upward with an equal and opposite reaction force. You see the pen fall. You *don't* see Earth accelerate toward the pen. Remember Newton's second law. If mass increases and force stays the same, acceleration decreases. The same force acts on both Earth and your pen. Since Earth has such a large mass, its acceleration is so small that you don't notice it.

Do Action-Reaction Forces Cancel?

You have learned that two equal forces acting in opposite directions on an object cancel each other out and produce no change in motion. So why don't the action and reaction forces in Newton's third law of motion cancel out as well?

Action and reaction forces do not cancel out because they act on different objects. The swimmer in **Figure 3** exerts a backward action force on the water. The water exerts an equal but opposite forward reaction force on her hands. The action and reaction forces act on different objects—the action force acts on the water and the reaction force acts on her hands.

Unlike the swimmer and the water, the volleyball players in **Figure 4** both exert a force on the *same* object—the volleyball. Each player exerts a force on the ball equal in strength but opposite in direction. The forces on the volleyball are balanced. The ball does not move toward one player or the other.

did you know?

Newton's third law of motion explains why rockets accelerate in space, even though there is no water or air to push off of. Inside rockets, gas is produced. When the rockets push that gas backward out of the rocket, a reaction force occurs that pushes the rocket forward.

Forces on hands

Force on ball

Force on ball

FIGURE 4 ....

Action-Reaction Forces

All the horizontal forces on the volleyball cancel out.

✎ **Apply Concepts** In the dog illustration above, use Newton's third law of motion to draw and label any missing force arrows for all the objects.

What Makes a Bug Go *Splat*?

How do objects react to forces?

FIGURE 5 ....

VIRTUAL LAB Splat! A bug has just flown into the windshield of an oncoming car. The car must have hit the bug much harder than the bug hit the car, right? **Apply Concepts** Use Newton's laws of motion to make sense of the situation and answer the questions.

A

Buzz!

In order for the bug to fly through the air, a force has to push the bug forward. Identify this force. How does the bug produce it? (*Hint:* Think back to how a swimmer moves through the water.)

_____

_____

_____

_____

The bug was at rest on a tree when it saw the car and decided to fly toward it. If the bug has a mass of 0.05 kg and accelerates at 2 m/s², what's the net force on the bug?

_____

10 - LG - SP

B

Vroom!

The driver hates killing bugs. When she saw one coming toward the windshield, she braked suddenly and hoped it would get out of the way. (Sadly, it did not.) When she hit the brakes, she felt that she was thrown forward. Use one of Newton's laws to explain why.

_____

_____

_____

_____

_____

C

Splat!

The unfortunate bug hits the windshield with a force of 1 N. If you call this the action force, what is the reaction force? Does the car hit the bug any harder than the bug hits the car? Use one of Newton's laws to explain why or why not.

_____

_____

_____

_____

_____

Compare the forces on the bug and the car again. Use another one of Newton's laws to explain why the bug goes _splat_ and the car keeps going, without noticeably slowing down.

_____

_____

_____

_____

🔑 Assess Your Understanding

2a. Identify A dog pulls on his leash with a 10-N force to the left, but doesn't move. Identify the reaction force.

_____

_____

_____

b. ANSWER THE BIG ? Using all three of Newton's laws, explain how objects react to forces.

_____

_____

_____

_____

_____

_____

_____

_____

_____

_____

_____

_____

_____

_____

_____

got it? ···

○ **I get it!** Now I know that Newton's third law of motion states that _____

_____

_____

_____

○ **I need extra help with** _____

_____

_____

🖉 _Go to_ MY SCIENCE ⓢ COACH _online for help with this subject._

369

Momentum

What Is an Object's Momentum?
PS.10b, PS.10d

MY PLANET DIARY

FUN FACTS

Air Hockey Science

Whoosh—you've just scored a goal! The puck is about to go back into play. How can you keep the puck out of your goal and get it back into your opponent's? One of the factors you have to consider is momentum. Momentum is a physical quantity that all moving objects have. If you know about momentum, you can predict how an object will act when it collides with other objects. With some quick scientific thinking, you can get the puck to bounce all over the table and back into your opponent's goal!

Answer the questions below.

1. Why might it be better to try to bounce a puck off the wall rather than shoot it straight into your opponent's goal?

_____

_____

_____

_____

2. Where else could it be helpful to know how objects act after colliding?

_____

_____

_____

_____

> PLANET DIARY Go to **Planet Diary** to learn more about momentum.

 Do the Inquiry Warm-Up *How Pushy Is a Straw?*

Vocabulary
- momentum
- law of conservation of momentum

Skills
↩ Reading: Identify the Main Idea
△ Inquiry: Calculate

What Is an Object's Momentum?

Is it harder to stop a rolling bowling ball or a rolling marble? Does your answer depend on the velocities of the objects? All moving objects have what Newton called a "quantity of motion." Today it's called momentum. **Momentum** (moh MEN tum) is a characteristic of a moving object that is related to the mass and the velocity of the object. **The momentum of a moving object can be determined by multiplying the object's mass by its velocity.**

Momentum = Mass × Velocity

Since mass is measured in kilograms and velocity is measured in meters per second, the unit for momentum is kilograms times meters per second (kg·m/s). Like velocity, acceleration, and force, momentum is described by both a direction and a strength. The momentum of an object is in the same direction as its velocity.

The more momentum a moving object has, the harder it is to stop. For example, a 0.1-kg baseball moving at 40 m/s has a momentum of 4 kg·m/s in the direction it's moving.

Momentum = 0.1 kg × 40 m/s

Momentum = 4 kg·m/s

But a 1,200-kg car moving at the same speed as the baseball has a much greater momentum: 48,000 kg·m/s. The velocity of an object also affects the amount of momentum it has. For example, a tennis ball served by a professional tennis player has a large momentum. Although the ball has a small mass, it travels at a high velocity.

Science Standards of Learning

PS.10b Investigate and understand Newton's laws of motion.

PS.10d Investigate and understand technological applications of work, force, and motion.

Word Origins *Momentum* comes from the Latin word *movere*. Based on the definition of momentum, which of these is the definition of *movere*?
○ to spin
○ to move
○ to sit

apply it!

Calculate In each question below, calculate the desired quantity.

❶ The lioness has a mass of 180 kg and a velocity of 16 m/s to the right. What is her momentum?

_____

_____

_____

❷ The warthog has a mass of 100 kg. What does the warthog's speed have to be for it to have the same momentum as the lioness?

_____

_____

371

🔁 **Identify the Main Idea**
Circle a sentence that relates the main idea of this section to two colliding cars. Then underline two supporting examples.

FIGURE 1 ....
▶ **INTERACTIVE ART** **Conservation of Momentum**
✏️ **Calculate** Complete the equations describing the momentum of each collision. Identify the direction in each case.

Conservation of Momentum Imagine you're driving a go-cart. If you ran into another go-cart that was at rest and got stuck to it, what do you think would happen to your momentum? Before you hit the other go-cart, your momentum was just your mass times your velocity. How has the additional mass changed that momentum? It actually hasn't changed it at all!

A quantity that is conserved is the same after an event as it was before. The **law of conservation of momentum** states that, in the absence of outside forces like friction, the total momentum of objects that interact does not change. The amount of momentum two cars have is the same before and after they interact.

🔑 **The total momentum of any group of objects remains the same, or is conserved, unless outside forces act on the objects.**

Before → 4 m/s
100 kg
Momentum = 400 kg·m/s to the right
Total momentum = _____ kg·m/s _____

→ 2 m/s
100 kg
Momentum = 200 kg·m/s to the right

"Non-Sticky" Collisions
Look at this example of a collision. When two objects of the same mass don't stick together and outside forces (such as friction) are negligible, the objects just trade velocities. The car that is going faster before the collision will end up slowing down, and the car that is going slower before the collision will end up speeding up.

After → 2 m/s

→ 4 m/s

Momentum = _____ kg·m/s to the right
Total momentum = _____ kg·m/s _____

Momentum = _____ kg·m/s to the right

"Sticky" Collisions

Sometimes objects end up sticking together during a collision. These two cars, which have the same mass, got tangled together after they collided. Since the green car was at rest and had a momentum of zero, only the blue car had any momentum before the collision. After they collided and stuck together, the cars shared that momentum. The total momentum of the two cars stayed the same.

Before

 4 m/s   0 m/s

100 kg   100 kg

Momentum = _____ kg·m/s to the right   Momentum = _____ kg·m/s

Total momentum = _____ kg·m/s _____

After

 ?

Total mass = _____

Total momentum = _____ kg·m/s _____

What must the velocity be? _____

Lab zone® Do the Quick Lab *Colliding Cars.*

🔑 Assess Your Understanding

1a. Explain How can a heavy moving van have the same momentum as a small motorcycle?

_____

_____

_____

_____

_____

_____

b. Calculate What is the momentum of a 750-kg car traveling at a velocity of 25 m/s?

_____

c. Infer The total momentum of two marbles before a collision is 0.06 kg·m/s. No outside forces act on the marbles. What is the total momentum of the marbles after the collision?

_____

_____

got it? ....

○ **I get it!** Now I know that momentum is conserved unless _____

_____

○ **I need extra help with** _____

Go to **MY SCIENCE COACH** *online for help with this subject.*

Free Fall and Circular Motion

  What Is Free Fall?
PS.10b, PS.10d

  What Keeps a Satellite in Orbit?
PS.10b, PS.10c, PS.10d

my planet diary

Finding Yourself

The GPS (Global Positioning System) is a "constellation" of satellites that orbit 10,600 miles above Earth. The GPS makes it possible for people with ground receivers to pinpoint their geographic location. The first GPS satellites were placed in orbit in 1978. These early satellites were expected to operate for approximately five years. Newer satellites have an expected lifespan of seven to eight years.

GPS Satellites in Orbit

Years	Number of GPS Satellites Launched	Number of Operating GPS Satellites
1978–1982	6	6
1983–1987	4	8
1988–1992	17	21
1993–1997	12	27
1998–2002	5	28
2003–2007	11	31

SCIENCE STATS

Interpret Data Use the data in the table to answer the questions below.

1. What is the total number of satellites launched from 1978 to 2007? How many were still operating as of 2007?

_____

_____

_____

2. How many satellites stopped operating between 2003 and 2007?

_____

_____

_____

> PLANET DIARY Go to **Planet Diary** to learn more about the GPS.

 Do the Inquiry Warm-Up What Makes an Object Move in a Circle?

Vocabulary
- free fall
- satellite
- centripetal force

Skills
- Reading: Relate Cause and Effect
- Inquiry: Create Data Tables

What Is Free Fall?

When the only force acting on an object is gravity, the object is said to be in **free fall.** The force of gravity causes the object to accelerate. **Free fall is motion where the acceleration is caused by gravity.** When something falls on Earth, there is fluid friction from the air around it. This friction acts against gravity, reducing the acceleration of falling objects. Air friction increases as an object falls. If an object falls for long enough, increased air friction will reduce its acceleration to zero. The object will continue to fall, but it will fall at a constant velocity.

Near the surface of Earth, the acceleration due to gravity is 9.8 m/s^2. If there were no air friction, a falling object would have a velocity of 9.8 m/s after one second and 19.6 m/s after two seconds. Since air friction reduces acceleration, an object falling on Earth for one second will actually have a velocity that is less than 9.8 m/s.

FIGURE 1 ....

Free Fall
The photo shows a tennis ball and a crumpled piece of paper of different masses as they fall during a fraction of a second. If the only force acting on them were gravity, they would fall at exactly the same rate and line up perfectly. However, air friction is also present. Air friction has a greater effect on the paper's acceleration than on the tennis ball's acceleration. This causes the tennis ball to fall faster.

Science Standards of Learning

PS.10b Investigate and understand Newton's laws of motion.

PS.10d Investigate and understand technological applications of work, force, and motion.

do the math!

Create Data Tables
Suppose you had a chamber with no air, eliminating the force of air friction. Complete the table below for an object that is dropped from rest. Remember the formula Velocity = Acceleration × Time. The acceleration due to gravity is 9.8 m/s^2.

Time (s)	Velocity (m/s)
0	
1	
2	
3	
4	

 Do the Quick Lab *Which Lands First?*

Assess Your Understanding

got it? ....

O I get it! Now I know that free fall is _____

_____

O I need extra help with _____

Go to MY SCIENCE COACH online for help with this subject.

↻ **Relate Cause and Effect**
On the next page, underline the effect a centripetal force has on an object's motion. Circle the effect of turning off a centripetal force.

What Keeps a Satellite in Orbit?

Objects don't always fall down in straight lines. If you throw a ball horizontally, the ball will move away from you while gravity pulls the ball to the ground. The horizontal and vertical motions act independently, and the ball follows a curved path toward the ground. If you throw the ball faster, it will land even farther in front of you. The faster you throw an object, the farther it travels before it lands.

Satellite Motion This explains how satellites, which are objects that orbit around other objects in space, follow a curved path around Earth. What would happen if you were on a high mountain and could throw a ball as fast as you wanted? The faster you threw it, the farther away it would land. But, at a certain speed, the curved path of the ball would match the curved surface of Earth. Although the ball would keep falling due to gravity, Earth's surface would curve away from the ball at the same rate. The ball would fall around Earth in a circle, as shown in Figure 2.

FIGURE 2 ·······

Satellite Motion

A satellite launched from Earth enters orbit because the curve of its path matches the curved surface of Earth.

✎ **Make Models** On the picture at the right, draw arrows representing the gravitational force on the ball at each point.

[CHALLENGE] Explain why Earth's atmosphere would prevent this baseball from ever actually being thrown into orbit. Why is this not a problem for satellites?

_____

_____

_____

🔑 **Satellites in orbit around Earth continuously fall toward Earth, but because Earth is curved they travel around it.** In other words, a satellite is a falling object that keeps missing the ground! It falls around Earth rather than onto it. Once it has entered a stable orbit, a satellite does not need fuel. It continues to move ahead due to its inertia. At the same time, gravity continuously changes the satellite's direction. Most satellites are launched at a speed of about 7,900 m/s. That's more than 17,000 miles per hour!

Centripetal Force

Many manufactured satellites orbit Earth in an almost circular path. Recall that an object traveling in a circle is accelerating because it constantly changes direction. If an object is accelerating, a force must be acting on it. A force that causes an object to move in a circular path is a **centripetal force** (sen TRIP ih tul). The word *centripetal* means "center-seeking." Centripetal forces always point toward the center of the circle an object is moving in. If you could turn off a centripetal force, inertia would cause the object to fly off in a straight line. For example, the string of a yo-yo being swung in a circle provides a centripetal force. Cutting the string would cut off the centripetal force, and the yo-yo would fly off in a straight line.

apply it!

Identify What is creating the centripetal force in each situation below?

❶ A tetherball swinging around a pole

_____

❷ Mars orbiting around the sun

_____

❸ A child standing on a merry-go-round

_____

Lab zone® Do the Quick Lab *Orbiting Earth.*

🔑 Assess Your Understanding

1a. Identify What is the force that causes objects to move in circles?

_____

b. Predict If Earth's gravity could be turned off, what would happen to satellites that are currently in orbit? Explain your reasoning.

_____

_____

_____

_____

got it?

○ **I get it!** Now I know that satellites stay in orbit because _____

_____

_____

○ **I need extra help with** _____

_____

Go to **my science COACH** *online for help with this subject.*

10 Study Guide

Changes in motion are caused by _____. _____ laws describe these changes in motion.

LESSON 1 The Nature of Force

🔑 Like velocity and acceleration, a force is described by its strength and by the direction in which it acts.

🔑 A nonzero net force causes a change in the object's motion.

Vocabulary
• force • newton
• net force

LESSON 2 Friction and Gravity

🔑 Two factors that affect the force of friction are the types of surfaces involved and how hard the surfaces are pushed together.

🔑 Two factors affect the gravitational attraction between objects: their masses and distance.

Vocabulary
• friction • sliding friction
• static friction • fluid friction
• rolling friction • gravity
• mass • weight

LESSON 3 Newton's Laws of Motion

🔑 Objects at rest will remain at rest and objects moving at a constant velocity will continue moving at a constant velocity unless they are acted upon by nonzero net forces.

🔑 The acceleration of an object depends on its mass and on the net force acting on it.

🔑 If one object exerts a force on another object, then the second object exerts a force of equal strength in the opposite direction on the first object.

Vocabulary
• inertia

LESSON 4 Momentum

🔑 The momentum of a moving object can be determined by multiplying the object's mass by its velocity.

🔑 The total momentum of any group of objects remains the same, or is conserved, unless outside forces act on the objects.

Vocabulary
• momentum
• law of conservation of momentum

LESSON 5 Free Fall and Circular Motion

🔑 Free fall is motion where the acceleration is caused by gravity.

🔑 Satellites in orbit around Earth continuously fall toward Earth, but because Earth is curved they travel around it.

Vocabulary
• free fall • satellite • centripetal force

Review and Assessment

LESSON 1 The Nature of Force

1. When a nonzero net force acts on an object, the force

  a. changes the motion of the object.

  b. must be greater than the reaction force.

  c. does not change the motion of the object.

  d. is equal to the weight of the object.

2. The SI unit of force is the _____

3. **Calculate** What is the net force on the box? Be sure to specify direction.

15 N ➡

⬅ 10 N

_____

LESSON 2 Friction and Gravity

4. Friction always acts

  a. in the same direction as motion.

  b. opposite the direction of motion.

  c. perpendicular to the direction of motion.

  d. at a 30° angle to the direction of motion.

5. The factors that affect the gravitational force

between two objects are _____

_____

6. **List** What are two ways you can increase the frictional force between two objects?

_____

_____

7. **Write About It** Design a ride for an amusement park. Describe the ride and explain how friction and gravity will affect the ride's design.

LESSON 3 Newton's Laws of Motion

8. Which of Newton's laws of motion is also called the law of inertia?

  a. First   **b.** Second

  c. Third   **d.** Fourth

9. Newton's second law states that force is equal

to _____

10. **Interpret Diagrams** Look at the diagram below of two students pulling a bag of volleyball equipment. The friction force between the bag and the floor is 4 N. What is the net force acting on the bag? What is the acceleration of the bag?

➡ 10 N

➡ 15 N

10 kg

4 N ⬅

_____

_____

_____

_____

_____

11. **Apply Concepts** Suppose you are an astronaut making a space walk outside your space station and your jet pack runs out of fuel. How can you use your empty jet pack to get you back to the station?

_____

_____

_____

_____

_____

_____

CHAPTER

10 Review and Assessment

LESSON 4 Momentum

12. Momentum is calculated by multiplying

   a. mass times velocity. **b.** weight times mass.

   c. force times speed. **d.** inertia times force.

13. The SI unit of momentum is _____

14. **Explain** How can two objects of different masses have the same momentum?

_____
_____
_____
_____

15. **Design Experiments** Design an experiment in which you could show that momentum is not conserved in a collision between two marbles when friction is present.

_____
_____
_____
_____
_____
_____
_____
_____
_____
_____

16. Write About It Pick two sports. Explain how knowing about momentum could help you predict what will happen in the game when you watch these sports on TV.

LESSON 5 Free Fall and Circular Motion

17. Satellites remain in orbit around Earth because

   a. the moon's gravitational pull on them is equal to Earth's pull.

   b. no forces act on them.

   c. their motors keep them moving in circles.

   d. the curve of their paths as they fall matches the curve of Earth.

18. Centripetal forces always point _____

_____

19. **Calculate** Determine the velocity of an object that started from rest and has been in free fall for 10 seconds. Assume there is no air resistance.

_____
_____

APPLY THE BIG Q How do objects react to forces?

20. Forces are all around you. Describe an example of each of Newton's laws of motion that you experience before you get to school in the morning.

_____
_____
_____
_____
_____
_____
_____
_____
_____

Read each question and choose the best answer.

1 In the balloon diagram, the two forces don't cancel each other out because—

Force Force   Motion

A they are not equal

B they both act on the air

C they both act on the balloon

D they act on different objects

2 What force makes it less likely for a person to slip on a dry sidewalk than on an icy sidewalk?

F gravity

G friction

H inertia

J momentum

3 A 5-kg cat accelerates at a rate of 2 m/s². What is the net force acting on the cat?

A 10 N

B 7 N

C 3 N

D 2.5 N

4 According to Newton's first law, what will plates at rest on a tablecloth do when the tablecloth is pulled out from under them? (Ignore outside forces such as friction.)

F fly off the table and hit the ground

G accelerate with the tablecloth

H resist the change in motion and stay at rest

J accelerate in the opposite direction from the tablecloth

5 In a game of tug-of-war, you pull on the rope with a force of 100 N to the right and your friend pulls on the rope with a force of 100 N to the left. What is the net force on the rope?

A 200 N to the right

B 200 N to the left

C 0 N

D 100 N to the right

6 Earth exerts a downward force of 3,920 N on this 400-kg car, causing it to fall. What is the strength and direction of the force the car exerts on Earth?

F 3,920 N upward

G 3,520 N downward

H 400 N upward

J 9.8 N downward

safety restraints

Did you wear your seat belt the last time you rode in a car? Seat belts are safety restraints designed to protect you from injury while you travel in a moving vehicle, whether you stop suddenly to avoid a crash or are stopped suddenly by a crash.

Without a seat belt, inertia would cause the driver and passengers in a car that suddenly stopped to continue traveling forward. Without a restraint, a 75-kilogram driver driving at 50 km/h would experience 12,000 newtons of force in a crash! A safety restraint prevents that forward motion and keeps the driver and passengers safe.

Safety harnesses and seat belts are available in many different designs. Most seat belts are three-point harnesses. Five- and seven-point harnesses are used in vehicles like race cars and fighter jets.

Race car drivers travel at higher speeds than most drivers experience. A five-point harness provides extra security at these high speeds. ▼

Debate It Most states have laws that require drivers and passengers to wear seat belts. Research the seat belt laws in your state, and participate in a class debate about whether the seat belts are strong enough.

 PS.1k

SUPERLUBRICITY

Get a Grip!

There is a substance that doesn't play by the rules of friction. You might be surprised to know it is graphite—the same material found in your pencils, and it has a quality called superlubricity!

When two pieces of graphite slide across each other, if the layers are properly arranged, friction almost disappears. This property makes graphite an excellent dry lubricant. Unlike oils and water- or silicon-based lubricants, graphite won't wet or damage the materials being lubricated.

Scientists are studying graphite because, while they can observe superlubricity, they still can't really describe how it works. Studies are being done to figure out the models of superlubricity, or how it works in different situations.

Test It Find more information about graphite and superlubricity. Design an experiment using lead (which contains graphite) from your pencils to test the friction of graphite sliding across other materials. Keep track of your results and present your findings in a series of graphs and charts.

 PS.1b, PS.1g, PS.1j, PS.1l

Colored scanning tunneling micrograph of the surface of graphite. The hexagonal pattern of the graphite surface is related to the way the carbon atoms are arranged. ▼

Graphite is a form of carbon. When it is properly prepared, two layers of graphite can slide across each other with almost no friction. ▶

HOW CAN A MECHANIC LIFT A RACE CAR?

THE BIG ? How do machines make it easier to do work?

This Formula 1 race car is waved into the pit, where a group of mechanics is ready to replace the tires. Formula 1 race cars are heavy—they must have a mass of at least 605 kg, including the driver. The pit crew can't lift the car or replace the tires by hand, so they use many tools to help get the job done. With the right tools, the pit crew can quickly get their car back into the race. **Develop Hypotheses** **How does a mechanic lift up a heavy race car?**

> **UNTAMED SCIENCE** Watch the **Untamed Science** video to learn more about work and machines.

_____

_____

_____

_____

_____

Work and Machines

11 Getting Started

Check Your Understanding

1. **Background** Read the paragraph below and then answer the question.

Charles wants to move his bed across the room, but the **weight** of the bed is too great for him to lift it. However, he can generate enough **force** to push the bed.

> A **force** is a push or pull exerted on an object.
>
> **Weight** is a measure of the force of gravity on an object.

- What forces are acting on the bed as Charles pushes it across the floor?

_____

_____

> MY READING WEB If you had trouble completing the question above, visit **My Reading Web** and type in *Work and Machines.*

Vocabulary Skill

Identify Multiple Meanings Some familiar words have more than one meaning. Words you use every day may have different meanings in science. Look at the different meanings of the words below.

Word	Everyday Meaning	Scientific Meaning
work	*n.* A job or responsibility Example: She carried her backpack to work every day.	*n.* The product of a force and the distance over which that force is exerted Example: It takes twice as much work to lift a suitcase 2 meters as it does to lift it 1 meter.
machine	*n.* A motorized device Example: A washing machine contains a large rotating basin.	*n.* Any device that makes work easier Example: A wheelbarrow is a machine that lets you lift more weight than you normally could.

2. **Quick Check** Circle the sentence below that uses the scientific meaning of the word *work.*
   - Jim did **work** on the bed to move it out of his room.
   - Tina had a lot of **work** to do at the end of the semester.

work

simple machine

inclined plane

pulley

Chapter Preview

LESSON 1
- work
- joule
- power
- watt

↻ **Identify Supporting Evidence**
△ **Calculate**

LESSON 2
- machine
- input force
- output force
- mechanical advantage
- efficiency

↻ **Compare and Contrast**
△ **Predict**

LESSON 3
- simple machine
- inclined plane
- wedge
- screw
- lever
- fulcrum

↻ **Relate Cause and Effect**
△ **Infer**

LESSON 4
- pulley
- wheel and axle
- compound machine

↻ **Summarize**
△ **Classify**

▷ VOCAB FLASH CARDS For extra help with vocabulary, visit **Vocab Flash Cards** and type in *Work and Machines.*

Work and Power

UNLOCK
THE BIG
?

🔑 **How Is Work Defined?**
PS.10c, PS.10d

🔑 **What Is Power?**
PS.1g, PS.10c, PS.10d

my planeT DiaRY

Feats of Strength

You've heard of weight-lifting, but bus-pulling? People have made a sport out of pulling huge objects using their muscles—sometimes their ears! Talk about extreme sports!

Manjit Singh used his ears to drag this double-decker bus for 5 meters. David Huxley pulled an airplane for more than 90 meters, landing him in the *Guinness World Records* book. These competitors have certainly worked hard to get to the top.

FUN FACT

Answer the questions below.

1. What factors might have affected how much work these competitors did?

_____

_____

2. Name an everyday task that you would consider to be a lot of work.

_____

_____

▶ PLANET DIARY Go to **Planet Diary** to learn more about feats of strength.

Do the Inquiry Warm-Up
Pulling at an Angle.

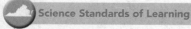
Science Standards of Learning

PS.10c Investigate and understand work, force, mechanical advantage, efficiency, and power.

PS.10d Investigate and understand technological applications of work, force, and motion.

How Is Work Defined?

If you push a child on a swing, you are doing work on the child. If you pull your books out of your backpack, you do work on your books. In scientific terms, you do **work** any time you exert a force on an object that causes the object to move some distance.

🔑 **Work is done on an object when the object moves in the same direction in which the force is exerted.**

Vocabulary
- work
- power
- joule
- watt

Skills
- Reading: Identify Supporting Evidence
- Inquiry: Calculate

No Work Without Motion Suppose you push on a car that is stuck in the mud. You certainly exert a force on the car, so it might seem as if you do work. But if the force you exert does not make the car move, you are not doing any work on it. To do work on an object, the object must move some distance as a result of your force. If the object does not move, no work is done, no matter how much force is exerted.

Force in the Same Direction Think about carrying your backpack to school in the morning. You know that you exert a force on your backpack when you carry it, but you do not do any work on it. To do work on an object, the force you exert must be in the same direction as the object's motion. When you carry an object while walking at constant velocity, you exert an upward force on the object. The motion of the object is in the horizontal direction. Since the force is vertical and the motion is horizontal, you don't do any work.

Figure 1 shows three different ways to move a cello. You can lift it off the ground and carry it, you can push it parallel to the ground, or you can pull it at an angle to the ground. The weight of the cello is the same in each situation, but the amount of work varies.

FIGURE 1 ··

Force, Motion, and Work
The amount of work that you do on something depends on the direction of your force and the object's motion. ✎ **Describe** Suppose you are moving a rolling suitcase. Describe three ways of moving it that require different amounts of work.

The lifting force is not in the direction of the motion, so no work is done.

Force

Direction of motion

The force acts in the same direction as the motion, so the maximum work is done.

Direction of motion

Force

Only the horizontal part of the force does work to move the cello case.

Direction of motion

Force

Part that does no work

Part that does the work

Two factors affect the amount of work April does to hand her friend an instrument: the force she must apply and the distance she must apply the force through.

FIGURE 2 ·····················

> INTERACTIVE ART **Amount of Work**

When April lifts a trumpet or a tuba up the stairs, she does work.

✏ **Draw Conclusions** If April's friend wanted to reduce the amount of work April needed to do to hand the trumpet to him, where could he stand? Circle the step(s). If the stage were higher, what would happen to the total amount of work required to lift the trumpet from the floor to the stage?

---

did you **know?** ·····················

Participants in the Empire State Building Run-Up race up the skyscraper's stairs. For a 500 N person to climb 1,576 steps (320 m) it takes 160,000 J of work. That's enough work to lift an elephant over 3 m!

Calculating Work Look at **Figure 2**. Which do you think involves more work: lifting a 40-newton tuba up three steps (about 0.5 meters), or lifting a 5-newton trumpet up the same three steps? Your common sense may suggest that lifting a heavier object requires more work than lifting a lighter object. This is true. But is it more work to lift an instrument up three steps or up to the top story of a building? As you might guess, moving an object a greater distance requires more work than moving the same object a shorter distance.

The amount of work you do depends on both the amount of force you exert and the distance the object moves. **The amount of work done on an object can be determined by multiplying force times distance.**

$$\text{Work} = \text{Force} \times \text{Distance}$$

When you lift an object, the upward force you exert must be at least equal to the object's weight. So, to lift the trumpet, you would have to exert a force of 5 newtons. The distance you lift the trumpet is 0.5 meters. The amount of work you do on the trumpet can be calculated using the work formula.

$$\text{Work} = \text{Force} \times \text{Distance}$$

$$\text{Work} = 5 \text{ N} \times 0.5 \text{ m}$$

$$\text{Work} = 2.5 \text{ N·m}$$

To lift the tuba, you would have to exert a force of 40 newtons. So the amount of work you do would be 40 newtons × 0.5 meters, or 20 N·m. You do more work to lift the heavier object.

When force is measured in newtons and distance in meters, the SI unit of work is the newton-meter (N•m). This unit is also called a **joule** (JOOL) in honor of James Prescott Joule, a physicist who studied work in the mid-1800s. One joule (J) is the amount of work you do when you exert a force of 1 newton to move an object a distance of 1 meter. It takes 2.5 joules of work to lift the trumpet up three steps. Lifting the tuba the same distance requires 20 joules of work.

apply it!

The climber on the right does work on his equipment as he carries it up the mountain.

❶ On a warm day, the climber does 3,000 J of work to get his pack up the mountain. On a snowy day, he adds equipment to his pack. If he climbs to the same height, he would do (more/less/the same amount of) work.

❷ If the climber's pack stayed the same weight and the climber only climbed halfway up, he would do (more/less/the same amount of) work.

❸ **Calculate** How much work does the climber do on his pack if his pack weighs 90 N and he climbs to a height of 30 m?

_____

❹ **CHALLENGE** On a different trip, the climber's pack weighs twice as much and he climbs twice as high. How many times more work does he do on this pack than the one in question 3?

_____

Do the Quick Lab
What is Work?

🔑 Assess Your Understanding

1a. Describe A waiter carries a 5-newton tray of food while he walks a distance of 10 meters. Is work done on the tray? Why or why not?

_____

_____

_____

b. Explain You're holding your dog's leash and trying to stand still as he pulls on the leash at an angle. You move forward. (All of/Some of/None of) his force does work on you.

c. Calculate How much work do you do when you push a shopping cart with a force of 50 N for a distance of 5 m?

_____

got it? ....

○ I get it! Now I know that work is _____

○ I need extra help with _____

    Go to MY SCIENCE COACH *online for help with this subject.*

Science Standards of Learning

PS.1g Construct and interpret data tables showing the independent and dependent variables, derived quantities, and the number of trials.

PS.10c Investigate and understand work, force, mechanical advantage, efficiency, and power.

PS.10d Investigate and understand technological applications of work, force, and motion.

Identify Supporting Evidence Underline details and examples that support the main idea of this section.

What Is Power?

If you carry a backpack up a flight of stairs, the work you do is the same whether you walk or run. The amount of work you do on an object is not affected by the time it takes to do the work. But scientists keep track of how fast work is done with a rate called power.

Power is the rate at which work is done. **Power equals the amount of work done on an object in a unit of time.** You need more power to run up the stairs with your backpack than to walk because it takes you less time to do the same work.

You can think of power in another way. An object that has more power than another object does more work in the same time. It can also mean doing the same amount of work in less time.

Calculating Power

Whenever you know how fast work is done, you can calculate power. Power is calculated by dividing the amount of work done by the amount of time it takes to do the work. This can be written as the following formula.

$$\text{Power} = \frac{\text{Work}}{\text{Time}}$$

Since work is equal to force times distance, you can rewrite the equation for power as follows.

$$\text{Power} = \frac{\text{Force} \times \text{Distance}}{\text{Time}}$$

FIGURE 3 ....

Work and Power

April carried her moving boxes up a flight of stairs. Notice how much time it took her.

Estimate Suppose April ran instead. Fill in the second panel to show how much time it would take her.

Power Units

You may have heard car advertisements mention horsepower. The term isn't misleading. It's the same kind of power you just learned how to calculate. When work is measured in joules and time in seconds, the SI unit of power is the joule per second (J/s). This unit is also known as the watt (W). One joule of work done in one second is one **watt** of power. In other words, 1 J/s = 1 W. A watt is very small, so power is often measured in larger units such as kilowatts or horsepower. One kilowatt (kW) equals 1,000 watts. One horsepower equals 746 watts.

Vocabulary Identify Multiple Meanings What is the scientific meaning of *power*?

_____

_____

_____

do the math!

When a tow truck pulls a car, it applies a force over a distance. Work is done in a horizontal direction. **Calculate** Complete the table by calculating the power of the tow truck in each case.

Recall the formula for power is

$$\text{Power} = \frac{\text{Work}}{\text{Time}}$$

If a tow truck does 10,000 J of work in 5 seconds, then the power of the truck is calculated as follows.

$$\text{Power} = \frac{10,000 \text{ J}}{5 \text{ s}} = 2,000 \text{ W}$$

Tow Truck Power

Work (J)	Time (s)	Power (W)
120,000	60	_____
69,000	30	_____
67,500	45	_____

Lab zone® Do the Quick Lab *Investigating Power.*

Assess Your Understanding

got it? ....

○ I get it! Now I know that power _____

_____

○ I need extra help with _____

Go to my science coach online for help with this subject.

Understanding Machines

UNLOCK THE BIG ?

🔑 **What Does a Machine Do?**
PS.10c, PS.10d

🔑 **What Is Mechanical Advantage?**
PS.1i, PS.1j, PS.10c, PS.10d

🔑 **What Is Efficiency?**
PS.10c, PS.10d

MY PLANET DIARY

FUN FACT

Sticks and Stones

When you need to peel an apple or open a can of soup, you reach for the right tool to do the job.

Some animals use items such as sticks and rocks to make finding or eating their food easier. For example, woodpecker finches and capuchin monkeys use sticks to get food out of places they can't reach. Sea otters and Egyptian vultures both use rocks as tools. Otters use rocks to pry shellfish away from other rocks. Egyptian vultures use their beaks to pick up rocks and break open eggs to eat.

Communicate Discuss these questions with a partner. Write your answers below.

1. How does the rock make it easier for the chimpanzee in the photo to crack open nuts?

_____

_____

_____

_____

_____

2. What human tools would you use to do the same job?

_____

_____

_____

> PLANET DIARY Go to **Planet Diary** to learn more about tools.

Do the Inquiry Warm-Up
Is It a Machine?

Vocabulary

- machine
- input force
- output force
- mechanical advantage
- efficiency

Skills

⟳ Reading: Compare and Contrast

△ Inquiry: Predict

What Does a Machine Do?

What do you picture when you hear the word *machine*? You may think of machines as complex gadgets with motors, but a machine can be as simple as a ramp. **Machines** are devices that allow you to do work in an easier way. Machines do not reduce the amount of work you do. Instead, they just change the way you do work. In **Figure 1,** April does the same amount of work to move her speaker onto the stage whether or not she uses a ramp. The ramp makes that work easier. 🔑 **A machine makes work easier by changing at least one of three factors: the amount of force you exert, the distance over which you exert your force, or the direction in which you exert your force.**

Input Versus Output When you do work, the force you exert is called the **input force.** You exert your input force over the input distance. In **Figure 1B,** April's input force is the force she uses to pull the speaker up the ramp. The input distance is the length of the ramp. The machine exerts the **output force** over the output distance. The weight of the speaker is the output force. The height of the ramp is the output distance. Input force times input distance equals input work. Output force times output distance equals output work. Since machines do not reduce the work you do, your output work can never be greater than your input work.

Science Standards of Learning

PS.10c Investigate and understand work, force, mechanical advantage, efficiency, and power.

PS.10d Investigate and understand technological applications of work, force, and motion.

FIGURE 1 ·····························

Using Machines

Using a ramp makes it easier for April to move the speaker onto the stage.

✏️ **Interpret Diagrams** In Figure 1B, draw a line that represents April's output distance and an arrow that represents her output force.

A Without a machine, your input force is the same as your output force, and your input distance is the same as your output distance.

Force

Distance

Input force

Input distance

B A ramp allows you to exert a smaller input force, but your input distance increases.

FIGURE 2 ·······································

Making Work Easier

The devices shown all make work easier in different ways. The arrows on the photos show how the machines change input work.

Input force

Output force

Input distance

Output distance

Changing Force In some machines, the output force is *greater* than the input force. How can this happen? Recall the formula for work: **Work = Force × Distance**. If the amount of work stays the same, a decrease in force means an increase in distance. So if a machine allows you to use less input force to do the same amount of work, you must apply that smaller input force over a greater distance.

You see machines that work like this every day. How hard would it be to turn on a faucet that didn't have a handle? Since the handle is wider than the shaft of the faucet, your hand turns a greater distance than it would if you turned the shaft directly. Turning the handle a greater distance allows you to use less force.

Changing Distance In some machines, the output force is less than the input force. This kind of machine allows you to exert your input force over a shorter distance. In order to apply a force over a shorter distance, you need to apply a greater input force. When do you use this kind of machine? Think of a pair of chopsticks. When you use chopsticks to eat, you move the hand holding the chopsticks a short distance. The other end of the chopsticks moves a greater distance, allowing you to pick up and eat a large piece of food with a small movement.

> Complete the equation below. Be sure to describe each quantity as *large* or *small*.

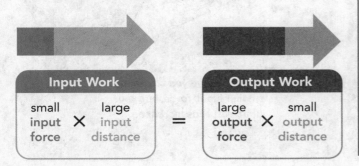

Input Work			Output Work	
small **input force**	× large **input distance**	=	large **output force**	× small **output distance**

Input Work			Output Work	
_____ _____	× small **input distance**	=	small **output force**	× _____ _____

Input
direction

Output
direction

Changing Direction
Some machines don't change either force or distance. The photo above shows a machine called a *pulley* attached to a bucket. (You'll learn more about pulleys soon.) The pulley doesn't increase input force or distance. However, by changing the direction of the input force, the pulley makes it much easier to move the bucket to the top of a building—you can just pull down on the rope. Without a pulley, you would have to carry the bucket up a ladder or staircase. A flagpole rigging is also a pulley.

Complete the equation below. Be sure to describe each quantity as *large* or *small*.

Input Work			Output Work	
___ × ___	=	___ × ___		

Lab® zone Do the Quick Lab
Going Up.

Assess Your Understanding

1a. List Name two examples of machines for which the output force is greater than the input force.

_____

_____

b. Apply Concepts Suppose that you use a pair of chopsticks and apply a force of 1 N over a distance of 0.01 m. How much work do you do? If the output force of the chopsticks is only 0.5 N, how far do the tips of the chopsticks move?

_____

_____

got it?...

○ **I get it!** Now I know that machines make work easier by _____

_____

_____

○ **I need extra help with** _____

Go to MY SCIENCE ⓢ COACH *online for help with this subject.*

🔄 **Compare and Contrast** On these two pages, underline the sentences that explain how to distinguish among machines based on their mechanical advantages.

FIGURE 3 ·····················

Mechanical Advantage
Drums are tuned by tightening and loosening bolts. Drum keys make the bolts easier to turn.
✏️ **Identify Draw an arrow for the key's output force.**

What Is Mechanical Advantage?

You've just learned how to describe machines using words, but you can also describe machines with numbers. A machine's **mechanical advantage** is the number of times a machine increases a force exerted on it. 🔧 **The ratio of output force to input force is the mechanical advantage of a machine.**

$$\text{Mechanical advantage} = \frac{\text{Output force}}{\text{Input force}}$$

Increasing Force When the output force is greater than the input force, the mechanical advantage of a machine is greater than 1. You exert an input force of 10 newtons on a can opener, and the opener exerts an output force of 30 newtons. The mechanical advantage of the can opener is calculated below.

$$\frac{\text{Output force}}{\text{Input force}} = \frac{30 \text{ N}}{10 \text{ N}} = 3$$

The can opener triples your input force!

Increasing Distance When a machine increases distance, the output force is less than the input force. The mechanical advantage is less than 1. If input force is 20 newtons and the output force is 10 newtons, the mechanical advantage is shown below.

$$\frac{\text{Output force}}{\text{Input force}} = \frac{10 \text{ N}}{20 \text{ N}} = 0.5$$

Your input force is cut in half, but your input distance is doubled.

When April provides an input force of 10 N, the drum key provides an output force of 15 N.

Input force

Is the output force acting in the same direction as the input force? _____

Calculate the mechanical advantage of the drum key.

Since the drum key increases April's input force, is her input distance greater or smaller than the key's output distance?

THE DEAD ELECTRONS

Changing Direction What can you predict about the mechanical advantage of a machine that changes the direction of the force? If only the direction changes, input force will be the same as the output force. The mechanical advantage will always be 1.

do the math!

The graph shows input and output force data for three different ramps. Use the graph to answer the questions below. (The actual ramps are not pictured. Do not confuse the lines in the graph with the ramps themselves!)

1 **Read Graphs** If an 80 N input force is exerted on Ramp 2, what is the output force?

_____

2 **Interpret Data** Find the slope of the line for each ramp.

3 **Draw Conclusions** Why does the slope represent each ramp's mechanical advantage?

Mechanical Advantages of Ramps

4 **Graph** On the graph above, plot a line for a ramp that has a mechanical advantage of 3.

5 CHALLENGE **Predict** Which ramp is the steepest? How do you know?

_____

_____

_____

_____

_____

Lab zone Do the Quick Lab
Mechanical Advantage.

🔑 Assess Your Understanding

got it? ···

O **I get it!** Now I know that mechanical advantage _____

_____

O **I need extra help with** _____

Go to MY SCIENCE ⓢ COACH *online for help with this subject.*

Science Standards of Learning

PS.10c Investigate and understand work, force, mechanical advantage, efficiency, and power.

PS.10d Investigate and understand technological applications of work, force, and motion.

What Is Efficiency?

So far you have assumed that the work you put into a machine is exactly equal to the work done by the machine. In an ideal situation, this would be true. In real situations, however, the output work is always less than the input work.

Overcoming Friction
If you have ever tried to cut something with rusty scissors, you know that a large part of your work is wasted overcoming the friction between the parts of the scissors.

All machines waste some work overcoming the force of friction. The less friction there is, the closer the output work is to the input work. The **efficiency** of a machine compares output work to input work. Efficiency is expressed as a percentage. The higher the percentage, the more efficient the machine is. If you know the input work and output work for a machine, you can calculate a machine's efficiency.

Calculating Efficiency
 To calculate the efficiency of a machine, divide the output work by the input work and multiply the result by 100 percent. This is summarized by the following formula.

$$\text{Efficiency} = \frac{\text{Output work}}{\text{Input work}} \times 100\%$$

Vocabulary Identify Multiple Meanings Underline the scientific definition of *efficiency* in the text. Then write a sentence that uses the everyday meaning of *efficient*.

_____

_____

_____

_____

_____

1 Calculate the efficiency of this bicycle if the input work to turn the pedals is 45 J and the output work is 30 J. Show your calculations.

_____

_____

_____

_____

2 Predict What will happen to the efficiency of the bike after the gears have been cleaned and the chain has been oiled?

_____

_____

Real and Ideal Machines A machine with an efficiency of 100 percent would be an ideal machine. Since all machines lose work to friction, ideal machines do not exist. All machines have an efficiency of less than 100 percent.

How does this affect mechanical advantage? *Ideal* mechanical advantage is your input distance divided by the machine's output distance. It is often related to the measurements of a machine. What you have calculated so far (output force divided by input force) is *actual* mechanical advantage. If machines were ideal and input work was equal to output work, ideal and actual mechanical advantages would be equal. Because of friction, actual mechanical advantage is always less than ideal mechanical advantage.

FIGURE 4 ....
> REAL-WORLD INQUIRY

An Ideal Machine?
The balls of this Newton's cradle may swing for a long time, but they will eventually come to rest.

✎ **Communicate** With a partner, discuss where in this machine work is lost due to friction. Circle these locations on the photo and explain your reasoning.

Lab® zone

Do the Quick Lab
Friction and Efficiency.

🔑 Assess Your Understanding

2a. Relate Cause and Effect Real machines have an efficiency of less than 100% because some work is wasted to overcome _____

b. Predict What happens to the efficiency of a bicycle as it gets rusty? What must you do to maintain the same amount of output work?

_____

_____

got it? ....

○ **I get it!** Now I know that efficiency _____

_____

○ **I need extra help with** _____

Go to MY SCIENCE ⓢ COACH online for help with this subject.

UNLOCK THE BIG ?

🔑 **How Do Inclined Planes Work?**
PS.10c, PS.10d

🔑 **How Are Levers Classified?**
PS.1m, PS.10c, PS.10d

my PLANET DiaRY

Is It a Machine?

Which objects in the photo below are machines? If you guessed the truck and the motorbike, you're correct—but not completely! Remember, a device doesn't have to be complicated or motorized in order to be a machine. Look between the truck and the motorbike. The ramp is a machine. Look at the person rolling the bike up the ramp. His hands hold the handlebars. His knees bend to help him walk. These are examples of simple machines. The motorbike and the truck contain many simple machines. There are dozens of machines in this photo, not just the two with motors.

MISCONCEPTIONS

Communicate Discuss these questions with a partner. Then write your answers below.

1. What kind of work is made easier by the ramp in the picture?

_____

_____

_____

2. What are other examples of ramps that you have seen or used?

_____

_____

> PLANET DIARY Go to **Planet Diary** to learn more about everyday machines.

Lab zone® Do the Inquiry Warm-Up *Inclined Planes and Levers.*

Vocabulary
- simple machine • inclined plane • wedge
- screw • lever • fulcrum

Skills
↻ Reading: Relate Cause and Effect
△ Inquiry: Infer

How Do Inclined Planes Work?

Machines can be as simple as chopsticks or as complex as motor-bikes. Any complex machine can be broken down into smaller build-ing blocks called simple machines. A **simple machine** is the most basic device for making work easier. Three closely related simple machines—the inclined plane, the wedge, and the screw—form the inclined plane family.

Inclined Plane Lifting a heavy object such as a motorbike is much easier with a ramp. A ramp is an example of a simple machine called an inclined plane. An **inclined plane** is a flat, sloped surface.

How It Works **An inclined plane allows you to exert your input force over a longer distance.** As a result, the input force needed is less than the output force. The input force you use on an inclined plane is the force with which you push or pull an object along the slope. The inclined plane's output force is equal to the object's weight.

Mechanical Advantage You can determine the ideal mechanical advantage of an inclined plane by dividing the length of the incline by its height.

Science Standards of Learning

PS.10c Investigate and understand work, force, mechanical advantage, efficiency, and power.

PS.10d Investigate and understand technological applications of work, force, and motion.

apply it!

❶ Imagine you were pushing a wheelchair up the ramps in the drawing above. Which would be the hardest to use? Why?

_____

❷ Calculate the ideal mechanical advantage of each ramp using the following formula.

$$\text{Ideal mechanical advantage} = \frac{\text{Length of ramp}}{\text{Height of ramp}}$$

_____

_____

❸ The ramp with the (smallest/greatest) mechanical advantage is the steepest.

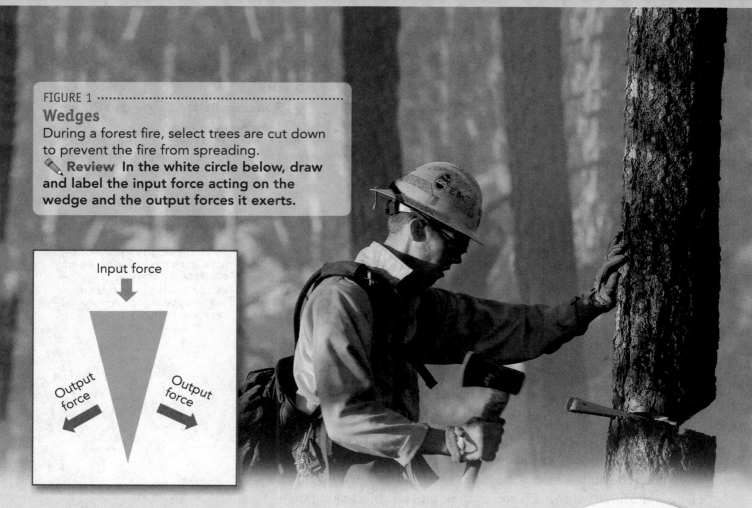

FIGURE 1

Wedges

During a forest fire, select trees are cut down to prevent the fire from spreading.

✏️ **Review** In the white circle below, draw and label the input force acting on the wedge and the output forces it exerts.

Input force

Output force

Output force

Wedge

If you've ever sliced an apple with a knife or pulled up a zipper, you are familiar with another simple machine known as a wedge. A **wedge** is a device that is thick at one end and tapers to a thin edge at the other end.

How It Works Think of a wedge as an inclined plane (or two back-to-back inclined planes) that moves. 🔑 **When you use a wedge, instead of moving an object along the inclined plane, you move the inclined plane itself.** For example, when an ax is used to split wood, the ax handle exerts a force on the blade of the ax, which is the wedge. That force pushes the wedge down into the wood. The wedge in turn exerts an output force at a 90° angle to its slope, splitting the wood in two.

Mechanical Advantage The ideal mechanical advantage of a wedge is determined by dividing the length of the wedge by its width. The longer and thinner a wedge is, the greater its mechanical advantage. When you sharpen a knife, you make the wedge thinner. This increases its mechanical advantage. That is why sharp knives cut better than dull knives.

$$\text{Ideal mechanical advantage} = \frac{\text{Length of wedge}}{\text{Width of wedge}}$$

Calculate the ideal mechanical advantage of the firefighter's wedge if it is 4 cm wide and 22 cm long.

_____

_____

Screw

Like a wedge, a **screw** is a simple machine that is related to the inclined plane. A screw can be thought of as an inclined plane wrapped around a cylinder.

How It Works When you twist a screw into a piece of wood, you exert an input force on the screw. **The threads of a screw act like an inclined plane to increase the distance over which you exert the input force.** As the threads of the screw turn, they exert an output force on the wood. Friction holds the screw in place. Other examples of screws include bolts, drills, and jar lids.

Mechanical Advantage Think of the length around the threads of a screw as the length of an inclined plane and the length of the screw as the height of an inclined plane. The ideal mechanical advantage of the screw is the length around the threads divided by the length of the screw—just as the ideal mechanical advantage of an inclined plane is its length divided by its height. The closer together the threads of a screw are, the greater the mechanical advantage.

FIGURE 2 ·······································

Screws

The diagram below shows a screw with ten threads.
✎ **Calculate** What is the mechanical advantage of the screw on the left? CHALLENGE On the smooth screw next to it, draw in the threads to make a screw that is the same length but would be easier to screw into a piece of wood. There is a hint in the text. Find it and circle it.

Input force turns.

Length of thread stretched out = 24 cm

3 cm

Output force is down.

$$\text{Ideal mechanical advantage} = \frac{\text{Length around threads}}{\text{Length of screw}}$$

_____

_____

Lab zone® Do the Lab Investigation *Angling for Access.*

Assess Your Understanding

1a. List List three closely related simple machines in the inclined plane family. _____

_____

b. Explain A simple inclined plane makes work easier by decreasing the input (force/distance) required to move the object.

c. Compare and Contrast Name one way inclined planes and screws are similar and one way they are different.

_____

_____

_____

_____

_____

got it? ·····································

○ **I get it!** Now I know that inclined planes _____

_____

○ **I need extra help with** _____

Go to **MY SCIENCE ⓢ COACH** online for help with this subject.

How Are Levers Classified?

Have you ever ridden on a seesaw or used a spoon to eat your food? If so, then you are already familiar with another simple machine called a lever. A **lever** is a rigid bar that is free to pivot, or rotate, on a fixed point. The fixed point that a lever pivots around is called the **fulcrum.**

How It Works To understand how levers work, think about using a spoon. Your wrist acts as the fulcrum. The bowl of the spoon is placed near your food. When you turn your wrist, you exert an input force on the handle, and the spoon pivots on the fulcrum. As a result, the bowl of the spoon digs in, exerting an output force on your food.

Science Standards of Learning

PS.1m Construct and use models and simulations to illustrate and explain phenomena.

PS.10c Investigate and understand work, force, mechanical advantage, efficiency, and power.

PS.10d Investigate and understand technological applications of work, force, and motion.

⟳ **Relate Cause and Effect**
The How It Works paragraph describes the use of a spoon. Underline the cause and the effect in this paragraph.

FIGURE 3 ···

Levers

A seesaw is a type of lever in which the fulcrum is located halfway between the input and output forces.

✎ **Make Models** In the space to the left, draw a diagram of a seesaw. Label the fulcrum, the input force, and the output force. CHALLENGE The diagrams below show levers in which the fulcrum is not centered. Write the name of a machine that matches each diagram.

Output force   Input force   Fulcrum

Output force   Input force   Fulcrum

Mechanical Advantage

Using a lever like a spoon doesn't increase your input force or change the direction of your input force. Instead, it increases your input distance. When you use a spoon, you only have to move the handle a short distance in order to scoop up food over a longer distance. However, you need to apply a greater force than you would have without the spoon.

The ideal mechanical advantage of a lever is determined using the following formula.

$$\text{Ideal mechanical advantage} = \frac{\text{Distance from fulcrum to input force}}{\text{Distance from fulcrum to output force}}$$

In the case of the spoon, the distance from the fulcrum to the input force is less than the distance from the fulcrum to the output force. This means that the mechanical advantage is less than 1.

Types of Levers

When a spoon is used as a lever, the input force is located between the fulcrum and the output force. But this is not always the case. 🔑 **Levers are classified according to the location of the fulcrum relative to the input and output forces.** The three different classes of levers are explained on the next page.

apply it!

A hockey stick is an example of a lever. Your shoulder acts as the fulcrum of the lever. The output force is exerted where the stick hits the puck. You exert the input force where your bottom hand grips the stick. What is the mechanical advantage of a hockey stick

1 that is gripped at point D and hits the puck at point A? _____

2 that is gripped at point D and hits the puck at point B? _____

3 **Infer** Would the mechanical advantage of a hockey stick ever be greater than 1? Explain.

_____

_____

_____

_____

_____

_____

407

FIGURE 4

▶ ART IN MOTION Three Classes of Levers

The three classes of levers differ in the positions of the fulcrum, input force, and output force. ✏ **Interpret Diagrams** Draw and label the fulcrum, input force, and output force on the second-class and third-class lever photographs.

First-Class Levers

First-class levers change the direction of the input force. They also increase force or distance. Force increases if the fulcrum is closer to the output force. Distance increases if the fulcrum is closer to the input force. Examples of first-class levers include seesaws and scissors.

Second-Class Levers

Second-class levers increase force. They do not change the direction of the input force. Examples include doors, nutcrackers, and bottle openers. The mechanical advantage of second-class levers is always greater than 1.

Third-Class Levers

Third-class levers increase distance, but do not change the direction of the input force. Examples include spoons, shovels, and baseball bats. The mechanical advantage of third-class levers is always less than 1.

If you find this one tricky, look for help on the previous page!

FIGURE 5 ··

Levers in the Body

Levers can be found throughout your body. ✎ **Classify** In the last two panels of the diagram, draw an arrow representing the output force. Then identify the class of lever for each part of the body.

Your biceps muscle provides the input force. The output force is used to lift your arm.

The muscles in the back of your neck provide an input force, and the resulting output force tilts your chin back.

Your calf muscle provides an input force, and the resulting output force raises your body and moves it slightly forward.

Lab zone® Do the Quick Lab *Modeling Levers.*

🗝 Assess Your Understanding

2a. Describe Describe how each class of lever makes work easier.

_____

_____

_____

_____

b. Calculate What is the mechanical advantage of a lever with 2 m between the input force and the fulcrum and 1 m between the output force and the fulcrum? _____

c. Infer What class(es) of lever could the lever from the previous question be? Explain.

_____

_____

_____

_____

_____

_____

_____

_____

got it? ··

○ I get it! Now I know that levers are classified by _____

_____

○ I need extra help with _____

Go to **MY SCIENCE ⓢ COACH** *online for help with this subject.*

409

Putting Machines Together

UNLOCK
THE BIG
?

🔑 **What Simple Machines Make Use of Turning?**
PS.10c, PS.10d

🔑 **How Does a Compound Machine Do Work?**
PS.10c, PS.10d

my planet diary

DISCOVERY

Lidar Alert

One of the oldest forms of transportation in the world—the sailboat—may benefit from new technology: a mobile lidar station. Lidar (short for light detection and ranging) stations sense wind speed and direction using laser beams. The new station, developed by Chinese scientists, fits on a bus that can be parked near bodies of water. Sailors need to know about wind speed and direction to position their sails. With the information they gather from these new lidar stations and the simple machines they use to control their sails, sailors can greatly improve their chances of navigating safely and winning races.

Answer the questions below.

1. Why might sailboat makers incorporate simple machines into their designs?

_____

_____

2. What is another example of pairing advanced technology with simple machines?

_____

_____

_____

▷ PLANET DIARY Go to **Planet Diary** to learn more about boating.

Lab
zone® Do the Inquiry Warm-Up *Machines That Turn.*

Vocabulary
- pulley
- wheel and axle
- compound machine

Skills
- Reading: Summarize
- Inquiry: Classify

What Simple Machines Make Use of Turning?

If you have ever pulled a suitcase with wheels that were stuck, you know that it is easier to move the suitcase when the wheels can turn. **Two simple machines take advantage of turning: the pulley and the wheel and axle.**

How a Pulley Works When you raise a sail on a sailboat, you are using a pulley. A **pulley** is a simple machine made of a grooved wheel with a rope or cable wrapped around it. You use a pulley by pulling on one end of the rope. This is the input force. At the other end of the rope, the output force pulls up on the object you want to move. The grooved wheel turns. This makes it easier to move the rope than if it had just been looped over a stick. To move an object some distance, a pulley can make work easier in two ways. It can decrease the amount of input force needed to lift the object. It can also change the direction of your input force. For example, when you pull down on a flagpole rope, the flag moves up.

Science Standards of Learning

PS.10c Investigate and understand work, force, mechanical advantage, efficiency, and power.

PS.10d Investigate and understand technological applications of work, force, and motion.

Summarize In one or two sentences, summarize what you have learned on this page.

_____

_____

_____

_____

FIGURE 1 ....

Simple Machines in Sailboats

You can find many simple machines on a sailboat. Below are some diagrams of different parts of a sailboat. **Classify Circle the machines on the diagram that you think are pulleys.**

FIGURE 2 ···

> INTERACTIVE ART **Types of Pulleys**

Pulley systems are classified by the number and position of the wheels they contain. ✎ **Classify** Go back to Figure 1 and check your answers. Next to each pulley, label its type.

Mechanical advantage = 1

Mechanical advantage = 2

Mechanical advantage = 3

Fixed Pulley

A fixed pulley changes the direction of force but not the amount applied.

Movable Pulley

A movable pulley decreases the amount of input force needed. It does not change the direction of the force.

Block and Tackle

A block and tackle is a pulley system made up of fixed and movable pulleys.

Types of Pulleys

A pulley that you attach to a structure is a fixed pulley. Fixed pulleys are used at the tops of flagpoles. A movable pulley is attached directly to the object you are attempting to move. Construction cranes often use movable pulleys. Combining fixed and movable pulleys makes a pulley system called a block and tackle. The direction of the input force of a block and tackle could be either up or down depending on the arrangement of the rope and pulleys. The ideal mechanical advantage of a pulley or pulley system is equal to the number of sections of rope that support the object. Don't include the rope on which you pull downward though, because it does not support the object.

apply it!

The pulley system shown here allows the painter to raise or lower himself.

1 Label Suppose the painter pulls down on the rope with just enough force to lift himself. Draw and label arrows to indicate the direction of the input and output forces. Draw one of the arrows longer to indicate which force is greater.

2 Interpret Diagrams The mechanical advantage of this pulley system is _____.

3 CHALLENGE What is the benefit of combining fixed and movable pulleys in a system like this one?

_____

_____

_____

_____

How a Wheel and Axle Works

You use a screwdriver to tighten screws because it is much easier to turn the handle instead of turning the screw itself. A simple machine made of two connected objects that rotate about a common axis is called a **wheel and axle**. The object with the larger radius is the wheel. In a screwdriver, the handle is the wheel and the shaft is the axle. When you turn the wheel, the axle rotates. The axle exerts a larger output force over a shorter distance.

If you apply force to the axle, your output force will be less than your input force. However, it will be exerted over a greater distance. This is how a paddle wheel on a boat works. The boat's motor turns an axle that turns the boat's wheel, pushing the boat forward a greater distance.

Mechanical Advantage

The ideal mechanical advantage of a wheel and axle is the radius of the wheel divided by the radius of the axle. (A radius is the distance from the outer edge of a circle to the circle's center.) The greater the ratio of the wheel radius to the axle radius, the greater the advantage.

> Ideal mechanical advantage = $\dfrac{\text{Radius of wheel}}{\text{Radius of axle}}$
>
> The blue screwdriver has a handle radius of 1.5 cm and a shaft radius of 0.25 cm. What is its mechanical advantage? _____
>
> ✏ Classify Go back to Figure 1 and recheck your answers. If you spot a wheel and axle, draw a box around it.

FIGURE 3 ·······························

Wheel and Axle

The screwdrivers have the same shaft radius. The blue screwdriver has a larger handle radius.

✏ **Infer Circle the screwdriver with the greater mechanical advantage.**

Output force
Input force
Axle
Wheel radius
Axle radius
Wheel

Lab zone® Do the Quick Lab *Building Pulleys.*

🔑 Assess Your Understanding

1a. List List two examples of a wheel and axle. Which of your examples has the greater mechanical advantage?

_____

_____

b. Apply Concepts You exert a 100-N force on a pulley system to lift 300 N. What's the mechanical advantage of this system? How many sections of rope support the weight?

_____

_____

got it?·······························

○ **I get it!** Now I know that pulleys and wheels and axles _____

○ **I need extra help with** _____

Go to **MY SCIENCE** ⓢ **COACH** online for help with this subject.

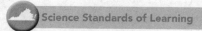
Science Standards of Learning

PS.10c Investigate and understand work, force, mechanical advantage, efficiency, and power.
PS.10d Investigate and understand technological applications of work, force, and motion.

How Does a Compound Machine Do Work?

Suppose you and your neighbors volunteer to clean up a local park. Will the job be easier if just a few people help or if everyone in the neighborhood works together? Getting a job done is usually easier if many people work on it. Similarly, doing work can be easier if more than one simple machine is used. A machine that combines two or more simple machines is called a **compound machine.**

🔑 **Within a compound machine, the output force of one simple machine becomes the input force of another simple machine.** Think about a stapler. The handle is a lever. Each tip of a staple acts as a wedge. Suppose the lever has a mechanical advantage of 0.8 and the wedge has mechanical advantage of 2. If you input a force of 10 N on the lever, the output force of the lever will be 8 N. That 8 N becomes the input force of the wedge, and the final output force is 8 N times 2, or 16 N.

Recall that mechanical advantage is output force divided by input force. The mechanical advantage of the stapler is 16 N divided by 10 N, or 1.6. There is another way to calculate this value. You can multiply the mechanical advantages of the stapler's component machines, the lever (0.8) and the wedge (2). The ideal mechanical advantage of a compound machine is the product of the ideal mechanical advantages of the simple machines that it consists of.

FIGURE 4

Compound Machines
A compound machine consists of two or more simple machines. ✎ **Identify** In the photo at the left, circle and identify three simple machines that make up the apple peeler.

If the mechanical advantages of the component machines in the peeler are 2, 3, and 12, what is the overall mechanical advantage of the apple peeler?

_____

EXPLORE THE BIG ?

How Can I Get That Up There?

How do machines make it easier to do work?

FIGURE 5 ·······································

Piano movers use compound machines to get their job done. ✏ **Calculate the mechanical advantage (MA) of each simple machine in the compound machine.** (The simple machine mounted on the truck has an inner radius of 0.05 m and an outer radius of 0.25 m.) What is the overall mechanical advantage?

Type of Machine:
_____
_____
MA = _____

Type of Machine:
_____
MA = _____

Type of Machine:
_____
MA = _____

Lab zone® Do the Quick Lab *Machines in the Kitchen.*

🔑 Assess Your Understanding

2a. Calculate What is the mechanical advantage of a pencil sharpener made from a wheel and axle with a mechanical advantage of 3 and a wedge with a mechanical advantage of 4?

_____

b. ANSWER THE BIG ? Explain how simple and compound machines make it easier to do work.

_____
_____
_____

_____
_____
_____

got it?

○ **I get it!** Now I know that compound machines _____
_____

○ **I need extra help with** _____

Go to MY SCIENCE ⓢ COACH *online for help with this subject.*

415

Work is done when a _____ is applied in the direction of motion.

_____ make it easier to do work.

LESSON 1 Work and Power

🔑 Work is done on an object when the object moves in the same direction in which the force is exerted.

🔑 The amount of work done on an object can be determined by multiplying force times distance.

🔑 Power equals the amount of work done on an object in a unit of time.

Vocabulary
• work • joule • power • watt

LESSON 2 Understanding Machines

🔑 A machine makes work easier by changing force, distance, or direction.

🔑 The ratio of output force to input force is the mechanical advantage of a machine.

🔑 To calculate the efficiency of a machine, divide the output work by the input work and multiply the result by 100 percent.

Vocabulary
• machine • input force • output force
• mechanical advantage • efficiency

LESSON 3 Inclined Planes and Levers

🔑 Three closely related simple machines—the inclined plane, the wedge, and the screw—form the inclined plane family.

🔑 Levers are classified according to the location of the fulcrum relative to the input and output forces.

Vocabulary
• simple machine • inclined plane
• wedge • screw • lever • fulcrum

LESSON 4 Putting Machines Together

🔑 Two simple machines make use of turning: the pulley and the wheel and axle.

🔑 Within a compound machine, the output force of one simple machine becomes the input force of another simple machine.

Vocabulary
• pulley
• wheel and axle
• compound machine

Review and Assessment

LESSON 1 Work and Power

1. The amount of work done on an object is found by multiplying

    a. force times distance.   **b.** force times time.

    c. power times efficiency.   **d.** speed times time.

2. The rate at which work is done is called

    _____

3. **Calculate** You go rock climbing with a pack that weighs 70 N and you reach a height of 30 m. How much work did you do to lift your pack? If you finished the climb in 10 minutes (600 s), what was your power?

    _____

    _____

    _____

4. **Apply Concepts** What do automobile makers mean when they say their cars are more powerful than their competitors' cars?

    _____

    _____

    _____

5. Write About It Your friend's parents tell him that he needs to do more work around the house. How can your friend use science to explain to them that he does plenty of work just by going through his daily activities?

LESSON 2 Understanding Machines

6. One way a machine can make work easier is by

    a. increasing force   **b.** decreasing time

    c. increasing work   **d.** reducing work

7. The actual mechanical advantage of any machine is its _____ divided by its _____

8. **Solve Problems** You and your friends are building a treehouse, and you need a machine to get a heavy load of wood from the ground to the top of the tree. You set up a pulley system that allows you to pull down on a rope to lift the wood up. You end up able to lift a load you normally couldn't. In what way(s) does your machine make work easier?

    _____

    _____

    _____

    _____

9. **Control Variables** You are designing an experiment to test the efficiency of different bikes. What variables do you have to control?

    _____

    _____

    _____

10. **Relate Cause and Effect** You push on an old skateboard with a force of 20 N. The output force is only 10 N. What is the skateboard's efficiency? How would the efficiency change if the old, rusty ball bearings were replaced with new ones?

    _____

    _____

    _____

LESSON 3 Inclined Planes and Levers

11. Which of these is an example of a simple machine from the inclined plane family?

    a. baseball bat   **b.** jar lid

    c. bottle opener   **d.** wheelbarrow

12. The fixed point that a lever pivots around is called the _____

13. Interpret Diagrams Which ramp has the greater ideal mechanical advantage?

Ramp Y — 4.0 m — 0.5 m

Ramp Z — 3.0 m — 1.0 m

_____

_____

_____

14. Make Judgments Your friend wants to design a wheelbarrow with an ideal mechanical advantage of 5,000. Do you think your friend should consider a different design? Explain.

_____

_____

_____

15. math! On a separate sheet of paper, draw one example of each of the three different classes of levers. For each lever, measure the distance between the fulcrum and the input force, the distance between the fulcrum and the output force, and calculate the ideal mechanical advantage.

LESSON 4 Putting Machines Together

16. Which of these is an example of a wheel and axle?

    a. axe   **b.** seesaw

    c. doorknob   **d.** flagpole rigging

17. A _____ is a system that consists of at least one fixed pulley and one movable pulley.

18. Apply Concepts A circular faucet handle is an example of a wheel and axle. How could you increase the mechanical advantage of a circular faucet handle?

_____

_____

_____

 APPLY THE BIG ?

How do machines make it easier to do work?

19. This paper cutter is a compound machine. How does it make cutting paper easier? What simple machines make up the paper cutter? Describe how they interact.

_____

_____

_____

_____

_____

_____

Virginia SOL Test Prep

Read each question and choose the best answer.

1 The table below shows the input work and output work for four different pulleys. Which pulley has the highest efficiency?

Work of Different Pulleys

Pulley	Input Work	Output Work
Fixed pulley A	20,000 J	8,000 J
Fixed pulley B	20,000 J	10,000 J
Movable pulley	20,000 J	12,000 J
Block and tackle	20,000 J	16,000 J

A Fixed pulley A
B Fixed pulley B
C Movable pulley
D Block and tackle

2 Why does it take more work to carry a 22-N bag of birdseed to the third floor of a house than it takes to move a 16-N bag of cat food to the second floor of a house?

F Work equals distance divided by force and the birdseed requires less force to lift it.

G The force exerted on the birdseed is not the direction of motion.

H The cat food has less mass than the birdseed.

J The birdseed has greater mass and has to be moved farther.

3 The *best* scientific definition of a machine is—

A it is a timesaving device that uses motors and gears

B it changes the amount of input force

C it makes work easier by changing force, distance, or direction

D it can either be simple or compound

4 Which of the following will increase the ideal mechanical advantage of a wheel and axle?

F increasing the wheel's radius
G decreasing the wheel's radius
H increasing the axle's radius
J increasing the wheel's radius and the axle's radius equally

5 Which activity describes work being done on an object?

A walking a dog on a leash
B lifting a bag of groceries
C holding an umbrella still
D pressing a stamp onto an envelope

6 Why would an engineer design a road to wind around a mountain rather than go straight up the side?

F to increase the mechanical advantage
G to decrease the mechanical advantage
H to increase the input force
J to increase the output force

Good Things Come in Small Packages

Imagine a tiny machine that works right inside your cells, delivering medication to specific sites. Scientists are working to build just such machines. Nanomachines, or nanites, are machines whose size is measured in nanometers. One nanometer is equivalent to one billionth (10^{-9}) of a meter. That's pretty tiny—smaller than most people can imagine. In comparison with these tiny machines, red blood cells, which have a diameter of about 7 micrometers (7×10^{-6} of a meter), look huge!

So how do these tiny machines work? Most nanomachines are made of gold or platinum. They use cylindrical carbon molecules or hydrogen peroxide for fuel. Scientists hope that nanomachines will one day use the fuel of a patient's cell to do work.

Some tube-shaped nanomachines convert energy from light into chemical energy and then into mechanical energy to do work. These machines are injected into human cancer cells in the dark. Before they are injected, the tiny machines are loaded with medicine. When scientists expose the machines to light, a chemical reaction causes a wagging motion inside the tube, which releases the medication in exactly the right spot.

Research It Scientists are working to develop a "submarine" nanomachine. How is this new machine different from other medical nanomachines? Draw the submarine and describe its functions.

This image shows an artist's idea of how a nanite might look as it helps fight cancer in the body. ▼

 PS.1k, PS.1m, PS.6b

A new SET OF WHEELS

Students at the Massachusetts Institute of Technology (MIT) have the chance to help 20 million people by taking a class called Wheelchair Design in Developing Countries.

Over the semester, students will learn how to build a wheelchair. They will also study the needs of people who use wheelchairs in developing countries. What's the real test? Designing devices that will actually improve people's lives!

Analyze It Look at the wheelchairs in the photo. Create a graphic organizer in which you identify things someone would need a wheelchair to do, and how a wheelchair feature could meet that need. For example, the user might need to go up or down a steep hill, so the chair should have good brakes and should not be too heavy. Identify and evaluate the scientific knowledge and concepts students may need to apply when creating their wheelchairs.

 PS.1k, PS.1m, PS.1n, PS.10d

SCIENCE ATHLETES
Let the Games Begin

Every year, students from all over the country compete to be the best at everything from chemistry to robot building. What is this scientific pageant of skill and achievement? It's the Science Olympiad™!

In the Mission Possible event, teams of students work all year to invent, design, and build a Rube Goldberg® machine. A Rube Goldberg® machine is a compound machine designed to accomplish a very simple task—and makes you laugh in the process.

◀ This Rube Goldberg® machine takes over 20 steps to perform three tasks. It selects, crushes, and pitches a can into a recycling bin.

Make It Work Divide your class into teams and compete in your own Mission Possible event in which you invent a complex machine to perform a simple task. Score each team's creation!

 PS.1m, PS.10d

WHAT
MAKES THESE
SNOWBOARDERS
"FLY"
DOWNHILL?

How is energy conserved in a transformation?

These women are competing in the sport of snowboard cross. They "fly" down a narrow course, filled with jumps, steep sections, and ramps. Disaster looms at every turn. If they don't crash into each other or fall, then the first one across the finish line wins.

Develop Hypotheses What do you think makes these snowboarders go so fast?

_____

_____

_____

_____

_____

> **UNTAMED SCIENCE** Watch the **Untamed Science** video to learn more about energy.

Energy

Science Standards of Learning

PS.1c, PS.1j, PS.1k, PS.1m, PS.1n,
PS.6a, PS.6b, PS.10c, PS.10d

12 Getting Started

Check Your Understanding

1. Background Read the paragraph below and then answer the question.

> Michael pulls his brother in a wagon. Suddenly, Michael's dog jumps on his brother's lap. Michael continues to pull the wagon, but it is more difficult now. The added **mass** of the dog means that Michael has to generate more **force** to accelerate the wagon to the same **speed**.

> **Mass** is a measure of the amount of matter in an object.
>
> A **force** is a push or pull.
>
> The **speed** of an object is the distance the object travels per unit of time.

- Why is it harder to pull the wagon with the dog in it?

_____

_____

> **MY READING WEB** If you had trouble completing the question above, visit **My Reading Web** and type in *Energy*.

Vocabulary Skill

Identify Multiple Meanings Some familiar words may have different meanings in science. Look at the different meanings of the words below.

Word	Everyday Meaning	Scientific Meaning
energy	*n.* the ability to be active or take part in a vigorous activity **Example:** She had enough *energy* to run for miles.	*n.* the ability to do work or cause change **Example:** The wind can move objects because it has *energy*.
power	*n.* the ability to influence others **Example:** The coach has a lot of *power* over his young athletes.	*n.* the rate at which work is done **Example:** A truck's engine has more *power* than a car's engine.

2. Quick Check Review the sentences below. Then circle the sentence that uses the scientific meaning of the word *energy*.

- A puppy has too much *energy* to be inside the house all day.
- A wrecking ball has enough *energy* to knock down a building.

kinetic energy

gravitational potential energy

600 N

400 N

mechanical energy

energy transformation

Chapter Preview

LESSON 1

- energy
- kinetic energy
- potential energy
- gravitational potential energy
- elastic potential energy

↻ **Relate Cause and Effect**

△ **Calculate**

LESSON 2

- mechanical energy
- nuclear energy
- thermal energy
- electrical energy
- electromagnetic energy
- chemical energy

↻ **Identify the Main Idea**

△ **Classify**

LESSON 3

- energy transformation
- law of conservation of energy

↻ **Identify Supporting Evidence**

△ **Infer**

> VOCAB FLASH CARDS   For extra help with vocabulary, visit **Vocab Flash Cards** and type in *Energy.*

What Is Energy?

- ## How Are Energy, Work, and Power Related?
  PS.6a, PS.10c
- ## What Are Two Types of Energy?
  PS.1j, PS.6a, PS.10c

MY PLANET DIARY

Wind Farms

Did you know that wind can be used to produce electricity? A wind farm is a group of very large windmills, or turbines, placed in a location that gets a lot of wind. The energy of the wind causes the propellers of the turbines to spin. The turbines are connected to generators. When the turbines are spinning, the generators produce electricity. The amount of electricity produced depends on the size of the propellers, the number of turbines, and the strength of the wind.

FUN FACT

Write your answer to the question below.

Analyze Costs and Benefits What are some advantages and disadvantages of using wind energy to create electricity?

_____

_____

_____

_____

_____

> PLANET DIARY Go to **Planet Diary** to learn more about energy.

Lab zone® Do the Inquiry Warm-Up
How High Does a Ball Bounce?

Science Standards of Learning

PS.6a Investigate and understand potential and kinetic energy and how they can be transferred and transformed.

PS.10c Investigate and understand work, force, mechanical advantage, efficiency, and power.

How Are Energy, Work, and Power Related?

Did you put a book in your backpack this morning? If so, then you did work on the book. Recall that work is done when a force moves an object. The ability to do work or cause change is called **energy**.

Work and Energy When you do work on an object, some of your energy is transferred to that object. You can think of work as the transfer of energy. When energy is transferred, the object upon which the work is done gains energy. Energy is measured in joules—the same units as work.

Vocabulary
- energy • kinetic energy • potential energy
- gravitational potential energy • elastic potential energy

Skills
↻ **Reading:** Relate Cause and Effect
△ **Inquiry:** Calculate

Power and Energy You may recall that power is the rate at which work is done. ➤ **Since the transfer of energy is work, then power is the rate at which energy is transferred, or the amount of energy transferred in a unit of time.**

$$\text{Power} = \frac{\text{Energy Transferred}}{\text{Time}}$$

Different machines have different amounts of power. For example, you could use either a hand shovel or a snowblower, like the one in **Figure 1,** to remove snow from your driveway. Each transfers the same amount of energy when it moves the snow the same distance. However, you could move the snow faster using a snowblower than a hand shovel. The snowblower has more power because it transfers the same amount of energy to the snow in less time.

FIGURE 1 ....
Power
The snowblower has more power than the person with the hand shovel.

✎ **Apply Concepts** You could use an elevator or the stairs to lift a box to the tenth floor. Which has greater power? Why?

_____

_____

_____

_____

_____

_____

_____

Lab zone Do the Lab Investigation
Can You Feel the Power?

➤ Assess Your Understanding

got it? ....

○ **I get it!** Now I know that since the transfer of energy is work, then power is _____

_____

_____

○ **I need extra help with** _____

Go to **my science** ⊙ **COACH** online for help with this subject.

Science Standards of Learning

PS.1j Make valid conclusions after analyzing data.

PS.6a Investigate and understand potential and kinetic energy and how they can be transferred and transformed.

PS.10c Investigate and understand work, force, mechanical advantage, efficiency, and power.

What Are Two Types of Energy?

Moving objects, such as the vehicles shown in **Figure 2,** have one type of energy. A rock perched on the edge of a cliff or a stretched rubber band has another type of energy. 🔑 **The two basic types of energy are kinetic energy and potential energy.** Whether energy is kinetic or potential depends on the motion, position, and shape of the object.

Kinetic Energy
A moving object can do work when it strikes another object and moves it. For example, a swinging hammer does work on a nail as it drives the nail into a piece of wood. The hammer has energy because it can do work. The energy an object has due to its motion is called **kinetic energy.**

Factors Affecting Kinetic Energy The kinetic energy of an object depends on both its speed and its mass. Suppose you are hit with a tennis ball that has been lightly tossed at you. It probably would not hurt much. What if you were hit with the same tennis ball traveling at a much greater speed? It would hurt! The faster an object moves, the more kinetic energy it has.

Kinetic energy also increases as mass increases. Suppose a tennis ball rolls across the ground and hits you in the foot. Compare this with getting hit in the foot with a bowling ball moving at the same speed as the tennis ball. The bowling ball is much more noticeable because it has more kinetic energy than a tennis ball. The bowling ball has more kinetic energy because it has a greater mass.

FIGURE 2 ·······················

> ART IN MOTION **Kinetic Energy**

The kinetic energy of an object depends on its speed and mass.

✏️ **Use the diagram to answer the questions.**

1. **Interpret Diagrams** List the vehicles in order of increasing kinetic energy.

   _____

   _____

   _____

2. **Explain** Describe another example of two objects that have different kinetic energies. Explain why their kinetic energies are different.

   _____

   _____

   _____

   _____

   _____

   _____

Calculating Kinetic Energy You can use the following equation to solve for the kinetic energy of an object.

$$\text{Kinetic energy} = \tfrac{1}{2} \times \text{Mass} \times \text{Speed}^2$$

For example, suppose a boy is pulling a 10-kg wagon at a speed of 1 m/s.

$$\text{Kinetic energy of wagon} = \tfrac{1}{2} \times 10 \text{ kg} \times (1 \text{ m/s})^2$$

$$= 5 \text{ kg·m}^2/\text{s}^2 = 5 \text{ joules}$$

$$\text{Note that } 1 \text{ kg·m}^2/\text{s}^2 = 1 \text{ joule}$$

Do changes in speed and mass have the same effect on the kinetic energy of the wagon? No—changing the speed of the wagon will have a greater effect on its kinetic energy than changing its mass by the same factor. This is because speed is squared in the kinetic energy equation. For example, doubling the mass of the wagon will double its kinetic energy. Doubling the speed of the wagon will quadruple its kinetic energy.

Relate Cause and Effect
What has a greater effect on an object's kinetic energy—doubling its mass or doubling its speed? Explain.

_____
_____
_____
_____
_____
_____

do the math!

A girl and her dog are running. The dog has a mass of 20 kg. The girl has a mass of 60 kg.

1 Calculate Suppose both the dog and the girl run at a speed of 2 m/s. Calculate both of their kinetic energies.

Kinetic energy of dog =

Kinetic energy of girl =

2 Calculate Suppose the dog speeds up and is now running at a speed of 4 m/s. Calculate the dog's kinetic energy.

Kinetic energy of dog =

3 Draw Conclusions Are your answers to Questions 1 and 2 reasonable? Explain.

_____
_____
_____
_____
_____

Review Write the SI unit for each quantity in the table.

Quantity	SI Unit
Force	_____
Height	_____
Work	_____
Mass	_____
Energy	_____

Potential Energy

An object does not have to be moving to have energy. Some objects have energy as a result of their shapes or positions. When you lift a book up to your desk from the floor or compress a spring by winding a toy, you transfer energy to it. The energy you transfer is stored, or held in readiness. It might be used later if the book falls or the spring unwinds. Energy that results from the position or shape of an object is called **potential energy.** This type of energy has the potential to do work.

Gravitational Potential Energy

Potential energy related to an object's height is called **gravitational potential energy.** The gravitational potential energy of an object is equal to the work done to lift it to that height. Remember that work is equal to force multiplied by distance. The force you use to lift the object is equal to its weight. The distance you move the object is its height above the ground. You can calculate an object's gravitational potential energy using this equation.

$$\text{Gravitational potential energy} = \text{Weight} \times \text{Height}$$

For example, suppose a book has a weight of 10 newtons (N). If the book is lifted 2 meters off the ground, the book has 10 newtons times 2 meters, or 20 joules, of gravitational potential energy.

FIGURE 3 ·······································

Gravitational Potential Energy

The rock climbers have gravitational potential energy.

Use the diagram to answer the questions.

1. **Identify** Circle the rock climber with the greatest potential energy. Calculate this potential energy. The height to be used is at the rock climber's lowest foot.

   _____

   _____

   _____

   _____

   _____

2. **CHALLENGE** Where would the rock climbers at the top have to be to have half as much potential energy?

   _____

   _____

   _____

Height (m)

6 m —
5 m — 600 N
4 m —
3 m —
2 m — 600 N
1 m —

400 N
400 N

Elastic Potential Energy An object has a different type of potential energy due to its shape. **Elastic potential energy** is the energy associated with objects that can be compressed or stretched. For example, when the girl in **Figure 4** presses down on the trampoline, the trampoline changes shape. The trampoline now has potential energy. When the girl pushes off of the trampoline, the stored energy sends the girl upward.

FIGURE 4 ··

Elastic Potential Energy
The energy stored in a stretched object, such as the trampoline, is elastic potential energy.

✏ **Interpret Diagrams** Rank the amount of elastic potential energy of the trampoline from greatest to least. A ranking of one is the greatest. Write your answers in the circles. Then explain your answers in the space to the right.

_____
_____
_____
_____
_____
_____
_____

 ® **Do the Quick Lab** *Mass, Velocity, and Kinetic Energy.*

⊙ Assess Your Understanding

1a. Identify The energy an object has due to its motion is called (kinetic/potential) energy. Stored energy that results from the position or shape of an object is called (kinetic/potential) energy.

b. Summarize What are the two factors that affect an object's kinetic energy?

_____

c. Apply Concepts What type of energy does a cup sitting on a table have? Why?

_____
_____
_____
_____

got it? ··

○ **I get it!** Now I know that the two basic types of energy are _____

_____

○ **I need extra help with** _____

Go to **my science ⊙ coach** online for help with this subject.

Forms of Energy

UNLOCK THE BIG

🔑 **How Can You Find an Object's Mechanical Energy?**
PS.6a, PS.6b

🔑 **What Are Other Forms of Energy?**
PS.6a, PS.6b

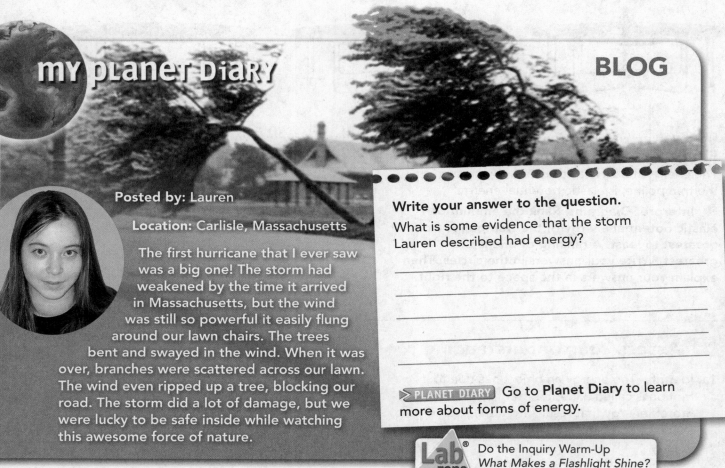

mY planet Diary

BLOG

Posted by: Lauren

Location: Carlisle, Massachusetts

The first hurricane that I ever saw was a big one! The storm had weakened by the time it arrived in Massachusetts, but the wind was still so powerful it easily flung around our lawn chairs. The trees bent and swayed in the wind. When it was over, branches were scattered across our lawn. The wind even ripped up a tree, blocking our road. The storm did a lot of damage, but we were lucky to be safe inside while watching this awesome force of nature.

Write your answer to the question.
What is some evidence that the storm Lauren described had energy?

_____

_____

_____

_____

_____

▶ PLANET DIARY Go to **Planet Diary** to learn more about forms of energy.

Lab® zone Do the Inquiry Warm-Up *What Makes a Flashlight Shine?*

 Science Standards of Learning

PS.6a Investigate and understand potential and kinetic energy and how they can be transferred and transformed.

PS.6b Investigate and understand mechanical, chemical, electrical, thermal, radiant, and nuclear energy and how they can be transferred and transformed.

How Can You Find an Object's Mechanical Energy?

What do a falling basketball, a moving car, and a trophy on a shelf all have in common? They all have mechanical energy. The form of energy associated with the motion, position, or shape of an object is called **mechanical energy.**

Vocabulary
- mechanical energy
- nuclear energy
- thermal energy
- electrical energy
- electromagnetic energy
- chemical energy

Skills
- Reading: Identify the Main Idea
- Inquiry: Classify

Calculating Mechanical Energy

An object's mechanical energy is a combination of its potential energy and its kinetic energy. For example, the basketball in **Figure 1** has both potential energy and kinetic energy. The higher the basketball moves, the greater its potential energy. The faster the basketball moves, the greater its kinetic energy. You can find an object's mechanical energy by adding together the object's kinetic energy and potential energy.

Mechanical energy = Potential energy + Kinetic energy

Sometimes an object's mechanical energy is its kinetic energy or potential energy only. A car moving along a flat road has kinetic energy only. A trophy resting on a shelf has gravitational potential energy only. But both have mechanical energy.

Potential energy = 20 J
Kinetic energy = 2 J
Mechanical energy =

B

FIGURE 1 ·······························
Mechanical Energy
The basketball has mechanical energy because of its speed and position above the ground.

✎ Calculate Solve for the mechanical energy of the basketball at point A and point B.

A

Potential energy = 12 J
Kinetic energy = 10 J
Mechanical energy =
_____

✎ **Draw Conclusions** Why does the ball's gravitational potential energy increase from points A to B?

_____
_____
_____
_____
_____
_____

433

Mechanical Energy and Work An object with mechanical energy can do work on another object. In fact, you can think of mechanical energy, like all forms of energy, as the ability to do work. For example, a basketball does work on the net as it falls through the hoop. The net moves as a result. The more mechanical energy an object has, the more work it can do.

apply it!

The bowling ball does work on the pins when it hits them.

1 Why is the bowling ball able to do work?

_____
_____
_____
_____

2 How should you throw the ball to maximize the amount of work it does on the pins?

_____
_____
_____
_____
_____
_____
_____

3 CHALLENGE In the type of bowling shown in the photo, the ball has a mass of 7.0 kg. In candlepin bowling, the ball has a mass of about 1.0 kg. Does the ball with the greater mass always have the greater mechanical energy? Explain.

_____
_____
_____
_____
_____

Lab zone® Do the Quick Lab *Determining Mechanical Energy.*

Assess Your Understanding

1a. Define Mechanical energy is the form of energy associated with the_____ , _____ , or _____ of an object.

b. Calculate At a certain point the kinetic energy of a falling apple is 5.2 J and its potential energy is 3.5 J. What is its mechanical energy?

_____

c. Infer If an object's mechanical energy is equal to its potential energy, how much kinetic energy does the object have? Explain.

_____
_____
_____
_____
_____

got it? ....

○ **I get it!** Now I know you can find an object's mechanical energy by _____
_____

○ **I need extra help with** _____

Go to MY SCIENCE ⓢ COACH online for help with this subject.

What Are Other Forms of Energy?

So far, you have read about energy that involves the motion, position, or shape of an object. But an object can have other forms of kinetic and potential energy. These other forms are associated with the particles that make up objects. These particles are far too small to see with the naked eye. **Forms of energy associated with the particles of objects include nuclear energy, thermal energy, electrical energy, electromagnetic energy, and chemical energy.**

Nuclear Energy All objects are made up of particles called atoms. The region in the center of an atom is called the nucleus. A type of potential energy called **nuclear energy** is stored in the nucleus of an atom. Nuclear energy is released during a nuclear reaction. One kind of nuclear reaction, known as nuclear fission, occurs when a nucleus splits. A nuclear power plant, like the one shown in **Figure 2,** uses fission reactions to produce electricity. Another kind of reaction, known as nuclear fusion, occurs when the nuclei of atoms fuse, or join together. Nuclear fusion reactions occur constantly in the sun, releasing huge amounts of energy. Only a tiny portion of this energy reaches Earth as heat and light.

Science Standards of Learning

PS.6a Investigate and understand potential and kinetic energy and how they can be transferred and transformed.

PS.6b Investigate and understand mechanical, chemical, electrical, thermal, radiant, and nuclear energy and how they can be transferred and transformed.

Identify the Main Idea
Underline the main idea under the red heading Nuclear Energy.

FIGURE 2 ····························
Nuclear Energy
Controlled nuclear fission reactions occur at some power plants. Nuclear fusion reactions occur in the sun.

✎ **Compare and Contrast** Use the Venn diagram to compare and contrast nuclear fission and nuclear fusion.

Nuclear Fission   Both   Nuclear Fusion

Thermal Energy The particles that make up objects are constantly in motion. This means that they have kinetic energy. These particles are arranged in specific ways in different objects, so they also have potential energy. The total kinetic and potential energy of the particles in an object is called **thermal energy.**

The higher the temperature of an object, the more thermal energy the object has. For example, suppose you heat a pot of water. As heat is applied to the water, the particles in the water move faster on average. The faster the particles move, the greater their kinetic energy and the higher the temperature. Therefore, a pot of water at 75°C, for example, has more thermal energy than the same amount of water at 30°C.

Electrical Energy When you receive a shock from a metal doorknob, you experience electrical energy. The energy of electric charges is **electrical energy.** Depending on whether the charges are moving or stored, electrical energy can be a form of kinetic or potential energy. Lightning is a form of electrical energy. You rely on electrical energy from batteries or electrical lines to run devices such as computers, handheld games, and digital audio players.

FIGURE 3 ·······························
> INTERACTIVE ART **Forms of Energy**
Many objects in this restaurant have more than one form of energy.

✏ Classify **Circle three objects. Describe two forms of energy each object has.**

Electromagnetic Energy

The light you see is one type of electromagnetic energy. **Electromagnetic energy**, also called radiant energy, is a form of energy that travels through space in waves. The source of these waves is vibrating electric charges. These waves do not require a medium, so they can travel through a vacuum, or empty space. This is why you can see the sun and stars.

The microwaves you use to cook your food and the X-rays doctors use to examine patients are also types of electromagnetic energy. Other forms of electromagnetic energy include ultraviolet rays, infrared (or heat) waves, and radio waves. Cell phones send and receive messages using microwaves.

Chemical Energy

Chemical energy is in the foods you eat, in the matches you use to light a candle, and even in the cells of your body. **Chemical energy** is potential energy stored in chemical bonds. Chemical bonds are what hold atoms together. Often when these bonds are broken, this stored energy is released. For example, bonds are broken in your cells and release energy for your body to use.

Vocabulary Identify Multiple Meanings Review the multiple meaning words in the Getting Started section and complete the sentence. During a lightning storm, electric charges move between the clouds and the ground, releasing stored

_____

Lab zone® Do the Quick Lab *Sources of Energy.*

🔑 Assess Your Understanding

2a. Explain Why do the particles of objects have both kinetic and potential energy?

_____

_____

_____

_____

_____

_____

b. Classify The energy you get from eating a peanut butter and jelly sandwich is in the form of _____ energy.

got it? ....

○ **I get it!** Now I know the forms of energy associated with the particles of objects include _____

_____

_____

○ **I need extra help with** _____

Go to MY SCIENCE ⓢ COACH *online for help with this subject.*

Energy Transformations and Conservation

UNLOCK THE BIG ?

🔑 **How Are Different Forms of Energy Related?**
PS.6a, PS.6b

🔑 **What Is the Law of Conservation of Energy?**
PS.1j, PS.1m, PS.6a, PS.6b, PS.10d

my planet Diary

Science Day at the Amusement Park

During science days at Great America Amusement Park™ in Santa Clara, California, the park becomes a giant laboratory! Here is how one investigation might work. You choose a ride like the Drop Tower, which drops you 68 meters in less than four seconds, or the Fire Fall, which contains a series of vertical twists and turns. You observe how your speed and height change during the ride. Then you use your observations to learn about transformations between potential and kinetic energy.

FIELD TRIP

Write your answer to the question below.

How do you think energy is transformed in the Drop Tower?

_____

_____

_____

_____

_____

▶ PLANET DIARY Go to **Planet Diary** to learn more about energy transformations.

Lab zone® Do the Inquiry Warm-Up *What Would Make a Card Jump?*

Science Standards of Learning

PS.6a Investigate and understand potential and kinetic energy and how they can be transferred and transformed.

PS.6b Investigate and understand mechanical, chemical, electrical, thermal, radiant, and nuclear energy and how they can be transferred and transformed.

How Are Different Forms of Energy Related?

What does flowing water have to do with electricity? In a hydro-electric power plant, the mechanical energy of moving water is transformed into electrical energy. 🔑 **All forms of energy can be transformed into other forms of energy.** A change from one form of energy to another is called an **energy transformation.** Some energy changes involve single transformations, while others involve many transformations.

Vocabulary
- energy transformation
- law of conservation of energy

Skills
↻ Reading: Identify Supporting Evidence
△ Inquiry: Infer

Single Transformations Sometimes, one form of energy needs to be transformed into another to get work done. For example, a toaster transforms electrical energy to thermal energy to toast your bread. A cell phone transforms electrical energy to electromagnetic energy that travels to other phones.

Your body transforms the chemical energy in food to the mechanical energy you need to move your muscles. Chemical energy in food is also transformed to the thermal energy your body uses to maintain its temperature.

Multiple Transformations Often, a series of energy transformations is needed to do work. For example, the mechanical energy used to strike a match is transformed first to thermal energy. The thermal energy causes the particles in the match to release stored chemical energy, which is transformed to more thermal energy and to the electromagnetic energy you see as light.

In a car engine, another series of energy conversions occurs. Electrical energy produces a spark. The thermal energy of the spark releases chemical energy in the fuel. The fuel expands as it is broken down into smaller particles. The expansion of the fuel produces pressure on parts of the car. The increased pressure eventually causes the wheels to turn, transforming chemical energy into mechanical energy.

↻ **Identify Supporting Evidence**
Underline the energy transformation that must occur for you to talk on your cell phone.

apply it!

A series of energy transformations must occur for you to ride your bike. Write the forms of energy involved in each transformation.

Reactions occur within the sun to transform _____ energy into _____ energy.

Plants transform _____ energy into _____ energy.

Your body transforms _____ energy into _____ energy to maintain your body temperature.

Your body also transforms _____ energy into _____ energy when you ride your bike.

Kinetic and Potential Energy

The transformation between potential and kinetic energy is one of the most common energy transformations. For example, when you stretch a rubber band, you give it elastic potential energy. If you let it go, the rubber band flies across the room. When the rubber band is moving, it has kinetic energy. The potential energy of the stretched rubber has transformed to the kinetic energy of the moving rubber band. Transformations between kinetic and potential energy can also occur in any object that rises or falls. A falling object, a pendulum, and a pole vault are all examples of these transformations.

Falling Object A transformation between potential and kinetic energy occurs in the ball in **Figure 1.** As the height of the ball decreases, it loses potential energy. At the same time, its kinetic energy increases because its speed increases. Its potential energy is transformed into kinetic energy.

Pendulum A pendulum like the one in **Figure 2** swings back and forth. At the highest point in its swing, the pendulum has no movement. As it swings downward, it speeds up. The pendulum is at its greatest speed at the bottom of its swing. As the pendulum swings to the other side, its height increases and its speed decreases. At the top of its swing, it comes to a stop again.

FIGURE 1 ·····························

Falling Ball

The ball was photographed at equal time intervals as it fell.

✎ **Interpret Photos** How can you tell that the ball's kinetic energy is increasing?

_____

_____

_____

_____

_____

_____

FIGURE 2 ·····························

▷ **INTERACTIVE ART** **Pendulum**

A continuous transformation between potential and kinetic energy occurs in a pendulum. ✎ **Interpret Diagrams** Label the type of energy the pendulum has at positions A, B, and C.

Pole Vault The pole-vaulter in **Figure 3** starts out by running forward. When the pole-vaulter plants the pole to jump, his speed decreases and the pole bends. As the pole straightens out, the pole-vaulter is lifted high into the air. Once he is over the bar, the pole-vaulter's speed increases as he falls toward the safety cushion.

FIGURE 3 ·······························

Pole Vault
Energy transformations enable this athlete to vault more than 6 meters into the air.

✎ Sequence **Identify the main forms of energy present at points A through D.**

A

B

C

D

Lab® zone Do the Quick Lab
Soaring Straws.

🔑 Assess Your Understanding

1a. Define A change in one form of energy to another form of energy is called a(n)

_____

b. Relate Cause and Effect When you turn on an

iron, _____ energy is transformed

into _____ energy.

c. Apply Concepts Describe the energy transformation that occurs in a waterfall.

_____

_____

_____

_____

got it? ··

○ **I get it!** Now I know that all forms of energy can be transformed into _____

_____

○ **I need extra help with** _____

Go to **MY SCIENCE ⑤ COACH** *online for help with this subject.*

PS.1j Make valid conclusions after analyzing data.

PS.1m Construct and use models and simulations to illustrate and explain phenomena.

PS.6a Investigate and understand potential and kinetic energy and how they can be transferred and transformed.

PS.6b Investigate and understand mechanical, chemical, electrical, thermal, radiant, and nuclear energy and how they can be transferred and transformed.

What Is the Law of Conservation of Energy?

Once you set a pendulum in motion, does it swing forever? No, it does not. Then what happens to its energy? Is the energy destroyed? Again, the answer is no. The **law of conservation of energy** states that when one form of energy is transformed to another, no energy is lost in the process. 🔑 **According to the law of conservation of energy, energy cannot be created or destroyed.** The total amount of energy is the same before and after any transformation. If you add up all of the new forms of energy after a transformation, all of the original energy will be accounted for. So what happens to the energy of the pendulum once it stops moving?

Conserving Energy While You Ride

How is energy conserved in a transformation?

FIGURE 4

> **VIRTUAL LAB** Transformations between potential and kinetic energy occur during a roller coaster ride. ✎ **Use what you have learned about energy transformations to answer Questions 1–3.**

1. **Interpret Diagrams** The roller coaster starts from rest at the top of the first hill. Shade in the bars to show approximately how much potential and kinetic energy the coaster has at each point. Assume that none of the coaster's mechanical energy is transformed to thermal energy. Also assume that no electrical energy is used to move the coaster.

Potential

Kinetic

CYCLONE

Potential

Kinetic

Potential

Kinetic

As the pendulum swings, it encounters friction at the pivot of the string and from the air through which it moves. Whenever a moving object experiences friction, some of its kinetic energy is transformed into thermal energy. So the mechanical energy of the pendulum is not destroyed. It is transformed to thermal energy.

The fact that friction transforms mechanical energy to thermal energy should not surprise you. After all, you take advantage of such thermal energy when you rub your cold hands together to warm them up. Friction is also the reason why no machine is 100 percent efficient. You may recall that the output work of any real machine is always less than the input work. This reduced efficiency occurs because some mechanical energy is always transformed into thermal energy due to friction.

did you know? ....

When ancient animals and plants died, the chemical energy they had stored was trapped within their remains. This trapped energy is the chemical energy found in coal.

2. **Infer** Suppose you had taken thermal energy into account in Step 1. Would the total length of the shaded portion of the bars increase, decrease, or stay the same as as result?

○ Increase ○ Decrease ○ Stay the same

3. **CHALLENGE** Why is the first hill of a roller coaster always the tallest?

_____

_____

_____

| Potential | | | | |
| Kinetic | | | | |

| Potential | | | | |
| Kinetic | | | | |

Lab zone ® Do the Quick Lab
Law of Conservation of Energy.

🔑 **Assess Your Understanding**

2. **ANSWER THE BIG ?** How is energy conserved in a transformation?

_____

_____

_____

_____

got it? ....

○ **I get it!** Now I know that according to the law of conservation of energy, energy _____

_____

○ **I need extra help with** _____

Go to **my science** ⑤ **COACH** *online for help with this subject.*

REVIEW THE BIG ?

The total amount of _____ is the same before and after any transformation.

LESSON 1 What Is Energy?

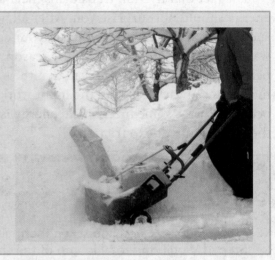

🔑 Since the transfer of energy is work, then power is the rate at which energy is transferred, or the amount of energy transferred in a unit of time.

🔑 The two basic types of energy are kinetic energy and potential energy.

Vocabulary
• energy
• kinetic energy
• potential energy
• gravitational potential energy
• elastic potential energy

LESSON 2 Forms of Energy

🔑 You can find an object's mechanical energy by adding together the object's kinetic energy and potential energy.

🔑 Forms of energy associated with the particles of objects include nuclear energy, thermal energy, electrical energy, electromagnetic energy, and chemical energy.

Vocabulary
• mechanical energy   • nuclear energy   • thermal energy
• electrical energy   • electromagnetic energy
• chemical energy

LESSON 3 Energy Transformations and Conservation

🔑 All forms of energy can be transformed into other forms of energy.

🔑 According to the law of conservation of energy, energy cannot be created or destroyed.

Vocabulary
• energy transformation
• law of conservation of energy

Review and Assessment

LESSON 1 What Is Energy?

1. When you stretch a rubber band, you give it

  a. kinetic energy.   **b.** electrical energy.

  c. potential energy.   **d.** chemical energy.

2. To calculate power, divide the amount of energy transferred by _____

3. Compare and Contrast In the illustration below, which vehicle has the greatest kinetic energy? Explain your answer.

_____

_____

_____

4. Apply Concepts If a handsaw does the same amount of work on a log as a chainsaw does, which has more power? Why?

_____

_____

_____

_____

5. math! A 1,350-kg car travels at 12 m/s. What is its kinetic energy?

_____

_____

_____

LESSON 2 Forms of Energy

6. What is the energy stored in the nucleus of an atom called?

  a. electrical energy   **b.** chemical energy

  c. thermal energy   **d.** nuclear energy

7. An object's mechanical energy is the sum of its

_____

8. Classify When you heat a pot of water over a flame, what form of energy is added to the water?

_____

The graph shows the kinetic energy of a 500-N diver during a dive from a 10-m platform. Use the graph to answer Questions 9 and 10.

9. Read Graphs How does the diver's kinetic energy change as the diver falls? Why?

_____

_____

_____

10. Calculate What is the diver's gravitational potential energy just before the dive?

_____

_____

_____

LESSON 3 **Energy Transformations and Conservation**

11. As a car skids to a stop, friction transforms kinetic energy to

   a. thermal energy.   **b.** potential energy.

   c. chemical energy.   **d.** electrical energy.

12. The law of conservation of energy states that

_____

_____

_____

_____

13. Classify Describe the energy transformation that occurs in a digital clock.

_____

_____

_____

14. Apply Concepts Explain why a spinning top will not remain in motion forever.

_____

_____

_____

_____

15. Infer Why does a bouncing ball rise to a lower height with each bounce?

_____

_____

_____

_____

_____

_____

_____

16. Write About It An eagle flies from its perch in a tree to the ground to capture and eat its prey. Describe its energy transformations.

APPLY THE BIG
How is energy conserved in a transformation?

17. The golfer in the photo is taking a swing. The golf club starts at point A and ends at point E. (1) Describe the energy transformations of the club from points A to E. (2) The kinetic energy of the club at point C is more than the potential energy of the club at point B. Does this mean that the law of conservation of energy is violated? Why or why not?

_____

_____

_____

_____

_____

_____

_____

_____

_____

_____

_____

Virginia SOL Test Prep

Read each question and choose the best answer.

1 The table gives the kinetic and potential energy of a 6-kg cat doing various activities.

Activity	Kinetic Energy (J)	Potential Energy (J)
Running	200	0
Leaping	150	100
Climbing a tree	3	300
Sleeping on a chair	0	30

During which activity does the cat have the greatest mechanical energy?

A climbing a tree

B leaping

C running

D sleeping on a chair

2 **Why does wind have energy?**

F It can change direction.

G It can do work.

H It moves through space as waves.

J It is electrically charged.

3 **What is the SI unit used to express gravitational potential energy?**

A newton

B kilowatt

C horsepower

D joule

4 **What causes a pendulum to eventually slow down and stop swinging?**

F friction

G kinetic energy

H weight

J potential energy

5 **Which energy transformation takes place when wood is burned?**

A Nuclear energy is transformed to thermal energy.

B Thermal energy is transformed to electrical energy.

C Chemical energy is transformed to thermal energy.

D Mechanical energy is transformed to thermal energy.

6 **A large pendulum at a science museum is set in motion at the beginning of the day. The table shows how its speed at the bottom of the swing changes during the day. Based on the data in the table, which of the following *best* describes the change in the height of the pendulum's swing from 8:00 a.m. to 2:00 p.m.?**

Time	Speed at Bottom of Swing (m/s)
8:00 a.m.	2.2
10:00 a.m.	1.9
12:00 p.m.	1.7
2:00 p.m.	1.6

F The height of the pendulum's swing increases over time.

G The height of the pendulum's swing does not change.

H The height of the pendulum's swing decreases over time.

J The height of the pendulum's swing first increases and then decreases over time.

TECH & DESIGN

Museum of Science

CHARGE IT!

Top Cap
(Positive Terminal)

Cathode Tab

Separator

Steel Can
(Negative Terminal)

Anode

Cathode

Anode Tab

Have you ever noticed how many batteries you use every day? There are batteries in cars, flashlights, cell phones, laptop computers, and even bug zappers! Discarded batteries add up to a lot of waste. Fortunately, rechargeable batteries can help keep the energy flowing and reduce the number of batteries that get thrown out. Can you imagine how many nonrechargeable batteries a cell phone would go through in a month?

Batteries transform chemical energy into electrical energy. To refuel a rechargeable battery, you plug it into a power source—such as an outlet in the wall. The electrical energy reverses the chemical changes, storing the electrical energy as chemical energy. The battery is once again "charged up" and ready to go!

Research It Gasoline-powered cars and hybrid cars have rechargeable batteries. Research how the batteries in gasoline-powered cars and hybrid cars are recharged.

PS.1k

▲ The inside of this rechargeable battery has three long thin layers. A separator separates a positive electrode from a negative electrode. Using the battery causes lithium ions to move from the positive material to the negative one. Applying an electrical charge moves the ions back to the positive electrode.

Museum of Science

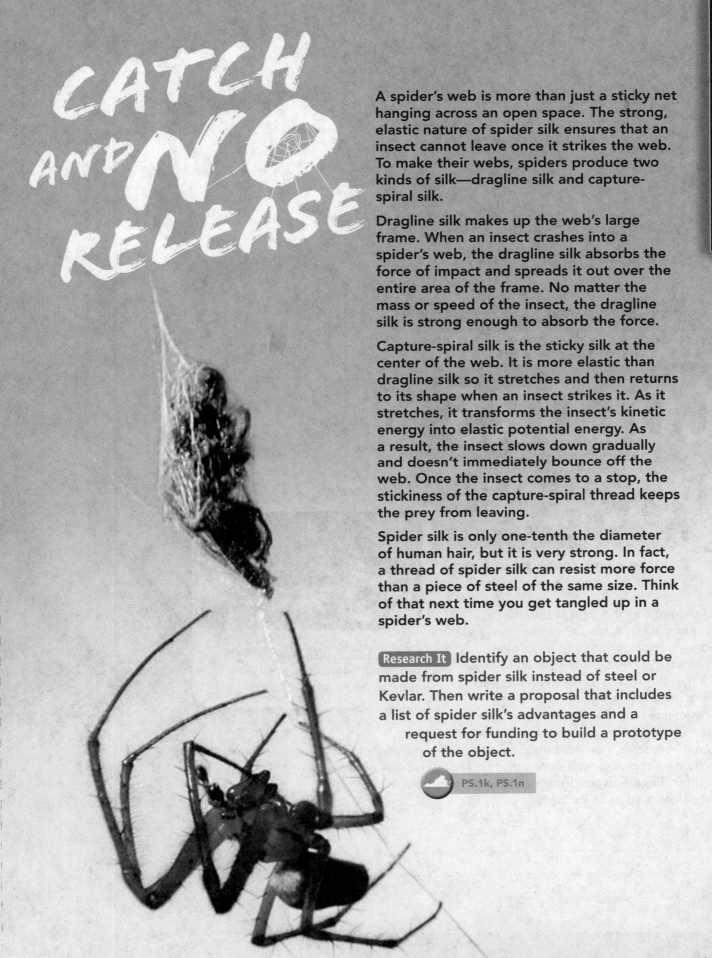

CATCH AND NO RELEASE

A spider's web is more than just a sticky net hanging across an open space. The strong, elastic nature of spider silk ensures that an insect cannot leave once it strikes the web. To make their webs, spiders produce two kinds of silk—dragline silk and capture-spiral silk.

Dragline silk makes up the web's large frame. When an insect crashes into a spider's web, the dragline silk absorbs the force of impact and spreads it out over the entire area of the frame. No matter the mass or speed of the insect, the dragline silk is strong enough to absorb the force.

Capture-spiral silk is the sticky silk at the center of the web. It is more elastic than dragline silk so it stretches and then returns to its shape when an insect strikes it. As it stretches, it transforms the insect's kinetic energy into elastic potential energy. As a result, the insect slows down gradually and doesn't immediately bounce off the web. Once the insect comes to a stop, the stickiness of the capture-spiral thread keeps the prey from leaving.

Spider silk is only one-tenth the diameter of human hair, but it is very strong. In fact, a thread of spider silk can resist more force than a piece of steel of the same size. Think of that next time you get tangled up in a spider's web.

Research It Identify an object that could be made from spider silk instead of steel or Kevlar. Then write a proposal that includes a list of spider silk's advantages and a request for funding to build a prototype of the object.

PS.1k, PS.1n

449

WHAT MIGHT THESE COLORS MEAN?

THE BIG

How does heat flow from one object to another?

The image at the right is called a thermogram. A special camera measures the electromagnetic radiation of an object and creates a temperature "map." A thermographic camera can be used to find people in a fire, detect when a racehorse might be injured, and spot tumors in humans. By noticing excessive heat in motors, transformers, and pumps, the camera can detect equipment problems before they fail, saving millions of dollars.

Infer **Since a thermogram shows temperature, what might the colors you see indicate?**

_____

_____

_____

_____

> **UNTAMED SCIENCE** Watch the **Untamed Science** video to learn more about heat.

Thermal Energy and Heat

Science Standards of Learning

PS.1b, PS.1j, PS.1k, PS.1m, PS.1n,
PS.6b, PS.7a, PS.7c, PS.7d

13 Getting Started

Check Your Understanding

1. **Background** Read the paragraph below and then answer the question.

Kiera is swimming in the ocean. Since she is moving, she has **kinetic energy.** Energy is measured in **joules.** Her brother, who swims at the same speed but has more mass, has more kinetic energy. If he slows down, he will have the same amount of kinetic energy as Kiera. While swimming, she notices that it is easier to float in salt water because it has a higher **density** than fresh water.

Kinetic energy is energy an object has due to its motion.

A **joule** is a unit of work equal to one newton-meter.

Density is the ratio of the mass of a substance to its volume.

• What are the two ways you can increase kinetic energy?

_____

> **MY READING WEB** If you had trouble completing the question above, visit **My Reading Web** and type in *Thermal Energy and Heat.*

Vocabulary Skill

Identify Multiple Meanings Some words have several meanings. Words you use every day may have different meanings in science.

Word	Everyday Meaning	Scientific Meaning
conductor	*n.* the director of an orchestra **Example:** The *conductor* signaled to the musicians to begin playing.	*n.* a material that conducts heat well **Example:** Metal is a good *conductor*.
heat	*v.* to make warm or hot **Example:** The fireplace began to *heat* the room.	*n.* thermal energy moving from a warmer object to a cooler object **Example:** When the door was left open, *heat* transferred from the warm room to the cool air outside.

2. **Quick Check** Circle the sentence below that uses the scientific meaning of the word *conductor*.

• The *conductor* got a standing ovation after the concert.

• It is easier to cook eggs in a pan that is a good *conductor*.

	MON	TUES	WED
			temperature
	25°	26°	24°
	18°	19°	17°

convection

radiation

conduction

Chapter Preview

LESSON 1
- temperature
- Fahrenheit scale
- Celsius scale
- Kelvin scale
- absolute zero
- heat

↻ Identify Supporting Evidence

△ Communicate

LESSON 2
- convection
- convection current
- radiation
- conduction

↻ Compare and Contrast

△ Infer

LESSON 3
- conductor
- insulator
- specific heat
- thermal expansion

↻ Identify the Main Idea

△ Calculate

> VOCAB FLASH CARDS For extra help with vocabulary, visit **Vocab Flash Cards** and type in *Thermal Energy and Heat.*

453

LESSON 1

Temperature, Thermal Energy, and Heat

🔑 **What Determines the Temperature of an Object?**
PS.1b, PS.6b, PS.7a

🔑 **What Is Thermal Energy?**
PS.1m, PS.6b, PS.7d

MY PLANET DIARY

Nature's Bathtub

Could you take a hot bath outside, with no ceramic bathtub or running water? This is possible in hot springs all over the world. Hot springs occur when underground water heated by Earth bubbles up and collects in pools on Earth's surface. The water in a hot spring can reach above 50°C (122°F). By contrast, a hot shower is about 43°C (110°F). Visitors use these hot springs to relax.

FUN FACT

Answer the question below.
What other daily household functions could be done without running water or electricity?

_____

_____

_____

_____

_____

▷ **PLANET DIARY** Go to Planet **Diary** to learn more about geothermal energy.

> **Lab zone** Do the Inquiry Warm-Up *How Cold Is the Water?*

 Science Standards of Learning

PS.1b Accurately measure temperature.

PS.6b Investigate and understand thermal energy and how it can be transferred and transformed.

PS.7a Investigate and understand Celsius and Kelvin temperature scales and absolute zero.

What Determines the Temperature of an Object?

You may have used a thermometer to take your temperature when you were sick. **Temperature** is a measure of how hot or cold something is compared to a reference point. (One reference point is the freezing point of water.) What makes an object hot or cold?

Vocabulary

- temperature
- Celsius scale
- absolute zero
- Fahrenheit scale
- Kelvin scale
- heat

Skills

- Reading: Identify Supporting Evidence
- Inquiry: Communicate

Recall that all moving objects have kinetic energy. Matter is made up of tiny particles that are always moving, so these particles have kinetic energy. 🔑 **Temperature is a measure of the average kinetic energy of the particles in an object.** As an object heats up, its particles move faster. As a result, both the average kinetic energy of the particles and the temperature increase.

The United States uses the **Fahrenheit scale** to measure temperature. Most countries use the **Celsius scale.** You can use an equation to convert between scales, but it's simpler to estimate using thermometers like the one in **Figure 1.** Temperatures that line up, like 32°F and 0°C, are equivalent. Many scientists use the **Kelvin scale.** Celsius and Fahrenheit scales are divided into degrees. The Kelvin scale is divided into kelvins (K). A temperature change of 1 K is the same temperature change as 1°C. Zero kelvins, or **absolute zero,** is the lowest temperature possible. At absolute zero, particles have no kinetic energy. Zero K is equal to −273°C.

did you know?

When Anders Celsius invented the Celsius scale, he had 100°C as the *freezing* point of water and 0°C as its *boiling* point.

MON	TUES	WED	THURS	FRI
25°	26°	24°	25°	24°
18°	19°	17°	17°	18°

FIGURE 1

> ART IN MOTION **Temperature Scales**

The chart above shows a weather report, but it does not identify the temperature scale.

✏️ **Interpret Diagrams** Explain why this report would mean something different in Japan than it would in the United States. Fill in the thermometer to show one of the temperatures in Celsius. What is this equivalent to in Fahrenheit?

_____

_____

_____

_____

_____

Lab zone Do the Lab Investigation *Build Your Own Thermometer.*

🔑 Assess Your Understanding

got it?

- ○ I get it! Now I know that temperature is related to _____

  _____

- ○ I need extra help with _____

  Go to **my science COACH** online for help with this subject.

455

⊙ **Identify Supporting Evidence** Since thermal energy is the total energy of all the particles in an object, it depends on multiple factors. Underline sentences that support this idea.

What Is Thermal Energy?

Different objects at the same temperature can have different amounts of energy. To understand this, you need to know about thermal energy and about heat. Temperature, thermal energy, and heat are closely related, but they are not the same thing.

Thermal Energy Temperature is a measure of the average kinetic energy of the individual particles in an object. However, it is not a measure of the total amount of energy in an object. **Thermal energy is the total energy of all the particles in an object.** It depends on the temperature of an object, the number of particles in it, and how those particles are arranged. This lesson will focus on the first two factors.

The more particles an object has at a given temperature, the more thermal energy it has. For example, a 1-liter pot of tea at 75°C has more thermal energy than a 0.2-liter mug of tea at 75°C because the pot contains more tea particles. On the other hand, the higher the temperature of an object, the more thermal energy the object has. Therefore, if two 1-liter pots of tea have different temperatures, the pot with the higher temperature has more thermal energy.

The total amount of thermal energy an object has depends on its temperature and how many particles it contains.

❶ **Identify** In the top two panels, circle the chicken pot pie that contains more thermal energy.

❷ **Apply Concepts** In the last panel, draw in and record the temperature of three pies that have more thermal energy than the one on the left.

100°C   200°C

200°C   200°C

200°C   _____°C   _____°C   _____°C

Heat You might say that an object contains heat, but, strictly speaking, it does not. Objects contain thermal energy. **Heat** is the *transfer* of thermal energy from a warmer object to a cooler object. The warmer object will cool down, and the cooler object will warm up until they are the same temperature. When this happens, heat stops transferring. Heat is measured in the units of energy—joules.

Vocabulary Write a sentence that uses the scientific meaning of *heat*.

_____

_____

FIGURE 2 ••••••••••••••••••••••

> **VIRTUAL LAB** **Heat**
When you hold your hand over a plate of food, you will feel warmth if heat transfers into you and cold if heat transfers out of you.

✎ **Communicate** In the photo, draw arrows to show the direction of heat transfer for at least two foods. Would your hand feel warmer over some foods than over others? What characteristics of the food might affect how warm or cold your hand feels? Discuss your ideas with a partner.

_____

_____

 Do the Quick Lab *Temperature and Thermal Energy.*

🔑 Assess Your Understanding

1a. List What are two factors that determine an object's thermal energy?

_____

_____

b. CHALLENGE Object A has less thermal energy than Object B, but heat flows from Object A to Object B. What conditions would make this possible?

_____

_____

got it?

○ **I get it!** Now I know that the thermal energy in an object is defined as _____

_____

_____

_____

_____

○ **I need extra help with** _____

Go to **my science** ⓢ **COACH** *online for help with this subject.*

The Transfer of Heat

🔑 **How Is Heat Transferred?**
PS.6b, PS.7c, PS.7d

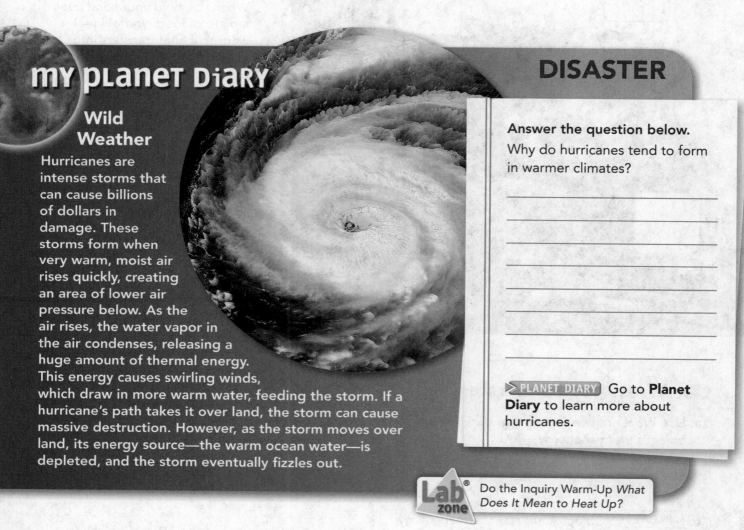

MY PLANET DIARY

DISASTER

Wild Weather

Hurricanes are intense storms that can cause billions of dollars in damage. These storms form when very warm, moist air rises quickly, creating an area of lower air pressure below. As the air rises, the water vapor in the air condenses, releasing a huge amount of thermal energy. This energy causes swirling winds, which draw in more warm water, feeding the storm. If a hurricane's path takes it over land, the storm can cause massive destruction. However, as the storm moves over land, its energy source—the warm ocean water—is depleted, and the storm eventually fizzles out.

Answer the question below.
Why do hurricanes tend to form in warmer climates?

_____

_____

_____

_____

_____

_____

_____

_____

> PLANET DIARY Go to **Planet Diary** to learn more about hurricanes.

Lab zone Do the Inquiry Warm-Up *What Does It Mean to Heat Up?*

🏴 **Science Standards of Learning**

PS.6b Investigate and understand thermal energy and how it can be transferred and transformed.

PS.7c Investigate conduction, convection, and radiation.

PS.7d Investigate and understand thermal energy transfer.

How Is Heat Transferred?

Heat is transferring around you all the time. If it wasn't, nothing would ever change temperature. Heat doesn't transfer randomly. It travels only in one direction and by three different methods. 🔑 **Heat is transferred from warmer areas to cooler areas by conduction, convection, and radiation.**

Vocabulary

- convection • convection current
- radiation • conduction

Skills

⟳ Reading: Compare and Contrast

△ Inquiry: Infer

Convection

Convection is a type of heat transfer that occurs only in fluids, such as water and air. When air is heated, its particles speed up and move farther apart. This makes the heated air less dense. The heated air rises to float on top of the denser, cooler air. Cooler air flows into its place, heats up, and rises. Previously heated air cools down, sinks, and the cycle repeats. This flow creates a circular motion known as a **convection current.** Convection currents in air cause wind and weather changes.

Radiation

Radiation is the transfer of energy by electromagnetic waves. Radiation is the only form of heat transfer that does not require matter. You can feel the radiation from a fire without touching the flames. The sun's energy travels to Earth through 150 million kilometers of empty space.

Conduction

Conduction transfers heat from one particle of matter to another within an object or between two objects. The fast-moving particles in the floor of the oven collide with the slow-moving particles in the uncooked pizza. This causes the pizza's particles to move faster, making the pizza hotter.

FIGURE 1 ....

Heat Transfer

A wood-fire pizza oven demonstrates three types of heat transfer.

✎ **Apply Concepts** Describe a heat transfer that occurs after the pizza comes out of the oven. What kind of transfer is it?

_____

_____

⟳ **Compare and Contrast**
Circle statements on the previous page that describe what the different types of heat transfer have in common. Underline their differences on this page.

459

Where Does Heat Transfer on This Beach?

How does heat flow from one object to another?

FIGURE 2 ···

> INTERACTIVE ART Heat transfer goes on all around you all the time, even on the beach. ✎ Apply Concepts Fill in the chart below to review the different types of heat transfer. Then, in the illustration, label at least one example of each type of heat transfer. Draw arrows to show how heat is being transferred in each example.

Type of Heat Transfer	Explanation
Conduction	
Convection	
Radiation	

Do the Quick Lab *Visualizing Convection Currents*.

apply it!

Cooking pots come in a variety of shapes and sizes, but you're much more likely to see a wide, squat pot like this

than a tall, narrow pot like this.

⚠ **Infer** Use conduction to explain why this is the case.

_____

_____

_____

_____

_____

_____

_____

🔑 Assess Your Understanding

1a. Classify What type of heat transfer occurs when eggs cook in a hot pan? Before toasters, people toasted bread by holding it over a fire. What type of heat transfer occurred then? Name the third type of heat transfer and an example of a food cooked by it.

_____

_____

b. ANSWER THE BIG ? How does heat flow from one object to another?

_____

_____

_____

_____

_____

got it? ....

○ **I get it!** Now I know that the three methods of heat transfer are _____

_____

○ **I need extra help with** _____

Go to **MY SCIENCE COACH** online for help with this subject.

Virginia
LESSON 3
Thermal Properties

UNLOCK THE BIG ?

🔑 **How Do Different Materials Respond to Heat?**
PS.1j, PS.6b, PS.7c, PS.7d

my planeт Diary

CAREER

Suiting Up

Comic book superheroes often wear special suits that allow them to fly or protect them from enemies. But there are some everyday heroes who wear suits that give them similar super-powers: astronauts! Whenever astronauts go outside a space station or ship, they put on suits that weigh hundreds of pounds. The suits enable them to survive in the wide temperature swings that occur in space. The suits are designed with a flexible insulating material to protect astronauts from extreme temperature swings, radiation, and low pressure in space. They also provide air to breathe, radio communication, and protection from micrometeoroids.

Communicate Answer the question below. Then discuss your answer with a partner.

You also use special clothing to stay warm. What materials do you use to stay warm?

_____

_____

_____

_____

▶ PLANET DIARY Go to **Planet Diary** to learn more about spacesuits.

 Do the Inquiry Warm-Up *Thermal Properties.*

🔵 Science Standards of Learning

PS.1j Make valid conclusions after analyzing data.

PS.6b Investigate and understand thermal energy and how it can be transferred and transformed.

PS.7c Investigate and understand conduction, convection, and radiation.

PS.7d Investigate and understand applications of thermal energy transfer.

How Do Different Materials Respond to Heat?

When you bake something in the oven, you use dishes made of glass, ceramics, or metal instead of plastic. Some materials can stand up to the heat of an oven better than others. Materials respond to heat in different ways. The thermal properties of an object determine how it will respond to heat.

Vocabulary
- conductor
- insulator
- specific heat
- thermal expansion

Skills
- ↻ Reading: Identify the Main Idea
- △ Inquiry: Calculate

Conductors and Insulators If you walk barefoot from your living room rug to the tile floor of your kitchen, you will notice that the tile feels colder than the rug. But the temperature of the rug and the tile are the same—room temperature! The difference has to do with how materials conduct heat. 🔑 **Some materials conduct heat well, while other materials do not.**

Conductors A material that conducts heat well is called a **conductor.** Metals such as silver are good conductors. Some materials are good conductors because of the particles they contain and how those particles are arranged. A good conductor, such as the tile floor, feels cold to the touch because heat easily transfers out of your skin and into the tile. However, heat also transfers out of conductors easily. A metal flagpole feels much hotter on a summer day than a wooden pole would in the same place because heat easily transfers out of the metal pole and into your hand.

Insulators A wooden pole and your living room rug are good insulators. **Insulators** are materials that do not conduct heat well. Other good insulators include air and wool. For example, wool blankets slow the transfer of heat out of your body.

FIGURE 1 ·····················

> ART IN MOTION **Conductors and Insulators**
Both conductors and insulators are useful in a kitchen. Conductors easily transfer heat to cook your food. Insulators stay cool enough to be handled.
✎ **Classify** Circle the conductors in the photo. Below, list objects in a kitchen that can act as insulators.

_____

_____

_____

_____

_____

Specific Heat Imagine running across hot sand toward the ocean. You run to the water's edge, but you don't go any farther—the water is too cold. How can the sand be so hot and the water so cold? After all, the sun heats both of them. The answer is that water requires more heat to raise its temperature than sand does.

When an object is heated, its temperature rises. But the temperature does not rise at the same rate for all objects. The amount of heat required to raise the temperature of an object depends on the object's chemical makeup. 🔑 **To change the temperature of different objects by the same amount, different amounts of thermal energy are required.**

The amount of energy required to raise the temperature of 1 kilogram of a material by 1 kelvin is called its **specific heat.** It is measured in joules per kilogram-kelvin, or J/(kg·K). A material with a high specific heat can absorb a great deal of thermal energy without a great change in temperature.

You can calculate thermal energy changes with a formula.

Energy Change = Mass × Specific Heat × Temperature Change

✏️ **Identify the Main Idea**
Circle the main idea on this page. Underline the sentences that support the main idea.

do the math!

You can calculate the amount of thermal energy gained by 2 kg of water as its temperature increases by 3 K.

Energy Change = Mass × Specific Heat × Temp. Change

Energy Change = 2 kg × 4,180 J/(kg·K) × 3 K

Energy Change = 25,080 J

Material	Specific Heat (J/(kg·K))
Copper	385
Water	4,180
Glass	837
Silver	235
Iron	450

① Calculate Use the formula and the table at the right to calculate how much energy is lost by 0.5 kg of silver that cools off by 2 K.

_____

② Interpret Tables How many times more energy must you transfer into a kilogram of glass than a kilogram of silver to raise their temperatures by the same amount?

_____

③ Draw Conclusions The seawater at a beach heats up more slowly than the sand on the beach does. The specific heat of water must be (greater than/less than) the specific heat of sand.

Thermal Expansion To loosen a jar lid, you can hold it under a stream of hot water. This works because the metal lid expands more than the glass does as it gets hotter. 🔑 **As the thermal energy of matter increases, its particles usually spread out, causing the substance to expand.** This is true for almost all matter. The expanding of matter when it is heated is known as **thermal expansion.** When matter is cooled, the opposite happens. Thermal energy is released. This causes the particles to slow down and move closer together. As matter cools, it usually decreases in volume, or contracts. Different materials expand and contract at different rates.

Power Lines

FIGURE 2 ··························

Thermal Expansion
Many objects are specifically designed to allow extra space for thermal expansion, such as road joints and train tracks.

✏️ **Predict Pick one of the examples. What might happen if thermal expansion was not considered when this object was designed?**

_____

_____

_____

_____

Road Joint

Train Track

Lab ® Do the Quick Lab
zone *Frosty Balloons.*

🔑 **Assess Your Understanding**

1a. Classify Foam picnic coolers keep food cold on a hot day. Is foam a conductor or an insulator? Explain.

_____

_____

_____

b. Calculate The specific heat of foam is about 1,200 J/(kg·K). How much heat does it take to raise the temperature of 1 kg of foam by 2 K?

_____

_____

_____

got it? ··························

○ **I get it!** Now I know that the way a material responds to heat depends on _____

_____

○ **I need extra help with** _____

Go to MY SCIENCE COACH *online for help with this subject.*

465

13 Study Guide

Heat flows from _____ **objects to** _____ **objects. The three methods of heat transfer are** _____.

LESSON 1 Temperature, Thermal Energy, and Heat

🔑 Temperature is a measure of the average kinetic energy of the particles in an object.

🔑 Thermal energy is the total energy of all the particles in an object.

Vocabulary
- temperature • Fahrenheit scale • Celsius scale
- Kelvin scale • absolute zero • heat

LESSON 2 The Transfer of Heat

🔑 Heat is transferred from warmer areas to cooler areas by conduction, convection, and radiation.

Vocabulary
- convection • convection current
- radiation • conduction

LESSON 3 Thermal Properties

🔑 Some materials conduct heat well, while other materials do not.

🔑 To change the temperature of different objects by the same amount, different amounts of thermal energy are required.

🔑 As the thermal energy of matter increases, its particles usually spread out, causing the substance to expand.

Vocabulary
- conductor • insulator • specific heat • thermal expansion

Review and Assessment

LESSON 1 Temperature, Thermal Energy, and Heat

1. What is the total energy of all the particles in an object called?

  a. chemical energy   **b.** thermal energy

  c. potential energy   **d.** mechanical energy

2. The temperature scale used in most of the world is the _____

3. Apply Concepts How does heat flow when you place an ice cube in your hand?

_____

_____

Use the illustration to answer the questions below.

A   30°C   B   30°C   C   60°C

100 g   200 g   200 g

4. Interpret Data Compare the average motion of the particles in the three containers. Explain your answer.

_____

_____

_____

_____

5. Draw Conclusions Compare the total amount of thermal energy in containers A and B. Explain your answer.

_____

_____

_____

LESSON 2 The Transfer of Heat

6. What is the process by which heat transfers from one particle of matter to another when the particles collide?

  a. conduction   **b.** convection

  c. expansion   **d.** radiation

7. A convection current is _____

_____

_____

_____

8. Classify Identify each example of heat transfer as conduction, convection, or radiation: opening the windows in a hot room; a lizard basking in the sun; putting ice on a sprained ankle.

_____

_____

9. Infer How can heat be transferred across empty space? Explain your answer.

_____

_____

_____

10. Make Judgments Suppose you try to heat your home using a fireplace in one of the rooms. Would a fan be helpful? Explain.

_____

_____

_____

_____

11. Write About It Explain why a school might ask teachers to keep the windows closed and the shades down during a heat wave.

LESSON 3 Thermal Properties

12. Suppose you want to know the amount of heat needed to raise the temperature of 2 kg of copper by 10°C. What property of the copper do you need to know?

    a. the thermal energy of the copper

    b. the temperature of the copper

    c. the specific heat of copper

    d. the melting point of copper

13. Wool is a good insulator, which means _____

_____

14. Apply Concepts When they are hung, telephone lines are allowed to sag. Explain why.

_____

_____

_____

15. Interpret Diagrams Why are two panes of glass used in the window shown below? (*Hint*: Air is an insulator.)

Glass

Air space

_____

_____

_____

16. math! Iron has a specific heat of 450 J/(kg·K). Design a set of three iron cooking pots. How much heat is required to increase the temperature of each pot by 100 K?

APPLY THE BIG ? **How does heat flow from one object to another?**

17. Suppose you were out camping and the weather turned cold. How would you keep warm? Explain each action you would take. Tell whether conduction, convection, or radiation is involved with each heat transfer.

_____

_____

_____

_____

_____

_____

_____

_____

_____

_____

_____

_____

Read each question and choose the best answer.

1 The temperature of four pies is shown below.

A

80°C

B

40°C

C

40°C

D

80°C

Which statement is true?

A   A and D have the same thermal energy.
B   C and D have the same thermal energy.
C   B has twice the thermal energy as C.
D   D has twice the thermal energy as A.

2 What does a thermometer measure?

F   temperature
G   thermal energy
H   heat
J   specific heat

3 Which statement describes the direction of heat flow?

A   Heat flows between two objects at the same temperature.
B   Thermal energy can only be absorbed by cool objects.
C   Heat flows from a warmer object to a cooler object.
D   Heat flows from a cooler object to a warmer object.

4 The specific heat of iron is 450 J/(kg·K). How much thermal energy must be transferred to 15 kg of iron to raise its temperature by 4.0 K?

F   450 J
G   2,700 J
H   5,400 J
J   27,000 J

5 Which of the following can be classified as a good conductor of thermal energy?

A   air
B   wood
C   silver
D   wool

6 Which type of heat transfer is occurring between the pot and the water shown in the image below?

F   convection
G   conduction
H   radiation
J   specific heat

Frontiers of Technology

Aerogel Windows

Close the Window!

Even when they are shut tight, windows can let as much as half of a building's heat out. Scientists at the National Aeronautics and Space Administration (NASA) are working on a new material that may make glass windows a thing of the past.

Aerogel is a nearly transparent solid made from silicon dioxide—the same ingredient found in sand and glass.

Unlike glass, aerogel is 99.8 percent air. This makes it the world's least dense solid. Yet it insulates 39 times better than the best fiberglass insulation.

Aerogel absorbs infrared radiation, stopping most forms of energy transfer, including heat. This should make it an amazing material for windows! Unfortunately, tiny pores scatter some of the visible light, which gives aerogel a blue haze.

NASA is researching ways to make aerogel truly transparent. That could prove to be the future of windows!

▲ Aerogel, the world's least dense solid, is nonflammable and absorbs heat.

Write About It Write an advertisement for aerogel windows or insulation. Be creative! Promote the idea that the government would give homeowners a rebate for installing a cutting-edge energy solution.

 PS.1k, PS.1n

THERMAL EXPANSION

Problem

metal roof expansion/contraction

force

stress cracking

stress cracking

Solution

expansion/contraction

expansion/contraction

no force

expansion joint

△ When a metal roof expands from the sun's heat, the expanding metal pushes against the concrete wall. An expansion joint adds space for the metal to expand.

Make Way for Heat

Sometimes when things heat up, it's time to get out. School board officials stopped construction on a Florida school when cement blocks in the building cracked. The school hired an architecture firm to explore the problem. An engineer discovered that thermal expansion was responsible for the damage. But where was the heat coming from?

The school was designed with a metal roofing system. When metal warms up, it expands. Concrete blocks attached to the metal should have been installed with expansion joints. These joints slip sideways as the metal expands. Unfortunately, there was no slip room over one of the entrances to the building. Something had to give—and it was the concrete blocks! Engineers fixed the problem by adding expansion joints to the roof of the building.

Building in a warm climate? Don't forget to account for thermal expansion!

Design It Do some research about thermal expansion and expansion joints. Make sketches of your own design for a building or bridge. Your design should use expansion joints to account for thermal expansion.

 PS.1k, PS.1m, PS.1n

↘ Even concrete cracks under pressure from thermal expansion.

HOW WOULD YOU DESCRIBE WAVES?

 THE BIG ?

What are the properties of waves?

Imagine a sunny day on a calm sea. It seems as if you can see to the edge of the world. Suddenly, the clouds roll in, and the waves begin to get larger and faster. Soon, you can barely see past the next wave. One after another, they batter the sailboat, making it pitch and roll like a wild roller coaster.

Draw Conclusions What are some features of waves?

_____

_____

_____

_____

_____

_____

> UNTAMED SCIENCE Watch the **Untamed Science** video to learn more about waves.

Characteristics of Waves

Science Standards of Learning

PS.1d, PS.1g, PS.1k, PS.1m, PS.1n, PS.8a,
PS.8b, PS.8c, PS.9a, PS.9b, PS.9c

14 Getting Started

Check Your Understanding

1. **Background** Read the paragraph below and then answer the question.

At a public pond, Lionel skips stones and tosses rocks into the water, sending waves in all directions. Nearby, Ali **floats** a wooden boat. Both boys observe the **properties** of the waves. The rocks make higher waves than the stones. They watch the **interaction** of the waves and the boat. The boat bounces violently as the higher waves travel under it.

Something **floats** if it moves or rests on the surface of a liquid without sinking.

The **properties** of something are its characteristic qualities or features.

Interaction is the combined action or effect that things have on each other.

- What example in the paragraph suggests that the properties of waves might affect a floating object?

_____

_____

_____

> **MY READING WEB** If you had trouble completing the question above, visit **My Reading Web** and type in *Characteristics of Waves.*

Vocabulary Skill

Identify Multiple Meanings Some words have more than one meaning. Consider the everyday and scientific meanings of the words below.

Word	Everyday Meaning	Scientific Meaning
reflection	*n.* serious thought or consideration	*n.* the bouncing back of a wave from a surface
frequency	*n.* the rate at which something occurs	*n.* the number of waves that pass a point in a certain time

2. **Quick Check** Circle in the chart the meaning of *reflection* as it is used in the following sentence: An echo is the *reflection* of a sound wave.

wave

amplitude

reflection

refraction

Chapter Preview

LESSON 1

- wave
- energy
- medium
- mechanical wave
- vibration
- transverse wave
- crest
- trough
- longitudinal wave
- compression
- rarefaction

🕑 **Summarize**
🔺 **Predict**

LESSON 2

- amplitude
- wavelength
- frequency
- hertz

🕑 **Identify the Main Idea**
🔺 **Calculate**

LESSON 3

- reflection
- refraction
- diffraction
- interference
- constructive interference
- destructive interference
- standing wave
- node
- antinode
- resonance

🕑 **Relate Cause and Effect**
🔺 **Observe**

> VOCAB FLASH CARDS For extra help with vocabulary, visit **Vocab Flash Cards** and type in *Characteristics of Waves.*

What Are Waves?

UNLOCK THE BIG ?

🔑 **What Forms Mechanical Waves?**
PS.8a, PS.8c, PS.9a

🔑 **What Are the Types of Mechanical Waves?**
PS.8a, PS.8c, PS.9a

my planet Diary

The Power of Waves

Where does the energy that powers your school come from? It may be from oil, gas, or coal. You also may have heard of using the sun or wind as energy sources. But did you know that ocean waves could be used as an energy source, too? Mechanical systems placed in the ocean or along the shore transform the energy from waves into electricity. Unlike oil, gas, or coal, the energy from ocean waves will not run out. Although wave energy technology is still very new, many scientists are optimistic about its possible use around the world.

FUN FACTS

Communicate Discuss this question with a partner. Write your answer below.

How might wave energy impact the environment? Consider both intended and unintended consequences.

_____

_____

_____

_____

_____

_____

> PLANET DIARY Go to **Planet Diary** to learn more about waves.

 Do the Inquiry Warm-Up
What Are Waves?

Vocabulary
- wave • energy • medium • mechanical wave
- vibration • transverse wave • crest • trough
- longitudinal wave • compression • rarefaction

Skills
- Reading: Summarize
- Inquiry: Predict

What Forms Mechanical Waves?

You have probably seen and felt water waves while swimming. But did you know that many kinds of waves affect you daily? Sound and light are very different from water waves, but they are waves, too.

Characteristics of Waves What is a wave? A **wave** is a disturbance involving the transfer of energy from place to place. In science, **energy** is defined as the ability to do work. For example, the energy of a water wave can lift an object on the water's surface as the wave passes under it. But after the wave passes, the water is calm again.

Most waves need something to travel through. For example, sound waves can travel through air, water, and even solid materials. Water waves travel along the surface of the water. A wave can even travel along an object, such as a rope. The material through which a wave travels is called a **medium.** Gases (such as air), liquids (such as water), and solids (such as ropes) can all act as mediums. Waves that require a medium to travel are called **mechanical waves.**

Science Standards of Learning

PS.8a Investigate and understand wavelength, frequency, speed, amplitude, rarefaction, and compression for sound waves.

PS.8c Investigate and understand the nature of compression waves for sound.

PS.9a Investigate and understand wavelength, frequency, speed, amplitude, crest, and trough of transverse waves.

Summarize On the notebook paper, summarize the text on this page in your own words.

CHALLENGE The news media, such as newspapers and television stations, carry current events worldwide. Explain how the way news travels is similar to the way a wave travels.

_____
_____
_____
_____

Waves and Energy
Energy is needed to make a wave. 🗝 **Mechanical waves form when a source of energy causes a medium to vibrate.** A **vibration** is a repeated back-and-forth or up-and-down motion. Moving objects have energy, which they can transfer to a medium to produce waves. For example, as you see in **Figure 1,** a motorboat's propeller can transfer energy to calm water. As a result, the particles that make up the water start to vibrate. The vibrations move through the water, resulting in a wave.

FIGURE 1 ....

Forming a Mechanical Wave
A source of energy in a medium can cause a mechanical wave to form.

✎ **Explain** Draw an arrow from each box to the correct part of the photo. Then tell your reason for each choice in the boxes.

Energy Source
Moving objects have energy.

_____
_____
_____

Vibration
When a vibration moves through a medium, a wave results.

_____
_____
_____

Medium
Mechanical waves form in mediums.

_____
_____
_____

Lab zone® Do the Quick Lab *What Causes Mechanical Waves?*

🗝 **Assess Your Understanding**

got it? ....

○ **I get it!** Now I know that a mechanical wave forms when _____
_____

○ **I need extra help with** _____

Go to **MY SCIENCE** 🔵 **COACH** online for help with this subject.

What Are the Types of Mechanical Waves?

Waves move through mediums in different ways. 🔑 **The three types of mechanical waves are transverse waves, longitudinal waves, and surface waves.** These waves are classified by how they move through mediums.

Transverse Waves When you make a wave on a rope, the wave moves from one end of the rope to the other. However, the rope itself moves up and down or from side to side, at right angles to the direction in which the wave travels. A wave that vibrates the medium at right angles, or perpendicular, to the direction in which the wave travels is called a **transverse wave.**

Making a transverse wave on a rope forms high and low points along the rope. A high point on a transverse wave is called a **crest,** and a low point is called a **trough** (trawf). In **Figure 2,** you can see that the red ribbon on the rope is first at a crest and then at a trough. As the wave moves through the rope, the ribbon moves up and down between crests and troughs. The dashed line shows the rope's position before it was moved. It is called the rest position.

Science Standards of Learning

PS.8a Investigate and understand wavelength, frequency, speed, amplitude, rarefaction, and compression for sound waves.

PS.8c Investigate and understand the nature of compression waves for sound.

PS.9a Investigate and understand wavelength, frequency, speed, amplitude, crest, and trough of transverse waves.

Vocabulary Identify Multiple Meanings The word *trough* has more than one meaning. Write two sentences that use the word, one showing its everyday meaning and one showing its scientific meaning.

_____

_____

_____

_____

FIGURE 2 ....

Motion in a Transverse Wave

When you shake out a bedsheet or move a rope up and down, you create a transverse wave.

✎ **Complete the tasks.**

1. **Identify** Label the crest, trough, and rest position.

2. **Relate Text and Visuals** Draw a vertical line through the purple arrows and a horizontal line through the blue arrow until it touches the vertical line. What angle did you draw?

Up

Direction of wave

Down

Longitudinal Waves

If you push and pull one end of a spring toy, you can produce a longitudinal wave like the one shown in **Figure 3**. Notice that the coils in the spring move back and forth in the same direction, or parallel, to the wave's motion. A **longitudinal wave** (lawn juh TOO duh nul) vibrates the medium in the same direction in which the wave travels. Also, notice how the spacing between the coils varies. Some coils are close together, while others are farther apart. An area where the coils are close together is called a **compression** (kum PRESH un). An area where the coils are spread out is called a **rarefaction** (rair uh FAK shun).

As compressions and rarefactions travel along the spring toy, each coil moves forward and then back. The energy travels from one end of the spring to the other, in the form of a wave. After the wave passes, each coil returns to its starting position.

FIGURE 3 ··

Motion in a Longitudinal Wave

Fixed points on a transverse wave vibrate up and down. Fixed points on a longitudinal wave, such as the one marked by the red ribbon, vibrate back and forth.

✎ **Interpret Diagrams** Label the areas of compression and rarefaction in the diagram.

Push

Rest position —

Pull

Direction of Wave ➡

apply it!

Sound waves are longitudinal waves. The picture shows an area of air as the compressions and rarefactions of a sound wave pass through it. The dots represent air particles.

❶ **Classify** Write an *R* in the rarefaction areas and a *C* in the compression areas.

❷ **Predict** Draw what the particles should look like in area Z.

Z

Direction of Wave ➡

Surface Waves Surface waves are combinations of transverse and longitudinal waves. This type of wave travels along a surface that separates two mediums. Ocean waves are the most familiar surface wave. An ocean wave travels at the surface between water and air. When a wave passes through water, the water (and anything on it) vibrates up and down, like a transverse wave on a rope. The water also moves back and forth slightly in the direction that the wave is traveling, like the coils of a spring. But unlike the coils of a spring, water does not compress. The up-and-down and back-and-forth movements combine to make each particle of water move in a circle, as you see in **Figure 4.**

FIGURE 4 ·····························
▶ ART IN MOTION **Waves Transfer Energy**
A wave moves the bottle in a circular motion. After the wave passes, the bottle returns to where it started.

✏ **Predict** In the empty box, draw what the next picture should look like.

Do the Quick Lab
Three Types of Waves.

🔑 Assess Your Understanding

1a. Review Compared to the direction it travels, at what angle does a transverse wave vibrate a medium?

_____

_____

b. Compare and Contrast How are transverse and longitudinal waves alike and different?

_____

_____

got it?

○ **I get it!** Now I know that the three types of mechanical waves are _____

_____

_____

_____

○ **I need extra help with** _____

Go to MY SCIENCE ⬢ COACH *online for help with this subject.*

LESSON 2

Properties of Waves

🔑 **What Are the Amplitude, Wavelength, Frequency, and Speed of a Wave?**
PS.1d, PS.8a, PS.8c, PS.9a

🔑 **How Are Frequency, Wavelength, and Speed Related?**
PS.1g, PS.8a, PS.9a

MY PLANET DIARY

DISCOVERY

The Sound of Romance

Bzzzzzzzzz! Bzzzzzzzzz! What's that noise? It's the sound of a mosquito buzzing in your ear. This distinct buzzing sound comes from sound waves formed as a mosquito beats its wings. Researchers recently discovered that the buzzing sound of female mosquitoes attracts male mosquitoes. When a male mosquito meets a female, he quickly adjusts his own buzz to match the frequency of the sound waves created by the female. Researchers think that this matched buzzing frequency aids in mosquito mating.

Communicate Discuss this question with a partner. Write your answer below.

What are two other animals you know of that make buzzing sounds?

_____

_____

_____

_____

_____

_____

▷ **PLANET DIARY** Go to **Planet Diary** to learn more about wave properties.

 Do the Inquiry Warm-Up *What Do Waves Look Like?*

Vocabulary
- amplitude • wavelength • frequency • hertz

Skills
Reading: Identify the Main Idea
Inquiry: Calculate

What Are the Amplitude, Wavelength, Frequency, and Speed of a Wave?

Waves may vary greatly. For example, waves can be long or short. They can carry a little energy or a lot of energy. They can be transverse or longitudinal. However, all waves have common properties—amplitude, wavelength, frequency, and speed. **Amplitude describes how far the medium in a wave moves. Wavelength describes a wave's length, and frequency describes how often it occurs. Speed describes how quickly a wave moves.**

Amplitude The height of a wave's crest depends on its amplitude. **Amplitude** is the maximum distance the medium vibrates from the rest position. For a water wave, this distance is how far the water particles move above or below the surface level of calm water. High waves have more energy than low waves. The more energy a wave has, the greater its amplitude.

A transverse wave is shown in **Figure 1.** Its amplitude is the maximum distance the medium moves up or down from its rest position. The amplitude of a longitudinal wave is a measure of how compressed or rarefied the medium becomes. When the compressions are dense, it means the wave's amplitude is large.

Science Standards of Learning

PS.1d Use metric rulers to gather data.

PS.8a Investigate and understand wavelength, frequency, speed, amplitude, rarefaction, and compression for sound waves.

PS.8c Investigate and understand the nature of compression waves for sound.

PS.9a Investigate and understand wavelength, frequency, speed, amplitude, crest, and trough of transverse waves.

FIGURE 1 ·····························

Amplitude

The amplitude of a transverse wave is the maximum distance the medium vibrates from the rest position.

✎ **Label the parts of the wave. Then answer the question.**

Measure What is the amplitude of the wave in centimeters?

_____

Rest position

FIGURE 2 ·······························

Properties of Waves

All waves have amplitude, wavelength, frequency, and speed.

✎ **Read the text on these pages before filling in the boxes and answering these questions.**

1. **Name** Which transverse wave has the shortest wavelength?

   _____

   _____

2. **Apply Concepts** If a transverse wave travels 10 meters in 5 seconds, what is its speed?

   _____

3. **Draw Conclusions** How does a shorter wavelength affect the frequency of a wave?

   _____

   _____

   _____

   _____

   _____

   _____

   _____

   _____

·············· ✎ ··············

🔵 **Identify the Main Idea** Read the text. Underline the main idea in each of the three sections.

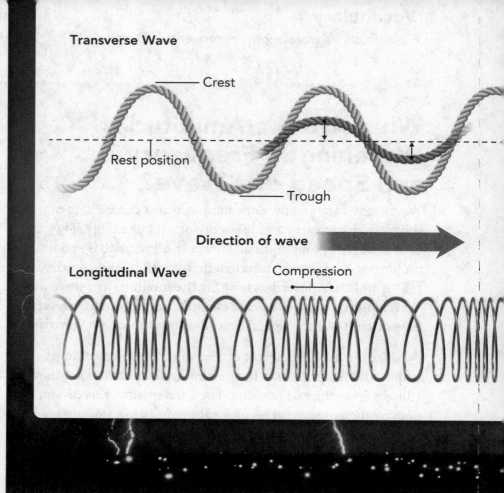

Transverse Wave

Crest

Rest position

Trough

Direction of wave

Longitudinal Wave   Compression

Wavelength A wave travels a certain distance before it starts to repeat. The distance between two corresponding parts of a wave is its **wavelength.** You can find the wavelength of a transverse wave by measuring the distance from crest to crest as shown in **Figure 2.** For a longitudinal wave, the wavelength is the distance between compressions.

Frequency The **frequency** of a wave is the number of waves that pass a given point in a certain amount of time. For example, if you make waves on a rope so that one wave passes by a point every second, the frequency is 1 wave per second. Move your hand up and down more quickly and you increase the frequency.

Frequency is measured in units called **hertz** (Hz), and is defined as the number of waves per second. A wave that occurs every second has a frequency of 1 wave per second (1/s) or 1 Hz. If two waves pass every second the frequency is 2 waves per second (2/s) or 2 Hz.

Which wave has the greater amplitude—yellow or blue?

_____

_____

One yellow wave passes this point each second, so the frequency is _____.

←Wavelength→

Amplitude

Wavelength

Two green waves pass this point each second, so the frequency is _____.

Wavelength

Rarefaction

Speed Different waves travel at different speeds. Think about watching a distant thunderstorm on a hot summer day. The thunder occurs the instant the lightning flashes, but the light and sound reach you seconds apart. This happens because light waves travel much faster than sound waves. In fact, light waves travel about a million times faster than sound waves!

The speed of a wave is how far the wave travels in a given amount of time. You can determine a wave's speed by dividing the distance it travels by the time it takes to travel that distance. Sound, for example, travels about 990 meters in 3 seconds in air when the temperature is 0°C. Therefore, its speed is 330 m/s in these conditions. As long as the temperature of the medium (air) doesn't change, the speed of sound will stay the same.

Do the Quick Lab
Properties of Waves.

🔑 Assess Your Understanding

got it? ....

○ I get it! Now I know that for any wave,

amplitude describes _____

_____,

wavelength describes _____,

frequency describes _____

_____,

and speed describes _____

_____

○ I need extra help with _____

Go to MY SCIENCE ⓢ COACH *online for help with this subject.*

485

How Are Frequency, Wavelength, and Speed Related?

You just learned that you can calculate the speed of a wave by dividing the distance it travels by the time it takes to travel that distance. But you can also calculate the speed of a wave if you know its wavelength and frequency. ⊶ **The speed, wavelength, and frequency of a wave are related by a mathematical formula.**

$$\text{Speed} = \text{Wavelength} \times \text{Frequency}$$

If you know two quantities in the formula, you can calculate the third quantity. For example, if you know a wave's speed and wavelength, you can calculate its frequency. If you know the speed and frequency, you can calculate the wavelength.

$$\text{Frequency} = \frac{\text{Speed}}{\text{Wavelength}}$$

$$\text{Wavelength} = \frac{\text{Speed}}{\text{Frequency}}$$

The speed of a wave remains constant if the medium, temperature, and pressure do not change. For example, all sound waves travel at the same speed in air at a given temperature and pressure. Even if a sound wave's frequency changes, its speed stays the same. So, if the frequency of a sound wave increases, its wavelength must decrease to maintain a constant speed.

do the math!

The table shows measurements of some properties of a sound wave in water and in air.

❶ **Calculate** Using what you know about the relationship between wavelength, frequency, and speed, fill in the table.

❷ **CHALLENGE** What can this table tell you about the speed of a wave?

Medium	Wavelength	Frequency	Speed
Water	_____	200 Hz	1500 m/s
Water	3.75 m	400 Hz	_____
Air (20°C)	10 m	_____	343 m/s
Air (20°C)	_____	17.15 Hz	343 m/s

_____

_____

_____

THE BIG ?

Ride the waves

What are the properties of waves?

FIGURE 3 ·······················

> INTERACTIVE ART The waves in some amusement park wave pools are controlled by regularly spaced bursts of air. Changing the timing and strength of these air bursts also changes the characteristics of the waves that result.

✏ **Predict** List and describe four wave characteristics. Which characteristic(s) do you think would change if the air bursts were stronger? Which would change if more air bursts came in a shorter amount of time? Explain.

_____

_____

_____

_____

_____

_____

_____

_____

_____

_____

_____

_____

Lab zone® Do the Quick Lab *What Affects the Speed of a Wave?*

🔑 Assess Your Understanding

1a. ANSWER THE BIG ? What are the properties of waves?

_____

_____

b. Calculate A wave's frequency is 2 Hz and its wavelength is 4 m. What is the wave's speed?

_____

got it?

○ **I get it!** Now I know that wavelength, frequency, and speed are related by the formula _____

_____

○ **I need extra help with** _____

Go to MY SCIENCE ⓢ COACH *online for help with this subject.*

Interactions of Waves

UNLOCK THE BIG Q?

🔑 **What Changes the Direction of a Wave?**
PS.9a, PS.9b, PS.9c

🔑 **What Are the Two Types of Wave Interference?**
PS.1m, PS.9a

🔑 **How Do Standing Waves Form?**
PS.1m, PS.8b, PS.9a

my planet diary

DISASTER

The Fall of Galloping Gertie

"My breath was coming in gasps; my knees were raw and bleeding, my hands bruised and swollen.... Safely back at the toll plaza, I saw the bridge in its final collapse and saw my car plunge into the Narrows."

This dramatic piece of writing is a witness's real-life account of the collapse of the Tacoma Narrows Bridge in Tacoma, Washington, on November 7, 1940.

Prior to its collapse, the suspension bridge was known for its swaying and rolling in the wind. This motion happened so regularly that the bridge was nicknamed "Galloping Gertie." Only four months after its construction, the bridge collapsed into the waters of Puget Sound during a windstorm. Although a disaster, Galloping Gertie's collapse became a valuable teaching tool for engineers.

Communicate **Discuss the following questions with a partner. Write your answers below.**

1. Why is "Galloping Gertie" an appropriate nickname for the bridge?

_____

_____

2. If you were an engineer studying this bridge collapse, what is one thing you would research?

_____

_____

Do the Inquiry Warm-Up *How Does a Ball Bounce?*

> PLANET DIARY Go to **Planet Diary** to learn more about waves interacting.

Vocabulary

- reflection • refraction • diffraction • interference
- constructive interference • destructive interference
- standing wave • node • antinode • resonance

Skills

- ⟳ Reading: Relate Cause and Effect
- △ Inquiry: Observe

What Changes the Direction of a Wave?

If you toss a ball against a wall, the ball bounces back in a new direction. Like a ball, waves can also change direction. ⌐○─ **Waves change direction by reflection, refraction, and diffraction.**

Reflection When a wave hits a surface, any part of the wave that cannot pass through the surface bounces back. This interaction with a surface is called **reflection.** Reflection happens often in your everyday life. When you looked in your mirror this morning you used reflected light to see yourself. The echo you hear when you shout in an empty gym is also a reflection.

In **Figure 1** you can see how light waves are reflected. All reflected waves obey the law of reflection.

> **Science Standards of Learning**
>
> **PS.9a** Investigate and understand wavelength, frequency, speed, amplitude, crest, and trough of transverse waves.
>
> **PS.9b** Investigate and understand the wave behavior of light.
>
> **PS.9c** Investigate and understand images formed by lenses and mirrors.

FIGURE 1 ···

The Law of Reflection
The law of reflection states that the angle of incidence equals the angle of reflection.

✎ **Explain** Read the sequence of steps, matching each step to its letter in the photo. If the angle of incidence is 45°, explain what the angle of reflection would be.

_____

_____

_____

_____

_____

_____

a Incoming wave A wave moving toward the surface at an angle.

b Angle of incidence The angle between the incoming wave and the normal.

c Normal A line perpendicular to the surface at the point where reflection occurs.

d Angle of reflection The angle between the reflected wave and the normal.

e Reflected wave A wave bouncing off the surface at an angle.

90° angle

Refraction Have you ever ridden a skateboard and gone off the sidewalk onto grass? If so, you know it's hard to keep moving in a straight line. The front wheel on the side moving onto the grass slows down. The front wheel still on the sidewalk continues to move fast. The difference in the speeds of the two front wheels causes the skateboard to change direction.

Like a skateboard that changes direction, changes in speed can cause waves to change direction. Look at **Figure 2.** When a wave enters a new medium at an angle, one side of the wave changes speed before the other side. This causes the wave to bend. Bending occurs because different parts of the wave travel at different speeds. **Refraction** is the bending of waves due to a change in speed.

Waves do not always bend when entering a new medium. No bending occurs if a wave enters a new medium at a right angle. Bending does not occur if the speed of the wave in the new medium is the same as the speed of the wave in the old medium.

....

↺ **Relate Cause and Effect**
In the second paragraph, circle the cause of refraction and underline the effect of refraction.

Beam of light

Air

Wave crests

FIGURE 2 ·······································

▷ VIRTUAL LAB **Refraction of Light Waves**
Light bends when it enters water at an angle because the side of the wave that enters the water first slows down before the other side does.

✎ **Relate Diagrams and Photos**
Suppose you shine a light into a corner of an empty pool. Why will a different spot be lit up if the pool is filled with water?

_____

_____

_____

_____

Water

Diffraction Waves sometimes bend around barriers or pass through openings. When a wave moves around a barrier or through an opening in a barrier, it bends and spreads out. These wave interactions are called **diffraction.** Two examples of diffraction are shown in **Figure 3.**

The Diffraction of Water Waves
Water waves diffract when they encounter canals or shorelines.

The waves bend around the barrier.

The waves spread out after passing through the narrow opening.

apply it!

Use the three pictures on the right to answer the questions.

1 **Observe** Under each picture, write how the waves are changing direction.

2 **Summarize** In what way are reflection, refraction, and diffraction similar?

_____

_____

_____

 Do the Lab Investigation *Making Waves.*

🔑 Assess Your Understanding

1a. Define What is diffraction?

_____

_____

_____

b. Classify A wave bends after entering a new medium. What type of interaction is this?

_____

_____

got it?

○ **I get it!** Now I know that a wave's direction can be changed by _____

_____

_____

○ **I need extra help with** _____

Go to **MY SCIENCE COACH** *online for help with this subject.*

did you know?

Interference is responsible for the iridescent colors seen in oil films, soap bubbles, and the feathers of some birds, like the common grackle. The structure of the bird's feathers creates the interference. The bright colors are only seen at specific angles of reflection.

FIGURE 4 ·······························

Constructive Interference

✎ **Infer** Explain what the black dotted line represents. Then tell what happens to the direction of each wave when the waves meet.

_____

_____

_____

_____

_____

_____

What Are the Two Types of Wave Interference?

Have you ever seen soccer balls collide? The balls bounce off each other because they cannot be in the same place at the same time. Surprisingly, this is not true of waves. Unlike two balls, two waves can overlap when they meet. **Interference** is the interaction between waves that meet. 🔑 **There are two types of interference: constructive and destructive.**

Constructive Interference Interference in which waves combine to form a wave with a larger amplitude than any individual wave's amplitude is called **constructive interference**. You can think of constructive interference as waves "helping each other," or adding their energies. For example, in **Figure 4,** when the crests of two waves overlap, they make a higher crest. If two troughs overlap, they make a deeper trough. In both cases, the amplitude of the combined crests or troughs increases.

❶ Two waves approach each other. The wave on the left has a greater amplitude.

❷ The crest's new amplitude is the sum of the amplitudes of the original crests.

❸ The waves continue on as if they had not met.

Destructive Interference Interference in which two waves combine to form a wave with a smaller amplitude than either original wave had is called **destructive interference.** Destructive interference can occur when the crest of one wave overlaps the trough of another wave. If the crest has a larger amplitude than the trough of the other wave, the crest "wins" and part of it remains. If the original trough had a larger amplitude than the crest of the other wave, the result is a trough. If a crest and trough have equal amplitudes, they will completely cancel as shown in **Figure 5.** Destructive interference is used in noise-canceling headphones to block out distracting noises in a listener's surroundings.

FIGURE 5 ···

> INTERACTIVE ART **Destructive Interference**

✎ ✐ Observe **Look at the pictures below. In the boxes, describe the steps of destructive interference.**

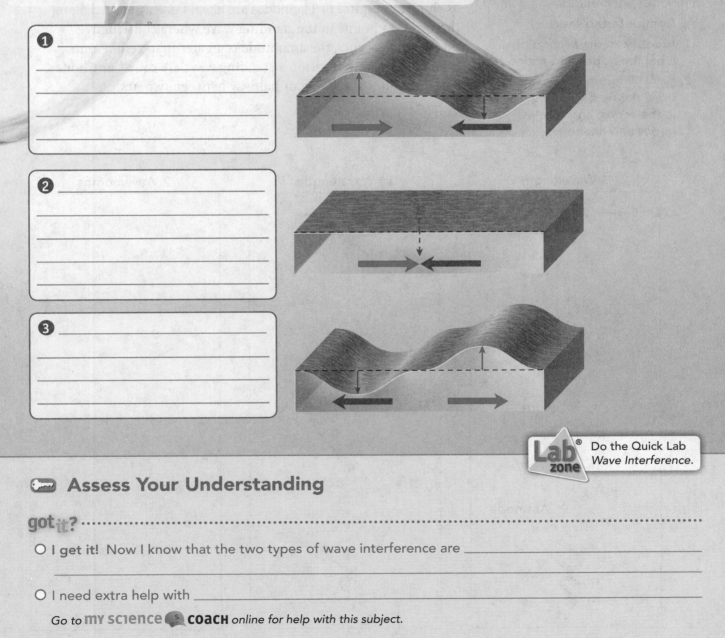

1 _____

2 _____

3 _____

Lab zone® Do the Quick Lab *Wave Interference.*

⚷ Assess Your Understanding

got it? ··

○ **I get it!** Now I know that the two types of wave interference are _____
_____

○ **I need extra help with** _____

Go to MY SCIENCE ⟞ COACH online for help with this subject.

FIGURE 6 ••••••••••••••••••••••••••••

Standing Waves

As the frequency of the standing wave increases, more nodes and antinodes are created.

✎ **Complete the tasks.**

1. **Identify** In the second box, label the nodes and antinodes.

2. **CHALLENGE** In the third box, draw the next standing wave in the series, and label its nodes and antinodes.

How Do Standing Waves Form?

If you tie a rope to a doorknob and shake the free end, waves will travel down the rope, reflect at the end, and come back. The reflected waves will meet the incoming waves and interference occurs. 🔑 **If the incoming wave and reflected wave have just the right frequency, they combine to form a wave that appears to stand still. This wave is called a standing wave.** A **standing wave** is a wave that appears to stand in one place, even though it is two waves interfering as they pass through each other.

Nodes and Antinodes In a standing wave, destructive interference produces points with zero amplitude, called **nodes,** as shown in **Figure 6.** The nodes are always evenly spaced along the wave. At points in the standing wave where constructive interference occurs, the amplitude is greater than zero. Points of maximum amplitude on a standing wave are called **antinodes.** The antinodes always occur halfway between two nodes.

1 Wavelength

Node

Antinode

$1\frac{1}{2}$ Wavelengths

2 Wavelengths

Resonance Have you ever pushed a child on a swing? At first the swing is difficult to push. But once it is going, you need only a gentle push to keep it going. This is because the swing has a natural frequency. Even small pushes that are in rhythm with the swing's natural frequency produce large increases in the swing's amplitude.

Most objects have at least one natural frequency of vibration. Standing waves occur in an object when it vibrates at a natural frequency. If a nearby object vibrates at the same frequency, it can cause resonance. **Resonance** is an increase in the amplitude of a vibration that occurs when external vibrations match an object's natural frequency.

The Tacoma Narrows Bridge, or "Galloping Gertie," may have collapsed because of resonance. Storm winds are said to have resonated with the natural frequency of the bridge. This caused the amplitude of the bridge's sway to increase until the bridge collapsed. You can see the result of the collapse in **Figure 7.**

FIGURE 7 ···

The Power of Resonance
Winds blew as fast as 67 km/h during the storm in which the Tacoma Narrows Bridge collapsed.

✎ **Redesign What might engineers do differently when designing a new bridge for this location?**

_____

_____

_____

Lab® zone
Do the Quick Lab
Standing Waves.

🔑 **Assess Your Understanding**

2a. Describe What causes resonance to occur?

_____

_____

b. ↻ **Relate Cause and Effect** What causes nodes to form in a standing wave?

_____

_____

_____

got it?

○ **I get it!** Now I know that standing waves form when _____

_____

_____

_____

○ I need extra help with _____

Go to **my science ⓢ coach** online for help with this subject.

CHAPTER

14 Study Guide

The basic properties of waves are _____, _____, _____, and _____.

LESSON 1 What Are Waves?

🔑 Mechanical waves form when a source of energy causes a medium to vibrate.

🔑 The three types of mechanical waves are transverse waves, longitudinal waves, and surface waves.

Vocabulary
• wave • energy • medium • mechanical wave • vibration • transverse wave • crest
• trough • longitudinal wave • compression • rarefaction

LESSON 2 Properties of Waves

🔑 Amplitude describes how far the medium in a wave moves. Wavelength describes a wave's length, and frequency describes how often it occurs. Speed describes how quickly a wave moves.

🔑 The speed, wavelength, and frequency of a wave are related by a mathematical formula:
Speed = Wavelength × Frequency.

Vocabulary
• amplitude • wavelength • frequency • hertz

LESSON 3 Interactions of Waves

🔑 Waves change direction by reflection, refraction, and diffraction.

🔑 There are two types of interference: constructive and destructive.

🔑 If the incoming wave and reflected wave have just the right frequency, they combine to form a wave that appears to stand still. This wave is called a standing wave.

Vocabulary
• reflection • refraction • diffraction • interference
• constructive interference • destructive interference • standing wave
• node • antinode • resonance

Review and Assessment

What Are Waves?

1. A wave transfers

   a. energy.   **b.** particles

   c. water.   **d.** air.

2. _____ form when a source of energy causes a medium to vibrate.

3. Classify Label the crest(s) and trough(s) on the transverse wave.

4. Compare and Contrast What is the difference between a transverse wave and a longitudinal wave?

_____

_____

_____

_____

_____

_____

5. Relate Cause and Effect Suppose ripples move from one side of a lake to the other. Does the water move across the lake? Explain.

_____

_____

_____

_____

_____

_____

Properties of Waves

6. The distance between two crests is a wave's

   a. amplitude.   **b.** wavelength.

   c. frequency.   **d.** speed.

7. The _____ of a wave is the number of waves that pass a given point in a certain amount of time.

This wave in the middle of the ocean was produced by an underwater earthquake. Use the diagram to answer Questions 8–10.

200,000 m

Speed 200 m/s

0.3 m

8. Interpret Diagrams What is the amplitude of the wave? What is its wavelength?

_____

_____

9. Calculate Find the frequency of the wave.

_____

_____

_____

10. math! How long would it take this wave to travel 5,000 km?

_____

_____

_____

_____

497

LESSON 3   Interactions of Waves

11. The bending of a wave due to a change in speed is called

    a. interference.   **b.** reflection.

    c. diffraction.   **d.** refraction.

12. _____ occurs when external vibrations match an object's natural frequency.

13. Predict Two waves are traveling toward each other. The crests from the waves meet. Describe what happens.

_____

_____

_____

_____

14. Draw Conclusions If you push a shopping cart and one wheel hits a rough patch of concrete, it is difficult to steer the cart in a straight line. Explain how this is similar to refraction of a wave as it enters a new medium.

_____

_____

_____

_____

_____

_____

15. [Write About It] Wave interaction occurs often in the environment. Describe three different ways that you could observe waves changing direction in an indoor swimming pool. Mention as many types of waves as possible.

APPLY ? THE BIG   What are the properties of waves?

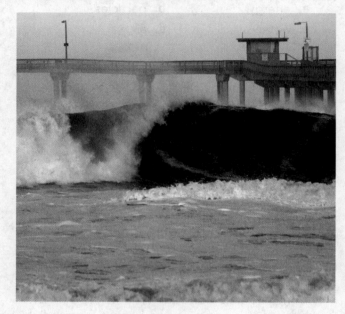

16. During a storm, a TV reporter says, "The ocean waves are 3 meters high. They are about 45 m apart and are hitting the shore every 15 seconds." Think about the four basic properties of waves and describe these ocean waves using the correct science words. (*Hint:* You will need to do some calculations first.)

_____

_____

_____

_____

_____

_____

_____

_____

_____

_____

_____

Read each question and choose the best answer.

1 Two waves approach each other as shown in the diagram below. What will be the amplitude of the wave produced when the crests from each wave meet?

A 20 cm   **B** 35 cm

C 15 cm   **D** 5 cm

2 When a wave enters a new medium at 60° and changes speed, the wave—

F does not bend because one side changes speed before the other side

G does not bend because the angle is less than 90°

H bends because both sides change speed at the same time

J bends because one side changes speed before the other side

3 The speed of a wave in a spring is 3 m/s. If the wavelength is 0.1 m, what is the frequency?

A 30 Hz   **B** 0.3 Hz

C 30 m/s   **D** 0.3 m/s

4 Which of the following is true about standing waves?

F Constructive interference produces points with zero amplitude.

G The nodes are unevenly spaced along the wave.

H The amplitude of antinodes is greater than nodes.

J Nodes are points of maximum energy on the wave.

5 What is the angle of incidence if a reflected wave bounces off a mirror at an angle of 65°?

A 25°

B 65°

C 90°

D 115°

6 Which of the following statements is true about the waves shown below?

F Wave A has a longer wavelength than Wave B.

G Wave A has lower frequency than Wave B.

H Wave A has a higher amplitude than Wave B.

J Wave A and Wave B have equal amplitudes.

Wall of Water

For as long as humans have sailed on the oceans, ships have disappeared without explanation. People chalked these losses up to bad luck and bad weather. A mysterious phenomenon, proven in 2004 to exist, may finally explain why some large ships are never seen again.

Waves in water usually behave like the other waves around them. Most waves in an area are about the same height and move at the same rate. Ocean waves are rarely more than 15 meters in height and usually form rolling hills of water. But freak monster waves can top 30 meters in height, forming huge walls of water!

Some monster waves form where two currents meet and their waves combine. The weather may be responsible for other monster waves. If an ordinary large wave travels at the same speed and in the same direction as the wind for more than 12 hours, the extra push from the wind can cause the wave to reach monster heights. Some monster waves seem to grow out of normal ocean wave patterns. Physicists theorize that these unstable waves absorb energy from the surrounding waves and grow to vast heights.

Most ships are not designed to withstand 30-meter-high waves, so it's no wonder that little has been found but wreckage. Fortunately, scientists are working on ways to protect ships and sailors in the face of these enormous destructive waves.

Model It Research how so-called monster waves focus and amplify the effects of surrounding waves. Use computer technology to create a diagram or to model the effects. Explain your diagram.

An *Operatic Superpower*

Can someone really break a glass by singing a high note? It may seem like a superpower, but the human voice does have the power to shatter a crystal wine glass! This feat is commonly credited to opera singers because they have very powerful and well-trained voices.

Many wine glasses are made of a type of glass called crystal. The molecules in a crystal glass are arranged in a repeating pattern that forms a repeating internal structure. If you tap a crystal object, you can hear a clear tone. That tone is the natural resonant frequency of vibration for that crystal. When the crystal is exposed to a sound at that frequency, the molecules of the crystal vibrate. When the glass vibrates too much, the shape of the glass distorts, which causes the glass to crack. The cracks expand very rapidly, and the crystal shatters.

A trained singer can reproduce the natural frequency of a crystal glass. If the singer can sing the tone of the crystal's natural frequency loudly enough, the singing can shatter the glass!

Design It Resonant frequencies can also be used to make music. Glass harps use wine glasses filled with varying amounts of water to create different notes. The player runs a moistened finger around the rim of each glass. The size of the glass and the amount of water determine which note sounds. Research to learn more about how glass harps work. Then design an experiment to test the amount of water needed to create different pitches. Create a one-page procedure for your experiment.

 PS.1k, PS.1m, PS.8b

HOW DOES MUSIC TRAVEL TO YOUR EARS?

What determines the pitch and loudness of sound?

As these New Orleans musicians play their instruments, vibrations travel through the air as sound waves. The audience hears the music when their ears detect the sound waves. **Infer** **How do you hear sound from a drum?**

_____

_____

_____

_____

_____

_____

_____

> **UNTAMED SCIENCE** Watch the **Untamed Science** video to learn more about sound.

Sound

Science Standards of Learning

PS.1g, PS.1i, PS.1j, PS.1k, PS.1m,
PS.1n, PS.8a, PS.8b, PS.8c, PS.8d

15 Getting Started

Check Your Understanding

1. **Background** Read the paragraph below and then answer the question.

> One morning, an earthquake occurs in California. The ground **vibrates** as **waves** travel out in all directions from the source of the earthquake. The rocks inside Earth are the **medium** that transmits the waves.

> To **vibrate** is to move back and forth.
>
> **Waves** are disturbances that carry energy from one place to another.
>
> A **medium** is a material through which a wave travels.

• What happens inside Earth during an earthquake?

_____

_____

▶ MY READING WEB If you had trouble completing the question above, visit **My Reading Web** and type in *Sound*.

Vocabulary Skill

Identify Multiple Meanings Some familiar words have more than one meaning. Words you use every day may have different meanings in science. Look at the different meanings of the words below.

Word	Everyday Meaning	Scientific Meaning
medium	*adj.* in the middle in quality, amount, or size **Example:** The boy is *medium* in size and build.	*n.* the material through which a wave travels **Example:** Air is a common *medium* for sound to travel through.
reflect	*v.* to express or show **Example:** Her skills in basketball *reflect* years of training.	*v.* to be bent or thrown back **Example:** The water waves *reflect* off the sides of the pool.

2. **Quick Check** Circle the sentence below that uses the scientific meaning of the word *reflect*.

• Her article *reflects* thorough research.
• Light waves *reflect* off the surface of a mirror.

density

pitch

decibel

intensity

Chapter Preview

LESSON 1
- density
  - Identify the Main Idea
  - Graph

LESSON 2
- pitch
- loudness
- intensity
- decibel
- Doppler effect
  - Compare and Contrast
  - Make Models

LESSON 3
- music
- fundamental tone
- overtone
  - Identify Supporting Evidence
  - Predict

LESSON 4
- ear canal
- eardrum
- cochlea
  - Relate Cause and Effect
  - Observe

LESSON 5
- echolocation
- ultrasound
- sonar
- sonogram
  - Ask Questions
  - Calculate

> VOCAB FLASH CARDS For extra help with vocabulary, visit **Vocab Flash Cards** and type in *Sound*.

The Nature of Sound

UNLOCK THE BIG **?**

🗝 **What Is Sound?**
PS.8a, PS.8c, PS.8d

🗝 **What Factors Affect the Speed of Sound?**
PS.1g, PS.1i, PS.1j, PS.8a, PS.8c, PS.8d

my planet diary

Thunder and Lightning

It's a hot, sticky summer day, and the sky is filled with dark clouds. Suddenly, a flash of light zigzags through the air! A few seconds later, you hear the loud crack of thunder.

The lightning you see causes the thunder you hear. The reason you see lightning before you hear thunder is because light travels much faster than sound. You can use this fact to figure out how close the storm is. After you see a flash of lightning, count off the seconds until you hear the thunder. Divide the number of seconds by five. The result gives the approximate distance (in miles) to the storm.

FUN FACTS

Write your answer to the question below.
You notice that the time between seeing the lightning and hearing the thunder is increasing. What does this mean?

_____

_____

_____

_____

_____

▷ **PLANET DIARY** Go to **Planet Diary** to learn more about the nature of sound.

Lab zone® Do the Inquiry Warm-Up
What Is Sound?

Science Standards of Learning

PS.8a Investigate and understand wavelength, frequency, speed, amplitude, rarefaction, and compression for sound waves.

PS.8c Investigate and understand the nature of compression waves for sound.

PS.8d Investigate and understand technological applications of sound.

What Is Sound?

Here is a riddle: If a tree falls in a forest and no one hears it, does the tree make a sound? To a scientist, a falling tree makes a sound whether someone hears it or not. When a tree falls, the energy with which it strikes the ground causes a disturbance. Particles in the ground and the air begin to vibrate, or move back and forth. The vibrations create a sound wave as the energy travels through two mediums—air and the ground. 🗝 **Sound is a disturbance that travels through a medium as a longitudinal wave.**

Vocabulary
- density

Skills
↻ Reading: Identify the Main Idea
△ Inquiry: Graph

Making Sound Waves

A sound wave begins with a vibration. Look at the drum shown in **Figure 1.** When the side of the drum (called the drumhead) is struck, it vibrates rapidly in and out. These vibrations disturb nearby air particles. Each time the drumhead moves outward, it pushes air particles together, creating a *compression*. When the drumhead moves inward, the air particles bounce back and spread out, creating a *rarefaction*. These compressions and rarefactions travel through the air as longitudinal waves.

How Sound Waves Travel

Like other mechanical waves, sound waves carry energy through a medium without moving the particles of the medium along. Each particle of the medium vibrates as the disturbance passes. When the disturbance reaches your ears, you hear the sound.

A common medium for sound is air. But sound can travel through solids and liquids, too. For example, when you knock on a solid wooden door, the particles in the wood vibrate. The vibrations make sound waves that travel through the door. When the waves reach the other side of the door, they make sound waves in the air.

Vocabulary Identify Multiple Meanings Review the multiple meanings of the words in the Getting Started section and answer the question. What is the material through which sound waves travel?

_____

FIGURE 1 ....
Sound Waves
As the drumheads vibrate, they create sound waves that travel through the air.

✎ **Interpret Diagrams** Label each box as a compression or a rarefaction. Explain how you knew what to label them.

_____

_____

_____

_____

Wavelength

Identify the Main Idea
Underline the main idea in the text under Diffraction of Sound Waves.

FIGURE 2 ·······························

Diffraction
Diffraction occurs when sound waves pass through an opening such as a doorway.

Identify Which diagram—A, B, or C—correctly shows what happens to sound waves when they pass through the doorway? Explain your answer.

_____

_____

_____

_____

_____

_____

_____

_____

Diffraction of Sound Waves Have you ever wondered why when you are sitting in a classroom you can hear your friends talking in the hallway before they walk through the doorway? You hear them because sound waves do not always travel in straight lines. Sound waves can diffract, or bend, around the edges of an opening, such as a doorway.

Sound waves can also diffract around obstacles or corners. This is why you can hear someone who is talking in the hallway before the person walks around the corner. The sound waves bend around the corner. Then they spread out so you can hear them even though you cannot see who is talking. Remember this the next time you want to tell a secret!

Classroom — Hallway — **A**
Classroom — Hallway — **B**
Classroom — Hallway — **C**

Lab zone® Do the Quick Lab *Understanding Sound.*

Assess Your Understanding

1a. Identify A sound wave carries _____ through a medium.

b. Compare and Contrast In a sound wave, the particles in the medium are close together in a (compression/rarefaction) and farther apart in a (compression/rarefaction).

c. Apply Concepts Explain why you can hear a ringing telephone through a closed door.

_____

_____

_____

_____

got it? ···

○ **I get it!** Now I know sound is _____

_____

○ **I need extra help with** _____

Go to **MY SCIENCE** s **COACH** online for help with this subject.

What Factors Affect the Speed of Sound?

Suppose you were in a stadium watching the baseball player in **Figure 3.** You might see the bat hit the ball before you hear the hit. It is possible to see an action before you hear it because sound travels much more slowly than light. At room temperature, about 20°C, sound travels through air at 342 m/s. This is nearly 900,000 times slower than the speed of light! But the speed of sound is not always 342 m/s. Sound waves travel at different speeds in different media. **The speed of sound depends on the temperature, stiffness, and density of the medium the sound travels through.**

Temperature In a given liquid or gas, sound travels more slowly at lower temperatures than at higher temperatures. Why? At lower temperatures, the particles of a medium move more slowly than at higher temperatures. It is more difficult for the particles to move, and they return to their original positions more slowly.

Science Standards of Learning

PS.1g Construct and interpret data tables showing the independent and dependent variables, derived quantities, and the number of trials.

PS.1i Construct and interpret frequency distributions, scatterplots, line plots, and histograms.

PS.1j Make valid conclusions after analyzing data.

PS.8a Investigate and understand wavelength, frequency, speed, amplitude, rarefaction, and compression for sound waves.

PS.8c Investigate and understand the nature of compression waves for sound.

PS.8d Investigate and understand technological applications of sound.

FIGURE 3

Speed of Sound in Air
How fast the sound of the bat hitting the ball travels depends on the air temperature. The data in the table show how the speed of sound in air changes with temperature.

✎ **Use the data to answer the questions.**

1. **Graph** Create a line graph. Plot temperature on the horizontal axis and speed on the vertical axis. Give the graph a title.

2. **Predict** What might the speed of sound be at 30°C? _____

Air Temperature (°C)	Speed (m/s)
−20	318
−10	324
0	330
10	336
20	342

509

Stiffness

Stiffness Years ago, Native Americans put their ears to the ground to find out if herds of bison or other animals were nearby. By listening for sounds in the ground they could hear the herds sooner than if they listened for sounds in the air. What is it about the state of the medium—solid, liquid, or gas—that determines the speed of sound?

The speed of sound depends on the stiffness of the medium. Sound travels more quickly in stiff media because when the particles of the medium are compressed, they quickly spread out again. For example, steel is stiffer than wood. If you knocked on both a wooden and steel door of the same thickness, the steel door would transmit the sound more easily. Sound also travels better over long distances in stiff media because sound waves lose energy more slowly than in less stiff media.

Solids are stiffer than liquids or gases. The particles in a solid are close together, so they bounce back and forth quickly as the compressions and rarefactions of the sound waves pass by. Most liquids are not as stiff as solids. So sound does not travel as fast in liquids as it does in solids. Gases are not very stiff. Sound generally travels the slowest in gases.

did you know?

An astronaut riding a vehicle on the surface of the moon would not hear the sound of the engine. Sound can travel only if there is a medium. There are no air molecules to compress or expand on the moon, so there is no sound.

do the math! Analyzing Data

The table shows the speed of sound in different media. Use the data to answer the following questions.

1 Interpret Tables In general, does sound travel faster in solids, liquids, or gases?

_____

2 Infer Which substance is stiffer—air or water?

_____

3 Infer What is the stiffest substance in the table?

_____

4 Apply Concepts Suppose you put your ear to a steel fence. You tell your friend to yell and tap the fence at the same time from far away. Which do you think that you will hear first, the yell or the tap? Why?

_____

_____

_____

_____

_____

5 [CHALLENGE] How many times faster does sound travel in a diamond than in air?

_____

_____

Speed of Sound	
Medium	Speed (m/s)
Gases (20°C)	
Air	342
Helium	977
Liquids (20°C)	
Mercury	1,450
Fresh water	1,482
Solids	
Lead	1,200
Plastic	1,800
Hardwood	4,000
Steel	5,200
Diamond	12,000

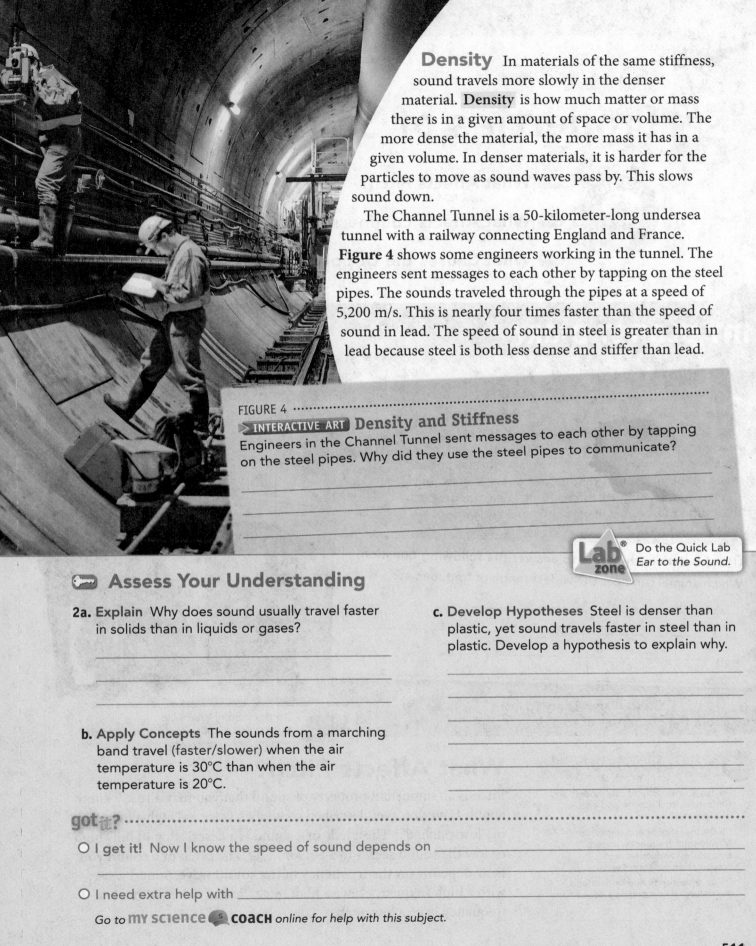

Density In materials of the same stiffness, sound travels more slowly in the denser material. **Density** is how much matter or mass there is in a given amount of space or volume. The more dense the material, the more mass it has in a given volume. In denser materials, it is harder for the particles to move as sound waves pass by. This slows sound down.

The Channel Tunnel is a 50-kilometer-long undersea tunnel with a railway connecting England and France. **Figure 4** shows some engineers working in the tunnel. The engineers sent messages to each other by tapping on the steel pipes. The sounds traveled through the pipes at a speed of 5,200 m/s. This is nearly four times faster than the speed of sound in lead. The speed of sound in steel is greater than in lead because steel is both less dense and stiffer than lead.

FIGURE 4 ·······

▶ **INTERACTIVE ART** **Density and Stiffness**
Engineers in the Channel Tunnel sent messages to each other by tapping on the steel pipes. Why did they use the steel pipes to communicate?

_____
_____
_____

Lab zone® Do the Quick Lab
Ear to the Sound.

🔑 Assess Your Understanding

2a. Explain Why does sound usually travel faster in solids than in liquids or gases?

_____
_____

b. Apply Concepts The sounds from a marching band travel (faster/slower) when the air temperature is 30°C than when the air temperature is 20°C.

c. Develop Hypotheses Steel is denser than plastic, yet sound travels faster in steel than in plastic. Develop a hypothesis to explain why.

_____
_____
_____
_____
_____
_____
_____

got it? ···

○ **I get it!** Now I know the speed of sound depends on _____
_____

○ **I need extra help with** _____

Go to **MY SCIENCE** 🅢 **COACH** _online for help with this subject._

Properties of Sound

UNLOCK THE BIG ?

🔑 **What Affects Pitch?**
PS.1m, PS.8a, PS.8c

🔑 **What Affects Loudness?**
PS.1g, PS.1j, PS.8a, PS.8c

🔑 **What Causes the Doppler Effect?**
PS.8a, PS.8c, PS.8d

MY PLANET DIARY

Silent Call

To get a dog's attention, a dog trainer blows into a small whistle. But you don't hear a thing. Dogs can hear frequencies well above the human range of hearing. Frequency is measured in hertz (Hz), or the number of sound waves a vibrating object gives off per second. A higher frequency means that the sound has a higher pitch. The table compares the range of frequencies that humans and various animals can hear.

Use the data in the table to answer the following question.

Which animal can hear the widest range of frequencies?

_____

_____

_____

_____

> PLANET DIARY Go to **Planet Diary** to learn more about the properties of sound.

SCIENCE STATS

Animal	Range of Hearing (in Hertz)
Human	20–20,000
Dog	67–45,000
Mouse	1,000–91,000
Cat	45–64,000
Bullfrog	100–2,500
Elephant	16–12,000

Lab zone Do the Inquiry Warm-Up
How Does Amplitude Affect Loudness?

What Affects Pitch?

Pitch is an important property of sound that you may already know about. Have you ever described someone's voice as "high-pitched" or "low-pitched"? The **pitch** of a sound is a description of how high or low the sound seems to a person. 🔑 **The pitch of a sound you hear depends on the frequency of the sound wave.** Sound waves with a high frequency have a high pitch. Sound waves with a low frequency have a low pitch.

Vocabulary

- pitch • loudness • intensity • decibel
- Doppler effect

Skills

↻ Reading: Compare and Contrast
△ Inquiry: Make Models

The frequency of a sound wave depends on how fast the source of the sound is vibrating. For example, when you speak or sing, air from your lungs rushes past your vocal cords, making them vibrate. This produces sound waves. To sing specific pitches, or notes, you use muscles in your throat to stretch or relax your vocal cords. When your vocal cords stretch, they vibrate more quickly as the air rushes by them. This creates higher-frequency sound waves that have higher pitches. When your vocal cords relax, lower-frequency sound waves with lower pitches are produced.

Frequency is measured in hertz (Hz). For example, a frequency of 50 Hz means 50 vibrations per second. A trained soprano voice can produce frequencies higher than 1,000 Hz. A bass singer can produce frequencies lower than 80 Hz. Young people can normally hear sounds with frequencies between 20 Hz and 20,000 Hz.

FIGURE 1 ....

Pitch

The female soprano singer sings high notes and the male bass singer sings low notes.

△ **Make Models In the bubble above the bass singer, draw lines to represent the frequency of the sound wave for a low note. Then explain your drawing.**

_____

_____

_____

_____

Lab zone   Do the Lab Investigation *Changing Pitch.*

⚷ Assess Your Understanding

got it? ....

○ **I get it!** Now I know the pitch of a sound that you hear depends on _____
_____

○ **I need extra help with** _____

  Go to **my science** ⒮ **coach** *online for help with this subject.*

FIGURE 2 ···································

Intensity

Sound waves spread out as they travel away from the source.

🖉 **Interpret Diagrams** Rank the intensity of a sound wave at the three locations. A ranking of 1 is the greatest. Write your answers in the boxes. Explain your answers.

_____

_____

_____

_____

_____

_____

What Affects Loudness?

Loudness is another important property of sound. You probably already know about loudness. For example, the closer you are to a sound, the louder it is. Also, a whisper in your ear can be just as loud as a shout from a block away. **Loudness** describes your awareness of the energy of a sound. 🔑 **The loudness of a sound depends on the energy and intensity of the sound wave.**

Energy If you hit a drum lightly, you hear a sound. If you hit the drum harder, you hear a louder sound. Why? When you hit a drum harder, you transfer more energy to it. This causes the amplitude, or the distance the drumhead moves from its rest position, to increase. A sound source vibrating with a large amplitude produces a sound wave with a large amplitude. Recall that the greater the amplitude of a wave, the more energy it has. So the more energy a sound wave has, the louder it sounds.

Intensity If you were to move closer to the stage shown in **Figure 2,** the voices of the performers would sound louder. Why? Close to the sound source, a sound wave covers a small area. As a wave travels away from the source, it covers more area. The total energy of the wave, however, stays the same. Therefore, the closer a sound wave is to its source, the more energy it has in a given area. The amount of energy a sound wave carries per second through a unit area is its **intensity**. A sound wave of greater intensity sounds louder.

Measuring Loudness The loudness of different sounds is compared using a unit called the **decibel** (dB). The table in the Apply It below compares the loudness of some familiar sounds. The loudness of a sound you can barely hear is about 0 dB. A 10-dB increase in loudness represents a tenfold increase in the intensity of the sound. For example, a 10-dB sound is ten times more intense than a 0-dB sound. A 20-dB sound is 100 times more intense than a 0-dB sound and ten times more intense than a 10-dB sound. Sounds louder than 100 dB can cause damage to your ears, especially if you listen to those sounds for long periods of time. For this reason, airport workers, like the one shown to the right, wear hearing protection.

apply it!

Use the table to answer the questions.

❶ Which sounds louder, a rock concert or a jet plane at takeoff?_____

❷ Which sounds could be dangerous to your ears?

_____

_____

❸ **Calculate** How much more intense is a 20-dB whisper than the threshold of human hearing?

_____

❹ [CHALLENGE] How much more intense is a 90-dB hair dryer than 60-dB street traffic?

_____

Measuring Loudness	
Sound	Loudness (dB)
Threshold of human hearing	0
Whisper	15–20
Normal conversation	40–50
Busy street traffic	60–70
Hairdryer	80–90
Rock concert	110–120
Headphones at peak volume	120
Jet plane at takeoff	120–160

Lab zone ® Do the Quick Lab *Listen to This.*

🔑 Assess Your Understanding

1a. Review The amount of energy a sound wave carries per second through a unit area is its

_____

b. Describe The intensity of a sound wave (increases/decreases) with distance.

c. Calculate An 80-dB sound is _____ times more intense than a 60-dB sound.

got it?

○ **I get it!** Now I know that the loudness of a sound depends on _____

_____

_____

○ **I need extra help with** _____

Go to my science ⓢ coach *online for help with this subject.*

Compare and Contrast
The waves in front of a moving sound source have a (shorter/longer) wavelength. The waves behind a moving sound source have a (shorter/longer) wavelength.

What Causes the Doppler Effect?

Have you ever listened to the siren of a firetruck on its way to a fire? If so, then you probably noticed that as the truck goes by, the pitch of the siren drops. But the pitch of the siren stays constant for the firefighters in the truck. The siren's pitch changes only if it is moving toward or away from a listener.

The change in frequency of a wave as its source moves in relation to an observer is called the **Doppler effect.** If the waves are sound waves, the change in frequency is heard as a change in pitch. The Doppler effect is named after the Austrian scientist Christian Doppler (1803–1853). **The Doppler effect occurs because the motion of the source causes the waves to either get closer together or spread out.**

Figure 3 shows how sound waves from a moving source behave. Each time the siren sends out a new wave, the firetruck moves ahead in the same direction as the waves in front of the truck. This causes the waves to get closer together. Because the waves are closer together, they have a shorter wavelength and a higher frequency as they reach observers in front of the truck. As the truck moves away, it travels in the opposite direction of the sound waves behind it. This causes the waves to spread out. Because they spread out, the waves have a longer wavelength and a lower frequency as they reach the observers behind the truck.

FIGURE 3 ....

> ART IN MOTION **The Doppler Effect**
As the firetruck speeds by, observers hear a change in the pitch of the siren. **Identify Circle the answer that describes the pitch that the observers hear.**

People behind the firetruck hear a (lower/higher) pitch than the firefighters in the truck hear.

People standing in front of the firetruck hear a (lower/higher) pitch than the firefighters in the truck hear.

FIRE DEPARTMENT

How Your Headphones Work

EXPLORE THE BIG ?

What determines the pitch and loudness of sound?

FIGURE 4 ....

> INTERACTIVE ART Headphones turn an electrical signal into sound waves.

❶ An electrical signal travels up a wire.

❷ The electrical signal causes a magnet to vibrate.

❸ The magnet is attached to a thin cone of material. The vibrating cone sends sound waves through the air.

Cone

Magnet

Wire

⤵ **Compare and Contrast** Compare how a drum and headphones produce sounds of higher pitch and greater loudness.

_____

_____

_____

_____

_____

_____

_____

Lab zone® Do the Quick Lab *Pipe Sounds.*

🔑 Assess Your Understanding

2. ANSWER THE BIG ? What determines the pitch and loudness of sound?

_____

_____

_____

_____

_____

got it?

◯ **I get it!** Now I know that the Doppler effect occurs because _____

_____

_____

◯ **I need extra help with** _____

Go to MY SCIENCE COACH online for help with this subject.

517

Music

UNLOCK THE BIG ?

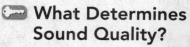 **What Determines Sound Quality?**

PS.1j, PS.8a, PS.8b, PS.8c, PS.8d

MY PLANET DIARY

BLOG

Posted by: Jameel

Location: Orlando, Florida

I play an instrument called the French horn. The French horn has valves, a bell, a mouthpiece, and three keys. It is interesting how pitch affects the music that I make. While I was practicing, the music sounded out of tune. I realized I hadn't tuned the instrument, so I slid the tuning valve up and down until I got the right pitch. I like to play my instrument because it enhances my hand/eye coordination. I also love the sound of the music when I play it right.

Write your answers to the questions below.

1. What does it mean to tune an instrument?

_____

_____

_____

2. The musicians in a marching band do not tune their instruments until they are outside. Why do you suppose this is?

_____

_____

> PLANET DIARY Go to **Planet Diary** to learn more about music.

 Lab zone Do the Inquiry Warm-Up *What Is Music?*

What Determines Sound Quality?

Most people agree on what is and what is not music. **Music** is a set of notes that combine in patterns that are pleasing. Noise, on the other hand, usually has no pleasing patterns. When you describe a sound as pleasant or unpleasant, you are describing sound quality. The sound quality of music depends on the instruments making the music. **The sound quality of musical instruments results from blending a fundamental tone with its overtones.**

Vocabulary
- music • fundamental tone
- overtone

Skills
- Reading: Identify Supporting Evidence
- Inquiry: Predict

Fundamental Tones and Overtones To understand sound quality, consider the example of a guitar string. As the string vibrates, waves travel along the string and reflect back, setting up a standing wave. Standing waves occur in all musical instruments when they are played. In a trumpet, for example, standing waves occur in a vibrating column of air.

A standing wave can occur only at specific frequencies, which are called natural frequencies. The lowest natural frequency is called the **fundamental tone.** The higher natural frequencies are called overtones. **Overtones** have frequencies that are two, three, or more times the frequency of the fundamental tone.

Most instruments produce several natural frequencies at once. The fundamental tone determines what note you hear. Each instrument produces different overtones, so the blending of the fundamental tones and overtones produces different sound qualities. The size, shape, and material of the instrument determine which overtones are loudest. For example, strumming a guitar's strings forces the guitar's hollow body to vibrate and resonate with the natural frequencies of the guitar strings. Resonance increases the amplitude of the vibration, increasing the loudness of the guitar.

Identify Supporting Evidence Underline the reason that the sound quality of a guitar is different from that of a trumpet.

apply it!

A guitar can produce a fundamental tone of 262 Hz. The diagrams show how the fundamental tone and the first two overtones combine to produce the unique sound for a guitar string.

1 Calculate What are the frequencies of the first and second overtones?

Frequency of first overtone = _____

Frequency of second overtone = _____

2 Explain What determines which overtone will be loudest?

_____

_____

3 CHALLENGE Which overtone will be loudest? Why?

_____

Fundamental tone

+

First overtone

+

Second overtone

=

Resulting sound wave

Groups of Musical Instruments

How does a musician control the sounds produced by a musical instrument? To control pitch, the musician changes the fundamental tones. To control loudness, the musician changes the energy of the vibrations. The way pitch and loudness are controlled varies among the groups of instruments.

Stringed Instruments

Stringed instruments include the guitar, violin, cello, and double bass. The strings of these instruments produce sound by vibrating when they are plucked or rubbed with a bow. To create louder sounds, the musicians pluck the strings harder or press the bow harder against the strings. To vary the pitch, the musicians change the length of the vibrating string. They do this by placing their fingers on different places along the string as they play. A short string produces a higher-pitched sound than a long string. The material, thickness, and tightness of a string also affect the pitch it produces.

FIGURE 1 ·····························
Violin
The musician creates sound by rubbing the bow across the strings.

✎ **Interpret Photos** Insert an arrow in the box above to indicate in what direction the musician should move his finger to create a higher-pitched sound.

Percussion Instruments

Percussion instruments include the drums, bells, cymbals, and xylophone. These instruments vibrate when struck. To create louder sounds, the musician hits the instrument harder. The pitch of these instruments depends on the material from which they are made, the size of the instrument, and the part of the instrument that is played. For example, a large drum produces a lower pitch than a small drum.

FIGURE 2 ·····························
Drums
The musicians create sound by hitting the drums.

✎ **Identify** Circle the drum that would produce the highest pitch.

Wind Instruments

Wind instruments include the trumpet, trombone, clarinet, and flute. These instruments create sound when the musician blows on or across the mouthpiece. This causes the air column inside the instrument to vibrate. The musician creates a louder sound by blowing harder. The musician changes pitch by changing the length of the air column. A shorter air column produces a higher pitch than a longer air column. In many wind instruments, the musician changes the length of the air column by pressing keys or valves. In the trombone, the musician changes the length of the air column by moving a slide either closer to or farther away from the mouthpiece.

FIGURE 3 ··

Trombone

The musician creates sound by blowing into the mouthpiece.

Predict If the musician pushes the slide away from her, what will happen to the pitch of the trombone? Why?

_____

_____

_____

_____

Slide

Lab® zone Do the Quick Lab *How Can You Change Pitch?*

🔑 Assess Your Understanding

1a. List What are the three groups of musical instruments?

_____

b. Classify What types of instruments are a bell, a whistle, and a banjo?

_____

_____

_____

got it?

○ **I get it!** Now I know the sound quality of a musical instrument results from _____

_____

_____

○ **I need extra help with** _____

Go to MY SCIENCE ⬤ COACH *online for help with this subject.*

521

Virginia

LESSON

4 Hearing Sound

UNLOCK THE BIG

🔑 **How Do Your Ears Work?**

PS.1m, PS.8a, PS.8c, PS.8d

my planet diary

MISCONCEPTION

Misconception: Deaf people are not able to sense music.

Did you know that Beethoven composed many great works after he lost his hearing? Like all musicians, Beethoven could read music and hear it being played in his mind. But Beethoven may have been able to appreciate music in ways that musicians with normal hearing cannot. A recent study has shown that deaf people can sense vibrations in the same area of the brain that is used to hear. These vibrations create a pattern that they recognize and enjoy.

Deaf musicians can also feel vibrations in different parts of their bodies. The famous solo percussionist Evelyn Glennie performs barefoot so that she can better feel the vibrations in the floor. She also notices changes in the density of the air around her.

Write your answers to the questions below.

1. What senses are used to feel music?

_____

2. Describe an example of how you have felt the vibrations from music.

_____

_____

_____

> PLANET DIARY Go to **Planet Diary** to learn more about hearing sound.

Lab® Do the Inquiry Warm-Up
Hearing Sound

Vocabulary
- ear canal • eardrum
- cochlea

Skills
↻ Reading: Relate Cause and Effect
△ Inquiry: Observe

How Do Your Ears Work?

The library is quiet. You are doing your homework. Suddenly, a door slams shut. Startled, you turn in the direction of the sound. Your ears detected the sound waves produced by the slamming door. But how exactly did your brain receive the information?

 Your ear gathers sound waves and sends information about sound to your brain. Your ear has three main sections: the outer ear, the middle ear, and the inner ear. Each section has a different function. The outer ear funnels sound waves, the middle ear transmits the waves inward, and the inner ear converts sound waves into a form that travels to your brain.

apply it!

One of the functions of your ears is to locate the direction of sounds.

❶ Ask your partner to sit in a chair with eyes closed.

❷ △ Observe Tap two pencils together in different locations around your partner's head and face. Ask your partner to identify what direction the sounds come from. Record the locations where the taps are easily identified. Record the locations where the taps are harder to identify.

_____
_____
_____
_____
_____

❸ Switch places with your partner and repeat steps 1 and 2.

❹ **Draw Conclusions** Discuss which sounds were easily located. Suggest an explanation for your observations.

_____
_____
_____
_____
_____
_____
_____
_____
_____
_____
_____
_____
_____

Outer Ear

The first section of your ear is the outer ear. The outermost part of your outer ear looks and acts like a funnel. It collects sound waves and directs them into a narrow region called the **ear canal.** Your ear canal is a few centimeters long and ends at the eardrum. The **eardrum** is a small, tightly stretched, drumlike membrane. The sound waves make your eardrum vibrate, just as a drum vibrates when you strike it.

② **Middle Ear**

Behind the eardrum is the middle ear. The middle ear contains the three smallest bones in your body—the hammer, the anvil, and the stirrup. The hammer is attached to the eardrum. When the eardrum vibrates, the hammer does too. The hammer then transmits vibrations first to the anvil and then to the stirrup.

Hammer Anvil Stirrup Auditory nerve

FIGURE 1 ·······························

The Human Ear

The ear has three main sections: the outer ear, the middle ear, and the inner ear.

✎ **Answer the following questions.**

1. **Name** Label the ear canal, eardrum, and cochlea.

2. **Identify** Circle each section of the ear. Draw a line from each circle to its matching text box.

3. CHALLENGE Which structure provides evidence that sound can travel through liquids? Explain.

_____

_____

_____

_____

③ **Inner Ear**

A membrane separates the middle ear from the inner ear, the third section of the ear. When the stirrup vibrates against this membrane, the vibrations pass into the cochlea. The **cochlea** (KAHK lee uh) is a liquid-filled cavity shaped like a snail shell. The cochlea contains more than 10,000 tiny structures called hair cells. These hair cells have hairlike projections that float in the liquid of the cochlea. When vibrations move through the liquid, the hair cells move, causing messages to be sent to the brain through the auditory nerve. The brain processes these messages and tells you that you've heard sound.

Hearing Loss When hearing loss occurs, a person may have difficulty hearing soft sounds or high-pitched sounds. Hearing loss can occur suddenly if the eardrum is damaged or punctured. (Imagine trying to play a torn drum!) For this reason, it is dangerous to put objects into your ear, even to clean it. Hearing loss can also occur gradually. As a person gets older, some hair cells in the cochlea die and do not grow back. People with this kind of hearing loss often have difficulty hearing high-frequency sounds. Extended exposure to loud sounds can also damage hair cells.

For some types of hearing loss, hearing aids can restore some ability to hear. Some hearing aids amplify sounds entering the ear. Others can amplify specific frequencies that a person has lost the ability to hear. For severe forms of hearing loss, a cochlear implant replaces the entire function of the ear. A cochlear implant contains a sound processor, an implant, and electrodes, as shown in **Figure 2.** The sound processor turns sound waves into an electrical signal. The implant transmits the signal to the electrodes. The electrodes stimulate the auditory nerve directly instead of the damaged cochlea.

⌖ **Relate Cause and Effect**
Underline three causes of hearing loss.

Implant

Sound processor

Electrodes

FIGURE 2 ···
A Cochlear Implant
A cochlear implant can restore the ability to hear.

✎ **Explain** How does a cochlear implant replace the function of the ear?

_____

_____

_____

_____

Lab zone ® Do the Quick Lab *Design and Build Hearing Protectors.*

🔑 **Assess Your Understanding**

1a. List What are the three sections of the ear?

_____

_____

b. Interpret Diagrams What happens to a sound wave as it enters your ear canal?

_____

_____

got it?

○ **I get it!** Now I know the function of your ear is

_____

_____

_____

○ **I need extra help with** _____

Go to MY SCIENCE ⓢ COACH *online for help with this subject.*

Using Sound

🔑 **How Do Animals and People Use Sound?**
PS.1n, PS.8a, PS.8c, PS.8d

MY PLANET DIARY

CAREERS

Marine Scientist

Why are marine scientists in Sarasota Bay, Florida, spying on dolphins? Dolphins send out a series of high-frequency clicks to navigate and find food. They whistle to communicate with each other. The scientists are recording underwater sounds in the bay. They are also noting dolphin sightings. They will use the data to determine how boat noise in the bay affects dolphin behavior.

Boat noise, underwater drilling, and sonar devices used by the military have all been shown to affect dolphins, porpoises, and whales. For this reason, it is a rich area of research for marine scientists.

Write your answer to the question below.

Make Judgments How do you think boat noise could affect the dolphins in the bay?

_____

_____

_____

_____

_____

_____

_____

▷ PLANET DIARY Go to **Planet Diary** to learn more about echolocation and ultrasound technologies.

 Do the Inquiry Warm-Up *How Can You Use Time to Measure Distance?*

 Science Standards of Learning

PS.1n Use current applications of physical science concepts.

PS.8a Investigate and understand wavelength, frequency, speed, amplitude, rarefaction, and compression for sound waves.

PS.8c Investigate and understand the nature of compression waves for sound.

PS.8d Investigate and understand technological applications of sound.

How Do Animals and People Use Sound?

Have you ever shouted into a canyon or a cave and then waited for the echo? An echo is a reflected sound wave. When a sound wave hits a surface that it cannot pass through, it may reflect. Some practical uses of sound, including echolocation and ultrasound technologies, are based on the fact that sound reflects off surfaces.

Vocabulary

- echolocation • ultrasound
- sonar • sonogram

Skills

- Reading: Ask Questions
- Inquiry: Calculate

1

3

Echolocation Many animals find it easy to move around in dark places. This is because they use echolocation. **Echolocation** (EK oh loh KAY shun) is the use of reflected sound waves to determine distances or to locate objects. **Some animals, including bats and dolphins, use echolocation to navigate and find food.**

Sound waves with frequencies above the normal human range of hearing are called **ultrasound.** The prefix *ultra-* means "beyond." Bats use ultrasound waves with frequencies up to 100,000 Hz to move around and hunt. As a bat flies, it sends out short pulses of ultrasound waves. The waves reflect off objects and return to the bat's ears, as shown in **Figure 1.** The time it takes for the sound waves to return tells the bat how far it is from obstacles or prey.

Dolphins use ultrasound waves with frequencies up to 150,000 Hz to hunt and move around in murky, deep water. The sound waves travel through the water and reflect off fish or other prey. Dolphins sense the reflected sound waves through their jawbones.

2

FIGURE 1 ....
Echolocation
A bat uses echolocation to hunt.

✎ **Answer the following questions**.

1. **Relate Diagrams and Photos** In each of the steps, describe how the bat locates its prey.

2. **Explain** Why would the bat have to continue to send out sound waves as it gets closer to its prey?

✎ **Ask Questions** Before reading about ultrasound technologies, ask yourself a *What* or *How* question. Then answer your question.

_____

_____

_____

_____

_____

_____

✎ **Vocabulary** Identify Multiple Meanings Review the multiple meanings of the words in the Getting Started section and complete the sentence. A sonar device detects sound waves

after they _____ off objects.

Ultrasound Technologies

Unlike animals, people cannot send out pulses of ultrasound to help them move around in the dark. But people sometimes need to explore places they cannot easily reach, such as deep under water or inside the human body. 🔑 **People use ultrasound technologies, such as sonar and ultrasound imaging, to observe things that they cannot see directly.**

Sonar A system that uses reflected sound waves to detect and locate objects under water is called **sonar.** The word *sonar* comes from the initial letters of **so**und **n**avigation **a**nd **r**anging. "Navigation" means finding your way around on the ocean (or in the air). "Ranging" means finding the distance between objects. People use sonar to determine the depth of water, to map the ocean floor, and to locate objects such as sunken ships and schools of fish.

A sonar device sends a burst of ultrasound waves that travel through the water. When the sound waves strike an object or the ocean floor, they reflect. The sonar device detects the reflected waves. A computer in the sonar device measures the time it takes for the sound waves to go out and return. Then it uses the following equation to solve for the total distance that sound travels.

$$\text{Distance} = \text{Speed of sound in water} \times \text{Time}$$

To solve for how far away the object is you must divide the total distance by two. This is because sound waves travel out and return.

apply it!

A sonar device sends out sound waves to detect a sunken ship.

1 **Calculate** Suppose the sonar device detects the reflected sound waves 10.0 seconds later. The speed of sound in salt water is 1,530 m/s. How far down is the sunken ship?

_____

_____

_____

_____

_____

2 **CHALLENGE** The *Titanic* is located nearly 3,800 meters below the surface of the ocean. How much time would it take for the sound waves to travel to the *Titanic* and back to the surface?

_____

_____

_____

Ultrasound Imaging Doctors use ultrasound imaging to look inside the human body. An ultrasound imaging device sends ultrasound waves into the body. Then it detects the reflected sound waves. Different parts of the body, such as bones, muscles, the liver, or the heart, reflect sound differently. The device uses the reflected waves to create a picture called a **sonogram.** A doctor can use sonograms to diagnose and treat many medical conditions.

The technician in **Figure 2** is using an ultrasound imaging device to examine a fetus. The technician holds a small probe on the pregnant woman's abdomen. The probe sends out very high frequency ultrasound waves (about 4 million Hz). By analyzing the reflected sound waves, the device builds up a sonogram. The sonogram can show the position of the fetus. Sonograms can also show if there is more than one fetus. In addition to a still picture, ultrasound imaging can produce a video of the fetus.

FIGURE 2 ···
> REAL-WORLD INQUIRY **Ultrasound in Medicine**
An ultrasound imaging device creates a sonogram of a fetus.

✎ **Explain** How does an ultrasound imaging device work?

_____
_____
_____
_____
_____

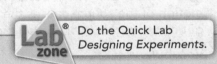 Do the Quick Lab
Designing Experiments.

🔑 **Assess Your Understanding**

1a. Define _____ is the use of reflected sound waves to determine distances or to locate objects.

b. Compare and Contrast How is sonar similar to ultrasound imaging? How is it different?

_____
_____
_____
_____
_____
_____
_____

got it?

○ I get it! Now I know that animals use

echolocation to _____

_____

and humans use ultrasound technologies to

_____

_____

○ I need extra help with _____

Go to **MY SCIENCE ⓢ COACH** *online for help with this subject.*

15 Study Guide

REVIEW THE BIG ?

The pitch of a sound depends on the_____ of the sound wave. The loudness of a sound depends on the _____ and _____ of the sound wave.

LESSON 1 The Nature of Sound

🔑 Sound is a disturbance that travels through a medium as a longitudinal wave.

🔑 The speed of sound depends on the temperature, stiffness, and density of the medium the sound travels through.

Vocabulary
• density

LESSON 2 Properties of Sound

🔑 The pitch of a sound you hear depends on the frequency of the sound wave.

🔑 The loudness of a sound depends on the energy and intensity of the sound wave.

🔑 The Doppler effect occurs because the motion of the source causes the waves to either get closer together or spread out.

Vocabulary
• pitch • loudness • intensity • decibel
• Doppler effect

LESSON 3 Music

🔑 The sound quality of musical instruments results from blending a fundamental tone with its overtones.

Vocabulary
• music
• fundamental tone
• overtone

LESSON 4 Hearing Sound

🔑 Your ear gathers sound waves and sends information about sound to your brain.

Vocabulary
• ear canal
• eardrum
• cochlea

LESSON 5 Using Sound

🔑 Some animals, including bats and dolphins, use echolocation to navigate and find food.

🔑 People use ultrasound technologies, such as sonar and ultrasound imaging, to observe things that they cannot see directly.

Vocabulary
• echolocation
• ultrasound
• sonar
• sonogram

Review and Assessment

The Nature of Sound

1. What term describes how much matter or mass there is in a given volume?

   a. stiffness   **b.** density

   c. temperature   **d.** diffraction

2. If you increase the temperature of a liquid or gas, a sound wave will travel _____

3. Summarize What three properties of a medium affect the speed of sound?

_____

_____

4. Make Models In the circles below, draw the air particles in a compression and rarefaction of the same sound wave.

 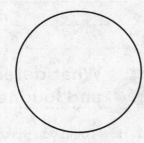

    Compression   Rarefaction

5. Relate Cause and Effect Why is a vibration of an object necessary for a sound wave to form?

_____

_____

_____

_____

6. Infer Thunder and lightning happen at the same time. Explain why you see the lightning before you hear the thunder.

_____

_____

_____

LESSON 2 **Properties of Sound**

7. What property of sound describes your awareness of the energy of a sound?

   a. loudness   **b.** intensity

   c. pitch   **d.** elasticity

8. As a sound wave travels, its intensity decreases because _____

_____

9. Interpret Diagrams Look at the sound waves coming from the two speakers. Which speaker cone is vibrating faster? How do you know?

_____

_____

_____

10. Relate Cause and Effect As a car drives past a person standing on a sidewalk, the driver keeps a hand on the horn. How does the pitch of the horn differ for the driver and the person standing on the sidewalk?

_____

_____

_____

_____

11. Write About It Explain how listening to your headphones at too high a volume can cause just as much damage to your ears as the sounds at a rock concert.

15 Review and Assessment

LESSON 3 Music

12. What term describes the lowest natural frequency of the source of a sound?

  a. overtone   **b.** standing wave

  c. fundamental tone   **d.** pitch

13. The quality of sound that a musical instrument produces is the result of _____

_____

_____

14. Apply Concepts A trumpet player pushes down on one of the valves to produce a lower note. How did the length of the air column in the trumpet change? Explain.

_____

_____

_____

_____

LESSON 4 Hearing Sound

15. What part of the ear contains thousands of hair cells that transmit sound?

  a. cochlea   **b.** middle ear

  c. ear canal   **d.** eardrum

16. The middle ear contains the three smallest bones in the body, which are called the

_____, the _____,

and the _____

17. Infer Sometimes a very loud sound or physical contact with an object can tear the eardrum. How would this affect hearing? Why?

_____

_____

_____

_____

LESSON 5 Using Sound

18. What system uses reflected sound waves to detect and locate objects under water?

  a. sonogram   **b.** ultrasound imaging

  c. diffraction   **d.** sonar

19. Some animals use _____

to navigate by sensing reflected sound waves.

20. math! Suppose it takes 6.0 seconds for a sound wave to travel to the bottom of the ocean and back to the surface. If the speed of sound in salt water is 1,530 m/s, how deep is the ocean at this point?

_____

_____

_____

_____

 What determines the pitch and loudness of sound?

21. How could you make sounds of different pitch and loudness with the two drums?

_____

_____

_____

_____

_____

Virginia SOL Test Prep

Read each question and choose the best answer.

1 The table below compares the loudness of several different sounds.

How many times more intense is the sound of a jet engine than the sound of loud thunder?

A 2   B 10

C 20   D 100

2 Fishing boats use sonar to locate schools of fish. What characteristic of sound is most important for this application of sonar?

F Sound waves reflect off some surfaces.

G Sound waves diffract around corners.

H Sound waves interfere when they overlap.

J Sound waves spread out from a source.

3 A trumpet and a piano can both play the same note, but the sound qualities are very different. Why does the sound quality depend on the instrument that produces it?

A Each instrument produces a different fundamental tone.

B Each instrument produces different overtones.

C The amplitude of the notes is different.

D The intensity of the sound is different.

4 Why does sound intensity decrease as the distance from the source increases?

F Most of the energy is absorbed by the particles of the medium.

G The same amount of energy is spread out over a larger area.

H The frequency increases as distance from the source increases.

J The energy of the sound wave decreases.

5 What is the function of the inner ear?

A The inner ear vibrates when sound waves strike it.

B The inner ear converts vibrations into signals that travel to the brain.

C The inner ear increases the frequency of sound waves.

D The inner ear transmits sound waves from the ear canal to the cochlea.

6 Sounds with frequencies above the normal human range of hearing are called—

F subsonic

G hypersonic

H overtones

J ultrasounds

7 As a ambulance speeds by, observers hear a change in the pitch of its siren. This is an example of—

A the Doppler effect

B echolocation

C resonance

D diffraction

CAN YOU HEAR ME NOW?

CRASH! BANG! BEEP BEEP! In cities all across the world, noise pollution is part of everyday life. Noise pollution is loud, distracting sound.

There are many different types of noise pollution. Some of the most common are residential noise, road traffic noise, and air traffic noise. Residential noise pollution occurs in places where people live. It includes noisy neighbors, high-pitched car alarms, and power tools from renovations. Road traffic noise pollution is common at busy intersections or on highways. Helicopters and airplanes cause air traffic noise pollution. Air traffic noise is especially troublesome for people who live or work near airports.

Too much noise can cause hearing loss, lack of sleep, and increased stress. Studies show that students who go to school in areas that have high levels of noise pollution have lower test scores. The noise affects students' ability to concentrate.

More than 100 million Americans are regularly exposed to noise levels higher than 55 decibels—the common standard for background noise levels. As a result, governments are passing laws to reduce noise pollution.

Write About It Write a letter to your town or city council. Identify and explain what the impact of noise pollution is on the people in your town or city. Describe your ideas about how to reduce noise in your area.

PS.1j

NOISY Occupations

Settings and costumes can make a film interesting to watch. But think for a moment about watching a car chase without the sounds of traffic, tires squealing, or motors revving. The scene might look great, but it would be less thrilling.

Several people work to create the sound effects in a movie.

Foley artists create the background noises that make a scene convincing. They create everyday sounds such as footsteps or jingling keys. They also create less ordinary noises, such as punching noises. These noises might not be very obvious, but you would notice if they weren't there.

Sound mixers record all sound effects and dialogue. If all of the sounds were recorded at the same time scenes were filmed, you wouldn't be able to hear a thing the actors were saying—the wrong noises would be loud and cover the speech. So sound mixers record the dialogue and effects separately and mix them together in the studio.

Sound effects editors make sure that everyone follows the sound plan for the film, and that all of the noises happen at the right time in a way that works.

Record It Work in a small group to record an audio track. Design a solution for sounds you have to "fake." For example, how would you make a sound for something dropping from the roof? Play your track for the class—can they tell what is happening?

 PS.1k, PS.1m, PS.1n, PS.8d

HOW DO SCANS "SEE" YOUR BRAIN?

What kinds of waves make up the electromagnetic spectrum?

It might look like a colorful wig, but this image shows the nerve pathways of the brain. Using machines that read energy from our bodies, doctors can see how and when different areas of the brain are active without surgery or radiation.

When your brain performs a task, such as remembering a phone number, blood circulation to that part of your brain increases. The scan recognizes that activity.

Infer What might the colors of this brain scan mean?

_____

_____

_____

_____

_____

▶ UNTAMED SCIENCE Watch the **Untamed Science** video to learn more about electromagnetic waves.

Electromagnetic Waves 10

Science Standards of Learning

PS.1c, PS.1e, PS.1j, PS.1k, PS.1n,
PS.9a, PS.9b, PS.9d, PS.9e

16 Getting Started

Check Your Understanding

1. **Background** Read the paragraph below and then answer the question.

Have you ever stepped in a large puddle? When your foot hits the water, it transfers energy to the water, creating a **wave.** The **medium,** water, **vibrates** with the transfer of energy. The water ripples around your foot.

A **wave** is a disturbance that transfers energy from place to place.

The material through which a wave travels is the **medium.**

To **vibrate** is to move in a repeated back-and-forth or up-and-down motion.

• What caused the water to vibrate?

_____

_____

> **MY READING WEB** If you had trouble completing the question above, visit **My Reading Web** and type in *Electromagnetic Waves.*

Vocabulary Skill

Greek Word Origins Some science words in this chapter contain word parts with Greek origins. The table below lists some of the Greek words from which the vocabulary words come.

Greek Word	Meaning of Greek Word	Example
mikro-	small	microwaves, *n.* electromagnetic radiation with short wavelengths and high frequencies
-skopion	for seeing or observing	spectroscope, *n.* instrument used to see different colors of light
photos	light	photon, *n.* packet of light energy

2. **Quick Check** Circle the word part in *spectroscope* that tells you its meaning has to do with viewing.

electromagnetic wave

Magnetic field

Electric field

polarized light

thermogram

X-rays

Chapter Preview

LESSON 1
- electromagnetic wave
- electromagnetic radiation
- polarized light
- photoelectric effect
- photon

  ↻ **Identify the Main Idea**
  ▲ **Calculate**

LESSON 2
- electromagnetic spectrum
- radio waves
- microwaves
- radar
- infrared rays
- thermogram
- visible light
- ultraviolet rays
- X-rays
- gamma rays

  ↻ **Summarize**
  ▲ **Communicate**

LESSON 3
- amplitude modulation
- frequency modulation

  ↻ **Compare and Contrast**
  ▲ **Interpret Data**

> VOCAB FLASH CARDS For extra help with vocabulary, visit **Vocab Flash Cards** and type in *Electromagnetic Waves.*

The Nature of Electromagnetic Waves

UNLOCK THE BIG ?

🔑 **What Makes Up an Electromagnetic Wave?**
PS.9d

🔑 **What Models Explain How Electromagnetic Waves Behave?**
PS.9a, PS.9b

MY PLANET DIARY *for* Virginia

Posted by: Justin
Location: King George, Virginia

Electromagnetic waves are used in everyday life. Some examples are phones, iPods, scales, and super computers. Imaging machines such as MRIs, CAT scans, X-rays, and ultrasound allow us to detect abnormalities in the body. Electromagnetic waves help us with jobs, school, and medical problems. They make life easier by shortening time needed to do things. Phones allow us to speak to relatives in different states. Super computers help us monitor the shuttles in space.

BLOG

Read the following questions. Write your answers below.

1. How do electromagnetic waves make Justin's life easier?

_____
_____
_____

2. How do you use electromagnetic waves in your everyday life?

_____
_____

▷ **PLANET DIARY** Go to **Planet Diary** to learn more about electromagnetic waves.

 Do the Inquiry Warm-Up *How Fast Are Electromagnetic Waves?*

Science Standards of Learning

PS.9d Investigate and understand the electromagnetic spectrum.

What Makes Up an Electromagnetic Wave?

As you sit at your desk and read this book, you are surrounded by waves you cannot see or hear. There are radio waves, microwaves, infrared rays, visible light, ultraviolet rays, and tiny amounts of X-rays and gamma rays. These waves are all electromagnetic waves.

Vocabulary
- electromagnetic wave
- electromagnetic radiation
- polarized light
- photoelectric effect
- photon

Skills
- Reading: Identify the Main Idea
- Inquiry: Calculate

Characteristics of Electromagnetic Waves

An **electromagnetic wave** is a transverse wave that involves the transfer of electric and magnetic energy. **An electromagnetic wave is made up of vibrating electric and magnetic fields that move through space or some medium at the speed of light.**

An electromagnetic wave can begin with the movement of charged particles, all of which have electric fields around them. As the particles change speed or direction, a vibrating electric field is created, which in turn produces a vibrating magnetic field. The vibrating magnetic field creates a vibrating electric field. The electric and magnetic fields produce each other repeatedly. The result is an electromagnetic wave, shown in **Figure 1.** Note that the two fields vibrate at right angles to one another.

Energy The energy that electromagnetic waves transfer through matter or space is called **electromagnetic radiation.** Electromagnetic waves do not require a medium such as air, so they can transfer energy through a vacuum, or empty space.

FIGURE 1 ·····················
Electromagnetic Wave
An electromagnetic wave travels through space at the speed of light—about 300,000 kilometers per second.

✎ Calculate How long will it take sunlight to travel the 150 million kilometers to Earth? Use a calculator to solve the problem.

_____

_____

_____

Electric field

Magnetic field

Direction of wave

90°

Fields are at right angles to each other.

Lab zone®   Do the Quick Lab *What Is an Electromagnetic Wave Made Of?*

⚷ Assess Your Understanding

got it? ····························

○ I get it! Now I know that electromagnetic waves are made of _____

_____

○ I need extra help with _____

Go to MY SCIENCE ⟨s⟩ COACH *online for help with this subject.*

PS.9a Investigate and understand wavelength, frequency, speed, amplitude, crest, and trough of transverse waves.

PS.9b Investigate and understand the wave behavior of light.

Identify the Main Idea

Circle the main idea in the first paragraph. Underline the details.

What Models Explain How Electromagnetic Waves Behave?

Two different models are needed to explain the behavior of electromagnetic waves. A wave model best explains many of the behaviors, but a particle model best explains others. Light is an electromagnetic wave. It has many properties of waves but can also act as though it is a stream of particles.

Wave Model of Light When light passes through a polarizing filter, it has the properties of a wave. An ordinary beam of light consists of waves that vibrate in all directions. A polarizing filter acts as though it has tiny slits aligned in only one direction. The slits can be horizontal or vertical. When light enters a polarizing filter, only some waves can pass through it. The light that passes through is called **polarized light.**

To help you understand the wave model, think of light waves like transverse waves on a rope. They vibrate in all directions. If you shake a rope through a fence with vertical slits, only waves that vibrate up and down will pass through, as shown in **Figure 2.** The other waves are blocked. A polarizing filter acts like the slits in a fence. It allows only waves that vibrate in one direction to pass through it.

FIGURE 2

VIRTUAL LAB **Light as a Wave**
A polarizing filter acts like the slits in a fence.

✎ **Predict Explain how light waves that pass through horizontal slits vibrate.**

_____

_____

_____

_____

A A fence, or filter, with vertical slits allows only waves that vibrate up and down to pass through.

B Vertical waves cannot pass through a fence, or filter, with horizontal slits.

apply it!

The picture shows the light from a flashlight shining on the lenses of two pairs of polarized sunglasses.

1 **Identify** Label the polarizing filters and the polarized light.

2 **CHALLENGE** Why will the polarized light not pass through the second sunglass lens?

_____

_____

Particle Model of Light Sometimes light behaves like a stream of particles. For example, when a beam of high frequency light shines on some metals, it causes tiny particles to move. These particles are called electrons. Sometimes light can even cause an electron to move so much that it is knocked out of the metal, as shown in **Figure 3.** This is called the **photoelectric effect.** This effect can be explained by thinking of light as a stream of tiny packets, or particles, of energy. Each packet of light energy is called a **photon.** For the effect to occur, each photon must contain enough energy to knock an electron free from the metal.

FIGURE 3 ·····························
The Photoelectric Effect
Photons hitting a metal surface knock out electrons.

Dim blue light or ultraviolet rays

Metal plate

Lab zone® Do the Quick Lab *Waves or Particles?*

🔑 Assess Your Understanding

1a. Define A _____ is a tiny packet of energy.

b. Describe What does a polarizing filter do?

_____

_____

_____

got it?

○ **I get it!** Now I know that the models that explain how electromagnetic waves behave are _____

_____

○ **I need extra help with** _____

Go to my science **COACH** *online for help with this subject.*

Waves of the Electromagnetic Spectrum

🔑 **How Do Electromagnetic Waves Compare?**
PS.9a, PS.9d

🔑 **What Makes Up the Electromagnetic Spectrum?**
PS.1c, PS.1e, PS.9a, PS.9d, PS.9e

my planet diary

DISCOVERY

Hey, Where Did It Go?

What would you do if you had an invisibility cloak? This idea might not be as far-fetched as it sounds. Scientists have actually been working on creating a way to make objects invisible! Researchers have created a device that can change the direction of microwaves, so that they flow around a test object. This rerouting causes the object to look invisible at microwave frequencies. Unfortunately, people cannot see microwaves, which means the object isn't invisible to us. But, who knows, maybe one day you'll be able to put on one of these "cloaks" and move around completely unseen!

Answer the question below.

If a device like this is developed for visible light, how do you think a scientist who studies animals in nature might use it?

_____

_____

_____

_____

_____

_____

▶ PLANET DIARY Go to **Planet Diary** to learn more about the electromagnetic spectrum.

 Do the Inquiry Warm-Up *What Is White Light?*

Vocabulary
- electromagnetic spectrum • radio waves • microwaves
- radar • infrared rays • thermogram • visible light
- ultraviolet rays • X-rays • gamma rays

Skills
- Reading: Summarize
- Inquiry: Communicate

How Do Electromagnetic Waves Compare?

Can you imagine trying to take a photo with a radio or heating your food with X-rays? Light, radio waves, and X-rays are all electromagnetic waves. But each has properties that make it more useful for some purposes than others. **All electromagnetic waves travel at the same speed in a vacuum, but they have different wavelengths and different frequencies.** A vacuum is a space that contains no air or other gas.

Visible light is the only range of wavelengths your eyes can see. Your radio detects radio waves, which have much longer wavelengths than visible light. X-rays, on the other hand, have much shorter wavelengths than visible light.

For waves in any medium, as the wavelength decreases, the frequency increases. Waves with the longest wavelengths have the lowest frequencies. Waves with the shortest wavelengths have the highest frequencies. The higher the frequency of a wave, the higher its energy.

Science Standards of Learning

PS.9a Investigate and understand wavelength, frequency, speed, amplitude, crest, and trough of transverse waves.

PS.9d Investigate and understand the electromagnetic spectrum.

FIGURE 1 ·····························

Comparing Electromagnetic Waves
Different types of electromagnetic waves have different wavelengths.

✎ **Complete these tasks.**

1. **Label** Write the names *visible light*, *radio waves*, and *X-rays* in the correct boxes on the diagram.

2. **Draw Conclusions** Which wave has the highest energy? Explain.

_____

_____

_____

_____

Lab zone® Do the Quick Lab *Differences Between Waves.*

🔑 Assess Your Understanding

got it? ···

○ I get it! Now I know that electromagnetic waves have different _____

_____ but the same _____

○ I need extra help with _____

Go to my science ⓢ coach *online for help with this subject.*

Science Standards of Learning

PS.1c Convert among metric units and apply appropriate prefixes.

PS.1e Express numbers in scientific notation where appropriate.

PS.9a Investigate and understand wavelength, frequency, speed, amplitude, crest, and trough of transverse waves.

PS.9d Investigate and understand the electromagnetic spectrum.

PS.9e Investigate and understand technological applications of light.

What Makes Up the Electromagnetic Spectrum?

There are many different types of electromagnetic waves. The complete range of electromagnetic waves placed in order of increasing frequency is called the **electromagnetic spectrum.** 🔑 **The electromagnetic spectrum is made up of radio waves, microwaves, infrared rays, visible light, ultraviolet rays, X-rays, and gamma rays.** The full spectrum is shown in **Figure 2.**

Radio Waves Electromagnetic waves with the longest wavelengths and the lowest frequencies are **radio waves.** Radio waves are used in broadcasting to carry signals for radio programs. A broadcast station sends out radio waves at certain frequencies. Your radio picks up the radio waves and converts them into an electrical signal. The electrical signal is then converted into sound.

FIGURE 2 ···

The Electromagnetic Spectrum
The electromagnetic spectrum can be broken up into different categories.

✎ **Interpret Diagrams Use the word bank to fill in the boxes in the diagram. Do microwaves or ultraviolet waves have longer wavelengths? Which have higher frequencies?**

_____

_____

_____

Word Bank

Shortest wavelength   Longest wavelength
Highest frequency   Lowest frequency

Visible light

| Radio waves | Microwaves | Infrared rays | Ultra-violet rays | X-rays | Gamma rays |

Microwaves **Microwaves** have shorter wavelengths and higher frequencies than radio waves do. When you think about microwaves, you probably think of microwave ovens that cook and heat food. But microwaves have many other uses, including cellular phone communication and radar.

Radar stands for **ra**dio **d**etection **an**d **r**anging. **Radar** is a system that uses reflected microwaves to detect objects and measure their distance and speed. To measure distance, a radar device sends out microwaves that reflect off an object. The time it takes for the reflected waves to return is used to calculate the object's distance. To measure speed, a radar device uses the Doppler effect. For example, suppose a police radar gun sends out microwaves that reflect off a car. Because the car is moving, the frequency of the reflected waves is different from the frequency of the original waves. The difference in frequency is used to calculate the car's speed.

apply it!

Radio stations are broadcast in two different frequency ranges. The ranges are the kilohertz range (kHz) for AM stations and the megahertz range (MHz) for FM stations. The prefix *kilo-* means "thousand"; *mega-* means "million."

1 Interpret Data What is the frequency range of the AM band on the radio? Of the FM band?

_____

_____

2 Interpret Photos Approximately what frequencies are being tuned in on each band?

_____

_____

3 CHALLENGE The units kHz and MHz stand for kilohertz and megahertz, respectively. If 1 MHz = 1000 kHz and 1 kHz = 1000 Hz, what is the frequency, in Hz, of a signal broadcast on 99.7 FM? Express your answer in scientific notation.

_____

_____

FM frequency Range in MHz

AM frequency Range in kHz

Vocabulary Greek Word **Origins** The prefix *thermo-* comes from the Greek word *thermos* which means "warm or hot." How does this meaning relate to the definition of *thermogram*?

_____

_____

_____

_____

Infrared Rays If you turn on an electric stove's burner, you can feel it warm up before the heating element starts to glow. The invisible heat you feel is infrared radiation, or infrared rays. **Infrared rays** are electromagnetic waves with wavelengths shorter than those of microwaves. They have higher frequencies and therefore more energy than microwaves. Because you can feel the energy of infrared rays as heat, these rays are often called heat rays. Heat lamps have bulbs that give off mainly infrared rays. They are used to keep things warm, such as food in a cafeteria or young animals in an incubator.

Most objects give off some infrared rays. Warmer objects give off infrared rays with more energy and higher frequencies than cooler objects. An infrared camera uses infrared rays instead of visible light to take pictures called thermograms. A **thermogram** is an image that shows regions of different temperatures in different colors, as shown in **Figure 3**.

FIGURE 3 ·······························

The Uses of Infrared Rays
Infrared rays are used in devices such as heat lamps and TV remote controls.

✎ **Complete these tasks.**

1. **Interpret Diagrams** List the labeled areas on the thermogram from hottest to coolest.

Heat lamp

2. **Identify** Where do you think this heat lamp is being used?

_____

_____

_____

Thermogram

37.0°C

35

30

25

21.7°C

Visible light waves with the longest wavelengths appear red in color.

The shortest wavelengths of visible light appear violet in color.

Sequence What are the colors of the visible spectrum in order, starting with red?

_____

_____

_____

_____

Interpret Photos Which color has the highest frequency?

_____

_____

FIGURE 4 ·······································

The Visible Spectrum

Refraction of white light from the sun by raindrops separates the light into the colors of the visible spectrum.

✎ **Answer the questions in the boxes to the left and below.**

◀ Communicate Talk with a partner. Describe other times when you have seen the visible spectrum.

_____

_____

_____

_____

_____

_____

Visible Light Electromagnetic waves that you can see are called **visible light.** They make up only a small part of the electromagnetic spectrum. Visible light waves have shorter wavelengths and higher frequencies than infrared rays.

Visible light that appears white is actually a mixture of many colors. Recall that light waves bend, or refract, when they enter a new medium. So, when white light passes through rain drops, a rainbow can result, like the one in **Figure 4.**

Ultraviolet Rays Electromagnetic waves with wavelengths just shorter than those of visible light are called **ultraviolet rays.** Ultraviolet rays have higher frequencies than visible light, so they carry more energy. The energy of ultraviolet rays can damage or kill living cells. For example, too much exposure to ultraviolet rays can burn your skin and over time may cause skin cancer. However, small doses of ultraviolet rays are useful. They cause skin cells to produce vitamin D, which is needed for healthy bones and teeth.

FIGURE 5 ·······················

Lead Apron

X-rays are often used to look at bones and teeth.

✎ **Explain** Why does a dentist cover you with a lead apron to take X-rays of your teeth?

_____

_____

_____

_____

·················✎·················

🔄 **Summarize** In your own words, write a summary of the section about gamma rays.

X-rays Electromagnetic waves with wavelengths just shorter than those of ultraviolet rays are **X-rays.** Their frequencies are just a little higher than ultraviolet rays. Because of their high frequencies, X-rays carry more energy than ultraviolet rays and can penetrate most matter. Dense matter, such as bone or lead, absorbs X-rays so they do not pass through. Therefore, X-rays are used to make images of bones and teeth. However, too much exposure to X-rays can cause cancer. See **Figure 5.**

X-rays can also be used in industry and engineering. Engineers can use an X-ray image of a steel or concrete structure to find cracks. Dark areas on the X-ray film show the cracks.

Gamma Rays Electromagnetic waves with the shortest wavelengths and highest frequencies are **gamma rays.** Since they have the greatest amount of energy, gamma rays are the most penetrating of electromagnetic waves. Because of their penetrating ability, these rays are used to examine the body's internal structures. A patient can be injected with a fluid that emits gamma rays. Then, a gamma-ray detector can form an image of the inside of the body.

Some radioactive substances and certain nuclear reactions produce gamma rays. Some objects in space emit bursts of gamma rays. However, these rays are blocked by Earth's atmosphere. Astronomers think that explosions of distant stars produce these gamma rays.

X-rays

Surfing the Spectrum

What kinds of waves make up the electromagnetic spectrum?

FIGURE 6 ....

> INTERACTIVE ART The electromagnetic spectrum includes many kinds of waves.

✎ **Complete the activities.**

1. **Identify** Label each kind of wave on the electromagnetic spectrum.

2. **Classify** Circle the name of the highest energy waves.

3. **Apply Concepts** On the notebook page, describe the uses of two kinds of waves.

Types of Waves

Radio
waves

Lab
zone® Do the Quick Lab *Parts of the Electromagnetic Spectrum.*

🗝 Assess Your Understanding

1a. Explain How do ultraviolet rays help your bones and teeth?

_____

_____

_____

b. ANSWER
THE BIG
? What kinds of waves make up the electromagnetic spectrum?

_____

_____

_____

_____

got it? ....

○ **I get it!** Now I know the electromagnetic spectrum is made up of _____

_____

○ **I need extra help with** _____

Go to **MY SCIENCE** ⓢ **COACH** online for help with this subject.

Wireless Communication

UNLOCK THE BIG ?

🔑 **How Do Radio Waves Transmit Information?**
PS.1c, PS.9a, PS.9d

🔑 **How Does a Cell Phone Work?**
PS.9a, PS.9d

🔑 **How Does Satellite Communication Work?**
PS.9a, PS.9d

MY PLANET DiARY

Teens and Their Cell Phones

How do teens feel about cell phones? Researchers asked some teens to take a survey so that they could learn about teens' cell-phone usage. How do these results compare with your own ideas?

- 45 percent believe that having a cell phone is the key to their social life.

- Having a cell phone makes 78 percent feel safe when they're not at home.

- When asked to select additional features for a basic cell phone, 71 percent chose a music player.

- More than half use cell phones to check e-mail.

- Nearly half said they could send text messages while blindfolded!

 Lab zone® Do the Inquiry Warm-Up *How Can Waves Change?*

FUN FACTS

Answer the questions below.

1. Who would find these results useful? Why?

_____

_____

_____

_____

_____

2. What do you think is the most important use of a cell phone?

_____

_____

▶ PLANET DIARY Go to **Planet Diary** to learn more about wireless communication.

Vocabulary
- amplitude modulation
- frequency modulation

Skills
- Reading: Compare and Contrast
- Inquiry: Interpret Data

How Do Radio Waves Transmit Information?

You are in the car on a long road trip and switch on the radio to listen to some music. In an instant, your favorite song is coming through the car's speakers. How do radio broadcasts reach you?

Broadcasting Radio waves carry, or transmit, signals for radio programs. Charged particles vibrating inside transmission antennas produce radio waves. Transmission antennas send out, or broadcast, radio waves in many directions. **Radio waves carry information from the antenna of a broadcasting station to the receiving antenna of your radio.** Look at **Figure 1.**

Science Standards of Learning

PS.1c Convert among metric units and apply appropriate prefixes.

PS.9a Investigate and understand wavelength, frequency, speed, amplitude, crest, and trough of transverse waves.

PS.9d Investigate and understand the electromagnetic spectrum.

FIGURE 1 ·······································
How a Radio Works
Radios tune in radio wave signals broadcast by antennas located at radio stations.

✏ **Sequence** In the circles, number the steps to show the correct order of events that results in hearing a broadcast.

The electronic signal comes out of your radio as sound.

Radio waves strike your radio's antenna and are picked up.

In the interior of the radio, radio waves are converted into an electronic signal.

At the radio station, electronics convert music into radio waves that are then broadcast by a large antenna.

FIGURE 2

> **INTERACTIVE ART** **Radio Waves**
Radio stations transmit signals by changing a radio wave's amplitude or frequency.

✎ **Interpret Diagrams** Under each type of wave, write the wave property that is constant.

AM Waves

FM Waves

Broadcasting Signals

Radio stations broadcast signals in two frequency bands. These bands are amplitude modulation (AM) and frequency modulation (FM).

Amplitude Modulation A method of broadcasting signals by changing the amplitude of a wave is called **amplitude modulation.** AM signals travel as changes, or modulations, in the amplitude of the wave. The frequency of an AM wave is constant.

AM radio waves have relatively long wavelengths and low frequencies and energy. They are easily reflected back to Earth's surface by Earth's ionosphere, a region of charged particles high in the atmosphere. Therefore, AM radio stations can be broadcast over long distances.

Frequency Modulation **Frequency modulation** is a method of broadcasting signals by changing the frequency of a wave. FM signals travel as changes in the frequency of the wave. The amplitude of an FM wave is constant.

FM waves have higher frequencies and more energy than AM waves. FM waves pass through the ionosphere instead of being reflected back to Earth. Therefore, they do not travel as far on Earth's surface as AM waves. However, FM waves usually produce better sound quality than AM waves. **Figure 2** shows FM waves and AM waves.

✎ **Compare and Contrast**
Complete the Venn diagram to compare AM and FM radio waves.

AM Waves   FM Waves

do the math! Analyzing Data

The table shows the frequencies assigned by the Federal Communications Commission (FCC) for various radio channels.

1 Interpret Data Which broadcast uses the highest-frequency range? Which uses the lowest-frequency range?

_____
_____
_____
_____
_____

Broadcast Frequencies

Type of Broadcast	Frequency Range	Converted Frequency Range
AM radio	535 kHz to 1,605 kHz	
Amateur radio	1,800 kHz to 1,900 kHz	
FM radio	88 MHz to 108 MHz	

2 CHALLENGE Convert each given frequency range into units of hertz. (*Hint:* 1 kHz = 1000 Hz, and 1 MHz = 1,000,000 Hz.) Write your answers in the table.

The Radio Spectrum

In addition to AM and FM broadcasts, radio waves are used for many types of communication. The FCC assigns different radio frequencies for different uses. Radio stations use one part of the radio spectrum. Taxi and police radios are assigned separate sets of frequencies. Amateur radio frequencies are assigned for people who operate radios as a hobby. Because the signals all have different assigned frequencies, they travel without interfering.

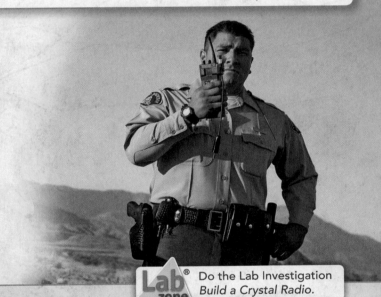

Lab zone® Do the Lab Investigation *Build a Crystal Radio.*

Assess Your Understanding

1a. Identify What wave property is changed when AM radio signals are broadcast?

_____
_____

b. Apply Concepts Longer wavelengths bend more easily around obstacles such as mountains. In a hilly countryside, will you be more likely to hear an AM or FM station?

_____
_____

got it?

○ I get it! Now I know that radio waves _____
_____
_____

○ I need extra help with _____

Go to **MY SCIENCE COACH** online for help with this subject.

How Does a Cell Phone Work?

Cellular telephones, or cell phones, are an important part of your daily life. However, they only work if they are in a cellular system. The cellular system works by dividing regions into many small cells, or geographical areas, as shown in **Figure 3**. Each cell has one or more towers that relay signals to a central hub.

Cell phones transmit and receive signals using high-frequency microwaves. Though the process needed to complete a cell phone call looks complicated, the entire process happens so quickly it seems to be instantaneous. In addition to making phone calls, cell phones have many different uses. They can be used to send text messages, browse the Internet, and take photos.

A

1 When you place a cell-phone call, the phone sends out microwaves, which are tagged with a number unique to your phone.

2 A tower picks up the microwaves and transfers the signal to a hub.

3 The hub channels and transmits the signal to a receiver. The receiver may be another tower or another hub, depending on the distance between the two phones.

4 The tower or hub transmits the signal to the receiving cell phone.

FIGURE 3 ....

> ART IN MOTION **Using a Cell Phone**

The quality of your cell-phone calls depends on the terrain and how close your phone is to a cell-phone tower or a central hub.

✎ **Apply Concepts** Suppose you make a call from location B to a friend at location C. Draw the path the signal could travel to complete the call. Explain what would likely happen if you made a cell call from location A.

_____

_____

_____

B

C

5 The receiving phone rings when it picks up the signal.

Lab zone® Do the Quick Lab *How Cell Phones Work.*

🔑 **Assess Your Understanding**

2a. Infer What happens if your cell phone is far away from a tower?

_____

_____

_____

b. Draw Conclusions Your cell phone sends out a signal at a specific frequency. What will happen if a cell phone next to you also uses this frequency?

_____

_____

_____

got it? ....

○ **I get it!** Now I know that cell phones work

by _____

_____

○ **I need extra help with** _____

Go to my science ⓢ coach *online for help with this subject.*

Compare and Contrast
In the paragraphs to the right, underline the sentences that compare satellite communication with another form of electronic communication.

How Does Satellite Communication Work?

Satellites orbiting Earth send information around the world. Communications satellites work like the receivers and transmitters of a cellular phone system. **Communications satellites receive radio, television, and telephone signals and relay the signals to receivers on Earth.** Because a satellite can "see" only part of Earth at any time, more than one satellite is needed for any purpose.

Satellite Phone Systems Several companies offer satellite phone systems. Radio waves from one phone are sent up to a communications satellite. The satellite transmits the waves back to the receiving phone on Earth. With this kind of phone, you can call anywhere in the world, but it costs more than using a cell phone.

Satellite Television Systems Television networks and cable companies use communications satellites. Television signals are sent up to satellites. The satellites then relay the signals to places around the world. Television signals from satellites are often scrambled. Customers of satellite companies need a satellite dish antenna like the one shown in **Figure 4** to pick up the signals and a decoding box to unscramble the signals.

FIGURE 4 ·······································
Satellite Dishes
Dish-shaped antennas receive signals for television programs from satellites.

✏ **Infer** Satellite dishes point to a fixed location in the sky. What does this tell you about the position of the satellite?

_____

_____

_____

Global Positioning System The Global Positioning System (GPS) is a system of navigation originally designed for the military. GPS uses a network of 24 satellites that broadcast radio signals to Earth. These signals carry information that tells you your exact location on Earth's surface, or even in the air. Anybody with a GPS receiver can pick up these signals. GPS receivers can be found in cars, airplanes, boats, and even cell phones.

Signals from four out of 24 GPS satellites are used to determine your position. The signals from three satellites tell you where you are on Earth's surface. The signal from the fourth satellite tells you how far above Earth's surface you are.

GPS unit in car

GPS satellite

FIGURE 5 ···

> ART IN MOTION **Uses of Satellites**
Modern communication uses satellites in different ways.

✎ **Summarize Complete the table by summarizing how satellites are used in each type of communication.**

System	Summary
Global Positioning System	
Satellite Phone System	
Television Satellites	

Lab zone ® Do the Quick Lab *How Does GPS Work?*

⚷ **Assess Your Understanding**

got it? ···

○ I get it! Now I know that satellites work by _____

_____

○ I need extra help with _____

Go to **my science** s **COACH** online for help with this subject.

The electromagnetic spectrum is made up of radio waves, _____, _____, visible light, _____, _____, and gamma rays.

LESSON 1 The Nature of Electromagnetic Waves

🔑 An electromagnetic wave is made up of vibrating electric and magnetic fields that move through space or some medium at the speed of light.

🔑 Two different models are needed to explain the behavior of electromagnetic waves. A wave model best explains many of the behaviors, but a particle model best explains others.

Vocabulary
- electromagnetic wave   • electromagnetic radiation
- polarized light   • photoelectric effect   • photon

LESSON 2 Waves of the Electromagnetic Spectrum

🔑 All electromagnetic waves travel at the same speed in a vacuum, but they have different wavelengths and different frequencies.

🔑 The electromagnetic spectrum is made up of radio waves, microwaves, infrared rays, visible light, ultraviolet rays, X-rays, and gamma rays.

Vocabulary
- electromagnetic spectrum   • radio waves   • microwaves   • radar
- infrared rays   • thermogram   • visible light   • ultraviolet rays
- X-rays   • gamma rays

LESSON 3 Wireless Communication

🔑 Radio waves carry information from the antenna of a broadcasting station to the receiving antenna of your radio.

🔑 Cell phones transmit and receive signals using high-frequency microwaves.

🔑 Communications satellites receive radio, television, and telephone signals and relay the signals to receivers on Earth.

Vocabulary
- amplitude modulation   • frequency modulation

Review and Assessment

LESSON 1 The Nature of Electromagnetic Waves

1. An electromagnetic wave consists of

  a. AM and FM waves.

  b. electrons and protons.

  c. electric and magnetic fields.

  d. particles of a medium.

2. The _____ model of light describes the behavior of light when it acts as a stream of photons.

3. Compare and Contrast Explain how polarized light is different from non-polarized light.

_____

_____

_____

_____

_____

4. Observe How do you know that electromagnetic waves can travel through a vacuum?

_____

_____

_____

5. **Write About It** Suppose you go shopping for sunglasses with a friend. He likes a pair of sunglasses labeled *polarized lenses*. Using what you learned in this lesson, explain to him how polarizing sunglasses work.

LESSON 2 Waves of the Electromagnetic Spectrum

6. The electromagnetic waves with the longest wavelengths and lowest frequencies are

  a. radio waves.   **b.** infrared rays.

  c. X-rays.   **d.** gamma rays.

7. _____ is the only type of electromagnetic wave that you can see.

Use the graph below to answer Questions 8 and 9.

Ultraviolet Rays During a Day

8. Interpret Graphs What is the amount of ultraviolet rays at 8 P.M.?

_____

9. Infer What is the cause of the peak in the graph line at 12 P.M.?

_____

_____

10. Classify Night vision goggles allow you to see warm objects in a dark environment. Which type of electromagnetic wave do they detect?

_____

_____

Wireless Communication

11. What is the ionosphere?

   a. a type of AM radio wave

   b. a region of charged particles
      in Earth's atmosphere

   c. the region of a cell-phone network

   d. a type of FM radio wave

12. Cell phones transmit and receive signals using

_____

13. Make Models An AM wave is shown below.
Draw an FM wave in the space provided.

AM wave

FM wave

14. Apply Concepts Explain how the Global
Positioning System works.

_____

_____

_____

_____

_____

15. [Write About It] You are going on a car trip with
your family across the United States. To your
brother's surprise, the AM radio station that
your family is listening to is coming from a city
1,000 kilometers away. Explain to him how this
is possible. Be sure to describe how the ionosphere affects AM radio transmissions.

 APPLY THE BIG ? **What kinds of waves make
up the electromagnetic
spectrum?**

16. Many everyday technologies with which you
come in contact use electromagnetic waves.
Choose four objects from the picture below
and describe the kinds of electromagnetic
waves that they use. List your answer in
order of increasing energy of the waves
each object uses.

_____

_____

_____

_____

_____

_____

_____

_____

Read each question and choose the best answer.

1 What would you add to the picture below so that light does not hit the final screen?

A another light bulb

B a filter with horizontal slits

C a filter with vertical slits

D none of the above

2 Ultraviolet rays from the sun are able to reach Earth's surface because—

F they require air to travel through

G they have less energy than infrared rays

H they have lower frequency than visible light

J they can travel through empty space

3 Which of the following groups of electromagnetic waves is listed correctly in order of increasing energy?

A X-rays, visible light, radio waves

B radio waves, visible light, X-rays

C infrared rays, visible light, radio waves

D visible light, gamma rays, X-rays

4 Radar is a system that—

F detects objects and measures their speed

G kills bacteria

H carries AM signals

J searches for hidden objects

5 AM radio waves are able to travel farther than FM radio waves because—

A AM waves produce better sound quality

B AM waves are reflected by Earth's ionosphere

C AM waves are faster than FM waves

D AM waves have constant amplitude

6 Which *best* explains the process that produces rainbows like the one shown below?

F X-rays and radio waves interfere with each other.

G Radio waves are reflected by the Earth's ionosphere.

H Gamma rays pass through the Earth's atmosphere.

J Visible light is refracted by water droplets in the air.

Channel Surfin'
on an
Infrared WAVE

You have access to an entire world of entertainment and information at the push of a button, and you don't have to leave your chair. When you push the buttons on your remote control, it uses infrared light (an invisible part of the electromagnetic spectrum) to send signals to an electronic device.

When you press a button on a TV remote control, it sends out pulses of infrared light. These pulses contain a binary code. A binary code consists of a combination of the numbers 1 and 0. Each command on the remote control has a different binary code. For example, on one type of remote the command for "channel up" is 001 0000. The command for "channel down" is 001 0001. The TV's microprocessor, or the brain of the TV, interprets and carries out the correct command.

So why doesn't that remote control turn on the CD player or the microwave? To avoid interference from other infrared light sources, such as the sun and fluorescent light bulbs, each remote control uses a specific wavelength for its signals. As a result, other electronic devices won't respond to the infrared signals from the TV remote control.

START 0 0 1 0 0 1 0 0 0 0 0 STOP

Volume Up   Device Address

Research It Research how a remote control can use both infrared light and radio frequencies. Design a device that uses both types of waves and explain how the device works and how it can be used.

 PS.1k, PS.1n, PS.9e

Museum of Science

Healing With MAGNETISM?

Magnetism is a powerful force with many uses. One claim is that it can relieve pain. The idea is that the magnetic field of a copper bracelet ionizes blood traveling through the wearer's wrist. This is supposed to change the electronic charge in the molecules of the blood. Supporters claim that the newly ionized blood improves circulation and oxygen flow. But what is really going on?

Doctors have done studies to test the claims made about these bracelets. A placebo is a control substance in experiments—something that looks like the material being tested, but doesn't do anything to the subject. In these studies, some patients wore ionic bracelets and others wore placebo bracelets, which looked the same but were not ionic. Doctors found no statistical difference in the pain relief from wearing an ionic bracelet versus a placebo bracelet. That means the bracelets don't work, but people experience pain relief because they believe the bracelets work. It's mind over matter!

Test It Find several sources presenting claims about magnetic bracelets. Write a letter to a friend who is considering buying one of these bracelets. Evaluate the claims made in the ads, and help your friend make an informed decision.

 PS.1j

▲ Manufacturers claim that this bracelet can improve circulation. Does this seem likely based on what you know about biology and magnetism?

565

WHY
CAN YOU SEE
A CITY
IN THIS
SCULPTURE?

How does light interact with matter?

Cloud Gate, a 110-ton sculpture in Chicago, Illinois, is made of highly polished stainless steel. The buildings that you see in the sculpture are a reflection of the city of Chicago.

Predict **If you were standing directly in front of this sculpture, what would you see? Explain your answer.**

_____

_____

_____

_____

_____

_____

> UNTAMED SCIENCE Watch the **Untamed Science** video to learn more about light.

Light

Science Standards of Learning

PS.1j, PS.1k, PS.1m, PS.1n, PS.9a,
PS.9b, PS.9c, PS.9e

Check Your Understanding

1. Background Read the paragraph below and then answer the question.

Jamal wakes up early to write a term paper. As the sun rises, it **transmits** sunlight through the window. The light **reflects** off of his computer screen, making it difficult for him to read the words he types. He pulls down the window shade knowing it will **absorb** some of the light.

> To **transmit** is to pass something from one place to another.
>
> To **reflect** is to throw something back.
>
> To **absorb** is to take something in or soak it up.

• Why does the window create a problem for Jamal?

_____

_____

> **MY READING WEB** If you had trouble completing the question above, visit **My Reading Web** and type in *Light*.

Vocabulary Skill

Use Prefixes A prefix is a word part that is added at the beginning of a root or base word to change its meaning. Knowing the meaning of prefixes will help you figure out new words.

Prefix	Meaning	Example
micro-	small, tiny	microscope
tele-	distant, operating at a distance	telescope
con-	together with, jointly	concave mirror, convex mirror
trans-	through	translucent

2. Quick Check Choose the word from the table that best completes the sentence.

You need a _____ to view the planets in any detail.

pigment

plane mirror

mirage

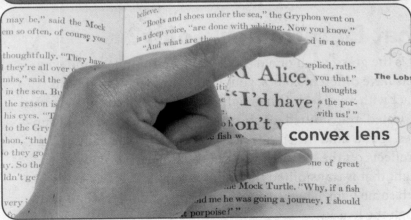

convex lens

Chapter Preview

LESSON 1

- transparent • translucent
- opaque • primary color
- secondary color
- complementary color • pigment

🔄 **Identify the Main Idea**
△ **Predict**

LESSON 2

- ray • regular reflection • image
- diffuse reflection • plane mirror
- virtual image • concave mirror
- optical axis • focal point
- real image • convex mirror

🔄 **Compare and Contrast**
△ **Classify**

LESSON 3

- index of refraction • mirage
- lens • concave lens
- convex lens

🔄 **Ask Questions**
△ **Interpret Data**

LESSON 4

- cornea • pupil • iris • retina
- rods • cones • optic nerve
- nearsighted • farsighted

🔄 **Sequence**
△ **Observe**

LESSON 5

- camera • telescope
- refracting telescope • objective
- eyepiece • reflecting telescope
- microscope

🔄 **Relate Text and Visuals**
△ **Infer**

> VOCAB FLASH CARDS For extra help with vocabulary, visit **Vocab Flash Cards** and type in *Light*.

LESSON

1 Light and Color

What Determines Color?
PS.1n, PS.9a, PS.9b, PS.9e

How Do Colors Combine?
PS.9b, PS.9e

my planet diary

FUN FACTS

Why Is the Sky Blue?

Why does the sky look blue on a clear, sunny day? The answer has to do with the nature of light.

The sun gives off white light. White light is made up of many colors. The different colors of light have different wavelengths. Red light has a longer wavelength than blue light. As the sun's light passes through our atmosphere, gas molecules in the air scatter the sunlight. The blue wavelengths get scattered the most, so the sky appears blue!

Communicate Discuss this question with a classmate. Then write your answer below.

The water droplets in clouds scatter all of the wavelengths of visible light equally. How does this explain why clouds are white?

_____
_____
_____
_____

> PLANET DIARY Go to **Planet Diary** to learn more about color.

Lab zone Do the Inquiry Warm-Up *How Do Colors Mix?*

What Determines Color?

Why is the grass green or a daffodil yellow? To understand why objects have different colors, you need to know how light can interact with an object. When light strikes an object, the light can be reflected, transmitted, or absorbed. Think about a pair of sunglasses. If you hold the sunglasses in your hand, you can see light that reflects off the lenses. If you put the sunglasses on, you see light that is transmitted through the lenses. The lenses also absorb some light. That is why objects appear darker when seen through the lenses.

Vocabulary

- transparent • translucent • opaque • primary color
- secondary color • complementary color • pigment

Skills

↺ Reading: Identify the Main Idea

△ Inquiry: Predict

Classifying Materials

Lenses, like all objects, are made of different materials. Most materials can be classified as transparent, translucent, or opaque based on what happens to light that strikes the material.

A material that transmits most of the light that strikes it is called **transparent.** Light passes through a transparent material without being scattered. This allows you to see clearly what is on the other side. Water, air, and clear glass are all transparent materials. In **Figure 1,** the window shown in the photo is partially fogged up by condensation. The center of the window, where the condensation has been wiped away, is transparent. The fogged-up part of the window is translucent. A **translucent** (trans LOO sunt) material scatters the light that passes through it. You can usually see something behind a translucent object, but the details are blurred. Wax paper and frosted glass are translucent materials.

A material that reflects or absorbs all of the light that strikes it is called **opaque** (oh PAYK). You cannot see through opaque materials because light cannot pass through them. In **Figure 1,** the wood and snow shown in the photo are opaque. Metals and tightly woven fabric are other examples of opaque materials.

> ✎
> ↺ **Identify the Main Idea**
> Underline the main idea under the red heading Classifying Materials.

FIGURE 1 ·····························

Types of Materials

The windows contain transparent, translucent, and opaque sections. ✎ Relate Diagrams and Photos **Suppose the ball was placed behind the three-sectional window below. Draw what you would see inside the dashed circle.**

Transparent

Translucent

Opaque

Vocabulary Prefixes How does knowing the meaning of the prefix *trans-* help you remember what happens to light that strikes a translucent object?

_____

_____

_____

_____

Opaque Objects

The color of an opaque object depends on the wavelengths of light that the object reflects. Every opaque object absorbs some wavelengths of light and reflects others. 🔑 **The color of an opaque object is the color of the light it reflects.** For example, look at the apple shown at the top of **Figure 2**. The apple appears red because it reflects red wavelengths of light. The apple absorbs the other colors of light. The leaf looks green because it reflects green light and absorbs the other colors.

Objects can appear to change color if you view them in a different color of light. In red light, the apple appears red because there is red light for it to reflect. But the leaf appears black because there is no green light to reflect. In green light, the leaf looks green but the apple looks black. And in blue light, both the apple and the leaf look black.

Transparent and Translucent Objects

Materials that are transparent or translucent allow only certain colors of light to pass through them. They reflect or absorb the other colors. 🔑 **The color of a transparent or translucent object is the color of the light it transmits.** For example, when white light shines through transparent blue glass, the glass appears blue because it transmits blue light.

White light

FIGURE 2 ·······································

> VIRTUAL LAB **Color of an Opaque Object**

The color an apple appears to be depends on the color of the light that strikes it. ✎ **Infer Circle the correct answers in the text below each apple.**

The apple appears red because it (absorbs/reflects) red light. The leaves look black because they (absorb/reflect) red light.

The apple appears black because it (absorbs/reflects) green light. The leaves look green because they (absorb/reflect) green light.

The apple appears black because it (absorbs/reflects) blue light. The leaves look black because they (absorb/reflect) blue light.

Transparent or translucent materials are used to make color filters. For example, a red color filter is red because it allows only red light to pass through it. When you look at an object through a color filter, the color of the object may appear different than when you see the object in white light.

The lenses in sunglasses are often color filters. For example, lenses tinted yellow are yellow filters. When you put on those sunglasses, some objects appear to change color. The color you see depends on the color of the filter and on the color of the object as it appears in white light.

White light

apply it!

Predict Imagine looking at the beach ball at the right through a red, green, or blue filter. Predict how each section of the beach ball would appear. In the diagrams below, label each section of the beach ball with its corresponding color.

Red filter	Green filter	Blue filter

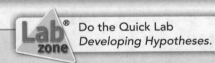
Do the Quick Lab
Developing Hypotheses.

Assess Your Understanding

1a. Identify A(n) _____ object reflects or absorbs all the light that strikes it.

b. Apply Concepts A person wearing a blue shirt is standing in sunlight. What color(s) of light does the shirt reflect? What color(s) of light does the shirt absorb?

_____

_____

c. Predict Suppose you are wearing green-tinted glasses. What color would a blue shirt appear through these glasses? _____

FIGURE 3 ··

Primary Colors of Light

The primary colors of light are red, green, and blue. A television produces many colors using only the primary colors of light. ✎ **Identify** Check off the primary color(s) that will produce the color in each circled part of the TV screen.

Red   Green   Blue

☐ ☐ ☐ = Red

☐ ☐ ☐ = White

☐ ☐ ☐ = Yellow

Magenta

Red

White   Yellow

Blue   Cyan   Green

Mixing light

List at least three examples of mixing light.

_____

_____

_____

_____

_____

_____

How Do Colors Combine?

Color is used in painting, photography, theater lighting, and printing. People who work with color must learn how to produce a wide range of colors using just a few basic colors. Three colors that can combine to make any other color are called **primary colors.** Two primary colors combine in equal amounts to produce a **secondary color.**

Mixing Light The primary colors of light are red, green, and blue. 🔲 **When the three primary colors of light are combined in equal amounts, they produce white light.** If they are combined in different amounts, the primary colors can produce other colors. For example, red and green combine to form yellow light. Yellow is a secondary color of light because two primary colors produce it. The secondary colors of light are yellow (red + green), cyan (green + blue), and magenta (red + blue). **Figure 3** shows the primary and secondary colors of light.

A primary and a secondary color can combine to make white light. Any two colors that combine to form white light are called **complementary colors.** Yellow and blue are complementary colors, as are cyan and red, and magenta and green.

A television produces many colors using only the primary colors of light. The picture on a TV screen is made up of little bars of red, green, and blue light. By varying the brightness of each colored bar, the television can produce thousands of different colors.

Mixing Pigment How does an artist produce the many shades of colors you see in a painting? Inks, paints, and dyes contain **pigments,** or colored substances that are used to color other materials. Pigments absorb some colors and reflect others. The color you see is the result of the colors that a particular pigment reflects.

Mixing colors of pigments is different from mixing colors of light. As pigments are added together, fewer colors of light are reflected and more are absorbed. The more pigments that are combined, the darker the mixture looks.

Cyan, yellow, and magenta are the primary colors of pigments. **When the three primary colors of pigments are combined in equal amounts, they produce black.** By combining pigments in varying amounts, you can produce many other colors. If you combine two primary colors of pigments, you get a secondary color, as shown in **Figure 4.** The secondary colors of pigments are red, green, and blue.

FIGURE 4 ⋯⋯⋯⋯⋯⋯⋯⋯⋯⋯⋯⋯

Primary Colors of Pigment
Oil painters use a tray called a *palette* to hold and mix pigments. ✏ Identify **Write the names of the primary colors that combine to produce the secondary color at the end of each statement.**

_____ + _____ = red

_____ + _____ = green

_____ + _____ = blue

Do the Lab Investigation *Changing Colors.*

Assess Your Understanding

2a. Identify What are the primary colors of light? What are the primary colors of pigment?

_____
_____
_____
_____

b. Compare and Contrast The result of mixing the primary colors of light in equal amounts is the color _____. The result of mixing the primary colors of pigment in equal amounts is the color _____.

got it? ⋯⋯⋯⋯⋯⋯⋯⋯⋯⋯⋯⋯⋯⋯⋯

○ **I get it!** Now I know that to produce white light you combine _____
_____

○ **I need extra help with** _____

Go to MY SCIENCE ⓢ COACH *online for help with this subject.*

Reflection and Mirrors

UNLOCK
THE BIG
?

What Are the Kinds of Reflection?
PS.9b, PS.9c

What Types of Images Do Mirrors Produce?
PS.1n, PS.9b, PS.9c, PS.9e

my planet Diary

DISCOVERY

Periscope

In a submarine hidden beneath the ocean's surface, a captain peered into a long tube to see possible threats in the sea and air above. This sight tube, called a periscope, was designed by the Frenchman Marie Davey in 1854. Davey's periscope contained two mirrors, one placed at each end of a vertical tube. The mirrors were set parallel to each other and at 45 degrees to the vertical. The reflective surfaces faced each other. When light from an object on the surface reflected downward, an image appeared to the eye. People in submerged submarines could see what was above them!

Write your answer to the question below.

Imagine you are in a submerged submarine looking through a periscope. What are some things you might see?

_____

_____

_____

_____

_____

> PLANET DIARY Go to **Planet Diary** to learn more about mirrors.

Lab zone® Do the Inquiry Warm-Up *How Does Your Reflection Wink?*

Science Standards of Learning

PS.9b Investigate and understand the wave behavior of light.

PS.9c Investigate and understand images formed by lenses and mirrors.

What Are the Kinds of Reflection?

Why do you see a reflection of yourself in a mirror but not on a page of your textbook? To answer this question, you need to understand how a surface reflects light. To show how light reflects, you can represent light waves as straight lines called **rays.** You may recall that light obeys the law of reflection—the angle of reflection equals the angle of incidence. 🔑 **The two ways in which a surface can reflect light are regular reflection and diffuse reflection.**

Vocabulary
- ray
- regular reflection
- image
- diffuse reflection
- plane mirror
- virtual image
- concave mirror
- optical axis
- focal point
- real image
- convex mirror

Skills
- Reading: Compare and Contrast
- Inquiry: Classify

Regular reflection occurs when parallel rays of light hit a smooth surface. All of the light rays reflect at the same angle because of the smooth surface. So you see a clear image. An **image** is a copy of the object formed by reflected or refracted rays of light. Shiny surfaces such as metal, glass, and calm water produce regular reflection.

Diffuse reflection occurs when parallel rays of light hit an uneven surface. Each light ray obeys the law of reflection but hits the surface at a different angle because the surface is uneven. Therefore, each ray reflects at a different angle. You either don't see an image or the image is not clear. Most objects reflect light diffusely. This is because most surfaces are not smooth. Even surfaces that appear to be smooth, such as a piece of paper, have small bumps that reflect light at different angles.

FIGURE 1 ·····································

Diffuse and Regular Reflection

✏ **Identify** Label the kind of reflection that occurs on each surface.

Do the Quick Lab
Observing.

🔑 Assess Your Understanding

got it? ·····································

- ○ **I get it!** Now I know the two kinds of reflection are _____

  _____

- ○ **I need extra help with** _____

  Go to **my science** 🔎 **coach** *online for help with this subject.*

Science Standards of Learning

PS.1n Use current applications of physical science concepts.

PS.9b Investigate and understand the wave behavior of light.

PS.9c Investigate and understand images formed by lenses and mirrors.

PS.9e Investigate and understand technological applications of light.

What Types of Images Do Mirrors Produce?

Have you ever looked at yourself in the curved mirrors of a fun house? If so, you know that your image looks different than it does in a flat mirror. Your image may look tall and skinny at one point and short and wide at another point. To understand why your image changes, you need to learn about the types of mirrors.

Plane Mirror Did you look into a mirror this morning to brush your teeth? If you did, you probably used a plane mirror. A **plane mirror** is a flat sheet of glass that has a smooth, silver-colored coating on one side. Often this coating is on the back of the glass to protect it from damage. When light strikes a mirror, the coating reflects the light. Because the coating is smooth, regular reflection occurs and a clear image forms. The image you see in a plane mirror is a **virtual image**—an image that forms where light seems to come from. "Virtual" describes something that does not really exist. Your image appears to be behind the mirror, but you can't reach behind the mirror and touch it.

🔑 **A plane mirror produces a virtual image that is upright and the same size as the object.** But the image is not quite the same as the object. The left and right of the image are reversed. For example, when you look in a mirror, your right hand appears to be a left hand in the image.

Plane Mirror

Pretend your friend has never seen her image in a plane mirror. How would you describe to her the similarities and differences between her image and the real her?

_____

_____

_____

_____

_____

_____

_____

_____

FIGURE 2 ··

Image in a Plane Mirror

A plane mirror forms a virtual image. The reflected light rays appear to come from behind the mirror, where the image forms.

✏️ **Interpret Photos** Is the raised hand in the image an image of the dancer's left hand or her right hand? Explain.

_____

_____

Image   Plane mirror   Object

Concave Mirrors A mirror with a surface that curves inward like the inside of a bowl is a **concave mirror. Figure 3** shows how a concave mirror can reflect parallel rays of light so that they meet at a point. Notice that the rays of light shown are parallel to the optical axis. The **optical axis** is an imaginary line that divides a mirror in half, much like the equator that divides Earth into northern and southern halves. The point at which rays parallel to the optical axis reflect and meet is called the **focal point.**

The type of image that is formed by a concave mirror depends on the location of the object. 👄 **Concave mirrors can produce real or virtual images.** A **real image** forms when light rays actually meet. If the object is farther away from the mirror than the focal point, the reflected rays form a real image. Unlike a virtual image, a real image can be projected on a surface such as a piece of paper. Real images are upside down. A real image may be smaller, larger, or the same size as the object.

If an object is between the mirror and the focal point, the reflected rays form a virtual image. Virtual images formed by a concave mirror are always larger than the object. Concave mirrors produce the magnified images you see in a makeup mirror.

Concave mirror

FIGURE 3 ·······································
Concave Mirror
A concave mirror reflects rays of light parallel to the optical axis back through the focal point. The figures below show how a concave mirror can produce both real and virtual images.

The type of image that is formed by a concave mirror depends on the location of the object.

✏️ **Describe** How does the image compare to the object in each of the diagrams?

_____

_____

_____

_____

_____

_____

_____

_____

Compare and Contrast

Compare and contrast the shape of a convex mirror and a concave mirror.

_____

_____

_____

_____

Convex Mirrors A mirror with a surface that curves outward is called a **convex mirror.** **Figure 4a** shows how convex mirrors reflect parallel rays of light. The reflected rays spread out but appear to come from a focal point behind the mirror. The focal point of a convex mirror is the point from which the rays appear to come. 🔑 **A convex mirror produces a virtual image that is always smaller than the object.**

Perhaps you have seen this warning on a car mirror: "Objects in mirror are closer than they appear." Convex mirrors are used in cars as passenger-side mirrors. The advantage of a convex mirror is that it allows you to see a larger area than you can with a plane mirror. The disadvantage is that the image is reduced in size. As a result, the image appears to be farther away than it actually is. The driver must understand this and adjust for it.

FIGURE 4 ••

▶ INTERACTIVE ART **Convex Mirror**

a. Light rays parallel to the optical axis reflect as if they came from the focal point behind a convex mirror.

b. CHALLENGE **Extend the two reflected rays behind the mirror to where they intersect. This is the top of the virtual image. Draw the image.**

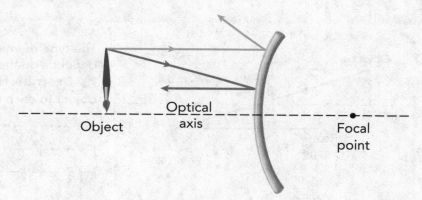

Complete the table to review the different types of images formed by mirrors.

Mirror	Location of Object	Is the image real or virtual?	Is the image upright or upside down?	What is the size of the image compared to the object?
Plane	Anywhere			
Concave	Farther than the focal point			
	Closer than the focal point			
Convex	Anywhere			

apply it!

Each of the photos shows an application of a curved mirror. A bus driver uses the mirror in the top photo to check for traffic. A boy uses the mirror in the bottom photo to put in contact lenses.

1 ▲ **Classify** Which type of curved mirror is in the top photo?_____

2 ▲ **Classify** Which type of curved mirror is in the bottom photo?_____

3 Explain Why is the mirror in the top photo more useful than a plane mirror for checking traffic?

_____

_____

_____

4 Explain Why is the mirror in the bottom photo more useful than a plane mirror for putting in contact lenses?

_____

_____

_____

Lab zone Do the Quick Lab *Mirror Images.*

🔑 Assess Your Understanding

1a. Define A(n) _____ is a copy of an object formed by reflected or refracted rays of light.

b. ▲ **Classify** A _____ mirror can form real and virtual images. _____ and _____ mirrors form only virtual images.

c. Apply Concepts Which type of mirror would you use if you wanted to project an image on a screen? Why?

_____

_____

_____

got it? ....

○ **I get it!** Now I know that the two types of images produced by mirrors are real _____

_____

○ **I need extra help with** _____

    Go to **MY SCIENCE** 🔹 **COACH** *online for help with this subject.*

Refraction and Lenses

UNLOCK THE BIG ?

🔑 **What Causes Light Rays to Bend?**
PS.1j, PS.1n, PS.9a, PS.9b, PS.9e

🔑 **What Determines the Type of Image Formed by a Lens?**
PS.1n, PS.9b, PS.9c

MY PLANET DIARY

Isaac Newton

Sir Isaac Newton (1642–1727) may be best known as the man who came up with the theory of gravity. But Newton, who was born in England, made numerous other important contributions to both math and science, including defining the laws of motion and co-founding the field of calculus. In the 1660s, Newton investigated the laws of light and color. In his famous book *Opticks*, he describes how he passed sunlight through a prism to prove that white light consists of many colors. Newton was knighted in 1705 and was the first scientist to be buried at Westminster Abbey.

BIOGRAPHY

Communicate Write your answers to the questions below. Then discuss your answers with a partner.

1. How did Newton prove that sunlight consists of many colors?

_____

_____

2. Describe a discovery that you made through experimentation.

_____

_____

_____

_____

_____

> PLANET DIARY Go to **Planet Diary** to learn more about lenses.

Lab zone® Do the Inquiry Warm-Up *How Can You Make an Image Appear?*

Vocabulary
- index of refraction • mirage • lens
- concave lens • convex lens

Skills
- ⟳ Reading: Ask Questions
- △ Inquiry: Interpret Data

What Causes Light Rays to Bend?

A fish tank can play tricks on your eyes. If you look through the side of a fish tank, a fish seems closer than if you look at it from the top. If you look through the corner of the tank, you may see the same fish twice. Look at **Figure 1.** You see one image of the fish through the front of the tank and another through the side. The two images appear in different places! How can this happen?

Refraction can cause you to see something that may not actually be there. As you look at a fish in a tank, the light coming from the fish to your eye bends as it passes through three different mediums. The mediums are water, the glass of the tank, and air. As the light passes from one medium to the next, it is refracted. ⟲ **When light rays enter a new medium at an angle, the change in speed causes the rays to bend.**

Science Standards of Learning

PS.1j Make valid conclusions after analyzing data.

PS.1n Use current applications of physical science concepts.

PS.9a Investigate and understand wavelength, frequency, speed, amplitude, crest, and trough of transverse waves.

PS.9b Investigate and understand the wave behavior of light.

PS.9e Investigate and understand technological applications of light.

FIGURE 1 ·······························

Optical Illusion in a Fish Tank

There is only one fish in this tank, but refraction makes it look as though there are two.

✎ **Communicate** Discuss with a classmate some other examples of how the appearance of objects in water is different than in the air. Describe these examples below.

_____

_____

_____

_____

_____

_____

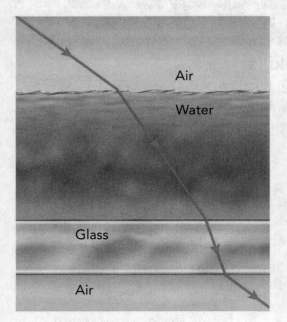

FIGURE 2
Refraction of Light
The light ray bends as it passes through different mediums.
✏️ **Interpret Diagrams** **In which medium does light travel the fastest?**

Refraction in Different Mediums
Some mediums cause light to bend more than others. **Figure 2** shows how the path of a light ray changes as it passes from one medium to another. When light passes from air into water, the light slows down. Light slows down again and bends even more when it passes from water into glass. When light passes from glass back into air, the light speeds up. Notice that the ray that leaves the glass is traveling in the same direction as it was before it entered the water. Light travels fastest in air, a little slower in water, and slower still in glass.

Glass causes light to bend more than either air or water does. Another way to say this is that glass has a higher index of refraction than either air or water. The **index of refraction** of a medium is a measure of how much a light ray bends when it enters that medium. The higher the index of refraction of a medium, the more it bends light. The index of refraction of water is 1.33. The index of refraction of glass is about 1.5. So light is bent more by glass than by water.

do the math! Analyzing Data

Bending Light
The table shows the index of refraction of some common mediums. **Use the data to answer the following questions.**

❶ **Interpret Data** Which medium causes the greatest change in the direction of a light ray that enters at an angle?

❷ **Interpret Data** According to the table, which tend to bend light more, solids or liquids?

❸ **Predict** Would you expect light to bend if it entered corn oil at an angle after it traveled through glycerol? Explain.

Index of Refraction	
Medium	**Index of Refraction**
Air (gas)	1.00
Water (liquid)	1.33
Ethyl alcohol (liquid)	1.36
Quartz (solid)	1.46
Corn oil (liquid)	1.47
Glycerol (liquid)	1.47
Glass, crown (solid)	1.52
Sodium chloride (solid)	1.54
Zircon (solid)	1.92
Diamond (solid)	2.42

Prisms and Rainbows Recall that when white light enters a prism, each wavelength is refracted by a different amount. The longer the wavelength, the less the wave is bent by a prism. Red, with the longest wavelength, is refracted the least. Violet, with the shortest wavelength, is refracted the most. This difference in refraction causes white light to spread out into the colors of the spectrum—red, orange, yellow, green, blue, and violet.

The same process occurs in water droplets suspended in the air. When white light from the sun shines through the droplets, a rainbow may appear. The water droplets act like tiny prisms, refracting and reflecting the light and separating the colors.

EXPLORE
THE BIG
?

Water + Light = A Rainbow

How does light interact with matter?

FIGURE 3 ....

> ART IN MOTION

A rainbow forms when light is reflected and refracted by water droplets suspended in the air. The diagram shows the path of a light ray that strikes a water droplet. ✎ Interpret Diagrams **Use the diagram to answer the questions.**

What happens to each color of light at point B?

_____

_____

_____

Why does light separate out into its colors at point A?

_____

_____

_____

A

B

C   Water droplet

What happens to each color of light at point C?

_____

_____

_____

585

_____

_____

_____

FIGURE 4 ·································
Mirage
The puddles and reflections on the road are mirages.

Mirages

You're traveling in a car on a hot day, and you notice that the road ahead looks wet. Yet when you get there, the road is dry. Did the puddles dry up? No, the puddles were never there! You saw a **mirage** (mih RAHJ)—an image of a distant object caused by refraction of light. The puddles on the road are light rays from the sky that are refracted to your eyes.

Figure 4 shows a mirage. Notice that there appears to be a reflection of the vehicle in the road. The air just above the road is hotter than the air higher up. Light travels faster in hot air. So light rays from the vehicle that travel toward the road are bent upward by the hot air. Your brain assumes that these rays traveled in a straight line. So the rays look as if they have reflected off a smooth surface. What you see is a mirage.

Lab® zone
Do the Quick Lab *Bent Pencil.*

Assess Your Understanding

1a. Identify A material's _____ is a measure of how much a ray of light bends when it enters that material from air.

b. Predict If a glass prism were in a medium with the same index of refraction, would it separate white light into different colors? Explain.

_____

_____

_____

c. ANSWER THE BIG ? How does light interact with matter?

_____

_____

_____

_____

_____

_____

got it? ··

○ **I get it!** Now I know that the reason light rays bend when they enter a new medium at an angle is because _____

○ **I need extra help with** _____

Go to MY SCIENCE COACH online for help with this subject.

What Determines the Type of Image Formed by a Lens?

Any time you look through binoculars, a camera, or eyeglasses, you are using lenses to bend light. A **lens** is a curved piece of glass or other transparent material that refracts light. A lens forms an image by refracting light rays that pass through it. Like mirrors, lenses can have different shapes. 🔑 **The type of image formed by a lens depends on the shape of the lens and the position of the object.**

Science Standards of Learning

PS.1n Use current applications of physical science concepts.

PS.9b Investigate and understand the wave behavior of light.

PS.9c Investigate and understand images formed by lenses and mirrors.

Concave Lenses A **concave lens** is thinner in the center than at the edges. When light rays traveling parallel to the optical axis pass through a concave lens, they bend away from the optical axis and never meet. A concave lens can produce only virtual images because parallel light rays passing through the lens never meet.

Look at the book to the right. Notice that the words seen through the lens appear smaller than the words outside of the lens. The words seen through the lens are virtual images. A concave lens always produces a virtual image that is upright and smaller than the object. **Figure 5a** shows how a concave lens forms an image. The image is located where the light rays appear to come from.

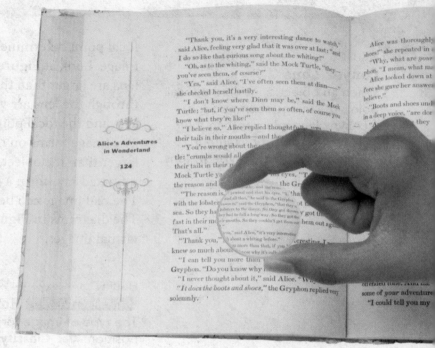

FIGURE 5 ·······································
Concave Lens

a. A concave lens produces a virtual image that is upright and smaller than the object.

Object | Focal point | Image | Focal point

b. ✎ **Apply Concepts** Locate this object's image. Extend the two light rays straight back to the same side of the lens as the object. The point where they intersect is the location of the image. Draw the image.

Focal point | Object | Focal point

Convex Lenses

A **convex lens** is thicker in the center than at the edges. As light rays parallel to the optical axis pass through a convex lens, they are bent toward the center of the lens. The rays meet at the focal point of the lens and continue to travel beyond. The more curved the lens, the more it refracts light. A convex lens acts like a concave mirror, because it focuses rays of light.

An object's position relative to the focal point determines whether a convex lens forms a real or virtual image. Look at **Figure 6.** Notice that the words seen through the lens are larger than the words outside of the lens. The words seen through the lens are virtual images. When an object is between the lens and the focal point, the refracted rays form a virtual image. The image forms on the same side of the lens as the object and is larger than the object. If the object is outside of the focal point, the refracted rays form a real image on the other side of the lens. The real image can be smaller, larger, or the same size as the object. The diagrams in **Figure 7** show how a convex lens forms real and virtual images.

FIGURE 6 ·······································

Convex Lens

When an object is inside the focal point, the image seen through a convex lens is larger than the object. ✎ **Identify Name a device that uses this type of lens.**

_____

_____

Lenses

List some devices that use lenses.

_____

_____

_____

_____

_____

_____

FIGURE 7 ··

⟩ INTERACTIVE ART **How a Convex Lens Works**

The type of image formed by a convex lens depends on the object's position. ✎ **Classify Label which image is virtual and which image is real.**

apply it!

Convex lens

Concave lens

1 Interpret Photos These photos show parallel rays of light passing through a convex lens and a concave lens. Why do you suppose a convex lens is called a converging lens and a concave lens is called a diverging lens?

_____

_____

_____

2 Review Complete the Lenses and Mirrors table. Use the table to answer Question 3.

3 Summarize A convex lens acts like a _____ mirror. A concave lens acts like a _____ mirror.

4 CHALLENGE Suppose a convex lens and a concave mirror are underwater. Compared to the way they work in air, which one do you expect will be more affected by the water? Why?

_____

_____

_____

Lenses and Mirrors

Type of Mirror or Lens	Real, Virtual, or Both Types of Images	Upright, Inverted, or Both Types of Images
Concave Mirror	Both	_____
Convex Mirror	_____	Upright
Concave Lens	_____	_____
Convex Lens	_____	_____

Lab zone® Do the Quick Lab _Looking at Images._

🔑 Assess Your Understanding

2a. Define A _____ is a curved piece of glass or other transparent material that refracts light.

b. Compare and Contrast Describe the shapes of a concave lens and a convex lens.

_____

_____

_____

c. Make Generalizations Use **Figure 7** to explain how you can you tell whether a convex lens will produce a real or virtual image.

_____

_____

_____

_____

got it?

○ **I get it!** Now I know that the type of image formed by a lens depends on _____

_____

○ **I need extra help with** _____

_Go to_ **MY SCIENCE ⓢ COACH** _online for help with this subject._

Seeing Light

UNLOCK
THE BIG
?

🔑 **How Do You See Objects?**

PS.1n, PS.9b, PS.9c, PS.9e

my planeт diary

MISCONCEPTION

Misconception: You can see in total darkness as long as your eyes adjust to the darkness.

Fact: It is impossible to see objects in total darkness. If there is some light, such as light from a street lamp or moonlight, we can see objects because the light reflects off the objects and enters our eyes. In these low light conditions, our eyes adjust to let more light in. It can take 10 to 30 minutes for this to happen.

Evidence: If a person is in a completely dark environment, such as a deep cave, he or she cannot see objects.

Communicate Write your answers to the questions below. Then discuss your answers with a partner.

1. How do you suppose your eyes adjust to let in more light?

_____

_____

_____

2. Think of an experiment to test whether or not humans can see in complete darkness.

_____

_____

_____

_____

> PLANET DIARY Go to **Planet Diary** to learn more about the human eye.

 Do the Inquiry Warm-Up *Can You See Everything With One Eye?*

Vocabulary

- cornea • pupil • iris • retina • rods • cones
- optic nerve • nearsighted • farsighted

Skills

↻ Reading: Sequence
△ Inquiry: Observe

How Do You See Objects?

The first rule of baseball or softball is to keep your eye on the ball. As the ball moves near or far, your eyes must adjust continuously to keep it in focus. Fortunately, your eyes can change focus automatically. The eye is a complex structure with many parts. Each part plays a role in vision. **You see objects when a process occurs that involves both your eyes and your brain.**

Light Enters the Eye Light enters the eye through the transparent front surface called the **cornea** (KAWR nee uh). The cornea protects the eye. It also acts as a lens to help focus light rays.

After passing through the cornea, light enters the pupil, the part of the eye that looks black. The **pupil** is an opening through which light enters the inside of the eye. In dim light, the pupil becomes larger to allow in more light. In bright light, the pupil becomes smaller to allow in less light. The **iris** is a ring of muscle that contracts and expands to change the size of the pupil. The iris gives the eye its color. In most people the iris is brown; in others it is blue, green, or hazel.

Science Standards of Learning

PS.1n Use current applications of physical science concepts.
PS.9b Investigate and understand the wave behavior of light.
PS.9c Investigate and understand images formed by lenses and mirrors.
PS.9e Investigate and understand technological applications of light.

apply it!

The photographs show the same pupil exposed to different amounts of light.

❶ **Identify** Label which pupil is in dim light and which pupil is in bright light.

❷ **Explain** Why does the size of the pupil change?

_____

_____

❸ △ **Observe** Work with a classmate. Cover one of your eyes with your hand for several seconds. Then remove your hand. Your classmate should observe what happens to your pupil. Switch roles. Record your observations.

_____

_____

_____ light

_____ light

✐ **Sequence** A sequence is the order in which the steps in a process occur. As you read, complete the flowchart to show how you see objects.

How You See Objects

1. Light enters the eye.

2. _____

3. _____

4. _____

An Image Forms After entering the pupil, the light passes through the lens. The lens is a convex lens that refracts light to form an image on the lining of your eyeball. Muscles, called ciliary muscles, hold the lens in place behind the pupil. When you focus on a distant object, the ciliary muscles relax, and the lens becomes longer and thinner. When you focus on a nearby object, the muscles contract, and the lens becomes shorter and fatter.

When the cornea and the lens refract light, an upside-down image is formed on the retina. The **retina** is a layer of cells that lines the inside of the eyeball. (Cells are the tiny structures that make up living things.) **Rods** are cells that contain a pigment that responds to small amounts of light. The rods allow you to see in dim light. **Cones** are cells that respond to color. They may detect red light, green light, or blue light. Cones respond best in bright light. Both rods and cones help change images on the retina into signals that then travel to the brain.

A Signal Goes to the Brain The rods and cones send signals to the brain along a short, thick nerve called the **optic nerve.** The optic nerve begins at the blind spot, an area of the retina that has no rods or cones. Your brain interprets the signals from the optic nerve as an upright image. It also combines the two images from your eyes into a single three-dimensional image.

FIGURE 1

The Human Eye

The human eye is a complex structure with many parts that allow you to see.

✐ **Identify** Use the words in the word bank to identify the parts of the eye.

Word Bank

Ciliary muscles
Cornea
Iris
Lens
Optic nerve
Pupil
Retina

Blood vessels

Correcting Vision If the eyeball is slightly too long or too short, the image on the retina is out of focus. Fortunately, wearing glasses or contact lenses can correct this type of vision problem.

A **nearsighted** person can see nearby things clearly, but objects at a distance are blurred. The eyeball is too long, so the lens focuses the image in front of the retina. To correct this, a concave lens in front of the eye spreads out light rays before they enter the eye. As a result, the image forms on the retina.

A **farsighted** person can see distant objects clearly, but nearby objects appear blurry. The eyeball is too short, so the image that falls on the retina is out of focus. A convex lens corrects this by bending light rays toward each other before they enter the eye. An image then focuses on the retina.

 Diagnose the Patient! Read each patient's chart. Circle the diagnosis. Write in the type of lens needed in each case.

Patient: Iris Green
Age: 11 years old
Reason for visit: having trouble reading the board

Diagnosis: Nearsightedness/Farsightedness

Focal point in front of retina

Correction: Eyeglasses with _____ lenses.

Focal point on retina

Patient: Cornealis Brown
Age: 14 years old
Reason for visit: routine eye exam

Diagnosis: Nearsightedness/Farsightedness

Focal point behind the retina

Correction: Eyeglasses with _____ lenses.

Focal point on retina

Lab zone® Do the Quick Lab *True Colors*.

🔑 Assess Your Understanding

1a. Sequence The part of the eye that light enters first is called the _____

b. Explain How is an image formed on the retina?
_____
_____
_____

got it?

○ **I get it!** Now I know that seeing objects is a process that involves both _____
_____

○ **I need extra help with** _____
_____

Go to MY SCIENCE ⬢ COACH online for help with this subject.

Using Light

🔑 **How Do Cameras, Telescopes, and Microscopes Work?**

PS.1n, PS.9b, PS.9c, PS.9e

my planet Diary

SCIENCE STATS

F-Numbers

Have you ever seen numbers such as F1.0, F1.4, or F2.8 on the LCD screen of a digital camera? These numbers are called *f-numbers*. F-numbers tell the size of the lens opening on the camera. The larger the f-number is, the smaller the lens opening is. By changing the f-number, a photographer can change the amount of light the lens lets in. The table shows the amount of light let in (relative ability to gather light) for different f-numbers.

Communicate Use the data in the table to answer these questions. Discuss your answers with a partner.

1. How does the relative light-gathering ability of a lens change as the f-number increases?

_____

_____

2. Suppose you want to take a picture in very low light. Which f-number would you use and why?

_____

_____

_____

F-number	Relative Ability to Gather Light
1.0	32×
1.4	16×
2.0	8×
2.8	4×
4.0	2×
5.6	1

▶ PLANET DIARY Go to **Planet Diary** to learn more about optical instruments.

Lab zone® Do the Inquiry Warm-Up *How Does a Pinhole Camera Work?*

Vocabulary
- camera
- telescope
- refracting telescope
- objective
- eyepiece
- reflecting telescope
- microscope

Skills
- Reading: Relate Text and Visuals
- Inquiry: Infer

How Do Cameras, Telescopes, and Microscopes Work?

A microscope helps you see objects that are nearby. But another type of optical (or light-using) instrument, a telescope, helps you see objects that are far away. Three common types of optical instruments are cameras, telescopes, and microscopes.

Cameras A **camera** records an image of an object. A film camera records the image on film. A digital camera records the image electronically on a sensor. Both types of cameras follow the same basic principle. 🔑 **The lenses in a camera focus light to form a real, upside-down image in the back of the camera.** In many cameras, the lenses automatically move closer to or away from the film or sensor until the image is focused.

To take a photo with a digital camera, you press halfway down on a button called the shutter release. The camera automatically adjusts the amount of light that hits the sensor by changing the size of its opening. The camera also adjusts the amount of time that the sensor is exposed to light. When you press all the way down on the shutter release, the camera records the final image. The camera stores the final images so that you can transfer them to a computer.

Shutter release

Lenses

Object

apply it!

The diagram shows the structure of a digital camera.

1 Interpret Diagrams What happens to each light ray as it passes through the lenses?

_____

2 Identify On what part of the camera does an image form?

_____

3 Infer Draw the image of the tree in the box to the right.

✏️
Relate Text and Visuals
What is the purpose of the eyepiece in both types of telescopes and the microscope?

- ⚪ to shrink the image
- ⚪ to magnify the image
- ⚪ to gather light
- ⚪ to reflect light

Telescopes Distant objects are difficult to see because light from them has spread out by the time it reaches your eyes. Your eyes are too small to gather much light. A **telescope** forms enlarged images of distant objects. 🔑 Telescopes use lenses or mirrors to collect and focus light from distant objects. The most common use of telescopes is to study objects in space.

Figure 1 shows the two main types of telescopes: refracting telescopes and reflecting telescopes. A **refracting telescope** consists of two convex lenses, one at each end of a tube. The larger lens is called the objective. The **objective** gathers the light coming from an object and focuses the rays to form a real image. The convex lens close to your eye is called the eyepiece. The **eyepiece** magnifies the image so you can see it clearly. The image seen through the refracting telescope is upside down.

A **reflecting telescope** uses a large concave mirror to gather light. The mirror collects light from distant objects and focuses the rays to form a real image. A small, plane mirror inside the telescope reflects the image to the eyepiece. The images you see through a reflecting telescope are upside down, just like the images seen through a refracting telescope.

FIGURE 1 ·······

▷ **INTERACTIVE ART** **Reflecting and Refracting Telescopes**
Both reflecting and refracting telescopes gather light from distant objects such as Mars, shown above. ✏️ **Identify** Label the type of lens or mirror in each part of the diagrams.

Eyepiece

Light rays

Focal point of both lenses

Light rays

Eyepiece

Refracting Telescope

Reflecting Telescope

Microscopes To look at small, nearby objects, you would use a microscope. A **microscope** forms enlarged images of tiny objects. 🔑 **A microscope uses a combination of lenses to produce and magnify an image.** For example, the microscope that is shown in **Figure 2** uses two convex lenses to magnify an object, or specimen. The specimen is placed near the objective. The objective forms a real, enlarged image of the specimen. Then the eyepiece enlarges the image even more.

Eyepiece
(convex lens)

Light rays

Objective
(convex lens)

Slide with
specimen

Light source

FIGURE 2 ··············
Microscope
This microscope uses a combination of lenses to form enlarged images of tiny objects.

✏️ CHALLENGE **The objects below have been enlarged by a microscope. Try to guess what they are.** *(The answers are upside down below.)*

From left to right: human hair, leaf, insect (louse)

Lab zone ® Do the Quick Lab
What a View!

🔑 Assess Your Understanding

1a. Review A _____ forms enlarged images of distant objects. A _____ forms enlarged images of tiny objects. A _____ records an image of an object.

b. Classify A pair of binoculars has two lenses in each tube. Which type of optical instrument are the binoculars most similar to?

_____

_____

got it? ···

○ **I get it!** Now I know that telescopes, microscopes, and cameras use _____

_____

○ **I need extra help with** _____

Go to MY SCIENCE 🔍 COACH *online for help with this subject.*

REVIEW
THE BIG
?

When light interacts with matter, it can be _____, _____, or _____.

LESSON 1 Light and Color

🔑 The color of an opaque object is the color of the light it reflects. The color of a transparent or translucent object is the color of the light it transmits.

🔑 When the three primary colors of light are combined in equal amounts, they produce white light. When the three primary colors of pigment are combined in equal amounts, they produce black.

Vocabulary
- transparent
- translucent
- opaque
- primary color
- secondary color
- complementary color
- pigment

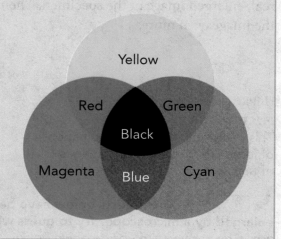

LESSON 2 Reflection and Mirrors

🔑 The two ways in which a surface can reflect light are regular reflection and diffuse reflection.

🔑 The three common types of mirrors are plane, concave, and convex.

Vocabulary
- ray
- regular reflection
- image
- diffuse reflection
- plane mirror
- virtual image
- concave mirror
- optical axis
- focal point
- real image
- convex mirror

LESSON 3 Refraction and Lenses

🔑 When light rays enter a new medium at an angle, the change in speed causes them to bend.

🔑 The type of image formed by a lens depends on the shape of the lens and the position of the object.

Vocabulary
- index of refraction
- mirage
- lens
- concave lens
- convex lens

LESSON 4 Seeing Light

🔑 You see objects when a process occurs that involves both your eyes and your brain.

Vocabulary
- cornea
- pupil
- iris
- retina
- rods
- cones
- optic nerve
- nearsighted
- farsighted

LESSON 5 Using Light

🔑 Three common optical instruments are cameras, telescopes, and microscopes.

Vocabulary
- camera
- telescope
- refracting telescope
- objective
- eyepiece
- reflecting telescope
- microscope

Review and Assessment

LESSON 1 Light and Color

1. A type of material that reflects or absorbs all of the light that strikes it is called

   a. translucent.   **b.** transparent.

   c. reflective.   **d.** opaque.

2. Colors that combine to make any other color are called _____

3. Classify Do the colors shown below represent colors of pigments or light? Explain.

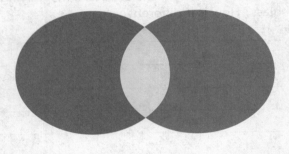

_____

_____

_____

4. Compare and Contrast Why do you see the petals of a rose as red and the leaves as green? Explain.

_____

_____

_____

_____

_____

5. [Write About It] Helena works in the lighting crew for a theater. She needs to create a red spotlight on the stage. Kimi is a painter. He wants to create red paint for the background in a new painting. Use the terms *primary color* and *complementary color* to explain what color or combinations of colors each person must use. Explain any differences you note.

LESSON 2 Reflection and Mirrors

6. What type of reflection describes how light reflects off an uneven surface?

   a. real reflection   **b.** concave reflection

   c. diffuse reflection   **d.** regular reflection

7. Light rays obey the law of reflection, which states that _____

_____

_____

8. Draw Use a ruler to draw how the parallel light rays reflect off each mirror below.

9. Classify Name the kind(s) of mirror(s) that can produce only virtual images.

_____

10. Apply Concepts Can a plane mirror produce a real image? Explain.

_____

_____

_____

_____

17 Review and Assessment

LESSON 3 Refraction and Lenses

11. A curved piece of glass or other transparent material that is used to refract light is called a

    a. prism.   **b.** lens.

    c. mirage.   **d.** mirror.

12. A _____ lens can produce only virtual images because parallel light rays passing through the lens never meet.

13. math! Quartz has an index of refraction of 1.46. Diamond has an index of refraction of 2.42. In which material does a light ray entering from air slow down more? Explain.

_____

_____

_____

_____

_____

LESSON 4 Seeing Light

14. What is the ring of muscle that changes the size of the eye's pupil?

    a. iris   **b.** retina

    c. cornea   **d.** cone

15. A _____ person has trouble seeing things nearby.

16. Apply Concepts How are your eyes able to clearly see both near and distant objects?

_____

_____

_____

_____

_____

LESSON 5 Using Light

17. What is a device that helps you see very small, nearby objects more clearly?

    a. telescope   **b.** camera

    c. microscope   **d.** binoculars

18. A _____ telescope gathers light with a concave mirror.

19. Compare and Contrast How is a microscope similar to a convex lens used as a magnifying glass? How is it different?

_____

_____

_____

_____

 How does light interact with matter?

20. Explain why the beam of light changes direction when it enters the water.

_____

_____

_____

Read each question and choose the best answer.

1 The diagram below shows a periscope, a tool used to see objects not in the viewer's direct line of sight.

If you want to build a periscope, what measurement is *most* important?

A the width of the two mirrors
B the distance between the two mirrors
C the angle of the two mirrors
D the length of the tube

2 The index of refraction for water is 1.33 and for glass it is 1.5. What happens to the speed of light when light travels from glass into water?

F It increases.
G It decreases.
H It remains the same.
J It depends on the angle of incidence.

3 A convex lens can produce a real or a virtual image. Which type of mirror is *most similar* to a convex lens?

A concave mirror
B convex mirror
C plane mirror
D none of the above

4 You view an American flag through sunglasses that are tinted green. What colors do you see?

F green and blue
G red and black
H blue and red
J black and green

5 Which of the following describes looking at an object through a translucent material?

A You see the object clearly but it is upside down.
B You do not see the object at all.
C You see the object but its details are blurred.
D You see the object very clearly.

6 Which of the following statements about the light ray as it travels through the different mediums is true?

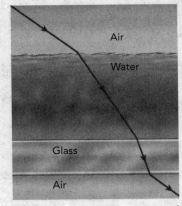

F Light slows down more when passing from glass to air than when passing from air to water.
G Water causes light to bend more than glass does.
H Light travels the fastest through water.
J Light slows down when passing from water to glass.

601

SeeingDouble

Isaac Newton built the first model for a reflecting telescope in 1688.

Binoculars are really a set of two telescopes—one for each eye—that magnify distant objects. When scientists want to look at something even farther away, they can now turn to the world's largest pair of binoculars: the Large Binocular Telescope (LBT) on Mount Graham in Arizona.

The 120-million-dollar LBT is the world's most powerful optical telescope. It provides scientists with pictures and data of a huge area of space. The LBT has two massive mirrors that work together. Each mirror has a diameter of 8.4 meters! The mirrors gather light and allow scientists to look deeper into the universe than ever before. In fact, the LBT provides the same resolution as a 22.8-meter telescope—that's about as big as two school buses! It also has a larger field for collecting images than any single telescope, allowing scientists to see more.

Design It Research how mirrors work in a reflecting telescope. Make a model or draw a diagram of how a reflecting telescope works. Show how the angles of reflection would work with the mirrors placed at two different angles. Which angles will work best? Present your model or drawing to your class.

PS.1k, PS.1m, PS.9c, PS.9e

The world's largest binoculars peer into space. ▶

Hiding in Plain Sight

The South African dwarf chameleon has mastered the art of the quick change! This lizard can change the color of its skin in response to light, temperature, and other environmental factors.

Each of the four layers of the dwarf chameleon's skin plays a role in its brilliant appearance. The top layer is clear, so light passes right through it. The second layer has cells that contain a yellow pigment. The third layer doesn't have a specific color—it has cells that scatter light. The way these cells scatter light is similar to the way Earth's atmosphere scatters light, reflecting blue light especially well. The bottom layer of a dwarf chameleon's skin contains a pigment called melanin, which absorbs red light. Hormones control how the melanin is arranged in this layer. The melanin moves in response to light, temperature, and other environmental factors. As the melanin moves, the color of the chameleon's skin changes.

The chameleon's color results from the combination of the reflected light from the underlying layers of skin. When mostly blue light reflected from the third layer combines with light from the yellow layer, the chameleon is bright green.

The third layer of the dwarf chameleon's skin reflects blue light, which combines with the yellow in the second layer to make the chameleon appear bright green. ▼

Model It Use a piece of clear plastic wrap, yellow plastic wrap, a small prism, and white or blue paper to model the top three layers of the chameleon's skin. Does changing the angle of the prism change the color you see through the layers of "skin"? Draw a diagram of your model, and describe how changing the color of the bottom layer and the angle of the prism change the colors you see.

PS.1m, PS.9b

WHY ARE THE PEOPLE IN THIS BUILDING SAFE FROM LIGHTNING?

 How does an electric circuit work?

Lightning strikes Earth more than 100 times every second. Buildings can be protected from lightning strikes with tall metal poles called lightning rods. When lightning strikes, it is more likely to hit the rod than the building. A lightning strike can flow through the rod and into metal wires that are connected to the ground. This prevents the building from being damaged and anyone inside from being injured.

Communicate **How is a lightning bolt like the electricity that runs through power lines? Discuss this with a partner.**

_____

_____

_____

_____

> **UNTAMED SCIENCE** Watch the **Untamed Science** video to learn more about electricity.

Electricity

Science Standards of Learning

PS.1a, PS.1k, PS.1m, PS.1n, PS.6b, PS.11a, PS.11d

18 Getting Started

Check Your Understanding

1. Background Read the paragraph below and then answer the question.

When you lift up a basketball, you apply a **force** to it. The **energy** you use to lift it gets transferred to the ball as gravitational **potential energy.** The higher you lift the ball, the more energy you use and the more gravitational potential energy the ball gains.

> A **force** is a push or pull exerted on an object.
>
> **Energy** is the ability to do work or cause change.
>
> **Potential energy** is the stored energy that results from the position or shape of an object.

- What happens to the ball's gravitational potential energy if it is dropped?

_____

▶ MY READING WEB If you had trouble completing the question above, visit **My Reading Web** and type in *Electricity.*

Vocabulary Skill

Latin Word Origins Many science words in English come from Latin. For example, the word *solar*, which means "of the sun," comes from the Latin *sol*, which means "sun."

Latin Word	Meaning of Latin Word	Example
circuitus	going around	circuit, *n.* a complete, unbroken path
currere	to run	current, *n.* a continuous flow
insula	island	insulator, *n.* a material through which charges cannot flow

2. Quick Check Choose the word that best completes the sentence.

- An electric _____ is formed by the movement of electric charges from one place to another.

static electricity

static discharge

electric circuit

Ohm's law

$$\text{Resistance} = \frac{\text{Voltage}}{\text{Current}}$$

Chapter Preview

LESSON 1
- electric force
- electric field
- static electricity
- conservation of charge
- friction
- conduction
- induction
- polarization
- static discharge

↻ **Relate Cause and Effect**
△ **Draw Conclusions**

LESSON 2
- electric current
- electric circuit
- conductor
- insulator
- voltage
- resistance

↻ **Ask Questions**
△ **Classify**

LESSON 3
- Ohm's law
- series circuit
- parallel circuit

↻ **Compare and Contrast**
△ **Make Models**

LESSON 4
- power
- short circuit
- third prong
- grounded
- fuse
- circuit breaker

↻ **Summarize**
△ **Calculate**

> **VOCAB FLASH CARDS** For extra help with vocabulary, visit **Vocab Flash Cards** and type in *Electricity.*

Electric Charge and Static Electricity

UNLOCK THE BIG **?**

🔑 **How Do Charges Interact?**
PS.11a

🔑 **How Does Charge Build Up?**
PS.1a, PS.1n, PS.11a

my planet Diary

Force Fields

Misconception: Force fields exist only in science fiction stories.

Fact: Force fields are an important part of your everyday life.

You're actually sitting in a force field right now! A force field exists around any object that repels or attracts other objects. A giant gravitational force field surrounds Earth. This field keeps you from floating off into space. Earth's magnetic field makes compass needles point north. You make your own force field every time you get shocked when you reach for a doorknob!

MISCONCEPTIONS

Answer the questions below.

1. A gravitational field keeps you on Earth. What other uses might force fields have?

_____

_____

2. Describe how a different science fiction invention could be rooted in real science.

_____

_____

▶ **PLANET DIARY** Go to **Planet Diary** to learn more about force fields.

Lab zone
Do the Inquiry Warm-Up *Can You Move a Can Without Touching It?*

Vocabulary
- electric force • electric field • static electricity
- conservation of charge • friction • conduction
- induction • polarization • static discharge

Skills
↻ **Reading: Relate Cause and Effect**
△ **Inquiry: Draw Conclusions**

How Do Charges Interact?

 Science Standards of Learning

PS.11a Investigate and understand static electricity, current electricity, and circuits.

You're already late for school and one of your socks is missing! You finally find it sticking to the back of your blanket. How did that happen? The explanation has to do with electric charges.

Types of Charge Atoms contain charged particles called electrons and protons. If two electrons come close together, they push each other apart. In other words, they repel each other. Two protons behave the same way. If a proton and an electron come close together, they attract one another. Protons attract electrons because the two have opposite electric charges. The charge on a proton is positive (+). The charge on an electron is negative (−).

The two types of electric charges interact in specific ways, as you see in **Figure 1.** 🔑 **Charges that are the same repel each other. Charges that are different attract each other.** The interaction between electric charges is called electricity. The force between charged objects is called **electric force.**

FIGURE 1 ···

Repel or Attract?
✏️ Draw Conclusions **On each sphere, write if it has a positive (+) or a negative (−) charge. Compare your answers with a group. Can you tell for sure which spheres are positively charged and which are negatively charged? What conclusions can you draw?**

_____

_____

_____

_____

Electric Fields You may have heard of a gravitational field, which is the space around an object (such as a planet) where the object's gravitational force is exerted. Similarly, an electric field extends around a charged object. An **electric field** is a region around a charged object where the object's electric force is exerted on other charged objects. Electric fields and forces get weaker the farther away they are from the charge.

An electric field is invisible. You can use field lines to represent it, as shown in **Figure 2**. A field line shows the force that would be exerted on a positive charge at any point along that line. Positive charges are repelled by positive charges and attracted to negative charges, so field lines point away from positive charges and toward negative charges. Single charges have straight field lines, since a positive charge will be repelled away from or attracted to it in a straight line. When multiple charges are present, each charge exerts a force. These forces combine to make more complicated field lines.

FIGURE 2 ·······························

Electric Fields
Field lines show the direction of the force acting on a positive charge.

✏️ **Answer the questions.**

1. **Identify** Identify which charge is positive and which charge is negative.

2. **Interpret Diagrams** The boxes on the electric field are the same size. How many field lines are inside the white box?

_____

3. **Interpret Diagrams** The blue box is closer to the charges. How many field lines are in this box?

_____

4. **Draw Conclusions** What is the relationship between the number of field lines in an area and the strength of the electric force?

_____

_____

_____

Do the Quick Lab
Drawing Conclusions.

🔑 **Assess Your Understanding**

got it? ·······························

○ I get it! Now I know that the way electric charges interact depends on _____

_____

○ I need extra help with _____

Go to MY SCIENCE ⑤ COACH *online for help with this subject.*

610 Electricity

How Does Charge Build Up?

Most objects have no overall charge. An atom usually has as many electrons as it has protons, so each positive charge is balanced by a negative charge. This leaves the atom uncharged, or neutral.

An uncharged object can become charged by gaining or losing electrons. If an object loses electrons, it is left with more protons than electrons. It has an overall positive charge. If an object gains electrons, it will have an overall negative charge. The buildup of charges on an object is called **static electricity.** In static electricity, charges build up on an object, but they do not flow continuously.

Science Standards of Learning

PS.1a Safely use equipment.

PS.1n Use current applications of physical science concepts.

PS.11a Investigate and understand static electricity.

FIGURE 3 ·······························

Charge Buildup

Rubbing two objects together can produce static electricity.

✎ **Interpret Photos** Circle the phrases that best complete the statements. Follow the directions to draw how the charges are arranged in each photo.

❶ The balloon is (positively/ negatively/not) charged. The balloon (attracts/repels/neither attracts nor repels) the girl's hair.

❷ Rubbing the balloon allows more electrons to move onto the balloon. The balloon is now (positively/negatively) charged. **Draw what the charges on the balloon look like now.**

❸ The (positive/negative) charges in the girl's hair are now attracted to the negative charges on the balloon. **Draw how the charges on the balloon are arranged now.**

611

Charging Objects Charges are neither created nor destroyed. This is a rule known as the law of **conservation of charge.** An object can't become charged by destroying or creating its own electrons. If one object loses electrons, another object must pick them up. 🔑 **There are four methods by which charges can redistribute themselves to build up static electricity: by friction, by conduction, by induction, and by polarization.**

Charging by Friction

When two uncharged objects are rubbed together, some electrons from one object can move onto the other object. The object that gains electrons becomes negatively charged. The object that loses electrons becomes positively charged. Charging by **friction** is the transfer of electrons from one uncharged object to another by rubbing the objects together.

Charging by Conduction

When a charged object touches another object, electrons can be transferred. Charging by **conduction** is the transfer of electrons from one object to another by direct contact. Electrons transfer from the object that has more negative charge to the object that has more positive charge. A positively charged object, like the metal ball, gains electrons when an uncharged person touches it. The girl starts out neutral, but electrons move from her hair, through her arm, to the ball. This leaves her hair positively charged, and the strands repel each other.

Charging by Induction and by Polarization

Electrons can react to the electric field of a charged object without touching the object itself. In some materials, like metals, electrons can easily leave their atoms. When a metal object is close to a negatively charged object, electrons are repelled by the field and move away from it. The close end of the metal object becomes positively charged, and the far end becomes negatively charged. The opposite happens if the other object is positively charged. This process is called **induction**.

In other materials, like the bits of paper in this photo, electrons move only within their own atoms. The electrons react to electric fields, resulting in individual atoms having charged ends that are attracted to charged objects. This is called **polarization**. Charges don't transfer between objects in polarization or induction, so neither method changes the *overall* charge of objects. *Parts* of objects end up charged in opposite ways.

FIGURE 4 ···

> ART IN MOTION **Moving Electrons**

✎ **Explain** In each image at the left, draw how the charges are arranged in each step. Use arrows to show movement.

🅐 When the girl's sock rubs the carpet, electrons move from the carpet onto her sock. This causes an overall negative charge on the sock. **What method of charge redistribution is this? Explain.**

_____

_____

🅑 Charges move from the girl's foot to the rest of her body. **What method of charge redistribution is this? Explain.**

_____

_____

🅒 The electrons in the girl's fingertip produce an electric field that repels the electrons on the doorknob. The electrons on the doorknob move away from the finger. One end of the doorknob becomes positively charged. **What method of charge redistribution is this? Explain.**

_____

_____

Machines called Van de Graaff generators can create lightning bolts indoors!

Static Discharge

If your hair becomes charged and sticks up after you remove a sweater, it doesn't stay that way forever. Positively charged objects gradually gain electrons from the air. Negatively charged objects gradually lose electrons to the air. The objects eventually become neutral again. The loss of static electricity as electric charges transfer from one object to another is called **static discharge.**

Static discharge often produces a spark. Moving electrons can heat the air around their path until it glows. The glowing air is the spark you see. The tiny spark you may have felt or seen when near a doorknob is an example of static discharge. Sparks from discharge happen more frequently during winter. This is because objects hold on to charge better in dry air. In humid weather, water collects on the surfaces of objects. The water picks up charge from the objects, so they don't stay charged as long as they would in dry weather.

apply it!

Draw Conclusions Anyone who works with computers has to be aware of static discharge. Even small discharges can damage electrical equipment.

❶ What activities should you avoid to prevent static discharge while working on a computer?

_____

_____

_____

_____

_____

❷ What should the conditions of the room you are in be like?

_____

_____

_____

Lightning bolts are an example of static discharge. During thunderstorms, air swirls violently. Water droplets within the clouds become charged. Electrons move from areas of negative charge to areas of positive charge, producing an intense spark. That spark is lightning.

Some lightning reaches Earth. Negative charges at the bottoms of storm clouds create an electric field. This causes Earth's surface to become positively charged through induction. Electrons jump between the clouds and Earth's surface, producing a giant spark of lightning as they travel through the air.

↪ **Relate Cause and Effect**
Pick one example of cause and effect in this section. Underline the cause, and then circle the effect that results.

FIGURE 5 ·····················

Static Discharge
Lightning is just a much bigger version of the sparks you feel when you shock yourself on a doorknob.

✎ **Relate Text and Visuals** In the white circles, draw how positive and negative charges are arranged during a lightning strike.

Lab zone Do the Quick Lab
Sparks Are Flying.

🔑 **Assess Your Understanding**

1a. Describe What happens to an object's atoms when the object becomes positively charged?

_____

_____

b. [CHALLENGE] Explain how you could use a piece of silk and a glass rod to attract a stream of tap water.

_____

_____

_____

_____

got **it?** ·····················

○ **I get it!** Now I know that the four methods of building up static electricity are _____

_____

_____

_____

○ I need extra help with _____

Go to MY SCIENCE ⑤ COACH *online for help with this subject.*

Virginia LESSON 2

Electric Current

UNLOCK THE BIG Q?

🔑 **How Is Electric Current Made?**
PS.11a

🔑 **How Do Conductors Differ From Insulators?**
PS.1n, PS.11d

🔑 **What Affects Current Flow?**
PS.11a, PS.11d

MY PLANET DIARY

Be a Superconductor—of Science!

John Vander Sande wants your city to run more efficiently. A company he cofounded is working to replace old power lines with materials that let electric current flow more efficiently. These materials are called superconductors. Superconductors are often found in lab equipment, as shown at the left, but companies like Vander Sande's are finding other uses for them. Vander Sande didn't start his career working with power lines. He began his work in materials science as a professor at the Massachusetts Institute of Technology (MIT). He got into superconducting by chance after hearing about discoveries at a lecture by one of his colleagues. He encourages everyone to stay open to opportunities in science, because they can pop up anywhere at any time.

CAREERS

Answer the question below.

Describe an instance in your life when hearing something by chance led to a new opportunity.

_____

_____

_____

_____

_____

_____

> **PLANET DIARY** Go to Planet Diary to learn more about superconductors.

Lab zone® Do the Inquiry Warm-Up *How Can Current Be Measured?*

Science Standards of Learning

PS.11a Investigate and understand static electricity, current electricity, and circuits.

How Is Electric Current Made?

Dozens of sushi dishes ride along a conveyor belt in **Figure 1.** The conveyer belt carries full dishes past customers and carries empty plates back to the kitchen. You might be wondering what a conveyor belt of rice, vegetables, and fish could possibly have to do with electricity. Like the sushi plates, electric charges can be made to move in a confined path.

Vocabulary
- electric current
- electric circuit
- conductor
- insulator
- voltage
- resistance

Skills
- Reading: Ask Questions
- Inquiry: Classify

Flow of Electric Charges Lightning releases a large amount of electrical energy. However, the electric charge from lightning doesn't last long enough to power your radio or your TV. These devices need electric charges that flow continuously. They require electric current.

Recall that static electric charges do not flow continuously. **When electric charges are made to flow through a material, they produce an electric current.** Electric current is the continuous flow of electric charges through a material. The amount of charge that passes through a wire in a given period of time is the rate of electric current. The unit for the rate of current is the ampere, named for André Marie Ampère, an early investigator of electricity. The name of the unit is often shortened to amp or A. The number of amps describes the amount of charge flowing past a given point each second.

FIGURE 1 ....

Electric Current
The conveyor belt represents a current. If it represented a greater current, more plates would pass by you in the same amount of time. One way for this to occur would be for the belt to go faster.

✎ **Make Models** Suppose the belt couldn't go faster. Draw a different way a greater current could be represented.

FIGURE 2 ·····························

Circuits

Just like charges in a wire, people can move around in circuits. One possible jogging circuit is outlined in this photo.

✎ **Interpret Photos** Trace another possible circuit. What could break this circuit?

_____

_____

_____

_____

Current in a Circuit The electric currents that power your computer and music player need very specific paths to work. In order to maintain an electric current, charges must be able to flow continuously in a loop. A complete, unbroken path that charges can flow through is called an **electric circuit.**

Someone jogging along the roads in **Figure 2** is moving like a charge in an electric circuit. If the road forms a complete loop, the jogger can move in a continuous path. However, the jogger cannot continue if any section of the road is closed. Similarly, if an electric circuit is complete, charges can flow continuously. If an electric circuit is broken, charges will not flow.

Electric circuits are all around you. All electrical devices, from toasters to televisions, contain electric circuits.

Lab® **zone** Do the Quick Lab *Producing Electric Current.*

🗝 Assess Your Understanding

1a. Review What is the unit of current?

_____

b. Predict What could break the circuit between your home and an electric power plant?

_____

got it?

○ **I get it!** Now I know that electric current is made of _____

_____

○ **I need extra help with** _____

Go to MY SCIENCE ⬤ᔆ COACH *online for help with this subject.*

How Do Conductors Differ From Insulators?

Science Standards of Learning

PS.1n Use current applications of physical science concepts.

PS.11d Investigate and understand conductors, semiconductors, and insulators.

Charges can flow more easily through some materials than others. A **conductor** is a material through which charge can flow easily. Electrons can move freely, allowing conductors to be charged by induction. Metals, such as copper, are good conductors.

Wires are surrounded by insulators. **Insulators** are materials, such as rubber, that do not allow charges to flow. However, electrons can move around within their own atoms, allowing for polarization. They can also be stripped off when charging by friction.

Semiconductors are materials that behave sometimes as conductors and sometimes as insulators. Pure silicon acts like an insulator, but when other elements are added, it behaves like a conductor. Silicon is a semiconductor found in most electronic devices.

The difference between conductors and insulators comes from how strongly electrons are attached to atoms. 🔑 **The atoms in conductors have loosely bound electrons that can move freely. Electrons in insulators cannot move freely among atoms.**

✏️ 🔎 **Ask Questions** Current, conductors, and insulators all show up in your daily life. Write down a question about one of these topics that you would like answered.

_____

_____

_____

apply it!

All objects are made up of conductors or insulators, not just the ones you usually see in electronic devices.

1 Identify The gloves that electricians wear when working on power lines should be made out of (insulating/conducting) materials.

2 Classify Circle the conductors in these photos. Be careful—only parts of some items are conductors!

Lab zone ® Do the Quick Lab *Conductors and Insulators.*

🔑 **Assess Your Understanding**

got it?

○ **I get it!** Now I know that conductors and insulators are different because of _____

_____

○ **I need extra help with** _____

Go to **MY SCIENCE** 🅢 **COACH** *online for help with this subject.*

Science Standards of Learning

PS.11a Investigate and understand static electricity, current electricity, and circuits.

PS.11d Investigate and understand conductors, semiconductors, and insulators.

What Affects Current Flow?

Suppose you are on a water slide at an amusement park. You climb the steps, sit down, and whoosh! The water current carries you down the slide. Electric charges flow in much the same way water moves down the slide. 🔑 **Current flow is affected by the energy of the charges and the properties of the objects that the charges flow through.**

Water Currents

A completely horizontal water slide wouldn't be much fun. A water slide that was only a few centimeters tall wouldn't be much better. Water slides are exciting because of gravitational potential energy. (Remember that gravitational potential energy is the energy an object has because of its height above the ground.) As the water falls down the slide, its potential energy is converted into kinetic energy. The water speeds up, since speed increases as kinetic energy increases. The higher the slide, the more potential energy the water starts with and the faster it will end up moving. At the bottom of the slide, the water has no potential energy. It has all been converted to kinetic energy. The water gains potential energy as it is pumped back to the top, starting the ride again.

✏️ **How could the current through a water slide be interrupted?**

_____

_____

Electric Currents

Electric currents flow through wires like water through pipes. Charges flow because of differences in electric potential energy. Potential energy from an energy source (like a battery) gets converted into different forms of energy. If a circuit contains a light bulb, its potential energy is converted into light and heat. The charges flow back to the energy source and the process restarts.

✏️ **Slides convert gravitational potential energy into kinetic energy. What do circuits convert electric potential energy into?**

_____

FIGURE 3 ·······························

▶ **INTERACTIVE ART** **Currents**

Water currents have many things in common with electric currents. The table at the right summarizes these similarities.

✏️ **Make Models** Complete the table.

	Water Current	Electric Current
Current is made up of moving	water	charges
Potential energy is converted into	_____	heat, light
The energy source for the circuit is a	_____	battery

Voltage

The *V* on a battery stands for volts, which is the unit of voltage. **Voltage** is the difference in electric potential energy *per charge* between two points in a circuit. (Electric potential energy per charge is also called electric potential.) This energy difference causes charges to flow. Because the voltage of a battery is related to energy per charge, it doesn't tell you how much total energy the battery supplies. A car battery and eight watch batteries both supply 12 volts, but eight watch batteries can't run a car. Each charge has the same amount of energy, but the car battery can provide that energy to many more charges. This results in a higher *total* energy. You can compare voltage to gravitational potential energy *per kilogram*. **Figure 4** shows the difference between total energy and energy per kilogram.

FIGURE 4 ··

Voltage

The total electric potential energy a charge has depends on voltage, just as the gravitational potential energy a person has depends on his or her height above the ground. Total gravitational potential energy is the energy per kilogram times the number of kilograms, and total electric potential energy is the energy per charge times the number of charges.

✎ **Interpret Diagrams Answer the questions.**

1. In the boxes, calculate the amount of gravitational potential energy each person has.

2. Which two people represent batteries with the same voltage?

3. Draw boxes around the two people who represent batteries that supply the same total amount of energy.

4. Gravitational potential energy per kilogram decreases as you go down the slide. This is like decreasing (voltage/total potential energy).

①

Mass: 50 kg
Height: 20 m
Energy/kg: 200 J/kg
Total Energy:

_____

②

Mass: 100 kg
Height: 10 m
Energy/kg: 100 J/kg
Total Energy:

_____
_____

③

Mass: 50 kg
Height: 10 m
Energy/kg: 100 J/kg
Total Energy:

_____
_____

FIGURE 5 ··

Dimensions and Resistance

The length and diameter of a straw determine how difficult it is to drink through it. Similarly, the length and diameter of a wire determine how difficult it is for charge to flow through it.

✎ **Interpret Photos Which of the straws in the photo would be the hardest to drink with? Explain. Is this straw like a wire with high or low resistance?**

_____

_____

_____

_____

_____

Resistance The amount of current in a circuit depends on more than voltage. Current also depends on the resistance of the circuit. **Resistance** is the measure of how difficult it is for charges to flow through an object. The greater the resistance, the less current there is for a given voltage. The unit of measure of resistance is the ohm (Ω).

The four factors that determine the resistance of an object are diameter, length, material, and temperature. Objects with different characteristics have different resistances. If more than one path is available, more current will flow through the path that has the lower resistance.

Diameter

Milk flows more easily through a wide straw than it does through a narrow straw. Current flows more easily through a wide wire than through a narrow wire.

✎ **How does a wire's diameter affect its electrical resistance? Explain.**

_____

_____

_____

_____

Length

You may have noticed that it is easier to drink milk through a short straw than through a long straw. Similarly, short wires have less resistance than long wires.

✎ **How does an object's length affect its electrical resistance?**

_____

_____

_____

_____

FIGURE 6 ···

Materials and Resistance

When power lines fall down during storms, the workers repairing them must be careful to avoid electric shocks.

✏ **Solve Problems** What should workers wear while doing the job? What should they avoid wearing?

_____

_____

_____

_____

Temperature

The electrical resistance of most materials increases as temperature increases. As the temperature of most materials decreases, resistance decreases as well.

✏ **Why would it be useful to keep power lines cool in the summer?**

_____

_____

_____

_____

Material

Some materials have electrons that are tightly held to their atoms. They have a high resistance because it is difficult for charges to move. Other materials have electrons that are loosely held to their atoms. They have a low resistance because charges can move through them easily.

✏ **Do conductors or insulators have a lower resistance? Explain.**

_____

_____

_____

_____

 Do the Quick Lab *Modeling Potential Difference.*

🔑 Assess Your Understanding

2a. List List the four factors that determine the resistance of an object.

_____

_____

b. CHALLENGE Battery A supplies 500 charges. Each charge has 2 J of energy. Battery B supplies 50 charges, each of which has 4 J of energy. Which battery supplies more total energy? Which has a higher voltage?

_____

_____

got it? ··

○ **I get it!** Now I know that current is affected by _____

○ **I need extra help with** _____

Go to **MY SCIENCE COACH** online for help with this subject.

623

Electric Circuits

UNLOCK THE BIG Q?

🔑 **What Did Ohm Discover?**
PS.1n, PS.11a, PS.11d

🔑 **What Is a Circuit Made Of?**
PS.1m, PS.6b, PS.11a, PS.11d

my planet diary

Lights Out

One winter night, a string of bright lights adorning a store window catches your eye. As you look, one bulb suddenly goes out, yet the others stay on! How can that be?

Normally, when a light bulb burns out, it breaks the flow of current through a circuit. But many holiday lights are on circuits that provide more than one possible path for the electric current to follow. This type of circuit provides a path for the current to flow even if one component goes bad. So if one light bulb burns out, the rest of the lights remain lit.

FUN FACTS

Communicate Discuss these questions with a partner and then answer them below.

1. What other devices have you used that can keep working even if one part stops working?

_____

_____

_____

2. When could it be useful to have a device turn off completely if one part breaks?

_____

_____

_____

▶ PLANET DIARY Go to **Planet Diary** to learn more about circuits.

Lab zone® Do the Inquiry Warm-Up
Do the Lights Keep Shining?

Vocabulary

- Ohm's law
- series circuit
- parallel circuit

Skills

- Reading: Compare and Contrast
- Inquiry: Make Models

What Did Ohm Discover?

In the 1800s, Georg Ohm performed many experiments on electrical resistance. **Ohm found that the current, voltage, and resistance in a circuit are always related in the same way.**

Ohm's Observations Ohm set up a circuit with a voltage between two points on a conductor. He measured the resistance of the conductor and the current between those points. Then he changed the voltage and took new measurements.

Ohm found that if the factors that affect resistance are held constant, the resistance of most conductors does not depend on the voltage across them. Changing the voltage in a circuit changes the current but does not change the resistance. Ohm concluded that conductors and most other devices have a constant resistance regardless of the applied voltage.

> **Science Standards of Learning**
>
> **PS.1n** Use current applications of physical science concepts.
>
> **PS.11a** Investigate and understand static electricity, current electricity, and circuits.
>
> **PS.11d** Investigate and understand conductors, semiconductors, and insulators.

FIGURE 1 ···

> VIRTUAL LAB **Circuit Relationships**

The work Ohm did on circuits in the 1800s still applies to almost all electric circuits today. The mathematical relationship he found between the components in a circuit holds true for circuits in everyday devices such as cell phones.

✎ **Interpret Data** Suppose you use various cell phone parts to perform experiments similar to Ohm's. You come up with the following data table. Use the data to predict the relationship that Ohm found.

Voltage (V)	Current (A)	Resistance (Ω)
6.0	2.0	3.0
6.0	1.5	4.0
6.0	1.0	6.0
4.2	2.0	2.1
4.2	0.7	6.0
4.2	1.4	3.0

_____

_____

Ohm's Law

Ohm's Law Ohm created a law that describes how voltage, current, and resistance are related. **Ohm's law** says that resistance in a circuit is equal to voltage divided by current. This relationship can be represented by an equation.

$$\text{Resistance} = \frac{\text{Voltage}}{\text{Current}}$$

The units are ohms (Ω) = volts (V) ÷ amps (A). One ohm is equal to one volt per amp. You can rearrange Ohm's law to solve for voltage when you know current and resistance.

$$\text{Voltage} = \text{Current} \times \text{Resistance}$$

You can use the formula to see how changes in resistance, voltage, and current are related. For example, what happens to current if voltage is doubled without changing the resistance? For a constant resistance, if voltage is doubled, current doubles as well.

do the math!

1 Calculate A multimeter is a device that can measure the current in a circuit. Use the reading on the multimeter and the battery to find the voltage and current in this circuit. Calculate the resistance of the bulb.

_____

2 Calculate Batteries gradually lose voltage. A circuit contains 2 ohms of resistance and an old 9-volt battery. Four amps of current run through the circuit. What is the actual voltage?

_____

3 Predict Suppose you tripled the voltage in a circuit but kept the resistance constant. The current in the circuit would be (triple/the same as/a third of) the original current.

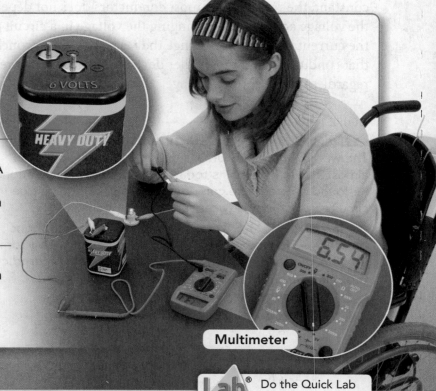

Multimeter

Lab zone® Do the Quick Lab *Ohm's Law.*

🔑 Assess Your Understanding

got it? ....

○ **I get it!** Now I know that Ohm's Law _____

_____

○ **I need extra help with** _____

Go to MY SCIENCE 🔵 **COACH** *online for help with this subject.*

What Is a Circuit Made Of?

Objects that use electricity contain circuits. **All electric circuits have these basic features: devices that run on electrical energy, sources of electrical energy, and conducting wires.**

- Batteries and power plants are examples of energy sources. They supply the voltage that causes current to flow. When the energy source is a battery, current flows from the positive end to the negative end.
- Energy is always conserved in a circuit. Electrical energy doesn't get used up. It gets transformed into other forms of energy, such as heat, light, mechanical, and sound energy. Appliances such as toasters transform electrical energy. These devices resist current, so they are represented in a circuit as resistors.
- Electric circuits are connected by conducting wires. The conducting wires complete the path of the current. They allow charges to flow from the energy source to the device that runs on electric current and back to the energy source.
- A switch is often included to control the current. Opening a switch breaks the circuit, which shuts off the device.

All the parts of a circuit are shown in **Figure 2.** Each part in the photograph is represented in the diagram by a simple symbol.

Science Standards of Learning

PS.1m Construct and use models and simulations to illustrate and explain phenomena.

PS.6b Investigate and understand mechanical, chemical, electrical, thermal, radiant, and nuclear energy and how they can be transferred and transformed.

PS.11a Investigate and understand static electricity, current electricity, and circuits.

PS.11d Investigate and understand conductors, semiconductors, and insulators.

FIGURE 2 ··

Circuit Diagrams

A symbol in a circuit diagram represents a part of the circuit.

✎ **Make Models** Draw the circuit diagram for a circuit with two resistors, two batteries, and a switch.

Series Circuits

Compare and Contrast On these two pages, underline differences between series and parallel circuits. Below, list their similarities.

_____

_____

_____

_____

_____

Series Circuits If all the parts of an electric circuit are connected one after another along one path, the circuit is called a **series circuit.** A series circuit has only one path for the current to take.

A series circuit is very simple to design and build, but it has some disadvantages. What happens if a light bulb in a series circuit burns out? A burned-out bulb is a break in the circuit, and there is no other path for the current to take. So if one light goes out, the other lights go out as well.

Another disadvantage of a series circuit is that the light bulbs in the circuit become dimmer as more bulbs are added. Think about what happens to the overall resistance of a series circuit as you add more bulbs. The resistance increases. Remember that for a constant voltage, if resistance increases, current decreases. If you add light bulbs to a series circuit without changing the voltage, the current decreases. The bulbs burn less brightly.

FIGURE 3 ·································

Series Circuits
The number of bulbs in a series circuit affects each bulb's brightness. Remember that voltage = current × resistance.

✎ **Answer the questions below.**

1. **Make Models** Draw the circuit diagram for the circuit in the photo.

2. **Relate Cause and Effect** If the voltage of the battery were doubled, what would happen to the current through each of the bulbs? How would this affect the brightness of the bulbs?

_____

_____

_____

3. **Predict** If the voltage of the battery were doubled **and** three more bulbs were added, what would happen to the current and the brightness of the bulbs?

_____

_____

_____

_____

Parallel Circuits In a **parallel circuit,** different parts of the circuit are on separate branches. There are several paths for current to take. Each bulb is connected by a separate path from the battery and back to the battery.

What happens if a light burns out in a parallel circuit? If there is a break in one branch, charges can still move through the other branches. So if one bulb goes out, the others remain lit. Switches can be added to each branch to turn lights on and off without affecting the other branches.

What happens to the resistance of a parallel circuit when you add a branch? The overall resistance actually *decreases.* As new branches are added to a parallel circuit, the electric current has more paths to follow, so the overall resistance decreases. Remember that for a given voltage, if resistance decreases, current increases. The additional current travels along each new branch without affecting the original branches. So as you add branches to a parallel circuit, the brightness of the light bulbs does not change.

FIGURE 4 ·····················

Parallel Circuits

A floor lamp with multiple bulbs can be represented with the same circuit diagram as the circuit at the left. You can turn each bulb on and off individually.

✎ Make Models **On the circuit diagram, draw where the switches must be for a lamp like this. If the lamp is lit as it is in the photo below, trace the path(s) in the circuit through which current flows.**

EXPLORE THE BIG ?

How is my house

WIRED?

How does an electric circuit work?

FIGURE 5 ▶INTERACTIVE ART Your home is full of electrical devices. When you turn one device on or off, it does not affect other appliances. This means that your home contains a (series/parallel) circuit. Since the devices in your home are part of complete circuits, each device must have a wire running into it and one running out of it.

✎ Mark each circuit element with its symbol (resistor, switch, or energy source). Draw in the appropriate connecting wires. Then answer the questions on the notepaper on the next page.

Key

Symbol	Name
——	Wires
—•⁄°—	Switch
⌇⌇⌇	Resistor
⊣⊢	Energy source

1. The kitchen lights are wired in series. How could you know this without seeing the wiring?

_____

_____

2. CHALLENGE Are there any incomplete circuits in the illustration? If so, where are they? How do you know there is an incomplete circuit there?

_____

_____

Lab® Do the Lab
zone Investigation
Build a Flashlight.

Assess Your Understanding

1a. Classify A (series/parallel) circuit has only one path for current to flow through.

b. ANSWER THE BIG How does an electric circuit work?

_____

_____

got it?

○ I get it! Now I know that electric circuits must contain _____

_____

○ I need extra help with _____

Go to my science ⓢ COACH online for help with this subject.

Electric Power and Safety

UNLOCK THE BIG ?

🔑 **How Do You Calculate Electric Power and Energy?**
PS.1n, PS.11a

🔑 **How Can Electric Shocks Be Prevented?**
PS.11a, PS.11d

MY PLANET DIARY

DISCOVERY

A Bright Idea

Forget about being *in* the spotlight—with LED clothing you can *be* the spotlight! LEDs, or light-emitting diodes, are small light bulbs. What's special about LEDs is that they can be just as bright as the regular bulbs in your home while using much less energy. Regular bulbs waste a lot of electrical energy by converting it into heat. A dress like this one made out of regular bulbs would be much too hot to wear! As scientists work to make LEDs cheaper, they could go from dresses in fashion shows to lamps in your house. This would lower your electric bill and help the environment.

Answer the question below.
What other electrical devices could be made more efficient with LEDs?

_____

_____

_____

_____

_____

▶ PLANET DIARY Go to **Planet Diary** to learn more about LEDs.

Lab zone® Do the Inquiry Warm-Up *How Can You Make a Bulb Burn More Brightly?*

Science Standards of Learning

PS.1n Use current applications of physical science concepts.
PS.11a Investigate and understand static electricity, current electricity, and circuits.

How Do You Calculate Electric Power and Energy?

All electrical appliances transform electrical energy into other forms. Hair dryers transform electrical energy into thermal energy to dry your hair. An amplifier that a guitar player uses transforms electrical energy into sound. A washing machine transforms electrical energy into mechanical energy. The rate at which energy is transformed from one form to another is known as **power.** The unit of power is the watt (W).

Vocabulary
- power • short circuit
- third prong • grounded
- fuse • circuit breaker

Skills
- ↻ **Reading: Summarize**
- △ **Inquiry: Calculate**

Power Ratings
You are already familiar with different amounts of electric power. The power rating of a bright light bulb, for example, might be 100 W. The power rating of a dimmer bulb might be 60 W. The brighter bulb transforms (or uses) electrical energy at a faster rate than the dimmer bulb.

Calculating Power
The power of a light bulb or appliance depends on two factors: voltage and current.

🔑 **Power is calculated by multiplying voltage by current.**

$$\text{Power} = \text{Voltage} \times \text{Current}$$

The units are watts (W) = volts (V) × amperes (A). The equation can also be rearranged to let you solve for current if you know power and voltage.

$$\text{Current} = \frac{\text{Power}}{\text{Voltage}}$$

↻ **Summarize** Summarize what you have learned from these two pages.

_____

_____

_____

_____

_____

_____

_____

_____

do the math! ─ TECH & DESIGN ─

Many appliances around your home are labeled with their power ratings. In the United States, standard wall outlets supply 120 volts.

△ **Calculate Determine the current running through each of these appliances. (The toaster has been done for you.)**

$$\text{Current} = \frac{\text{Power}}{\text{Voltage}}$$

$$7.08 \text{ A} = \frac{850 \text{ W}}{120 \text{ V}}$$

Paying for Electrical Energy

The electric bill that comes to your home charges for the month's energy use, not power. Power tells you how much energy an appliance uses in a certain amount of time. 🔑 **The total amount of energy used is equal to the power of the appliance multiplied by the amount of time the appliance is used.**

$$\text{Energy} = \textbf{Power} \times \text{Time}$$

Electric power is usually measured in thousands of watts, or kilowatts (kW). To go from watts to kilowatts, you divide by 1,000. Time is measured in hours. A common unit of electrical energy is the kilowatt-hour (kWh).

$$\text{Kilowatt-hours} = \textbf{Kilowatts} \times \text{Hours}$$

A refrigerator averages a power of 0.075 kW (75 W). Knowing that, you can calculate how much energy it will use in one month (about 720 hours).

$$\text{Energy} = \textbf{0.075 kW} \times 720 \text{ hours}$$

$$\text{Energy} = 54 \text{ kWh}$$

FIGURE 1 ·······························
▶ REAL-WORLD INQUIRY
Electrical Energy
There are devices that let you measure the energy usage of electronic devices.

✏️ **Apply Concepts** Pick an appliance from the previous page. Use the notebook to answer the questions.

1. What would the monitor display if the appliance you picked was plugged in for three hours?

2. CHALLENGE Calculate the power rating for the appliance that is plugged into the meter at the left. Assume that it has been running for three hours.

Do the Quick Lab
Calculating Electric Power and Energy Use.

🔑 Assess Your Understanding

1a. Review The power of an appliance can be found by multiplying _____ by _____.

b. Calculate How much energy does an 850 W toaster consume if it is used for 1.5 hours over the course of a month?

_____
_____

got it?

○ **I get it!** Now I know that electric power and energy depend on _____
_____

○ **I need extra help with** _____

Go to MY SCIENCE ⬤ᵛ COACH *online for help with this subject.*

How Can Electric Shocks Be Prevented?

A **short circuit** is a connection that allows current to take the path of least resistance. Touching a frayed wire causes a short circuit, since current can flow through the person rather than through the wire. Since the new path has less resistance, the current can be very high. Many bodily functions, such as heartbeat, breathing, and muscle movement, are controlled by electrical signals. Because of this, electric shocks can be fatal.

 Shocks can be prevented with devices that redirect current or break circuits. Ground wires connect the circuits in a building directly to Earth, giving charges an alternate path in the event of a short circuit. The **third prong** you may have seen on electrical plugs connects the metal parts of appliances to the building's ground wire. Any circuit connected to Earth in this way is **grounded.**

The circuits in your home also contain devices that prevent circuits from overheating, since overheated circuits can result in fires. **Fuses** are devices that melt if they get too hot. This breaks the circuit. **Circuit breakers** are switches that will bend away from circuits as they heat up. Unlike fuses, which break when they are triggered, circuit breakers can be reset.

Science Standards of Learning

PS.11a Investigate and understand static electricity, current electricity, and circuits.

PS.11d Investigate and understand conductors, semiconductors, and insulators.

FIGURE 2 ···

Fuses

Fuses are often found in appliances such as coffee makers. A fuse will melt and break, cutting off the circuit, before the appliance can get so hot that it catches fire.

✎ **Infer** What other electronic devices may contain fuses? Explain your reasoning.

_____

_____

_____

 Do the Quick Lab
Electric Shock and Short Circuit Safety.

🔑 Assess Your Understanding

got it? ···

○ **I get it!** Now I know that electric safety devices _____

_____

_____

○ **I need extra help with** _____

Go to MY SCIENCE ⓢ COACH *online for help with this subject.*

18 Study Guide

The basic features of an electric circuit are _____
_____
_____

LESSON 1 Electric Charge and Static Electricity

🔑 Charges that are the same repel each other. Charges that are different attract each other.

🔑 There are four methods by which charges can redistribute themselves to build up static electricity: by friction, by conduction, by induction, and by polarization.

Vocabulary
- electric force   • electric field
- static electricity   • conservation of charge
- friction   • conduction
- induction   • polarization   • static discharge

LESSON 2 Electric Current

🔑 When electric charges are made to flow through a material, they produce an electric current.

🔑 The atoms in conductors have loosely bound electrons that can move freely. Electrons in insulators cannot move freely among atoms.

🔑 Current flow is affected by the energy of the charges and the properties of the objects that the charges flow through.

Vocabulary
- electric current   • electric circuit
- conductor   • insulator   • voltage   • resistance

LESSON 3 Electric Circuits

🔑 Ohm found that the current, voltage, and resistance in a circuit are always related in the same way.

🔑 All electric circuits have the same basic features: devices that are run by electrical energy, sources of electrical energy, and conducting wires.

Vocabulary
- Ohm's law   • series circuit   • parallel circuit

LESSON 4 Electric Power and Safety

🔑 Power is calculated by multiplying voltage by current.

🔑 The total amount of energy used is equal to the power of the appliance multiplied by the amount of time the appliance is used.

🔑 Shocks can be prevented with devices that redirect current or break circuits.

Vocabulary
- power   • short circuit   • third prong
- grounded   • fuse   • circuit breaker

Review and Assessment

LESSON 1 Electric Charge and Static Electricity

1. What type of charge transfer occurs when two objects are rubbed together?

a. friction

b. induction

c. conduction

d. polarization

2. The transfer of electrons from a cloud to the ground during a lightning strike is an example of _____

3. Apply Concepts Draw the electric field for a single positive charge. Be sure to show which way the field lines point.

4. Relate Cause and Effect Explain what happens to the electrons in a metal object when it is held near a negatively charged object. What happens to the overall charge of the metal object?

_____

_____

_____

_____

_____

 5. Write About It A park needs a sign to tell visitors what to do during a thunderstorm. Write a paragraph that explains why standing under a tall tree during a thunderstorm is dangerous.

LESSON 2 Electric Current

6. Which of these objects is an insulator?

a. gold ring

b. copper coin

c. glass rod

d. steel fork

7. An electric current is _____

_____

8. Classify The appliances in your home can be made of several different materials. What kinds of materials are the wires made of? What kinds of materials surround the wire for safety?

_____

9. Infer Copper wires carry electric current from power plants to users. How is the resistance of these power lines likely to vary during the year in an area that has very hot summers? Explain.

_____

_____

_____

_____

10. Make Models Water will not flow down a flat slide because there is no potential energy difference between the two ends. How could this situation be represented in an electric circuit? Explain your reasoning.

_____

_____

_____

_____

LESSON 3 Electric Circuits

11. Lisa built an electric circuit. When she added a second light bulb, the first bulb became dimmer. What type of circuit did Lisa build?

   a. series   **b.** parallel

   c. open   **d.** short

12. According to Ohm's law, the resistance in a circuit can be determined by _____

_____

Use the diagram below to answer Questions 13 and 14.

13. Predict Will any of the bulbs light if you open the switch? Explain.

_____

_____

14. Control Variables Which bulbs would continue to shine if Bulb 1 broke? Which would shine if Bulb 2 broke instead? Explain.

_____

_____

_____

_____

15. math! Most homes contain 120-V outlets. Suppose you have lamps with resistances of 120 Ω, 144 Ω, and 240 Ω. Predict which one will draw the most current. Check your prediction by calculating the current that runs through each lamp.

LESSON 4 Electric Power and Safety

16. What unit is used to measure electric power?

   a. ampere (A)   **b.** volt (V)

   c. watt (W)   **d.** ohm (Ω)

17. An appliance's total electrical energy consumption is calculated by _____

_____

18. Infer If you touch an electric wire and get a shock, what can you infer about the resistance of your body compared to the resistance of the circuit?

_____

_____

_____

19. Calculate A device draws 40 A of current and has a 12-V battery. What is its power?

_____

APPLY THE BIG ❓ How does an electric circuit work?

20. Identify the parts that make up the circuit in a laptop computer. Describe what happens inside the circuit when the computer is on.

_____

_____

_____

_____

_____

_____

_____

_____

_____

_____

_____

Virginia SOL Test Prep

Read each question and choose the best answer.

1 Which of the following is a valid interpretation of the graph?

Cost of Using Household Appliances

A   The voltage is highest in Appliance 1.

B   Appliance 1 uses the most power.

C   During one month, a family pays more to run Appliance 1 than Appliance 2.

D   Appliance 1 draws the least current.

2 Your alarm clock has a voltage of 120 V and a resistance of 1200 Ω. What current does the alarm clock draw?

F   0.10 A

G   10.0 A

H   12.0 A

J   100 A

3 You want to build a device that can conduct current but will be safe if touched by a person. Which of the following pairs of materials could you use?

A   glass to conduct and rubber to insulate

B   copper to conduct and silver to insulate

C   sand to conduct and plastic to insulate

D   silver to conduct and plastic to insulate

4 How does a fuse prevent electrical fires?

F   by providing a path for excess charges to get to the ground

G   by melting if the current gets too high

H   by reducing the voltage supplied to electrical devices

J   by storing potential energy for later use

5 What happens when an object is rubbed against another object to charge by friction?

A   Electrons are transferred from one object to another.

B   Electrons in one of the objects disappear.

C   Electrons in one object suddenly become negatively charged.

D   Electrons are created by the friction between the objects.

6 Suppose you created a series circuit with 3 bulbs. What would happen if you added a fourth bulb?

F   The overall resistance of the circuit would increase and the bulbs would become brighter.

G   The overall resistance of the circuit would decrease and the bulbs would become brighter.

H   The overall resistance of the circuit would increase and the bulbs would become dimmer.

J   The overall resistance of the circuit would decrease and the bulbs would become dimmer.

SOMETHING for NOTHING

▲ This complicated device can supposedly harness free energy.

The race is on to find a new, cheap energy source. Any online search for "free energy" will find a lot of Web sites. These sites promise clean, free electricity if you buy or invest in their devices.

But can they back up their promises? Many sites suggest that the power companies have conspired against the people who have discovered and invented these free-energy devices. One site even claims that there is a fourth law of motion. This fourth law is an extension of Newton's Third Law of Motion. If every action has an equal and opposite reaction, the site claims, then that reaction can power the original action.

Debate It Some free-energy devices claim to be able to generate electricity using a perpetual motion machine. Some claim to harness latent heat from the air. Some claim to use magnets. Research how energy is generated, and evaluate these claims. Debate as a class whether it is possible to have truly free energy.

 PS.1k, PS.6b

Does free electricity really exist? Some people say yes.

▼ In 1913, Nikola Tesla patented a turbine that ran off of steam. Many people have tried to find a way to use Tesla's engine to generate free electricty.

Going GREEN

Every time you turn on a light, you are using energy. We know this, but we don't always think about where the energy comes from. In most cases, that energy has come from fossil fuels, extracted from the ground, refined, and burned for their energy, in a process that causes a lot of pollution. Some scientists and government policymakers are exploring green (environmentally friendly) sources of energy.

According to the U.S. Environmental Protection Agency (EPA), green energy comes from technologies that don't produce waste products that will harm the environment. This includes resources like solar power and wind power, as well as geothermal energy from hot springs under the Earth's crust.

Reduced air pollution is just one of many benefits of green energy. Green energy also lowers greenhouse gas emissions and can cost less for consumers—like your family! Going green also creates jobs. Having many different sources makes the energy grid more stable. If one source stops working, we will still be able to get energy from other sources. What's not to love? Unfortunately, green energy technologies are expensive to develop.

▲ The flow of water is a renewable resource. But hydroelectric dams can damage habitats by changing the course of rivers.

Debate It Research the benefits and costs of developing green energy technologies. Organize a classroom debate about the costs and benefits of green energy. Be prepared to argue both sides of the issue.

 PS.1k, PS.1n, PS.6b

HOW CAN THIS TRAIN MOVE WITHOUT TOUCHING THE TRACK?

How are electricity and magnetism related?

This type of train is called a maglev, or magnetic levitation train, and operates at speeds of 430 km/h (about twice as fast as a conventional train). It does not have a traditional engine, which means it does not give off any pollutants. Instead, the maglev train uses electricity in the track to power magnets that propel the train forward and levitation magnets to keep the train floating about 10 mm above the track.

Draw Conclusions How can this train move without touching the track?

_____

_____

_____

_____

> UNTAMED SCIENCE Watch the **Untamed Science** video to learn more about magnetism and electromagnetism.

Magnetism and Electromagnetism

19 Getting Started

Check Your Understanding

1. **Background** Read the paragraph below and then answer the question.

While Chung works, his computer shuts down. Both the street and his house are dark, so he knows there is no **electricity**. A fallen tree has snapped an electric wire. The wire was the **conductor** that brought him power. Chung reaches for the light switch, but then remembers that no **electric current** will flow when he turns it on.

Electricity is a form of energy sometimes created by the movement of charged particles.

A material through which charges can easily flow is a **conductor.**

Electric current is the continuous flow of electric charges through a material.

- How can electricity be restored to Chung's house?

_____

_____

> **MY READING WEB** If you had trouble completing the question above, visit **My Reading Web** and type in *Magnetism and Electromagnetism.*

Vocabulary Skill

Use Context to Determine Meaning Science books often use unfamiliar words. Look for context clues in surrounding words and phrases to figure out the meaning of a new word. In the paragraph below, look for clues to the meaning of *magnetic force.*

The attraction or repulsion between magnetic poles is **magnetic force.** A force is a push or pull that can cause an object to change its motion. A magnetic force is produced when magnetic poles interact.

Example	Magnetic force
Definition	*n.* attraction or repulsion between magnetic poles
Explanation	Force is a push or pull.
Other Information	Magnetic force is produced when magnetic poles interact.

2. **Quick Check** In the paragraph above, circle the explanation of the word *force.*

magnetic pole

magnetic field lines

electromagnet

generator

Chapter Preview

LESSON 1
- magnet
- magnetism
- magnetic pole
- magnetic force
- ↺ **Summarize**
- △ **Infer**

LESSON 2
- magnetic field
- magnetic field lines
- compass
- magnetic declination
- ↺ **Identify the Main Idea**
- △ **Observe**

LESSON 3
- electromagnetism
- solenoid
- electromagnet
- ↺ **Relate Cause and Effect**
- △ **Predict**

LESSON 4
- galvanometer
- electric motor
- ↺ **Sequence**
- △ **Graph**

LESSON 5
- electromagnetic induction
- direct current
- alternating current
- generator
- transformer
- ↺ **Ask Questions**
- △ **Make Models**

> **VOCAB FLASH CARDS** For extra help with vocabulary, visit **Vocab Flash Cards** and type in *Magnetism and Electromagnetism.*

LESSON

1 What Is Magnetism?

UNLOCK THE BIG

🔑 **What Are the Properties of Magnets?**
PS.11

🔑 **How Do Magnetic Poles Interact?**
PS.1n, PS.11

my PLaNeT DiaRY

Crocodile Sense

Crocodiles are threatened animals. So, if they are not protected, they may become endangered and then disappear altogether. However, in Florida, many crocodiles live where people do, so they threaten people's safety.

To keep both people and crocodiles safe, biologists tried to move crocodiles away from people. But there was a problem. Crocodiles use Earth's magnetic field to help them navigate. Whenever they relocated a crocodile, it eventually returned, if it was not killed on the way back. But then the biologists heard that scientists in Mexico had taped a magnet to each side of a crocodile's head before relocating it. They thought that the magnets would interfere with the crocodile's ability to use Earth's magnetic field to find its way back. Biologists here did the same thing. So far, it has been successful.

FUN FACTS

Communicate Discuss the following questions with a partner. Write your answers below.

Why do you think it is important to relocate crocodiles?

_____

_____

_____

_____

_____

> **PLANET DIARY** Go to Planet Diary to learn more about magnetism.

Do the Inquiry Warm-Up
Natural Magnets.

Science Standards of Learning

PS.11 Investigate and understand basic principles of magnetism.

What Are the Properties of Magnets?

Imagine that you're in Shanghai, China, zooming along in a maglev train propelled by magnets. Your 30-kilometer trip from the airport to the city station takes less than eight minutes. The same trip in a taxi would take about an hour.

Vocabulary
- magnet
- magnetism
- magnetic pole
- magnetic force

Skills
- Reading: Summarize
- Inquiry: Infer

Magnets When you think of magnets, you might think about the objects that hold notes to your refrigerator. But magnets can be large, like the one in **Figure 1.** They can be small like those on your refrigerator, in your wallet, on your kitchen cabinets, or on security tags at a store. A **magnet** is any material that attracts iron and materials that contain iron.

Discovering Magnets Magnets have many modern uses, but they are not new. The ancient Greeks discovered that a rock called magnetite attracted materials containing iron. The rocks also attracted or repelled other magnetic rocks. The attraction or repulsion of magnetic materials is called **magnetism.**

Magnets have the same properties as magnetite rocks. ⚷ Magnets attract iron and materials that contain iron. Magnets attract or repel other magnets. In addition, one end of a magnet will always point north when allowed to swing freely.

FIGURE 1 ·······················
What's Wrong With This Picture?
Most people would not expect the powerful magnet used at a metal scrap yard to be able to pick up wood.

✎ **Explain** Use what you know about magnets to explain why this scene is impossible.

_____
_____
_____
_____
_____

✎

⟲ **Summarize** Summarize the properties of magnetite.

_____
_____
_____

Lab zone® Do the Lab Investigation *Detecting Fake Coins.*

⚷ Assess Your Understanding

got it? ·······························

○ **I get it!** Now I know that three properties of magnets are that magnets _____
_____
_____

○ **I need extra help with** _____

Go to **my science ⑤ coach** *online for help with this subject.*

South pole

How Do Magnetic Poles Interact?

Science Standards of Learning

PS.1n Use current applications of physical science concepts.

PS.11 Investigate and understand basic principles of magnetism.

Any magnet, no matter what its size or shape, has two ends. Each one is called a **magnetic pole.** The magnetic effect of a magnet is strongest at the poles. The pole of a magnet that points north is labeled the *north pole*. The other pole is labeled the *south pole*. A magnet always has both a north pole and a south pole.

Magnetic Interactions What happens if you bring two magnets together? The answer depends on how you hold the poles of the magnets. If you bring the north pole of one magnet near the south pole of another, the two unlike poles attract one another. However, if you bring two north poles together, the like poles move away from each other. **Magnetic poles that are unlike attract each other, and magnetic poles that are alike repel each other.** You can see how bar magnets interact in **Figure 2.**

FIGURE 2 ··

ART IN MOTION **Attraction and Repulsion**
These pairs of magnets show how magnetic poles interact.

✎ **Relate Text and Visuals** Draw and label what happens when two south poles are near each other.

North pole

Unlike poles attract.	Like poles repel.	_____
S N N N	S N N S	

Magnetic Force The attraction or repulsion between magnetic poles is **magnetic force.** A force is a push or a pull that can cause an object to move. A magnetic force is produced when magnetic poles come near each other and interact. Any material that exerts a magnetic force is a magnet.

Train car

S
N

Repulsive force

apply it!

Train car

Guideway

Magnets

Guideway

The maglev train you read about earlier depends on magnetic force to float above the guideway, or track. The magnetic force is produced by magnets in the bottom of the train and in the guideway.

1 **Infer** For the train to float, which pole of the guideway's magnet should face the north pole of the train car's magnet?

_____

2 CHALLENGE List some advantages of the fact that the train does not touch the guideway.

_____

_____

Lab zone

Do the Quick Lab
Magnetic Poles.

🔑 Assess Your Understanding

1a. Identify What areas of a magnet have the strongest magnetic effect?

_____

_____

_____

b. Relate Cause and Effect How can two magnets demonstrate magnetic force?

_____

_____

_____

got it? ....

○ **I get it!** Now I know that magnetic poles that are unlike _____

and magnetic poles that are alike _____

○ **I need extra help with** _____

Go to MY SCIENCE ⓢ COACH online for help with this subject.

Magnetic Fields

UNLOCK THE BIG Q?

🔑 **What Is a Magnetic Field's Shape?**
PS.1n, PS.11

🔑 **What Is Earth's Magnetic Field Like?**
PS.1h, PS.11

MY PLANET DIARY

Cow Magnets

You probably know that cows eat grass. Did you know that they also eat metal? When cows graze, they may ingest metal objects that contain iron such as nails, wires, and old cans. If the metal is sharp, it could pierce the cow's stomach, causing infection, illness, or even death.

To ensure that their cows are safe, farmers have their cows swallow a magnet. Once inside the cow's stomach, the magnet attracts the iron in the metal that the cow eats. This keeps the metal from moving around and possibly puncturing other organs. One magnet can protect a cow for life.

FUN FACTS

Read the following questions. Write your answers below.

1. Why is it dangerous for a cow to eat metal?

_____

_____

_____

_____

2. As a farmer, what else could you do to keep metal objects from harming the cows?

_____

_____

▶ **PLANET DIARY** Go to **Planet Diary** to learn more about magnetic fields.

 Lab zone® Do the Inquiry Warm-Up *Predict the Field.*

Vocabulary
• magnetic field • magnetic field lines
• compass • magnetic declination

Skills
↻ Reading: Identify the Main Idea
△ Inquiry: Observe

What Is a Magnetic Field's Shape?

You know that a magnetic force is strongest at the poles of a magnet. But magnetic force is not limited to the poles. It is exerted all around a magnet. The area of magnetic force around a magnet is known as its **magnetic field.** Because of magnetic fields, magnets can interact without even touching.

Science Standards of Learning

PS.1n Use current applications of physical science concepts.

PS.11 Investigate and understand basic principles of magnetism.

Representing Magnetic Field Lines
Figure 1 shows the magnetic field of a bar magnet. The **magnetic field lines** are shown in purple. Magnetic field lines are lines that map out the invisible magnetic field around a magnet. 🔑 **Magnetic field lines spread out from one pole, curve around the magnet, and return to the other pole.** The lines form complete loops from pole to pole and never cross. Arrowheads indicate the direction of the magnetic field lines. They always leave the north pole and enter the south pole. The closer together the lines are, the stronger the field. Magnetic field lines are closest together at the poles.

FIGURE 1 ··

Magnetic Field Lines

Magnetic fields are invisible, but you can represent a field using magnetic field lines.

✏️ **Complete the tasks below.**

1. **Relate Text and Visuals** In the boxes, identify where the magnetic field is strong and where it is weak.

2. **CHALLENGE** Forces that affect objects without touching them are called *field* forces. Is gravity a field force? Explain.

_____

_____

_____

FIGURE 2 ···

> **INTERACTIVE ART** **Magnetic Fields**

Different magnetic pole arrangements will produce different magnetic fields.

✎ **Make Models** In the box below each diagram, draw the corresponding magnetic field lines with arrowheads to show direction.

A Single Magnetic Field Although you cannot see a magnetic field, you can see its effects. **Figure 2A** shows iron filings sprinkled on a sheet of clear plastic that covers one magnet. The magnetic forces of the magnet act on the iron filings and align them along the invisible magnetic field lines. The result is that the iron filings form a pattern similar to magnetic field lines.

Combined Magnetic Fields When the magnetic fields of two or more magnets overlap, the result is a combined field. **Figures 2B** and **2C** show the effects of magnetic force on iron filings when the poles of two bar magnets are brought near each other. Compare the pattern of a north-north pole arrangement and a north-south pole arrangement. The fields from two like poles repel each other. But the fields from unlike poles attract each other, forming a strong field between the magnets.

C Combined Magnetic Field, North-South

S N

S N

apply it!

When magnets come together, you can feel magnetic forces.

1 **Observe** You hold two refrigerator magnets and push them toward each other. What will you observe that lets you know that the fields of the magnets are interacting?

_____

_____

_____

2 **Develop Hypotheses** Why might a magnet that sticks to your refrigerator be unable to pick up a faraway paper clip?

_____

_____

_____

_____

_____

Lab zone® Do the Quick Lab
Spinning in Circles.

🔑 Assess Your Understanding

1a. Define What is a magnetic field?

_____

_____

_____

_____

b. Describe Describe the magnetic field of a south-south pole arrangement.

_____

_____

_____

_____

got it? ···

○ **I get it!** Now I know that a magnetic field's shape is _____

_____

_____

○ **I need extra help with** _____

Go to **MY SCIENCE** Ⓢ **COACH** *online for help with this subject.*

✏️

🔄 **Identify the Main Idea**
What is the main idea in the Earth's Core section?

_____

_____

_____

_____

_____

What Is Earth's Magnetic Field Like?

People have used compasses as tools for navigation for centuries. A **compass** is a device that has a magnet on a needle that spins freely. It is used for navigation because its needle usually points north. But why does that happen? In the late 1500s an Englishman, Sir William Gilbert, proved that a compass behaves as it does because Earth acts as a giant magnet. 🔑 **Just like a bar magnet, Earth has a magnetic field around it and two magnetic poles.** So, the poles of a magnetized compass needle align themselves with Earth's magnetic field. See Earth's magnetic field in **Figure 3**.

Earth's Core Earth's core is a large sphere of metal that occupies Earth's center. The core is divided into two parts—the outer core and the inner core. The outer core is made of hot swirling liquid iron. The motion of this iron creates a magnetic field similar to the magnetic field of a bar magnet.

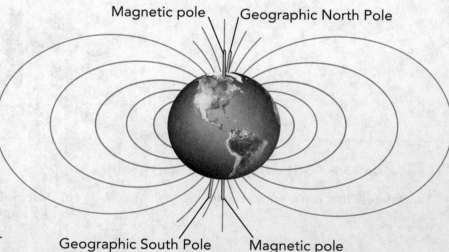

FIGURE 3 ··········
Earth's Magnetic Field
Magnetized compass needles usually align with Earth's magnetic field and point north. This allows hikers and travelers to orient their maps correctly.

✏️ **Explain** Why might a compass not work correctly when it is near a strong magnet?

_____

_____

_____

_____

_____

_____

did you
know? ·····················

The magnetic pole in the Northern Hemisphere is actually a magnetic south pole! Compasses point north because the magnetic north pole of a compass needle is attracted to the magnetic south pole in the Northern Hemisphere.

Earth's Magnetic Poles You know that Earth has geographic poles. But Earth also has magnetic poles that are located on Earth's surface where the magnetic force is strongest. As you just saw in **Figure 3**, the magnetic poles are not in the same place as the geographic poles. Suppose you could draw a line between you and the geographic North Pole. Then imagine a second line drawn between you and the magnetic pole in the Northern Hemisphere. The angle between these two lines is the angle between geographic north and the north to which a compass needle points. This angle is known as **magnetic declination.**

The magnetic declination of a location changes. Earth's magnetic poles do not stay in one place as the geographic poles do.

do the math!

The last expedition to directly observe the pole's location was in May 2001. The map shows estimated positions after 2001.

1 Calculate What is the total distance the pole traveled from 1948 to 2001?

_____

_____

_____

2 Interpret Data What was the mean speed of the pole's movement from 1948 to 2001? What was the mode?

_____

_____

Magnetic North Pole Movement

Year of Reading	Distance Moved Since Previous Reading (km)
1948	420
1962	150
1972	120
1984	120
1994	180
2001	287

 Lab zone Do the Quick Lab *Earth's Magnetic Field.*

Assess Your Understanding

got it? ....

O **I get it!** Now I know that Earth has a magnetic field _____

O **I need extra help with** _____

Go to MY SCIENCE COACH *online for help with this subject.*

Virginia

LESSON

3

Electromagnetic Force

UNLOCK THE BIG Q?

🔑 **How Are Electric Currents and Magnetic Fields Related?**
PS.11b

🔑 **What Is a Magnetic Field Produced by a Current Like?**
PS.11b, PS.11c

🔑 **What Are the Characteristics of Solenoids and Electromagnets?**
PS.1n, PS.11b, PS.11c

MY PLANET DIARY

FUN FACTS

More Than Just Plastic

How do plastic cards with stripes, such as your library card, work? The black stripe on the back of the card is made up of tiny magnetic particles. Information can be recorded on the stripe. When a card is swiped through a card-reading machine, the cardholder's information is relayed from the card to a computer or sent to a place for verification.

If the card is placed near magnetic material, the arrangement of the magnetic particles on the stripe can get rearranged. Once this happens, the card becomes useless because it no longer holds the cardholder's information. If you are ever given a credit card to use, make sure you keep it away from magnets or else you may leave the store empty-handed!

Communicate Discuss the question with a partner. Then write your answer below.

List types of cards that have a magnetic stripe.

_____

_____

_____

_____

_____

_____

▷ **PLANET DIARY** Go to **Planet Diary** to learn more about electromagnetic force.

 Lab zone® Do the Inquiry Warm-Up *Electromagnetism.*

Vocabulary
- electromagnetism
- electromagnet
- solenoid

Skills
↻ Reading: Relate Cause and Effect
△ Inquiry: Predict

How Are Electric Currents and Magnetic Fields Related?

Science Standards of Learning

PS.11b Investigate and understand the relationship between a magnetic field and an electric current.

You know that a magnet has a magnetic field. But did you know that an electric current produces a magnetic field? In 1820, the Danish scientist Hans Christian Oersted (UR STED) accidentally discovered this fact. He was teaching a class at the University of Copenhagen. During his lecture he produced a current in a wire just like the current in a battery-powered flashlight. When he brought a compass near the wire, he observed that the compass needle changed direction.

Oersted's Experiment Oersted could have assumed that something was wrong with his equipment, but instead he decided to investigate further. So he set up several compasses around a wire. With no current in the wire, all of the compass needles pointed north. When he produced a current in the wire, he observed that the compass needles pointed in different directions to form a circle. Oersted concluded that the current had produced a magnetic field around the wire. Oersted's results showed that magnetism and electricity are related.

Cause	Effect
There is no current in the wire.	_____ _____ _____ _____
_____ _____ _____ _____	The compass needles pointed in different directions to form a circle.

✏️

↻ **Relate Cause and Effect**
Use the information about Oersted's experiment to complete the chart.

Electric Current and Magnetism

Oersted's experiment showed that wherever there is electricity, there is magnetism. 🔑 **An electric current produces a magnetic field.** This relationship between electricity and magnetism is called **electromagnetism.** Although you cannot see electromagnetism directly, you can see its effect. That is, a compass needle moves when it is in a magnetic field produced by an electric current, as you can see in **Figure 1**.

FIGURE 1 ....

Moving Compass Needles
These photographs show you how an electric current produces a magnetic field.

✏️ **Interpret Photos** In the boxes, explain what is happening to the compass needles when the current in the wire is turned on or off.

Without current

With current

🔑 Assess Your Understanding

1a. Explain What did Oersted conclude?

_____

_____

_____

b. 🔄 **Relate Cause and Effect** How does a current affect a compass?

_____

_____

Lab zone ® Do the Quick Lab *Electric Current and Magnetism.*

got it? ....

○ **I get it!** Now I know that an electric current produces a _____

○ **I need extra help with** _____

Go to **MY SCIENCE COACH** online for help with this subject.

What Is a Magnetic Field Produced by a Current Like?

Science Standards of Learning

PS.11b Investigate and understand the relationship between a magnetic field and an electric current.

PS.11c Investigate and understand electromagnets, motors, and generators, and their uses.

The magnetic field produced by a current has a strength and a direction. The field can be turned on or off, have its direction reversed, or have its strength changed. To turn a magnetic field produced by a current on or off, you turn the current on or off. To change the direction of the magnetic field, you reverse the direction of the current.

There are two ways to change the strength of a magnetic field. First, you can increase the amount of current in the wire. Second, you can make a loop or coil in the wire. The magnetic field around the wire forms a circle. When you make a loop in a wire, the magnetic field lines bunch close together inside the loop. This strengthens the magnetic field. Every additional loop strengthens the magnetic field even more. **Figure 2** shows three different ways to change the characteristics of a magnetic field.

FIGURE 2 ···

Change Magnetic Field Characteristics

✏️ **Interpret Diagrams** Write the ways used to change the magnetic fields in diagrams A and B. In diagram C, draw a picture to show a third way to change magnetic fields and describe it.

A

B

C

Wire   Magnetic field   Current

Bunched magnetic field

Lab zone ® Do the Quick Lab *Magnetic Fields From Electric Current.*

🔑 Assess Your Understanding

got it? ···

○ **I get it!** Now I know that the magnetic field produced by a current can be changed by _____

_____

○ **I need extra help with** _____

Go to **my science** ⓢ **coach** online for help with this subject.

Science Standards of Learning

PS.1n Use current applications of physical science concepts.

PS.11b Investigate and understand the relationship between a magnetic field and an electric current.

PS.11c Investigate and understand electromagnets, motors, and generators, and their uses.

What Are the Characteristics of Solenoids and Electromagnets?

You know that you can strengthen the magnetic field around a wire with a current by coiling the wire. **Both solenoids and electromagnets use electric current and coiled wires to produce strong magnetic fields.**

Solenoids By running current through a wire which is wound into many loops, you strengthen the magnetic field in the center of the coil as shown in **Figure 3**. A coil of wire with a current is called a **solenoid.** The two ends of a solenoid act like the poles of a magnet. However, the north and south poles change when the direction of the current changes.

Electromagnets If you place a material with strong magnetic properties inside a solenoid, the strength of the magnetic field increases. This is because the material, called a ferromagnetic material, becomes a magnet. A solenoid with a ferromagnetic core is called an **electromagnet.** Both the current in the wire and the magnetized core produce the magnetic field of an electromagnet. Therefore, the overall magnetic field of an electromagnet is much stronger than that of a solenoid. An electromagnet is turned on and off by turning the current on and off.

FIGURE 3 ···

> REAL-WORLD INQUIRY **A Solenoid and an Electromagnet**

An electromagnet is a solenoid with a ferromagnetic core.

✎ Interpret Diagrams **Explain how the diagram shows you that the magnetic field of the electromagnet is stronger than that of the solenoid on its own.**

_____

_____

Solenoid

Electromagnet

Regulating Strength You can increase the strength of an electromagnet in four ways. First, you can increase the current in the solenoid. Second, you can add more loops of wire to the solenoid. Third, you can wind the coils of the solenoid closer together. Finally, you can use a material that is more magnetic than iron for the core. Alnico is such a material.

Using Electromagnets Electromagnets are very common. They are used in electric motors, earphones, and many other everyday objects. Electromagnets are even used in junkyards to lift old cars and other heavy steel objects.

Vocabulary Use Context to Determine Meaning Underline clues in the text that help you determine the meaning of *alnico*.

apply it!

An electromagnet makes a doorbell ring. A pushed button closes the circuit and turns on the electromagnet. Current flows through the electromagnet, producing a strong magnetic field.

Energy source — Current — Electromagnet — Bell — Steel bar — Spring — Button — Clapper

1 Predict What effect will the magnetic field have on the steel bar? The clapper?

_____

_____

_____

2 CHALLENGE What turns off the electromagnet?

_____

Lab zone ® Do the Quick Lab *Electromagnet.*

🔑 Assess Your Understanding

2a. Define What is a solenoid?

_____

_____

b. Apply Concepts What are four ways to make an electromagnet stronger?

_____

_____

_____

_____

got it?

○ **I get it!** Now I know that both solenoids and electromagnets _____

_____

_____

_____

_____

○ **I need extra help with** _____

Go to MY SCIENCE ⓢ COACH *online for help with this subject.*

Electricity, Magnetism, and Motion

UNLOCK THE BIG

🔑 **How Is Electrical Energy Transformed Into Mechanical Energy?**
PS.6b, PS.11b

🔑 **How Does a Galvanometer Work?**
PS.1i, PS.11b, PS.11c

🔑 **What Does an Electric Motor Do?**
PS.6b, PS.11b, PS.11c

MY PLANET DIARY

Miniature Motor

In 1960, scientist and California Institute of Technology (Caltech) professor Richard Feynman publicly offered a prize of $1,000 to the first person to build an electric motor no larger than 0.3969 cubic millimeters. A Caltech graduate named William McLellan accepted the challenge. He used a toothpick, microscope slides, fine hairs from a paintbrush, and wires only 1/80th of a millimeter wide to build the world's smallest motor. McLellan showed his tiny motor to Feynman and collected the $1,000 prize. Scientists today have found many uses for tiny motors in products such as high-definition televisions, cars, and ink-jet printers.

A tiny motor capable of producing high-resolution, DVD-quality images.

DISCOVERY

Communicate **Work with a partner to answer the question.**

What might be some other uses of tiny motors?

_____

_____

_____

_____

_____

▶ PLANET DIARY Go to **Planet Diary** to learn more about electric motors.

Do the Inquiry Warm-Up *How Are Electricity, Magnets, and Motion Related?*

Science Standards of Learning

PS.6b Investigate and understand mechanical, chemical, electrical, thermal, radiant, and nuclear energy and how they can be transferred and transformed.

PS.11b Investigate and understand the relationship between a magnetic field and an electric current.

How Is Electrical Energy Transformed Into Mechanical Energy?

What do trains, fans, microwave ovens, and clocks have in common? The answer is that these objects, along with many other everyday objects, use electricity. In addition, all these objects move or have moving parts. How does electricity produce motion?

Vocabulary
- galvanometer
- electric motor

Skills
- Reading: Sequence
- Inquiry: Graph

Energy and Motion As you know, magnetic force can produce motion. For example, magnets move together or apart when they are close. You also know that an electric current in a wire produces a magnetic field. So, a magnet can move a wire with a current, just as it would move another magnet. The direction of movement depends on the direction of the current. See **Figure 1**.

The ability to move an object over a distance is called energy. The energy associated with electric currents is called electrical energy. The energy an object has due to its movement or position is called mechanical energy.

Energy Transformation Energy can be transformed from one form into another. ◯ **When a wire with a current is placed in a magnetic field, electrical energy is transformed into mechanical energy.** This transformation happens when the magnetic field produced by the current causes the wire to move.

FIGURE 1 ·······························
Producing Motion
A wire with a current can be moved by a magnet.

✎ **Complete the tasks.**

1. **Identify** What affects the direction of the wire's movement?

_____

_____

2. **Classify** In each box, write down the type of energy that is being pointed out.

Wire moves down

Wire moves up

Lab® zone | Do the Quick Lab
Can a Magnet Move a Wire?

◯— Assess Your Understanding

got it? ···

○ I get it! Now I know that when a wire with a current is placed in a magnetic field, electrical energy

_____

○ I need extra help with _____

Go to my science ◯ coach *online for help with this subject.*

PS.1i Construct and interpret scatterplots.

PS.11b Investigate and understand the relationship between a magnetic field and an electric current.

PS.11c Investigate and understand electromagnets, motors, and generators, and their uses.

⊘ **Sequence** In the second paragraph on this page, underline and number the steps that explain how a galvanometer works.

FIGURE 2 ⋯⋯⋯⋯⋯⋯⋯⋯⋯⋯⋯⋯⋯⋯⋯

How a Galvanometer Works

✎ **Answer the questions about a galvanometer.**

1. **Predict** What would happen if the current flowed in the opposite direction?

_____

_____

2. **Interpret Diagrams** Where does the needle point when there is no current?

_____

_____

How Does a Galvanometer Work?

You have learned that a straight wire with a current moves when it is placed in a magnetic field. But what happens if you place a loop of wire with a current in a magnetic field? Look at **Figure 2.** The current in one side of the loop flows in the opposite direction than the current in the other side of the loop. The direction of the current determines the direction in which the wire moves. Therefore, the sides of the loop move in opposite directions. Once each side has moved as far up or down as it can go, it will stop moving. As a result, the loop can rotate only a half turn.

Inside a Galvanometer The rotation of a wire loop in a magnetic field is the basis of a galvanometer. A **galvanometer** is a device that measures small currents. ⊙ **An electric current turns the pointer of a galvanometer.** In a galvanometer, an electromagnet is suspended between opposite poles of two permanent magnets. The electromagnet's coil is attached to a pointer, as you can see in **Figure 2.** When a current is in the electromagnet's coil, it produces a magnetic field. This field interacts with the permanent magnet's field, causing the coil and the pointer to rotate. The distance the loops and the pointer rotate depends on the amount of current in the wire.

A Because the current on each side of the wire loop flows in different directions, one side of the loop moves down as the other side moves up. This causes the loop to rotate.

B An electromagnet turns the pointer to indicate the amount of current present.

To energy source

Uses of Galvanometers

A galvanometer has a scale that is marked to show how much the pointer turns for a known current. You can use the galvanometer to measure an unknown current. Galvanometers are useful in everyday life. For example, electricians use them in their work. Some cars use them as fuel gauges. Galvanometers are also used in lie detectors to measure how much current a person's skin conducts. People who are stressed sweat more. Water conducts electricity. Therefore, their moist skin conducts more electric current.

do the math!

This data from a galvanometer show the current conducted by a person's skin. The current is measured in microsiemens, a unit used to measure small amounts of electricity.

Minutes	0	4	8	12	16	20
Microsiemens	5	7	3	1	8	10

1. **Graph** Use the data in the table to plot points on the graph.

2. **CHALLENGE** What would a point at (24, 12) tell you about the person?

_____

_____

_____

_____

_____

_____

Skin Current

Graph with x-axis labeled "Time (Minutes)" with values 0, 4, 8, 12, 16, 20, 24 and y-axis labeled "Current (Microsiemens)" with values 2, 4, 6, 8, 10, 12.

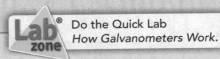

Do the Quick Lab
How Galvanometers Work.

🔑 Assess Your Understanding

1a. Review What does a galvanometer measure?

_____

b. Relate Cause and Effect What causes the pointer to move in a galvanometer?

_____

_____

got it?

○ **I get it!** Now I know that a galvanometer works by using _____

_____

○ **I need extra help with** _____

Go to **MY SCIENCE** ⓢ **COACH** *online for help with this subject.*

665

Science Standards of Learning

PS.6b Investigate and understand mechanical and electrical energy and how they can be transformed.

PS.11b Investigate and understand the relationship between a magnetic field and an electric current.

PS.11c Investigate and understand motors and their uses.

What Does an Electric Motor Do?

Have you ever wondered how a remote-controlled car moves? A remote-controlled car's wheels are turned by a rod, or axle, which is connected to an electric motor. An **electric motor** is a device that uses an electric current to turn an axle. 🔌 **An electric motor transforms electrical energy into mechanical energy.**

Look at **Figure 3** to read about the parts of a motor.

If current only flowed in one direction through the armature, the armature could only rotate a half a turn. However, the brushes and commutator enable the current in the armature to change direction. Current always flows from the positive to the negative terminal of a battery. The current in the armature is reversed each time the commutator moves to a different brush. This causes the side of the armature that just moved up to move down. The side that just moved down will move up. The armature rotates continuously. See **Figure 4**.

FIGURE 3 ··

Parts of a Motor

A simple electric motor contains four parts.

✏️ Observe **Which part of an electric motor must be attached directly to the energy source?**

Permanent magnets produce a magnetic field. This causes the armature to turn.

The **commutator** consists of two semicircular pieces of metal. It conducts current from the brushes to the armature.

Brushes conduct current to the rest of the commutator. They do not move.

The **armature** is a loop of wire that current flows through.

FIGURE 4 ···

> INTERACTIVE ART **How a Motor Works**

The magnetic field around the armature interacts with the field of the permanent magnet, allowing the armature to turn continuously. The direction of the current determines which way the armature turns.

✎ **Infer** Based on the direction the armature is turning in each diagram, draw arrows showing the direction of the current.

The current is in opposite directions on each side of the armature causing one side to move up while the other side moves down.

The commutator rotates with the armature. The direction of current reverses with each half turn so the armature spins continuously.

Lab zone® Do the Quick Lab *Parts of an Electric Motor.*

🔑 Assess Your Understanding

2a. Define What is an electric motor?

_____

_____

_____

_____

b. Summarize What makes the armature turn continuously?

_____

_____

got it?

○ **I get it!** Now I know that an electric motor transforms _____

_____

_____

○ **I need extra help with** _____

Go to my science ⓢ coach *online for help with this subject.*

Electricity From Magnetism

UNLOCK THE BIG **?**

🔑 **How Can an Electric Current Be Produced in a Conductor?**
PS.11b, PS.11c, PS.11d

🔑 **How Does a Generator Work?**
PS.1m, PS.6b, PS.11b, PS.11c

🔑 **What Does a Transformer Do?**
PS.1j, PS.1m, PS.11b, PS.11c

MY PLANET DIARY

CAREERS

MRI Technologist

Does working in the medical field interest you? Are you good at operating devices? Do you have a knack for soothing anxious people? If you answered yes, you should think about becoming an Magnetic Resonance Imaging (MRI) technologist.

When a patient is put into an MRI machine, radio waves and magnetic fields are used to create images of the patient's internal structures. The doctors use these detailed pictures to determine what is wrong with the patient. The MRI technologist's responsibilities include operating the MRI machine, comforting nervous patients, and maintaining patient confidentiality. You can become an MRI technologist by completing a bachelor's degree program, an associate's degree program, or a certificate program.

Read the following question. Write your answer below.

What do you think might happen to the MRI image if you wore metal jewelry while in the MRI machine? Why?

_____
_____
_____
_____

▶ PLANET DIARY Go to **Planet Diary** to learn more about electricity from magnetism.

Lab zone

Do the Inquiry Warm-Up
Electric Current Without a Battery.

Vocabulary
- electromagnetic induction
- alternating current
- direct current
- generator
- transformer

Skills
↻ Reading: Ask Questions
△ Inquiry: Make Models

How Can an Electric Current Be Produced in a Conductor?

An electric motor uses electrical energy to produce motion. Can motion produce electrical energy? In 1831, scientists discovered that moving a wire in a magnetic field can cause an electric current. This current allows electrical energy to be supplied to homes, schools, and businesses all over the world.

To understand how electrical energy is supplied by your electric company, you need to know how current is produced. A magnet can make, or induce, current in a conductor, such as a wire, as long as there is motion. An electric current is induced in a conductor when the conductor moves through a magnetic field. Generating electric current from the motion of a conductor through a magnetic field is called **electromagnetic induction.** Current that is generated in this way is called induced current.

Science Standards of Learning

PS.11b Investigate and understand the relationship between a magnetic field and an electric current.

PS.11c Investigate and understand electromagnets, motors, and generators, and their uses.

PS.11d Investigate and understand conductors.

↻ **Ask Questions** Read the paragraph. Then write two questions that you still have about producing electric current.

_____
_____
_____
_____
_____
_____
_____
_____
_____
_____
_____
_____
_____

Induction of Electric Current Michael Faraday and Joseph Henry each found that motion in a magnetic field will induce a current. Either the conductor can move through the magnetic field, or the magnet can move. In **Figure 1,** a conductor, the coil of wire, is connected to a galvanometer, forming a closed circuit. If the coil and the magnet do not move, the galvanometer's pointer does not move. However, when either the wire coil or the magnet moves, the galvanometer registers a current. Moving the coil or the magnet induces the current without any voltage source. The direction of an induced current depends on the direction that the coil or magnet moves. When the motion is reversed, the direction of the current also reverses.

FIGURE 1 ·······························

Motion Produces a Current

Electric current is induced in a wire whenever the magnetic field around it is changing. The field changes when either the magnet or the wire moves.

✎ **Complete the tasks.**

1. **Describe** Under each diagram, label the direction of the current using *clockwise* or *counterclockwise*.

2. **CHALLENGE** Make a general statement that relates the motion of the circuit (up or down) to the direction of the current (clockwise or counterclockwise).

_____
_____
_____
_____
_____
_____
_____
_____

Moving Coil

Coil moves up ⬆

Galvanometer

Magnetic field

Coil moves down ⬇

Coil

Moving Magnet

Magnet moves up ⬆

Magnetic field

Magnet moves down ⬇

Alternating and Direct Current

A current with charges that flow in one direction is called **direct current,** or DC. A battery produces direct current when a battery is placed in a circuit and charges flow in one direction. They move from one end of the battery, around the circuit, and into the other end of the battery.

If a wire in a magnetic field changes direction repeatedly, the induced current also keeps changing direction. A constantly reversing current is called **alternating current,** or AC. You could induce alternating current by moving either the coil or the magnet up and down repeatedly in the **Figure 1** circuit.

Alternating current has a major advantage over direct current. An AC voltage can be easily raised or lowered. This means that a high voltage can be used to send electrical energy over great distances. Then the voltage can be reduced to a safer level for everyday use. The electric current in the circuits in homes, schools, and other buildings is alternating current. Look at **Figure 2** to learn about how electricity has changed over time.

1882
Direct Current ————
Thomas Edison opens a generating plant in New York City. It serves an area of about 2.6 square kilometers.

1888
Alternating Current ————
Nikola Tesla receives patents for a system of distributing alternating current.

Today
Direct and Alternating Current
An electric car runs on direct current from its battery. However, alternating current is needed to charge the battery.

1860

1880

Today

FIGURE 2 ··
The History of Electricity
The work of several scientists brought electricity from the laboratory into everyday use.

✎ **Draw Conclusions** Why do you think we use alternating current today?

_____

 Do the Quick Lab *Inducing an Electric Current.*

🔑 Assess Your Understanding

1a. Describe How can you use a magnet to induce a current?

_____

_____

b. Classify Give an example of an electronic appliance that runs on AC and one that runs on DC.

_____

_____

got it? ···

○ **I get it!** Now I know that electric current is induced when _____

_____

○ **I need extra help with** _____

Go to MY SCIENCE ⓢ COACH online for help with this subject.

Science Standards of Learning

PS.1m Use models to illustrate and explain phenomena.

PS.6b Investigate and understand mechanical and electrical energy and how they can be transformed.

PS.11b Investigate and understand the relationship between a magnetic field and an electric current.

PS.11c Investigate and understand generators and their uses.

FIGURE 3 ·····································

> INTERACTIVE ART **How a Generator Works**

In a generator, an armature rotates in a magnetic field to induce a current.

✎ **Describe** Write what each part of the generator does in the boxes.

How Does a Generator Work?

An electric **generator** is a device that transforms mechanical energy into electrical energy. 🔑 **A generator uses motion in a magnetic field to produce current.**

In **Figure 3,** you can see how an AC generator works. Turn the crank, and the armature rotates in the magnetic field. As the armature rotates, one side of it moves up as the other moves down. This motion induces a current in the armature. Slip rings turn with the armature. The turning slip rings allow current to flow into the brushes. When the brushes are connected to a circuit, the generator can be used as an energy source.

The electric company uses giant generators to produce most of the electrical energy you use each day. Huge turbines turn the armatures of the generators. Turbines are circular devices with many blades. They spin when water, steam, or hot gas flows through them. This turns the armatures, which generates electric current.

Slip Ring

Armature

Brush

Crank

EXPLORE THE BIG ?

ZAP!

How are electricity and magnetism related?

FIGURE 4 ··
Wind-up cell phone chargers are small generators that let you charge your cell phone anywhere.

✎ **Analyze Models and Systems** Complete the tasks below.

When I turn the crank of the wind-up cell phone charger, or generator, I turn an armature in a(n) _____.
This generates a(n) _____ in the wire, which powers the phone.

If you connect the output wires of the charger to a battery, _____ will flow through the armature, producing a _____. The permanent magnet in the charger will then cause the armature to _____. Draw what you will observe that lets you know this is happening.

Lab zone ® Do the Quick Lab *How Generators Work.*

🔑 Assess Your Understanding

2a. Review What is one way to induce an electric current?

_____

_____

_____

b. ANSWER THE BIG ? How are electricity and magnetism related?

_____

_____

_____

_____

got it? ···

○ **I get it!** Now I know a generator produces current by _____
_____

○ **I need extra help with** _____

Go to **my science** s **COACH** *online for help with this subject.*

What Does a Transformer Do?

The electrical energy generated by electric companies is transmitted over long distances at very high voltages. However, in your home, electrical energy is used at much lower voltages. Transformers change the voltage so you can use electricity.

🔑 **A transformer is a device that increases or decreases voltage.** A **transformer** consists of two separate coils of insulated wire wrapped around an iron core. The primary coil is connected to a circuit with a voltage source and alternating current. The secondary coil is connected to a separate circuit that does not contain a voltage source. The changing current in the primary coil produces a changing magnetic field. This changing magnetic field induces a current in the secondary coil.

The change in voltage from the primary coil to the secondary coil depends on the number of loops in each coil. In step-up transformers, as shown in **Figure 5,** the primary coil has fewer loops than the secondary coil. Step-up transformers increase voltage. In step-down transformers, the primary coil has more loops. Voltage is reduced. The greater the difference between the number of loops in the primary and secondary coils in a transformer, the more the voltage will change. The relationship is a ratio.

$$\frac{\text{voltage}_{\text{primary}}}{\text{voltage}_{\text{secondary}}} = \frac{\text{coils}_{\text{primary}}}{\text{coils}_{\text{secondary}}}$$

$$\frac{120\text{ v}}{6\text{ v}} = 20$$

In this transformer, the voltage in the primary coil is twenty times higher than the voltage in the secondary coil. This means there are twenty times as many loops in the primary coil as there are in the secondary coil. If the primary coil has forty loops, then the secondary coil has two.

FIGURE 5 ·····································

Transformers

A step-up transformer, like the one shown below, is used to help transmit electricity from generating plants. Step-down transformers are used in power cords for some small electronics.

✏️ **Make Models** Draw wire loops to show both the primary and secondary coils of this step-down transformer.

This kind of plug contains a step-down transformer.

Step-Up Transformer

Primary coil   Secondary coil

Step-Down Transformer

do the math!

Transforming Electricity

The illustration shows how transformers change voltage between the generating plant and your home. For each transformer in the illustration below, state whether it is a step-up or step-down transformer.

In the boxes, calculate the ratio of loops in the primary coil to loops in the secondary coil.

Transformer

Transformer

Transformer

Generating plant

11,000 V

240,000 V

High-voltage transmission lines

2,400 V

120 V

Lab zone® Do the Quick Lab
How Transformers Work.

🔑 Assess Your Understanding

3a. Identify Which coil has more loops in a step-down transformer?

_____
_____
_____

b. Infer Why do some appliances have step-down transformers built in?

_____
_____
_____

got it? ....

○ **I get it!** Now I know a transformer is a device used to _____

_____

○ I need extra help with _____

Go to my science ⑤ coach *online for help with this subject.*

19 Study Guide

REVIEW THE BIG ?

_____ in a wire produces a _____
and movement of a wire through a _____
produces _____.

LESSON 1 What Is Magnetism?

🔑 Magnets attract iron and materials that contain iron. Magnets attract or repel other magnets. In addition, one end of a magnet will always point north when allowed to swing freely.

🔑 Magnetic poles that are unlike attract each other, and magnetic poles that are alike repel each other.

Vocabulary
• magnet
• magnetism
• magnetic pole
• magnetic force

LESSON 2 Magnetic Fields

🔑 Magnetic field lines spread out from one pole, curve around the magnet, and return to the other pole.

🔑 Like a bar magnet, Earth has a magnetic field around it and two magnetic poles.

Vocabulary
• magnetic field
• magnetic field lines
• compass
• magnetic declination

LESSON 3 Electromagnetic Force

🔑 An electric current produces a magnetic field.

🔑 The magnetic field produced by a current can be turned on or off, reverse direction, or change its strength.

🔑 Both solenoids and electromagnets use electric current and coiled wires to produce strong magnetic fields.

Vocabulary
• electromagnetism • solenoid • electromagnet

LESSON 4 Electricity, Magnetism, and Motion

🔑 By placing a wire with a current in a magnetic field, electrical energy can be transformed into mechanical energy.

🔑 An electric current turns the pointer of a galvanometer.

🔑 An electric motor transforms electrical energy into mechanical energy.

Vocabulary
• galvanometer • electric motor

LESSON 5 Electricity From Magnetism

🔑 An electric current is induced in a conductor when the conductor moves through a magnetic field.

🔑 A generator uses motion in a magnetic field to produce current.

🔑 A transformer is a device that increases or decreases voltage.

Vocabulary
• electromagnetic induction • direct current
• alternating current • generator • transformer

Review and Assessment

LESSON 1 What Is Magnetism?

1. A magnet is attracted to a soup can because the can has
   a. a south pole.
   b. a north pole.
   c. a magnetic field.
   d. iron in it.

2. Any magnet, no matter its shape, has two ends, and each one is called a _____

3. **Predict** What will happen to a bar magnet suspended from a string when it swings freely?

_____

_____

_____

4. **Interpret Diagrams** In the diagram, what do the arrows represent? Explain your answer.

_____

_____

_____

_____

5. **Design Experiments** If two magnets' poles are not labeled, how can you tell which poles are the same and which are different?

_____

_____

_____

LESSON 2 Magnetic Fields

6. A compass works because its magnetic needle
   a. points east.
   b. spins freely.
   c. points west.
   d. repels magnets.

7. _____ map out the magnetic field around a magnet.

8. **Make Models** How is Earth like a magnet?

_____

_____

_____

9. **Draw Conclusions** Look at the diagram below. Is the left magnetic pole a north or south pole? Explain your answer.

_____

_____

_____

10. **Write About It** Imagine that you are the early inventor of the compass. Write an advertisement for your product that tells explorers how a compass works.

LESSON 3 Electromagnetic Force

11. The relationship between electricity and magnetism is called

a. electrical energy.　　**b.** induced current.

c. electromagnetism.　**d.** ferromagnetism.

12. A coil of wire with a current is called

a _____

13. Relate Cause and Effect You have a magnetic field produced by a current. What would you do to change the direction and increase the strength of the field?

_____

_____

_____

_____

_____

LESSON 4 Electricity, Magnetism, and Motion

14. Electrical energy is transformed into mechanical energy in a

a. motor.　　　　**b.** solenoid.

c. transformer.　**d.** electromagnet.

15. A galvanometer is a device that

measures _____

16. Compare and Contrast How is a motor similar to a galvanometer? How is it different?

_____

_____

_____

_____

_____

_____

LESSON 5 Electricity From Magnetism

17. A device that changes the voltage of alternating current is a

a. transformer.　**b.** motor.

c. generator.　　**d.** galvanometer.

18. Generating a current by moving a conductor in a magnetic field is _____

_____

19. Write About It You are a television news reporter covering the opening of a new dam that will help to generate electrical energy. Write a short news story describing how the dam transforms mechanical energy from the motion of the water into electrical energy.

APPLY THE BIG ? How are electricity and magnetism related?

20. A crane in a junkyard may have an electromagnet to lift heavy metal objects. Explain how electricity and magnetism work in an electromagnet so that a crane can lift heavy metal objects.

_____

_____

_____

_____

_____

_____

_____

_____

_____

Virginia SOL Test Prep

Read each question and choose the best answer.

1 The graph below shows how a solenoid's loops affect its magnetic field strength. Predict the strength of a 12-loop solenoid.

Strength of a Solenoid

A 300 gauss   B 600 gauss

C 700 gauss   D 1200 gauss

2 What happens when a magnet moves through a coil of wire?

F The magnet loses magnetism.

G A current is induced in the wire.

H A current is induced in the magnet.

J Electrical energy is transformed into mechanical energy.

3 To measure the current induced by moving a wire through a magnetic field, which piece of equipment would a scientist need?

A a galvanometer

B a transformer

C an insulated wire

D an LED

4 You can increase a step-up transformer's voltage—

F with a power source connected to the primary coil

G with a source connected to the secondary coil

H by increasing the number of loops in the primary coil

J by increasing the number of loops in the secondary coil

5 How could you modify a solenoid to produce a stronger magnetic field?

A Remove loops from the solenoid.

B Convert the solenoid to an electromagnet by adding a ferromagnetic core.

C Wind the loops farther apart.

D Decrease the current in the solenoid.

6 Three electromagnets are illustrated in the diagram below. Order the electromagnets from strongest magnetic field to weakest magnetic field.

A   B   C

F A, C, B

G B, C, A

H C, A, B

J A, B, C

MAGNETIC PICTURES

Now, instead of using X-rays, doctors use magnets to look in detail at systems inside the body. ▼

Doctors can look inside your body to detect infection, bleeding, or tumors in the brain—without surgery or high-energy radiation that can damage tissues. They can get very detailed views of ligaments, tendons, and muscles that reveal injuries. They can find breast cancers that mammograms miss, and they can map areas of low blood flow after a heart attack. How do they do this? They use Magnetic Resonance Imaging (MRI).

MRI machines use powerful electromagnets, radio waves, and computers to take pictures of the inside of bodies. This process works because human bodies contain so much water. First, the large magnet in the MRI machine aligns the hydrogen atoms in the water molecules within the field. Then, the machine emits a radio frequency pulse that spins all of the hydrogen atoms the same way. The hydrogen atoms release energy in the form of a radio signal as they return to their normal positions, and computers can turn that signal into pictures. Healthy tissues respond differently to the magnet than unhealthy or damaged tissues.

Research It MRI scanning rooms have strict rules about what is allowed inside because metal objects can become deadly. Research the safety concerns for MRI use on humans. Then write a safety brochure to share your findings.

PS.1k, PS.1n, PS.11b, PS.11c

▲ This MRI of a healthy brain shows both hemispheres in bright pink and the cerebellum in green.

A SHOCKING MESSAGE!

In the 1830s, before the telephone had been invented, people were experimenting with ways to communicate across long distances. Samuel Morse and Alfred Vail discovered that it was possible to use an electromagnet to send a signal through cheap wire.

The electromagnet is part of an electric circuit. On one end of the wire is a telegraph switch. Closing the switch completes the circuit, sending an electric current through the wire. Opening the switch stops the current. On the other end of the wire is a telegraph with an electromagnet, a metal key, and a metal plate. As the electric current flows through the electromagnet, a magnetic field forms.

The metal key is then attracted to the metal plate. The sender can close and open the switch quickly, making a short clicking sound called a "dot" on the other end. Or, the sender can hold the switch closed and create a longer sound, called a "dash." Leaving the switch open for a moment comes across as a "space," or a break in the sounds.

This pattern of dots, dashes, and spaces became a new tool for communicating without using voices—Morse code. Telegraph operators could spell out words and phrases. Three dots, followed by three dashes, followed by three dots, for example, is the Morse code signal for SOS, or help!

Signal It Work with a partner to find resources that will help you construct your own electromagnetic telegraph machine! Predict which materials will best conduct a signal, and then verify your predictions by building a model.

PS.1m, PS.1n, PS.11b, PS.11c

APPENDIX A

Safety Symbols

These symbols warn of possible dangers in the laboratory and remind you to work carefully.

 Safety Goggles Wear safety goggles to protect your eyes in any activity involving chemicals, flames or heating, or glassware.

 Lab Apron Wear a laboratory apron to protect your skin and clothing from damage.

 Breakage Handle breakable materials, such as glassware, with care. Do not touch broken glassware.

 Heat-Resistant Gloves Use an oven mitt or other hand protection when handling hot materials such as hot plates or hot glassware.

 Plastic Gloves Wear disposable plastic gloves when working with harmful chemicals and organisms. Keep your hands away from your face, and dispose of the gloves according to your teacher's instructions.

 Heating Use a clamp or tongs to pick up hot glassware. Do not touch hot objects with your bare hands.

 Flames Before you work with flames, tie back loose hair and clothing. Follow instructions from your teacher about lighting and extinguishing flames.

 No Flames When using flammable materials, make sure there are no flames, sparks, or other exposed heat sources present.

 Corrosive Chemical Avoid getting acid or other corrosive chemicals on your skin or clothing or in your eyes. Do not inhale the vapors. Wash your hands after the activity.

 Poison Do not let any poisonous chemical come into contact with your skin, and do not inhale its vapors. Wash your hands when you are finished with the activity.

 Fumes Work in a well-ventilated area when harmful vapors may be involved. Avoid inhaling vapors directly. Only test an odor when directed to do so by your teacher, and use a wafting motion to direct the vapor toward your nose.

 Sharp Object Scissors, scalpels, knives, needles, pins, and tacks can cut your skin. Always direct a sharp edge or point away from yourself and others.

 Animal Safety Treat live or preserved animals or animal parts with care to avoid harming the animals or yourself. Wash your hands when you are finished with the activity.

 Plant Safety Handle plants only as directed by your teacher. If you are allergic to certain plants, tell your teacher; do not do an activity involving those plants. Avoid touching harmful plants such as poison ivy. Wash your hands when you are finished with the activity.

 Electric Shock To avoid electric shock, never use electrical equipment around water, or when the equipment is wet or your hands are wet. Be sure cords are untangled and cannot trip anyone. Unplug equipment not in use.

 Physical Safety When an experiment involves physical activity, avoid injuring yourself or others. Alert your teacher if there is any reason you should not participate.

 Disposal Dispose of chemicals and other laboratory materials safely. Follow the instructions from your teacher.

 Hand Washing Wash your hands thoroughly when finished with an activity. Use soap and warm water. Rinse well.

 General Safety Awareness When this symbol appears, follow the instructions provided. When you are asked to develop your own procedure in a lab, have your teacher approve your plan before you go further.

APPENDIX B

Using a Laboratory Balance

The laboratory balance is an important tool in scientific investigations. Different kinds of balances are used in the laboratory to determine the masses and weights of objects. You can use a triple-beam balance to determine the masses of materials that you study or experiment with in the laboratory. An electronic balance, unlike a triple-beam balance, is used to measure the weights of materials.

The triple-beam balance that you may use in your science class is probably similar to the balance illustrated in this Appendix. **To use the balance properly, you should learn the name, location, and function of each part of the balance you are using. What kind of balance do you have in your science class?**

The Triple-Beam Balance

The triple-beam balance is a single-pan balance with three beams calibrated in grams. The back, or 100-gram, beam is divided into ten units of 10 grams each. The middle, or 500-gram, beam is divided into five units of 100 grams each. The front, or 10-gram, beam is divided into ten units of 1 gram each. Each of the units on the front beam is further divided into units of 0.1 gram. What is the largest mass you could find with a triple-beam balance?

The following procedure can be used to find the mass of an object with a triple-beam balance:
1. Place the object on the pan.
2. Move the rider on the middle beam notch by notch until the horizontal pointer on the right drops below zero. Move the rider back one notch.
3. Move the rider on the back beam notch by notch until the pointer again drops below zero. Move the rider back one notch.
4. Slowly slide the rider along the front beam until the pointer stops at the zero point.
5. The mass of the object is equal to the sum of the readings on the three beams.

Pan

Riders

Pointer (at zero)

Beams

TRIPLE BEAM BALANCE
700 SERIES 800 SERIES
2610g CAPACITY 5 lb 2 oz

APPENDIX C

Periodic Table of the Elements

Key
- Metal
- Metalloid
- Nonmetal

Group

Period

1										
1 H Hydrogen 1.0079										

Lanthanides

| 57 La Lanthanum 138.91 | 58 Ce Cerium 140.12 | 59 Pr Praseodymium 140.91 | 60 Nd Neodymium 144.24 | 61 Pm Promethium (145) | 62 Sm Samarium 150.4 | 63 Eu Europium 151.96 | 64 Gd Gadolinium 157.25 |

Actinides

| 89 Ac Actinium (227) | 90 Th Thorium 232.04 | 91 Pa Protactinium 231.04 | 92 U Uranium 238.03 | 93 Np Neptunium (237) | 94 Pu Plutonium (244) | 95 Am Americium (243) | 96 Cm Curium (247) |

Many periodic tables include a zigzag line that separates the metals from the nonmetals. Metalloids, found on either side of the line, share properties of both metals and nonmetals.

18

	2
	He
	Helium
	4.0026

13	**14**	**15**	**16**	**17**	
5	6	7	8	9	10
B	**C**	**N**	**O**	**F**	**Ne**
Boron	Carbon	Nitrogen	Oxygen	Fluorine	Neon
10.81	12.011	14.007	15.999	18.998	20.179
13	14	15	16	17	18
Al	**Si**	**P**	**S**	**Cl**	**Ar**
Aluminum	Silicon	Phosphorus	Sulfur	Chlorine	Argon
26.982	28.086	30.974	32.06	35.453	39.948

12

30	31	32	33	34	35	36
Zn	**Ga**	**Ge**	**As**	**Se**	**Br**	**Kr**
Zinc	Gallium	Germanium	Arsenic	Selenium	Bromine	Krypton
65.38	69.72	72.59	74.922	78.96	79.904	83.80
48	49	50	51	52	53	54
Cd	**In**	**Sn**	**Sb**	**Te**	**I**	**Xe**
Cadmium	Indium	Tin	Antimony	Tellurium	Iodine	Xenon
112.41	114.82	118.69	121.75	127.60	126.90	131.30
80	81	82	83	84	85	86
Hg	**Tl**	**Pb**	**Bi**	**Po**	**At**	**Rn**
Mercury	Thallium	Lead	Bismuth	Polonium	Astatine	Radon
200.59	204.37	207.2	208.98	(209)	(210)	(222)
112	113	114	115	116	117	118
Cn	***Uut**	***Uuq**	***Uup**	***Uuh**	***Uus**	***Uuo**
Copernicium	Ununtrium	Ununquadium	Ununpentium	Ununhexium	Ununseptium	Ununoctium
(277)	(284)	(289)	(288)	(292)		(294)

*The discoveries of elements 113 and above have not yet been officially confirmed.

Atomic masses in parentheses are those of the most stable isotopes.

65	66	67	68	69	70
Tb	**Dy**	**Ho**	**Er**	**Tm**	**Yb**
Terbium	Dysprosium	Holmium	Erbium	Thulium	Ytterbium
158.93	162.50	164.93	167.26	168.93	173.04

97	98	99	100	101	102
Bk	**Cf**	**Es**	**Fm**	**Md**	**No**
Berkelium	Californium	Einsteinium	Fermium	Mendelevium	Nobelium
(247)	(251)	(252)	(257)	(258)	(259)

APPENDIX D

List of Chemical Elements

Name	Symbol	Atomic Number	Atomic Mass†
Actinium	Ac	89	(227)
Aluminum	Al	13	26.982
Americium	Am	95	(243)
Antimony	Sb	51	121.75
Argon	Ar	18	39.948
Arsenic	As	33	74.922
Astatine	At	85	(210)
Barium	Ba	56	137.33
Berkelium	Bk	97	(247)
Beryllium	Be	4	9.0122
Bismuth	Bi	83	208.98
Bohrium	Bh	107	(264)
Boron	B	5	10.81
Bromine	Br	35	79.904
Cadmium	Cd	48	112.41
Calcium	Ca	20	40.08
Californium	Cf	98	(251)
Carbon	C	6	12.011
Cerium	Ce	58	140.12
Cesium	Cs	55	132.91
Chlorine	Cl	17	35.453
Chromium	Cr	24	51.996
Cobalt	Co	27	58.933
Copernicium	Cn	112	(277)
Copper	Cu	29	63.546
Curium	Cm	96	(247)
Darmstadtium	Ds	110	(269)
Dubnium	Db	105	(262)
Dysprosium	Dy	66	162.50
Einsteinium	Es	99	(252)
Erbium	Er	68	167.26
Europium	Eu	63	151.96
Fermium	Fm	100	(257)
Fluorine	F	9	18.998
Francium	Fr	87	(223)
Gadolinium	Gd	64	157.25
Gallium	Ga	31	69.72
Germanium	Ge	32	72.59
Gold	Au	79	196.97
Hafnium	Hf	72	178.49
Hassium	Hs	108	(265)
Helium	He	2	4.0026
Holmium	Ho	67	164.93
Hydrogen	H	1	1.0079
Indium	In	49	114.82
Iodine	I	53	126.90
Iridium	Ir	77	192.22
Iron	Fe	26	55.847
Krypton	Kr	36	83.80
Lanthanum	La	57	138.91
Lawrencium	Lr	103	(262)
Lead	Pb	82	207.2
Lithium	Li	3	6.941
Lutetium	Lu	71	174.97
Magnesium	Mg	12	24.305
Manganese	Mn	25	54.938
Meitnerium	Mt	109	(268)
Mendelevium	Md	101	(258)
Mercury	Hg	80	200.59
Molybdenum	Mo	42	95.94
Neodymium	Nd	60	144.24
Neon	Ne	10	20.179
Neptunium	Np	93	(237)
Nickel	Ni	28	58.71
Niobium	Nb	41	92.906
Nitrogen	N	7	14.007
Nobelium	No	102	(259)
Osmium	Os	76	190.2
Oxygen	O	8	15.999
Palladium	Pd	46	106.4
Phosphorus	P	15	30.974
Platinum	Pt	78	195.09
Plutonium	Pu	94	(244)
Polonium	Po	84	(209)
Potassium	K	19	39.098
Praseodymium	Pr	59	140.91
Promethium	Pm	61	(145)
Protactinium	Pa	91	231.04
Radium	Ra	88	(226)
Radon	Rn	86	(222)
Rhenium	Re	75	186.21
Rhodium	Rh	45	102.91
Roentgenium	Rg	111	(272)
Rubidium	Rb	37	85.468
Ruthenium	Ru	44	101.07
Rutherfordium	Rf	104	(261)
Samarium	Sm	62	150.4
Scandium	Sc	21	44.956
Seaborgium	Sg	106	(263)
Selenium	Se	34	78.96
Silicon	Si	14	28.086
Silver	Ag	47	107.87
Sodium	Na	11	22.990
Strontium	Sr	38	87.62
Sulfur	S	16	32.06
Tantalum	Ta	73	180.95
Technetium	Tc	43	(98)
Tellurium	Te	52	127.60
Terbium	Tb	65	158.93
Thallium	Tl	81	204.37
Thorium	Th	90	232.04
Thulium	Tm	69	168.93
Tin	Sn	50	118.69
Titanium	Ti	22	47.90
Tungsten	W	74	183.85
Uranium	U	92	238.03
Vanadium	V	23	50.941
Xenon	Xe	54	131.30
Ytterbium	Yb	70	173.04
Yttrium	Y	39	88.906
Zinc	Zn	30	65.38
Zirconium	Zr	40	91.22

†Numbers in parentheses give the mass number of the most stable isotope.

APPENDIX E

Probeware in the Science Classroom

Probeware is scientific equipment that uses sensors, or probes, to make data collection faster and easier. There are different probes to measure everything from pH and dissolved oxygen of water to temperature and the pressure of air. The probes collect data and can be connected to hand-held devices, laptops, or desktop computers that record and display the data.

These probes are connected to a hand-held device that records the data.

These students are using probeware to test the water quality of a stream.

Probeware is a powerful scientific tool because probes record data continuously, giving you more data to work with than you could record yourself. Because the technology is portable, you also can measure and record data out in the field. Rather than bringing water samples back from a lake, for example, you can test the pH and dissolved oxygen of the water right there. All the information is stored on the device.

The other major benefit of probeware is that it can display the data it collects and records in a variety of graphical forms. With the press of a button, software can present the data as any kind of table or graph that you choose, letting you spend more time analyzing your results instead of creating tables and graphs yourself.

Probeware was used to generate this line graph for an experiment involving respiration and CO_2 levels. It displays the results of three runs of the experiment on the same graph.

GLOSSARY

A

absolute zero The temperature at which no more energy can be removed from matter. (455)
cero absoluto Temperatura a cuyo punto ya no se puede extraer energía de la materia.

acceleration The rate at which velocity changes. (334)
aceleración Ritmo al que cambia la velocidad.

accuracy How close a measurement is to the true or accepted value. (56)
exactitud Cuán cerca está una medida del valor verdadero o aceptado.

acid A substance that tastes sour, reacts with metals and carbonates, and turns blue litmus red. (301)
ácido Sustancia de sabor agrio que reacciona con metales y carbonatos, y que vuelve rojo el papel de tornasol azul.

activation energy The minimum amount of energy needed to start a chemical reaction. (271)
energía de activación Cantidad mínima de energía que se necesita para iniciar una reacción química.

alkali metal An element in Group 1 of the periodic table. (180)
metal alcalino Elemento en el Grupo 1 de la tabla periódica.

alkaline earth metal An element in Group 2 of the periodic table. (180)
metal alcalinotérreo Elemento en el Grupo 2 de la tabla periódica.

alloy A mixture of two or more elements, at least one of which is a metal. (239)
aleación Mezcla de dos o más elementos, uno de los cuales es un metal.

alpha particle A particle given off during radioactive decay that consists of two protons and two neutrons. (197)
partícula alfa Partícula liberada durante la desintegración radiactiva que tiene dos protones y dos neutrones.

alternating current Current consisting of charges that move back and forth in a circuit. (671)
corriente alterna Corriente de cargas eléctricas que se mueven hacia delante y hacia atrás en un circuito.

amorphous solid A solid made up of particles that are not arranged in a regular pattern. (130)
sólido amorfo Sólido constituido por partículas que no están dispuestas en un patrón regular.

amplitude 1. The height of a transverse wave from the center to a crest or trough. **2.** The maximum distance the particles of a medium move away from their rest positions as a longitudinal wave passes through the medium. (483)
amplitud 1. Altura de una onda transversal desde el centro a una cresta o un valle. **2.** Máxima distancia del desvío de las partículas de un medio, desde sus posiciones de reposo, al ser atravesado por una onda longitudinal.

amplitude modulation A method of transmitting signals by changing the amplitude of a radio wave. (554)
amplitud modulada Método de transmisión de señales al cambiar la amplitud de una onda de radio.

analyzing Evaluating data to reach a conclusion about an experiment. (8)
analizar Evaluar datos para llegar a una conclusión acerca de un experimento.

anomalous data Data that do not fit with the rest of a data set. (59)
datos anómalos Información que no encaja con los otros datos de un conjunto de datos.

antinode A point of maximum amplitude on a standing wave. (494)
antinodo Punto de máxima amplitud de una onda estacionaria.

atom The basic particle from which all elements are made; the smallest particle of an element that has the properties of that element. (98)
átomo Partícula básica de la que todos los elementos están formados; partícula más pequeña de un elemento, que tiene las propiedades de ese elemento.

atomic mass The average mass of all the isotopes of an element. (169)
masa atómica Promedio de la masa de todos los isótopos de un elemento.

atomic number The number of protons in the nucleus of an atom. (166)
número atómico Número de protones en el núcleo de un átomo.

average speed The overall rate of speed at which an object moves; calculated by dividing the total distance an object travels by the total time. (328)
velocidad media Índice de velocidad general de un objeto en movimiento; se calcula dividiendo la distancia total recorrida por el tiempo total empleado.

_____ **B** _____

base A substance that tastes bitter, feels slippery, and turns red litmus paper blue. (303)
base Sustancia de sabor amargo, escurridiza y que vuelve azul el papel de tornasol rojo.

beta particle A fast-moving electron that is given off as nuclear radiation. (197)
partícula beta Electrón de movimiento rápido producido como radiación nuclear.

bias A subjective belief that affects a person's attitude toward something; an error in the design of an experiment that affects the results of the experiment. (22)
predisposición Creencia subjetiva que afecta la actitud de una persona acerca de algo; un error en el diseño de un experimento que afecta los resultados del experimento.

boiling Vaporization that occurs at and below the surface of a liquid. (139)
ebullición Evaporación que ocurre en y bajo la superficie de un líquido.

boiling point The temperature at which a liquid boils. (139)
punto de ebullición Temperatura a la cual hierve un líquido.

Boyle's law A principle that describes the relationship between the pressure and volume of a gas at constant temperature. (148)
ley de Boyle Principio que describe la relación entre la presión y el volumen de un gas a una temperatura constante.

_____ **C** _____

camera An optical instrument that uses lenses to focus light, and film or an electronic sensor to record an image of an object. (595)
cámara Instrumento óptico que usa lentes para enfocar la luz, y película o un sensor electrónico para grabar la imagen de un objeto.

catalyst A material that increases the rate of a reaction by lowering the activation energy. (275)
catalizador Material que aumenta la velocidad de una reacción al disminuir la energía de activación.

Celsius scale The temperature scale on which water freezes at 0°C and boils at 100°C. (455)
escala Celsius Escala de temperatura en la que el punto de congelación del agua es 0°C y el punto de ebullición es 100°C.

centripetal force A force that causes an object to move in a circle. (377)
fuerza centrípeta Fuerza que hace que un objeto se mueva circularmente.

Charles's law A principle that describes the relationship between the temperature and volume of a gas at constant pressure. (146)
ley de Charles Principio que describe la relación entre la temperatura y el volumen de un gas a una presión constante.

chemical bond The force of attraction that holds two atoms together. (98)
enlace químico Fuerza de atracción que mantiene juntos a dos átomos.

chemical change A change in which one or more substances combine or break apart to form new substances. (111)
cambio químico Cambio en el cual una o más sustancias se combinan o se descomponen para formar sustancias nuevas.

chemical energy A form of potential energy that is stored in chemical bonds between atoms. (115)
energía química Forma de energía potencial almacenada en los enlaces químicos de los átomos.

chemical equation A short, easy way to show a chemical reaction, using symbols. (258)
ecuación química Forma corta y sencilla de mostrar una reacción química usando símbolos.

chemical formula Symbols that show the elements in a compound and the ratio of atoms. (99)
fórmula química Símbolos que muestran los elementos de un compuesto y la cantidad de átomos.

chemical property A characteristic of a substance that describes its ability to change into different substances. (94)
propiedad química Característica de una sustancia que describe su capacidad de convertirse en sustancias diferentes.

chemical symbol A one- or two-letter representation of an element. (171)
símbolo químico Representación con una o dos letras de un elemento.

GLOSSARY

chemistry The study of the properties of matter and how matter changes. (93)
química Estudio de las propiedades de la materia y de sus cambios.

circuit breaker A reusable safety switch that breaks the circuit when the current becomes too high. (635)
interruptor de circuito Interruptor de seguridad reutilizable que corta un circuito cuando la corriente es demasiado alta.

classifying The process of grouping together items that are alike in some way. (6)
clasificar Proceso de agrupar objetos con algún tipo de semejanza.

closed system A system in which no matter is allowed to enter or leave. (263)
sistema cerrado Sistema en el cual la materia no puede entrar ni salir.

cochlea A fluid-filled cavity in the inner ear that is shaped like a snail shell and lined with receptor cells that respond to sound. (524)
cóclea Cavidad llena de fluido situada en el oído interno, con forma de caracol, forrada de células receptoras que responden a los sonidos.

coefficient A number in front of a chemical formula in an equation that indicates how many molecules or atoms of each reactant and product are involved in a reaction. (265)
coeficiente En un ecuación, número delante de una fórmula química que indica cuántas moléculas o átomos de cada reactante y producto intervienen en una reacción.

colloid A mixture containing small, undissolved particles that do not settle out. (289)
coloide Mezcla que contiene partículas pequeñas y sin disolver que no se depositan.

compass A device with a magnetized needle that can spin freely; a compass needle always points north. (654)
brújula Instrumento con una aguja imantada que puede girar libremente; la aguja siempre apunta hacia el norte.

complementary colors Any two colors that combine to form white light. (574)
colores complementarios Dos colores cualesquiera que se combinan para crear luz blanca.

compound A substance made of two or more elements chemically combined in a specific ratio, or proportion. (99)
compuesto Sustancia formada por dos o más elementos combinados químicamente en una razón o proporción específica.

compound machine A device that combines two or more simple machines. (414)
máquina compuesta Dispositivo que combina dos o más máquinas simples.

compression 1. Stress that squeezes rock until it folds or breaks. **2.** The part of a longitudinal wave where the particles of the medium are close together. (480)
compresión 1. Fuerza que oprime una roca hasta que se pliega o se rompe. **2.** Parte de una onda longitudinal en la que las partículas del medio están muy próximas unas con otras.

concave lens A lens that is thinner in the center than at the edges. (587)
lente cóncava Lente que es más fina en el centro que en los extremos.

concave mirror A mirror with a surface that curves inward. (579)
espejo cóncavo Espejo cuya superficie se curva hacia dentro.

concentrated solution A mixture that has a lot of solute dissolved in it. (293)
solución concentrada Mezcla que tiene muchos solutos disueltos en ella.

concentration The amount of one material in a certain volume of another material. (274)
concentración Cantidad de un material en cierto volumen de otro material.

condensation The change in state from a gas to a liquid. (140)
condensación Cambio del estado gaseoso al estado líquido.

conduction 1. The transfer of thermal energy from one particle of matter to another. **2.** A method of charging an object by allowing electrons to flow from one object to another object through direct contact. (459)
conducción 1. Transferencia de energía térmica de una partícula de materia a otra. **2.** Método de transferencia de electricidad que consiste en permitir que los electrones fluyan por contacto directo de un cuerpo a otro.

conductor 1. A material that conducts heat well. **2.** A material that allows electric charges to flow. (463)
conductor 1. Material que puede conducir bien el calor. **2.** Material que permite que las cargas eléctricas fluyan.

cones Cells in the retina that respond to and detect color. (592)
conos Células en la retina que responden y detectan el color.

conservation of charge The law that states that charges are neither created nor destroyed. (612)
conservación de carga eléctrica Ley que establece que las cargas no se crean ni se destruyen.

constructive interference The interference that occurs when two waves combine to make a wave with an amplitude larger than the amplitude of either of the individual waves. (492)
interferencia constructiva Interferencia que ocurre cuando se combinan ondas para crear una onda con una amplitud mayor a la de cualquiera de las ondas individuales.

controlled experiment An experiment in which only one variable is manipulated at a time. (22)
experimento controlado Experimento en el cual sólo se manipula una variable a la vez.

convection The transfer of thermal energy by the movement of a fluid. (459)
convección Transferencia de energía térmica por el movimiento de un líquido.

convection current The movement of a fluid, caused by differences in temperature, that transfers heat from one part of the fluid to another. (459)
corriente de convección Movimiento de un líquido ocasionado por diferencias de temperatura y que transfiere calor de un área del líquido a otra.

convex lens A lens that is thicker in the center than at the edges. (588)
lente convexa Lente que es más gruesa en el centro que en los extremos.

convex mirror A mirror with a surface that curves outward. (580)
espejo convexo Espejo cuya superficie se curva hacia fuera.

cornea The transparent tissue that covers the front of the eye. (591)
córnea Tejido transparente que cubre la parte delantera del ojo.

corrosion The gradual wearing away of a metal element due to a chemical reaction. (179)
corrosión Desgaste progresivo de un elemento metal debido a una reacción química.

corrosive The way in which acids react with some metals so as to wear away the metal. (301)
corrosivo Forma en que los ácidos reaccionan con algunos metales y los desgastan.

covalent bond A chemical bond formed when two atoms share electrons. (227)
enlace covalente Enlace químico que se forma cuando dos átomos comparten electrones.

crest The highest part of a transverse wave. (479)
cresta Parte más alta de una onda transversal.

crystal A solid in which the atoms are arranged in a pattern that repeats again and again. (224)
cristal Cuerpo sólido en el que los átomos siguen un patrón que se repite una y otra vez.

crystalline solid A solid that is made up of crystals in which particles are arranged in a regular, repeating pattern. (130)
sólido cristalino Sólido constituido por cristales en los que las partículas están colocadas en un patrón regular repetitivo.

D

data Facts, figures, and other evidence gathered through observations. (12)
dato Hechos, cifras u otra evidencia reunida por medio de observaciones.

decibel (dB) A unit used to compare the loudness of different sounds. (515)
decibelio (dB) Unidad usada para comparar el volumen de distintos sonidos.

decomposition A chemical reaction that breaks down compounds into simpler products. (268)
descomposición Reacción química que descompone los compuestos en productos más simples.

density The measurement of how much mass of a substance is contained in a given volume. (50)
densidad Medida de la masa de una sustancia que tiene un volumen dado.

dependent variable The factor that changes as a result of changes to the independent variable in an experiment; also called responding variable. (21)
variable dependiente Factor que cambia a causa de los cambios de la variable independiente de un experimento; también se denomina variable de respuesta.

destructive interference The interference that occurs when two waves combine to make a wave with an amplitude smaller than the amplitude of either of the individual waves. (493)
interferencia destructiva Interferencia que ocurre cuando dos ondas se combinan para crear una onda con una amplitud menor a la de cualquiera de las ondas individuales.

GLOSSARY

diatomic molecule A molecule consisting of two atoms. (188)
molécula diatómica Molécula que tiene dos átomos.

diffraction The bending or spreading of waves as they move around a barrier or pass through an opening. (491)
difracción Desviación de las ondas al desplazarse alrededor de una barrera o atravesar una abertura.

diffuse reflection Reflection that occurs when parallel rays of light hit an uneven surface and all reflect at different angles. (577)
reflexión difusa Reflexión que ocurre cuando rayos de luz paralelos tocan una superficie rugosa y se reflejan en diferentes ángulos.

dilute solution A mixture that has only a little solute dissolved in it. (293)
solución diluida Mezcla que sólo tiene un poco de soluto disuelto en ella.

direct current Current consisting of charges that flow in only one direction in a circuit. (671)
corriente directa Corriente de cargas eléctricas que fluyen en una sola dirección en un circuito.

directly proportional A term used to describe the relationship between two variables whose graph is a straight line passing through the point (0, 0). (147)
directamente proporcional Término empleado para describir la relación entre dos variables cuya gráfica forma una línea recta que pasa por el punto (0, 0).

distance The length of the path between two points. (325)
distancia Medida del espacio entre dos puntos.

Doppler effect The change in frequency of a wave as its source moves in relation to an observer. (516)
efecto Doppler Cambio en la frecuencia de una onda a medida que la fuente se mueve en relación al observador.

double bond A chemical bond formed when atoms share two pairs of electrons. (228)
enlace doble Enlace químico formado cuando los átomos comparten dos pares de electrones.

ductile A term used to describe a material that can be pulled out into a long wire. (178)
dúctil Término usado para describir un material que se puede estirar hasta crear un alambre largo.

E

ear canal A narrow region leading from the outside of the human ear to the eardrum. (524)
canal auditivo Región estrecha que conecta el exterior del oído humano con el tímpano.

eardrum The small, tightly stretched drumlike membrane that separates the outer ear from the middle ear, and that vibrates when sound waves strike it. (524)
tímpano Membrana pequeña, extendida y tensa como la de un tambor que separa el oído externo del oído medio y que vibra cuando la golpean las ondas sonoras.

echolocation The use of reflected sound waves to determine distances or to locate objects. (527)
ecolocación Uso de ondas sonoras reflejadas para determinar distancias o para localizar objetos.

efficiency The percentage of input work that is converted to output work. (400)
eficacia Porcentaje de trabajo aportado que se convierte en trabajo producido.

elastic potential energy The energy of stretched or compressed objects. (431)
energía elástica potencial Energía de los cuerpos estirados o comprimidos.

electric circuit A complete, unbroken path through which electric charges can flow. (618)
circuito eléctrico Trayecto completo y continuo a través del cual pueden fluir las cargas eléctricas.

electric current The continuous flow of electric charges through a material. (617)
corriente eléctrica Flujo continuo de cargas eléctricas a través de un material.

electric field The region around a charged object where the object's electric force is exerted on other charged objects. (610)
campo eléctrico Región alrededor de un objeto cargado, donde su fuerza eléctrica interactúa con otros objetos cargados eléctricamente.

electric force The force between charged objects. (609)
fuerza eléctrica Fuerza entre cuerpos cargados eléctricamente.

electric motor A device that transforms electrical energy to mechanical energy. (666)
motor eléctrico Instrumento que convierte la energía eléctrica en energía mecánica.

electrical conductivity The ability of an object to carry electric current. (178)
conductividad eléctrica Capacidad de un objeto para cargar corriente eléctrica.

electrical energy The energy of electric charges. (436)
energía eléctrica Energía de las cargas eléctricas.

electromagnet A magnet created by wrapping a coil of wire with a current running through it around a core of material that is easily magnetised. (660)
electroimán Imán creado al enrollar una espiral de alambre, por la cual fluye una corriente eléctrica, alrededor de un núcleo de material que se magnetiza fácilmente.

electromagnetic energy The energy of light and other forms of radiation, which travels through space as waves. (437)
energía electromagnética Energía de la luz y otras formas de radiación, que viaja a través del espacio en forma de ondas.

electromagnetic induction The process of generating an electric current from the motion of a conductor through a magnetic field. (669)
inducción electromagnética Proceso por el cual se genera una corriente eléctrica a partir del movimiento de un conductor a través de un campo magnético.

electromagnetic radiation The energy transferred through space by electromagnetic waves. (541)
radiación electromagnética Energía transferida a través del espacio por ondas electromagnéticas.

electromagnetic spectrum The complete range of electromagnetic waves placed in order of increasing frequency. (546)
espectro electromagnético Gama completa de ondas electromagnéticas organizadas de menor a mayor frecuencia.

electromagnetic wave 1. A wave made up of a combination of a changing electric field and a changing magnetic field. **2.** A wave that can transfer electric and magnetic energy through the vacuum of space. (541)
onda electromagnética 1. Onda formada por la combinación de un campo eléctrico cambiante y un campo magnético cambiante. **2.** Onda que puede transferir energía eléctrica y magnética a través del vacío del espacio.

electromagnetism The relationship between electricity and magnetism. (658)
electromagnetismo Relación entre la electricidad y el magnetismo.

electron A tiny, negatively charged particle that moves around the outside of the nucleus of an atom. (162)
electrón Partícula pequeña de carga negativa que se mueve alrededor del núcleo de un átomo.

electron dot diagram A representation of the valence electrons in an atom, using dots. (213)
esquema de puntos por electrones Representación del número de electrones de valencia de un átomo, usando puntos.

element A pure substance that cannot be broken down into other substances by chemical or physical means. (97)
elemento Sustancia que no se puede descomponer en otras sustancias por medios químicos o físicos.

empirical evidence Data and observations that are collected through scientific processes and that explain a particular observation. (12)
evidencia empírica Datos y observaciones que se recopilan a través de procesos científicos y que explican una observación particular.

endothermic change A change in which energy is absorbed. (115)
cambio endotérmico Cambio en el que se absorbe energía.

endothermic reaction A reaction that absorbs energy. (256)
reacción endotérmica Reacción que absorbe energía.

energy The ability to do work or cause change. (426)
energía Capacidad para realizar un trabajo o producir cambios.

energy level A region of an atom in which electrons of the same energy are likely to be found. (164)
nivel de energía Región de un átomo en la que es probable que se encuentren electrones con la misma energía.

energy transformation A change from one form of energy to another; also called an energy conversion. (438)
transformación de la energía Cambio de una forma de energía a otra; también se le llama conversión de energía.

enzyme 1. A type of protein that speeds up a chemical reaction in a living thing. **2.** A biological catalyst that lowers the activation energy of reactions in cells. (275)
enzima 1. Tipo de proteína que acelera una reacción química de un ser vivo. **2.** Catalizador biológico que disminuye la energía de activación de las reacciones celulares.

GLOSSARY

estimate An approximation of a number based on reasonable assumptions. (55)
estimación Aproximación de un número basada en conjeturas razonables.

evaporation The process by which molecules at the surface of a liquid absorb enough energy to change to a gas. (139)
evaporación Proceso mediante el cual las moléculas en la superficie de un líquido absorben suficiente energía para pasar al estado gaseoso.

evidence Observations and conclusions that have been repeated. (29)
evidencia Observaciones y conclusiones que se han repetido.

exothermic change A change in which energy is released. (115)
cambio exotérmico Cambio en el que se libera energía.

exothermic reaction A reaction that releases energy, usually in the form of heat. (256)
reacción exotérmica Reacción que libera energía generalmente en forma de calor.

eyepiece A lens that magnifies the image formed by the objective. (596)
ocular Lente que aumenta la imagen formada por el objetivo.

F

Fahrenheit scale The temperature scale on which water freezes at 32°F and boils at 212°F. (455)
escala Fahrenheit Escala de temperatura en la que el punto de congelación del agua es 32°F y el punto de ebullición es 212°F.

farsighted Having the condition in which a person can see distant objects clearly and nearby objects as blurry. (593)
hipermetropía Condición en la que una persona ve con claridad los objetos lejanos y ve borrosos los objetos cercanos.

feedback Output that changes a system or allows the system to adjust itself. (71)
retroalimentación Salida que cambia un sistema o permite que éste se ajuste.

field Any area outside of the laboratory. (77)
campo Cualquier área fuera del laboratorio.

fluid Any substance that can flow. (131)
fluido Cualquier sustancia que puede fluir.

fluid friction Friction that occurs as an object moves through a fluid. (357)
fricción de fluido Fricción que ocurre cuando un cuerpo se mueve a través de un fluido.

focal point The point at which light rays parallel to the optical axis meet, or appear to meet, after being reflected (or refracted) by a mirror (or a lens). (579)
punto de enfoque Punto en el que se encuentran, o parecen encontrarse, los rayos de luz paralelos al eje óptico después de reflejarse (o refractarse) en un espejo (o lente).

force A push or pull exerted on an object. (351)
fuerza Empuje o atracción que se ejerce sobre un cuerpo.

free fall The motion of a falling object when the only force acting on it is gravity. (375)
caída libre Movimiento de un objeto que cae cuando la única fuerza que actúa sobre éste es la gravedad.

freezing The change in state from a liquid to a solid. (138)
congelación Cambio del estado líquido al sólido.

frequency The number of complete waves that pass a given point in a certain amount of time. (484)
frecuencia Número de ondas completas que pasan por un punto dado en cierto tiempo.

frequency modulation A method of transmitting signals by changing the frequency of a wave. (554)
frecuencia modulada Método de transmisión de señales mediante el cambio de la frecuencia de una onda.

friction **1.** The force that two surfaces exert on each other when they rub against each other. **2.** The transfer of electrons from one uncharged object to another uncharged object by rubbing. (355)
fricción **1.** Fuerza que dos superficies ejercen una sobre la otra al frotarse. **2.** Transferencia de electrones al frotarse un cuerpo no cargado con otro cuerpo no cargado.

fulcrum The fixed point around which a lever pivots. (406)
fulcro Punto fijo en torno al cual gira una palanca.

fundamental tone The lowest natural frequency of an object. (519)
tono fundamental Frecuencia natural más baja de un cuerpo.

fuse A safety device with a thin metal strip that will melt if too much current passes through a circuit. (635)
fusible Elemento de seguridad que tiene una tira metálica delgada que se derrite si una corriente demasiado fuerte pasa por un circuito.

G

galvanometer A device that uses an electromagnet to detect small amounts of current. (664)
galvanómetro Instrumento que usa un electroimán para detectar la intensidad de una pequeña corriente.

gamma rays Electromagnetic waves with the shortest wavelengths and highest frequencies. (197, 550)
rayos gamma Ondas electromagnéticas con la menor longitud de onda y la mayor frecuencia.

gas A state of matter with no definite shape or volume. (133)
gas Estado de la materia sin forma ni volumen definidos.

generator A device that transforms mechanical energy into electrical energy. (672)
generador eléctrico Instrumento que convierte la energía mecánica en energía eléctrica.

graph A picture of information from a data table; shows the relationship between variables. (63)
gráfica Representación visual de la información de una tabla de datos; muestra la relación entre las variables.

gravitational potential energy Potential energy that depends on the height of an object. (430)
energía gravitatoria potencial Energía potencial que depende de la altura de un cuerpo.

gravity The attractive force between objects; the force that moves objects downhill. (359)
gravedad Fuerza que atrae a los cuerpos entre sí; fuerza que mueve un cuerpo cuesta abajo.

grounded Allowing charges to flow directly from the circuit into the building's ground wire and then into Earth in the event of a short circuit. (635)
conectado a tierra Permitir que las cargas eléctricas fluyan directamente del circuito al cable a tierra del edificio y luego a la Tierra en caso de un cortocircuito.

group Elements in the same vertical column of the periodic table; also called family. (175)
grupo Elementos en la misma columna vertical de la tabla periódica; también llamado familia.

H

half-life The time it takes for half of the atoms of a radioactive element to decay. (199)
vida media Tiempo que toma descomponer la mitad de los átomos de un elemento radiactivo.

halogen An element found in Group 17 of the periodic table. (189)
halógeno Elemento del Grupo 17 de la tabla periódica.

heat The transfer of thermal energy from a warmer object to a cooler object. (457)
calor Transferencia de energía térmica de un cuerpo más cálido a uno menos cálido.

hertz (Hz) Unit of measurement for frequency. (484)
hercio (Hz) Unidad de medida de la frecuencia.

hydrogen ion A positively charged ion (H^+) formed of a hydrogen atom that has lost its electron. (307)
ión hidrógeno Ión de carga positiva (H^+) formado por un átomo de hidrógeno que ha perdido su electrón.

hydroxide ion A negatively charged ion made of oxygen and hydrogen (OH^-). (308)
ión hidróxido Ión de carga negativa formado de oxígeno e hidrógeno (OH^-).

hypothesis A possible explanation for a set of observations or answer to a scientific question; must be testable. (20)
hipótesis Explicación posible de un conjunto de observaciones o respuesta a una pregunta científica; se debe poder poner a prueba.

I

image A copy of an object formed by reflected or refracted rays of light. (577)
imagen Copia de un objeto formada por rayos de luz que se reflejan y se refractan.

inclined plane A simple machine that is a flat, sloped surface. (403)
plano inclinado Máquina simple que consiste en una superficie plana con pendiente.

independent variable The one factor that a scientist changes during an experiment; also called manipulated variable. (21)
variable independiente El único factor que un científico altera durante un experimento; también se denomina variable manipulada.

GLOSSARY

indicator A compound that changes color in the presence of an acid or a base. (302)
indicador Compuesto que cambia de color en presencia de un ácido o una base.

index of refraction A measure of the amount a ray of light bends when it passes from one medium to another. (584)
índice de refracción Medida de la inclinación de un rayo de luz cuando pasa de un medio a otro.

induction A method of redistributing the charge on an object by means of the electric field of another object; the objects have no direct contact. (613)
inducción Método de redistribuir la carga de un cuerpo haciendo uso del campo eléctrico de otro; los cuerpos no están en contacto directo.

inertia The tendency of an object to resist a change in motion. (363)
inercia Tendencia de un cuerpo de resistirse a cambios de movimiento.

inferring The process of making an inference, an interpretation based on observations and prior knowledge. (6)
inferir Proceso de hacer una inferencia; interpretación basada en observaciones y conocimientos previos.

infrared rays Electromagnetic waves with shorter wavelengths and higher frequencies than microwaves. (548)
rayos infrarrojos Ondas electromagnéticas con longitudes de onda más cortas y frecuencias más altas que las microondas.

inhibitor A material that decreases the rate of a reaction. (275)
inhibidor Material que disminuye la velocidad de una reacción.

input Material, energy, or information that goes into a system. (70)
entrada Material, energía o informacion que se agrega a un sistema.

input force The force exerted on a machine. (395)
fuerza aplicada Fuerza que se ejerce sobre una máquina.

instantaneous speed The speed of an object at one instant of time. (329)
velocidad instantánea Velocidad de un objeto en un instante del tiempo.

insulator 1. A material that does not conduct heat well. 2. A material that does not easily allow electric charges to flow. (463)
aislante 1. Material que no conduce bien el calor. 2. Material que no permite fácilmente que las cargas eléctricas fluyan.

intensity The amount of energy per second carried through a unit area by a wave. (514)
intensidad Cantidad de energía por segundo que transporta una onda a través de una unidad de área.

interference The interaction between waves that meet. (492)
interferencia Interacción entre dos o más ondas que se encuentran.

International System of Units (SI) A system of units used by scientists to measure the properties of matter. (45, 104)
Sistema Internacional de Unidades (SI) Sistema de unidades que los científicos usan para medir las propiedades de la materia.

inversely proportional A term used to describe the relationship between two variables whose product is constant. (149)
inversamente proporcional Término usado para describir la relación entre dos variables cuyo producto es constante.

ion An atom or group of atoms that has become electrically charged. (219)
ión Átomo o grupo de átomos que está cargado eléctricamente.

ionic bond The attraction between oppositely charged ions. (220)
enlace iónico Atracción entre iones con cargas opuestas.

ionic compound A compound that consists of positive and negative ions. (220)
compuesto iónico Compuesto que tiene iones positivos y negativos.

iris The ring of muscle that surrounds the pupil and regulates the amount of light entering the eye; gives the eye its color. (591)
iris Disco de músculo que rodea la pupila y regula la cantidad de luz que entra al ojo; da color al ojo.

isotope An atom with the same number of protons and a different number of neutrons from other atoms of the same element. (167)
isótopo Átomo con el mismo número de protones y un número diferente de neutrones que otros átomos del mismo elemento.

J

joule The amount of work you do when you exert a force of 1 newton to move an object a distance of 1 meter. (391)
julio Cantidad de trabajo que se produce al aplicar una fuerza de 1 newton para mover un objeto una distancia de 1 metro.

K

Kelvin scale The temperature scale on which zero is the temperature at which no more energy can be removed from matter. (455)
escala Kelvin Escala de temperatura en la cual el cero es la temperatura a cuyo punto no se puede extraer más energía de la materia.

kinetic energy Energy that an object has due to its motion. (428)
energía cinética Energía que tiene un cuerpo debido a su movimiento.

L

law of conservation of energy The rule that energy cannot be created or destroyed. (442)
ley de conservación de la energía Regla que dice que la energía no se puede crear ni destruir.

law of conservation of mass The principle that the total amount of matter is neither created nor destroyed during any chemical or physical change. (113)
ley de conservación de la masa Principio que establece que la cantidad total de materia no se crea ni se destruye durante cambios químicos o físicos.

law of conservation of momentum The rule that in the absence of outside forces the total momentum of objects that interact does not change. (372)
principio de la conservación del momento Regla que establece que, en ausencia de fuerzas externas, la cantidad de movimiento total de los cuerpos que se relacionan no cambia.

lens 1. The flexible structure that focuses light that has entered the eye. **2.** A curved piece of glass or other transparent material that is used to refract light. (587)
lente 1. Estructura flexible que enfoca la luz que entra al ojo. **2.** Trozo curvo de vidrio u otro material transparente que se usa para refractar la luz.

lever A simple machine that consists of a rigid bar that pivots about a fixed point. (406)
palanca Máquina simple que consiste en una barra rígida que gira en torno a un punto fijo.

linear graph A line graph in which the data points yield a straight line. (64)
gráfica lineal Gráfica en la cual los puntos de los datos forman una línea recta.

liquid A state of matter that has no definite shape but has a definite volume. (131)
líquido Estado de la materia que no tiene forma definida pero sí volumen definido.

longitudinal wave A wave that moves the medium in a direction parallel to the direction in which the wave travels. (480)
onda longitudinal Onda que mueve al medio en una dirección paralela a la dirección en la que se propaga la onda.

loudness Perception of the energy of a sound. (514)
volumen Percepción de la energía de un sonido.

luster The way a mineral reflects light from its surface. (178)
lustre Manera en la que un mineral refleja la luz en su superficie.

M

machine A device that changes the amount of force exerted, the distance over which a force is exerted, or the direction in which force is exerted. (395)
máquina Dispositivo que altera la cantidad de fuerza ejercida, la distancia sobre que se ejerce la fuerza, o la dirección en la que se ejerce la fuerza.

magnet Any material that attracts iron and materials that contain iron. (647)
imán Material que atrae hierro o materiales que contienen el hierro.

magnetic declination The angle between geographic north and the north to which a compass needle points. (655)
declinación magnética Ángulo (en una ubicación particular) entre el norte geográfico y el polo magnético ubicado en el hemisferio norte de la Tierra.

magnetic field The region around a magnet where the magnetic force is exerted. (651)
campo magnético Área alrededor de un imán donde actúa la fuerza magnética.

GLOSSARY

magnetic field lines Lines that map out the magnetic field around a magnet. (651)
líneas del campo magnético Líneas que representan el campo magnético alrededor de un imán.

magnetic force A force produced when magnetic poles interact. (649)
fuerza magnética Fuerza que se produce cuando hay actividad entre los polos magnéticos.

magnetic pole The ends of a magnetic object, where the magnetic force is strongest. (648)
polo magnético Extremo de un cuerpo magnético, donde la fuerza magnética es mayor.

magnetism The force of attraction or repulsion of magnetic materials. (647)
magnetismo Poder de atracción o repulsión de los materiales magnéticos.

malleable A term used to describe material that can be hammered or rolled into flat sheets. (178)
maleable Término usado para describir materiales que se pueden convertir en láminas planas por medio de martillazos o con un rodillo.

mass A measure of how much matter is in an object. (48)
masa Medida de cuánta materia hay en un cuerpo.

mass number The sum of protons and neutrons in the nucleus of an atom. (167)
número de masa Suma de los protones y neutrones en el núcleo de un átomo.

matter Anything that has mass and takes up space. (93)
materia Cualquier cosa que tiene masa y ocupa un espacio.

mean The numerical average of a set of data. (58)
media Promedio numérico de un conjunto de datos.

mechanical advantage The number of times a machine increases a force exerted on it. (398)
ventaja mecánica Número de veces que una máquina amplifica la fuerza que se ejerce sobre ella.

mechanical energy Kinetic or potential energy associated with the motion or position of an object. (432)
energía mecánica Energía cinética o potencial asociada con el movimiento o la posición de un cuerpo.

mechanical wave A wave that requires a medium through which to travel. (477)
onda mecánica Onda que necesita un medio por el cual propagarse.

median The middle number in a set of data. (58)
mediana Número del medio de un conjunto de datos.

medium The material through which a wave travels. (477)
medio Material a través del cual se propaga una onda.

melting The change in state from a solid to a liquid. (137)
fusión Cambio del estado sólido a líquido.

melting point The temperature at which a substance changes from a solid to a liquid; the same as the freezing point, or temperature at which a liquid changes to a solid. (137)
punto de fusión Temperatura a la que una sustancia cambia de estado sólido a líquido; es lo mismo que el punto de congelación (la temperatura a la que un líquido se vuelve sólido).

meniscus The curved upper surface of a liquid in a column of liquid. (49)
menisco Superficie superior curva de un líquido en una columna de líquido.

metal A class of elements characterized by physical properties that include shininess, malleability, ductility, and conductivity. (177)
metal Clase de elementos caracterizados por propiedades físicas que incluyen brillo, maleabilidad, ductilidad y conductividad.

metallic bond An attraction between a positive metal ion and the electrons surrounding it. (235)
enlace metálico Atracción entre un ión metálico positivo y los electrones que lo rodean.

metalloid An element that has some characteristics of both metals and nonmetals. (191)
metaloide Elemento que tiene algunas características de los metales y de los no metales.

metric system A system of measurement based on the number 10. (45)
sistema métrico Sistema de medidas basado en el número 10.

microscope An instrument that makes small objects look larger. (597)
microscopio Instrumento que permite que los objetos pequeños se vean más grandes.

microwaves Electromagnetic waves that have shorter wavelengths and higher frequencies than radio waves. (547)
microondas Ondas electromagnéticas con longitudes de onda más cortas y frecuencias más altas que las ondas de radio.

mirage An image of a distant object caused by refraction of light as it travels through air of varying temperature. (586)
espejismo Imagen de un objeto distante causada por la refracción de la luz cuando viaja por el aire a temperaturas cambiantes.

mixture Two or more substances that are together in the same place but their atoms are not chemically bonded. (100)
mezcla Dos o más sustancias que están en el mismo lugar pero cuyos átomos no están químicamente enlazados.

mode The number that appears most often in a list of numbers. (58)
moda Número que aparece con más frecuencia en una lista de números.

model A representation of a complex object or process, used to help people understand a concept that they cannot observe directly. (69)
modelo Representación de un objeto o proceso complejo que se usa para explicar un concepto que no se puede observar directamente.

molecular compound A compound that is composed of molecules. (229)
compuesto molecular Compuesto que tiene moléculas.

molecule A neutral group of two or more atoms held together by covalent bonds. (98)
molécula Grupo neutral de dos o más átomos unidos por medio de enlaces covalentes.

momentum The product of an object's mass and velocity. (371)
momento Producto de la masa de un cuerpo multiplicada por su velocidad.

motion The state in which one object's distance from another is changing. (322)
movimiento Estado en el que la distancia entre un cuerpo y otro va cambiando.

music A set of sounds or notes combined in ways that are pleasing. (518)
música Conjunto de sonidos o notas que se combinan de una manera agradable.

N

nearsighted Having the condition in which a person can see nearby objects clearly and distant objects as blurry. (593)
miopía Condición en la que una persona ve con claridad los objetos cercanos y ve borrosos los objetos lejanos.

neutralization A reaction of an acid with a base, yielding a solution that is not as acidic or basic as the starting solutions were. (310)
neutralización Reacción de un ácido con una base, que produce una solución que no es ácida ni básica, como lo eran las soluciones originales.

neutron A small particle in the nucleus of the atom, with no electrical charge. (165)
neutrón Partícula pequeña en el núcleo del átomo, que no tiene carga eléctrica.

newton A unit of measure that equals the force required to accelerate 1 kilogram of mass at 1 meter per second per second. (351)
newton Unidad de medida equivalente a la fuerza necesaria para acelerar 1 kilogramo de masa a 1 metro por segundo cada segundo.

net force The overall force on an object when all the individual forces acting on it are added together. (352)
fuerza neta Fuerza total que se ejerce sobre un cuerpo cuando se suman las fuerzas individuales que actúan sobre él.

noble gas An element in Group 18 of the periodic table. (190)
gas noble Elemento del Grupo 18 de la tabla periódica.

node A point of zero amplitude on a standing wave. (494)
nodo Punto de amplitud cero de una onda estacionaria.

nonlinear graph A line graph in which the data points do not fall along a straight line. (64)
gráfica no lineal Gráfica lineal en la que los puntos de datos no forman una línea recta.

nonmetal An element that lacks most of the properties of a metal. (185)
no metal Elemento que carece de la mayoría de las propiedades de un metal.

nonpolar bond A covalent bond in which electrons are shared equally. (231)
enlace no polar Enlace covalente en el que los electrones se comparten por igual.

GLOSSARY

nuclear energy The potential energy stored in the nucleus of an atom. (435)
energía nuclear Energía potencial almacenada en el núcleo de un átomo.

nuclear reaction A reaction involving the particles in the nucleus of an atom that can change one element into another element. (195)
reacción nuclear Reacción en la que intervienen las partículas del núcleo de un átomo que puede transformar un elemento en otro.

nucleus 1. In cells, a large oval organelle that contains the cell's genetic material in the form of DNA and controls many of the cell's activities. **2.** The central core of an atom which contains protons and neutrons. **3.** The solid core of a comet. (163)
núcleo 1. En las células, orgánulo grande y ovalado que contiene el material genético de la célula en forma de ADN y que controla muchas de las funciones celulares. **2.** Parte central del átomo que contiene los protones y los neutrones. **3.** Centro sólido de un cometa.

O

objective 1. A lens that gathers light from an object and forms a real image. **2.** Describes the act of decision-making or drawing conclusions based on available evidence. (596)
objetivo 1. Lente que reúne la luz de un objeto y forma una imagen real. **2.** Describe el acto de tomar una decisión o llegar a una conclusión basándose en la evidencia disponible.

objective reasoning Reasoning based on evidence. (14)
razonamiento objetivo Razonamiento basado en la evidencia.

observing The process of using one or more of your senses to gather information. (5)
observar Proceso de usar uno o más de tus sentidos para reunir información.

Ohm's law The law that states that resistance in a circuit is equal to voltage divided by current. (626)
ley de Ohm Regla que establece que la resistencia en un circuito es equivalente al voltaje dividido por la corriente.

opaque A type of material that reflects or absorbs all of the light that strikes it. (571)
material opaco Material que refleja o absorbe toda la luz que llega a él.

open system A system in which matter can enter from or escape to the surroundings. (263)
sistema abierto Sistema en el que la materia puede escapar a sus alrededores o entrar desde ahí.

opinion An idea about a situation that is not supported by evidence. (29)
opinión Idea sobre una situación que la evidencia no sustenta.

optic nerve Short, thick nerve that carries signals from the eye to the brain. (592)
nervio óptico Nervio corto y grueso que lleva señales del ojo al cerebro.

optical axis An imaginary line that divides a mirror in half. (579)
eje óptico Recta imaginaria que divide un espejo por la mitad.

outlier An abnormal or irregular data point; a point on a graph that is clearly not part of the trend. (64)
valor atípico Punto de datos anormal o irregular; punto en una gráfica que se aleja demasiado de los valores esperados.

output Material, energy, result, or product that comes out of a system. (70)
salida Material, energía, resultado o producto que un sistema produce.

output force The force exerted on an object by a machine. (395)
fuerza desarrollada Fuerza que una máquina ejerce sobre un cuerpo.

overtone A natural frequency that is a multiple of the fundamental tone's frequency. (519)
armónico Frecuencia natural que es un múltiplo de la frecuencia del tono fundamental.

P

parallel circuit An electric circuit in which different parts of the circuit are on separate branches. (629)
circuito paralelo Circuito eléctrico en el que las distintas partes del circuito se encuentran en ramas separadas.

percent error A calculation used to determine how accurate, or close to the true value, an experimental value really is. (60)
error porcentual Cálculo usado para determinar cuán exacto, o cercano al valor verdadero, es realmente un valor experimental.

period 1. A horizontal row of elements in the periodic table. 2. One of the units of geologic time into which geologists divide eras. (174)
período 1. Fila horizontal de los elementos de la tabla periódica. 2. Una de las unidades del tiempo geológico en las que los geólogos dividen las eras.

periodic table An arrangement of the elements showing the repeating pattern of their properties. (170)
tabla periódica Configuración de los elementos que muestra el patrón repetido de sus propiedades.

pH scale A range of values used to indicate how acidic or basic a substance is; expresses the concentration of hydrogen ions in a solution. (308)
escala de pH Rango de valores que se usa para indicar cuán ácida o básica es una sustancia; expresa la concentración de iones hidrógeno de una solución.

photoelectric effect The ejection of electrons from a substance when light is shined on it. (543)
efecto fotoeléctrico Expulsión de electrones de una sustancia al ser iluminada.

photon A tiny particle or packet of light energy. (543)
fotón Partícula diminuta o paquete de energía luminosa.

physical change A change that alters the form or appearance of a material but does not make the material into another substance. (109, 252)
cambio físico Cambio que altera la forma o apariencia de un material, pero que no convierte el material en otra sustancia.

physical property A characteristic of a pure substance that can be observed without changing it into another substance. (94)
propiedad física Característica de una sustancia pura que se puede observar sin convertirla en otra sustancia.

pigment 1. A colored chemical compound that absorbs light. 2. A colored substance used to color other materials. (575)
pigmento 1. Compuesto químico que absorbe luz. 2. Sustancia de color que se usa para teñir otros materiales.

pitch A description of how a sound is perceived as high or low. (512)
tono Descripción de un sonido que se percibe como alto o bajo.

plane mirror A flat mirror that produces an upright, virtual image the same size as the object. (578)
espejo plano Espejo liso que produce una imagen virtual vertical del mismo tamaño que el objeto.

polar bond A covalent bond in which electrons are shared unequally. (231)
enlace polar Enlace covalente en el que los electrones se comparten de forma desigual.

polarization The process through which electrons are attracted to or repelled by an external electric field, causing the electrons to move within their own atoms. (613)
polarización Proceso por el cual un campo eléctrico externo atrae o repele a los electrones y hace que éstos se muevan dentro de su átomo.

polarized light Light that has been filtered so that all of its waves are parallel to each other. (542)
luz polarizada Luz que se ha filtrado de manera que sus ondas queden paralelas unas con otras.

polyatomic ion An ion that is made of more than one atom. (220)
ión poliatómico Ión formado por más de un átomo.

potential energy The energy an object has because of its position; also the internal stored energy of an object, such as energy stored in chemical bonds. (430)
energía potencial Energía que tiene un cuerpo por su posición; también es la energía interna almacenada de un cuerpo, como la energía almacenada en los enlaces químicos.

power The rate at which one form of energy is transformed into another. (392)
potencia Rapidez de la conversión de una forma de energía en otra.

precipitate A solid that forms from a solution during a chemical reaction. (254)
precipitado Sólido que se forma de una solución durante una reacción química.

precision How close a group of measurements are to each other. (56)
precisión Cuán cerca se encuentran un grupo de medidas.

predicting The process of forecasting what will happen in the future based on past experience or evidence. (7)
predecir Proceso de pronosticar lo que va a suceder en el futuro, basándose en evidencia o experiencias previas.

pressure The force pushing on a surface divided by the area of that surface. (134)
presión Fuerza que actúa contra una superficie, dividida entre el área de esa superficie.

GLOSSARY

primary color One of three colors that can be used to make any other color. (574)
color primario Uno de los tres colores que se pueden usar para hacer cualquier color.

process A sequence of actions in a system. (70)
proceso Secuencia de acciones en un sistema.

product A substance formed as a result of a chemical reaction. (252)
producto Sustancia formada como resultado de una reacción química.

protons Small, positively charged particles that are found in the nucleus of an atom. (163)
protones Partículas pequeñas de carga positiva que se encuentran en el núcleo de un átomo.

pseudoscience A set of beliefs that may make use of science but whose conclusions and predictions are not based on observation, objective reasoning, or scientific evidence. (15)
pseudociencia Conjunto de creencias que pueden basarse en la ciencia, pero cuyas conclusiones no se derivan de la observación, el razonamiento objetivo o la evidencia científica.

pulley A simple machine that consists of a grooved wheel with a rope or cable wrapped around it. (411)
polea Máquina simple que consiste en una rueda con un surco en el que yace una cuerda o cable.

pupil The opening in the center of the iris through which light enters the inside of the eye. (591)
pupila Apertura en el centro del iris por donde entra la luz al ojo.

Q

qualitative observation An observation that deals with characteristics that cannot be expressed in numbers. (5)
observación cualitativa Observación que se centra en las características que no se pueden expresar con números.

quantitative observation An observation that deals with a number or amount. (5)
observación cuantitativa Observación que se centra en un número o cantidad.

R

radar A system that uses reflected radio waves to detect objects and measure their distance and speed. (547)
radar Sistema que usa ondas de radio reflejadas para detectar cuerpos y medir su distancia y velocidad.

radiation The transfer of energy by electromagnetic waves. (459)
radiación Transferencia de energía por medio de ondas magnéticas.

radio waves Electromagnetic waves with the longest wavelengths and lowest frequencies. (546)
ondas de radio Ondas electromagnéticas con las longitudes de onda más largas y las frecuencias más bajas.

radioactive dating The process of determining the age of an object using the half-life of one or more radioactive isotopes. (199)
datación radiactiva Proceso para determinar la edad de un objeto usando la vida media de uno o más isótopos radiactivos.

radioactive decay The process in which the nuclei of radioactive elements break down, releasing fast-moving particles and energy. (195)
desintegración radiactiva Proceso de descomposición del núcleo de un elemento radiactivo que libera partículas de movimiento rápido y energía.

radioactivity The spontaneous emission of radiation by an unstable atomic nucleus. (196)
radiactividad Emisión espontánea de radiación por un núcleo atómico inestable.

range The difference between the greatest value and the least value in a set of data. (58)
rango Diferencia entre el mayor y el menor valor de un conjunto de datos.

rarefaction The part of a longitudinal wave where the particles of the medium are far apart. (480)
rarefacción Parte de una onda longitudinal donde las partículas del medio están muy apartadas entre sí.

ray A straight line used to represent a light wave. (576)
rayo Línea recta que se usa para representar una onda de luz.

reactant A substance that enters into a chemical reaction. (252)
reactante Sustancia que interviene en una reacción química.

reactivity The ease and speed with which an element combines, or reacts, with other elements and compounds. (179)
reactividad Facilidad y rapidez con las que un elemento se combina, o reacciona, con otros elementos y compuestos.

real image An upside-down image formed where rays of light meet. (579)
imagen real Imagen invertida formada en el punto de encuentro de los rayos de luz.

reference point A place or object used for comparison to determine if an object is in motion. (323)
punto de referencia Lugar u objeto usado como medio de comparación para determinar si un objeto está en movimiento.

reflecting telescope A telescope that uses a curved mirror to collect and focus light. (596)
telescopio de reflexión Telescopio que usa un espejo curvado para captar y enfocar la luz.

reflection The bouncing back of an object or a wave when it hits a surface through which it cannot pass. (489)
reflexión Rebote de un cuerpo o una onda al golpear una superficie que no puede atravesar.

refracting telescope A telescope that uses convex lenses to gather and focus light. (596)
telescopio de refracción Telescopio que usa lentes convexas para captar y enfocar la luz.

refraction The bending of waves as they enter a new medium at an angle, caused by a change in speed. (490)
refracción Cambio de dirección de las ondas al entrar en un nuevo medio con un determinado ángulo, y a consecuencia de un cambio de velocidad.

regular reflection Reflection that occurs when parallel rays of light hit a smooth surface and all reflect at the same angle. (577)
reflexión regular Reflexión que ocurre cuando rayos de luz paralelos chocan contra una superficie lisa y se reflejan en el mismo ángulo.

repeated trial A repetition of an experiment to gather additional data and determine whether the experiment's results support the hypothesis. (24)
prueba repetida Repetición de un experimento para recopilar datos adicionales y determinar si los resultados de un experimento sustentan la hipótesis.

replacement A reaction in which one element replaces another in a compound or when two elements in different compounds trade places. (268)
sustitución Reacción en la que un elemento reemplaza a otro en un compuesto o en la que se intercambian dos elementos de diferentes compuestos.

replication An attempt to repeat a scientist's experiment by a different scientist or group of scientists. (25)
replicación Intento, por parte de un científico o grupo de científicos, de repetir el experimento de otro científico.

resistance The measurement of how difficult it is for charges to flow through an object. (622)
resistencia Medida de la dificultad de una carga eléctrica para fluir por un cuerpo.

resonance The increase in the amplitude of a vibration that occurs when external vibrations match an object's natural frequency. (495)
resonancia Aumento en la amplitud de vibración que ocurre cuando vibraciones externas corresponden con la frecuencia natural de un cuerpo.

retina The layer of receptor cells at the back of the eye on which an image is focused. (592)
retina Capa de células receptoras de la parte posterior del ojo donde se enfoca una imagen.

rods Cells in the retina that detect dim light. (592)
bastones Células de la retina que detectan la luz tenue.

rolling friction Friction that occurs when an object rolls over a surface. (357)
fricción de rodamiento Fricción que ocurre cuando un cuerpo rueda sobre una superficie.

S

salt An ionic compound made from the neutralization of an acid with a base. (311)
sal Compuesto iónico formado por la neutralización de un ácido con una base.

satellite 1. An object that orbits a planet. **2.** Any object that orbits around another object in space. (376)
satélite 1. Cuerpo que orbita alrededor de un planeta. **2.** Cualquier cuerpo que orbita alrededor de otro cuerpo en el espacio.

GLOSSARY

saturated solution A mixture that contains as much dissolved solute as is possible at a given temperature. (295)
solución saturada Mezcla que contiene la mayor cantidad posible de soluto disuelto a una temperatura determinada.

science A way of learning about the natural world through observations and logical reasoning; leads to a body of knowledge. (5)
ciencia Estudio del mundo natural a través de observaciones y del razonamiento lógico; conduce a un conjunto de conocimientos.

scientific explanation A generalization that makes sense of observations by using logical reasoning. (26)
explicación científica Generalización que usa el razonamiento lógico para darle sentido a las observaciones.

scientific inquiry The ongoing process of discovery in science; the diverse ways in which scientists study the natural world and propose explanations based on evidence they gather. (19)
indagación científica Proceso continuo de descubrimiento en la ciencia; diversidad de métodos con los que los científicos estudian el mundo natural y proponen explicaciones del mismo basadas en la evidencia que reúnen.

scientific literacy The knowledge and understanding of scientific terms and principles required for evaluating information, making personal decisions, and taking part in public affairs. (29)
conocimiento científico Conocimiento y comprensión de los términos y principios científicos necesarios para evaluar información, tomar decisiones personales y participar en actividades públicas.

scientific notation A mathematical method of writing numbers using powers of ten. (59)
notación científica Método matemático de escritura de números que usa la potencia de diez.

screw A simple machine that is an inclined plane wrapped around a central cylinder to form a spiral. (405)
tornillo Máquina simple que consiste en un plano inclinado enrollado alrededor de un cilindro central para formar una espiral.

secondary color Any color produced by combining equal amounts of any two primary colors. (574)
color secundario Color producido al combinar iguales cantidades de dos colores primarios cualesquiera.

semiconductor A substance that can conduct electric current under some conditions. (191)
semiconductor Sustancia que puede conducir una corriente eléctrica bajo ciertas condiciones.

series circuit An electric circuit in which all parts are connected one after another along one path. (628)
circuito en serie Circuito eléctrico en el que todas las partes se conectan una tras otra en una trayectoria.

short circuit A connection that allows current to take the path of least resistance. (635)
cortocircuito Conexión que permite que la corriente siga el camino de menor resistencia.

significant figures All the digits in a measurement that have been measured exactly, plus one digit whose value has been estimated. (57)
cifras significativas En una medida, todos los dígitos que se han medido con exactitud, más un dígito cuyo valor se ha estimado.

simple machine The most basic device for making work easier, these are the smaller building blocks for complex machines. (403)
máquina simple Aparatos sencillos que facilitan el trabajo; son los componentes de las máquinas compuestas.

skepticism An attitude of doubt. (11)
escepticismo Actitud de duda.

sliding friction Friction that occurs when one solid surface slides over another. (356)
fricción de deslizamiento Fricción que ocurre cuando una superficie sólida se desliza sobre otra.

slope The steepness of a graph line; the ratio of the vertical change (the rise) to the horizontal change (the run). (332)
pendiente Inclinación de una gráfica lineal; la razón del cambio vertical (el ascenso) al cambio horizontal (el avance).

solenoid A coil of wire with a current. (660)
solenoide Bobina de alambre con una corriente.

solid A state of matter that has a definite shape and a definite volume. (129)
sólido Estado en el que la materia tiene forma y volumen definidos.

solubility A measure of how much solute can dissolve in a given solvent at a given temperature. (295)
solubilidad Medida de cuánto soluto se puede disolver en un solvente a una temperatura dada.

solute The part of a solution that is dissolved by a solvent. (287)
soluto Parte de una solución que se disuelve en un solvente.

solution A mixture containing a solvent and at least one solute that has the same properties throughout; a mixture in which one substance is dissolved in another. (287)
solución Mezcla que contiene un solvente y al menos un soluto, y que tiene propiedades uniformes; mezcla en la que una sustancia se disuelve en otra.

solvent The part of a solution that is usually present in the largest amount and dissolves a solute. (287)
solvente Parte de una solución que, por lo general, está presente en la mayor cantidad y que disuelve a un soluto.

sonar A system that uses reflected sound waves to locate and determine the distance to objects under water. (528)
sónar Sistema que usa ondas sonoras reflejadas para detectar y localizar objetos bajo agua.

sonogram An image formed using reflected ultrasound waves. (529)
sonograma Formación de una imagen usando ondas de ultrasonido reflejadas.

specific heat The amount of heat required to raise the temperature of 1 kilogram of a material by 1 kelvin, which is equivalent to 1°C. (464)
calor específico Cantidad de calor que se requiere para elevar la temperatura de 1 kilogramo de un material en 1°C.

speed The distance an object travels per unit of time. (327)
rapidez Distancia que viaja un objeto por unidad de tiempo.

standing wave A wave that appears to stand in one place, even though it is two waves interfering as they pass through each other. (494)
onda estacionaria Onda que parece permanecer en un lugar, y que en realidad es la interferencia de dos ondas que se atraviesan.

static discharge The loss of static electricity as electric charges transfer from one object to another. (614)
descarga estática Pérdida de la electricidad estática cuando las cargas eléctricas se transfieren de un cuerpo a otro.

static electricity A buildup of charges on an object. (611)
electricidad estática Acumulación de cargas eléctricas en un cuerpo.

static friction Friction that acts between objects that are not moving. (356)
fricción estática Fricción que actúa sobre los cuerpos que no están en movimiento.

subjective reasoning Reasoning based on personal feelings or values. (14)
razonamiento subjetivo Razonamiento basado en los sentimientos o los valores personales.

sublimation The change in state from a solid directly to a gas without passing through the liquid state. (141)
sublimación Cambio del estado sólido directamente a gas, sin pasar por el estado líquido.

subscript A number in a chemical formula that tells the number of atoms in a molecule or the ratio of elements in a compound. (222)
subíndice Número en una fórmula química que indica el número de átomos que tiene una molécula o la razón de elementos en un compuesto.

substance A single kind of matter that is pure and has a specific set of properties. (93)
sustancia Tipo único de materia que es pura y tiene propiedades específicas.

surface tension The result of an inward pull among the molecules of a liquid that brings the molecules on the surface closer together; causes the surface to act as if it has a thin skin. (132)
tensión superficial Resultado de la atracción hacia el centro entre las moléculas de un líquido, que hace que las moléculas de la superficie se acerquen mucho, y que la superficie actúe como si tuviera una piel delgada.

suspension A mixture in which particles can be seen and easily separated by settling or filtration. (289)
suspensión Mezcla en la cual las partículas se pueden ver y separar fácilmente por fijación o por filtración.

synthesis A chemical reaction in which two or more simple substances combine to form a new, more complex substance. (268)
síntesis Reacción química en la que dos o más sustancias simples se combinan y forman una sustancia nueva más compleja.

system 1. A group of parts that work together as a whole. **2.** A group of related parts that work together to perform a function or produce a result. (70)
sistema 1. Partes de un grupo que trabajan en conjunto. **2.** Grupo de partes relacionadas que trabajan conjuntamente para realizar una función o producir un resultado.

GLOSSARY

T

telescope An optical instrument that forms enlarged images of distant objects. (596)
telescopio Instrumento óptico que provee ampliaciones de los cuerpos lejanos.

temperature How hot or cold something is; a measure of the average energy of motion of the particles of a substance; the measure of the average kinetic energy of the particles of a substance. (114)
temperatura Cuán caliente o frío es algo; medida de la energía de movimiento promedio de las partículas de una sustancia; medida de la energía cinética promedio de las partículas de una sustancia.

thermal conductivity The ability of an object to transfer heat. (178)
conductividad térmica Capacidad de un objeto para transferir calor.

thermal energy The total kinetic and potential energy of all the particles of an object. (114, 436)
energía térmica Energía cinética y potencial total de las partículas de un cuerpo.

thermal expansion The expansion of matter when it is heated. (465)
expansión térmica Expansión de la materia cuando se calienta.

thermogram An image that shows regions of different temperatures in different colors. (548)
termograma Imagen que muestra regiones de distintas temperaturas con distintos colores.

third prong The round prong of a plug that connects any metal pieces in an appliance to the safety grounding wire of a building. (635)
tercera terminal Terminal redondeado de un enchufe que conecta cualquier pieza de metal de un artefacto con el cable a tierra de un edificio.

tracer A radioactive isotope that can be followed through the steps of a chemical reaction or industrial process. (200)
trazador Isótopo radiactivo que se puede seguir mediante los pasos de una reacción química o un proceso industrial.

transformer A device that increases or decreases voltage, which often consists of two separate coils of insulated wire wrapped around an iron core. (674)
transformador Aparato que aumenta o disminuye el voltaje, que consiste de dos bobinas de alambre aislado y devanado sobre un núcleo de hierro.

transition metal One of the elements in Groups 3 through 12 of the periodic table. (181)
metal de transición Uno de los elementos de los Grupos 3 a 12 de la tabla periódica.

translucent A type of material that scatters light as it passes through. (571)
material traslúcido Material que dispersa la luz cuando ésta lo atraviesa.

transparent A type of material that transmits light without scattering it. (571)
material transparente Material que transmite luz sin dispersarla.

transverse wave A wave that moves the medium at right angles to the direction in which the wave travels. (479)
onda transversal Onda que desplaza a un medio perpendicularmente a la dirección en la que viaja la onda.

triple bond A chemical bond formed when atoms share three pairs of electrons. (228)
enlace triple Enlace químico formado cuando los átomos comparten tres pares de electrones.

trough The lowest part of a transverse wave. (479)
valle Parte más baja de una onda transversal.

U

ultrasound Sound waves with frequencies above 20,000 Hz. (527)
ultrasonido Ondas sonoras con frecuencias mayores de 20,000 Hz.

ultraviolet rays Electromagnetic waves with wavelengths shorter than visible light but longer than X-rays. (549)
rayos ultravioleta Ondas electromagnéticas con longitudes de onda más cortas que la luz visible pero mas largas que los rayos X.

V

valence electrons The electrons that are in the highest energy level of an atom and that are involved in chemical bonding. (213)
electrones de valencia Electrones que tienen el nivel más alto de energía de un átomo y que intervienen en los enlaces químicos.

vaporization The change of state from a liquid to a gas. (139)
vaporización Cambio del estado de líquido a gas.

velocity Speed in a given direction. (330)
velocidad Rapidez en una dirección dada.

vibration A repeated back-and-forth or up-and-down motion. (478)
vibración Movimiento repetido hacia delante y hacia atrás o hacia arriba y hacia abajo.

virtual image An upright image formed where rays of light appear to come from. (578)
imagen virtual Imagen vertical que se forma desde donde parecen provenir los rayos de luz.

viscosity A liquid's resistance to flowing. (132)
viscosidad Resistencia a fluir que presenta un líquido.

visible light Electromagnetic radiation that can be seen with the unaided eye. (549)
luz visible Radiación electromagnética que se puede ver a simple vista.

voltage The difference in electrical potential energy per charge between two places in a circuit. (621)
voltaje Diferencia en el potencial eléctrico que hay entre dos áreas de un circuito.

volume The amount of space that matter occupies. (49, 105)
volumen Cantidad de espacio que ocupa la materia.

—————————— **W** ——————————

watt The unit of power when one joule of work is done in one second. (393)
vatio Unidad de potencia equivalente a un julio por segundo.

wave 1. A disturbance that transfers energy from place to place. **2.** The movement of energy through a body of water. (477)
onda 1. Perturbación que transfiere energía de un lugar a otro. **2.** Movimiento de energía por un fluido.

wavelength The distance between two corresponding parts of a wave, such as the distance between two crests. (484)
longitud de onda Distancia entre dos partes correspondientes de una onda, por ejemplo la distancia entre dos crestas.

wedge A simple machine that is an inclined plane that moves. (404)
cuña Máquina simple que consiste de un plano inclinado que se mueve.

weight A measure of the force of gravity acting on an object. (48, 103)
peso Medida de la fuerza de gravedad que actúa sobre un objeto.

wheel and axle A simple machine that consists of two attached circular or cylindrical objects that rotate about a common axis, each one with a different radius. (413)
rueda y eje Máquina simple que consiste en dos objetos circulares o cilíndricos unidos, de diferente radio, que giran en torno a un eje común.

work Force exerted on an object that causes it to move. (388)
trabajo Fuerza que se ejerce sobre un cuerpo para moverlo.

—————————— **X** ——————————

X-rays Electromagnetic waves with wavelengths shorter than ultraviolet rays but longer than gamma rays. (550)
rayos X Ondas electromagnéticas con longitudes de onda más cortas que los rayos ultravioleta pero más largas que los rayos gamma.

INDEX

Page numbers for key terms are printed in **boldface** type.

A

Absolute zero, 455
Acceleration, 334, 335–340
    due to gravity, 375
    graphing, 338–339
    and Newton's Second Law of
    Motion, 364–365
Accuracy, 56
Acids, 301, 302
    measuring pH, 308
    neutralization, **310,** 311
    in solution, 307
Actinides, 182
Action-reaction forces, 366–367
Activation energy, 271, 272, 275
Air. *See* Atmosphere
Alkali metals, 180, 216
Alkaline earth metals, 180
Alloys, 239
Alpha particles, 197, 198
Alternating current (AC), 671
Aluminum, 182
Ammonia, 98
Amorphous metal, 245
Amorphous solids, 130
Ampere (A), 626, 633
Amplitude, 483, 484–485
    increasing and decreasing,
    492–493
    of radio waves, 554
Amplitude modulation (AM), 554
Analyzing, 8
Anomalous data, 59
Antinodes of waves, 494
Application of skills
    Apply It!, 17, 24, 31, 50, 59, 65,
    72, 77, 95, 97, 106, 111, 138,
    163–164, 171, 179, 186, 191,
    215, 223–224, 227, 238, 252,
    261, 268, 274, 287, 297, 305,
    309, 324, 327, 329, 353, 358,
    371, 377, 391, 400, 403, 405,
    407, 412, 434, 439, 456, 461,
    480, 491, 515, 519, 523, 528,
    543, 547, 573, 581, 589, 591,
    595, 614, 619, 649, 653, 661
    Do the Math!, 151, 675
        analyze data, 555, 584
        apply concepts, 265, 510
        calculate, 7, 46, 115, 134,
        199, 273, 294, 337, 365, 393,
        429, 464, 486, 497, 626, 633,
        655, 675

        control variables, 149
        create data tables, 375
        draw conclusions, 115, 399,
        429, 464
        evaluate impact on society, 7
        explain, 46, 291
        graph, 23, 149, 230, 257,
        399, 665
        infer, 510
        interpret data, 181, 257, 291,
        399, 555, 584, 655
        interpret tables, 464, 510
        make generalizations, 149
        predict, 230, 399, 584, 626
        read graphs, 23, 181, 257,
        291, 399
    Science Matters
        Aerogel Windows, 470
        An Antiuniverse?, 123
        Aquanauts, 87
        Can You Be Clean and
        Green?, 281
        Can You Hear Me Now?, 534
        Catch and No Release, 449
        Channel Surfin' on the
        Infrared Wave, 564
        Charge It!, 448
        Discovery of the Elements,
        206
        Elements of the Human
        Body, 207
        Engineering Solutions, 39
        Going Green, 641
        Good Things Come in Small
        Packages, 420
        Growing Snow, 155
        Healing with Magnetism?,
        565
        Hiding in Plain Sight, 603
        Limestone and Acid
        Drainage, 316
        Long Ago in a Faraway Land,
        122
        Look, Ma, Warm Hands, 280
        Magnetic Pictures, 680
        A New Set of Wheels, 421
        Noisy Occupations, 535
        An Operatic Superpower,
        501
        Pharmacists: Chemists at
        Work, 244
        The Race for Speed, 344
        The Race To Be Faster, 86
        Safety Restraints, 382
        Sci-Fi Metal, 245
        Science Athletes Let the
        Games Begin, 421
        Scuba Diving, 154
        Seeing Double, 602
        Seismic-Safe Buildings, 38
        A Shocking Message!, 681

        A Shocking State, 155
        Something for Nothing, 640
        Stop Sign, 345
        The Superhero of Glues, 245
        Superlubricity, 383
        Thermal Expansion, 471
        Vinegar, 317
        Wall of Water, 500
Apply It!. *See* Application of skills
Art conservation scientist, 92
Assessment
    Assess Your Understanding, 9,
    13, 16–17, 20, 25, 27, 29, 31,
    33, 46, 53, 57, 61, 67, 69, 71,
    75, 80–81, 95, 99, 101, 105,
    107, 110, 113, 117, 130, 132,
    135, 138, 140, 143, 145, 147,
    149, 164, 167, 170, 173, 175,
    179, 183, 186, 193, 196, 198,
    201, 217, 221, 223, 225, 228,
    230, 233, 235, 239, 253, 257,
    261, 267, 269, 272, 275, 289,
    291, 294, 299, 305, 309, 311,
    325, 329, 331, 333, 337, 339,
    351, 353, 358, 361, 363, 365,
    369, 373, 375, 377, 391, 393,
    397, 399, 401, 405, 409, 413,
    415, 427, 431, 434, 437, 441,
    443, 455, 457, 461, 465, 478,
    481, 485, 487, 491, 493, 495,
    508, 511, 513, 515, 517, 521,
    525, 529, 541, 543, 545, 551,
    555, 557, 559, 573, 575, 577,
    581, 586, 589, 593, 597, 610,
    615, 618–619, 623, 626, 631,
    634–635, 647, 649, 653, 655,
    658–659, 661, 663, 665, 667,
    671, 673, 675
    Review and Assessment, 35–36,
    83–84, 119–120, 151–152,
    203–204, 241–242, 277–278,
    313–314, 341–342, 379–380,
    417–418, 445–446, 467–468,
    497–498, 531–532, 561–562,
    599–600, 637–638, 677–678
    Study Guide, 34, 82, 118, 150,
    202, 240, 276, 312, 340, 378,
    416, 444, 466, 496, 530, 560,
    598, 636, 676
    Virginia SOL Test Prep, 37, 85,
    121, 153, 205, 243, 279, 315,
    343, 381, 419, 447, 469, 499,
    533, 563, 601, 639, 679
Assumptions, testing, 74
Atmosphere, 185
Atomic mass, 169, 171
Atomic mass units (amu), 166
Atomic number, 166, 171, 214
Atoms, 96, 98, **161,** 162–167
    Bohr's model, 163

bonded, 227–233, 255
cloud model, 164
and conservation of mass, 262–265
Dalton's atomic theory, 161
and elements, 213–217
and ions, 219–225
isotopes, 167
and metals, 234–239
modern model, 165–167
particle charges and masses, 165–166
and periodic table, 168, **170**, 171–175
Rutherford's model, 162–163
Thomson's model, 162
See also Molecules
Average speed, 328

B

Balanced and unbalanced forces, 375
Balances, electronic and triple-beam, 48
Bar graphs, 63
Bases, 303, 304
    measuring pH, 308
    neutralization, 304, 306, **310,** 311
    in solution, 308
Becquerel, Henri, 196
Beta particles, 197, 198
Bias, experimental, 22
Big Idea, xxxviii, 40, 88, 124, 156, 208, 246, 282, 318, 346, 384, 422, 450, 472, 502, 536, 566, 604, 642
Big Question
    Answer the Big Question, 33, 61, 117, 193, 233, 267, 299, 331, 369, 415, 443, 461, 487, 517, 551, 586, 631, 673
    Apply the Big Question, 36, 84, 120, 152, 204, 242, 278, 314, 342, 380, 418, 446, 468, 498, 532, 562, 600, 638, 678
    Chapter Opener, 1, 41, 89, 125, 157, 209, 247, 283, 319, 347, 385, 423, 451, 473, 503, 537, 567, 605, 643
    Explore the Big Question, 33, 60, 116, 142, 192, 232, 266, 298, 331, 368, 415, 442, 460, 487, 517, 551, 585, 630, 673
    Review the Big Question, 34, 82, 118, 150, 202, 240, 276, 312, 340, 378, 416, 444, 466, 496,

530, 560, 598, 636, 676
    Unlock the Big Question, 4, 10, 18, 28, 44, 54, 62, 68, 76, 92, 96, 102, 108, 128, 136, 144, 160, 168, 176, 184, 194, 212, 218, 226, 234, 250, 258, 270, 286, 292, 300, 306, 322, 326, 334, 350, 354, 362, 370, 374, 388, 394, 402, 410, 426, 432, 438, 454, 458, 462, 482, 488, 506, 512, 518, 522, 526, 540, 544, 552, 570, 576, 582, 590, 594, 608, 616, 624, 632, 646, 650, 656, 662, 668
Binoculars, 602
Bohr, Niels, 163–164
Boiling, 136, **139**
Boiling point, 139, 224, 229, 291
Bonds. *See* Chemical bonds; Ionic bonds and compounds
Boyle, Robert, 148
Boyle's law, 148, 149

C

Calcium, 180
Calculating
    acceleration, 336, 364–365
    current, voltage, and resistance, 626
    efficiency, 400
    electric energy, 634
    electric power, 632–633
    energy change, 464
    kinetic energy, 429, 433
    mechanical advantage, 398, 403–405, 407, 413–415
    mechanical energy, 433
    net force, 352, 365
    potential energy, 430, 433, 621
    power, 392–393, 427
    slope, 332
    speed, 327–329
    work, 390–391, 396–397
Cameras, 594, **595**
Carbon, 166, 268
    family of nonmetals, 187
    isotopes, **167**
Carbonates, 302
Carbon dioxide, 98–99, 232, 259
Careers in science
    art conservation scientist, 92
    chemical engineer, 39
    chemist, 244
    coastal restoration project manager, 54
Catalysts, 275
Categorical data, 63

Cell phones, 552, 556–558
Celsius (C), 53
Celsius scale, 455
Census, 62
Centimeter (cm), 47
Centripetal force, 377
Chadwick, James, 165
Changes of state, 109–116
Charge. *See* Electric charge
Charles, Jacques, 144, 146
Charles's law, 146, 147
Chemical bonds, 98, 208, **213,** 245
    and chemical changes, 253
    covalent, **227,** 228–233
    electron sharing, 227
    ionic compounds, 218–225
    metallic, **235,** 236–239
    molecular compounds, 229–230
    polar and nonpolar, **231,** 232–233
    single, double, and triple, 228
    and valence electrons, **213,** 214–217, 219–220
Chemical changes, 111, 112–113, 195, **252,** 253–255
    combustion, electrolysis, oxidation, and tarnishing, 112
Chemical compounds. *See* Compounds
Chemical elements. *See* Elements
Chemical energy, 115, 437, 448
Chemical engineer, 39
Chemical equations, 258, 259–265
Chemical formulas, 99, 222, 259
Chemical properties, 92, **94**
    of acids and bases, 301–304
    of matter, 94–95, 251
    of metals, 179
    of nonmetals, 186
Chemical reactions, 250–275
    activation energy, **271,** 272, 275
    catalysts and inhibitors, **275**
    and conservation of mass, 262–267
    described by equations, **258,** 259–265
    described by properties, 251–253
    endothermic and exothermic, **256,** 266, 272, 280
    identifying, 254–257
    open and closed systems, **263**
    rate of, 273–275
    reactants and products, **252,** 260, 274
    synthesis, decomposition and replacement, **268,** 269
Chemical symbols, 171
Chemist, 244

INDEX

Page numbers for key terms are printed in **boldface** type.

Chemistry, 93
Circuit. *See* Electric circuit
Circuit breakers, 635
Circular motion, 374–377
Classifying, 6
Classifying matter, 96–101
Closed systems, 263
Cloud model of atoms, 164
Coastal restoration project manager, 54
Cochlea, 524
Cochlear implant, 525
Coefficients, 265
Colloids, 289
Color, 570–575, 582
    combining, 574–575
    material of objects viewed, 571–575
    primary, 574
    of visible light, 549
    white light, 570, 574
Combustion, 112
Communication, scientific, 25
Compass, 654
Complementary colors, 574
Complex systems, modeling, 73
Compound machines, 414, 421
Compounds, 99, 212
    ionic, 218, **220,** 221–225
    molecular, **229,** 230
    nonmetal, 186
    polar and nonpolar, 296
    See also DNA
Compression (waves), 480, 507
Concave lens, 587
Concave mirror, 579
Concentrated solutions, 293
Concentration
    of reactants, **274**
    of solutions, 293–294
Condensation, 140, 142
Conduction, 459, 460–461, **612**
Conductivity, 94
    electrical, **178,** 191, 225, 229, 238
    of solutions, 291
    thermal, **178,** 237
Conductors, 463, 619
    and magnetic fields, 669–671
    superconductors, 616
Cones (eyes), 592
Conservation. *See* Environmental issues
Conservation of charge, 612
Conservation of energy, 442, 443

Conservation of mass, 113, 262, 263–267
Conservation of momentum, 372, 373
Constructive interference, 492
Controlled experiments, 22
Convection, 459, 460–461
Convection currents, 459
Convex lens, 588
Convex mirror, 580
Copernicus, Nicolaus, 322
Cornea, 591
Corrosion, 179, 301
Covalent bonds, 227, 228–233
    double and triple, **228**
    polar and nonpolar, **231,** 232–233
Crest of waves, 479
Crystalline solids, 130
Crystals, 208, **224**
    metal, 235–236
Cubic centimeter (cm³), 49, 105
Cubic meter (m³), 105
Curie, Marie, 196
Curie, Pierre, 196
Current. *See* Electric current

D

Dalton, John, 161
Data, 12, 23
Decibel (dB), 515
Decomposition reactions, 268, 269
Democritus, 161
Density, 50, 51, 102, **106,** 107, **511**
Dependent variables, 21, 63
Designing experiments, 22–25
Destructive interference, 493, 494
Diatomic molecules, 188
Did You Know?, 6, 64, 74, 104, 141, 178, 223, 262, 296, 323, 367, 390, 443, 455, 492, 510, 549, 585, 614, 654
Diffraction, 491
    of sound waves, 508
Diffuse reflection, 577
Digital Learning
    Apply It, 17, 31, 47, 59, 73, 93, 107, 137, 175, 223, 225, 237, 259, 269, 273, 287, 295, 303, 327, 331, 353, 359, 377, 403, 415, 433, 457, 479, 515, 519, 523, 543, 547, 575, 587, 591, 611, 619, 661
    Art in Motion, 97, 99, 197, 231, 271–272, 323, 355, 407–408, 428–429, 455, 463, 479, 516–517,

557, 559, 583, 585, 611, 613, 648–649
    Do the Math, 21, 115, 133, 149, 181, 199, 229, 255, 263, 273, 291, 293, 335, 365, 375, 393, 399, 429, 487, 509, 635, 655, 665, 675
    Interactive Art, 5, 8, 59–60, 64, 70–71, 111, 113, 115–116, 133, 148–149, 165–166, 171, 173, 214, 219–220, 231–232, 251–252, 263, 266, 290–291, 295, 298, 307–308, 332–333, 339, 352–353, 371–372, 389–390, 411–412, 435–436, 439–440, 459–460, 487, 493, 509, 511, 517, 547, 551, 553–554, 579–580, 587–588, 595–596, 620–621, 627, 630, 651–652, 667, 672–673
    My Reading Web, 2–3, 42–43, 90–91, 126–127, 158–159, 210–211, 248–249, 284–285, 320–321, 348–349, 386–387, 424–425, 452–453, 474–475, 504–505, 538–539, 568–569, 606–607, 644–645
    My Science Coach, 9, 13, 15–17, 19–20, 25, 27, 29, 31, 33, 35, 46–47, 53, 55, 57, 61, 63, 67, 69, 71, 73, 75, 77, 80–81, 83, 95, 99, 101, 105, 107, 109–111, 113, 117, 119, 129–130, 132, 135, 138–141, 143, 145, 147, 149, 151, 161, 164–165, 167, 169, 171, 173, 175, 177, 179, 181, 183, 185–187, 193, 195–199, 201, 217, 221, 223, 225, 227–230, 233, 235, 237, 239, 241, 253, 257, 261, 267, 269, 272, 275, 289, 291, 294, 299, 301, 303, 305, 309, 311, 313, 325, 329, 331, 333, 337, 339, 341, 351, 353, 359, 361, 363, 365, 367, 369, 373, 375, 377, 379, 391, 393, 395, 397, 399, 401, 405, 407, 409, 413, 415, 417, 427, 431, 434–435, 437, 441, 443, 445, 455, 457, 461, 465, 467, 477–478, 481, 483, 485, 487, 491, 493, 495, 497, 507–508, 511, 513, 515, 517, 521, 525, 529, 531, 541, 543, 545, 551, 555, 557, 559, 561, 573, 575, 577, 579, 581, 586, 589, 593, 597, 599, 609–610, 615, 617–619, 621, 623, 626–627, 631, 634–635, 637, 647, 649, 653, 655, 657, 659, 661, 663, 665, 667, 669, 671, 673, 675, 677

Planet Diary, 4–5, 10–11, 18–19, 28–29, 44–45, 54–55, 62–63, 68–69, 76–77, 92–93, 96–97, 102–103, 108–109, 128–129, 136–137, 144–145, 160–161, 168–169, 176–177, 184–185, 194–195, 212–213, 218–219, 226–227, 234–235, 250–251, 258–259, 270–271, 286–287, 292–293, 300–301, 306–307, 322–323, 326–327, 334–335, 350–351, 354–355, 362–363, 370–371, 374–375, 388–389, 394–395, 402–403, 410–411, 426–427, 432–433, 438–439, 454–455, 458–459, 462–463, 477, 482–483, 488–489, 506–507, 513, 518–519, 522–523, 526–527, 540–541, 544–545, 552–553, 570–571, 576–577, 582–583, 590–591, 594–595, 608–609, 616–617, 624–625, 632, 646–647, 650–651, 656–657, 662–663, 668–669

Real-World Inquiry, 11–12, 33, 187, 401, 485, 527, 529, 633–634, 660–661

Untamed Science, xxxviii, 1, 40–41, 88–89, 124–125, 156–157, 208–209, 246–247, 282–283, 318–319, 346–347, 384–385, 422–423, 450–451, 473, 502–503, 536–537, 566–567, 604–605, 642–643

Virtual Lab, 21–22, 45, 103, 105, 107, 141–142, 192, 213, 216, 255–256, 310–311, 338–339, 367–368, 442–443, 457, 489–490, 542–543, 571–572, 625

Vocab Flash Cards, 3, 43, 91, 127, 159, 211, 249, 285, 321, 349, 387, 425, 453, 505, 539, 569, 607, 645

Dilute solutions, 293
Dirac, Paul, 123
Direct current (DC), 671
Direction, changing, 335, 397, 399
Directly proportional variables, 147
Discharge, static, 614
Distance, 325
   and gravity, 360
   and speed, 327
   and work, 390–391, 396, 398
Distillation, 101
DNA, 185
Do the Math!. *See* Application of skills
Doppler effect, 516
Double bonds, 228

Double replacement reactions, 268
Ductility, 178, 237

E

Ear, 523–525
Ear canal, 524
Eardrum, 524
Earthquakes, 38
Echolocation, 527
Efficiency of machines, 400, 401
Elastic potential energy, 431
Electrical conductivity, 178, 191, 238
   ionic compounds, 225
   molecular compounds, 229
   of solutions, 291
Electrical energy, 436
   and mechanical energy, 662–663, 672–673
   and motion, 663–667, 669–670, 672
Electric charge, 608–615
   buildup, 611–613
      by friction and conduction, 612
      by induction and polarization, 613
   conservation of, **612**
   discharge, 614–615
   and electric fields, 610
   of molecular compounds, 231
   positive and negative, 609–610
Electric circuit, 618, 624–631
   current, voltage, and resistance, 625–626
   parts of, 627
   series and parallel, **628–629,** 630–631
Electric current, 617, 618–623
   alternating (AC) and direct (DC), **671**
   in circuits, 618
   and electric power, 633
   flow, 620–623
   and generators, 672–673
   induced, 669–671
   and magnetic fields, 657–659, 669–671
   and Ohm's law, 625–626
Electric fields, 610
Electric force, 609
Electricity
   charge, 608–615
   circuits, **618,** 624–631
   cost of, 632, 634, 640
   current, 616, **617,** 618–623

   delivering, 674–675
   and magnetic fields, 657–661
   and mechanical energy, 662–667
   power, **632,** 633–634
   producing, 669–673
   safety, 635
   static, **611**
Electric motors, 662, 666, 667
Electric power, 632, 633–634
Electrolysis, 112
Electromagnetic energy, 437
   electromagnetic induction, **669,** 670–671
   electromagnetism, **658**
   electromagnets, **660,** 661
Electromagnetic radiation, 459, 536, **541**
Electromagnetic spectrum, 546, 547–551
Electromagnetic waves, 541
   cell phones, 552, 555–556
   characteristics, 541, 545
   gamma rays, **550**
   infrared rays, **548**
   microwaves, **547**
   particle model of light, 543
   radio waves, **546,** 553–555
   satellite communications, 558–559
   ultraviolet rays, **549**
   usefulness, 540
   visible light, **549**
   wave model of light, 542
   X-rays, **550**
   See also Radiation; Wave
Electron, 162, 163–166
   energy levels, **164**
   valence, **213,** 214–217, 219–220, 235
   See also Atoms
Electron dot diagram, 213
Elements, 97, 98–99, 168–201
   and atoms, 96
   chemistry of, 212–217
   discovery of, 206
   in human body, 207
   hydrogen, 217
   lanthanides and actinides, 182
   metalloids, **191,** 217
   metals, **177,** 178–183, 216, 234–239
   noble gases, **190,** 215
   nonmetals, **185,** 186–189, 216
   radioactive, 194–201
   table, 172–173, 686
   transuranium, 183
   See also Periodic table
Empedocles, 97
Empirical evidence, 12, 13
Endothermic change, 115

INDEX

Page numbers for key terms are printed in **boldface** type.

Endothermic reactions, 256, 266, 272

Energy, 114–115, **426**, 427–449, **477**
  activation, **271**, 272, 275
  chemical, 114, 256, **437**, 448
  conservation of, **113**, **442**, 443
  electrical, **436**, 634, 663–673
  electromagnetic, **437**
  and electromagnetic radiation, **541**
  and heat transfer, 458–465
  kinetic, **428**, 429, 440
  and matter, 114–115
  mechanical, **432**, 433–434, 662–663, 672–673
  potential, **430**, 431
  and power, 427
  thermal, **114**, 115, 137, 178, **436**, 454–457
  transformation of, 114–115, **438**, 439–441, 448–449
  and wave amplitude, 483–485, 514
  and work, 426, 434
  See also Energy sources; Kinetic energy; Potential energy
Energy level (electrons), 164
Energy sources, 478
  renewable, 426, 448
  waves, 476
  wind, 426
Environmental issues
  acid run-off, 316
  alternative power sources, 426, 476, 640–641
  biodegradable cleaners, 281
  energy conservation, 470
  fishery management, 86
  rechargeable batteries, 448
  recycling, 176
Enzymes, 275
Equations. *See* Calculating
Equations, chemical, 258, 259–265
Estimate, 55
Evaluating information, 28–33
Evaporation, 101, **139**
Evidence, 29
Exothermic change, 115
Exothermic reactions, 256, 266, 272, 280
Experiments, controlled, 22
  collecting and interpreting data, 23
  communicating results, 25
  designing, 21–22
  drawing conclusions, 24

Eye, 591–593
Eyepiece (telescopes), 596

_____ F _____

Fahrenheit scale, 455
Faraday, Michael, 670
Farsighted vision, 593
Feedback, in scientific systems, 71
Ferromagnetic core, 660
Field, 77
Filtration, 101
Fission, nuclear, 435
Flammability, 95, 251
Flexibility, 94
Fluid, 131
Fluid friction, 357
Fluorine, 227
Focal point, 579
Foley artists, 535
Force, 350, **351**, 356–383
  and acceleration, 364–365
  action-reaction, 366–367
  balanced and unbalanced, 375
  centripetal, **377**
  electric, **609**
  free fall, **375**, 376–377
  friction, 354–358, **355**, 383
  gravity, 354, **359**, 360–361
  inertia, 362–363, 382
  input and output, 395–399
  and momentum, **371**, 372–373
  and motion, 350, 352–353
  net, 352, **352**
  strength and direction, 351
  weight and mass, 361
  and work, **388**, 389–391, 396, 398
  See also Machines
Force fields, 608
Forensics, 111
Fossil dating, 199
Free fall, 375, 376–377
Freezing, 94, **138**
Frequency, 484, 486
  and Doppler effect, **516**
  of electromagnetic waves, 545–551, 554
  natural, 495, 501, 519
  and pitch, **512**, 513
  of standing waves, 494
Frequency distributions, 66–67
Frequency modulation (FM), 554
Friction, 355, 356–358, 383, **612**
  fluid, **357**
  overcoming, 400

  rolling, **357**
  sliding, **356**
  static, **356**
Fuel. *See* Energy sources
Fuel cells, 266–267
Fulcrum, 406
Fundamental tones, 519
Fuses, 635
Fusion, nuclear, 435

_____ G _____

Galvanometer, 664, 665
Gamma rays, 197, 198, 200–201, **550**
Gases, 133, 134–135, 144–149
  pressure, **134**, 144–145, 148–149, 154
  solubility, 296–297
  temperature, 135, 144–147
  volume, 133, 146–149
Generators, 672, 673
Global Positioning System (GPS), 559
Gram (g), 48
Grams per cubic centimeter (g/cm³), 50
Grams per milliliter (g/ml), 50
Graph, 63, 64–67
  categorical and numerical data, 63
  histogram, 67
  line and bar, 63
  line plot, 66
  linear and nonlinear, **64**
  and outliers, **64**
  scatterplot, 65
Graphing
  acceleration, 338–339
  current, 665
  motion, 332–333
  speed, 333
Gravitational fields, 608
Gravitational potential energy, 430
Gravity, 354, **359**
  acceleration due to, 375
  mass and weight, 103–104, 360–361
  universal, 359
Grounded circuits, 635
Groups (periodic table), 175, 214–217

H

Half-life (radioactive isotopes), 199
Halite, 224
Halogens, 189, 216
Hearing, 522–525
Hearing loss, 523, 525, 534
Heat, 237, 280, **457**
    See also Thermal energy
Heat transfer, 457–465
    conductors and insulators, **463**
    convection, conduction, and radiation, **459,** 460–461
    impact of, 462–465, 471
    and specific heat, **464**
    and thermal expansion, **465,** 471
    and weather, 458–459
Henry, Joseph, 670
Hertz (Hz), 484, 513, 519, 529
Heterogeneous mixtures, 100
Histograms, 67
Homogeneous mixtures, 100
Human activities, impact of. *See* Environmental issues
Hydrochloric acid, 307
Hydrogen, 190, 217, 228
Hydrogen fuel cells, 266–267
Hydrogen ions (H⁺), 307, 308
Hydroxide ions (OH⁻), 308
Hypothesis, 20

I

Ice, 124, 137
Ideal machine, 401, 407
Images, 577
    real and virtual, 578–580
Inclined planes, 403, 404–405
Independent variables, 21, 63
Index of refraction, 584
Indicators of acids and bases, 302, 304, 308
Induction, 613
Inertia, 363, 382
    law of, 362–363
Inferring, 6
Infrared rays, 548, 564
Inhibitors of reactions, 275
Input, in scientific systems, 70
Input forces, 395, 396–399
Inquiry, scientific, 18, 19
Inquiry Skills. *See* Science Inquiry Skills
Instantaneous speed, 329
Insulators, 463, 619

Intensity of waves, 514
Interference, 492
International System of Units (SI). *See* SI (International System of Units)
Inversely proportional variables, 149
Ion, 219, 220
    and crystals, 224
    hydrogen, **307,** 308
    hydroxide, **308**
    polyatomic, **220,** 223
Ionic bonds and compounds, 218, **220,** 221–225
    and molecular compounds, 229–230
    naming, 223
    properties, 218, 224–225
    and solutions, 290–291, 296
Iris, 591
Irregular solids, volume of, 49, 105
Isotopes, 167
    radioactive, 194, 199–201

J

Joule (J), 391, 457
Julian, Percy Lavon, 10

K

Kelvin (K), 53, 147
Kelvin scale, 455
Kilogram (kg), 48, 104
Kilograms per cubic meter (kg/m³), 50
Kilometer (km), 47
Kilopascal (kPa), 134
Kilowatt (kW), 634
Kinetic energy, 428, 429
    and mechanical energy, 433
    and potential energy, 440
    and temperature, 455
    and thermal energy, 436
    transformation of, 440, 448

L

Lab Zone
    Inquiry Warm-Up, 4, 10, 18, 28, 44, 54, 62, 68, 76, 92, 96, 102, 108, 128, 136, 144, 160, 168, 176, 184, 194, 212, 218, 226, 234, 250, 258, 270, 286, 292,

300, 306, 322, 326, 334, 350, 354, 362, 370, 374, 388, 394, 402, 410, 426, 432, 438, 454, 458, 462, 476, 482, 488, 506, 512, 518, 522, 526, 540–541, 544, 552, 570, 576, 582, 590, 594, 608, 616, 624, 632, 646, 650, 656, 662, 668
    Lab Investigation, 25, 75, 107, 138, 179, 225, 257, 291, 329, 405, 427, 455, 491, 513, 555, 575, 631, 647
    Quick Lab, 9, 13, 16–17, 20, 27, 29, 31, 33, 46, 53, 57, 61, 67, 69, 71, 80–81, 95, 99, 101, 105, 110, 113, 117, 130, 132, 135, 140, 143, 145, 149, 164, 167, 170, 173, 175, 183, 186, 193, 196, 198, 201, 217, 221, 223, 228, 230, 233, 235, 239, 253, 261, 267, 269, 272, 275, 289, 294, 299, 305, 309, 311, 325, 331, 333, 337, 339, 351, 353, 361, 363, 365, 369, 373, 375, 377, 391, 393, 397, 399, 401, 409, 413, 415, 431, 434, 437, 441, 443, 457, 461, 465, 478, 481, 485, 487, 493, 495, 508, 511, 515, 517, 521, 525, 529, 541, 543, 545, 551, 557, 559, 573, 577, 581, 586, 589, 593, 597, 610, 615, 618–619, 623, 626, 634–635, 653, 655, 658–659, 661, 663, 665, 667, 671, 673, 675
Lanthanides, 182
Lavoisier, Antoine, 113, 262
Law of conservation of energy, 442, 443
Law of conservation of mass, 113, 262
Law of conservation of momentum, 372, 373
Law of inertia, 362–363
Law of universal gravitation, 359
Laws of motion, 362–367
    first (inertia), 362–363
    second (acceleration), 364–365
    third (action-reaction), 366–367
Length, measuring, 47
Lenses, 587, 588–589
    in cameras, 595
    concave, **587**
    convex, **588**
    in eyeglasses, 593
    in microscopes, 597
    in telescopes, 596
Levers, 406, 407–409
    classes of, 408

INDEX

Page numbers for key terms are printed in **boldface** type.

Light
    color, 570–575, 603
    and material of objects viewed, 571–575
    particle model of, 543
    polarized, **542**
    reflection and mirrors, 576–581
    refraction, 583–586
    refraction and lenses, 582–589
    seeing, 590–593
    speed of, 506
    and surface of objects, 577
    using, 594–597, 602
    visible, 545, **549**
    wave model of, 542
    white, 549, 570, 572, 574
    See also Electromagnetic waves
Lightning, 615
Line graphs, 63
Line plots, 66
Linear graphs, 64
Liquid crystal displays, 128
Liquids, 131, 132
    density, **106,** 107
    evaporation and distillation, 101
    vaporization and condensation, 139–140
    See also Solutions
Liter (L), 49, 105
Litmus paper, 302, 304
Longitudinal waves, 480
    amplitude, 483–485
    wavelength, 484
Loudness, 514, 515
    musical, 519–520
Luster, 94, **178,** 236

M

Machines, 395, 396–421
    compound, **414,** 421
    efficiency, **400,** 401
    input and output forces, 395–399
    mechanical advantage, **398,** 399, 407, 413, 415
    nanomachines, 420
    pulleys, 397
    simple, 394, 402, **403,** 404–413
        inclined plane, **403,** 404–405
        lever, **406,** 407–409
        pulley, 397, **411,** 412
        screw, **405**
        wedge, **404**
        wheel and axle, **413**

Magnetic attraction, 101
    of metals, 178
Magnetic declination, 655
Magnetic field, 608, 646, **651**
    of Earth, 654–655
    and electric current, 657–659, 669–673
    single and combined, 652–653
    See also Electromagnetic energy
Magnetic field lines, 651
Magnetic force, 649
Magnetic poles, 648
    of Earth, 655
Magnetic Resonance Imaging (MRI), 668, 680
Magnetic stripes, 656
Magnetism, 565, **647,** 648–649
    See also Electromagnetic waves
Magnets, 647
Making models, 6
Malleability, 178, 237
Manipulated variables, 21
Mass, 104, 360
    4, 359–360
    and acceleration, 364–365
    atomic, 166, **169,** 171
    conservation of, **113, 262,** 263–267
    and energy, 428
    and gravity, 359–360
    and inertia, 363
    measuring, **48,** 104
    and momentum, 371
    and weight, 103–104, 360–361
Mass number, 167
Math. *See* Application of skills
Mathematics, 54–61
    accuracy and precision, **56**
    calculating percent error, 60
    estimation, **55**
    mean, median, mode, and range, **58**
    reasonable and anomalous data, **59**
Matter, 93
    acids and bases, **301,** 302–311
    and antimatter, 123
    changes in, 108–115, 122, 137–143, 195, 251–255
    classifying, 96–101
    and energy, 114–115
    gases, **133,** 134–135, 144–149, 296–297
    liquids, **131,** 132, 139–140
    mass, **104,** 166, 169, 171
    measuring, 102–107
    properties of, 92–95, 251, 267, 301–304
    solids, **129,** 130, 137–138, 141

    solutions, 286–288, 290–297
    states of, 109, 128–135
    See also Atoms; Chemical bonds; Compounds; Elements; Molecules
Mean, 58
Measurement units
    adding, subtracting, and multiplying, 57
    Celsius (C), 53
    centimeter (cm), 47
    cubic centimeter (cm^3), 49, 105
    cubic meter (m^3), 105
    decibel (dB), 515
    gram (g), 48, 104
    gram per cubic centimeter (g/cm^3), 50
    gram per milliliter (g/mL), 50
    grams per cubic centimeter (g/cm^3), 106
    grams per milliliter (g/mL), 106
    hertz (Hz), 484, 513
    joule (J), 391, 457
    kelvin (K), 53
    kilogram (kg), 48, 104
    kilograms per cubic meter (kg/m^3), 50
    kilometer (km), 47
    kilopascal (kP), 134
    liter (L), 49, 105
    meter (m), 47
    metric system, **45**
    milligram (mg), 48
    milliliter (mL), 105
    millimeter (mm), 47
    newton (N), 48, 351
    pascal (P), 134
    second (s), 52
    SI (International System of Units), **45,** 46–53
    standard, 45
    time, 52
    volume, 49
    watt (W), 393, **393,** 633
    weight, 48
    See also SI (International System of Units)
Measuring, 44–53, 102–107
    density, 50, 106–107
    distance, 325
    electrical energy, 634
    electrical power, 633
    frequency, 484, 513
    heat, 457
    length, 47
    loudness, 515
    mass, 48, 104
    power, 393
    pressure, 134
    temperature, 53, 455
    volume, 105, 133

weight, 103
work, 391
See also Calculating
Mechanical advantage, 398, 399,
415
and efficiency, 400–401
of simple machines, 403–405,
407
Mechanical energy, 432, 433–434
and electric motors, 666–667
and electrical energy, 662–663,
672–673
and work, 434
Mechanical waves, 477
Median, 58
Mediums for waves, 477, 478
change of, 490
density, 511
for electromagnetic waves, 541
for light waves, 584–585
for sound waves, 507, 509–511
stiffness, 510
temperature, 509
Melting, 137, 142
Melting point, 137, 224, 229
Mendeleev, Dmitri, 168–170
Meniscus, 49
Metallic bonds, 235, 236–239
Metalloids, 191, 217
Metals, 177, 178–183
and acids, 301
alloys, 239
classifying, 180–183
glassy, 245
ions, 219
metallic bonds, **235,** 236–239
mixed group, 182
properties, 177–179, 235–239,
245
reactivity, **179,** 216
recycling, 176
transition, 181
Meter (m), 47
Metric system, 45
Microscopes, 597
Microwaves, 547
Middle ear, 524
Milligram (mg), 48
Milliliter (mL), 105
Millimeter (mm), 47
Mirage, 586
Mirrors, 576–580
concave, **579**
convex, **580**
plane, **578**
Mixed group metals, 182
Mixtures, 100, 101, 110, 286–289
classifying, 287–289
separating, 101

types of, 100
See also Colloids; Solutions;
Suspensions
Mode, 58
Models, 68, **69**
making, 6
of systems, 72–75
Molecular compounds, 229, 230
Molecules, 98, 227
diatomic, **188**
and molecular solutes, 290–291
polar bonding, 232–233
and surface tension, 132
See also Atoms
Momentum, 370, **371**
conservation of, **372,** 373
Monitoring earthquakes, 38
Monster waves, 500
Morse, Samuel, 681
Motion, 322, 323–345
acceleration, 334–340
circular, 374–377
and electrical energy, 663–667,
669–670, 672
and energy, 436
and forces. *See* Force
graphing, 332–333
measuring distance, 325
and momentum, 370–373
Newton's Laws, 362–369
and power, **392,** 393
relative, 324
speed, 326–329
velocity, 330
and work, **388,** 389–391
Music, 518, 519–521
fundamental tones and
overtones, **519**
instruments, 518, 520–521
My Planet Diary
Biography, 4, 10, 144, 582
Blog, 76, 108, 326, 432, 518, 540
Career, 54, 92, 354, 462, 526,
616, 668
Disaster, 270, 458, 488
Discovery, 18, 160, 234, 292,
410, 482, 544, 576, 632, 662
Field Trip, 102, 438
Fun Fact, 28, 128, 194, 212, 218,
226, 258, 306, 334, 370, 388,
394, 426, 454, 476, 506, 552,
570, 624, 646, 650, 656
Misconception, 44, 184, 286,
350, 402, 522, 590, 608
Profile, 250
Science and Technology, 68
Science Stat, 62, 96, 136, 176,
374, 512, 594
Voices from History, 168, 300,
322, 362

N

Nanometer, 96
Natural frequencies
fundamental tones and
overtones, **519**
resonance, **495,** 501
Nearsighted vision, 593
Net force, 352
Neutralization, 304, 306, **310,** 311
Neutrons, 165, 166–167
Newton (N), 48, **351,** 365, 382
Newton, Isaac, 582
**Newton's law of universal
gravity,** 359
Newton's laws of motion
first (inertia), 362–363
second (acceleration), 364–365
third (action-reaction), 366–367
Nitrogen, 228
in air, 184
family of nonmetals, 188
Nitrogen fixation, 188
Noble gases, 190, 215
Nodes of waves, 494
Noise pollution, 526, 534
Nonlinear graphs, 64
Nonmetals, 185, 186–189
covalent bonds, 227
families, 187–190
ions, 219
properties, 185–186
reactivity, 186, 216
Nonpolar bonds, 231, 232–233
Nonpolar compounds, 296
Nuclear energy, 201, **435**
Nuclear radiation, 197–198
uses of, 199–201
Nuclear reactions, 195
Nucleus, 163, 165
Numerical data, 63

O

Objective reasoning, 14
Objectives (telescopes), 596
Observing, 5
Oceans, 87
Ocean waves, 500
producing energy from, 476
Oersted, Hans Christian, 657
Ohm, George, 625
Ohm's law, 626
Onnes, Heike Kamerlingh, 234
Opaque materials, 571, 572
Open systems, 263

INDEX

Page numbers for key terms are printed in **boldface** type.

Opinion, **29**
Optical axis, **579**
Optic nerve, **592**
Outlier (graph data), **64**
Output, of scientific systems, **70**
Output forces, **395**, 396–399
Overtones, **519**
Oxidation, 112
Oxygen, 228, 253
    in air, 184
    family of nonmetals, 189
    molecular composition, 98

P

Palladium, 175
Parallel circuits, **629**
Particle accelerator, 183
Particle charges, 165–166
Particle masses, 166
Particle model of light, **543**
Particles
    in gases, 133–135
    in liquids, 131
    in solids, 129, 141
Pascal (Pa), **134**
Percent error, **60**
Period, **174**
Periodic table, 168, **170**, 171–175
    groups of, **175**, 214–217
    hydrogen in, 190
    metalloids, 191
    metals, 180–183
    noble gases, 190
    nonmetals, 187–189
    periods of, **174**
    table, 172–173, 684–685
    and valence electrons, 214–217
Petroleum, 281
Pharmacists, 244
PH scale, **308**, 309
Photoelectric effect, **543**
Photon, **543**
Physical change, **109**, 110, **252**, 254–255
Physical properties, **94**
    of acids and bases, 301–304
    of matter, 94–95, 251
    of metals, 178, 235–239, 245
    of nonmetals, 185
Pigments, **575**
Pitch, **512**, 513, 521
    musical, 520
Plane mirror, **578**

Planes, inclined, **403**, 404–405
Polar bonds, **231**, 232–233
Polar compounds, 296
Polarization, **613**
Polarized light, **542**
Polyatomic ions, **220**, 223
Potential energy, **430**, 431
    in kinetic energy, 440
    in mechanical energy, 433
    in thermal energy, 436
    transformation to kinetic energy, 440
Power, **392**, 393, 427
    electric, **632**, 633–634
Precipitate, **254**
Precision, **56**
Predicting, **7**
    from models, 72
Pressure
    air, 154
    of gases, **134**
    and solubility of gases, 296
    and temperature of gases, 144–145
    and volume of gases, 148–149
Primary colors, **574**
Prisms, 582, 585
Probeware, 53, 687
Process, of scientific systems, **70**
Process Skills. *See* Science Inquiry Skills
Products of chemical change, **252**, 253, 260
Properties
    of acids, 301–302
    of bases, 303–304
    changes in, 252–255
    of matter, 92–95, 251
    of metals, 177–179, 235–239, 245
    of nonmetals, 185–186
    of solutions, 298–299, 317
    See also Chemical properties; Physical properties
Protons, **163**, 165–167
Pseudoscience, 14, **15**
Pulleys, 397, **411**, 412
Pupil, **591**

Q

Qualitative observation, **5**
Quantitative observation, **5**

R

Radar, **547**
Radiant energy, 437
    See also Electromagnetic energy
Radiation, **459**, 460–461
Radioactive dating, **199**
Radioactive decay, **195**, 196–197
Radioactive elements, 194–201
Radioactive isotopes, 194, 199–201
Radioactive thermoelectric generators (RTGs), 194
Radioactivity, **196**, 197–198
    uses of, 199–201
Radio waves, 545, **546**, 553–555, 558–559
    broadcasting, 553–554
    radio spectrum, 555
Rainbows, 585
Range, **58**
Rarefaction (waves), **480**, 507
Rays, **576**
    gamma, **550**
    infrared, **548**, 564
    ultraviolet, **549**
    X-rays, **550**
Reactants, **252**
    in chemical change, 260, 274
Reactivity, **179**
    nonmetals, 186, 216
Reading Skills
    graphic organizers, 329, 336, 375, 393, 396, 430, 435, 460, 620, 657
        chart, 70, 486, 555, 559, 580, 589
        concept web, 487
        flow chart, 71, 73, 592
        Venn diagram, 93, 130, 435, 554
    reading/thinking support strategies
        apply concepts, 13–14, 22, 24, 46–47, 61, 67, 71, 83, 106, 110, 114, 119, 140, 151, 167, 183, 196, 198, 203, 221, 223, 227, 239, 242, 252, 255, 257, 265, 267, 278, 291, 293, 305, 313–314, 329, 333, 341, 367–368, 379, 397, 413, 417–418, 427, 431, 441, 445–446, 456, 459–460, 467–468, 480, 484, 489, 497–498, 508, 510–511, 532, 551, 555, 557, 562, 573, 581, 587, 599–600, 634, 637, 661
        define, 9, 48, 164, 196, 217, 287, 311, 337, 434, 441, 491,

529, 543, 581, 589, 653, 661, 667

describe, 14, 95, 99, 103, 132, 135, 164, 175, 261, 275, 294, 361, 389, 391, 409, 487, 495, 515, 543, 579, 615, 653, 670–672

discuss, 17

explain, 9, 46, 69, 75, 84, 97, 105, 130, 135, 138, 140–141, 167, 179, 190, 200–201, 217, 223, 239, 261, 269, 275, 291, 293, 324–325, 330, 337, 364, 373, 380, 391, 405, 428, 437, 478, 511, 519, 525, 527, 529, 550–551, 581, 591, 593, 613, 647, 654, 658

identify, 11, 19, 21, 25, 31, 50, 53, 59, 66, 71, 73, 80–81, 99, 101, 107, 117, 130, 138, 140, 143, 147, 149, 165, 183, 185–186, 198, 222, 239, 252, 261, 263, 288, 309, 323, 327, 329, 333, 351, 369, 377, 398, 414, 430–431, 437, 456, 479, 508, 516, 520, 524, 543, 548, 551, 555, 573–575, 577, 586, 588, 591–592, 595–596, 610, 619, 663, 675

identify faulty reasoning, 16

interpret diagrams, 56, 98, 113, 119, 129, 131, 133, 139, 148, 162, 213, 219, 227, 232, 269, 271, 289, 313, 360, 366, 379, 395, 408, 412, 418, 428, 431, 440, 442, 455, 468, 480, 497, 507, 514, 525, 531, 546, 548, 554, 584–585, 592, 595, 610, 621, 659–660, 664, 677

interpret graphs, 23, 65, 67, 149, 181, 257, 272, 291, 332–333, 341–342, 399, 445, 561

interpret photos, 8, 80, 100, 134, 178, 237, 252, 256, 259, 277, 323–324, 335, 440, 520, 547, 549, 578, 589, 611, 618, 622, 658

interpret tables, 61, 83, 119, 173, 214, 241, 259, 311, 464, 510

list, 193, 239, 257, 358, 379, 397, 405, 457, 521, 525, 623

make generalizations, 12, 27, 31, 46, 149, 186, 203, 311, 589

make judgments, 120, 418, 467, 526

mark text, 6, 19–21, 24, 32, 56, 63, 73, 81, 103, 115, 131, 148, 216, 236–238, 253, 288, 297, 330, 335, 360, 372–373, 377, 392, 398–400, 405–406, 435, 439, 456, 458–459, 464, 484–485, 490, 508, 519, 525, 542, 558, 571, 615, 629, 661, 664

name, 21, 45, 113, 132, 175, 412, 484, 524, 545

relate diagrams and photos, 137

review, 13, 27, 33, 46, 75, 99, 116, 142, 166, 170, 221, 225, 232–233, 253, 266, 289, 299, 305, 325, 365, 404, 430, 481, 497, 515, 589, 597, 618, 634, 665, 673

solve problems, 59, 111, 120, 277, 298, 417, 623

target reading skills

ask questions, 45, 183, 271, 366, 528, 586, 619, 669

compare and contrast, 35, 67, 93, 98, 119, 130, 132, 138–139, 151, 164–165, 173, 186, 193, 197–198, 231, 257, 275, 289, 304, 307, 324, 341, 398, 405, 435, 445, 459, 497, 508, 516–517, 529, 554, 558, 561, 575, 580, 589, 599–600, 678

identify main idea, 24, 56, 73, 103, 148, 236, 297, 335, 372, 435, 464, 484, 508, 542, 571, 654

identify supporting evidence, 7, 288, 330, 360, 392, 439, 456, 519

outline, 14

relate cause and effect, 63, 115, 131, 135, 140, 152, 200–201, 203, 216–217, 221, 225, 253, 274, 311, 361, 376, 401, 406, 417, 429, 441, 481, 490–491, 495, 525, 531, 615, 637, 649, 657–658, 665, 678

relate text and visuals, 78, 167, 170, 219, 352, 479, 527, 571, 596, 615, 648, 651

sequence, 53, 81, 290, 355, 441, 549, 553, 592–593, 664

summarize, 16–17, 22, 27, 29, 93, 191, 253, 265, 303, 411, 431, 477, 480, 491, 531, 550, 559, 589, 633, 647, 667

Real images, 579

Reasonable and anomalous data, 59

Rectangular solids, volume of, 49

Reference points, 323

Reflecting telescope, 596

Reflection, 489, 576–581
regular and diffuse, **577**

Refracting telescope, 596

Refraction, 490, 582–589
cause of, 582
in different mediums, 583
and lenses, 587–589
and mirages, 586
and prisms, 585

Regular reflection, 577

Relative motion, 324

Repeated trial, 24

Replacement reactions, 268, 269

Replication, 25

Resistance, 622, 623
and Ohm's law, 625–626

Resonance (waves), 495, 501

Resonance, sound, 519

Retina, 592

Rods (eyes), 592

Rolling friction, 357

Rutherford, Ernest, 162–163

S

Safety, 76–81
accident response, 81
in the field, 77, 80
in the lab, 76–79
preparation, 77

Safety symbols, 79, 682

Salts, 311

Satellite, 374, **376,** 377

Satellite communications, 558–559

Saturated solutions, 295, 297

Scatterplot graph, 65

Science, 5
and society, 28–33

Science Inquiry Skills
basic process skills
calculate, 7, 46, 49–50, 52, 55, 57, 60–61, 83, 104–107, 115, 199, 262, 277, 294–295, 297, 328–329, 331, 333, 337–338, 341, 353, 365, 371–373, 379–380, 391, 393, 405, 409, 415, 417, 429, 433–434, 445, 464–465, 486–487, 497, 515, 519, 528, 541, 626, 633–634, 638, 655, 675

classify, 6, 11, 21, 88, 95, 110, 119, 151, 156, 174, 191, 204, 238, 241–242, 251, 268–269, 277, 303, 309, 314, 318, 341, 356–358, 409, 411, 436–437, 445–446, 461, 463, 465, 467, 521, 551, 561, 581,

INDEX

Page numbers for key terms are printed in **boldface** type.

588, 597, 599, 619, 631, 637, 663, 671

communicate, 9–10, 25, 28, 44, 102, 110, 128, 144, 160, 168, 176–177, 184, 194–195, 218, 225–226, 231, 234, 238, 251, 326, 354, 394, 401–402, 457, 462, 476, 482, 488, 549, 570, 582–583, 590, 594, 604, 624, 646, 656, 662

create data tables, 358, 375

estimate, 55, 103, 107, 309, 392

graph, 23, 63–64, 66–67, 149, 230, 257, 275, 338–339, 509, 665

infer, 6, 13, 33, 35, 40, 48–49, 51, 60, 71, 75, 80, 84, 97, 124, 132, 145, 179, 183, 192, 204, 220, 224, 235, 241–242, 256, 267, 271, 282, 287, 289, 301, 304, 337, 363, 373, 407, 409, 434, 443, 446, 450, 461, 467, 492, 502, 510, 531–532, 536, 557–558, 561, 572, 595, 635, 637–638, 649, 667, 675

make models, 72, 110, 164, 260–261, 352, 376, 406, 513, 531, 562, 617, 620, 627–629, 637, 652, 674, 677

measure, 47–49, 308, 325, 331, 358, 483

observe, 5–6, 11, 50, 77, 112, 169, 186, 229, 255, 359, 491, 493, 523, 561, 591, 653, 666

predict, 50, 53, 73, 75, 109, 113, 139, 143, 146–147, 151, 161, 170–171, 175, 198, 204, 215, 230, 233, 274, 304–305, 313, 332, 336, 353, 361, 365, 377, 399–401, 465, 480–481, 509, 521, 542, 566, 573, 584, 586, 618, 626, 628, 638, 661, 664, 677

experimental methods

analyze experimental results, 24

analyze sources of error, 22, 30, 52

evaluate data reliability, 32, 36

identify experimental bias, 24, 30

relate evidence and explanation, 13, 203, 255

integrated process skills

control variables, 149, 299, 358, 417, 638

design experiments, 22, 25–26, 254, 263, 314, 358, 380, 677

develop hypotheses, xxxviii, 20, 297, 346, 384, 422, 511, 653

draw conclusions, 21, 60, 64–65, 95, 99, 115, 130, 147, 151, 241, 246, 269, 390, 399, 429, 433, 464, 467, 484, 523, 545, 557, 609–610, 614, 642, 671, 677

form operational definitions, 208

interpret data, 12, 31, 55, 66, 83, 152, 181, 223, 257, 261, 268, 278, 291, 309–310, 374, 399, 467, 547, 555, 584, 625, 655

pose questions, 9, 19–20, 36, 253, 305

technology design/evaluation

analyze costs and benefits, 426

evaluate impact on society, 7

redesign, 495

Science Literacy Skills

analyze models and systems, 74, 673

distinguish evidence and opinion, 29

evaluate scientific claims, 31

identify faulty reasoning, 15

Science Matters. *See* Application of skills

Scientific explanation, 26

Scientific inquiry and investigation, 4, 8–9, 18, **19**

designing and conducting experiments, 22–25

developing hypotheses, 20

elements of, 11–13

posing questions and defining problems, 19

Scientific literacy, 29, 30–31

finding and evaluating information, 28–33

Scientific notation, 59

Scientific thinking and skills, 4–9, 11–15

analyzing, classifying, and inferring, **8**

characteristics, 17

making models, 6

and nonscientific ways of knowing, 16

observing, 4, **5**

predicting, **7**

and pseudoscientific thinking, 14–15

skepticism, 11

and subjective and objective reasoning, **14**

Scientific tools

electronic and triple-beam balances, 48, 683

graphs, 63–65

mathematics, 54–61

measurement, 44–53, 687

models, 68–75

Scientists. *See* Careers in science

Screw, 405

Secondary colors, 574

Seismic waves, 38

Semiconductors, 191, 619

Series circuit, 628

Short circuit, 635

SI (International System of Units), 45, 46–53, **104, 325**

cubic meter (volume), 105

kelvin (temperature), 53

kilogram (mass), 48, 104

kilograms per cubic meter (density), 50

meter (length), 47

newton (weight), 48

second (time), 52

Sight, 591–593

Significant figures, 57

Silicon, 191

in semiconductors, 619

Simple machines, 394, 402, **403,** 404–413

inclined plane, **403,** 404–405

lever, **406,** 407–409

pulley, 397, **411,** 412

screw, **405**

wedge, **404**

wheel and axle, **413**

Simple systems, modeling, 73

Single replacement reactions, 268

Skepticism, 11

Sliding friction, 356

Slope, 332, 333

Society and science, 28–33

Solenoids, 660, 661

Solids, 129, 130

crystalline and amorphous, **130**

filtration, 101

melting and freezing, 137–138

sublimation, 141

Solubility, 295, 296–297

Solutes, 287, 290–291

Solutions

acids and bases in, 307–311, 316

boiling and freezing, 291

concentration, 293–294

conductivity, 291

dilute and concentrated, **293**

evaporation and distillation, 101, 110, 282, **287**, 288–295
formation of, 290–291
mixtures, 286–288
properties, 298–299, 317
saturated and unsaturated, **295**, 297
solubility, 295–297
solutes and solvents, **287**, 288, 290–291
supersaturated, 297
Solvents, 287, 288, 290–291, 296
Sonar, 528
Sonogram, 529
Sound waves, 482, 507–508
diffraction, 508
Doppler effect, **516**
echolocation, **527**
formation of, 507
frequency, 513
hearing, 522–525
impact of medium, 509–511
loudness, **514**, 515
movement of, 507
music, **518**, 519–521
noise pollution, 526, 534
pitch, **512**, 513
resonant frequency, 495, 501
sensing, 522
speed, 506, 509–511
ultrasound, **527**, 528–529
See also Wave
Specific heat, 178, **464**
Speed, 327, 328–329, 344, 485–486
average, **328**
calculating, **327**, 328–329
changing, 335
and energy, 428
instantaneous, **329**
of sound waves, 506, 509–511
Standing waves, 494, 519
States of matter, 95, 128–135
changes of, 109–116
gases, 133–135
liquids, 131–132
solids, 129–130
Static discharge, 614
Static electricity, 611
Static friction, 356
Stopwatches, 52
Strength, 388
See also Power
Subjective reasoning, 14
Sublimation, 141
Subscripts of chemical symbols, 222
Substances, 93
chemical changes in, 111–112, 252–253

physical changes in, 109–110
See also Matter
Superconductors, 234, 616
Supersaturated solutions, 297
Surface area of reactant, 273
Surface tension, 132
Surface waves, 481
amplitude, 483–485
Surfactants, 281
Suspensions, 289
Synthesis reaction, 268, 269
Systems, 70, 71–75

_____ **T** _____

Tarnishing, 112
Telegraph machines, 681
Telephone systems
cell, 552, 555–556
satellite, 559
Telescopes, 596, 602
Television systems
and remote control, 564
satellite, 559
Temperature, 114, 454, 455
of chemical reactions, 274
and electric current, 622–623
of gases, 135, 144–147
and kinetic energy, 455
measuring, 53
and pressure, 144–145
and solubility, 297
and sound waves, 509
and thermal energy, 115, **436,** 456–457
and volume, 146–147
Thermal conductivity, 178, 237
Thermal energy, 114, 115, 137, 178, **436**
and heat transfer, 458–465
and temperature, 456–457
Thermal expansion, 465, 471
Thermogram, 548
Thermometer, 53
Third prong, 635
Thomson, J.J., 162
Time, measuring, 52
Tracers, 200, 201
Transformation of energy, 438, 439–441, 663
and conservation of energy, 442–443
Transformers, 674, 675
Transition metals, 181
Translucent materials, 571, 572–573

Transparent materials, 571, 572–573
Transuranium elements, 183
Transverse waves, 479
amplitude, 483–485
electromagnetic, 542
wavelength, 484
Triple-beam balances, 48, 683
Triple bonds, 228
Trough (waves), 479
Turbines, 672

_____ **U** _____

Ultrasound, 527
Ultrasound technology, 528–529
Ultraviolet rays, 549
Unsaturated solutions, 295

_____ **V** _____

Vacuum, 541, 545
Vail, Alfred, 681
Valence electrons, 213, 214–217, 219–220, 235
Vaporization, 139, 142, 291
Variables, 21
directly proportional, **147**
inversely proportional, **149**
Velocity, 330, 371
Vibration, 478, 502
and sound waves, 507, 519
Virtual image, 578, 580
Viscosity, 132
Visible light, 545, 549
Vision, 591–593
Vocabulary Skills
high-use academic words, 42, 65, 210, 216, 222, 320, 327
identify multiple meanings, 2, 248, 254, 386, 393, 400, 424, 437, 452, 457, 474, 479, 504, 507, 528
identify related word forms, 284, 293
prefixes, 90, 100, 568, 572
suffixes, 126, 140
use context to determine meaning, 32, 644, 661
word origins (Greek or Latin), 158, 189, 348, 355, 371, 538, 548, 606, 623
Volt (V), 626
Voltage, 621
and electric power, 633
and Ohm's law, 625–626

INDEX

Page numbers for key terms are printed in **boldface** type.

and transformers, 674–675
Volume, 49, 105
    of gases, 133, 146–149
    measuring, 105, 133
    and pressure, 148–149
    and temperature, 146–147

——————— **W** ———————

Water
    density, 102
    melting and freezing, 94, 137–138, 142, 291
    molecular composition and bonding, 98, 228, 232–233
    pressure, 292
    snow crystals, 155
    as solvent, 287
    states of, 136
    vaporization and condensation, 139–140, 143
    waves, 476, 481, 483
Water current, 620
Watt (W), 393, 633
Wave, 477
    amplitude, **483,** 484–485
    change of direction
        by diffraction, **491**
        by reflection, **489**
        by refraction, **490**
    compression and rarefaction, **480,** 507
    electromagnetic. *See* Electromagnetic waves
    formation, 494–495, 507
    interference, constructive, **492**
    interference, destructive, **493**
    light. *See* Light
    longitudinal, **480**
    mechanical, **477**
    mediums for, 477
    producing energy from, 476
    properties of, 482–487
    resonance, **495,** 501, 519
    sound. *See* Sound waves
    sources of energy, 478
    speed of, 485–486, 509–511
    standing, **494**
    surface, 481
    transverse, **479**
    wavelength and frequency, 484–486
Wavelength, 484, 486
    of electromagnetic waves, 545–550
Wave model of light, 542

Weather
    and heat transfer, 458–459
    and static discharge, 615
Wedge, 404
Weight, 48, 103, 361
    and mass, 103–104, 360–361
    and potential energy, 430
Wheel and axle, 413
Work, 388, 389–391
    and energy, 426, 434
    and power, 392–393
    See also Machines

——————— **X** ———————

X-rays, 545, **550**

ACKNOWLEDGMENTS

Staff Credits

The people who made up the *Interactive Science* team—representing composition services, core design digital and multimedia production services, digital product development, editorial, editorial services, manufacturing, and production—are listed below:

Jan Van Aarsen, Samah Abadir, Ernie Albanese, Chris Anton, Zareh Artinian, Bridget Binstock, Suzanne Biron, Niki Birbilis, MJ Black, Nancy Bolsover, Stacy Boyd, Jim Brady, Katherine Bryant, Michael Burstein, Pradeep Byram, Jessica Chase, Jonathan Cheney, Arthur Ciccone, Allison Cook-Bellistri, Rebecca Cottingham, AnnMarie Coyne, Bob Craton, Chris Deliee, Paul Delsignore, Michael Di Maria, Diane Dougherty, Kristen Ellis, Kelly Engel, Theresa Eugenio, Amanda Ferguson, Jorgensen Fernandez, Kathryn Fobert, Alicia Franke, Louise Gachet, Julia Gecha, Mark Geyer, Steve Gobbell, Paula Gogan-Porter, Jeffrey Gong, Sandra Graff, Robert M. Graham, Adam Groffman, Lynette Haggard, Christian Henry, Karen Holtzman, Susan Hutchinson, Sharon Inglis, Marian Jones, Sumy Joy, Sheila Kanitsch, Courtenay Kelley, Chris Kennedy, Toby Klang, Greg Lam, Russ Lappa, Margaret LaRaia, Ben Leveillee, Thea Limpus, Charles Luey, Dotti Marshall, Kathy Martin, Robyn Matzke, John McClure, Mary Beth McDaniel, Krista McDonald, Tim McDonald, Rich McMahon, Cara McNally, Bernadette McQuilkin, Melinda Medina, Angelina Mendez, Maria Milczarek, Claudi Mimo, Mike Napieralski, Deborah Nicholls, Dave Nichols, William Oppenheimer, Jodi O'Rourke, Ameer Padshah, Lorie Park, Celio Pedrosa, Jonathan Penyack, Linda Zust Reddy, Jennifer Reichlin, Stephen Rider, Charlene Rimsa, Walter Rodriguez, Stephanie Rogers, Marcy Rose, Rashid Ross, Anne Rowsey, Logan Schmidt, Amanda Seldera, Laurel Smith, Nancy Smith, Ted Smykal, Emily Soltanoff, Cindy Strowman, Dee Sunday, Barry Tomack, Elizabeth Tustian, Patricia Valencia, Ana Sofia Villaveces, Stephanie Wallace, Amanda Watters, Christine Whitney, Brad Wiatr, Heidi Wilson, Heather Wright, Rachel Youdelman.

Illustrations

64 Steve McEntee; **65, 66, 67** Stephen Durke.

Photographs

Photo locators denoted as follows: Top (T), Center (C), Bottom (B), Left (L), Right (R), Background (Bkgd)

Cover, Front and Back
Jim Stroup/Virginia Tech

Front Matter
i Caitlin Mirra/Shutterstock; **vii** Eric Isselée/Fotolia; **ix** (TR) Michael C. York/©Associated Press; **x** (TR) Tom Schierlitz/Getty Images; **xi** (TR) Javier Trueba/Madrid Scientific Films; **xii** N A Callow/Science Source; **xiii** (TR) David Doubilet/National Geographic Image Collection; **xiv** (TR) Liane Cary/AGE Fotostock; **xv** (TR) Nutscode/T Service/Photo Researchers, Inc.; **xvi** (TR) Brian Snyder/Reuters Media; **xvii** (TR) Roland Weihrauch/AFP/Getty Images; **xviii** (TR) Max Rossi/Reuters Media; **xix** (TR) Corbis; **xx** (TR) ©Associated Press; **xxi** (TR) Don Carstens/Robertstock; **xxii** (TR) Cloud Gate, Millennium Park, Chicago(2004), Anish Kapoor. Photo ©2008 Kim Karpeles/Kim Karpeles Photography; **xxiii** (TR) Nick Suydam/Alamy Images; **xxiv** (TR) Corbis; **xxxii** (TC) iStockphoto.

Chapter 1
xxxviii Robert Postm/AGE Fotostock; **3** (BC) ©Edgewater Media/Shutterstock, (B) Daniel Templeton/Alamy Images, (T) Mark Humphrey/©Associated Press; **4** Copyright ©2006 by The National Academy of Sciences of the USA; **5** (Inset) Inga Spence/Getty Images, (R) Tom & Pat Leeson/Photo Researchers, Inc.; **6** (TL) USDA-NRCS PLANTS Database/USDA; **7** (BR) Greg Vaughn / Alamy; **8** Mark Humphrey/©Associated Press; **10** (B) Freerk Brouwer/Shutterstock, (CL) Indiana Historical Society; **14** (B) ©Edgewater Media/Shutterstock; **15** Babak Tafreshi/Photo Researchers, Inc.; **16** (TR) Untitled (1920), George Grosz. Oil on canvas. Collection Kunstsammlung Nordrhein-Westfalen, Duesseldorf, Germany/Photo by Erich Lessing/Art Resource, NY; **17** (CR) Walter C. Jaap/Sustainable Seas/R. Halley/Courtesy of USGS; **18** (B) NASA; **19** (B) Navnit/Shutterstock; **20** (BL) Radius Images/Photolibrary Group, Inc.; **21** (BR) Sam Yu/The Frederick News-Post/©Associated Press; **24** (Bkgrd) Patrick LaRoque/PhotoLibrary Group, Inc.; **26** light poet/Shutterstock; **27** John Dominis/PhotoLibrary Group, Inc.; **28** (C) Andrew Brookes/Corbis, (Bkgrd) MedicalRF/Photo Researchers, Inc.; **29** (CR) Daniel Templeton/Alamy Images, (CL) Jupiter Images; **31** (CL) Inspirestock/Jupiter Images; **32** (B) Haywiremedia/Dreamstime LLC, (T) Paul Burns/Getty Images; **33** (Bkgrd) Bodo Schieren/Alamy Images, (Bkgrd) Creatas Images/Jupiter Images; **34** (BL) Jupiter Images, (CR) Navnit/Shutterstock, (TL) Science Source/Photo Researchers, Inc.; **36** (CR) ©Barrie Rokeach/Alamy Images; **38** (Bkgrd) Bruce Leighty/Getty Images; **39** (T) Andreas Guskos/iStockphoto, (BR) Emrah Turudu/iStockphoto, (CL) Nancy Louie/iStockphoto.

Chapter 2
40 NASA Langley Research Center/NASA; **43** (BC) Dr. Ing. José Ignacio Alvarez-Hamelin, (TC) Stem Jems/Photo Researchers, Inc.; **45** (BR) Zhao Jianwei/©Associated Press; **46** (T) Image Source/Getty Images; **47** (Bkgrd) Barry Mansell/Nature Picture Library, (CR) Eric Isselée/Fotolia; **48** (L) Paul Burns/Getty Images; **49** (C) ©image100/SuperStock; **51** Kenneth Morris/ASP-Covered Images/Zuma Press, Inc.; **52** Contra Costa Newspapers/Tue Nam Ton/Zuma Press, Inc., (TL) Olga Lipatova/Shutterstock; **54** (B) Erik Zobrist/NOAA Restoration Center/National Oceanic and Atmospheric Administration, (BC) National Marine Fisheries Service/National Oceanic and Atmospheric Administration; **55** (TR) Amazon Images/Alamy, (BR) Stem Jems/Photo Researchers, Inc.; **57** (CR) Lukasz Kwapien/iStockphoto; **58** (T) Andy Levin/Alamy Images, (B) T-Design/Shutterstock; **59** (CR) Melvyn Longhurst/Alamy; **60** (CL) Science & Society Picture Library/Getty Images; **62** (B) Bernd Vogel/Corbis; **63** (BR) Chris Parypa/Alamy Images; **64** (B) Bill Curtsinger/National Geographic Image Collection; **65** (TR) Valery Rizzo/Alamy Images; **66** (CR) ©Adrian Sherratt/Alamy, (T) ©elfart/Alamy; **67** (TR) NASA, (Bkgrd) NASA Hubble Space Telescope Collection/

ACKNOWLEDGMENTS

NASA; **68** (BL) Oliver Burston/PhotoLibrary Group, Inc., (TR) Vladislav Ociacia/Alamy; **69** (CR) Dr. Ing. José Ignacio Alvarez-Hamelin; **70** (Bkgrd) Agence Zoom/Getty Images; **72** (B) Brian E. Small/VIREO; **74** (TR) creativex/Shutterstock; **75** (Bkgrd) Gary C. Tognoni/Shutterstock; **76** (TR) Martin Shields/Alamy Images, (CR) Originalpunkt/Shutterstock; **81** (CR) Chas/Shutterstock, (BL) Dave White/iStockphoto, (CL) Martin Darley/iStockphoto; **82** (CL) Chris Parypa/Alamy Images; **86** (Bkgrd, BCL) ©Associated Press, (TCL) Greg Huey/©Associated Press; **87** Brian J. Skerry/National Geographic Image Collection.

Chapter 3

88 (TR) Nordic Photos/PhotoLibrary Group, Inc.; **91** (BL) John Shaw/Science Source, (TL) Nigel Hicks/Dorling Kindersley/©DK Images; **92** (TCR) Nicolo Orsi Battaglini/Art Resource, NY, (CR) Scala/Ministero per i Beni e le Attività culturali/Art Resource, NY; **93** (BR) Katy Williamson/©DK Images, (BL) Nigel Hicks/Dorling Kindersley/©DK Images; **94** (B) ArabianEye/Getty Images, (BR) jlsohio/iStockphoto, (BC) Wave RF/Photolibrary Group, Inc.; **95** (C) Andy Crawford/©DK Images, (TC) Nicole Hill/Rubberball/Photolibrary Group, Inc.; **97** (BCR) ©DK Images, (CL) Ashok Rodrigues/iStockphoto, (CR) Judy Ledbetter/iStockphoto, (C) Thinkstock, (BL) webking/iStockphoto; **98** (C) Max Blain/Shutterstock; **99** (CC) Albert J. Copley/age Fotostock/PhotoLibrary Group, Inc., (C) Mark A. Schneider/Photo Researchers, Inc., (CR) Steve Gorton/©DK Images; **101** (CL) Charles D. Winters/Photo Researchers, Inc.; **102** (CR) Juergen Hasenkopf/Alamy Images, (B) Patrick Robert/Corbis; **104** (R) Mark Lennihan/©Associated Press; **107** (CL) ©The Granger Collection, NY, (CR) Charles D. Winters/Photo Researchers, Inc., (BCR) Harry Taylor/©DK Images, (TR) Steve Gorton/©DK Images; **108** (B) Entienou/iStockphoto; **109** (BR) Carolyn Kaster/©Associated Press; **110** (TL) Elena Schweitzer/iStockphoto; **111** (CR) Courtesy of North Carolina State Bureau of Investigation, Raleigh NC/North Carolina State Bureau of Investigation, (B) Rich Legg/iStockphoto; **112** (TL) Anthony Upton/PA Wire URN/©Associated Press; **114** (CL) Jonathan Hayward/©Associated Press, (BR) Umit Bektas/Reuters Media; **115** (CR) John Shaw/Science Source; **116** (B) Amr Nabil/©Associated Press, (TCR) AudsDad/iStockphoto, (T) Jakub Semeniuk/iStockphoto, (C) Matthew J. Sroka/Reading Eagle/©Associated Press; **117** (C) Jim Jurica/iStockphoto; **118** (TR) Nigel Hicks/Dorling Kindersley/©DK Images, (BR) Umit Bektas/Reuters Media; **122** (L) The Art Gallery Collection/Alamy Images; **123** (CR) American Institute of Physics/Photo Researchers, Inc., (B) Lawrence Berkeley National Laboratory/Science Photo Library/Photo Researchers, Inc.

Chapter 4

124 (B) Michael C. York/©Associated Press; **127** (TCL) BC Photography/Alamy, (BL) Charles Winters/Photo Researchers, Inc., (BCL) SuperStock; **128** (B) James M. Bell/Photo Researchers, Inc., (BC) Ryan Pyle/Corbis; **130** (CR) Mark A. Schneider/Photo Researchers, Inc., (CL) Sue Atkinson/Fresh Food Images/PhotoLibrary Group, Inc.; **132** (TL) BC Photography/Alamy; **133** (BR) Charles D. Winters/Photo Researchers, Inc.; **135** Frits Meyst/Adventure4ever; **136** (BL) Simon Butcher/Imagestate/PhotoLibrary Group, Inc.; **137** (BR) SuperStock; **138** (TR) Winfield Parks/National Geographic Image Collection; **141** (BC) Charles Winters/Photo

Researchers, Inc., (CR) Frank Greenaway/©DK Images, (B) Neal Preston/Corbis; **142** (BR) Andreas Kuehn/Getty Images, (CL) Michael S. Quinton/National Geographic Image Collection; **143** (CL) ©epa European Pressphoto Agency creative account/Alamy (BL) Kat Fahrer/Middletown Journal/©Associated Press, (TC) Odilon Dimier/Photolibrary Group, Inc.; **150** (CR) epa European Pressphoto Agency creative account/Alamy, (TR) Mark A. Schneider/Photo Researchers, Inc.; **152** (TCR) David Branch/©Associated Press; **154** (L) Sami Sarkis/Getty Images; **155** (TR) Stephen Lockett/Alamy Images, (BL) Ted Kinsman/Photo Researchers, Inc.

Chapter 5

156 (B) B2M Productions/Photolibrary Group, Inc.; **157** (TC) Klaus Guldbrandsen/Photo Researchers, Inc.; **159** (BCL) NASA/Photo Researchers, Inc., (TCL) Tom Schierlitz/Getty Images; **160** (BC) Nano-Tex, Inc./©Associated Press; **161** (B) Novastock/PhotoLibrary Group, Inc.; **162** (TL) Paul Blundell Photography/Fresh Food Images/PhotoLibrary Group, Inc.; **163** (TR) Iconotec/Photolibrary Group, Inc., (BR) Martin Bond/Photo Researchers, Inc.; **164** (BR, BL) Cole Vineyard/iStockphoto, (CR) Corey Radlund/Brand X Pictures/Photolibrary Group, Inc., (CR) Douglas Whyte/Corbis, (TL) Drew Hadley/iStockphoto, (CC) Harun Aydin/iStockphoto, (T) Milton Wordley/PhotoLibrary Group, Inc., (C) Steve Gorton and Gary Ombler/©DK Images, (TCR) Steve Gorton/©DK Images, (B) Wojtek Kryczka/iStockphoto; **166** (L) DLILLC/Corbis; (BC) William Steinecker; **168** (C) Portrait of Dmitry Ivanovich Mendeleyev (ca. 1865). Archives Larousse, Paris, France/Bridgeman Art Library; **169** (BL, BC) Copyright ©2008 Richard Megna/Fundamental Photographs, NYC, (BR) Copyright ©2008 Richard Megna/Fundamental Photographs, NYC; **171** (BL) ©DK Images; **174** (BR, BL, BC) Charles D. Winters/Photo Researchers, Inc.; **175** (C) Charles D. Winters/Photo Researchers, Inc., (BCR) Kim Kyung Hoon/Reuters Media, (TR) PjrStudio/Alamy Images; **176** (CR) Douglas Whyte/Corbis, (CC) Luis Carlos Torres/iStockphoto; **178** (TR) Charles D. Winters/Photo Researchers, Inc., (TL) Joel Arem/Photo Researchers, Inc., (BL) Keith Webber Jr./iStockphoto, (TC) László Rákoskerti/iStockphoto, (CL) Peter Spiro/iStockphoto; **179** (CR) Kai Schwabe/Photolibrary Group, Inc., (L) Tom Schierlitz/Getty Images; **180** (T) Bill Ross/PhotoLibrary Group, Inc., (BL) Living Art Enterprises, LLC/Photo Researchers, Inc.; **181** (BR) Science Source/Photo Researchers, Inc.; **182** (BL) Bullit Marquez/©Associated Press, (TC) Juerg Mueller/Keystone/©Associated Press; **183** (CR) Salvatore Di Nolfi/Keystone/©Associated Press; **184** (B) Rene Tillmann/©Associated Press; **185** (BR) Digital Art/Corbis; **186** (CR) Charles D. Winters/Photo Researchers, Inc.; **187** (BC) Lawrence Lawry/Photo Researchers, Inc.; **188** (B) Jim W. Grace/Photo Researchers, Inc.; **189** (TR) LWA/Dann Tardif/Photolibrary Group, Inc., (BR) Stockdisc/Photolibrary Group, Inc.; **190** (B) Julian Baum/Photo Researchers, Inc.; **191** (TR) David R. Frazier Photolibrary/Photo Researchers, Inc., (TR) NASA/Photo Researchers, Inc., (TL) Rosenfeld Images Ltd/Photo Researchers, Inc.; **192** (L) Peter Galbraith/iStockphoto; **194** (B) European Space Agency (ESA)/©Associated Press; **196** (CL) Rue des Archives/©The Granger Collection, NY; **199** (CR) Biophoto Associates/Photo Researchers, Inc.; **202** (CR) Lawrence Lawry/Photo Researchers, Inc., (BR) Rue des Archives/©The Granger Collection, NY; **206** (L) Ed Register/

ACKNOWLEDGMENTS

CNP/NewsCom; **358** (TR, CR) ©DK Images, (TCR) Clive Streeter/©DK Images, (TC) Steve Gorton/©DK Images; **359** (B) Darryl Leniuk/Getty Images; **361** (T) JPL/NASA; **362** (C) The Art Archive; **363** (R) Zuma Press, Inc.; **364** (B) David Trood/Getty Images; **365** (CR) Zuma Press, Inc.; **366** (TR) Grace Chiu/UPI/UPI United Press International, (TL) Mark J. Terrill/©Associated Press; **367** (BC) Kim Kyung Hoon/Reuters Media, (TR) Steve Helber/©Associated Press; **370** (B) Crista Jeremiason/Santa Rosa Press-Democrat; **371** (B) Jeremy Woodhouse/Getty Images; **374** (B) Tim Platt/Getty Images; **375** (C) Richard Megna/Fundamental Photographs, NYC; **376** (T) NASA; **377** (CR) UberFoto/Alamy; **378** (CR) Mark J. Terrill/©Associated Press; **381** (BR) Zuma Press, Inc.; **382** (BCL) Car Culture/Corbis, (B) Rick Fischer/Masterfile Corporation; **383** (CR) Colin Cuthbert/Photo Researchers, Inc., (BR) Harry Taylor/©DK Images.

Chapter 11

384 (B) Roland Weihrauch/AFP/Getty Images; **387** (TL) Javier Pierini/Getty Images, (BCL) Photolibrary Group, Inc., (BL) Yiorgos Karahalis/Reuters Media; **388** (C) John Stillwell/©Associated Press; **390** (BL) Laurie Noble/Digital Vision/Photolibrary Group, Inc.; **391** (TR) Javier Pierini/ Getty Images; **393** (C) Getty Images; **394** (BL) Justine Evans/ Alamy; **396** (TL) ©ThinkStock/SuperStock; **397** (TC) M. Lakshman/©Associated Press; **400** (B) Richard Hutchings/ PhotoEdit, Inc.; **401** (CL) James Shearman/Getty Images; **402** DiscountRamps; **403** (BL) Photolibrary Group, Inc.; **404** (T, CR) Seth A. McConnell/Rapid City Journal/©Associated Press; **405** (CR) ©DK Images; **406** (B) Ole Graf/Corbis; **407** (CR) Dave Sandford/Getty Images; **408** (BR) Douglas McFadd/©Associated Press, (CL) Steve Gorton/©DK Images; **410** (B) Robert F. Bukaty/©Associated Press; **413** (CR) ©DK Images, (BCR) Creatas/Photolibrary Group, Inc.; **416** (BR) Creatas/Photolibrary Group, Inc., (TR) Getty Images; **417** (CL) Javier Pierini/Getty Images; **418** (CR) Jupiter Images/Ablestock/Alamy; **419** (BR) Corbis/SuperStock; **420** (L) Coneyl Jay/Photo Researchers, Inc.; **421** (BL) Dave Umberger/©Associated Press; (TC) Courtesy of MIT Mobility Lab.

Chapter 12

422 (B) Max Rossi/Reuters Media; **425** (BL) Gilbert Iundt/ TempSport/Corbis, (BCL) Zuma Press, Inc.; **426** (B) Josiah Davidson/Getty Images; **427** (CR) DesignPics Inc./Photolibrary Group, Inc., (CL) PhotoLibrary Group, Inc.; **429** (BR) Zia Soleil/ Iconica/Getty Images; **432** (C) ©Associated Press; **433** (B) Heinz Kluetmeier/Sports Illustrated/Getty Images; **434** (T) Zuma Press, Inc.; **435** (B) PhotoLibrary Group, Inc.; **438** (CL) Michael Goulding/Orange County Register/Zuma Press, Inc.; **440** (L) Fundamental Photographs, NYC; **441** (T) Gilbert Iundt/ TempSport/Corbis; **443** (TR) Creatas/Thinkstock, (TCR) Niall Benvie/Nature Picture Library/Nature Picture Library; **444** (TR, CR) PhotoLibrary Group, Inc.; **446** (CR) Globus Brothers, NYC; **448** (BR) geopaul/iStockphoto; **449** (L) M. Brodie/Alamy

Chapter 13

450 (B) Nutscode/T Service/Photo Researchers, Inc.; **453** (TCL, BL) PhotoLibrary Group, Inc.; **454** (CL) Annette Soumillard/ Corbis; **455** (CR) Martin McCarthy/iStockphoto; **456** (BL) Lisa Svara/iStockphoto; **457** (CL) Acme Food Arts/Getty Images;

458 (C) GRIN/NASA; **459** (C) PhotoLibrary Group, Inc.; **462** (CR) GRIN/NASA; **463** (B) Vincent Leblic/PhotoLibrary Group, Inc.; **464** (T) Alberto Pomares/iStockphoto; **465** (CR) Chris Mattison/Alamy Images, (TR) Mark Lewis/Alamy Images, (C) Matt Meadows/Alamy Images; **466** (BR) Mark Lewis/Alamy Images, (TR) Martin McCarthy/iStockphoto; **468** (TR) Ariel Skelley/Corbis; **469** (BR) Martin Dohrn/Science Source; **470** (L) Science Source/Photo Researchers, Inc.; **471** (TR) Branko Miokovic/iStockphoto, (BL) Ekaterina Hashbarger/iStockphoto

Chapter 14

472 (B) Corbis; **475** (BCL) ©Richard Megna/Fundamental Photographs, (BL) Richard Megna/Fundamental Photographs, NYC, (TL) Sami Sarkis/Getty Images; **476** (B) Wen Zhenxiao/ ChinaFotoPress/Zuma Press, Inc.; **477** (BR) Adrian Lourie/ Alamy; **478** (C) Sami Sarkis/Getty Images; **480** (BR) Digital Vision/Alamy; **482** (BL) Kin Images/Getty Images, (B) Martin Siepmann/Alamy, (BC) Michael Durham/Nature Picture Library; **483** (R) David Pu'u/Corbis; **484** (T) Stockbyte/Getty Images; **486** (L) Chad Baker/Digital Vision/Getty Images, (CL) Moodboard/Corbis; **487** (T) Walter Bibikow/Danita Delimont Inc./Alamy Images; **488** (B) ©AP Images, (CR) Bettmann/ Corbis; **489** (BR) ©Richard Megna/Fundamental Photographs; **490** (TL) ©Matthias Kulka/Corbis, (CL) ©Richard Megna/ Fundamental Photographs, (CR) Nice One Productions/ Corbis, (B) Richard Megna/Fundamental Photographs, NYC; **491** (CR) ©DK Images, (TR, TL) Image downloaded from the Coastal Inlets Research Program web site, US Army Corps of Engineers, (BCR) Richard Megna/Fundamental Photographs, NYC; **492** (CL) Peter Steiner/Alamy Images, (B) Yamado Taro/ The Image Bank/Getty Images; **495** (R) Special Collections Division, University of Washington Libraries; **496** (BR) ©DK Images, (CL) David Pu'u/Corbis; **498** (TR) Earl S. Cryer/ UPI/Landov LLC; **500** (L) Photos 12/Alamy Images; **501** (L) Ablestock/Alamy.

Chapter 15

502 (T) Cheryl Gerber/©Associated Press; **505** (TCL) ©Associated Press, (TC) Aaron Haupt/Photo Researchers, Inc., (BCL) Caren Firouz/Reuters Media, (BL) Greg Baker/©Associated Press, (TR) Michael Clutson/Photo Researchers, Inc.; **506** (C) Digital Vision/Getty Images; **507** (BC) ©Associated Press; **509** (B) Andy King/©Associated Press; **510** (TL) Harrison H. Schmitt/Johnson space Center/ NASA; **511** (TL) Jim Byrnre/QA Photos; **512** (CR) Jean Frooms/ iStockphoto; **513** (CR) ©Associated Press, (CC) Clive Barda/ Arena-PAL Images; **514** (B) Greg Baker/©Associated Press; **515** (TR) Caren Firouz/Reuters Media; **517** (L) ©Associated Press; **518** (CL) AlexStar/iStockphoto, (TR) iStockphoto; **519** (CR) Marc Grimberg/Getty Images; **520** (C) AlexStar/ iStockphoto, (TR) Jorge Silva/Reuters Media, (BL) Mark Aronoff/Santa Rosa Press Democrat/Zuma Press, Inc.; **521** (CC) Jorge Silva/Reuters Media; **522** (CR) Clive Barda/ Arena-PAL Images; **525** (TR) AJPhoto/Photo Researchers, Inc.; **526** (C) Ralph Lee Hopkins/National Geographic Image Collection; **527** (TR) Stephen Dalton/Science Source; **529** (TR) Ric Feld/©Associated Press; **530** (TR) ©Associated Press, (CR) iStockphoto; **534** (B) Jason Verschoor/iStockphoto; **535** (T) Chris Lemmens/iStockphoto, (B) Yevgen Timashov/ iStockphoto.

Chapter 16

536 (B) Tom Barrick, Chris Clark/SGHMS/Photo Researchers, Inc.; **539** (BL) Don Carstens/Robertstock, (BCL) Nutscode/T Service/Photo Researchers, Inc.; **540** (C) J. A. Kraulis/©Masterfile Royalty-Free, (TR) Photography by Ward/Alamy Images; **542** (B) Benjamin Rondel/Corbis; **543** (T) ©DK Images; **544** (C) Arthur S. Aubry/Getty Images, (CL) Mode Images Limited/Alamy Images; **546** (R) AbleStock/Thinkstock; **547** (TR) Dave L. Ryan/Photolibrary/AGE Fotostock; **548** (CL) Joel Sartore/National Geographic/Getty Images, (BR) Nutscode/T Service/Photo Researchers, Inc.; **549** (T) Goodshoot/Corbis, (BR) Tom Arne Hanslien/Alamy Images; **550** (B) Don Carstens/Robertstock; **551** (T) Stocktrek Images, Inc./Alamy; **552** (B) Brand X Pictures/Jupiter Images; **554** (BL) Fuse/Jupiter Images; **555** (TR) Ablestock/Jupiter Images, (CR) Moodboard/Corbis; **558** (BL) Dana Hoff/Beateworks/Corbis; **560** (TR) ©DK Images, (CL) Goodshoot/Corbis; **563** (BR) Bloomimage/Corbis; **564** (L) Ngo Thye Aun/Shutterstock; **565** (B) Mark Thomas/Photo Researchers, Inc.

Chapter 17

566 (BC) Anish Kapoor, (B) Cloud Gate, Millennium Park, Chicago(2004), Anish Kapoor. Photo ©2008 Kim Karpeles/Kim Karpeles Photography; **569** (TCL) Corbis/Photolibrary Group, Inc., (BCL) David R. Frazier Photolibrary, Inc./Alamy, (TL) Glow Images/Photolibrary Group, Inc.; **570** (C) Dennis Flaherty/Getty Images; **571** (BR) Kevin Frayer/©Associated Press; **574** (TCL) ©Tom & Pat Leeson, (TL) Dmitry Kutlayev/iStockphoto; **575** (R) Glow Images/Photolibrary Group, Inc.; **577** (CR) LOETSCHER CHLAUS/Alamy; **578** (B) Corbis/Photolibrary Group, Inc.; **581** (TR) age Fotostock/SuperStock; **582** (B) Lawrence Lawry/Photo Researchers, Inc.; **585** (TR) Lawrence Lawry/Photo Researchers, Inc., (B) AFP/AFP/Getty Images; **586** (T) David R. Frazier Photolibrary, Inc./Alamy; **590** (B) Stephen Alvarez/National Geographic Image Collection; **591** (BR, BCR) Adam Hart-Davis/Photo Researchers, Inc.; **594** (BL) Niels van Gijn/Getty Images; **596** (CL) John Chumack/Photo Researchers, Inc.; **597** (CR, CL) Edward Kinsman/Photo Researchers, Inc., (CC) Markus Brunner/Imagebroker/PhotoLibrary Group, Inc.; **598** (BL) Adam Hart-Davis/Photo Researchers, Inc.; **600** (BR) Richard Megna/Fundamental Photographs, NYC; **602** (B) David Steele/Large Binocular Telescope Observatory; **603** (B) JupiterImages/Creatas/Alamy.

Chapter 18

604 (B) Nick Suydam/Alamy Images; **607** (TCL) Jim Ketsdever/©Associated Press; **608** (B) Kerry Hayes/20th Century Fox/The Kobal Collection/The Kobal Collection; **612** (TL) Dev Carr/Cultura/Photolibrary Group, Inc., (BC) Paul A. Souders/Corbis; **613** (TL) GIPhotoStock/Photo Researchers, Inc.; **614** (B) Jim Ketsdever/©Associated Press, (TL) Peter Menzel/Photo Researchers, Inc., (BC) Virgo Productions/Corbis; **616** (CL) Volker Steger/Photo Researchers, Inc.; **617** (B) ©2003 Universal/Everett Collection, Inc.; **618** (C) Google, Inc.; **619** (BL) Brandon Laufenberg/iStockphoto, (CR) Franc Podgor?ek/iStockphoto, (CC) Jill Fromer/iStockphoto, (BC) jo unruh/iStockphoto, (B) Julia Nichols/iStockphoto, (BCL) Linda King/iStockphoto; **622** (CR) Alan Keohane/©DK Images; **623** (BC) Enrique de la Osa/Reuters Media; **624** (B) Jeff Horner/©Associated Press; **625** (BR) iStockphoto; **629** (BR) Liquid Library/Thinkstock; **632** (C) Kim Kyung Hoon/Reuters Media; **633** (BR) Akirastock/iStockphoto, (BL) Gualtiero Boffi/iStockphoto, (T) magicinfoto/iStockphoto, (CR) pixhook/iStockphoto, (BC) Uyen Le/iStockphoto; **634** (CL) Emmeline Watkins/SPL/Photo Researchers, Inc.; **635** (BL) Jill Fromer/iStockphoto; **636** (TR) Paul A. Souders/Corbis; **637** (CR) pixhook/iStockphoto; **639** (BR) iStockphoto; **640** (BR) Bettmann/Corbis, (TL) Jerry Mason/Photo Researchers, Inc., (B) Silman Snozyk/PhotoLibrary Group, Inc.; **641** (TR) Earl Roberge/Photo Researchers, Inc., (B) Michael Peuckert/Alamy Images.

Chapter 19

642 (B) Liu Xiaoyang/Alamy Images; **645** (B) Shutterstock, (TL) Yiap Edition/Alamy Images; **646** (CL) Vikram Hoshing/Alamy; **647** (TC) /Alamy Images, (T) Galina Barskaya/Alamy, (C) Richard Baker/In Pictures/Corbis; **648** (BL, BC) Richard Megna/Fundamental Photographs, NYC, (T) Yiap Edition/Alamy Images; **649** (C) Amazing Images/Alamy; **650** (TR) Roger Harris/Science Source, (BL) DLI LLC/Corbis, (BC) Master Magnetics; **656** (BL) Novastock/Alamy Images; **661** (CR) Pictures by Rob/Alamy/Alamy; **662** (CR) Nikkytok/Shutterstock; (CL) Microvision, Inc. (C) Richard T. Nowitz/Photo Researchers, Inc.; **665** (TR) DreamPictures/Stone/Getty Images; **668** (B) Corbis, (CR) Peter Beck/Corbis; **671** (BR) Car Culture/Corbis, (CR) Clive Streeter/The Science Museum, London/©DK Images, (TR) Schenectady Museum/Hall of Electrical History Foundation/Corbis; **672** (B) Shutterstock; **675** (TR) Omri Waisman/Beateworks/Corbis; **676** (TR) Amazing Images/Alamy; **680** (BCL) Living Art Enterprises/Photo Researchers, Inc., (B) RubberBall Selects/Alamy; **681** (BL) North Wind Picture Archives, (BR) Steve Gorton/British Telecommunications/©DK Images.

this is your book

you can write in it

this is your book

you can write in it